THE
INTER-AMERICAN
SYSTEM

THE INTER-AMERICAN SYSTEM

Its Development
and Strengthening

**INTER-AMERICAN INSTITUTE OF
INTERNATIONAL LEGAL STUDIES**

1966
OCEANA PUBLICATIONS, INC. / DOBBS FERRY, NEW YORK

F 1402
I 61

EXPLANATORY NOTE

In March of 1964, at its Inaugural Meeting in Bogotá, Colombia, the INSTITUTE decided to bring out a publication that would contain the basic instruments of the inter-American system, with annotations. Even at that time, however, there already existed a movement to rebuild and strengthen the system, which gradually evolved into the idea of amending the Charter of the Organization of American States (OAS). A Special Inter-American Conference was recently convoked for this purpose and will meet during 1966.

The existence of this movement and its logical repercussions both within the Continent and outside it, made it appear advisable to revamp the planned publication and publish instead an analysis of the structure, functions and activities of the inter-American system, including the texts of its basic instruments. Only in this way would it be possible to accurately reflect the development and strengthening the inter-American system has undergone during the last few years, in nearly all the areas of inter-American cooperation. Also, only by means of an accurate reflection of reality, which today does not always coincide with the image proffered by the OAS Charter and other basic instruments, will it be possible to evaluate properly the movement for reform that is now under way.

In the preparation of this study the General Secretariat of the INSTITUTE received the cooperation of officials of the Pan-American Union, General Secretariat of the OAS, as well as of the Inter-American Development Bank. Its publication, in both English and Spanish, was made possible thanks to the funds made available to the INSTITUTE by the Ford Foundation.

F. V. García-Amador
Secretary-General

ABBREVIATIONS

International Conferences (1889-1928)

International Conferences of American States, 1889-1928, A Collection of the Conventions, Recommendations, Resolutions, etc. (Carnegie Endowment for International Peace, 1931).

International Conferences, 1st Sup., (1933-1940)

International Conferences of American States, First Supplement, 1933-1940 (Carnegie Endowment for International Peace, 1940).

International Conferences, 2nd Sup., (1942-1954)

International Conferences of American States, Second Supplement, 1942-1954 (Department of Legal Affairs, Pan American Union, 1958).

Applications, vol. 1

Inter-American Treaty of Reciprocal Assistance, Applications, Volume I, 1948-1959 (Pan American Union, General Secretariat, Organization of American States, 1964).

Applications, vol. 2

Inter-American Treaty of Reciprocal Assistance, Applications, Volume II, 1960-1964 (Pan American Union, General Secretariat, Organization of American States, 1964).

TABLE OF CONTENTS

Part One

STRUCTURE, FUNCTIONS, AND GENERAL ACTIVITIES

POSTSCRIPT

APPENDICES

Part One

Part Two

Part Three

Introduction

The inter-American system, which in 1965 celebrated its 75th anniversary, is not only the oldest regional organization, but also the one that has experienced the most notable degree of development and strengthening in its various spheres of activity. It had its beginning in a hemisphere where there existed from the outset a propitious environment for rapprochement and solidarity among peoples and governments. Favorable circumstances included a similar origin and historical evolution, geographic proximity and similarity of political institutions. In fact, all the states that function within the inter-American system were born of European colonialism. They struggled for many years to gain their freedom and independence, and once these were won they abandoned the monarchial institutions of the Old World and chose representative democracy as their form of government.

The Congress of Panama (1826)

During that period, particularly in its last stages, various ideas and proposals emerged in favor of forming a general confederation, designed to protect and consolidate their freedom and independence. The principal apostle and most active promoter of these aspirations for union and hemisphere solidarity was the Liberator Simón Bolívar, who for many years had cherished the ideal of a strong and united America under the shield of law and democracy. To carry out these aspirations, Bolívar sent notes to the governments of the newly independent republics, first in 1822 and again in 1824, to suggest to them that a "meeting of plenipotentiaries of the Americas" be held, for the purpose of establishing the proposed confederation. In his second note, written from Lima on December 7, 1824, two days before the Battle of Ayacucho, Bolívar eloquently explained his reasons for proposing this meeting, and he also made the following prediction: "The day that our plenipotentiaries exchange their powers, an immortal era will be established in the diplomatic history of the Americas."

Following many difficulties and delays, the meeting took place in Panama from June 22 to July 15, 1826, and was called "The First Congress of American States". Its chief purpose was to establish a great hemisphere confederation, composed of all the American nations, in order to consolidate the relations then existing between the new American states and give them solemn and lasting form by means of a treaty.

Representatives of Colombia (now Colombia, Ecuador, Panama, and Venezuela); Central America (now Costa Rica, Guatemala, Honduras, Nicaragua, and El Salvador); the United Mexican States, Peru, and observers from Great Britain and Holland attended that congress. Argentina, Bolivia, Brazil, and the United States of America also appointed delegates, but various obstacles prevented them from reaching Panama in time to participate in the meeting. Although Chile supported the Congress, it was unable, for constitutional reasons, to appoint its delegates in time for them to attend. It should be remembered that in those days land and sea transportation was very slow and difficult. For example, it took the delegate of Colombia 74 days to travel from Bogotá to Panama City.

The principal instrument signed at the Congress of Panama, on July 15, 1826, was the Treaty of Perpetual Union, League, and Confederation between the Republics of Colombia, Central America, Peru, and the United Mexican States, which crystallized the ideas of Bolívar and other heroes of the independence. The treaty did not enter into force because only Colombia ratified it. Nevertheless, the fact that a considerable number of delegates from the young American republics held a meeting in a period when international conferences were rare was in itself a great achievement.

Moreover that first inter-American diplomatic instrument set forth certain juridical principles and standards of international conduct that inspired and motivated other Hispano-American congresses held during the course of the nineteenth century, as well as the inter-American regional organization which was established in 1890, and in certain aspects even the League of Nations and the United Nations.

The Treaty of Panama of 1826 established a confederation of states, based on principles and procedures that would later become generally accepted. These included the establishment, as the principal organ of the confederation, of a general assembly in which all the federated states would be represented on a level of juridical equality and with full powers to conclude treaties designed to consolidate relations between the parties, to contribute to the maintenance of peace and the friendly solution of disputes that existed or that might arise between them, and to seek conciliation and mediation, either between the federated powers themselves or between them and one or more foreign powers. The treaty also provided for the mutual guarantee of the integrity of the respective territories; the obligation to cooperate toward the complete abolition of slavery; the codification of international law; the exclusion from the confederation of any member state that violated the treaty in regard to maintenance of the peace or respect for the decisions of the general assembly; and the establishment of hemisphere citizenship for citizens of the member states. At the Congress of Panama three additional instruments were signed, among them a convention that set a troop quota for each country, with a view to forming and maintaining a permanent army of 60,000 soldiers, and regulated the organization and direction of this army. It was thus, also in Panama, that the idea of an international force to guarantee the peace originated.[1]

Latin American Congresses

Following the Congress of Panama, efforts toward hemisphere confederation were continued at several congresses of a political nature, which were, in fact, extensions of the one held in Panama. These meetings included the one held in Lima in 1847-48; those in Santiago, Chile, and Washington, D.C. in 1856; and, finally, the second Lima meeting of 1864-65. All these stemmed from the concern of the new American states in the face of threats of reconquest by the former mother country and from a desire to organize a confederation or society of American nations to meet common dangers.

The first Congress of Lima was held from December 11, 1847 to March 1, 1848. It was attended by plenipotentiaries of Bolivia, Chile, Colombia, Ecuador, and Peru. As a result of its deliberations, the meeting adopted two treaties, one on confederation and the other on commerce and navigation; and two conventions, one on consular agents and the other on postal matters. The Treaty on Confederation, which was the most important instrument signed at that congress, represented a renewed effort to agree upon means to tighten the bonds between the new republics; to maintain their independence, sovereignty, and institutions; to unite their efforts and resources; and to arrange for the peaceful settlement of disputes that might arise among them. Although these treaties and conventions were not ratified by the signatory states, they once again made evident the constant interest of the new American republics in strengthening their solidarity.

The Governments of Chile, Ecuador, and Peru were represented at the Congress of Santiago (Chile 1856) during which, the Continental Treaty of Alliance and Reciprocal Assistance was signed on September 15.

That Treaty incorporated the same principles of continental

---

[1] On the documents relating to the Congress of Panama, including the complete text of the Treaty of Perpetual Union, League, and Confederation, see *International Conferences* (1889-1928), p. xix *et seq.*

solidarity and confederation that had been included in the instruments adopted in Panama in 1826 and at the first Congress of Lima in 1847-1848. Several months later, on November 9, 1856, inspired by the same ideas of collective defense, the plenipotentiaries of Costa Rica, Guatemala, Colombia, Honduras, Mexico, Peru, El Salvador, and Venezuela met in Washington and signed the Treaty of Alliance and Confederation, which was similar to the Continental Treaty of Chile. The meetings of plenipotentiaries in Santiago and in Washington to sign the two instruments mentioned above were not congresses strictly speaking, but they have been considered as such and are therefore included among the Latin American congresses of the nineteenth century. Although neither of the two treaties signed in Santiago and Washington was ratified, that fact did not prevent their serving as another reaffirmation of the ideal of political union that was inspiring the leaders of the Latin American republics.

The second Congress of Lima met in that capital from November 15, 1864 to March 12, 1865, and was attended by representatives of Argentina, Bolivia, Chile, Colombia, Ecuador, El Salvador, Guatemala, Venezuela, and Peru. It was convoked because of added threats arising in that period against the territorial integrity and democratic institutions of the new American states. The hemisphere situation at the time was all the more grave because the United States was in a state of civil war, and consequently, was in no position to take action in defense of democracy and liberty in the American nations. At the second Congress of Lima, four treaties were signed on union and defensive alliance; preservation of the peace between the American states; mails; and commerce and navigation. In the first treaty, another effort was made to establish an international army in the Americas and in the second a mechanism was created for the pacific settlement of disputes. Like the treaties signed at the first Congress of Lima those signed at the second were not ratified.

Dating from the second Congress of Lima, the international policy of the Latin American countries changed direction, largely because by that time the danger of reconquest of the former Spanish colonies had almost completely disappeared, and, consequently, there was no longer a pressing need to seek common defense and solidarity through union.

In the following years, serious problems arose in Latin America, among them, civil strife and wars between the sister countries, which, from the political standpoint, made all efforts toward hemisphere solidarity more difficult. From 1865 to 1889, the congresses held were exclusively juridical in nature. Held during that period were the Congress of Jurists at Lima (1877-1879), and the First South American Congress on Private International Law, Montevideo

(1888-1889). The purpose of these congresses, like that of the one held in the same capital in 1939-1940, was to codify the principles of private international law applicable in the Americas, in order to eliminate one of the causes of disputes between the states.

The Congress of Jurists in Lima opened on December 13, 1877, and closed on March 27, 1879. The following countries were represented: Argentina, Bolivia, Chile, Costa Rica, Ecuador, Peru, and Venezuela. Later, they were joined by representatives of Guatemala and Uruguay. The United States abstained from accepting the invitation because of differences between its legislation and that of the Latin America countries. The republican Government of Cuba, which at that time was fighting to gain its independence, was also invited, and although it had not yet been recognized, it was represented at the Congress on an equal footing with the representatives of the other governments.

The Congress adopted a treaty to establish uniform rules for the settlement of disputes in matters dealing with the civil status and the legal capacity of individuals; goods situated in the country, contracts signed in a foreign country and those signed by foreigners in the republic; succession; the competence of national courts over juridical acts performed outside of the republic and over acts by foreigners who do not reside therein; national jurisdiction over crimes committed in a foreign country and over crimes of falsification harmful to other states; the execution of sentences and other jurisdictional acts; and the legalization of letters rogatory and other instruments from a foreign country.

The first South American Congress on Private International Law met in Montevideo from August 25, 1888 to February 18, 1889, at the initiative of the Governments of Argentina and Uruguay. Besides these two countries, Bolivia, Brazil, Chile, Paraguay, and Peru were also represented. The work of the Congress consisted of approval of eight treaties and one protocol, as follows: Treaty on Procedural Law; Treaty on Literary and Artistic Copyright; Treaty on Patents of Invention; Treaty on Merchants' and Manufacturers' Trademarks; Treaty on International Penal Law; Treaty on International Civil Law; and an additional protocol fixing the general rules for applying the laws of any contracting state in the territory of the others.

This was the first serious effort in the Americas to codify private international law. Although the treaty adopted by the Congress of Jurists in Lima did not enter into force because only one country ratified it, the treaties of Montevideo have been ratified and are in effect in most of the signatory countries. The Treaty on International Penal Law contains a chapter on diplomatic asylum for political refugees, this being the first time in the Americas that common standards for diplomatic asylum were codified in an international treaty.[2]

The First International American Conference (Washington 1889-1890)

Toward the end of the nineteenth century, the ideas expressed in the congresses already mentioned began to find an echo in the United States and to evoke public opinion favorable to carrying them out. This was one of the reasons that prompted the Government of the United States, to invite, through its then Secretary of State James G. Blaine, the Latin American republics "to participate in a general congress, to be held in the city of Washington on the 24th day of November, 1882, for the purpose of considering and discussing the methods of preventing war between the nations of America." In his circular of November 29, 1881 Mr. Blaine also said: "The United States will enter into the deliberations of the Congress on the same footing as the other powers represented, and with the loyal determination to approach any proposed solution, not merely in its own interest or with a view to asserting its own power, but as a single member among many co-ordinate and co-equal States." For several reasons, however, the congress did not materialize as planned. Among these reasons were the assassination of President Garfield, which took place shortly after the note was sent; the replacement of Mr. Blaine as Secretary of State; and the War of the Pacific, between Chile on one side and Bolivia and Peru on the other.

Some years later, on June 7, 1884, the United States Congress passed a law creating a committee to make a careful study of the best methods to assure the closest international and commercial relations between the countries of the hemisphere. Since the results of this study, were favorable, the United States Congress passed a law on May 24, 1888, authorizing the President of the United States to invite the governments of the American republics to join the United States in holding a conference in Washington, for the purpose of discussing and recommending for adoption by their respective Governments some plan of arbitration for the settlement of disagreements and disputes that might thereafter arise between them, and for considering questions relating to the improvement of business intercourse and means of direct communication between said countries, and to encourage such reciprocal commercial relations as would be beneficial to all and secure more extensive markets for the products of each of the said countries.

---

[2] On the documentation relating to Latin American congresses, including the text of the principal instruments signed at them, see J. M. Yepes, *Del Congreso de Panamá a la Conferencia de Caracas, 1826-1954*, Caracas, 1955, 2 vols.

The invitation was sent out on July 13, 1888, and the meeting took place in Washington from October 2, 1889 to April 19, 1890, with the name of the "First International American Conference". At the time it was held, the Secretary of State was once again James G. Blaine, who had taken such an interest in improving relations between the American peoples.

Seventeen American republics, that is, all of those then in existence except the Dominican Republic, were represented at the First Conference. Cuba and Panama were not yet independent states. The Dominican Republic explained to the United States in a friendly way that it was not accepting the invitation because it had already concluded a treaty with that country in 1884 with reference to arbitration and commercial reciprocity. That treaty was then pending ratification by both parties.

A resolution was adopted at that first conference establishing an association under the title of "The International Union of American Republics" for the purpose of "prompt collection and distribution of commercial information." Also established at the same time, to represent the International Union, was "The Commercial Bureau of the American Republics", which would operate for the common good and would be supported by the participating countries. Thus, through the simple procedure of a mere resolution and with a modest budget of $36,000, the regional organization of the Americas came into being. At first, the functions of the Bureau were limited to compiling and publishing, through a bulletin, data and reports on the production, trade, and customs laws and regulations of the respective countries; and to providing the contracting countries with statistics on trade and with reports provided by any of the member countries.

The resolution in question was adopted on April 14, 1890, and since 1930, by decision of the Governing Board of the Pan American Union—now the Council of the Organization of American States—this date has been observed throughout the American republics as Pan American Day. Its purpose is to emphasize the political, legal, economic, and cultural ties that unite them.

In line with its objectives, the First Conference was devoted principally to laying the foundations for economic cooperation between the American states and to establishing a plan of arbitration for the peaceful settlement of disputes that might arise among them. For lack of ratifications, the treaty that incorporated this plan did not go into effect. Nevertheless, it served as a model for the adoption of similar procedures that were incorporated into later instruments, both in this hemisphere and elsewhere in the world. Also, it was at that conference that the idea of an inter-American bank was first brought up, although it was not finally carried out until 1959, the year the Inter-American Development Bank was created.

At the time the Washington conference was held in 1889-90, the population of the American republics was about 100 million; today it exceeds 415 million. The inter-American organization developed gradually after 1890, changing its organic structure and expanding its field of action at successive conferences. Because of existing problems and others involving relations between the states that frequently arose throughout the years, the advance was relatively slow, but as time went on, the inter-American system gradually and systematically became firmly rooted. Its progress during the first 58 years of its existence, that is, up to the Ninth Conference, at Bogotá (1948), which established the present structure and named it the Organization of American States, cannot be said to have been spectacular or extraordinary. Nevertheless, throughout that long period the organization never experienced a serious setback, but continued to move forward and positively in keeping with the requirements of the American regional community.[3]

The Second Conference (Mexico 1901-1902)

Eleven years after the American regional organization was established, the Second Conference took place in Mexico City, from October 22, 1901, to January 31, 1902, with the name of the Second International American Conference. At this conference, the Bureau established at the First Conference was reorganized and its name changed to "The International Bureau of the American Republics". The Bureau was to be directed by a Governing Board, composed of the diplomatic representatives of all the governments of the American republics accredited to the Government of the United States; its chairman was the United States Secretary of State. The post of Director of the Bureau was retained, and new duties were assigned to the Bureau. The conference adopted several resolutions, treaties, and conventions on pecuniary claims; extradition and protection against anarchism; practice of learned professions; formation of codes on public and private international law; protection of literary and artistic copyrights; exchange of official, scientific, literary, and industrial publications; patents of invention, industrial drawings, and models and trade marks; rights of aliens; and compulsory arbitration.

The Third Conference (Rio de Janeiro 1906)

The Third International American Conference was held in Rio de Janeiro from July 23 to August 27, 1906, with Cuba and Panama attending for the first time. The International Union of American

---

[3] On the treaties and conventions, resolutions and declarations adopted by the First and succeeding International American Conferences, as well as by the special conferences and early Meetings of Consultation of Ministers of Foreign Affairs, see *International Conferences of American States*, (1889-1928), First Supplement (1933-1940) and Second Supplement (1942-1954).

Republics and the Bureau that represented it were continued, with the Bureau remaining under the authority of the Governing Board established at the previous conference, but with broader and more precise functions.

A new Convention on Pecuniary Claims was adopted, in view of the fact that the previous one was due to expire in 1907 (five years from the date it was adopted); the earlier conventions on patents, trade marks, and literary and artistic copyright were changed and combined into a single convention; a convention was adopted establishing the status of naturalized citizens who again take up residence in their country of origin; and another to promote the codification of public and private international law.

The Fourth Conference (Buenos Aires 1910)

In 1910, the year in which many of the American republics, among them Argentina, celebrated the first centennial of their independence, the Fourth International American Conference was held in Buenos Aires from July 12 to August 30.

This conference maintained the International Union established at the First Conference, and continued at the Second and Third, but changed the name to the "Union of American Republics". The Bureau, serving as the agent of the organization, was renamed the "Pan American Union". Although the name "Pan American Union" was used for the first time at the Fourth Conference, the organization was actually a continuation of the one that had been established in 1890 on a more modest and restricted scale, which by 1910, had acquired greater scope and hemisphere importance. The Pan American Union was then given broader functions. The Governing Board remained the highest authority and administration was entrusted to a director, who thenceforth would be called the "Director General" and would be appointed by the Governing Board. It was also provided that there should be an Assistant Director, who, while also performing other duties, would act as Secretary of the Board.

This, then, is the origin of the name chosen by the Conference of Bogotá (1948) to designate the General Secretariat of the Organization of American States.

April 26, 1910, shortly before the Fourth Conference, saw the opening of the new Pan American Union building, since then known throughout the hemisphere as the "House of the Americas". This beautiful building, which since 1910 has been the headquarters of the inter-American organization, was built on land donated by the United States with funds contributed by the eminent U.S. philanthropist Andrew Carnegie, who was a delegate of his country at the First Conference in 1889-90. The other American republics contributed the funds needed to complete the building. The cornerstone laying ceremony, which took place on May 11, 1908, was attended by 5,000 people, who heard the following speakers: the President of the United States, Theodore Roosevelt; the United States Secretary of State, Elihu Root; the Ambassador of Brazil, Joaquim Nabuco, speaking for the Latin American countries; and Andrew Carnegie. Mr. Elihu Root, who was Secretary of State from 1905 to 1909 and Chairman of the Governing Board of the Union, and to whose initiative the building was largely due, closed his speech with these words: "May the structure now begun stand for many generations to come as the visible evidence of mutual respect, esteem, appreciation, and kindly feeling between the peoples of all the republics . . . and may all the Americas come to feel that for them this place is home . . . the product of a common effort and the instrument of a common purpose." Ambassador Nabuco of Brazil made the following remarks: ". . . There has never been a parallel for the sight which this ceremony presents—that of twenty-one nations, of different languages, building together a house for their common deliberations. The more impressive is the scene, as these countries, with all possible differences between them in size and population, have established their union on the basis of the most absolute equality."

The Fourth Conference adopted four conventions on: inventions, patents, designs, and industrial models; protection of trade-mark; literary and artistic copyright; and pecuniary claims. The first three conventions again separated these matters that at the previous conference had been combined into one convention. The fourth convention was a repetition of the one adopted in Mexico in 1902 and extended by the conference of Rio de Janeiro in 1906. At the Fourth Conference, the first attempt was made to adopt a convention for organizing the Pan American Union on a permanent basis. As will be seen later, the same effort was again made at the Sixth Conference, but the idea did not bear fruit until the Ninth in 1948. In the meantime, during this long period of 58 years, the inter-American organization functioned on the basis of resolutions adopted at the International American Conferences.

The Fifth Conference (Santiago, Chile 1923)

As agreed at the Fourth Conference, the Fifth International Conference of American States should have been convoked in 1915, but because of World War I, it did not meet until 1923. It was held at Santiago, Chile, from March 25 to May 3 of that year. The Fifth Conference confirmed the existence of the "Union of the Republics of the American Continent" and of the "Pan American Union" as its permanent organ. The functions of the latter were restated and its bases of organization enlarged. It was established that the governments of the American republics enjoy, as of right, representation at the International Conferences of American States and in the Pan American Union. Also, it was stipulated that the governments might appoint special representatives on the Governing Board; formerly, representation had been limited to the diplomatic representatives accredited to the Government of the United States.

The conference in Santiago, Chile approved a treaty, and three conventions and adopted numerous resolutions. The first instrument, "Treaty to Avoid or Prevent Conflicts between the American States", known as the "Gondra Pact", after its principal author, the Paraguayan statesman of that name, is especially important because it was the first positive effort to establish, on a contractual basis, a procedure for avoiding or preventing conflicts.

The three conventions approved by the conference were on publicity of customs documents; protection of commercial, industrial, and agricultural trade-marks and commercial names; and on uniformity of nomenclature for the classification of merchandise.

The Sixth Conference (Havana 1928)

As provided for at the previous one, the Sixth International Conference of American States was held at Havana five years later, from January 16 to February 20, 1928. This conference adopted a convention on the Pan American Union to give permanent status to the organization, but it never entered into force, since it was ratified by only 16 countries and required ratification by all 21 member countries of the Union. Foreseeing a possible delay in ratifying the convention, the conference passed a resolution maintaining in effect previous resolutions governing the Pan American Union.

The Havana Conference was very productive insofar as the number and quality of the conventions and resolutions adopted were concerned. Besides the convention on the Pan American Union, ten others were signed on the following matters: asylum, consular agents, diplomatic officials, status of aliens, maritime neutrality, duties and rights of states in the event of civil strife, treaties, commercial aviation, literary and artistic copyright (revision of the Buenos Aires convention), and private international law ("Bustamante Code").

The Seventh Conference (Montevideo 1933)

The Seventh International Conference of American States, considered to be one of the most important of those held up to that time, took place in Montevideo from December 3 to 26, 1933. This conference did not modify the statute of the Pan American Union but merely entrusted to the Eighth Conference a study of possible changes. The work of progressively improving the regional organization of the Americas had, in fact, been suspended at the Sixth Conference in 1928. As will later be noted, it was resumed provisionally at the conference in Mexico City in 1945 and was completed at the Bogotá Conference of 1948 with the adoption of the Charter of the Organization of American States.

Several conventions and numerous resolutions were adopted at the Montevideo Conference. The conventions dealt with the following matters: the nationality of women, nationality, extradition, political asylum, the teaching of history, and rights and duties of states. An additional protocol to the General Convention of Inter-American Conciliation of 1929 was also adopted. The convention on rights and duties of states was of special significance because it was the first inter-American instrument to establish the principle of non-intervention. Its Article 8 reads: "No state has the right to intervene in the internal or external affairs of another." Among others, it also sets forth the principle of juridical equality of states (Art. 4). The Convention on Political Asylum improved upon the convention of 1928, stipulating, among other things, that "the judgment of political delinquency concerns the State which offers asylum" and that "political asylum, as an institution of humanitarian character, is not subject to reciprocity." One of the most important of the 95 resolutions adopted at this conference has to do with good offices and mediation. Some of the other significant resolutions concerned economic, commercial, and tariff policy, commercial arbitration, promotion of tourist travel, codification of international law, industrial and agricultural use of international rivers, improvement of the conditions of the working classes, and agrarian reform.

Inter-American Conference for the Maintenance of Peace (Buenos Aires 1936)

Between the Seventh and Eighth Conferences, the Inter-American Conference for the Maintenance of Peace was held in Buenos Aires, from December 1 to 23, 1936. At that time, the statesmen of the Americas were fearful lest the peace of the Western Hemisphere be threatened, not so much by anything that might happen there as by the events then occurring with such ominous swiftness in other parts of the world, such as the rearmament of Germany, Japanese aggression in China, and the Italian invasion of Ethiopia. It was in that atmosphere that the President of the United States, Franklin D. Roosevelt, addressed a personal letter to the heads of state of all the Latin American republics, proposing that a conference be held "to determine how the maintenance of peace among the American Republics may best be safeguarded." Mr. Roosevelt pointed out that any steps taken in this direction would, at the same time, advance the cause of world peace. Consequently, the object of the conference was not only to seek measures to protect the hemisphere against any internal threats to the peace, but also to safeguard it from outside threats.

In considering the immediate problem of maintaining the peace, the conference was also faced with the problem of finding an adequate mechanism to coordinate inter-American activities to meet unforeseen events in the most effective way. The solution to this problem lay in the creation of a new procedure, that of consultation, which was further developed and perfected at successive conferences until its definitive adoption at Rio de Janeiro (1947) and at Bogotá (1948).

In addition to the Convention for the Maintenance, Preservation, and Reestablishment of Peace and an Additional Protocol relative to Non-Intervention, the Buenos Aires Conference approved nine other conventions, on the following subjects: prevention of controversies, good offices and mediation, fulfillment of the existing treaties between the American states, the Pan American highway, promotion of inter-American cultural relations, interchange of publications, facilities for artistic exhibitions, peaceful orientation of public instruction, and facilities for educational and publicity films. Among the resolutions adopted was a Declaration of Principles of Inter-American Solidarity and Cooperation, which stated that every act susceptible of disturbing the peace of America affects each and every country and justifies the initiation of the procedure of consultation.

The Eighth Conference (Lima 1938)

Two years later, from December 9 to 27, 1938, the Eighth International Conference of American States was held in Lima, Peru. This conference did not introduce new bases for reorganizing the Pan American Union but simply recommended to the Governing Board of the Union that it take certain measures that would better enable the organization to perform the new functions assigned to it by certain resolutions of the conference. Neither did the Eighth Conference adopt treaties or conventions, but only resolutions. Among these was the Declaration of the Principles of the Solidarity of America, known as the "Declaration of Lima", one of the most important statements in the history of inter-American relations.

At the time of the Eighth Conference in Lima, world confusion and instability had increased to the extent that an international conflict seemed inevitable. Taking that situation into account, the representatives of the American states met in the capital of Peru, determined to maintain the peace and solidarity of the hemisphere and, with this purpose in view, they adopted the Declaration of Lima. In this Declaration, the governments of the American states reaffirmed their continental solidarity and their purpose to collaborate in the maintenance of the principles upon which that solidarity was based, as well as their decision to maintain and defend these principles against all foreign intervention or activity that might threaten them. Moreover, in case the peace, security, or territorial integrity of any American republic was threatened by acts of any nature that might impair them, the governments proclaimed their common concern and their determination to make effective their solidarity, coordinating their respective sovereign wills by means of the procedure of consultation. The Declaration also established that the consultations provided for in inter-American peace instruments would be effected by meetings of the ministers of foreign affairs of the American republics, to be held in the various capitals of these countries in rotation and without protocolary character.

In addition to the Declaration of Lima, the following resolutions of the Eighth Conference should be mentioned: Declaration of American Principles; uniformity of commercial and civil law; perfection and coordination of inter-American peace instruments; defense of human rights; methods for the codification of international law; nonrecognition of the acquisition of territory by force; methods of preparing multilateral treaties, with respect to the matter of reservations; conservation of natural and historic sites; nature protection and wild life preservation; universal protection of intellectual property; relations with other international organizations; commercial arbitration; regulations governing labor contracts; the Pan American highway; and tourist travel.

The First Three Meetings of Consultation (1939, 1940 and 1942)

Less than a year after the Declaration of Lima was signed, the Second World War broke out in Europe. In view of this, the governments of the American states agreed to put into effect the procedures established in Buenos Aires and Lima, and on September 23, 1939, the First Meeting of Consultation of Ministers of Foreign Affairs opened in Panama. During the war, two other Meetings were held: the second in Havana, in 1940, and the third in Rio de Janeiro, in 1942. Because of the circumstances that surrounded their convocation, the first three Meetings of Consultation were devoted primarily to the juridical-political and military problems brought on by the war that were of immediate concern to the American republics. Some of these problems, such as that of subversive activities conducted by Axis agents, were the object of continual study throughout the three meetings. To counteract these subversive activities, a number of resolutions were passed, which together represented a system to safeguard the hemisphere against subversion. This is generally known as the system for the "political defense of the hemisphere". Moreover, each meeting concerned itself with those specific questions that had to be resolved at the time it was in session.

Thus, for example, the First Meeting gave particular attention to questions of neutrality, beginning with the "General Declaration of Neutrality of the American Republics", set forth in one of its resolutions. Perhaps one of the most important resolutions adopted in this respect, however, was the "Declaration of Panama", which, as a "measure of continental self-protection", set aside a broad area of waters on both sides of the hemisphere that the American republics, "as of inherent right," reserved "free from the commission of any hostile act by any non-American belligerent nation. . . ." The Second Meeting on the other hand, concerned itself mainly with strengthening the principle of hemispheric solidarity against acts of aggression and that of reciprocal assistance and cooperation for defense. Also of concern was improvement of the procedure of consultation. Another important resolution was the "Act of Habana Concerning the Provisional Administration of European Colonies and Possessions in the Americas", which declared that when islands or regions in the Americas then under the possession of non-American nations were in danger of becoming the subject of barter of territory or change of sovereignty, the American nations, taking into account the imperative need of hemisphere security and the desires of the inhabitants of the said islands or regions, could set up a regime of provisional administration for those islands or regions. The Third Meeting, moreover, recommended that the American republics sever diplomatic relations with Japan, Germany, and Italy. Through a second resolution on the same subject, the Meeting recommended the immediate adoption of measures necessary to halt all commercial and financial relations with the nations that signed the Tripartite Pact and the territories dominated by them.

Inter-American Conference on Problems of War and Peace (Mexico 1945)

In 1945, when the end of the war seemed in sight, the American states agreed to meet in Mexico City for an Inter-American Conference on Problems of War and Peace. The meeting was held from February 21 to March 8, with three fundamental aims in view: to study methods to hasten victory; to consider the coordination of the regional system with the future world organization; and to strengthen the inter-American system and the economic solidarity of the hemisphere.

With reference to the strengthening of the inter-American system, it was agreed that the activities of the regional organization should be reoriented to meet the requirements of the period. In view of the new ideas and theories regarding international organization, which were set forth in the Dumbarton Oaks Proposals and which later were given concrete form at the San Francisco Conference, and because of the serious economic problems and disturbances caused by the war, it was proposed to consolidate formally and permanently the 55 years of American regional juridical tradition. In keeping with this, certain transitory decisions were adopted, which appear in Resolution IX, entitled "Reorganization, Consolidation, and Strengthening of the Inter-American System".

Besides the aforementioned resolution, which referred exclusively to reorganization of the inter-American system, the conference in Mexico adopted Resolution VIII on "Reciprocal Assistance and American Solidarity", known as the "Act of Chapultepec". This resolution was to be in effect only during the state of war and until its provisions were included in a treaty that would give them permanent force, consistent with the United Nations Charter when this was established.

In addition to Resolutions VIII and IX which were the basis for the adoption in 1947 and 1948 of the two most important conventional instruments governing the inter-American system, the Mexico City Conference adopted many others, among which were the Declaration of Mexico, which reaffirms certain principles governing the relations between the states composing the American community; the Economic Charter of the Americas; other resolutions of an economic nature; one on the inter-American peace system; on international protection of the essential rights of man; and on general international organization. In this last resolution, the Secretary General of the conference was asked to transmit to the states that formulated the Dumbarton Oaks Proposals, to the other nations invited to the conference in San Francisco, and to the conference itself, the report and appended documents containing the views, comments, and suggestions that, in the judgment of the American republics presenting them, should be taken into consideration in drafting the definitive text of the Charter of the new international organization.

The United Nations Conference on International Organization opened in San Francisco on April 25, 1945, and closed on June 26, with the signing of the Charter of the United Nations and of the Statute of the new International Court of Justice. This conference was of special importance to the American republics, because on its decisions would largely depend whether the inter-American system for peace and security, developed by those countries over a period of 55 years, would be able to preserve its freedom of action, so essential to its effective functioning. The American republics were particularly concerned by the fact that within the world structure for the maintenance of peace the privilege of the veto was established for the so-called "great powers", which, they felt, might retard or even completely paralyze regional action.

When the text of the United Nations Charter was discussed at San Francisco, the member states of the American regional organization gave their support to the new international organization; but at the same time they insisted upon maintaining the free operation of their own system of peace and security. The problem raised by the position taken by that group of states was satisfactorily resolved after several weeks of intensive discussion, with the adoption of the provisions for "Regional Arrangements" (Chapter VIII) and particularly with the general acceptance of the formula that was incorporated into Article 51, which recognizes the inherent right of individual and collective self-defense. Acceptance was thereby given to the legitimacy of regional action with respect to the pacific settlement of disputes as well as with respect to collective security and, therefore, to the compatibility of such action with the principles and procedures governing both matters in the United Nations Charter.

The Inter-American Conference for the Maintenance of Continental Peace and Security (Rio de Janeiro 1947)

The results of the San Francisco conference considerably facilitated conclusion of the treaty called for in the Act of Chapultepec. After careful preparation on the part of the former Governing Board of the Pan American Union, the Inter-American Conference for the Maintenance of Continental Peace and Security met in Quitandinha, Brazil, from August 15 to September 2, 1947. Signing of the Inter-American Treaty of Reciprocal Assistance took place in Rio de Janeiro on the day that the conference closed. The Rio Treaty is still the basic instrument of collective security of the inter-American system, but it is not the only source of principles and rules governing the matter. The pertinent provisions of the Charter of the Organization of American States, signed the following year, introduced no substantial change in the system. On the other hand, the frequency with which the Rio Treaty has been applied has served to develop and strengthen the system of collective security. This is particularly true with reference to acts of aggression and to cases and circumstances that justify the exercise of individual and collective self-defense. For the present, it is enough to add that this development and strengthening has been made possible because of the sound juridical-political tradition on which rests the principle of inter-American solidarity in the face of extracontinental aggression, and because of the intrinsic flexibility that characterizes both the Rio Treaty and the Charter of the OAS.

The Conference on Reorganization of the Inter-American System (Bogotá 1948)

The following year, 1948, the Ninth International Conference of American States was held in Bogotá from March 30 to May 2, considered to be the most important event in the history of inter-American relations. Just as the conference at Quitandinha carried out Resolution VIII of the Mexico City Conference, that embodied the Act of Chapultepec, so did the Bogotá Conference comply with Resolution IX, referring to the reorganization, consolidation, and strengthening of the inter-American system.

The Bogotá Conference marked the end of one era and the beginning of another. The long period of 58 years of trial and practice in the development of inter-American cooperation and solidarity, begun in Washington in 1889-1890 with the First International Conference of American States, culminated in the results achieved at the Ninth Conference in 1948. That conference has been aptly described as a "constituent assembly", since it was there that the inter-American community was provided with the institutional framework it had lacked up to that time.

The principal instrument adopted at the Bogotá Conference was the Charter of the Organization of American States, which was prepared on the basis of a draft "Organic Pact", submitted by the Governing Board of the Pan American Union. In discussing the best way to give permanent effectiveness to the spirit and the letter of Resolution IX of Mexico, the authors of the Charter decided that the provisions relating to the structure and functions of the new organization should be preceded by a declaration of the postulates and basic principles that had thus far governed the inter-American system. Outstanding in this declaratory part of the Charter is Chapter III which defines the "fundamental rights and duties of States" with a scope and precision unparalleled in any other conventional instrument.

The Charter entered into force on December 13, 1951, when the Government of Colombia deposited the fourteenth instrument of ratification at the Pan American Union. Even before it entered into force, the Charter was applied provisionally, with respect to the organic structure and nomenclature of the Organization, by virtue of Resolution XL adopted at the Bogotá Conference.

In addition to the Charter, the following treaties and conventions were concluded at the Bogotá Conference: the American Treaty on Pacific Settlement (Pact of Bogotá), which codifies the various procedures for peaceful settlement that appeared in earlier treaties; the Economic Agreement of Bogotá, which establishes the essential principles that should orient the economic and social policy of the American states; the Inter-American Convention on the Granting of Political Rights to Women, which establishes that the right to vote and to be elected to national office should not be denied or abridged by reason of sex; and the Inter-American Convention on the Granting of Civil Rights to Women, by which the American states agreed to grant women the same civil rights that men enjoy.

In addition to these treaties and conventions, the Bogotá Conference adopted 46 resolutions, among which the following should be mentioned: the American Declaration of the Rights and Duties of Man; the Inter-American Charter of Social Guarantees; the Organic Statute of the Inter-American Commission of Women; the preservation and defense of democracy in America; colonies and occupied territories in America; and exercise of the right of legation.

Later Activities and Developments

As it has been possible to observe, it was during the three-year period between 1945 and 1948 that the inter-American system completely altered its traditional character. The bold and profound changes experienced by the system did not prevent it from continuing to evolve and become stronger as required for the full accomplishment of its new objectives. It has already been indicated that, with reference to collective security, this evolution and increasing strength of the system was truly significant. The same is now occurring in the field of economic and social cooperation. In both spheres of action, the causes and effects of this new evolutionary process coincide in substance. With reference to the first, political events and the great economic and social changes of these last few years have meant that the activities of the system have expanded to a degree that was not anticipated at the conferences of Mexico, Quitandinha, and Bogotá. With reference to the second, the performance of these activities has again made it necessary to adapt the institutional framework, in order to give the inter-American organs broader and more adequate powers. As is true in the field of collective security, the intrinsic flexibility of the instruments has made it possible to considerably develop and strengthen the mechanism of economic and social cooperation.

There is no point in pausing in the course of this *Introduction* to outline, however briefly, the activities of the system from 1948 to the present time, nor would it be fitting to explain the new structural and functional changes it has undergone during the course of recent years. For the present it is enough, perhaps, to point out that since the Third Meeting of Consultation of Ministers of Foreign Affairs (1942) seven others have been held—four according to the Charter of the OAS and three in application of the Rio Treaty— in addition to the ten occasions on which the Council of the Organization, likewise in application of this instrument, has acted provisionally as Organ of Consultation. Since the Bogotá Conference (1948) only the Tenth Inter-American Conference (Caracas 1954) and the First Special Inter-American Conference have been held, the latter for the purpose of establishing a procedure for the admission of new states into the OAS (Washington 1964). In conformity with its new structure and functions, the Inter-American Economic and Social Council (IA-ECOSOC) has now held its first three Annual Meetings at the Expert and Ministerial Levels (Mexico City 1962, Sao Paulo 1963, and Lima 1964), in addition to the special meeting held at Punta del Este, Uruguay, in 1961, to formally establish the Alliance for Progress. With a view to strengthening inter-American cooperation in this field, the Inter-American Development Bank (IDB) was set up in 1959, while in 1963 the Inter-American Committee on the Alliance for Progress (CIAP) was created as a special and permanent committee of the IA-ECOSOC. Finally, reference should be made to the specialized conferences that have been held in order to take up specific technical matters; the new activities of the inter-American specialized organizations; and the creation of new organs and entities, such as the Inter-American Nuclear Energy Commission, the Special Consultative Committee on Security, and the Inter-American Commission on Human Rights.

The Conference to Strengthen the System (Rio de Janeiro 1965)

At the initiative of some of the governments, the Council of the OAS, at the end of 1964, convoked the Second Special Inter-American Conference to consider, according to the text of the convocation, "various matters of fundamental importance in strengthening the inter-American system." Undeniably, the fact that a special meeting of the supreme organ of the OAS has been convoked for this purpose contradicts the emphasis this study places on the development and strengthening already undergone by the system. It is true that the specific objective assigned to the conference, together with the highly dramatic manner in which some political leaders and members of the press have treated its convocation, may well have given the general public an erroneous impression of the facts.

In the introduction to the report, prepared with a view to the conference to be held in November 1965, Dr. José A. Mora, Secretary General of the OAS, does not hide his concern in this respect and says: "I believe it would be a serious error for us to permit the public to form a false and negative image of the historic role which our regional system has played since the close of the last world war. The evolution and strengthening of the inter-American system in almost all its fields of activity have been so notable during the past five years that it would be difficult to find a parallel in any other international system or organization."[4] This does not imply that there is no room for improving or strengthening certain aspects of the system. In this connection, Dr. Mora observes: "It would, however, be unwise to create the wrong impression that our regional organization does not need structural or other changes. On the contrary, I think that this institution, like any other, can be strengthened even more to enable it to carry out its essential objectives. On the grounds of both conviction and duty I felt called last October to lay before the Council of the Organization and the peoples and governments represented therein a nine-point program, which I thought might serve to solve the problems confronting the inter-American system."

Along the same line, note should also be taken of the factor that actually determines the development and strengthening of an international organization. Here, it is fitting to quote the famous passage of the address given by former President Alberto Lleras Camargo of Colombia when he announced at the Tenth Inter-American Conference (1954) that he was resigning as Secretary General of the OAS:[5]

> As is true of any other international organization, the Organization in itself is neither good nor bad. It is what the member governments want it to be and nothing else. From a certain standpoint, the governments are the Organization; especially is this true in an organization such as ours, where, in its deliberative bodies, all the governments have an equal vote.
>
> The weaknesses of the Organization, if it has them, are weaknesses of the governments; weakness in their capacity to act in coordination and jointly with each other. The strength of the Organization, when it is evident, lies precisely in the action of the governments. If the Organization had structural defects that put it at the mercy of a minority of states or of a single state, the governments would still be justified in studying them and dealing with them as a matter apart, the character of which is no reflection on that of the member states. But, in our case, for good or for ill, the Organization is only a form of our conduct as states, and it if fares badly, we have no one to blame; neither can we right the wrongs by establishing new machinery, or by extravagantly expanding or stingily diminishing what we already have.

Thus the extraordinary development and strengthening experienced by the inter-American system during these recent years have been possible, primarily, because of the disposition of the governments to introduce the structural and other changes required by the

---

[4] *Report of the Secretary General of the Organization of American States to the Second Special Inter-American Conference*, Vol. 1, "Strengthening the Political, Juridical, and Institutional Aspects of the Inter-American System", OEA/Ser. E/XIII. 1 (Doc. 16) 14 April 1965.

[5] *Cf. Actas y Documentos de la Décima Conferencia Interamericana*, Vol. 1 (Conferences and Organizations Series No. 39 (Spanish)), p. 108.

inescapable demands of the regional community. In the same way, it will again become the exclusive responsibility of the governments to introduce into the system the changes that, in reality, are now required. The agenda of the Second Special Inter-American Conference is sufficiently broad to entertain the discussion of any question related to the institutional structure and to the functioning of the system, and to permit the taking of decisions at which the said governments are disposed to arrive.

Certain doubts must arise, however, in regard to the appropriateness of the vehicle chosen to improve and perfect the regional organization. To achieve such a purpose, the constructive willingness and aptitude of the member governments are not always enough. The profound reorganization applied to the inter-American system at the Bogotá Conference (1948) might not have been possible had it not been for the exceptional circumstances and requirements arising as a result of the ending of the war, as well as the careful and painstaking preparatory work that preceded that conference. In any case, what is sure is that the phenomenon has not been repeated. The new projections of the inter-American system and the great changes that have been introduced into its institutional structure since then, especially during the past five years, have not grown out of meetings convoked for the purpose, nor have they always resulted from meetings of the Inter-American Conference nor even from the Meetings of Consultation of Ministers of Foreign Affairs. They have been the result, as will be seen in the course of this study, of meetings of these and of other organs of lesser importance, whenever the need of reorienting the system and adapting it institutionally has arisen. These have been the occasions since Bogotá on which, in reality, the willingness and the readiness of the American governments to develop and strengthen their regional organization have been made clear.

PART ONE

Structure, Functions and General Activities

The inter-American system, in its present state of development, is a regional organization whose structure, functions and activities are highly complex. Part One has for its purpose, principally, the presentation of an overall panorama, which will facilitate the more detailed examination of the system in the two areas of its most intense activity: that of collective security and that of the economic and social development of Latin America.

Chapter I

Nature, Purposes, and Principles

As was stated in the *Introduction,* the objectives envisaged in the resolution on the "Reorganization, Consolidation and Strengthening of the Inter-American System", adopted at the Inter-American Conference on Problems of War and Peace held in Mexico City (1945), were achieved at the Ninth International Conference of American States, which convened in Bogotá three years later. The Conference drew up the Charter of the Organization of American States (OAS),[1] completing the work that had been done in the interim by the body then known as the Governing Board of the Pan American Union. Part One of the Charter defines the nature and basic purposes of the new Organization and states the principles on which it is being established. Although a complete picture of these three aspects of Part One cannot be provided without a detailed study of the present structure, functions, and activities of the Organization, it might be helpful to point out at this time the most salient features of Part One, which is the section that contains the dogma of the Bogotá Charter.

According to Article 1, "The American States establish by this Charter the international organization that they have developed to achieve an order of peace and justice, to promote their solidarity, to strengthen their collaboration and to defend their sovereignty, their territorial integrity, and their independence." It is evident that in this first provision of the Charter the Conference desired to establish the fact that, through it, the regional organization which had been developing in the past for the purpose of attaining objectives of common interest to the American States—that is to say, the inter-American system—was being inaugurated.

Is it mandatory, therefore, to identify with that system the Organization established by the Charter? After the aforesaid Conference was held, practically every inter-American institution was integrated into the new organization, in accordance with the decisions of the Mexico City Conference. The present situation, however, is not precisely the same. The OAS is no longer identifiable to the same degree with the inter-American system. Although it is continuing to absorb almost all inter-American relations, some of the latter fall, either

---

[1] The complete text of the OAS Charter appears in *Appendix 1,* p. 331, *infra.*

1

entirely or in part, within the sphere of activity of other agencies. The most outstanding example is the Inter-American Development Bank (IDB), but it is not the only one. There are other examples, not of "inter-American" agencies, but of Latin-American relations and machinery—such as those established for economic integration— that are so closely connected with the OAS programs and machinery that they cannot be considered as being outside of the inter-American institutional framework. Subject to corroboration in the course of this study, the idea that is being expressed is that after the Bogotá Conference, the inter-American system continued to develop, and that some of its relations and institutions transcend the structures and functions established at that time. Moreover, in the present stage of its development, the system is a complex of functions, mechanisms, and activities that are not strictly confined to the OAS and other inter-American and Latin American organizations. This phenomenon can be appreciated especially when considering the participation of extracontinental organizations and governments in the field of inter-American economic and social cooperation.[2]

As to the nature of the inter-American system, there is another aspect that it would be advisable to clarify. Article 1 of the Charter itself states that: "Within the United Nations, the Organization of American States is a regional agency." Article 4 speaks, within this same range of ideas, of the "regional obligations [of the OAS] under the Charter of the United Nations." The latter, however, only envisages the type of juridical connection or relation that appears to derive from the above-cited provisions of the Charter of the OAS in relation to the "specialized agencies", provided for in Article 57 of the U.N. Charter (which "shall be brought into relationship with the United Nations in accordance with the provisions of Article 63"), or in connection with the "regional arrangements or agencies for dealing with such matters relating to the maintenance of international peace and security as are appropriate for regional action," as provided in Chapter VIII of the Charter of the United Nations. Therefore, the provisions of Articles 1 and 4 of the Charter of Bogotá only have legal effect with respect to the functions and activities of the OAS in the field of regional peace and security.[3]

Of equal validity is the provision of Article 102, setting forth the primacy of the "rights and obligations of the Member States under the Charter of the United Nations." Since all the member states are likewise members of the world organization, Article 103 of the Charter of the United Nations is applicable. It states: "In the event of a conflict between the obligations of the Members of the United Nations

---

[2] In this regard see, particularly, Chapter II, 5 and p. 233, *infra*.
[3] On this particular see Chapter X, 35, *infra*.

under the present Charter and their obligations under any other international agreement, their obligations under the present Charter shall prevail." Naturally, this does not hinder the regional instruments from being interpreted and applied in ways that diverge, to a certain extent, from the letter and even the spirit of that Charter. Provided that the interpretations and applications are entirely justified by circumstances and by the collective needs of the states that are parties to the regional instrument, it would be inappropriate to invoke the primacy of the general instrument. To insist upon the contrary would mean that the natural development and strengthening process of regional communities would be paralyzed at precisely the historic moment at which these communities were fulfilling an exceptionally important mission in all phases of international life. In the specific case of the inter-American system, it would, moreover, mean that one of the most patent and characteristic realities of the development and strengthening process that has been achieved in recent years is not being recognized.

In Articles 2 and 3, the Charter of Bogotá provides for the entry of new member states into the OAS. The latter provides for the case of "any new political entity that arises from the union of several Member States," and the inclusion of this article in the Charter was the result, for the most part, of recognition of the possibility that the Central American States might establish themselves as a single political entity. The entry of the latter would cause the loss of individual membership status for each of the states that became a member of that entity. However, Article 2 merely states that: "All Member States that ratify the present Charter are Members of the Organization." The possibility that Canada and some of the former European colonies in the Americas might express their willingness to become members of the OAS, made it apparent that it was advisable to establish a procedure to that end. After prolonged preparatory study of the matter in the Council of the OAS,[4] the First Special Inter-American Conference was held in Washington in December 1964 for this specific purpose.

The "Act of Washington", which was signed at that Conference, establishes the procedure that is to be followed when a state desires to become a member of the OAS.[5] This instrument does not, however, limit itself merely to pointing out the procedural conditions and actions required for new members to enter the OAS. It also establishes the basic conditions that must be met. As to these conditions, they require that a new member seeking entry, in addition to being

---

[4] See the collection of documents of the Committee on Juridical-Political Affairs of the Council, OEA/Ser. G/VI, C/INF-352, 31 October 1963.

[5] See the complete text of the Act in *Appendix 3*, p. 351, *infra*.

"an independent American State," must formally state that it is willing to sign and ratify the Charter of the OAS and to fulfill all the obligations arising from its condition as member of the Organization, particularly the obligations of collective security, expressly mentioned in Articles 24 and 25 of the Charter. The preamble of the Act states, in this respect, that: "In accordance with those articles, the American states shall apply the measures and procedures established in the Inter-American Treaty of Reciprocal Assistance, for the purpose of fulfilling all the obligations arising from their condition as members of the Organization." It is evident, therefore, that although no more than the signing and ratification of the Charter is expressly required, the entry of a state into the Organization presupposes that the state will assume obligations that would not have to be fulfilled if that state were not a party to the instrument establishing the measures and procedures that are to be applied in matters of collective security. A third basic, or substantive, condition is that the Council of the OAS will abstain from making a decision on a request for admission when the applicant is a political entity whose territory, prior to the date on which the Act was signed, was subject in whole or in part to litigation or to a claim involving an extracontinental country and any or several member states of the OAS, until that controversy has been resolved by peaceful settlement.[6]

The "essential purposes" of the OAS are enumerated in Article 4 of the Charter. Those dealing with peace and security are set forth in paragraphs *a, b,* and *c.* According to paragraph *b,* the OAS proposes "to prevent possible causes of difficulties and to ensure the pacific settlement of disputes that may arise among the Member States," and according to paragraph *c*: "To provide for common action on the part of those States in the event of aggression." Article 5 *g* and Chapter IV set forth the principles and procedures established by the Charter for the fulfillment of the first of these purposes. As regards this matter, there is reiteration of the obligation to submit all international controversies to measures of peaceful settlement, including provision for a "special treaty" that will establish adequate procedures for the pacific settlement of disputes, "so that no dispute between American States shall fail of definitive settlement within a reasonable period" (Art. 23).[7] Article 5 *e* and *f,* and Chapter V, in turn, set forth the principles and procedures that the Charter establishes in the field of collective security. To this end, it states that: "Every act of aggression . . . against . . . an American State shall be considered an act of aggression against the other American States," and it sets forth the

---

[6] For the documents of the Conference see OEA/Ser. E/XII. 1.

[7] The "special treaty" referred to in Article 23 is the American Treaty on Pacific Settlement (Pact of Bogotá), signed at the Bogotá Conference. See Chapter V, 13, *infra.*

events or situations in which "the American States, in furtherance of the principles of continental solidarity or collective self-defense, shall apply the measures and procedures established in the special treaties on the subject" (Art. 25).[8]

Another of the purposes stated in Article 4 is: "To promote, by cooperative action, their economic, social and cultural development." The Charter also has various provisions dealing with this purpose of the OAS. Thus, in Chapter VI ("Economic Standards") it is stipulated that it is the duty of the member states to cooperate with one another. This is "in order to strengthen their economic structure, develop their agriculture and mining, promote their industry and increase their trade" (Art. 26). It is likewise interesting to point out that this Chapter also provides for consultation as a means of seeking the most suitable solution to problems that are brought up by a state whose economy "is affected by serious conditions that cannot be satisfactorily remedied by its own unaided effort" (Art. 27). Chapter VII deals with "Social Standards", and in it the statement is again made that it is the duty of the member states "to cooperate with one another to achieve just and decent living conditions for their entire populations" (Art. 28), and it is likewise agreed that it is desirable to develop their social legislation on certain specific bases (Art. 29). Chapter VIII deals with "Cultural Standards", and one of its articles provides that the member states agree to promote "the exercise of the right to education," on the specific bases set forth (Art. 30). In another article the member states agree "to facilitate free cultural interchange by every medium of expression" (Art. 31).

The fourth purpose set forth in Article 4 is "to seek the solution of political, juridical and economic problems that may arise among them" [the American states]. The terms in which this paragraph's concept are stated are so broad that they show that it was intended that no problem arising between the member states, regardless of its nature or the circumstances causing it, should be excluded from the OAS sphere of activity. The expression "among them" indicates, of course, that the problems envisaged are to be of an international nature. Many of those included fall within one or the other of the two aforesaid purposes. However, in practice, the action of the OAS has not always been limited to strictly international problems, inasmuch as it has also endeavored to settle some that were essentially of a domestic nature. Moreover, as an illustration of the economic and social problems expressly referred to in Chapter VI, mention should be made of those that are related to human rights and representative

---

[8] Strictly speaking, the only existing "special" treaty is the Inter-American Treaty of Reciprocal Assistance, signed at the conference held in Rio de Janeiro the previous year. See Chapter VI, 18, *infra.*, in particular.

democracy. In contrast to the Charter of the United Nations, one of whose purposes is to achieve international cooperation "in promoting and encouraging respect for human rights and for fundamental freedoms," the Charter of Bogotá does not specifically confer this function on the OAS. Nevertheless, the OAS has been performing duties of this nature with ever increasing efficiency, by authority of other provisions of the Charter itself, as will be duly shown.[9]

In contrast with the United Nations Charter, which says nothing on this matter, the OAS Charter establishes many important principles of international law. The difference can be attributed, in part, to the fact that the countries represented at the San Francisco Conference were advocates of various different political systems and partly to the strong political tradition that the American republics already possessed when they met at the Bogotá Conference. It was this same factor (of differences in political systems) that hindered the General Assembly of the United Nations from adopting, even in the form of a resolution, the draft declaration on the rights and duties of states that had been prepared by the International Law Commission. Moreover, one of the most outstanding features of the inter-American system has been precisely the fact that it has always rested upon the bases of an aggregate of postulates and principles. These have been constantly enunciated and reaffirmed in conference after conference. This fact is of such significance that it was explicitly mentioned by the Mexico City Inter-American Conference (1945), which stated: "The American states have been incorporating in their international law, since 1890, by means of conventions, resolutions, and declarations, the following principles. . . ."[10] This process culminated in the Charter of the OAS, the provisions of which collected, developed, and established the postulates and principles that have served as the basis of the inter-American system.

It should not appear strange, therefore, that in the Bogotá Charter the principles are set forth in terms that are much more explicit and precise than those of the San Francisco Charter. The principle dealing with the juridical equality of the states is a good example. While the U.N. Charter limits itself to stating that: "The Organization is based on the principle of the sovereign equality of all its Members," the OAS Charter defines this principle as fully as possible: "States are juridically equal, enjoy equal rights and equal capacity to exercise these rights, and have equal duties. The rights of each State depend, not upon its power to ensure the exercise thereof, but upon the mere fact of its existence as a person under international law" (Art. 6).

---

[9] See Chapter IV, *infra.*

[10] See the complete text of Resolution VIII, Reciprocal Assistance and American Solidarity, in *International Conferences,* 2nd Sup. (1942-1954), p. 66.

It should be noted, moreover, in this particular, that this formulation of the principle of equality is faithfully reflected in the structure of the regional organization, as well as in the regulatory provisions of its organs. It is also reflected, in ever more obvious ways, in the process of negotiating and adopting the great political decisions that are reached through these organs. In spite of the enormous imbalance of power among the member states of the OAS, it is undeniable that the actual observance of the principle of juridical equality has gradually increased, to a degree unsuspected by those who are not serious students of the inter-American system.

The principle of nonintervention, as expressed in the Charter of the OAS, is another example of the breadth and precision with which its provisions were conceived. Thus, Article 15 states that: "No State or group of States has the right to intervene, directly or indirectly, for any reason whatever, in the internal or external affairs of any other State. The foregoing principle prohibits not only armed force but also any other form of interference or attempted threat against the personality of the State or against its political, economic and cultural elements." The next Article forbids one of the most typical methods of intervention—so-called "economic aggression": "No State may use or encourage the use of coercive measures of an economic or political character in order to force the sovereign will of another State and obtain from it advantages of any kind." Powerful historic reasons, which need not be recalled at this time, were responsible for the decision to state this principle so explicitly and categorically in the Charter together with that on juridical equality. Unilateral intervention, which is what both articles envisage, was definitively proscribed, no matter what form it might assume. Nevertheless, this has not hindered the development and strengthening of the inter-American system in fields that have been historically considered as within the jurisdiction or domain reserved for the state. On the basis of other provisions of the Charter, the OAS has been able, legitimately, to carry out any action it has been required to take for the purpose of effectively achieving its established purposes. It has been possible, in this sense, to reconcile the old and just aspiration that established the principle of nonintervention with the new and equally justifiable principle of collective action.

The foregoing should suffice to show the juridical-political orientation of the principles on which the OAS was established. For the most part, they are formulated in terms of "the fundamental rights and duties of States" (Chapter III) which greatly ensures the observance and fulfillment of these fundamental rights and duties. As a final example, the provision dealing with human rights serves as a good illustration. The fact that the Charter does not limit itself—as it did in Article 5, *j*—to "proclaiming" these rights but, in another provision, concretely imposes upon the member states the duty to respect them—as is done in Article 13— is, clearly, the principle that has given viability to the system of collective action that the OAS is continuing to follow for the purpose of promoting respect for these rights and protecting them when a state fails to fulfill this basic duty that the Charter has imposed upon it. There will be occasion in the course of this study to examine this and other principles established by the Charter.

Chapter II

Structure and Competence of the Organs

In accordance with Article 32 of the Charter of the OAS, the Organization "accomplishes its purposes by means of: a) The Inter-American Conference; b) The Meeting of Consultation of Ministers of Foreign Affairs; c) The Council; d) The Pan American Union; e) The Specialized Conferences; and f) The Specialized Organizations."[1] In subsequent chapters, the Charter defines the structure, functions, and powers of each of these organs. In view of the nature and scope of the transformation that has taken place in the structure and competence of several of these organs, it would be advisable to begin by pointing out, along general lines at least, the nature of these changes. This is basic, as will soon be seen, since it is here that the principles that have led to the development and strengthening of the inter-American system can be found.

1. *The Inter-American Conference and the Meeting of Consultation*

Under the system of the Charter, the Inter-American Conference is the "supreme organ of the Organization of American States." As such, "It decides the general action and policy of the Organization and determines the structure and functions of its Organs, and has the authority to consider any matter relating to friendly relations among the American States. These functions shall be carried out in accordance with the provisions of this Charter and of other inter-American treaties" (Art. 33). Although, strictly speaking, there is only one Inter-American Conference, this organ has a dual character. It consists of the regular Conference (which, by virtue of Article 35, should meet every five years) and the special Conference, which may be held "in special circumstances and with the approval of two thirds of the American Governments." The Inter-American Conference, provided for in Article 111, which may be convened for the purpose of adopting amendments to the Charter has the character of the latter [special].

When the inter-American system was reorganized at Bogotá (1948), the Inter-American Conference was the organ that replaced

---

[1] See the organizational chart of the OAS in *Appendix 2*, p. 349, *infra.*

the International Conferences of American States, which had been held periodically from the time of the First Conference that convened in Washington, D.C. (1889-1890). The long periods elapsing between the meetings of this organ were incompatible with the dynamic developments of recent years. The Conference therefore gradually lost the position of special importance it had formerly held. Matters that were historically the responsibility of the Conference are now, for this reason, being considered by other organs of lower rank. Of even greater significance is the fact that these organs have been exercising the authority that is expressly reserved for the Conference by Article 33, namely, the power to decide the general action and policy of the Organization and to determine the structure and function of its organs. As to this, it should be noted that the anachronism of the Inter-American Conference has not in all cases been the result of the lapse of time between its meetings, nor of the fact that there has been no meeting since the Tenth Conference (1954), since the Eleventh has not yet been held. It is also the result of the fact that the matters of peace and security, and also, recently, of inter-American cooperation in the economic and social fields, have required consideration and action by organs that the governments have regarded as more capable of achieving the desired goals.

Because of its highly political level of membership the Meeting of Consultation of Ministers of Foreign Affairs has, naturally, been assuming the functions and powers of the Inter-American Conference in the field of peace and security. Actually, the establishment and perfecting of the consultation machinery since the Buenos Aires Conference (1936) show how, since then, it has become advisable to have a more suitable organ and more appropriate procedures for the solution of the problems that arise in this field. Nevertheless, when the Charter was drafted, the Meeting of Consultation was envisaged only "in order to consider problems of an urgent nature and of common interest to the American States, and to serve as the Organ of Consultation" (Art. 39). When the Meeting acts for this second purpose, it is invested with the functions and powers provided in the Inter-American Treaty of Reciprocal Assistance, some of which include powers beyond the scope of those conferred upon the Inter-American Conference. However, when the Meeting is acting for the first purpose mentioned in Article 39, it does not have explicit or concrete authority to carry out the duties assigned to it. Therefore, in spite of the highly specialized sphere of activity within which the Organ of Consultation may exercise its functions and powers, on the one hand, and the lack of explicit or concrete authority by the Meeting of Consultation convoked to consider problems of an urgent nature and of common interest, on the other hand, the Meeting has, in both cases, exercised powers in the nature of those that the Charter assigns to the Inter-American Conference as "the supreme organ".

It will become duly apparent that the Meeting, acting as Organ of Consultation, has introduced substantial changes in the collective security system envisaged by the Charter and the Treaty of Reciprocal Assistance. Some of these changes have consisted of the establishment of new organs and the extension of the powers of others. As to the latter, it should be pointed out that the Organ of Consultation has delegated to the Council of the OAS functions and powers that are reserved to it by authority of these two instruments. Also, while serving as Organ of Consultation, the Meeting of Consultation has made decisions involving the general action and policy of the Organization in matters of major importance. It is sufficient to mention, as an illustration, the measure excluding the government of a member state from participating in the inter-American system. When the Meeting has acted for the first of the purposes set forth in Article 39, it has not introduced structural changes or adopted resolutions of similar high importance dealing with the general activity and policy of the Organization. It has, however, created new organs and notably developed and strengthened the juridical-political order of the system, particularly in the field of peace and security and that of human rights and representative democracy.[2]

The so-called "informal meeting" of Ministers of Foreign Affairs developed on a parallel with these institutional changes. This new "organ" of the inter-American system has been closely linked to the idea that annual meetings of a high political level should be held to study the general situation of the regional community, including any matters of an extracontinental nature that affect the interests of the American countries. The possibility and advisability of holding meetings of this kind will be discussed at the Second Special Inter-American Conference. Although it would not be appropriate to anticipate what the nature and functions of these meetings would be, it will be useful to mention briefly the two of an informal nature that have been held in the past.

The first Informal Meeting of Ministers of Foreign Affairs met in Washington, D.C., on September 23 and 24, 1958, for the purpose of exchanging views on the world situation, studying the advisability of holding regular meetings of this kind, and considering how "Oper-

---

[2] Chapter XI, *infra,* contains a summary and evaluation of the changes made in the regional collective security system. With respect to the development and strengthening of the system in the field of human rights and representative democracy see, especially, Chapter IV, *infra.* Reference should also be made to the action of the Tenth Meeting of Consultation in the situation that arose in the Dominican Republic in April 1965. On the nature and scope of this action see Chapter IX, *infra.*

ation Pan America", as proposed by the Government of Brazil, might be carried forward. Immediately after the close of the Meeting, a special meeting of the Council of the Organization was held, with the participation of the Ministers of Foreign Affairs. This meeting resolved to study the advisability of holding informal meetings more often and of establishing a special committee to study new measures of economic cooperation. The following month, the Council appointed two Special Committees. The first was the one that drew up the proposed procedures to govern the holding of informal meetings. The second was the so-called "Committee of Twenty-one", which, at its final sessions, adopted the Act of Bogotá.[3]

The second Informal Meeting of Ministers of Foreign Affairs was held October 2 and 3, 1962, on the eve of the so-called "October crisis", for the purpose of studying the serious problems facing the Western Hemisphere at that time. Because of its informal nature, the Meeting did not take any decisions or pass any resolutions but limited itself to issuing a final communiqué to the press, recording the matters the Foreign Ministers had considered and their pertinent statements and observations. A few days later, the Council of the Organization took up the specific matters referred to in this communiqué and entrusted to several of its committees the study of certain of its parts. Several of these statements and observations played an important part in the meeting of the Organ of Consultation that was held three weeks later.[4]

2. *The Council and Its Organs*

There are two aspects to the matter of the institutional development and strengthening of the inter-American system in relation to the Council of the Organization and its organs (the Inter-American Economic and Social Council, the Inter-American Council of Jurists, and the Inter-American Cultural Council). On the one hand, organs of higher rank have conferred important powers upon it in the political field and in the field of collective security—fields in which previously it was authorized to intervene only to act provisionally as Organ of Consultation (Articles 52 of the Charter and 12 of the Inter-American Treaty of Reciprocal Assistance). On the other hand, in order to take care of the urgent matters of economic and social development in Latin America, the Council itself has introduced important structural changes that have, in turn, enabled one of its organs, in particular, and the Council itself, directly, to take decisions on the general action and policies of the Organization in that

---

[3] Concerning the work accomplished by this Committee of the OAS Council see p. 213, *infra*.

[4] See p. 162, *infra*.

field of inter-American cooperation. Although both phases of the matter will be duly discussed, it is advisable to make some general observations at this point.

As to the new powers conferred upon the Council of the OAS, it should be remembered that when the Charter of Bogotá was written it did not include any prohibition of the kind that appeared in the Convention and Resolution approved at the Havana Conference (1928) to the effect that what was then the Governing Board of the Pan American Union would have no functions of a political nature. It should be noted, moreover, that Article 50 of the Charter authorizes the Council to take cognizance "of any matter referred to it by the Inter-American Conference or the Meeting of Consultation of Ministers of Foreign Affairs." There was, therefore, no lack of a constitutional basis for conferring these powers. Along this same line of thought, it is likewise interesting to recall the efforts that were made at the Tenth Conference (1954) for the purpose of giving new powers to the Council and the resistance of the delegations that were still opposed to granting it political functions.[5] Although this opposition has not entirely disappeared, whatever remains no longer stands in the way of conferring functions of this kind on the Council, nor prevents it from performing some of the duties that the Charter has not expressly assigned to it.

As to the latter, the extraordinary development and strengthening of the machinery for inter-American cooperation in the economic and social field is the specific result of the initiative taken by the Council and, with its approval or consent, by one of its organs, the Inter-American Economic and Social Council (IA-ECOSOC). There was also a constitutional basis for this action—Article 64, b of the Charter —according to which the IA-ECOSOC is to act as coordinating agency for all official inter-American activities of an economic and social nature; and Article 27, which provides for consultation through this organ, for the purpose of seeking appropriate solutions when a state places its economic problems before IA-ECOSOC. As the result of a long process that will be reviewed in Part Three of this study, the Council instituted meetings of the IA-ECOSOC at the ministerial level, thus enabling it to become the vehicle through which the Alliance for Progress, one of the inter-American system's most important expressions of cooperative action and general policy, was established. In a certain sense, the establishment by the IA-ECOSOC itself of the Inter-American Committee on the Alliance for Progress

---

[5] The only result of these efforts was the approval of Resolution XLVI by the Conference, under which the Council was assigned the preparation, at the request of the governments, of draft agreements and other similar tasks. See the complete text of the resolution in *International Conferences*, 2nd Sup. (1942-1954), p. 324.

(CIAP), whose functions and powers conform to a new and essential reconstruction of the machinery provided in the Charter, was an even more daring step.[6]

3. The General Secretariat

According to Article 78 of the Charter, "The Pan American Union is the central and permanent Organ of the Organization of American States and the General Secretariat of the Organization. It shall perform the duties assigned to it in this Charter and such other duties as may be assigned to it in other inter-American treaties and agreements." As to the latter, the Pan American Union is also to: "Perform the functions entrusted to it by the Inter-American Conference, and the Meeting of Consultation of Ministers of Foreign Affairs" (Art. 83 f). By authority of these and other provisions of the Charter, this other organ of the OAS has also been developed and strengthened to a noteworthy degree since the time of the Bogotá Conference. In view of the role that the General Secretariat plays in the machinery and operation of a modern international organization, it is practically inevitable that there should be a certain parallel between its evolution and the development and strengthening of the political organs. This phenomenon has also occurred in the United Nations and other international organizations; it is a typical reflection, as well as an inevitable result, of the implicit or inherent powers of all international entities.

Therefore, the actual duties and powers exercised by the General Secretariat are not always to be found explicitly established in the Charter. Strictly speaking, this is also true of the General Secretariat of the United Nations. However, even when Article 99 of the San Francisco Charter is invoked—as has sometimes been done—according to which "The Secretary General may bring to the attention of the Security Council any matter which in his opinion may threaten the maintenance of international peace and security," actually, most of his initiatives and activities of the last decade have not involved the exercise of this power. In this sense, such initiatives and activities have transcended the functions and powers of a purely administrative and technical nature envisaged in the U.N. Charter. In any event, the Charter of the OAS does contain a provision that may be interpreted with a reasonable amount of latitude: "The Secretary General shall participate with voice, but without vote, in the deliberations of the Inter-American Conference, the Meeting of Consultation of Ministers of Foreign Affairs, the Specialized Conferences, and the Council and its organs" (Art. 81). It is clear that this provision does not explicitly or implicitly limit the matters in whose consideration

---

[6] Concerning this reshaping of the system see Chapter XIII, 40 and 41, *infra*.

the Secretary General may participate, nor the occasion or extent of his participation. Moreover, there is no other provision of the Charter limiting that power and responsibility of the General Secretariat of the OAS.[7]

The foregoing interpretation has been corroborated in actual practice. The documents prepared by the General Secretariat, at the request of the political organs or on its own initiative are, generally speaking, strictly technical in nature, but some have contained nuances, and at times even concrete opinions, that have been markedly political, without encountering any serious objections or reservations from the governments or their representatives in those organs.

As will be duly seen, the initiatives and activities referred to are in fields as sensitive as that of collective security against subversion of extracontinental origin. On various occasions the Secretary General has taken an active part in the work of reconstructing the inter-American machinery for economic and social cooperation.

The Secretary General also performed functions and tasks of a decidedly political nature on the occasion of the OAS action in the recent case of the Dominican Republic. With the intention of returning to this important institutional development of the central and permanent organ of the OAS in Chapter IX and of making a review and evaluation of the inter-American peace and security system in Chapter XI, for the moment it is enough to point out that among the functions and tasks entrusted to it by the Tenth Meeting of Consultation are those relating to the economic recovery and development of the country.

The Secretary General has been able to perform these and other important functions in the field of inter-American economic and social cooperation thanks, in part, to the wide area of his contractual authority. One year after the signing of the Charter, which, in Article 80, limits the role of the Secretary General to that of the "legal representative" of the Pan American Union, the Council of the OAS approved the Agreement on Privileges and Immunities of the Organization of American States which, in Article 9, provides that: "The Pan American Union, in exercising its functions as General Secretariat of the Organization of American States, shall have the capacity: a) to contract; b) to acquire and dispose of movable and immovable property; c) to institute legal proceedings."[8]

In 1960, the Council itself included a provision in the Regulations

---

[7] On this point see also the Regulations of the Pan American Union, OEA/Ser. D/I. 1, 5 September 1962.

[8] The complete text of the Agreement is in *Documents and Notes on Privileges and Immunities with Special Reference to the OAS*, Washington, D.C., Pan American Union, 1960.

of the Pan American Union by virtue of which: "The Secretary General may establish trust funds, reserve funds, and special funds, for the first two of which the approval of the Council shall be required. The purposes and limitations of these funds shall be defined in precise terms. Such funds shall be administered in separate accounts in accordance with these Regulations, except for special provisions that are established in specific cases" (Art. 85).[9]

By authority of this Article, the Secretary General signed various agreements with the United States Government for the purpose of carrying out the programs of the Alliance for Progress and, recently, pursuant to Article 6 of the Statutes of the Special Development Assistance Fund, he was authorized to receive the contributions from the member states and other sources. Moreover, in accordance with those Statutes, the Secretary General is responsible to the IA-ECOSOC for the administration of the Fund and the carrying out of its activities.[10]

4. The Specialized Conferences and Organizations

Article 93 of the Charter provides for the convening of Specialized Conferences "to deal with special technical matters or to develop specific aspects of inter-American cooperation, when it is so decided by the Inter-American Conference or the Meeting of Consultation of Ministers of Foreign Affairs; when inter-American agreements so provide; or when the Council of the Organization considers it necessary, either on its own initiative or at the request of one of its organs or of one of the Specialized Organizations." Pursuant to this provision, Specialized Conferences have been held on various matters such as agriculture, education, communications, ports, statistics, tourism, copyright, etc. One of these, held in the capital of the Dominican Republic, prepared the formula that was subsequently adopted by the International Law Commission and the First Conference on the Law of the Sea (Geneva 1958), for the purpose of defining the juridical nature of the continental shelf and submarine areas, which is included in Article 1 of the Convention dealing with this matter.

Meetings of this organ offer the advantage, particularly when they deal with juridical matters, of enabling all phases of a problem to be studied, so that practical and suitable solutions can be achieved. With this criterion in mind, the possibility of convoking another Specialized Conference on the agricultural and industrial use of the waters of international rivers and lakes is being considered. The convocation of this conference was first requested by the Brazilian Government and subsequently recommended by the Inter-American Council of Jurists.

---

[9] See OEA/Ser. D/I. 1 (1960).
[10] See the complete text of the Statutes in *Appendix 20*, p. 464, *infra*.

When the legal rules dealing with this matter are adopted, it will have to be kept in mind that the utilization of these waters is of great importance to the economic development of each country and also to the plans for regional development and integration.[11]

There were many official, semi-official, and private inter-American organizations in existence before the OAS Charter was signed. Because of this, the Bogotá Conference requested the Council of the OAS to study the situation and activities of these organizations in order to determine which among them met the requirements for becoming Specialized Organizations of the OAS, pursuant to the pertinent provisions of the Charter. In compliance with this request, the Council proceeded to make this study on a gradual basis, and, for the purpose, adopted certain standards based on Article 95 of the Charter.

These standards stipulate that to be considered a "specialized" organization, an agency should fulfill the following conditions: a) it should be intergovernmental, that is, an official entity made up of governments; b) it should be established by multilateral agreement, in other words, by agreement between governments; c) it should have a specific function; d) that function should be of a technical nature; e) its field of activities should be of common interest to the American states. After the Council of the Organization has determined that an international organization meets all these conditions, it signs an agreement with it for the purpose of determining the relations that should exist between the aforesaid organization and the OAS. At that time the organization is also placed on the register the Council maintains for this purpose.

After these two procedures have been carried out, the organization is recognized as specialized and operates within the framework of the following powers and obligations established by the Charter in Articles 53 and 95 to 101: a) it enjoys the fullest technical autonomy but it is to take into account the recommendations of the Council, in conformity with the provisions of the Charter; b) its relations with the Organization are determined by means of the aforesaid agreement with the Council; c) it submits periodic reports to the Council on the progress of its work and on its annual budget and expenses; d) it should establish cooperative relations with world agencies of the same character, in order to coordinate their activities; e) it should preserve its identity and status as an integral part of the Organization of American States, even when it performs regional functions of international agencies; and f) its geographic location should be determined after taking the interests of all the

---

[11] See Resolution I adopted by the Council of Jurists at its Fifth Meeting, San Salvador, January-February 1965, *Final Act*, OEA/Ser. C/IV. 5, CIJ-77.

American states into account. The Council has concluded agreements with the following organizations and has listed them in the Register of Specialized Inter-American Organizations on the basis of the aforesaid standards: the Pan American Health Organization; the Inter-American Children's Institute; the Inter-American Commission of Women; the Pan American Institute of Geography and History; the Inter-American Indian Institute; and the Inter-American Institute of Agricultural Sciences. A brief account of the history and work of each of these organizations will be given below.

The *Pan American Health Organization* (PAHO), was originally established by a resolution of the Second International American Conference held in Mexico City (1901-1902). It was later organized by the First Pan American Sanitary Conference of 1902 and reorganized at the Sixth in 1920, and in subsequent sanitary conferences. It is now governed by the Pan American Sanitary Code, signed at Havana in 1924, the Protocol to the Sanitary Code, signed at the same city in 1952, which amended the 1924 Code, and by a Constitution that was approved in 1961. On July 1, 1949, the PAHO signed an agreement with the World Health Organization (WHO) by virtue of which the Pan American Sanitary Conference, through the Directing Council of the PAHO, and the Pan American Sanitary Bureau, Secretariat of the PAHO, serve, respectively, as the Regional Committee and the Regional Office of the WHO in the Western Hemisphere, within the terms of the Constitution of the WHO. On May 23, 1950, the PAHO also signed an Agreement with the OAS, which recognized the PAHO as an Inter-American Specialized Organization and determined the relations between the two organizations.

According to the provisions of the PAHO Constitution, its basic purposes are the promotion and coordination of the efforts of the countries of the Western Hemisphere to fight disease, prolong life, and encourage the physical and mental improvement of their peoples. The PAHO achieves its purposes through the Pan American Sanitary Conference, which is the supreme authority, the Directing Council, which performs the functions the Conference delegates to it, acting in its name during the period between meetings, and which carries out the decisions and policies of the Conference; the Executive Committee, composed of seven member states, with administrative and advisory duties, and the Pan American Sanitary Bureau. The work of the PAHO covers a vast area, since it includes not only what it is performing as an Inter-American Specialized Organization but also its activities as the Regional Committee of the WHO in the Americas. Its headquarters is in Washington, D.C.[12]

---

[12] *Cf.* Basic Documents of the Pan American Health Organization, 5th ed., Doc. No. 47, Washington, D.C., 1963.

The *Inter-American Children's Institute* was established in 1927 under the name of the "American International Institute for the Protection of Childhood", by authority of the Fourth Child Congress, which was held in Santiago, Chile, in 1924. The present name was adopted in 1957 when its Statutes were revised. The original Agreement between the Institute and the Council of the OAS was signed in 1949 and amended in 1962 for the purpose of settling financial questions pertaining to the Institute and in order to bring it into closer relationship with other organs of the inter-American system. By means of the new Agreement, the Office of the Institute operates administratively as part of the General Secretariat of the OAS. Its activities and expenditures are, therefore, included in the program and budget of the Pan American Union. Its situation is similar to that of the Inter-American Commission of Women. As Specialized Organizations, both enjoy technical autonomy in carrying out their objectives but their secretariats are part of the General Secretariat of the OAS.

So that the 1957 Statutes of the Institute could be adapted to the provisions of the new 1962 Agreement, the Directing Council of the Institute prepared a new text, which it submitted to the Council of the OAS for consideration, and which was approved on June 18, 1963. According to these Statutes, the Institute has as its purpose to promote the study of the problems of maternity, childhood, adolescence, and the family in the American countries, and the adoption of measures conducive to their solution. The Institute achieves its goals by means of the Directing Council, which formulates its general policy and is responsible for the fulfillment of its responsibilities; the Pan American Child Congress, which meets every four years, and its Office. The Director of the Office and the other members of its staff are appointed by the Secretary General of the OAS. The Office provides technical and administrative services to the Congress and the Directing Council and carries out the work program of the Institute. Its headquarters is in Montevideo.[13]

The *Inter-American Commission of Women* was established by a resolution of the Sixth International Conference of American States (Havana 1928). The Bogotá Conference (1948) approved its Organic Statutes, which replaced the original resolution. The current Statutes were approved by the Tenth Conference (Caracas 1954). The purpose of the Commission is to work for the extension of civil, political, economic, and social rights to the women of the Americas; to study their problems and propose means of solving them. It carries out its purposes by means of its regular annual Assemblies and its

---

[13] *Cf.* Conferences and Organizations Series, No. 4, Washington, D.C., Pan American Union, and Doc. C-i-572 Rev.

special Assemblies, which formulate policy and establish the Commission's program of action; the Executive Committee, composed of the Chairman and the representatives of four countries elected for a two-year period, and the secretariat, which is part of the General Secretariat of the OAS. The Agreement between the Commission and the Council of the OAS was signed on June 16, 1953. The headquarters of the Commission is at the Pan American Union.[14]

The *Pan American Institute of Geography and History* was also established by authority of a resolution of the Havana Conference of 1928. The Fourth General Assembly of the Institute, held in Caracas in 1946, adopted new Statutes, based on the 1928 Resolution. In 1960, the Directing Council of the Institute, at its Fifth Meeting, prepared a draft amendment to the Organic Statutes of the Institute, for the purpose of adapting them to its new working conditions, and then decided to submit them to the Seventh General Assembly of the Institute, which was to meet in 1961, for approval. Prior to that time, however, the Statutes were submitted to the Council of the OAS, pursuant to Article V of the Agreement between the Institute and the Council, signed on January 12, 1949. The General Assembly, taking into account the observations of the aforesaid Council, approved the new Statutes on August 11, 1961.

The Institute's purpose is to promote, coordinate, and publicize studies on geography, cartography, history, and related sciences, and to promote cooperation between institutes operating in these fields. It achieves its purposes through the General Assembly, which is the supreme organ of the Institute; the Directing Council, which performs the duties of the Assembly in the period between its meetings, as regards administrative matters; the Commission on Cartography, Geography, and History, or any other Commissions the Assembly may establish, and the General Secretariat. The headquarters of the Institute is in Mexico City.[15]

The *Inter-American Institute of Agricultural Sciences* was established by a Convention that was opened for signature at the Pan American Union in 1944 and which went into effect that year. Its purposes are to encourage and promote the development of agricultural sciences in the member countries by means of research, teaching, and the dissemination of information on agricultural theory and practice and other related arts and sciences. It achieves its purposes through its Board of Directors, which is composed of the representatives of the member countries of the OAS on the Council of the Organization; through the Technical Advisory Council, whose mem-

---

[14] *Cf.* Conferences and Organizations Series, No. 35 (1954) and No. 25 (1953).

[15] *Cf. ibid.,* No. 3, 19.

bers are agricultural experts of the Contracting States; and through the General Secretariat.

A Protocol of Amendment to the Convention was opened for signature in 1958. Its purpose was to strengthen the agricultural activities of the OAS, primarily by changing the system of financial support for the maintenance of the Institute and also by changing the structure of the Board of Directors, so that its members would, preferably, be the General Directors, or officials of equal rank, of the Ministries of Agriculture. Because this Protocol never became effective, the Board of Directors approved a resolution on May 18, 1962, which temporarily changed the Institute's quota system by the adoption of the scale governing the financing of the Pan American Union, and which called for the convocation of an annual meeting of the Board of Directors, with the participation of high-ranking officials of the Ministries or Secretariats of Agriculture of the respective governments, or of special representatives appointed by those Ministries or Secretariats. The Institute has its headquarters in Turrialba, Costa Rica.[16]

The *Inter-American Indian Institute* was established by authority of the Convention approved at the First Inter-American Conference on Indian Life, held in Pátzcuaro, Mexico, in 1940. The establishment of the Institute had previously been recommended by the Eighth International Conference of American States (Lima 1938). Its purposes are to study the problems affecting the Indian groups of the respective member countries, which number 17 at the present time, and to establish cooperative bases for the solution of the problem of the Indian population of America. To this end, the Institute carries out a variety of projects and programs, holds meetings and conferences, and publishes a number of periodicals and special publications. The headquarters of the Institute is in Mexico City.[17]

5. *Other Inter-American Entities and Relations with International Organizations*

In addition to the Specialized Organizations that have just been mentioned, there are other inter-American entities that were established prior or subsequent to the Bogotá Conference (1948), including some established by the Organization of American States itself. Some have more or less close relations of a structural and functional nature with the OAS. These entities or agencies are: the Inter-American Development Bank (IDB); the Inter American Statistical Insti-

---

[16] *Cf.* Treaty Series No. 12, Washington, D.C., Pan American Union, 1958.
[17] See the *Report of the Secretary General 1963–June 1964,* Washington, D.C., Pan American Union, pp. 182-185.

tute; the Inter-American Defense Board; the Inter-American Peace Committee; the Inter-American Commission on Human Rights; and the Special Consultative Committee on Security. Except for the budget of the IDB, the budgets of these entities are included in the regular budget of the General Secretariat of the OAS, which is approved by the Council of the Organization. With the exception of the IDB and the Defense Board, the respective secretariats of these agencies are an integral part of the General Secretariat of the OAS and, therefore, their staffs are appointed by the Secretary General. Their individual Statutes, again with the exception of those of the IDB and the Board, and also those of the Statistical Institute, are approved by the Council of the Organization.

The functions and activities of these inter-American agencies will be examined in succeeding chapters of this study. As regards cooperative relations with "other American organizations of recognized international standing," provided for in Article 53, *d* of the Charter, the Council of the OAS has concluded official agreements with only two organizations: the Statistical Institute and the Association of the Pan American Railway Congress, which is a semi-official agency with headquarters in Buenos Aires. Nevertheless, under the rules and procedures established by the Council of the Organization in 1952, cooperative relations have been entered into with semi-official and nongovernmental inter-American organizations at the secretariat level, by means of notes exchanged between the Secretary General and the chief officials of the various agencies. These relations find expression chiefly in the exchange of documents and information and the mutual presentation of points of view on matters of common interest. In this respect, the Secretary General of the OAS, in his Report to the Second Special Inter-American Conference, pointed out that it would be desirable for the Council to broaden the aforesaid rules and procedures in order to give consultative status to some of these organizations, as is done in the United Nations, in the certainty that such a relationship would lead to much more effective collaboration in working for the objectives of the OAS.[18]

The Secretary General referred anew, for the aforesaid purpose, to the desirability of establishing a procedure to make it possible to obtain the counsel of an inter-American organ of parliamentary character. In his opinion, if there is to be better public understanding of the inter-American system in the member countries and more vigorous support of its work and accomplishments in their legislative bodies, it would be useful for the Conference to study the possibility of creating an advisory body of that nature. This could be given consultative status, with capacity to participate and present its points of

---

[18] *Cf.* OEA/Ser. E/XIII. 1, Doc. 16, vol. 1, p. 25.

view in meetings and conferences of the Organization. Such a body might well cooperate with existing agencies and with the Inter-American Regional Group of the World Interparliamentary Union, as well as with the new Latin American Parliament, in all undertakings designed to achieve common objectives.[19]

From the institutional standpoint, the IDB holds a special and outstanding position in the inter-American system. Although Part Three of this study will review its main activities, particularly with reference to the operative relationships and connections that it maintains with the OAS, for the moment it should be indicated that, by virtue of Article II, Section 1, a) of the Agreement Establishing the IDB (1959), only the member countries of the OAS can be members of this agency. The other formal relationships that exist between the two entities are indicated in the Charter of Punta del Este and other instruments of the Alliance for Progress, especially in the resolution of the Inter-American Economic and Social Council which created the CIAP. To these relationships, and as a result of them, are to be added those which they often have for the purpose of carrying out the objectives and programs of the Alliance.[20]

Even though the two current processes of Latin American economic integration have their own institutional framework, important connections and relationships exist between the Latin American integration organizations and the inter-American system. This is due, naturally, to the fact that economic integration constitutes an essential part of one program—that of the Alliance for Progress—which is a program of inter-American action.[21]

Finally, the Charter also calls for collaboration between the OAS and other international agencies (Arts. 53, e and 61). In accordance with these provisions, cooperative relationships have become established with many agencies of this kind, through formal agreements arrived at largely by decision of the Council of the Organization and the IA-ECOSOC. Likewise, in Article 100, the Charter authorizes the specialized inter-American agencies to establish cooperative relationships with world organizations of the same kind, in order to coordinate their activities. The only conditions governing the subject require that the world organizations have a similar character, and that the specialized inter-American agencies maintain their identity and position as an integral part of the Organization of American States, even when they are performing regional functions of international organi-

---

[19] *Ibid.*, p. 26.

[20] Concerning the activities of the IDB see, especially, Chapter XIII. 42. The complete text of the Agreement establishing the Bank appears in *Appendix 16*, p. 407, *infra.*

[21] With respect to the connections and relations with these Latin American agencies see Chapter XV, 54.

zations. The Council of the Organization is empowered to promote and facilitate this type of collaboration and, moreover, it may on its own initiative establish relationships with the United Nations and its specialized agencies.[22]

[22] Concerning the relations and formal agreements established to date, see Chapter XIII, 43. These relations and agreements do not always refer to activities relating to economic, social, and cultural cooperation. For example, on April 28, 1961, an exchange of notes between the OAS Secretary General and the Secretary General of ODECA agreed on exchanging information, publications, and documents relating to the development of programs of mutual interest in cultural, economic, social, and legal fields. At its Fifth Meeting, held in January-February 1965 in San Salvador, the Inter-American Council of Jurists recommended to the Council of the OAS that it take appropriate measures for the purpose of establishing cooperation between it and ODECA, through which the OAS might provide ODECA with technical assistance in the legal field, whenever the latter might so request.

Chapter III

Development and Codification of International Law

The development of international law and its codification constitute one of the fields of activity most closely connected with the historical course of the inter-American system. Indeed, this is an activity that has played a considerably more important role in the organization, functioning, and strengthening of that system than in any other international organization. In this connection, it is important to recall how the Liberator Simón Bolívar, in his famous "Thoughts on the Congress of Panama" written shortly before that meeting took place, foresaw that "The relations of the political societies would receive a code of public law as a rule of universal conduct," and thus "the New World would be made up of independent nations, all bound together by a common law which would determine their foreign relations. . . ."[1]

Following the Congress of Panama, as has been indicated in the *Introduction* to this study, the other Latin American Congresses of the nineteenth century, especially the Juridical Congress of Limà (1877-1879) and the South American Congress of Private International Law of Montevideo (1888-1889), devoted themselves to the task of establishing, through conventions, uniform rules to govern the relations among the states, particularly in matters of private international law.

The function that the development and codification of international law have played in the inter-American system is explained by the fruitful work the technical and political agencies of the system have done in this field. This work also explains the important contribution made by the American hemisphere to the development and codification of universal international law. Since it is impossible to examine any of these contributions here with the thoroughness that they deserve, we shall now give an account of the most outstanding mechanisms and activities, beginning with the first initiatives and efforts made by inter-American organizations.

---

[1] Simón Bolívar, *Un pensamiento sobre el Congreso de Panamá,* published on the occasion of the Second American Scientific Congress, Washington, D. C., 1916.

6. *Historical Outline of the Inter-American Contribution in this Field*

The results of the Congresses of Lima and Montevideo, mentioned above, were limited since not all the American republics were represented at them. The first efforts of a hemisphere-wide nature to promote the work of codification began at the Second International American Conference (Mexico City 1901-1902). By that time experience had shown that codification is in itself such a difficult, technical, and complex task that it can only be performed with the participation of experts who represent the various legal points of view of the hemisphere. This criterion was the one that inspired the Convention for the Formation of Codes on Public and Private International Law. That convention provided for the establishment of a Committee of Jurists, but since the convention did not obtain the necessary number of ratifications for it to enter into force, that committee never came into being.[2]

Nevertheless, at the Third Conference (Rio de Janeiro 1906) this effort was renewed, and a Convention on International Law was adopted, which in due course was ratified by 17 countries. That instrument created an International Commission of Jurists, to be composed of one representative from each of the signatory states, appointed by their respective governments. Two or more governments could appoint a single representative, but such representative would have but one vote. This stipulation was changed by a protocol signed at Washington on January 15, 1912, by virtue of which the representation of each state on the Commission was increased to two delegates, but still with only one vote per country. The function of the Commission was to prepare a draft Code of Private International Law and another of Public International Law regulating the relations between the American nations. In performing this work, the Commission was to give special attention to the subjects and principles that had been agreed upon in existing treaties and conventions, as well as to those that were incorporated in the national laws of the American states, or that tended to eliminate the causes of misunderstanding or conflicts between said states.[3]

The first meeting of the Commission was to be held in 1907, and the work distributed between two separate committees, in accordance with the double nature of the task entrusted to it, but since there was some delay in the ratification of the convention the meeting did not take place until 1912. At that first meeting 17 countries were represented. As a preliminary question, the method of work the Commission should follow was discussed. Some argued that the draft

---

[2] See the complete text of the convention in *International Conferences,* (1889-1928), p. 69.

[3] See the complete text of the convention *ibid.,* p. 144.

codes that had previously been circulated among the governments should be considered, with a view to adopting them in whole or in part, while others maintained that the meeting should limit itself to the organization of the tasks of the Commission, by dividing it into two subcommittees that would be entrusted with the preparation of draft codes, taking as a basis the drafts prepared by Dr. Epitácio Pessoa and Dr. Lafayette Rodrigues Pereira (Brazil). The latter viewpoint prevailed, with certain variations. Among others, it was agreed to divide the Commission into six subcommittees, on the following subjects: Maritime and Civil Warfare and foreign claims arising from each, in Rio de Janeiro; Public International Law in Time of Peace, in Santiago, Chile; Peaceful Solution of Conflicts and the Organization of International Tribunals, in Buenos Aires; the Legal Capacity and Status of Aliens, Domestic Relations and Succession of Property, in Montevideo; matters of private international law not included in the foregoing enumeration, including international penal law, in Lima; preparation of codes on maritime warfare and neutrality, in Washington, D.C.

In the preparation of the respective projects each subcommittee could ask the governments for detailed information on their internal legislation, judicial and administrative decisions, conventions, usages, international cases and their settlement, as well as the regulations that in the opinion of these governments would be most adequate with respect to the various subjects. The Commission limited itself at this first meeting to approval of its internal Regulations, of a chapter on extradition, and of a project concerning working methods. Of the six subcommittees, only those of Rio de Janeiro, Santiago, Montevideo, and Lima carried out preparatory work or prepared projects.[4]

The second meeting of the International Commission of Jurists was to have been held in 1914, but had to be postponed because of the war. The Fifth International Conference of American States (Santiago, Chile 1923), which had also been postponed because of the war, adopted a resolution by which the Commission of Jurists was reorganized and was requested to submit the results of its studies to the Sixth Conference, which was to be held in Havana in 1928. In the report presented to the Fifth Conference by the Juridical Committee (Second Committee), in submitting a draft resolution that was later adopted, concerning the future work of the International

---

[4] On the work accomplished to date, see Charles G. Fenwick, *International Law*, 3rd ed., 1948, p. 84; Alberto Ulloa, *Derecho Internacional Público*, 2nd ed., Lima, 1938, vol. 1, p. 66; Antonio Sánchez de Bustamante, *Derecho Internacional Público*, Havana, 1933, vol. 1, p. 104; *Report of the United States Delegates,* 62nd Congress, 3rd Session, Doc. No. 1343, Washington, D. C., 1913.

Commission of Jurists, the following conclusions were expressed:[5]

I. The Codification of International Law is desirable;
II. While it is true as regards Public International Law, that complete codification may not be practicable, there is nothing to prevent the gradual approximation to this end through conventions entered into between the countries of the Continent, embodying the principles upon which there is agreement;
III. The codification of private international law is desirable and practicable, provided it is possible to harmonize by means of conciliatory agreements, the differences of principle which proved an obstacle to the development of an important branch of such codification at the Congress of Montevideo and in the respective committee of the Congress which met at Rio de Janeiro;
IV. The advantage of the total or partial codification of international law has been demonstrated in this conference in the consideration of the various problems included in the agenda, but the complete solution thereof requires the cooperation of specialists, and the time and the environment of tranquility which are more characteristic of scientific bodies than of conferences entrusted with the consideration of such varied topics as is the present one.

In order to facilitate the task entrusted to the Commission of Jurists, the Governing Board of the Pan American Union, now the Council of the Organization of American States, in 1924 invited the American Institute of International Law, a nongovernmental organization, to cooperate in the work of codification of international law. The Institute accepted this invitation and submitted to the Governing Board a series of 30 draft conventions prepared by a group of distinguished jurists of the hemisphere, as a contribution to the preparation of a code of public international law. These drafts, which were preceded by a preamble and some general declarations, dealt with the following subjects: fundamental bases of international law; nations; recognition of new nations and new governments; declaration of rights and duties of nations; fundamental rights of the American republics; Pan American Union; national domain; rights and duties of nations in territories in dispute on the question of boundaries; jurisdiction; international rights and duties of natural and juridical persons; immigration; responsibility of governments; diplomatic protection; extradition; freedom of transit; navigation of international rivers; aerial navigation; treaties; diplomatic agents; consuls; exchange of publications; interchange of professors and students; maritime neutrality; pacific settlement; inter-American court of justice; measures of repression; and conquests.[6]

---

[5] Verbatim Record of the Plenary Sessions of the Fifth International Conference of American States, vol. 1, *Journal of Sessions,* Santiago, Chile, 1923, pp. 299-300.

[6] *Codification of American International Law: Projects of Conventions prepared by the American Institute of International Law,* Washington, D.C., Pan American Union, 1925.

The International Commission of Jurists held its second meeting in Rio de Janeiro in 1927. Among the projects submitted with respect to public international law were the draft Code of Public International Law by the Brazilian jurist Dr. Pessoa, submitted by Brazil to the Commission in 1912; the drafts that Dr. Alejandro Alvarez, in his capacity as Delegate of Chile, submitted to the Fifth Conference; the drafts prepared by the American Institute of International Law that are listed above; and in addition the drafts that, with regard to certain subjects, several delegations presented to the Institute at its meeting held in Montevideo.[7] With respect to private international law, the Commission had before it the following working documents: the conventions signed at the First South American Congress of Private International Law, Montevideo, 1888-1889; the draft Code of Private International Law by Dr. Lafayette Rodrigues Pereira, presented to the Commission at its 1912 meeting by the Brazilian Delegation; the projects prepared by the Fifth and Sixth Subcommittees of the first Commission, which met in Montevideo and in Lima, respectively; and the draft Code of Private International Law prepared at the request of the Pan American Union by the American Institute of International Law, which was the work of the Cuban jurist Dr. Antonio Sánchez de Bustamante.[8]

The Commission of Jurists prepared 12 drafts dealing with the following subjects: fundamental bases of international law; states, their existence, equality, and recognition; status of aliens; treaties; exchange of publications; exchange of professors and students; diplomatic agents; consuls; maritime neutrality; asylum; duties of states in case of civil war; and pacific solution of international conflicts.[9] In the field of private international law, the Commission approved, in addition to the draft code or convention, a draft agreement on the permanent technical organs to organize in the future the preliminary work for formulating and developing international law in America, and a resolution on the unification of legislations.[10]

The drafts formulated by the Commission were submitted to the Sixth Conference (Havana 1928), and served as a basis for the treaties and conventions signed on the following subjects: status of aliens; asylum; treaties; diplomatic officers; consular agents; maritime neutrality; duties and rights of states in the event of civil strife; and private international law ("Bustamante Code"). In addition to these instruments, the Conference approved a resolution on methods of codification that should be used in the future, which provided for

---

[7] Cf. Comisión Internacional de Jurisconsultos Americanos, Reunión de 1927, Ministry of Foreign Affairs of Brazil, Rio de Janeiro, 1927, vol. 4, p. 8.

[8] Ibid., p. 9.

[9] Ibid., p. 8.

[10] Ibid.

continuation of the International Commission of Jurists and the organization of three permanent committees, one in Rio de Janeiro on public international law, one in Montevideo on private international law, and one in Havana on comparative law and uniformity of legislations. This resolution, which was based on a draft agreement also prepared by the Commission of Jurists, also set forth in detail the functions to be performed by each permanent committee.[11]

Until the Havana Conference, the International Commission of Jurists was the only official agency in the field of codification, but at that conference the practice was started of multiplying the organs of codification and of dividing efforts, a tendency that was regularly followed until the Ninth Conference (Bogotá 1948). The Seventh Conference (Montevideo 1933) maintained the International Commission of Jurists and created a Committee of Experts for the codification of international law and provided for the establishment of national committees on codification, at the same time eliminating the three permanent committees established by the Sixth Conference.[12] In turn, the Inter-American Conference for the Maintenance of Peace (Buenos Aires 1936), in again revising the procedure, reestablished those three committees.[13] Later the Eighth International Conference of American States (Lima 1938), with the purpose of facilitating and expediting the work of codification, again revised the procedure, placing special stress on the coordination of the work of the various entities. As the last stage in the procedure, the International Conference of American Jurists was established to replace the International Commission of Jurists. The Conference was to be composed of jurists appointed by the American governments with plenipotentiary powers, and its function was "the revision, coordination, approval, modification or rejection of the drafts prepared by the Committee of Experts."[14]

As will have been noted, the ten years from 1928 to 1938 were characterized mainly by the reorganization of the machinery and procedures of codification, little substantive work being done except that carried out by the Committee of Experts, which will be referred to below. The mechanism and procedures, which went through changes down to the time of the Bogotá Conference in 1948, consisted in the following. The consideration of any topic susceptible of codification could be initiated by the permanent committees, the national committees, the Committee of Experts, or the governments them-

---

[11] See the complete texts of these instruments in *International Conferences,* (1889-1928), pp. 325-376, 415-436.

[12] See the complete text of Resolution LXX in *International Conferences,* 1st Sup. (1933-1940), p. 84.

[13] See the complete text of Resolution VI in *ibid.,* p. 145.

[14] See the complete text of Resolution XVII in *ibid.,* p. 246.

selves, but it was the function of the permanent committees to coordinate the various initiatives. These committees were to consult
the governments, through the national committees, on the topics considered susceptible of codification. If at least two thirds of the governments replied favorably, the permanent committee submitted a questionnaire to all of them, indicating the points with respect to each
subject under study that might eventually constitute bases for conventions, declarations, or uniform laws. The national committees were
to prepare doctrinal studies on international law and comparative
legislation and send the results to the permanent committees. These
committees, taking into account the replies, were then to prepare the
bases for such conventions, declarations, or uniform laws, and send
them to the Pan American Union, in order that it in turn might transmit them to the Committee of Experts. The drafts prepared by the
Committee of Experts were to be sent to the governments through
the Pan American Union. As a final stage in the work of codification, the International Conference of American Jurists had the aforementioned function of "revision, coordination, approval, modification or rejection of the drafts prepared by the Committee of Experts."
During that period, the total number of jurists members of the permanent official agencies of codification and unification exceeded
225.[15]

The Committee of Experts for the codification of international law
was organized in accordance with the procedure established in the
previously cited Resolution LXX of the Seventh Conference, entitled "Methods of Codification of International Law". It was originally composed of seven eminent jurists, but the number was increased to nine by Resolution XVII of the Eighth Conference, also
already mentioned. Once the members of the Committee were
selected, it met at the Pan American Union to carry out its task of
organizing, on a provisional basis, the work of codification of international law. It took certain decisions to advance the work and divided
among its members the study of the subjects entrusted to the Committee in 1936 by the Buenos Aires Conference so that it could submit the corresponding reports or drafts to the Eighth Conference,
to be held in 1938. Those subjects were: definition of the aggressor,
sanctions, and prevention of war; investigation, conciliation, and
arbitration; nationality; peace code; immunity of state-owned vessels;
and pecuniary claims.[16]

The Committee met again in Lima one month before the opening

---

[15] *Lista de Organismos Interamericanos Encargados de la Codificación, Uni-
ficación y Uniformidad del Derecho en América,* 5th ed., Washington, D.C., Pan
American Union, 1944.

[16] *Final Act of the First Meeting of the Committee of Experts on the Codification of International Law,* Washington, D.C., Pan American Union, 1937.

of the Eighth Conference to complete its work, and submitted to that conference reports and proposals on the following subjects: consideration of the rules concerning the codification of international law in America; definition of the aggressor and application of sanctions; peace code; investigation, conciliation, and arbitration; nationality; immunity of state-owned vessels; and pecuniary claims.[17] The Conference did not have time to discuss all these proposals, and decided to process them in various ways, in some cases referring them to one or another codifying agency, especially to the International Conference of American Jurists. The following topics were also referred to codifying agencies: recognition of belligerency, uniformity and improvement of the methods of preparation of multilateral treaties; nationality of juridical persons; and consolidation of the American peace agreements.[18]

The decisions taken by the Eighth Conference could not be put into effect because the events of the following year, with the outbreak of war in Europe, affected the normal course of the work of codification. The transportation difficulties created at that time made it necessary to postpone indefinitely the meetings of the codifying agencies, especially of the Committee of Experts. Meanwhile, the Inter-American Neutrality Committee was established by the First Meeting of Consultation of Ministers of Foreign Affairs (Panama City 1939). Its function was to study and formulate recommendations with respect to the problems of neutrality, in the light of experience and changing circumstances. This committee made various recommendations that served as the basis for many laws, decrees, and regulations enacted or issued by the governments of the American republics during the period in which they remained neutral. In addition, under the provisions of a resolution of the Second Meeting of Consultation (Havana 1940), the Committee prepared two draft conventions, one dealing with the juridical effects of the Security Zone established by the Declaration of Panama, and another, in partial form, on the principles and rules generally recognized in international law in matters of neutrality. While the work of this committee was not carried out in accordance with the resolutions on codification, it nevertheless constituted a valuable contribution to the work of codification.

The Third Meeting of Consultation, held in Rio de Janeiro in 1942, shortly after World War II had extended itself to the Ameri-

---

[17] *Diario de la Conferencia,* Lima, 1938, pp. 188, 243, 298, 351, 373, 444, 449.

[18] *Codification of International Law.* General Report on the Status of the Work Provided for in the Resolutions on the Codification of International Law and the Improvement and Coordination of Inter-American Peace Treaties, Washington, D.C., Pan American Union, Legal Division, 1944.

can hemisphere, changed the name of the Inter-American Neutrality Committee to "Inter-American Juridical Committee", and made it its function, among others, "to develop and coordinate the work of codifying international law, without prejudice to the duties entrusted to other existing organizations."[19] In performing its new functions, the Juridical Committee prepared various drafts and proposals, among which those it submitted to the Ninth Conference were outstanding. Indeed, its draft of an Inter-American Peace System constituted the basis for the American Treaty on Pacific Settlement ("Pact of Bogotá"), signed at that conference, and its draft Declaration of the International Rights and Duties of Man and draft American International Charter of Social Guarantees were the bases, respectively, for the American Declaration of the Rights and Duties of Man and the Inter-American Charter of Social Guarantees, adopted at the same conference. The Inter-American Juridical Committee was incorporated by the Charter of the Organization of American States into the new machinery of codification that is described below, acting as the permanent committee of the Inter-American Council of Jurists.

During World War II and prior to the Ninth Conference, when it was necessary to suspend the work of codification, aside from that partially done by the Juridical Committee, the time was used for taking inventory, that is, for studying the machinery then in existence, which many people considered slow and inefficient, in order to seek means of improving it. Despite the services rendered by the various codifying agencies in the period starting in 1928, and the results obtained thanks to that work, the conviction was becoming widespread that much could be accomplished if the machinery were changed. The most noticeable defects from which it suffered could be attributed to three main factors: a) the committees were made up of lawyers who could not devote all their time and attention to the work of codification; b) the members of the committees in many cases resided in different countries; and c) the functions performed by the various agencies duplicated one another in many respects. These factors made it impossible to establish the coordination necessary for doing a more intensive and efficient job.

As a result, opinion inclined toward the idea of creating a central agency of a permanent character, which could devote itself exclusively to the work of codification and make greater progress. The codifying agencies themselves shared this opinion. For example, the Committee of Experts on the Codification of International Law stated in the report that it rendered in 1938 to the Eighth Inter-American Conference that "the system of codification now in effect is suffering

---

[19] The origin and the activities of the Committee up to 1943 are described in an article published in the *Bulletin of the Pan American Union,* May 1943, pp. 268-274.

from excessive and unnecessary complexity, which, far from favoring and stimulating the work of codification, is harming and retarding it."[20] The Inter-American Juridical Committee, which because of its continuous operation did not suffer the disadvantages experienced by the other codifying agencies, expressed in 1945 the same point of view the Committee of Experts had stated. Performing functions conferred on it by the Third Meeting of Consultation, the Juridical Committee in 1945 formulated a recommendation on the reorganization of the agencies engaged in the codification of international law, in which it proposed the establishment of a central agency of a permanent character, capable of devoting all its time to the work of giving unity to the activities. In the report accompanying its recommendation, the Committee reached the conclusion that "before the work can be efficiently and systematically carried out, it will be necessary to coordinate the numerous agencies created from time to time by the American governments to undertake the work of codification."[21]

The question was considered by the American governments, and later it was studied by the Governing Board of the Pan American Union in accordance with Resolution IX of the Inter-American Conference on Problems of War and Peace (Mexico City 1945), entitled "Reorganization, Consolidation and Strengthening of the Inter-American System".[22] Drawing on past experience, the Governing Board drafted a new plan or procedure, substantially similar to that of the Juridical Committee, with the aim of being able to achieve more effective and more rapid results through the coordination of the activities in a central agency. The draft prepared by the Governing Board was submitted to the Ninth Conference, and served as a basis for consideration of the establishment of the Inter-American Council of Jurists. The Conference included provision for this council, as one of the three organs of the Council of the Organization, in the Charter of the Organization of American States.

The purpose of the Inter-American Council of Jurists, as set forth in Article 67 of the Charter, is "to serve as an advisory body on juridical matters; to promote the development and codification of public and private international law; and to study the possibility of

---

[20] Cf. Informe de la Comisión sobre la Organización del Sistema Interamericano referente al Establecimiento de un Consejo Interamericano de Jurisconsultos, Washington, D.C., Pan American Union, 1946.

[21] Cf. "Recommendation on a Reorganization of the Agencies Engaged in the Codification of International Law", prepared by the Inter-American Juridical Committee, in Recommendations and Reports, Official Documents 1942-1944, Rio de Janeiro, Imprensa Nacional, 1945.

[22] See the complete text of Resolution IX in International Conferences, 2nd Sup. (1942-1954), p. 69.

attaining uniformity in the legislation of the various American countries, insofar as it may appear desirable." The Council is assisted in the performance of its duties by the Inter-American Juridical Committee of Rio de Janeiro, which acts as its permanent committee, and the Department of Legal Affairs of the Pan American Union, which provides technical and administrative services both to the Council and to the Committee through its Codification Division. The Juridical Committee is composed of nine jurists, chosen by the Council of Jurists from panels presented by each of the nine countries selected for the purpose by the Inter-American Conference. The members of the Committee represent all member states of the Organization.

Since its establishment, the Inter-American Council of Jurists has met five times: in Rio de Janeiro 1950; in Buenos Aires 1953; in Mexico City 1956; in Santiago, Chile 1959; and in San Salvador 1965. In accordance with the terms of Article 70 of the Charter of the OAS and the Codification Plan adopted at the First Meeting of the Council and revised at the Fourth Meeting, the Council selects the topics to be studied, taking into account the recommendations made to it by the Inter-American Conference, the Meetings of Consultation, the Council of the Organization, or its own permanent committee. The Juridical Committee then makes the studies or preparatory works and transmits them to the governments through the General Secretariat. When it has received the observations of the governments, it proceeds to prepare definitive reports or drafts that are then submitted to the Council of Jurists for consideration, at its next meeting. The Juridical Committee may also undertake studies on its own initiative, when it considers them advisable, in which case the same procedure is followed. The reports or drafts that are adopted by the Inter-American Council of Jurists are sent to the General Secretariat so that they may be transmitted to the Council of the Organization, the governments, and, when appropriate, to the Inter-American Conference, to the Meeting of Consultation of Ministers of Foreign Affairs, or to a specialized conference.

At its First Meeting, the Council of Jurists considered several drafts prepared by its permanent committee, on such subjects as recognition of *de facto* governments, possible elimination of the use of passports, the inter-American court to protect human rights, the right of resistance, and the scope of the powers of the Council of the OAS. It also adopted the codification plan mentioned in the preceding paragraph. Under this plan, the Committee prepared studies and drafts on the following subjects, among others: strengthening and effective exercise of democracy; regimen of political asylees, exiles, and refugees (territorial asylum); diplomatic asylum; possibility of revising the Bustamante Code; international sale of personal

property; international cooperation in judicial procedures; territorial
waters and related questions; and nationality and status of stateless
persons.[23]

These studies and drafts were submitted to the Second Meeting of
the Council. The two draft conventions on territorial and diplomatic
asylum were approved with some modifications by the Council, and
were sent, through the Council of the OAS, to the Tenth Inter-
American Conference (Caracas 1954), which, after making some
additional modifications, adopted them as conventions. On the other
subjects, the Juridical Committee was requested to take certain steps
in order to advance their study and future consideration by the Council of Jurists.[24]

The Juridical Committee submitted to the Third Meeting, among
others, drafts on extradition; commercial arbitration; international
cooperation in judicial procedures; territorial waters and related questions; and reservations to multilateral treaties. On the subject of
commercial arbitration, the Council approved, with certain modifications, the draft uniform law on the subject prepared by the Committee.
This draft was transmitted to the governments with the recommendation that it be adopted in the local legislation, insofar as possible, in
accordance with the respective constitutional procedures.[25]

At its Fourth Meeting, the Council studied, among others, the
following subjects with respect to which its permanent committee had
also prepared studies or drafts: political offenses; convention on extradition; immunity of state-owned vessels; contribution of the American continent to the principles that govern the responsibility of the
state; and reservations to multilateral treaties. In addition to a draft
convention on extradition and a draft of rules on reservations to
multilateral treaties, the Council approved the draft convention on
human rights, which will be dealt with in the next chapter.[26] The
Fifth Meeting did not have occasion to approve any draft treaty or
convention, although it gave thorough consideration to the draft
convention on industrial and agricultural use of international rivers
and lakes prepared by the Juridical Committee, giving its support to
the proposals that had been made in the Council of the OAS with
respect to the convocation of an Inter-American Specialized Conference to deal with the various aspects of the topic as a whole. It
also adopted another resolution of great interest, as will be seen, with
respect to the future course of these activities of the inter-American
system.[27]

---

[23] *Final Act of the First Meeting,* CIJ-6.
[24] *Final Act of the Second Meeting,* CIJ-17.
[25] *Final Act of the Third Meeting,* CIJ-29.
[26] *Final Act of the Fourth Meeting,* CIJ-43.
[27] *Final Act of the Fifth Meeting,* CIJ-77.

7. *Evaluation of the Work Done and the Prospects for the Future*

The outstanding role the activities connected with the development and codification of international law have played in the organization and strengthening of the inter-American system was pointed out at the beginning of this chapter. The brief narrative above gives an idea, although incomplete, of the intensive work done in this field. In the broader field of international legislation, the table of treaties and other instruments that appears at the end of this volume will give a fuller idea of the notable evolution and diversity of inter-American written law.[28] In this direction, through a long historical process, a fine legal tradition has been maintained and strengthened that was initiated by Bolívar when he advocated that the independent nations of the New World should be "all bound together by a common law which would determine their foreign relations. . . ."

However, in evaluating the work done in the past, we should not overlook the future implications and prospects of the "development and codification of international law"—to continue to use, to the extent that this is appropriate, the term that traditionally has been used to refer to these activities. In this regard, the initiatives and accomplishments of inter-American codification, both at the private or scientific level and at the official and political level, have always been in response to the needs and interests that have required the formulation of legal rules. At present the same phenomenon is occurring. Now it is a question of the needs and interests originated by the economic and social development of Latin America, which are already raising problems of a legal and institutional nature whose solution is daily becoming more urgent. Indeed, the program of action outlined first by the Act of Bogotá (1960) and then by the Charter of Punta del Este (1961) in formally establishing the Alliance for Progress presupposes profound changes both in the internal legal structures and in the multilateral machinery; changes that are even explicitly foreseen in both instruments.[29] For this reason the Council of the OAS, in approving the agenda of the Fifth Meeting of the Inter-American Council of Jurists, included, at the suggestion of the Department of Legal Affairs of the General Secretariat, the topic "Programming of Studies on the International Aspect of Legal and Institutional Problems of the Economic and Social Development of Latin America". This topic was included in order to give the Council of Jurists an opportunity to explore the legal and institutional problems raised by the economic and social development of Latin America, with a view to determining what matters or subjects deserved research

---

[28] *Appendix 24,* p. 504, *infra.*

[29] The complete text of the Act of Bogotá and the Charter of Punta del Este appear in *Appendices 17* and *18,* pp. 437 and 443, respectively, *infra.*

and study.[30] The Council of the OAS had also taken into account an opinion of the Inter-American Juridical Committee, in which it deemed it "imperative to undertake a serious study of the juridical aspects of the Alliance for Progress."[31] In connection with this topic of the agenda, the Council of Jurists approved a long resolution recommending the establishment of machinery that would be entrusted with the task of studying the aforementioned problems. It is most interesting to note that the Council of Jurists recommended the holding of a joint meeting with the Inter-American Economic and Social Council (IA-ECOSOC), "in order to examine the economic and legal aspects of development."[32]

Meanwhile the IA-ECOSOC, at its Third Annual Meetings (Lima, November-December 1964), had included in the program and budget of the new Special Development Assistance Fund a program of activities directed toward examining various legal and institutional aspects of economic integration. One part of this program has to do with the Central American Common Market and includes a number of topics that appear in the research and study plan that was agreed upon at a seminar held a few months earlier under the auspices of the Inter-American Institute of International Legal Studies. The program of the Special Fund also included the holding of another seminar to program the study of the legal and institutional problems of the Latin American Free-Trade Association (LAFTA). This seminar, the preparation and organization of which was entrusted to the Institute, was held in Montevideo in the month of October 1965. With regard to this method of work, it is appropriate to emphasize the participation that is once more being given to nongovernmental institutions in the programming and execution of these activities. The advantages that can be obtained through this method were already noted in the decade of the twenties, when the Governing Board of the Pan American Union requested the collaboration of the American Institute of International Law to facilitate the codification tasks in which the official organizations were engaged during that period.

---

[30] Cf. OEA/Ser.G/IV, C-i-684 Rev. 2, October 1964. Also see the memorandum prepared by the Department of Legal Affairs on April 9 of that same year, OEA/Ser.G/VII-CA/JP/54 and Addendum of October 14 (Spanish only).

[31] Cf. Opinion on the Topic "Functioning and Activities of the Inter-American Juridical Committee", CIJ-72, November 1964.

[32] Cf. Resolution V in the Final Act of the Fifth Meeting, CIJ-77.

Chapter IV

Human Rights and
Representative Democracy

The activity of the inter-American system in these two fields is grounded in explicit commitments set forth in the Charter of the Organization of American States. Pursuant to Article 13, "Each State has the right to develop its cultural, political and economic life freely and naturally. In this free development, the State shall respect the rights of the individual and the principles of universal morality." Accordingly, the Bogotá Charter is the first contractual instrument that establishes respect for human rights as an obligation. Regarding representative democracy, the Charter of Bogotá states that "The solidarity of the American States and the high aims which are sought through it require the political organization of those States on the basis of the effective exercise of representative democracy". (Art. 5, d). Even though the fields under discussion are closely connected, considering the intimate relationship that exists between respect for human rights and the effective exercise of representative democracy,[1] the machinery, functions, and activities of the system in each field should be studied separately.

8. *Human Rights and the Inter-American System*

The promotion of respect for human rights and the fundamental freedoms and their international protection, is one of the increasingly important fields of activity of the inter-American system. Considering the political-juridical tradition of the American countries, from the time they gained their independence for the purpose of establishing a republican and democratic form of government, this is clearly understandable. At the end of World War II, when a universal movement sprang up in behalf of the "internationalization" of these rights and freedoms, the system was the first to take initiatives and realize

---

[1] See the Study prepared by the Inter-American Juridical Committee at the request of the Inter-American Council of Jurists (Doc. CIJ-52, 1960), and those prepared on the same topic by Dr. D. V. Sandifer, member of the Inter-American Commission on Human Rights, OEA/Ser.L/V/II.4, Doc. 21 (9 July 1962) and OEA/Ser.L/V/II.5, Doc. 3 (19 September 1962).

concrete achievements. Among these should be mentioned the resolution adopted by the Inter-American Conference on Problems of War and Peace (Mexico 1945), by authority of which the projected "draft charter" was to proclaim the obligation to observe the standards set forth in a "Declaration of the International Rights and Duties of Man".[2] This resolution was supplemented by another, in which the Conference, after proclaiming "the adherence of the American Republics to the principles established by international law for safeguarding the essential rights of man, and to declare their support of a system of international protection of these rights," requested the Inter-American Juridical Committee to prepare the aforesaid preliminary draft Declaration.[3]

When the Ninth International Conference of American States met in Bogotá in March 1948, it did not limit itself to stating in the Charter of the OAS that one of the basic duties of the state is to respect the rights of the individual. As a result of the decisions of the earlier conference, it adopted the "American Declaration of the Rights and Duties of Man".[4] The Bogotá Conference made a new proposal: that the Inter-American Court be created to guarantee the rights of man and the basic freedoms, and it charged the Juridical Committee to prepare a draft statute for this purpose.[5] In a report issued the following year, the Committee pointed out that "the lack of positive substantive law on the subject constitutes a serious obstacle to the drafting of a statute for the Court," and that it "would involve a radical transformation of the constitutional systems in effect." It therefore considered that it would be advisable first to prepare a convention on the matter.[6] For these and other political reasons, the question has been repeatedly postponed throughout the last decade, by the Inter-American Council of Jurists (1950 and 1953), as well as by the Tenth Inter-American Conference (1954) and the Council of the OAS.[7]

The favorable circumstances surrounding the Fifth Meeting of

[2] Cf. Resolution IX, Reorganization, Consolidation, and Strengthening of the Inter-American System, in International Conferences, 2nd Sup. (1942-1954), pp. 69-74.

[3] See the complete text of Resolution XL, International Protection of the Essential Rights of Man, ibid., p. 102.

[4] See the complete text of the Declaration in Appendix 8, p. 365, infra.

[5] See the complete text of Resolution XXXI, Inter-American Court to Protect the Rights of Man, International Conferences, 2nd Sup. (1942-1954), p. 270.

[6] Cf. "Informe sobre la Resolución XXXI de la Conferencia de Bogotá, noviembre de 1949", in Recomendaciones e Informes, Documentos Oficiales 1949-1953 (1955), p. 105.

[7] For a summary report on the background of this question, see Human Rights in the American States, Preliminary Edition, June 1960.

Consultation of Ministers of Foreign Affairs (Santiago, Chile, August 1959) eliminated some of the obstacles that had hindered action since the 1948 Bogotá Conference, thereby enabling decisions to be taken which renewed the process of development and strengthening of the inter-American system in this field. Actually, this had been the basic purpose behind the convocation of the meeting, as its Agenda revealed. In addition to decisions with respect to representative democracy, the meeting adopted the following resolution:

VIII
HUMAN RIGHTS

WHEREAS:

In the preamble to the Charter of the Organization of American States it is stated: "Confident that the true significance of American solidarity and good neighborliness can only mean the consolidation on this continent, within the framework of democratic institutions, of a system of individual liberty and social justice based on respect for the essential rights of man";

The furtherance of those rights is a part of the fundamental aims of solidarity of the American states, as set forth in the preambles to the Inter-American Treaty of Reciprocal Assistance and to the Charter of the Organization of American States, and is one of the means for achieving solidarity, as asserted as a precept in Article 5.j of the Charter and Resolution XXXII of the Ninth International Conference of American States;

In various instruments of the Organization of American States there has been set forth and repeated the rule that liberty, justice, and peace are based on recognition of the inherent dignity and the equal and inalienable rights of the individual;

It has been considered essential, as a fundamental corollary to this rule, that such rights be protected by a juridical system, so that men will not be driven to the extreme expedient of revolt against tyranny and oppression; and

The American states have constantly demanded in the United Nations the urgent approval of the covenants on civil and political rights and on economic, social, and cultural rights, which will give world-wide application to the 1948 Universal Declaration of Human Rights,

The Fifth Meeting of Consultation of Ministers of Foreign Affairs

DECLARES:

That eleven years after the proclamation of the American Declaration of the Rights and Duties of Man—progress having been made during the same period in both the United Nations and the union known as the Council of Europe, in the codification and methodical study of this field until today a satisfactory and promising point has been reached—the climate in this hemisphere is favorable to the conclusion of a convention; and therefore

RESOLVES:

I

1. That the Inter-American Council of Jurists proceed to prepare, at its Fourth Meeting, a draft Convention on Human Rights, referring this task, if it should not itself accomplish it, to the Council of the Organization of American States, which shall commission for this

purpose the Inter-American Juridical Committee, or the entity it considers appropriate; and that it likewise proceed to prepare a draft convention or draft conventions on the Creation of an Inter-American Court for the Protection of Human Rights and of other organizations appropriate for the protection and observance of those rights.

2. That the aforesaid drafts be submitted to the Eleventh Inter-American Conference and be transmitted to the governments 60 days prior to the opening of the Conference.

II

To create an Inter-American Commission on Human Rights, composed of seven members elected, as individuals, by the Council of the Organization of American States from panels of three names presented by the governments. The Commission, which shall be organized by the Council of the Organization and have the specific functions that the Council assigns to it, shall be charged with furthering respect for such rights.

The structure and activities of the Inter-American Commission on Human Rights, which was created by Part II of the resolution, will be studied in a subsequent section. With respect to Part I, the Inter-American Council of Jurists prepared the draft convention on human rights requested of it during its Fourth Meeting, held in Santiago during the two weeks following the Meeting of Consultation.

The draft convention contains 88 articles, divided into five Parts. Part I, Chapter I (Arts. 2-33) enumerates and defines the civil and political rights to be guaranteed. Part II (Art. 34) mentions the two organs that are to be responsible for ensuring the observance of the commitments and guaranteeing the exercise of the human rights contained in the Convention. These are: an Inter-American Commission for the Protection of Human Rights and an Inter-American Court of Human Rights. Part III, Chapter I (Arts. 35-57), refers to the organization of the Commission and the protection that it is empowered to give with respect to civil and political rights. Chapter II (Arts. 58-64) deals with the protection that is to be given to economic, social, and cultural rights. Part IV (Arts. 65-81) discusses the organization and functioning of the Inter-American Court of Human Rights. Lastly, Parts V and VI (Arts. 82-88) contain provisions of a general nature.[8]

The "protection of human rights" is one of the topics on the Agenda of the Second Special Inter-American Conference, along with the draft convention. In the report prepared for the Conference by the Inter-American Commission on Human Rights, the latter indicates that, after the draft convention was prepared, important steps were taken in the area, and points out, among others, the conclusion

---

[8] *Cf.* The complete text of the draft convention appears in the Final Act of the Fourth Meeting of the Inter-American Council of Jurists, CIJ-43, September 1959.

of the two studies made by the Third Committee of the General Assembly of the United Nations on the two draft covenants on human rights; the approval of four additional protocols to the European Convention, signed in Rome in 1950, which broadened its area of application and added new rights to the list of those that were originally protected; the approval of several draft conventions for the protection of specific rights; and the decisions of the European Court of Human Rights in important cases submitted to it for decision. Accordingly, the Commission suggested to the Conference the advisability of revising the Council of Jurists' draft convention in the light of the progress achieved in this field.[9] Moreover, in his report, the Secretary General of the OAS suggested that should the Conference not have time to study the proposal, it might transmit it to the Inter-American Commission on Human Rights, which, with the benefit of considerable experience in the field, could attach its pertinent observations prior to submission to the Council of the Organization. The Council would then be in a position to decide on the procedure to be followed, including the possibility of revising the present text according to the observations of the Commission and of the governments, and then opening the instrument for signature by the governments.[10]

9. *The Inter-American Commission on Human Rights*

In accordance with Part II of Resolution VIII of the Fifth Meeting of Consultation, *supra,* the OAS Council proceeded to prepare the Statute that established the Inter-American Commission on Human Rights and by which it has been governed since the election of its members in June 1960 and their formal installation in October of that year.[11] According to Article 1 of that Statute, the Commission "is an autonomous entity of the Organization of American States, the function of which is to promote respect for human rights." It is composed of seven members, nationals of the member states of the OAS, elected from a list made up of panels of three persons proposed for the purpose by the governments. The persons selected are to be of high moral character and recognized competence in the field of human rights. In accordance with the principle of collective representation, they "shall represent all the member countries of the Organization of American States and act in its name" (Art. 3). The members of the Commission are elected for a four-year term and its Chairman, who is elected by the Commission, holds office for two years (Art. 6).

---

[9] *Cf.* OEA/Ser.L/V/II.11, Doc. 5, Rev. 2, 15 October 1965, pp. 12-14.
[10] *Cf.* OEA/Ser.E/XIII.1/Doc. 16, vol. I, p. 49.
[11] See the complete text of the Statute in *Appendix 10,* p. 372, *infra.*

Before reviewing the activities of the Commission, it will be of interest to refer briefly to its fundamental structure and functions, that is, to the question of its competence. According to Article 9 of the Statute, the Commission has the following functions and powers:

a. To develop an awareness of human rights among the peoples of America;

b. To make recommendations to the Governments of the member states in general, if it considers such action advisable, for the adoption of progressive measures in favor of human rights within the framework of their domestic legislation and, in accordance with their constitutional precepts, appropriate measures to further the faithful observance of those rights;

c. To prepare such studies or reports as it considers advisable in the performance of its duties;

d. To urge the Governments of the member states to supply it with information on the measures adopted by them in matters of human rights;

e. To serve the Organization of American States as an advisory body in respect of human rights.

Article 10 states, moreover, that

In performing its assignment, the Commission shall act in accordance with the pertinent provisions of the Charter of the Organization and bear in mind particularly that, in conformity with the American Declaration of the Rights and Duties of Man, the rights of each man are limited by the rights of others, by the security of all, and by the just demands of the general welfare and the advancement of democracy.

Leaving for the present the evaluation of the progress achieved by the inter-American system in the field of both human rights and representative democracy, it should be noted that in the deliberations of the OAS Council at the time the Statute was being drawn up, careful study was given to the question of whether or not the Commission should be authorized to examine complaints or accusations made by private persons (individuals, groups or entities), and to process them according to special procedures. As may be observed from the quoted articles, the decision was against granting this competence. The legislative history of these articles also reveals opposition to the idea of the Commission making recommendations to the governments directly and individually. In spite of the Commission's lack of competence in this particular and the failure of the Council to act upon its request for wider powers, these limitations have been overcome in large measure in practice, owing to its liberal and progressive interpretation of its Statutes and the general approval with which its actions have met.[12] A brief summary of the Commission's actions will corroborate the above observations.

[12] In the aforesaid report submitted by the Inter-American Commission on Human Rights to the Second Special Inter-American Conference, the Commis-

The Situation Regarding Human Rights in the Dominican Republic

When the Commission began its work in October 1960, it received numerous communications denouncing serious and repeated violations of human rights in the Dominican Republic. Accordingly, it ordered the Secretariat to prepare a background document on the situation regarding human rights in that country, which it considered together with the new complaints or claims, some of which requested the Commission to go to Dominican territory. Upon its decision to visit the Dominican Republic to make a direct study of the situation in that country and to inquire into the denunciations, it requested and received the consent of the Dominican Government. During its stay in the country, from October 22 to 28, 1961, the Commission visited the capital city and the cities of La Vega, Moca, Santiago de los Caballeros, and San Francisco de Macorís, holding, in all these places, interviews with the civil authorities as well as with members of political, workers', and professional groups and private citizens.

On November 8, 1961, the Commission sent the Dominican Government a note regarding its direct verifications and observations in the course of its visit to the country. The note referred specifically to the activities of the so-called "paleros" [literally, those who beat others with a stick], and to the excesses by the police and other authorities at the time of the students' and workers' conflicts that occurred during the so-called "process of democratization", to the limitations on the exercise of freedom of expression, the lack of freedom for labor unions, and deportations of Dominican citizens for political reasons.[13]

During its Fourth Session (April 1962) the Commission approved a report based on the denunciations and information received from the time of its First Session and those obtained on its visit to Do-

---

sion states the following on this matter: "Through sound and correct interpretation of paragraphs b, c and d of Article 9 of the Statute, the Commission approved a resolution that was subsequently incorporated into its Regulations, whereby it is considered competent to take cognizance of written communications or claims that it receives involving alleged violations of human rights within the American states, and to transmit the pertinent parts thereof to the states interested, requesting them to supply the pertinent information and recommending to them that they adopt, in accordance with their respective constitutional precepts appropriate measures to further the faithful observance of those rights.

"Only one American state has objected to this interpretation, which has thus been firmly established, since it is derived from the natural meaning of the statutory precepts and the basic principle that governs the functioning of the Commission, namely, that it is the mandatory agency of the Organization of American States to promote respect for the human rights set forth in the American Declaration of the Rights and Duties of Man (Articles 1 and 2 of the Statute)." Cf. Document mentioned in Note 9, pp. 5-6.

[13] For a more detailed report on the activities of the Commission, see Appendix I of the report mentioned in Note 9, p. 18.

minican territory in October 1961. This report contains a summary of the Commission's activities in regard to this case, as well as a study of the violations of human rights. In that document the Commission concludes that the most flagrant violations were perpetrated during the regime of Generalissimo Rafael L. Trujillo and that, "While the situation with respect to human rights improved after July 1, 1961, and new legislation was passed containing reforms designed to bring this about, during the government of President Balaguer serious violations continued, as pointed out in this report. . . ."[14]

During its First Special Session (January 1963), the Commission considered the invitation extended by the Dominican Government for it to return to that country to complete the mission it had begun in 1961. Since five of its seven members had participated in the First Symposium on Representative Democracy held in Santo Domingo from December 17 to 22, 1962, which had afforded them an opportunity to observe the elections of December 20, 1962, and consequently to verify the progress made by the Dominican Republic in the field of human rights, the Commission considered it unnecessary to visit there and, on January 18, 1963, addressed a note to the Dominican Government recording its satisfaction with the situation regarding human rights in that country and with the exemplary conduct of the Dominican authorities and citizens during the aforementioned elections.

During its Sixth Session (April-May 1963), the Commission visited the Dominican Republic at the invitation of President Bosch, to study accusations made by the leaders of various opposition political parties regarding serious violations of human rights. For that purpose, the Commission spent from May 4 to 9 in the city of Santo Domingo, and after studying the reported incidents and the information furnished by the Government and the declarers, reached the following conclusions, which were transmitted to the Dominican Government by a note of May 20, 1963:

> 1. That it would refrain from qualifying the acts denounced in the aforementioned cable, and particularly the political aspects that such acts could imply, because of the conviction that the clarification of these acts properly belonged to the administration of justice of the Dominican Republic, and also because the Attorney General of the republic had informed the Commission that the investigation of these acts was in the stage of preliminary court proceedings; and
>
> 2. That the Commission clearly understood the full significance of the trust shown by the Dominican Government in inviting it to meet again in Santo Domingo, and that it hoped that the Dominican people would continue to enjoy the benefits of representative democracy recently re-

---

[14] *Cf. Report on the Situation Regarding Human Rights in the Dominican Republic,* OEA/Ser.L/V/II.4, Doc. 32, p. 33.

established, and of the human rights upon which the existence of democratic government depends.

As a result of the political events that occurred in the Dominican Republic in September 1963, the Commission again began to receive numerous communications or complaints regarding violations of human rights in that country and decided to ask the Dominican Government for the relevant information and to continue studying the situation.[15]

More recently, because of the events which took place in the Dominican Republic at the end of April, 1965, the Commission received a communication from the so-called "Constitutional Government" requesting it to go to that country to verify and adopt the necessary measures regarding the "abuses and assassinations committed by the troops of the Government of National Reconstruction." Similarly, the so-called "Government of National Reconstruction" called the attention of the Commission to the urgent necessity that existed for it to make an on-the-spot examination of the situation regarding human rights in that country. Furthermore, the OAS Secretary General, in a cable of May 25, 1965, to the President of the Tenth Meeting of Consultation of Ministers of Foreign Affairs, stated that he considered essential and urgent the presence in Santo Domingo of the Inter-American Commission on Human Rights.

Complying with the requests of both governments as well as the appeal of the Secretary General, the Commission went to Santo Domingo on June 1, 1965, and from that date maintained a representative there in order to attend to the numerous denunciations and complaints regarding violations of human rights which were submitted to it. In interviews with the authorities of those governments, both sides manifested their respect for the American Declaration of the Rights and Duties of Man, and furnished the Commission all the facilities necessary for the fulfillment of its mission. In view of these manifestations, the Commission convinced the two governments to sign a document by which they promised to respect the Declaration and to provide the Commission with the necessary facilities. The "Constitutional Government" signed the document on June 8, 1965, and the "Government of National Reconstruction" did the same on the following day.

In carrying out its mission, the Commission visited numerous prisons, both in the zone of the "Constitutional Government" and the "Government of National Reconstruction", and made several trips to the interior of the country. It took a number of steps to improve the condition of political prisoners or to free persons not being held on specific charges. The preliminary report regarding the

---

[15] *Cf.* Report of the Commission mentioned in Note 9, p. 30.

situation of human rights in the Dominican Republic, submitted by
the Chairman of the Commission for consideration by the members,
details the activities which were being undertaken. Some conclusions
of that report were:[16]

> 1. Overcrowding in some cells of prisons under the authority of the
> Government of National Reconstruction was the most negative scene
> observed by the Commission in its trip through the Dominican Republic.
> 2. Arrest for reasons of political vengeance or partisan rancor should
> be entirely avoided. The Commission knows of many cases in which
> those arrested were the victims of the hatred or passion of determined
> agents of authority, either for the purpose of holding them as hostages
> or in order to terrorize their families. This problem continues on both
> sides of the conflict.
> 3. The disappearance of persons arrested is another important phe-
> nomenon observed by the Commission. Many cases have been reported
> of persons arrested who were transferred from one prison to another
> without reaching their destination. This aspect should be investigated
> and prevented, particularly in the area under the authority of the Gov-
> ernment of National Reconstruction, where, because of the greater
> number of prisons and greater distances, a larger number of denun-
> ciations have been forthcoming.
> 4. The Commission has observed that despite the existence of written
> orders authorizing the visiting of prisoners by their families, some of
> them are unable to see their families because this is prevented by the
> prison guards.
> The Commission learned of cases in which the families of prisoners
> waited 30 and 40 consecutive days without seeing them, and even with-
> out being certain that they were receiving the clothes or meals they
> brought them.
> 5. The Commission has likewise observed that the wages of persons
> imprisoned for political reasons are withheld, with the result that their
> families are left in desperate circumstances.
> 6. The Commission observed that in some cases imprisoned persons
> were punished physically, in both factions, in flagrant violation of the
> right of the individual to physical integrity.

On June 23 the Chairman convoked a special meeting of the
Commission (Eleventh Session), for the purpose of determining the
specific tasks that it was responsible for undertaking in the Dominican Republic. During the meeting, which took place from July
21 to 23, a resolution was approved regarding the activities which
the Commission would continue to carry out until the establishment
of a Provisional Government. Concerning the work to be done in the
period between the establishment of the Provisional Government
and the installation of an elected government, another resolution was
approved authorizing the Chairman to maintain a representative of
the Commission in the Dominican Republic, provided that by

---

[16] See the Preliminary Report of the Chairman of the Commission on this new
action in the Dominican Republic, OEA/Ser.L/V/II.12, Doc. 2 Rev., 23 June
1965, *passim.*

virtue of the Institutional Act the Provisional Government agreed to the presence of the Commission, to promote respect for the human rights contained in the American Declaration of the Rights and Duties of Man, and considering especially strict adherence to Articles I, II, IV, IX, X, XVII, XVIII, XX, XXI, XXII, XXIII, XXIV, XXV, and XXVI of the Declaration.

Continuing the activity begun on June 1, 1965, during July and August the Commission visited the prisons of the country, going to many interior cities as well as the Isla Beata, in an attempt to achieve more humane treatment of the prisoners and obtain information about missing persons whose cases had been brought before the Commission. As a result of the steps taken by the Commission, more than 2,500 political prisoners were freed in the zone of the "Government of National Reconstruction", as well as more than 100 prisoners who were in the Fortaleza Ozama under the control of the "Constitutional Government".

The Institutional Act, which governs the Provisional Government, provides for the presence of the Commission in the country until the installation of the elected government. It also stipulates that the former will cooperate with the Commission to enable it to observe the fulfillment of the provisions of the Act in relation to human rights and fundamental freedoms.

The Situation Regarding Human Rights in Cuba

From the beginning of its work in October 1960, the Commission also received numerous communications denouncing serious and continuing violations of human rights in Cuba. In accordance with Article 9.d of the Statute and as provided in the Regulations, the Commission requested the government of that country to furnish the necessary information about the acts denounced.

At the Second Session (April 1961), the Commission received a substantial number of communications regarding the serious situation that existed in Cuba in connection with the Bay of Pigs invasion, and requesting it to use its good offices to prevent irreparable violations of human rights.

After careful consideration of the communications and a study of whether or not its powers enabled it to make recommendations to the Government of Cuba, the Commission concluded that it could do so, by virtue of its power to recommend the adoption of general measures within the framework of the legislation of each American state in favor of human rights, and to recommend to the member states the adoption, in accordance with their constitutional precepts, of appropriate measures to further the faithful observance of those rights (Article 9.b of the Statute). Likewise, by the authority vested in it by section d. of the same article, the Commission considered itself justified in requesting information from the Government of Cuba on measures which it adopted in the field of human rights in the current situation in the country. On April 24, 1961, the Commission transmitted the following communication to the Minister of Foreign Affairs of Cuba:[17]

> The Inter-American Commission on Human Rights, deeply concerned by communications it has received in which grave fear is expressed that your Excellency's Government may apply imminent and severe repressive measures in the present situation of Cuba that would not be in harmony with the fundamental respect for human rights prescribed by the Charter of the OAS and the American Declaration of the Rights and Duties of Man, is obedient to its duty, in accordance with the powers given in its Statute (Article 9.b), in recommending strongly to your Excellency's Government that any such measures be taken in accordance with respect for these rights, expressing confidence that this aspiration of the Commission will be satisfied in conformity with the terms of the Note which the Ministry of Foreign Affairs of Cuba addressed to the Commission on November 7, 1960.
>
> This Commission, in accordance with Article 9.d of its Statute, requests your Government to be good enough to send the Commission information on measures that it adopts in the field of human rights during the present situation.

In reply to the Commission's request for information, the Cuban Government stated that the Bay of Pigs prisoners had "received humanitarian treatment," and that the government would apply the laws in effect in Cuba "which is basically the same as legislation in force in other civilized countries, on territorial defense, and sovereignty with full rights and guarantees for the accused, . . ." It stated, moveover, that the Cuban people had been the victim of bombings and acts of armed aggression and formally requested that the Commission ask the United States "to suspend bombings, invasions and all acts of aggression . . . ."

The Commission decided, during its Third Session (October-November, 1961) to send the Cuban Government a note requesting information on the most urgent complaints and recommending that it adopt "progressive measures in favor of human rights." Earlier, the Commission had instructed its secretariat to prepare a document containing all the information available on the matter. This compilation entitled "Information on Respect for Human Rights in the Republic of Cuba", prepared for the exclusive use of the Commission, contained a summary of the political events that had taken place in Cuba since 1959; of the human rights protected by the Cuban Constitution and other laws, and an account of the communications and statements received by the Commission.

In view of the new communications or complaints received in April 1962 concerning the trials of the prisoners of the Bay of Pigs, and

---

[17] OEA/Ser.L/V/II.2, Doc. 24, p. 13.

requesting action by the Commission to prevent those prisoners from being sentenced to death, the Commission decided to address the Cuban Government on April 4, 1962, reminding it of its promise that those trials would be held "with full rights and guarantees for the accused." Similarly, the Commission referred to the obligation contained in Article 26 of the American Declaration of the Rights and Duties of Man and exhorted the Cuban Government to refrain from passing the death sentence on those tried.[18]

By cable of April 8, 1962, the Minister of Foreign Affairs of Cuba denied the Commission had the right to make recommendations and to suggest the application of "alien norms to matters in the internal jurisdiction of Cuba" and accused it of not having intervened when Cuban territory was invaded in 1961 by the "mercenaries now brought to justice," who, according to the Minister, were "in the service of a foreign power." The Commission, in its "Report on the Situation Regarding Human Rights in the Republic of Cuba", published during the Fourth Session, referred to those statements of the Cuban Foreign Minister, and declared that it did have competence to formulate recommendations to the governments of the American states in cases such as that of the trials of the prisoners of the Bay of Pigs. Moreover, in the same report, the Commission put on record its profound concern over the form of the proceedings against those prisoners, which, according to information received by it, was not in accord with the norms established in Article 26 of the American Declaration of the Rights and Duties of Man.[19]

During the same Fourth Session, the Commission studied the scope of Resolution VI of the Eighth Meeting of Consultation by which it was agreed to exclude the present Government of Cuba from participation in the inter-American system, and the position of the Commission with respect thereto. The Commission stated that in no case could it renounce its inescapable obligation to promote respect for human rights in all the member states of the Organization. Consequently, it resolved to continue to concern itself with the situation regarding human rights in Cuba and to continue to consider and to process, according to the regulations, the communications or complaints it received with respect to that country.

During the Fifth Session (September-October, 1962), the Commission considered the possibility of holding part of its meetings in

---

[18] Article XXVI of the Declaration establishes the following: "Every accused person is presumed to be innocent until proved guilty. Every person accused of an offense has the right to be given an impartial and public hearing, and to be tried by courts previously established in accordance with pre-existing laws, and not to receive cruel, infamous, or unusual punishment."

[19] See the *Report on the Situation Regarding Human Rights in the Republic of Cuba,* to which reference has been made, OEA/Ser.L/V/II.4, Doc. 30, *passim.*

Cuba, for the purpose of studying first-hand the situation regarding human rights. For this purpose, in accordance with Article 11.c of its Statute, it requested the Government of Cuba for permission to visit that country. The Government of Cuba never replied to this request.[20]

During 1962, the Commission received numerous communications denouncing the ill treatment suffered in Cuba by political prisoners and their families, and indicating that the situation appeared to be even more serious with regard to the women prisoners. Moreover, in several of these communications the Commission was asked to go to Miami, Florida to receive the testimony of many former political prisoners whose financial position did not permit them to travel to its permanent seat in Washington, D.C. Therefore, the Commission decided to transfer its seat temporarily to Miami and hold part of its First Special Session there. During five meetings held there beginning on January 20, interviews were granted to more than eighty persons, who furnished extensive documented information concerning the life and the conditions of the political prisoners in Cuba supplemented by evidence such as judicial certificates, photostatic copies, photographs, drawings, prisoners' uniforms, and some exhibits of the instruments used in the prisons by the political prisoners. Testimony was likewise presented regarding the existence of concentration camps, the living conditions therein, and the system of forced labor to which political prisoners were subjected.

On the basis of this information, the Commission prepared its "Report on the Situation of Political Prisoners and Their Relatives in Cuba", published in May 1963. This document contains one chapter with background information on the Commission's activities in this case, including the texts of the notes exchanged between the Commission and the Government of Cuba. Other chapters deal with the right to protection against arbitrary arrest, the situation of the political prisoners in Cuba, the situation of women in the political prisons, and the situation of the relatives of political prisoners. The Report contains these final considerations: "The Commission regrets that repeated requests for information addressed to the Cuban Government only received evasive replies in some cases and a complete absence of reply in others, as is described in Chapter I of this document. This has precluded the Commission from arriving at an opinion different from that which it could have if the substantial incorrectness of the denunciations received would have been proved." Furthermore, it stated that, "in carrying out its mandate 'to promote the respect for human rights' consecrated in the American Declaration

---

[20] *Cf.* OEA/Ser.L/V/II.4, Doc. 34, and OEA/Ser.L/V/II.5, Doc. 40, respectively.

of the Rights and Duties of Man, the Inter-American Commission on Human Rights would have desired that there could have been fulfilled in the case of Cuba the noble aspirations expressed in the Charter of the Organization of American States which proclaims the fundamental rights of the individual (Article 5.j) and the full observance of those rights and of the principles of universal morality (Art. 13)."[21]

At its Ninth Session (October 1964), the Commission decided to request the Cuban Government for information on several accusations received subsequently, which called for urgent attention. The note, dated October 22, 1964, referred specifically to the existence in Cuba of courts whose membership and functioning were in violation of human rights; to the review of sentences imposed on political prisoners for the purpose of increasing the penalties and to the unlawful treatment accorded to minors by the court and prison officials. The Cuban Government replied on November 4, pointing out that ". . . Cuba was arbitrarily excluded from the Organization of American States . . . and, therefore, there is no occasion for providing the information you request. The Organization of American States has no jurisdiction or competence, legally, factually, or morally, over a state that has illegally been deprived of its rights."

The Commission took cognizance of the Cuban Government's reply at its next session (March 1965) and decided to repeat its request for information and to point out, moreover, that the measure of exclusion taken by the Eighth Meeting of Consultation was directed at the "present Government of Cuba" and not at the Cuban State and that, furthermore, after carefully studying Resolution VI of the aforesaid Meeting of Consultation, the Inter-American Commission on Human Rights had stated that it could not, in any case, renounce its inescapable obligation to promote respect for human rights in all the member states of the Organization. The note, expressed in these terms, was sent to the Cuban Government on April 6, 1965.[22]

The Situation Regarding Human Rights in Haiti

During the Commission's ten sessions it took cognizance of the denunciations of repeated violations of human rights in the Republic of Haiti and requested that government to provide it with the pertinent information on those denunciations that were considered to be in order. That government furnished some information, which the Commission felt was insufficient, and restricted itself in other instances to denying that there were any violations of human rights in

---

[21] Cf. OEA/Ser.L/V/II.7, Doc. 4, 17 May 1963, passim.
[22] Cf. The Commission's reports on the work of its Ninth and Tenth Sessions, OEA/Ser.L/V/II.10, Doc. 21 and OEA/Ser.L/V/II.11, Doc. 19, respectively.

its territory. The Commission twice requested permission to visit Haitian territory for the purpose of studying the human rights situation on the spot. The government refused to permit the visit, alleging that it could be interpreted as a form of interference in the internal affairs of the republic. Since the communications the Commission had received contained denunciations regarding serious and repeated violations of human rights, it approved, at its Seventh Session (October 1963) a Report on the Situation Regarding Human Rights in Haiti, in which it recorded the following:[23]

> 1. That the request for information sent to the Government of Haiti by the Commission referred to serious and repeated violations of human rights in that country;
> 2. That the information supplied by the Government of Haiti did not relate to the complaints transmitted by the Commission in their entirety;
> 3. That, in some cases, the information supplied to the Commission by the Government of Haiti was incomplete, while in others the Government merely denied that human rights were violated in Haiti, but without supplying any information on the specific complaints transmitted by the Commission;
> 4. That on two occasions, September 26, 1962, and May 7, 1963, the Commission, in accordance with Article 11.c of its Statute, requested permission from the Government of Haiti to go to that country to study the situation regarding human rights;
> 5. That, on both occasions, the Government of Haiti refused the Commission the permission it requested, on the grounds that its visit might be interpreted as a form of interference in the internal affairs of the Republic of Haiti; and
> 6. That, on both occasions, the Commission made it expressly clear that it respected the sovereignty of Haiti, but that it was empowered by Article 11.c of its Statute to visit the territory of any American state, with prior consent of its government.

During its Ninth Session (October 1964), the Commission decided to address the Government of Haiti once more for the purpose of: a) repeating the request for information made in previous notes; b) transmitting the new claims, in which Haitian authorities were accused of serious violations of human rights; and c) requesting the Haitian Government, in the event that the accusations made were found to be true, to adopt progressive measures to promote the faithful observance of human rights.[24]

The Situation Regarding Human Rights in Other American Countries

The Commission has also acted on communications, complaints, or denunciations dealing with violations of human rights in other American countries. During its Eighth Session (April 1964), it studied documents relative to the situation in Ecuador, requesting

---

[23] *Cf.* OEA/Ser.L/V/II.8, Doc. 5, 19 November 1963.
[24] See the first of the reports mentioned in Note 22.

that government to provide it with the pertinent information, and instructing its Secretariat to prepare a background document on the situation regarding human rights in that country. The government provided the information on the alleged violations of human rights and invited the Commission to visit Ecuadorian territory to ascertain on the spot the degree of observance of human rights. The Commission decided that later, at an opportune time, it would consider the possibility of visiting that country.

Since the Seventh Session (October 1963), the Commission had received denunciations regarding violations of human rights in Guatemala. As a result of a request it made to the government of that country, it received some of the required data and entrusted to the Secretariat the preparation of a background document on the situation regarding human rights in that country.

During the latter part of 1963, the Commission received accusations regarding violations of human rights in Honduras. When the Commission requested the pertinent information, the Honduran Government replied by inviting it to send representatives to that country "in order to prove the falseness of the claims."

During its first seven sessions the Commission received communications regarding violations of human rights in Nicaragua. The information that it requested of the Nicaraguan Government was duly provided. In September 1962, the Commission again addressed that government and requested its consent to hold part of its session in the territory of that country. The consent was granted but the date for the trip was left pending. The dates suggested by the Commission were not accepted by the government. After the Seventh Session, very few communications were received and the Nicaraguan Government replied promptly to the Commission's requests for information.

From its First Session on, the Commission received accusations regarding violations of human rights in Paraguay. The information requested was provided by the government. During the Ninth Session, the Commission studied the possibility of having a subcommittee visit Paraguay and entrusted to its Secretariat the preparation of a draft report on the situation regarding human rights in that country.[25]

---

[25] See Appendix II of the report mentioned in Note 9, p. 35, with respect to these activities of the Commission. During its Tenth Session, the Commission authorized its Chairman to undertake the necessary steps before the Government of Paraguay to permit the visit of a Subcommittee. In April 1965, the Government, through its Ambassador in Chile, announced that it had extended authorization for the Chairman and Executive Secretary of the Commission to undertake the visit. This was completed in August 1965, on which occasion interviews were held with high authorities of the Paraguayan Government, trips were made

General Work Program

The Inter-American Commission on Human Rights, pursuant to Article 9.c of its Statute, also is "To prepare such studies or reports as it considers advisable in the performance of its duties." To this end, the Commission has established a work program that includes studies and reports that are, at this time, in various stages of development and which deal with the following subjects: political, economic, and social conditions of the American countries that may influence human rights; relationship between the respect for human rights and the effective exercise of representative democracy; improvement of electoral procedures and measures that should be taken to assure the effective practice of the right of suffrage; most effective measures for the judicial protection of human rights in the American states; measures designed to perfect and implement the rights to freedom of investigation, of opinion, and of the expression and dissemination of ideas; comparative study of the American Declaration of the Rights and Duties of Man, the Universal Declaration of Human Rights, and the corresponding constitutional texts of the American states; the "state of siege" in relation to human rights; situation of political refugees in the Americas.[26]

10. *Promotion of Representative Democracy*

The principle set forth in Article 5.d of the OAS Charter, quoted in the introduction to this chapter, has a long tradition in the inter-American system. It was first expressed at the Inter-American Conference held in Buenos Aires in 1936, which declared "the existence of a common democracy throughout America," based upon the form of government selected by the American republics.[27] This declaration of solidarity also established the basis for the development of the system for the "political defense" of the hemisphere; that is, the system for security against subversion, initiated in 1939 because of propaganda and other subversive activities inspired by the totalitarian ideologies of the Axis Powers.[28] It is likewise interesting to point out that in the Preamble to the Inter-American Treaty of Reciprocal Assistance (1947) it is recognized "That the obligation of mutual assistance and common defense of the American Republics is essen-

---

to several interior cities, information gathered regarding human rights and documentation obtained regarding complaints which had been addressed to the Commission.

[26] *Ibid.,* p. 35.

[27] See the complete text of the "Declaration of Principles of Inter-American Solidarity and Co-operation", in *International Conferences,* 1st Sup. (1933-1940), p. 160.

[28] On the development of the security system against subversion of extracontinental origin, see p. 113, *infra.*

tially related to their democratic ideals . . ." and that "peace is founded on justice and moral order and, consequently, . . . on the effectiveness of democracy. . . ."

After the Bogotá Conference (1948), the principle of representative democracy was called upon for various reasons and, at the same time, there were repeated efforts to make it more effective. The first initiative was taken by the Council of the OAS, acting provisionally as Organ of Consultation in the Caribbean Situation (1950). In one of the five resolutions adopted at that time, the Council pointed out that one of the factors that had contributed to the creation of a situation susceptible of disturbing the peace and security of the region was the presence of political refugees and exiles in various countries and, consequently, the problem of making the principle of representative democracy more effective.[29]

The relationship between the failure to observe this principle and the violations of human rights, on the one hand, and the political tensions that were affecting the peace of the hemisphere, on the other hand, was demonstrated in subsequent applications of the Inter-American Treaty of Reciprocal Assistance, and in certain actions by the Inter-American Peace Committee. As regards the former, it should be recalled that one of the decisions of the Organ of Consultation in the Situation between Haiti and the Dominican Republic (1963-1964) was "To urge the Government of Haiti to observe the principle of respect for human rights . . . inasmuch as compliance with that principle effectively contributes to the maintenance of peace and the diminution of international tensions. . . ."[30] As to the latter, in compliance with the express request of the Fifth Meeting of Consultation (1959), the Peace Committee prepared a special report in 1960 in which it studied "the relationship between violations of human rights or the non-exercise of representative democracy, on the one hand, and the political tensions that affect the peace of the hemisphere, on the other";[31] and in a report on its activities in one case it stated that it was evident that the violations of human rights in the Dominican Republic had increased the existing tensions in the Caribbean region.[32]

In view of the basic purpose for which it had been convoked, the aforementioned Meeting of Consultation adopted other resolutions designed to develop and strengthen the principle of representative democracy. Undoubtedly the most important of all the resolutions

---

[29] For other aspects of this resolution, see p. 129, *infra.*

[30] See the complete text of the resolution of July 16, 1963, p. 144, *infra.*

[31] *Cf.* OEA/Ser.G/VI, C./INF-699 (15 April 1960) The request of the Fifth Meeting of Consultation appears in its Resolution IV, the complete text of which is reproduced in *Appendix 14*, p. 402, *infra.*

[32] Regarding this action of the Committee, see p. 95, *infra.*

is the one known as the "Declaration of Santiago, Chile", which sets forth some of the essential attributes of the democratic system in the hemisphere. Among these are the following: "The governments of the American republics should be the result of free elections," "Perpetuation in power, or the exercise of power without a fixed term and with the manifest intent of perpetuation, is incompatible with the effective exercise of democracy."[33] The declaration was supplemented by Resolution IV of the Eighth Meeting of Consultation (1962) in which it is recommended that the governments of the American states "whose structure or acts are incompatible with the effective exercise of representative democracy hold free elections in their respective countries, as the most effective means of consulting the sovereign will of their peoples, to guarantee the restoration of a legal order based on the authority of the law and respect for the rights of the individual."[34] The Fifth Meeting entrusted to the Council of the OAS the preparation of a draft convention on "the effective exercise of representative democracy, and the establishment of the procedure and measures applicable thereto."[35] The draft was prepared a few months later and sent to the governments for their observations, but no other action was ever taken by the Council.[36]

In November 1963 concern over several *coups d'état* led the Council of the Organization to convoke, at the request of Costa Rica and Venezuela, a Meeting of Consultation pursuant to Article 39 of the Charter. The meeting was never held and was eventually cancelled because the matter it was convoked to discuss—the strengthening of representative democracy—had been included on the agenda of the Second Special Inter-American Conference.[37]

The occurrence of *coups d'état* and the problem of recognizing *de facto* governments are matters that have been accorded constant attention in the inter-American system, particularly since the Bogotá Conference (1948). In 1949, the Inter-American Juridical Committee (at the request of that conference and of the conference in Mexico City in 1945) prepared a draft and a report covering the

---

[33] See the complete text of the Declaration in *Appendix 9*, p. 370, *infra*.

[34] See the complete text of Resolution IV, Holding of Free Elections, in *Final Act* of the Eighth Meeting of Consultation, OEA/Ser.C/II.8 Corr., p. 10.

[35] See the complete text of Resolution IX, Effective Exercise of Representative Democracy, in the *Final Act* of the Fifth Meeting of Consultation, OEA/Ser. C/II.5, p. 11.

[36] See the documents of the OAS Council relative to the draft convention in OEA/Ser.E/XIII.1, Doc. 8.

[37] As to the documents relative to the convocation of this Meeting of Consultation see the *Report of the Committee on Preparations for the Meeting of Consultation of Ministers of Foreign Affairs on Representative Democracy*, OEA/Ser.E/XIII.1, Doc. 19, 10 March 1965.

most important aspects of the subject.[38] According to Article 1 of the draft,

> A de facto government has the right to be recognized whenever it fulfills the following conditions:
> a. Effective authority over the national territory, based on the acquiescence of the people manifested in an adequate manner;
> b. Ability and willingness to discharge the international obligations of the state.

As regards Article 1. a, the Juridical Committee made the following comments:

> The mere fact that a de facto government can demonstrate effective authority over the territory of the State is not sufficient to accredit it as a legal regime. This would, at the most, reveal the existence in the State of a governmental authority the effective power of which springs from the mere physical or material force of those who occupy such authority. For a government to be entitled to recognition, its authority must be supported by the will of the people, which is the only element that can impart legal force to a government which has come into power through a revolution or *coup d'état*. Although the form of expression of the popular will may vary according to circumstances in each particular case, it is nevertheless indispensable that the new government allow public opinion to manifest itself freely and fully: in short, that it duly respect the exercise of the fundamental rights and liberties of the individual. In this regard, the Committee has believed it timely to draw upon the principles affirmed in the Charter of the Organization of American States relating to this fundamental duty of the State.

When the First Meeting of the Inter-American Council of Jurists discussed the report and draft prepared by the Juridical Committee, it was unable to reach an agreement and decided to continue the study of the problem at the Second Meeting. At that time (Buenos Aires 1953), the Council of Jurists approved a resolution by which it agreed, after stating its reasons, "to reaffirm its adherence to the principles proclaimed in Resolution XXXV of the Ninth International Conference of American States regarding the exercise of the right of legation."[39]

In Resolution XXXV of the Bogotá Conference, on the Exercise of the Right of Legation, the following is stated:

> 1. That continuity of diplomatic relations among the American States is desirable.
> 2. That the right of maintaining, suspending or renewing diplomatic relations with another government shall not be exercised as a means of individually obtaining unjustified advantages under international law.

---

[38] *Cf.* Comité Jurídico Interamericano, *Recomendaciones e Informes, Documentos Oficiales, 1949-1953* (1955), p. 123.

[39] See the complete text of Resolution III, Recognition of *De Facto* Governments, in the *Final Act* of the Second Meeting of the Council of Jurists, Doc. CIJ-17, p. 10.

3. That the establishment or maintenance of diplomatic relations
with a government does not imply any judgment upon the domestic
policy of that government.

As is evident from the foregoing text, the conference proposed to
overcome the problem of the recognition of *de facto* governments by
adopting a policy conducive to a kind of tacit or automatic recognition. Nevertheless, in actual practice subsequent to Resolution
XXXV, the continuance of diplomatic relations with those governments was generally effected by the delivery of a note or, in any
event, by means of a verbal communication to the appropriate officials
of the new government, informing them of the willingness of the
other government to continue diplomatic relations. The last two
paragraphs of the resolution are clearly for the laudable purpose of
preventing recognition from being used as a means of intervening
in the internal or external affairs of a state.

Technical Assistance in Electoral Matters

It is appropriate at this time to mention a positive contribution
being made by the OAS in the promotion of the effective exercise of
representative democracy: the provision of technical assistance in the
electoral field. The Fifth Meeting of Consultation submitted to the
OAS Council a draft on this matter that was presented by the Delegation of Nicaragua, providing for the appointment of observers
for elections of high authorities upon request by the government of
a member state.[40] The OAS General Secretariat has provided technical cooperation in the electoral field to several American governments.

In January 1962, the Government of Costa Rica requested the
Secretary General of the Organization to send a direct technical
assistance mission to observe the presidential election that was to take
place in that country on February 4, 1962. Accordingly, three outstanding American citizens visited Costa Rica in February 1962 and
delivered their report directly to the President of that country. This
report was published with the authorization of the government.[41]

Pursuant to a request from the Government of the Dominican
Republic, in August 1961, a technical assistance mission provided
advisory services to that government on the essential legal requirements, regulations, and procedures, as well as the technical conditions
required for the preparation of free elections. In October 1961 the
technical mission sent its report directly to the Dominican Govern-

---

[40] See the complete text of Resolution X in the *Final Act* of the Fifth Meeting of Consultation, OEA/Ser.C/II.5, p. 12.

[41] Cf. *Report of the Technical Assistance Mission of the Organization of American States on the Presidential Elections in the Republic of Costa Rica,* Pan American Union, March 1962.

ment. It was later published by the General Secretariat with the authorization of that government.[42] It should be pointed out, moreover, that this same government, through the General Secretariat, invited a group of distinguished citizens of the hemisphere to observe the elections of December 20, 1962, and to participate, at the same time, in a symposium on representative democracy. The symposium was held from December 17 to 22, 1962, and the report prepared by it was published by the General Secretariat that same month.[43]

Complying with a request made by the Government of Nicaragua for a list recommending outstanding citizens of the hemisphere from which it might select three or four who would be invited to observe the elections of February 3, 1963, the OAS Secretary General provided that government with a list of distinguished American citizens. Three citizens selected from this list observed the aforesaid elections and transmitted their report directly to the Government of Nicaragua. In July 1963 the Government of Honduras requested the General Secretariat to send a technical assistance mission to assist it in electoral matters. The mission appointed for the purpose sent its report directly to the President of the Honduran Republic and the General Secretariat was subsequently authorized to publish it.[44]

11. Evaluation of the Progress Achieved in Both Fields

The promotion and protection of human rights and the fundamental freedoms, as well as the promotion of the effective exercise of representative democracy are fields of activity in which the inter-American system is being developed and strengthened to a truly noteworthy degree. For an overall appraisal of the progress achieved in both fields, a brief recapitulation of the most outstanding decisions and activities of the competent organs and an indication of the real meaning that should be attributed to them will suffice.

As to the promotion and protection of human rights and fundamental freedoms, progress has been possible, in large measure, due to the position that these rights and freedoms occupy in the Charter of the OAS. In contrast to the Charter of the United Nations, which provides only that it is the function of the international organization to promote respect for those rights and freedoms, with no obligation on the part of the member states to cooperate with the United Na-

---

[42] Cf. Report of the Technical Assistance Mission of the Organization of American States to the Dominican Republic on Electoral Matters, Pan American Union, November 1961.

[43] Cf. First Symposium on Representative Democracy. Final Report. Pan American Union, December 1962.

[44] Cf. Report of the Technical Assistance Mission of the Organization of American States to the Republic of Honduras on Electoral Matters, Pan American Union, October 1963.

tions in the performance of that function, Article 13 of the OAS Charter explicitly imposes upon the state the obligation to respect the rights of the human person. Thus, since an obligation of this kind is set forth in the constitutional instrument of the inter-American system, its agencies have had a solid foundation for carrying out, with ever-increasing efficiency, and not infrequently with marked audacity, the function of promoting respect for these rights and seeking their protection. The establishment of the Inter-American Commission on Human Rights was a highly important step in the process. There are two significant facts to be borne in mind here: first, that this Commission is composed not of government representatives but of persons who enjoy full autonomy in the fulfillment of their mission; and second, that the establishment of an inter-American agency invested with a function of this kind was not carried out by means of a convention, subject to formal approval by the governments.

The productive and effective work carried out by the Commission highlights the progress of the inter-American system in this field. In particular, it shows how the Commission, by its broad interpretation of its Statute, has made possible the full exercise, in written and oral statements and testimony, of the right of petition; that is, the right of individuals to have recourse to an international organization in protest against violations committed by governments, even their own government. This right is one for which the United Nations still aspires to obtain recognition. In this sense, as the Secretary General of the OAS also pointed out in his Report to the Second Special Inter-American Conference, it is undeniably an extraordinary accomplishment that the individual in the Americas has an international agency —completely autonomous and free of all government participation —to which he can resort to denounce violations of the rights and freedoms which the member states of the OAS have formally obligated themselves to respect.[45]

It is equally interesting to point out how the Commission's competence has developed with respect to its power to make recommendations to the governments. After having decided that it did have this power in relation to individual member states, the Commission has proceeded to formulate its conclusions and recommendations where there have been serious and repeated violations of human rights and has made those conclusions and recommendations public. This action has naturally made a great impact on public opinion and has helped appreciably to alleviate the situation in several countries.

The Secretary General's Report also points out the very important role played in this field by an inter-American agency composed of governmental representatives, the Inter-American Peace Committee.

---

[45] *Cf.* OEA/Ser.E/XIII.1, Doc. 16, vol. 1, p. 47.

In exercise of the new functions and powers conferred on it by Resolution IV of the Fifth Meeting of Consultation, when it took cognizance of the Peruvian Government's complaint against the Government of Cuba, the Peace Committee expressed the opinion that "The serious and systematic violation of human rights by the Government of Cuba not only constitutes one of the principal causes of the international tensions that now are affecting the peace of the Hemisphere but is in open contradiction to various instruments of the inter-American system, and particularly to the Charter of the Organization, Article 13 of which establishes that in the free development of its cultural, political and economic life, 'The State shall respect the rights of the individual. . . .'" It will be noted that in this part of the Peace Committee's report to the Eighth Meeting of Consultation it did not confine itself to dealing with the serious and systematic violation of human rights in Cuba as a cause of international tension, but considered it also as a situation in open contradiction to the OAS Charter and other inter-American instruments. Once again, the OAS goes further than the United Nations, whose organs refrain from condemning violations of human rights that do not produce a state of international tension.[46]

In spite of the progress that has been achieved in this field, it is clear that, as was stated in Resolution IX of the Eighth Meeting of Consultation, "There is pressing need for accelerating development in the hemisphere of the collective defense of human rights, so that this development may result in international legal protection of these rights." That meeting also resolved to recommend to the Council of the Organization "that it revise the Statute of the Inter-American Commission on Human Rights, broadening and strengthening the Commission's attributes and faculties to such an extent as to permit it effectively to further respect for these rights in the countries of the hemisphere." It is interesting to note, in this respect, that in another of the "whereas" clauses of Resolution IX, it is explicitly recognized that the "inadequacy" of the faculties and attributes conferred upon it by its Statute "have made it difficult for the Commission to fulfill its assigned mission."[47] It is therefore clear that, as the aforesaid report points out, compliance with this recommendation is increasingly urgent and necessary.

The Commission itself, in its Report to the Second Special Inter-American Conference, proposed the adoption of specific provisions to supplement its present Statute, amplifying and strengthening its

---

[46] *Ibid.*, p. 48. Regarding this action by the Inter-American Peace Committee, see p. 99, *infra*. The complete text of Resolution IV of the Fifth Meeting of Consultation appears in *Appendix 14*, p. 402, *infra*.

[47] *Ibid.*, pp. 48-49. See the complete text of Resolution IX in *Final Act* of the Eighth Meeting of Consultation, OEA/Ser.C/II.8 Corr., p. 16.

powers to the extent necessary for it to fulfill its mandate effectively.[48] In this regard, the Commission recommends that, in order to assure the observance of Articles 5.j, 13, 28, and 29 of the Charter, it should be authorized to process, in accordance with the procedure set forth below, communications that may be addressed to it by any person, group of persons, or any association recognized according to the laws of its country, in which a violation is alleged of any of the human rights specified in Articles I, IV, XVIII, XXV, XXVI of the American Declaration of the Rights and Duties of Man. The special procedure indicated by the Commission is:

> a. The Commission shall not process claims that are not presented within the period that it may, in its judgment, establish in its Regulations, or when there is no exhaustion of the remedies provided in the legislation of the respective state for the legal protection of the rights that it is alleged have been violated, except in case of notorious denial of justice.
>
> b. The Commission may request of the government to whose authorities the acts examined by the Commission are attributed any information that it may deem pertinent, as well as the necessary cooperation for preparing the corresponding reports.
>
> c. If a strong presumption or proof of a violation is found, the Commission shall prepare the corresponding report and make appropriate recommendations to the government concerned, even though it may not have provided information, so that they may be dealt with within the provisions of the domestic legislation of the country.
>
> d. If the government does not adopt the measures recommended within a reasonable period, the Commission may publish its report when in its opinion the violations claimed present maximum gravity and provided that publication is decided upon by the vote of an absolute majority of the members.

As was previously stated, the initiatives and measures taken with a view to ensuring the exercise of representative democracy have also had as their constitutional basis a principle established in the OAS Charter. When the Fifth Meeting of Consultation adopted the Declaration of Santiago, Chile, among other resolutions, and established in it the essential principles and attributes of "the democratic system in this hemisphere," it provided a basic impetus for the process of developing and strengthening the inter-American system in this field.

Within the framework of this process, the Eighth Meeting of Consultation's action in the case of the present Government of Cuba is of singular importance. The report that was presented to it by the Inter-American Peace Committee expressly points out the basic antagonism between the principle of representative democracy and the democratic system and "The identification of the Government of Cuba with the Marxist-Leninist ideology and socialism of the Soviet type." The concept that the adherence by any member of the OAS to

---

[48] *Cf.* Report cited in Note 9, p. 14.

Marxism-Leninism is incompatible with the inter-American system, with which 20 of the 21 participating governments agreed, was the primary basis for the exclusion of the present Government of Cuba (Resolution VI).[49] At the next meeting of the United Nations General Assembly, the Soviet and several Afro-Asian delegations objected to this action, inasmuch as it was based on the concept of the "incompatibility" of a system of government. Their objection demonstrated that, unlike the world organization, the regional organization requires the political structure of its members to adhere to the system of representative democracy. The presence of a totalitarian political structure is, by definition, antagonistic to and incompatible with the purposes and principles of the inter-American system. As the Secretary General of the OAS stated in the aforementioned report, it is, of course, not only the presence of Marxist-Leninist regimes that is being discussed but also that of any government "whose structure or acts are incompatible with the effective exercise of representative democracy," as stated by the Meeting of Consultation itself in Resolution IV, which recommended that governments in that situation hold free elections in their respective countries.

With further reference to the foregoing, it would be appropriate to make clear the true spirit and scope of Resolution IV. When the Eighth Meeting recommended that the governments hold free elections, it did so because it believed this to be the "most effective means of consulting the sovereign will of their peoples, to guarantee the restoration of a legal order based on the authority of the law and respect for the rights of the individual." Interpretation of this is made considerably easier if one takes into account the fact that the final clause of the preamble of the resolution mentions the principles expressed in the Declaration of Santiago, according to which, ". . . the governments of the American republics should be the result of free elections, and perpetuation in power, or the exercise of power without a fixed term and with the manifest intent of perpetuation, is incompatible with the effective exercise of democracy." In this respect, the failure to hold free elections does not appear by itself to be the essential or exclusive element of a government's incompatibility with the principle of the effective exercise of representative democracy. The interpretation that seems to derive most clearly from the pronouncements of both Meetings of Consultation appears to be that incompatibility stems from two conditions—that is, the failure to hold free elections and the perpetuation in power or the manifest intent of perpetuation in power.

---

[49] Regarding this action by the Inter-American Peace Committee see p. 97, *infra*. With respect to the application of the Inter-American Treaty of Reciprocal Assistance to which reference was made, including the complete text of Resolution VI, see p. 159, *infra*.

There is no need to stress the importance of a correct interpretation of the spirit and scope of Resolution IV, which expresses a reiterated position of the American governments on this subject. By way of illustration, it would be sufficient to recall one of the principal aspects of the matter: what the advent to power of *de facto* governments represents. As a matter of principle, there is no question but that this is an institution incompatible with the effective exercise of representative democracy. Nevertheless, according to the draft of the Inter-American Juridical Committee, mentioned in the preceding section, a government of that type "has the right to be recognized" when it meets certain conditions. Thus, in the opinion of the Committee, the question does not lie in denying a *de facto* government the right to be recognized, but in determining the conditions that it must meet in order to merit recognition. Its opinion must be kept in mind particularly because, in spite of the date on which the draft was published (1949), what the Committee appears to have been interested in was not so much the nature of the government as its conduct with respect to the exercise of human rights and fundamental freedoms.

Following this line of thought, it may be observed that the institution of *de facto* government, even when it is judged from the much more severe viewpoint of the effective exercise of representative democracy, is not intrinsically and necessarily incompatible with this principle. Both when it is the product of a revolutionary process in which the people have actively and directly participated, and when it is the result of a *coup d'état*, the new government may signify the overthrow of a falsely "democratic" and "constitutional" regime and the reestablishment of an order which will guarantee the respect for fundamental human rights and liberties, thereby making feasible the resumption of a genuinely constitutional and democratic process of government. Latin American experience in recent years has repeatedly demonstrated the grounds for this observation.[50]

Technical assistance in the field of elections has shown positive results in the effort to strengthen the principle of representative democracy. This was recognized by the First Symposium on Representative Democracy, which believed that "the American States should request that type of technical assistance of the Organization of American States, inasmuch as such assistance in no way constitutes interference or intervention in the internal affairs of the American nations. It is only logical that the Organization should provide technical assistance in a field as important as that of elections, in the same manner as it does in the social, economic, and cultural fields. The presence of technical missions of this type, and of observers,

---

[50] See the report by the Secretary General cited in Note 10, p. 50.

would undoubtedly guarantee, as far as possible, the honesty of the elections." The Symposium was also of the opinion "that countries having a clean democratic record will not object to having impartial observers present at the elections held on their territory. Costa Rica is an example. On the other hand, the Symposium feels that in requesting an OAS electoral technical assistance mission and in inviting observers to the elections of 20 December, the Dominican Republic demonstrated its faith in democratic electoral processes. It does not surprise the Symposium to note that dictatorial governments, invoking the principle of nonintervention, should impede or obstruct visits by the Inter-American Commission on Human Rights to their territories, or that they should consider requests for OAS electoral technical missions as contrary to that principle, and that, thereby, they should oppose activities which, as experience has demonstrated, strengthen the system of representative democracy."[51]

Respect for human rights and a faithful observance of the principle of representative democracy do not only have a very close relationship to each other, and the two together to international tensions, as has been indicated elsewhere. As has been mentioned there exists an equally close relationship with the system for the political defense of the hemisphere. With respect to the latter, it should be recalled that even in its first stage the system was not conceived merely as a series of preventive and repressive measures against subversive activity of extracontinental origin. In a report published at the end of the war, the Emergency Advisory Committee for Political Defense, which functioned in Montevideo from 1942 to 1948, pointed out that "it is an indispensable condition to securing the best practical results from the measures it recommends, that in all the American countries there exist a genuinely democratic regime, free from faults and weaknesses which would lower their resistance to the infiltration and development of totalitarian doctrines."[52] Subsequently, the Pan American Union, in examining that relationship in detail, especially as shown in the resolutions adopted by the Fourth Meeting of Consultation (1951), reiterated, in a report concerning the strengthening of internal security, that as long as attention is not given to the urgent need for strengthening and effectively exercising representative democracy "there will exist in the Americas a political and social environment always ready to receive the infiltration of anti-democratic ideas and, therefore, in which it will be difficult to resist the subversive action of international communism." The same report states that in adopting measures to oppose the subversive action of international communism, care must be taken "at the same

---

[51] See the report cited in Note 43.

[52] Cf. *Third Annual Report,* First Section, "A Study of Conditions Necessary to Assure Political Defense", Montevideo, 1947, p. 8.

time, guarding against any infringement on the rights of the human person or the basic democratic institutions of the American Republics. That is, guarding against the possibility that such ways and means be used to obstruct or suppress genuinely democratic expressions of opinion, activities or political aspirations completely foreign to international communism."[53]

Even though dealing with a subject that will be examined *in extenso* in Part Three of this study, one should not fail to make reference here to the progress that is being achieved with respect to economic, social, and cultural rights. In effect, the program for the development of Latin America formally adopted at Punta del Este (1961) presumes profound changes in economic and social structures, which, to the extent that they become realities, will overcome living conditions that are essentially incompatible with respect for human rights and fundamental freedoms. As will be seen, the Alliance for Progress does not consist merely of a program of economic development and social betterment, but also of a new concept of democracy; that is, a program that proposes profound structural changes on a basis of respect and support for democratic institutions.

The foregoing permits one to repeat that, both the promotion and protection of human rights and fundamental freedoms as well as the promotion of the exercise of representative democracy are areas of activity in which the inter-American system has shown a truly noteworthy degree of development and strength. There is nothing exaggerated in this affirmation, particularly if one takes into account, among other obstacles that had to be overcome, the traditional concept of national sovereignty and the strict interpretation that has usually been given to the principle of nonintervention. Without affecting the genuine and legitimate interests which these principles protect, it has been possible to intensify the international protection of those principles for which it has been necessary to admit the existence of a joint responsibility by the American republics. Neither human rights nor representative democracy are now matters of the exclusive competence of the state, regardless of what may be the circumstances under which a violation took place or the consequences that may have resulted. Both cases are matters which have transcended the national orbit and, therefore, neither sovereignty nor nonintervention are principles that can be opposed to a collective action, perfectly justifiable in the light of other equally established principles in the legal structure of the inter-American system.

---

[53] *Strengthening of Internal Security.* Report prepared in compliance with Resolution VIII, approved by the Fourth Meeting of Consultation of Ministers of Foreign Affairs. Washington, D. C., Pan American Union, 1953, pp. 87 and 89, respectively.

PART TWO

Pacific Settlement and Collective Security

In the inter-American system a close relationship exists between the pacific settlement of disputes and collective security, from an organic or structural point of view as much as from a procedural or operative one. It might be affirmed that in a sense they are two facets of a single, unique system of peace and security. The link between the two is established, in principle, in the Charter of the Organization of American States as well as in the Inter-American Treaty of Reciprocal Assistance, but the flexibility of these instruments has permitted it to be considerably developed and strengthened in practice. There are also important relations and links between the regional system and the system of peace and security of the United Nations, as will be shown later. The presentation in Part Two corresponds to these considerations.

Chapter V

Instruments and Machinery for Pacific Settlement

Chapter IV of the OAS charter deals with the "Pacific Settlement of Disputes", and therein are set forth the basic principles that rule the present inter-American system in this field. According to the final article of this chapter, "A special treaty will establish adequate procedures for the pacific settlement of disputes and will determine the appropriate means for their application, so that no dispute between American States shall fail of definitive settlement within a reasonable period." This "special treaty" foreseen in Article 23 is the American Treaty on Pacific Settlement or "Pact of Bogotá", signed at the Ninth International Conference of American States (Bogotá 1948). The Pact, in Articles I and II of which the obligation to "have recourse at all times to pacific procedures" is once again explicitly and categorically stipulated, was designed to replace the inter-American treaties and conventions that had been concluded during the previous 50-year period.

The inter-American peace system has other instruments and other machinery as well. The Inter-American Peace Committee, created earlier and apparently overlooked during the Bogotá Conference, is a permanent, autonomous body and its action is the most productive of all the mechanisms in the system. Brief mention might also be made of the mechanisms that have acted in an *ad hoc* manner, especially those created by the Organ of Consultation in application of the Inter-American Treaty of Reciprocal Assistance.

12. *Early Instruments for Peace*

The present system for the pacific settlement of disputes is a direct descendent of the group of inter-American instruments concluded prior to the Bogotá Conference (1948). However, of great importance also were the earlier efforts of the newly independent Latin American countries to establish methods and procedures to forestall disputes and assure their pacific settlement.

The first of those efforts appears in several dispositions of the Treaty of Perpetual Union, League, and Confederation, signed at the Congress of Panama (1826). Among the principal objects or functions of the General Assembly of Ministers Plenipotentiary set forth in Article 13 of the treaty was that of endeavoring "to secure conciliation, or mediation, in all questions which may arise between the allied powers, or between any of them and one or more powers foreign to the confederation, whenever threatened of a rupture, or engaged in war because of grievances, serious injuries, or other complaints." In addition, in Articles 16, 17, 18, and 19 the treaty established the parties' obligation to amicably compromise between themselves all differences and to seek a settlement through the assembly, whose decision would be obligatory if the parties had expressly agreed thereto. After setting forth the procedure to be followed to reach a pacific settlement, in accordance with the different circumstances foreseen in the treaty itself, Article 19 provided for the exclusion from the confederation of any party that commenced hostilities against another in violation of that procedure, or that failed to comply with the decisions of the assembly after having previously recognized them as obligatory.[1]

The obligation of resolving international disputes by peaceful means, particularly through arbitration, if direct negotiations had not led to a settlement, appears as a basic principle in the treaties signed after 1826 such as those of Lima (1848), and those of Santiago, Chile, and Washington, D.C., both of 1856. Special mention should be made of the treaty signed at the second Congress of Lima (1864-1865) on the "Conservation of Peace Among the Contracting American States". Article 1 of the treaty established the obligation not only of not having recourse to the use of arms as a means of settling differences, but also of employing "exclusively pacific means to terminate those differences, submitting them to the unappealable decision of an arbiter when they cannot be compromised in any other way." It is doubly interesting to note the other stipulation contained in Article 2: when the interested parties could not agree on the naming of an arbiter, this would be done by an assembly of plenipotentiaries appointed by the contracting states and at least equal in number to the majority of the said states. In the event that the interested parties were unable to agree about the procedure, Article 5 authorized the arbiter to establish it.[2]

When relating, however briefly, these interesting Latin American

---

[1] Cf. *International Conferences* (1889–1928), p. xxviii. With reference to the Congress of Panama and other aspects of the treaty see *Introduction,* p. iv, *supra.*

[2] Cf. J. M. Yepes, *Del Congreso de Panama a la Conferencia de Caracas, 1826–1954.* Caracas, 1955, vol. 1, p. 206. The complete text of the *Tratado de Lima* of January 23, 1865 appears on p. 258.

antecedents, another important one must be included: the Central American Court of Justice. The Court was created by a treaty signed by the five Central American countries on December 20, 1907, and functioned in the city of Cartago, Costa Rica during the ten years the treaty was in force. The most noteworthy characteristic of this first permanent tribunal lay in its competence to take cognizance "of the questions which individuals of one Central American country may raise against any of the other Contracting Governments, because of the violation of Treaties or Conventions, and other cases of an international character; no matter whether their own Government supports said claim or not; and provided that the remedies which the laws of the respective country provide against such violation shall have been exhausted or that denial of justice shall have been shown."

The Court's labors were most productive. Five questions of which it took cognizance were brought by individuals under the foregoing clause. The Bryan-Chamorro Treaty, between the United States and Nicaragua, by which the first obtained concessions for the construction of an interoceanic canal and the establishment of a naval base on the Gulf of Fonseca, gave rise to two international litigations; the second of these dealt with the juridical nature of the Gulf of Fonseca which borders on Nicaragua and two other Central American countries.[3]

Since the First International American Conference (1889-1890) the development and perfecting of the principles and mechanisms of pacific settlement were of constant concern, as is revealed by the numerous instruments adopted at various inter-American conferences. The first instrument of a conventional nature[4] was the Treaty on Compulsory Arbitration, signed on January 29, 1902 at the Second Conference. It stipulates the obligation of submitting to the decision of arbiters all controversies that exist or may arise and which diplomacy cannot settle, provided that in the exclusive judgment of any of the interested nations said controversies do not affect either the independence or the national honor (Art. 1). Article 3 contemplates recourse to the Permanent Court of Arbitration, created by the Convention of The Hague of July 29, 1899. In addition to establishing procedures of good offices and mediation, the treaty foresees the establishment of an International Commission of Inquiry for those

---

[3] Cf. Anales de la Corte de Justicia Centroamericana (1911), vol. 1, p. 3.

[4] The text of the following 12 instruments, as well as the reservations attached to them and the date of deposit of the respective instruments of adherence and ratification, are contained in Inter-American Peace Treaties and Conventions, 2nd ed. rev., Washington, D.C., Pan American Union, 1961 (Treaty Series No. 16). They are also included in The International Conferences of American States (1889–1954), 3 vols.

controversies arising from a difference of opinion on points of fact (Art. 13). The Treaty was signed by nine countries, ratified by six, and entered into force on January 31, 1903.

The next inter-American convention was signed on May 3, 1923 at the Fifth International Conference of American States. This is the Treaty to Avoid or Prevent Conflicts Between the American States, usually called the "Gondra Treaty". After condemning, in the preamble, "armed peace which increases military and naval forces beyond the necessities of domestic security and the sovereignty and independence of the States," Article I stipulates that all controversies which for any cause whatsoever may arise between two or more of the contracting parties and which it has been impossible to settle through diplomatic channels, or to submit to arbitration in accordance with existing treaties, shall be submitted for investigation and report to a five-member commission, composed of nationals of the American states, as provided in Article IV. Article III deals with the establishment of two permanent commissions, one with its seat in Washington and the other in Montevideo. The findings of the commission of inquiry will be considered as reports and will not have the value or force of judicial decisions or arbitral awards (Art. VI). All 21 republics signed or later adhered to the "Gondra Treaty" and 20 ratified it; it entered into force on October 8, 1924.

At the International Conference of American States on Conciliation and Arbitration, held in Washington from December 1928 to January 1929, three instruments of the type in reference were signed.[5] In one of these, the General Convention of Inter-American Conciliation, the obligation is established to submit to the procedure of conciliation all controversies of any kind which have arisen or may arise between the parties for any reason and which it may not have been possible to settle through diplomatic channels (Art. 1). According to Article 2, the Commission of Inquiry to be established pursuant to the provisions of Article IV of the "Gondra Treaty" shall likewise have the character of Commission of Conciliation, and according to Article 3, the Permanent Commissions established by virtue of Article III of the aforesaid treaty shall be bound to exercise conciliatory functions. The function of the Commission, as an organ of conciliation, is to procure the conciliation of the differences subject to its examination by endeavoring to effect a settlement between the parties (Art. 6), but its report and recommendations shall not

---

[5] The English, Spanish, Portuguese and French texts of these three instruments are included in *Proceedings of the International Conference of American States on Conciliation and Arbitration, held at Washington, December 10, 1928–January 5, 1929.* Washington, D.C., U.S. Government Printing Office, 1929, p. 634. English text also appears in *International Conferences* (1889–1928), pp. 455–462.

have the character of a decision nor an arbitral award and shall not
be binding on the parties in any respect (Art. 9). The Convention
was signed by the 20 countries participating in the Conference and
later ratified by 18, entering into force on November 15, 1929.

The second instrument signed at the Conference of Washington
was the General Treaty of Inter-American Arbitration. Article 1
stipulated obligatory arbitration of all differences of an international
character which have arisen or may arise between the contracting
parties by virtue of a claim of right made by one against the other
under treaty or otherwise, which it has not been possible to adjust
by diplomacy and which are juridical in their nature by reason of
being susceptible of decision by the application of the principles of
law. In the same article, the four categories established in Article 38
of the Statute of the then Permanent Court of International Justice
are considered as included among the questions of juridical character. Nevertheless, those controversies which are within the domestic jurisdiction of any of the parties and not controlled by international law, as well as those which affect the interest or refer to the
action of a state not a party to the treaty, are excepted from the stipulations of the treaty (Art. 2). The designation of an arbitrator or
tribunal depends on the agreement of the parties, according to Article
3, as does the formulation of a special agreement (Art. 4). The
award, duly pronounced and notified to the parties, settles the dispute
definitively and without appeal and the differences which arise with
regard to its interpretation or execution shall be submitted to the
decision of the court which rendered the award (Art. 7). Of the
20 signatory countries, 13 attached reservations primarily with regard
to the matters to be excluded from obligatory arbitration. The treaty
was ratified by 16 countries, 10 of these with reservations, and entered into force on October 28, 1929.

The Protocol of Progressive Arbitration is the third instrument
concluded at the Washington Conference. As a Protocol to the General Treaty of Inter-American Arbitration, signed like the other
instruments on January 5, 1929, it proposed to establish a procedure by which the exceptions or reservations attached to the General Treaty may from time to time be abandoned, thus progressively
extending the field of arbitration. Along with this proposal, explicitly
stated in the preamble of the Protocol, Article 1 stipulates that any
party to the General Treaty may at any time deposit with the Department of State of the United States of America an appropriate instrument evidencing that it has abandoned in whole or in part the exceptions from arbitration stipulated in the said treaty or the reservation
or reservations attached by it thereto. Only 10 countries ratified the
Protocol and it entered into force on the date on which each respective instrument of ratification was deposited.

On October 10, 1933 six Latin American countries signed the Anti-War Treaty of Non-Aggression and Conciliation, also known as the "Saavedra Lamas Pact", to which the remaining member states of the inter-American system as well as 11 European countries later adhered.[6] This instrument was intended to condemn wars of aggression and territorial acquisitions obtained by armed conquest, making the first impossible and establishing the invalidity of the second through the positive provisions of the treaty, in order to replace them with pacific solutions based on lofty concepts of justice and equality. In the preamble it is also stated that one of the most effective means of assuring the moral and material benefits which peace offers to the world is the organization of a permanent system of conciliation of international disputes.

Consequently, in Articles I and II wars of aggression are condemned and it is declared that the settlement of disputes of any kind shall be effected only by the pacific means which have the sanction of international law and that the contracting parties will not recognize any territorial arrangement which is not obtained by pacific means, nor the validity of the occupation or acquisition of territories that may be brought about by force of arms. Article IV stipulates the obligation to submit the disputes to the conciliation procedure established by the treaty and Article V sets forth the only limitations to the conciliation procedure which may be formulated at the time of signature, ratification or adherence. The treaty calls for the establishment of a conciliation commission, in the absence of a permanent conciliation commission or of some other international agency charged with this mission by virtue of previous treaties in effect, and determines the formation of the said commission (Art. VI). The report of the commission shall in no case have the character of a final decision or arbitral award, either with respect to the exposition or interpretation of the facts, or with regard to the considerations or conclusions of law (Art. X).

The majority of the countries that signed, adhered to, or ratified this treaty attached reservations, and it entered into force on the date of each respective adherence or ratification.

On December 26, 1933 the contracting parties of the General Convention of Inter-American Conciliation of January 5, 1929, represented at the Seventh International Conference of American States, signed an Additional Protocol to the said convention since they were convinced of the advantage of giving a permanent character to the committees of investigation and conciliation foreseen in Article

---

[6] The European countries that adhered to this treaty were Bulgaria, Czechoslovakia, Finland, Greece, Italy, Norway, Portugal, Rumania, Spain, Turkey and Yugoslavia.

2 of that convention. To this effect, Article 1 of the Additional Protocol establishes that each signatory of the "Gondra Treaty" shall name, as soon as possible, by means of a bilateral agreement, those members of the various commissions provided for in Article IV of the said treaty. The commissions so named shall have a permanent character and shall be called Commissions of Investigation and Conciliation. On the other hand, the commissions organized in fulfillment of Article III of the "Gondra Treaty" shall be called Permanent Diplomatic Commissions of Investigation and Conciliation (Art. 3). Articles 4 and 5 of the Protocol deal with the procedures for the organization of the respective commissions. The Protocol was signed by 13 countries, ratified by nine, and entered into force on March 10, 1935.

At the Inter-American Conference for the Maintenance of Peace, held in Buenos Aires in 1936, the remaining five inter-American instruments in reference were signed.[7] One of these is the Convention for the Maintenance, Preservation and Reestablishment of Peace, signed like the others on December 23, 1936.

This convention inaugurates the system or procedure of consultation, later developed and perfected in various conventional and other instruments. In this regard, Article I establishes that in the event the peace of the American republics is menaced, and in order to coordinate efforts to prevent war, any of the governments of the American republics signatory to the Treaty of Paris of 1928 or to the Treaty of Non-Aggression and Conciliation of 1933, shall consult with the other governments of the American republics which, in such event, shall consult together for the purpose of finding and adopting methods of peaceful cooperation. In further reference to this stipulation, Article II establishes that in the event of war, or a virtual state of war between American states, the governments represented at the Conference shall undertake without delay the necessary mutual consultations, in order to exchange views and to seek, within the obligations resulting from the pacts mentioned above and from the standards of international morality, a method of peaceful collaboration. The same article also foresees consultation in the event of an international war outside America which might menace the peace of the American republics, to determine the proper time and manner in which the signatory states, if they so desire, may eventually cooperate in some action tending to preserve the peace of the American Continent. The convention, which was ratified by 17 countries, entered into force on August 25, 1937.

The second instrument to emanate from the Conference of Buenos

---

[7] *International Conferences*, 1st Sup. (1933–1940), pp. 188–201. The English, Spanish and French texts of these five instruments were also contained in the pamphlet *Final Act of the Conference*, Buenos Aires, 1937.

Aires is an Additional Protocol Relative to Non-Intervention, concluded for the purpose of reaffirming the principle set forth in Article 8 of the Convention on Rights and Duties of States signed at the Seventh Conference, according to which "no state has the right to intervene in the internal or external affairs of another." Consequently, after declaring inadmissible the intervention, directly or indirectly, and for whatever reason, in the internal or external affairs of any of the contracting parties, Article 1 establishes that the violation of this provision shall give rise to mutual consultation, with the object of exchanging views and seeking methods of peaceful adjustment. Article 2 stipulates that every question concerning the interpretation of the Protocol, which it has not been possible to settle through diplomatic channels, shall be submitted to the procedure of conciliation provided for in the agreements in force, or to arbitration, or to judicial settlement. The Additional Protocol was ratified by 16 countries and entered into force on August 25, 1937.

The Treaty on the Prevention of Controversies was signed in order to adopt a preventive system for the consideration of possible causes of future controversies and their settlement by pacific means. In order to assure this objective, stated in the preamble, Article 1 of the Treaty sets forth the obligation to establish permanent bilateral mixed commissions composed of representatives of the signatory governments which shall in fact be constituted at the request of any of them. It shall be the duty of these commissions to study and propose, for the purposes set forth in the treaty, the additional or detailed lawful measures which it might be convenient to take in order to promote, as far as possible, the due and regular application of treaties in force between the respective parties (Art. 2). The treaty was ratified by 14 of the signatories and entered into force on July 29, 1937.

Also signed at the Conference of Buenos Aires was the Inter-American Treaty on Good Offices and Mediation since it was considered that, notwithstanding the pact concluded between the governments represented at the Conference, it was desirable to facilitate recourse to peaceful methods for the solution of controversies to an even greater degree. Articles I and II of the treaty stipulate the right to have recourse to the good offices or mediation of an eminent citizen of any other American country, and the Pan American Union was charged with the preparation of a list on the basis of the names given by each government of two citizens selected from among the most eminent by reason of their high character and juridical learning. Articles III, IV and V refer to the procedure to be followed in setting in motion the mechanism established by the treaty. It was ratified by 15 countries and entered into force on July 29, 1937.

The fifth and final instrument concluded at Buenos Aires was the Convention to Coordinate, Extend and Assure the Fulfillment of the Existing Treaties Between the American States. With that purpose, and recognizing the need for placing the greatest restrictions upon resort to war, the Convention reaffirms, in Article 1, the obligations entered into to settle, by pacific means, controversies of an international character that may arise between them. Article 2 stipulates that in all matters which affect peace on the Continent the consultation and cooperation provided for in the Convention for the Maintenance, Preservation and Reestablishment of Peace signed on the same date will be carried out, having as their object to assist, through the tender of friendly good offices and of mediation, the fulfillment by the American republics of existing obligations for pacific settlement. The remaining articles stipulate the method or procedure to be followed when a controversy arises or hostilities break out. The convention was ratified by 14 of the signatories and entered into force on November 24, 1938.

13. *The American Treaty on Pacific Settlement ("Pact of Bogotá")*

In spite of the specific purpose of the fifth instrument concluded at the Conference of Buenos Aires, the Eighth International Conference of American States, held in Lima only two years later, considering that "The juridical measures to prevent war in America are scattered in numerous treaties, conventions, pacts and declarations which it is necessary to coordinate into an organized and harmonious unified instrument," resolved that the various projects submitted in the course of its deliberations be classified by the Pan American Union and transmitted by it to each of the American governments with a request for its opinion and proposals so that the International Conference of American Jurists might undertake to prepare a "Peace Code" and render a detailed report of its labors at the next International Conference of American States.[8] In 1943 the then Governing Board of the Pan American Union requested the Inter-American Juridical Committee to prepare a coordinated draft Peace Convention. In accordance with this request, the Committee studied existing inter-American agreements as well as the projects presented at the Conference of Lima and prepared two drafts.[9]

The question entered a new phase as a result of Resolution XXXIX of the Inter-American Conference on Problems of War and Peace, held in Mexico City in the spring of 1945. Once again it was recommended that the Inter-American Juridical Committee undertake the immediate preparation of a draft "Inter-American Peace

[8] See the complete text of Resolution XV in *International Conferences,* 1st Sup. (1933–1940), p. 244.
[9] *Cf.* Comité Jurídico Interamericano, *Recomendaciones e Informes, Documentos Oficiales, 1945–1947,* Rio de Janeiro, 1950, p. 37.

System", which would coordinate the continental agreements for the prevention and pacific solution of controversies.[10] The Committee, therefore, prepared a third draft in September of that year which was transmitted to the American governments for their observations. On this basis, the Committee drafted a second text which was sent to the Governing Board in November 1947. In this latter text the Committee, changing an earlier opinion, decided on a system of obligatory arbitration for differences of any nature, juridical or not, that in the opinion of one of the parties it had not been possible to resolve by one of the procedures of mediation, investigation, or conciliation established in the same draft.[11] In the report accompanying the aforesaid text the Committee recalled Resolution X of the Conference at which the Inter-American Treaty of Reciprocal Assistance was signed, in which it was recommended that at the Ninth International Conference of American States, to be held at Bogotá in 1948, "there be studied with a view to approval, institutions which may give effectiveness to a pacific system of security and among them compulsory arbitration for any dispute which may endanger peace and which is not of a juridical nature."[12]

It was against this background and on the basis of this documentation that the Bogotá Conference proceeded to draw up the American Treaty on Pacific Settlement or "Pact of Bogotá".[13] After lengthy discussion about the nature and scope of arbitration, the Conference leaned toward and later decided in favor of a system that had not been foreseen in any of the instruments or drafts known prior to that date. The new system established obligatory judicial settlement as the definitive method for the solution of controversies. The said settlement was to be achieved through the International Court of Justice and in accordance with its Statute. Arbitration, on the other hand, would only be obligatory when the Court declared itself to be without jurisdiction to hear the controversy. Therefore, when examining the general outline of the system for peaceful settlement established in the Pact, as is done here, it should be pointed out, above all, that by virtue of Article XXXI the High Contracting Parties "declare that they recognize, in relation to any other American State, the juris-

---

[10] See the complete text of Resolution XXXIX in *International Conferences,* 2nd Sup. (1942-1954), p. 100.

[11] *Cf.* Comité Jurídico Interamericano, *op. cit.,* p. 161 and p. 173.

[12] See the complete text of Resolution X in *International Conferences,* 2nd Sup. (1942-1954), p. 154.

[13] The complete text of the "Pact of Bogotá", as well as the reservations attached and the date of deposit of the respective ratifications, appears in *Appendix 12,* p. 387, *infra.* For the Spanish, French, and Portuguese texts see OEA Documentos Oficiales OEA/Ser. A/3 (SEPF), Serie sobre Tratados No. 17, Washington, D.C., 1961.

diction of the Court as compulsory *ipso facto,* without the necessity of
any special agreement so long as the present Treaty is in force, in all
disputes of a juridical nature that arise among them concerning. . . ."
There follow the four categories of disputes listed in paragraph 2
of Article 36 of the Statute of the International Court of Justice.[14]
In this sense, the pact itself constitutes an unconditional declaration
of the type foreseen in that article.

The foregoing notwithstanding, the compulsory nature of the
judicial settlement is subject, to be precise, to the fact that the conciliation procedure established in the pact or by the decision of the
parties has not led to a solution and, in addition, that the said parties
have not agreed on an arbitral procedure. Only in these circumstances
may one of the parties exercise its right to have recourse to the Court
and the other, therefore, be subject to its jurisdiction (Art. XXXII).
The optional nature of the procedure of arbitration, to which Chapter Five of the pact refers, is expressly established in Article
XXXVIII. Now, according to Article XXXIX the submission of the
controversy to arbitration, in accordance with the procedure set forth
in that chapter, becomes compulsory in the event the Court declares
itself to be without jurisdiction to hear and adjudge the controversy
for any reason other than those mentioned in Article XXXIV. As
distinguished from previous inter-American instruments, for the
purposes of both Articles XXXIX and XXXVIII, once the procedure of arbitration is initiated, there are provisions to avoid the failure
of the arbitration due to disagreement between the parties either on
the constitution of the tribunal or the drawing up of the special agreement.

The motives for which the Court may decline to exercise its jurisdiction are those referring to matters regarding which, by virtue of
Articles V, VI and VII, the application of this and the other procedures set forth in the pact is excluded. Although Article V is the
only one in which the submission to the Court of the preliminary
question is expressly stipulated, Article XXXIII contains a general
provision that if there is no agreement as to the Court's jurisdiction
over a controversy, the Court shall first decide that question.

In addition, the order in which the pacific procedures are established in the treaty, which besides the ones mentioned also include
good offices and mediation as well as investigation as an integral
part of the conciliation procedure, does not signify that the parties
may not have recourse to the one they consider most appropriate in

---

[14] These four categories are as follows: "a. The interpretation of a treaty;
b. Any question of international law; c. The existence of any fact which, if
established, would constitute the breach of an international obligation; d. The
nature or extent of the reparation to be made for the breach of an international
obligation."

each case, or that they should use all these procedures, or that any of them have preference over others except as expressly provided (Art. III). However, once any pacific procedure has been initiated, whether by agreement between the parties or in fulfillment of the treaty or a previous pact, no other procedure may be commenced until that procedure is concluded (Art. IV). Chapter Six deals with the failure to carry out the obligations imposed by a decision of the International Court of Justice or by an arbitral award, in which case a Meeting of Consultation of Ministers of Foreign Affairs is to be called to agree upon appropriate measures to ensure the fulfillment of the judicial decision or arbitral award, prior to having recourse to the United Nations Security Council. Finally, Chapter Seven authorizes the parties concerned in the solution of a controversy, by agreement, to petition, through the Council of the OAS, the General Assembly or the Security Council of the United Nations to request an advisory opinion of the International Court of Justice on any juridical question.

In accordance with the objectives of the Pact of Bogotá, as can be noted at the beginning of this section, Article XVIII establishes that, as the treaty enters into force through the successive ratifications of the High Contracting Parties, the treaties, conventions, and protocols listed in the article and examined in the previous section, shall cease to be in force with respect to them.

Granted the compulsory nature of the system of pacific settlement established in the American Treaty on Pacific Settlement, it is natural to expect not only that a certain number of reservations would be attached—the majority of which exclude its application to disputes about specific matters—but also that many countries would delay their ratification or would refuse to ratify it.[15] Both the reservations attached to the treaty and the small number of ratifications deposited caused the inclusion in the agenda of the Tenth Inter-American Conference, held in Caracas in 1954, of a study of the possibility of revising the treaty. This idea sprang from various states' desire to seek a way to introduce changes in the treaty that would provide a solution, as far as possible, to the difficulties raised by the different articles to which reservations were attached. The subject was too complex, however, and the Conference merely agreed that the Council of the Organization should conduct an inquiry among the member states to ascertain the suitability of and the appropriate opportunity for, proceeding to revise the treaty. If the decision were affirmative, the Inter-American Council of Jurists and its permanent committee, the Inter-American Juridical Committee, were to study the possibility of revising the pact and to formulate preliminary drafts of various

---

[15] The ten countries that have ratified are: Brazil, Costa Rica, Dominican Republic, El Salvador, Haiti, Honduras, Mexico, Nicaragua, Panama, and Uruguay.

texts which might be accepted. In accordance with Resolution XCIX of Caracas, the results of these studies and drafts prepared by both bodies were to be transmitted to the Council of the Organization so that it might prepare a report and pertinent proposals for submission to the Eleventh Inter-American Conference.[16]

The Council began the inquiry called for and set October 1, 1954 as the date by which the governments were to send their replies. This period was extended several times in view of the few countries that answered, and by early 1957 only 12 governments had done so. Those in favor of the revision were Brazil, Ecuador, the United States of America and Venezuela; those opposed, Chile, Mexico and Peru. The opinion of the remaining governments regarding the revision depended on various conditions. In these circumstances, it was evident that the majority of the American governments did not favor the revision of the pact and, therefore, on March 6, 1957, the Council of the Organization decided to declare that the result of the inquiry carried out during the period from June 16, 1954 to February 4, 1957 was that the majority of the governments of the member states did not emit a favorable opinion regarding the suitability of, and appropriate opportunity for, revising the American Treaty on Pacific Settlement, and to declare terminated the inquiry ordered by the Tenth Inter-American Conference.[17]

Along with this inquiry and also on instructions received from the Tenth Inter-American Conference, the Council of the Organization carried out another inquiry on a question closely related to the peace system established by the Pact of Bogotá. The Eighth Conference (Lima 1938) had declared "That it is the firm purpose of the States of the American Continent to establish an Inter-American Court of International Justice, whenever these States may recognize the possibility of doing so with complete assurance of success; and that in the meantime the study of an adequate statute on which international justice in America may rest should be encouraged."[18] The Tenth Conference resolved that the Council of the Organization should ascertain the position of each of the member states with respect to the idea of constituting an Inter-American Court of Justice, and that, in the event a majority pronounced favorably upon it, the Inter-American Council of Jurists and its permanent committee should prepare a preliminary draft statute for the aforesaid court,

[16] See the complete text of Resolution XCIX in *International Conferences*, 2nd Sup. (1942–1954), p. 439.

[17] For further details regarding the inquiry see the Report submitted to the Council by the Committee on Juridical–Political Affairs, OEA/Ser.E/XIII. 1/Doc. 5, 1 March 1965.

[18] See the complete text of Resolution XXV in *International Conferences*, 1st Sup. (1933–1940), p. 253.

keeping in mind the studies that had been made for that purpose, including the draft presented for consideration to the Conference by the Government of El Salvador.[19]

The Council of the Organization began this inquiry on June 14, 1954 and gave the governments until October 1 to answer. The period was extended several times but by April 24, 1964 only eight governments had replied. Cuba, Ecuador and El Salvador were in favor of establishing the Court. The Government of Brazil, without opposing the idea of establishing the Court, made its support conditional, subject to the structure given it and its relation to the inter-American system of pacific settlement. The Government of Mexico expressed the opinion that the establishment of the Court was not of immediate urgency and Argentina, Chile and the United States of America opposed it. In spite of these results, the Council resolved to consult the governments once again before declaring the inquiry terminated, and this time received replies from the Governments of the United States, Venezuela, El Salvador and Brazil. The three which had replied previously ratified their positions and the Government of Venezuela stated that it considered premature the establishment of the said Court but that, nevertheless, as the Government of Mexico had also stated, if the majority were in favor, it would reconsider its position. Consequently, at the meeting held on November 25, 1964, the Council decided to declare that the result of the inquiry was that three governments were in favor, six made objections and the majority did not express any opinion on the advisability of constituting an Inter-American Court of Justice.[20]

14. *The Inter-American Peace Committee*

As it was conceived of by the Second Meeting of the Ministers of Foreign Affairs of the American Republics for Consultation (1940), this Committee was to "have the duty of keeping constant vigilance to insure that States between which any dispute exists or may arise, of any nature whatsoever, may solve it as quickly as possible, and of suggesting, without detriment to the methods adopted by the parties or to the procedures which they may agree upon, the measures and steps which may be conducive to a settlement." Aside from this general description of the functions and attributes of the Committee, Resolution XIV limited itself to recommending to the then Govern-

---

[19] See the complete text of Resolution C in *International Conferences,* 2nd Sup. (1942–1954), p. 440.

[20] See the Report of the Committee on Juridical-Political Affairs of the Council, in which the replies of the governments appear as appendices, OEA/ Ser. G/IV, C-i-688 Rev., 25 November 1964.

ing Board of the Pan American Union that it organize the Committee with representatives of five countries.[21]

The Committee was established by the Governing Board on December 4, 1940 and since then has had its seat in Washington. It was installed on July 31, 1948 by the Chairman of the Council of the Organization and carried out its activities in accordance with provisional bases of action under the name "Inter-American Committee on Methods for the Peaceful Solution of Conflicts", until July 6 of the following year. On May 24, 1950 the Committee approved the Statutes that it had prepared and sent them to the governments. These Statutes governed its activities until May 9, 1956, when the Council of the Organization gave its approval to new Statutes, which are still in force.[22]

Both Statutes broadened the Committee's functions and attributes and, therefore, make it possible to define more precisely its juridical nature. Viewed in the light of Resolution XIV, the Committee is a body that is to promote and facilitate the pacific settlement of disputes or controversies that exist or may arise between the states, suggesting to them the "measures and steps" conducive to such settlement. In this sense, the Committee itself is not a method or procedure of pacific settlement, such as the traditional ones (mediation, investigation, conciliation, etc.) but merely a vehicle by which such methods or procedures are suggested to the parties in a dispute. The *sui generis* character of the Committee is accentuated, to put it thus, when one bears in mind the additional power conferred on it by its Statutes, particularly the first ones, that is: that of being able to "offer its good services to facilitate a solution to the dispute." This second power, as well as the new powers and attributes later conferred on the Committee by the Fifth Meeting of Consultation, as pointed out later, have permitted it to participate more actively and directly in the settlement itself of the dispute or controversy and, consequently, to contribute much more effectively to its solution.

From the point of view of the Committee's competence and, therefore, the efficiency of its operation, it is of interest to point out that in accordance with the earlier Statutes of 1950 the Committee could "take action at the request of any American State, when the recourse of direct negotiations has been exhausted, when none of the other customary procedures of diplomacy or of pacific settlement is in process or when existing circumstances render negotiation impracticable." In addition, when the case was submitted by "directly in-

---

[21] See the complete text of Resolution XIV in *International Conferences,* 1st Sup. (1933–1940), p. 360.

[22] The complete text of the Statutes in force appears in *Appendix 13*, p. 399, *infra.*

terested" parties, the consent of the other party or parties was not required in order for the Committee to take action.[23] The new Statutes (1956), however, considerably restricted these attributes of the Committee by stipulating that only a state directly concerned in the dispute or controversy may request it to take action and, also, that it will take up the case only with "the prior consent of the Parties." It is obvious that these substantial limitations on the competence of the Committee present, intrinsically, serious obstacles to the performance of the functions stated in Resolution XIV.

The Committee itself appears to have admitted this fact in its report to the Fifth Meeting of Consultation (1959). In effect, referring to the new Statutes approved by the Council, it stated the following:

> The Committee wishes to state that since May 9, 1956, the date on which the new statute entered into force, no case has been submitted to it for consideration, which leads to the deduction that the governments have preferred to utilize other procedures of the inter-American system to settle problems or resolve situations that have arisen between them. The Committee considers that this fact may be due to the changes introduced into the statute referred to in section II of this report.[24]

The Committee's position was shared by various delegations and one, the Ecuadorian Delegation, presented a draft resolution charging the Council of the Organization with the revision of the present Statutes, "for the purpose of restoring to that agency the powers needed to attain the objectives that inspired its creation. . . ." However, the Meeting of Consultation transmitted the Ecuadorian draft resolution to the Inter-American Juridical Committee for its study and a report. The Committee abstained from making a judgment on the substance and limited itself to expressing "that the American governments must decide the question according to the greater or lesser success obtained respectively by applying the statutes of 1950 or those of 1956—a success or failure which it is obviously not for the Juridical Committee to assess in any way."[25]

The Fifth Meeting of Consultation had been called to consider the situation of international tension in the Caribbean area in its general and multiple aspects. The second point on its agenda was the effec-

---

[23] The earlier Statutes of the Committee are included in the Appendices of the Committee's report to the Second Special Inter-American Conference, OEA/ Ser. L/III/II.10, 31 March 1965.

[24] Section II referred to the changes the new Statutes caused in the functioning of the Committee. Cf. Report of the Inter-American Peace Committee to the Fifth Meeting of Consultation, Doc. 5, 6 August 1959.

[25] Cf. Study by the Inter-American Juridical Committee of the Proposal of Ecuador Concerning the Inter-American Peace Committee Pursuant to Resolution VI of the Fifth Meeting of Consultation of Ministers of Foreign Affairs, OEA/ Ser. E/XIII. 1/ Doc. 6, 1 March 1965.

tive exercise of representative democracy and the respect for human rights. Considering that the Inter-American Peace Committee was "a permanent entity and an appropriate one for assisting in the realization of the aforesaid purposes," the meeting resolved, without changing the present Statutes, to confer new functions and powers on the Committee. Specifically, it was entrusted with the study of the following three questions:[26]

a. Methods and procedures to prevent any activities from abroad designed to overthrow established governments or provoke instances of intervention or aggression as contemplated in instruments such as the Convention on Duties and Rights of States in the Event of Civil Strife, without impairment to: (i) the rights and liberties of political exiles recognized in the Convention on Territorial Asylum; (ii) the American Declaration of the Rights and Duties of Man; and (iii) the national constitutions of the American states;

b. The relationship between violations of human rights or the nonexercise of representative democracy, on the one hand, and the political tensions that affect the peace of the hemisphere, on the other; and

c. The relationship between economic underdevelopment and political instability.

Regarding the powers granted the Committee for the performance of these new duties, it is of interest to point out that Resolution IV authorized it to act "at the request of governments or on its own initiative." As was previously indicated, and will be corroborated below, this allowed the Committee once again to act with the intensity and efficacy that characterized it during the period when it was governed by its first Statutes.

Despite the previously mentioned fact that the Inter-American Peace Committee apparently was overlooked during the conference at which the inter-American system was completely overhauled, its relations and links with the other organs of the OAS have been very close and frequent. Many of these links and relations are foreseen in the three instruments which govern the Committee. Others, however, have been established in the course of the Committee's activities, especially in cases of applications of the Inter-American Treaty of Reciprocal Assistance. As far as the first are concerned, since its creation the Committee has been required to report to the Inter-American Conference and to the Meetings of Consultation regarding its activities. In accordance with its first Statutes, the Chairman was also to transmit this information to the Secretary General of the OAS and to the Security Council, in compliance with Article 54 of the United Nations Charter.

In accordance with its present Statutes, the Committee has also

---

[26] See the complete text of Resolution IV of the Fifth Meeting of Consultation in *Appendix 14,* p. 402, *infra.*

presented reports to the Council of the Organization and to the Council acting provisionally as Organ of Consultation. These reports reveal the close relationships and links which have existed between the Council and the Committee as well as the latter's important role in certain cases handled by the former, above all when the Council was acting provisionally as Organ of Consultation. Besides, the Council continues to elect the members of the Committee. The General Secretariat of the OAS provides the secretariat services and working facilities required for the functioning of the Committee.

15. *Brief Summary of the Committee's Activities (1948-1956)*

The activities of the Inter-American Peace Committee summarized in this section were governed, first, by the provisional bases of action, and later by the Statutes it approved on May 24, 1950. This distinction is made because of the changes in its competence and functioning brought about by the new Statutes approved by the Council on May 9, 1956. The following section contains an outline of the Committee's actions since 1959, both in accordance with Resolution IV of the Fifth Meeting of Consultation and in the two cases in which it acted in accordance with the new Statutes.

The Inter-American Peace Committee acted for the first time in the situation that had arisen between the Dominican Republic and Cuba in 1948. On August 13 the Dominican Government requested its services to help find a solution for the situation between it and the Government of Cuba. After advising the latter of the request, the Committee held several meetings, both alone and with the representatives of the parties. The situation had been caused by the activities of Dominican exiles. This first action by the Committee terminated with the agreement of the parties that direct negotiation was the most appropriate method for settling the situation, to which they attested in the document signed on September 9, 1948 by the representatives of the parties and the members of the Committee.[27]

On March 24, 1949 the Committee met again to take cognizance of a note from the Government of Haiti relative to a dispute that had arisen between it and the Government of the Dominican Republic, also caused by the activities of exiles, and in which it requested the Committee's services to assist in finding a solution to the situation. After informing the Dominican Government of the request and holding several meetings with the representatives of the parties, the Committee decided to send a delegation to visit both countries.

---

[27] This document appears as Appendix C of the *Second Report of the Inter-American Peace Committee Submitted to the Tenth Inter-American Conference*, Doc. 11, SG-11, 3 February 1954.

On its return to Washington the delegation informed the Committee regarding its activities and presented the text of a joint declaration that had been approved by the Foreign Ministries of both parties. At a joint meeting of the Committee and representatives of the parties on June 9, an act was signed by the representatives of the parties and the members of the Committee in which the two governments declared, among other things, that they would not tolerate in their respective territory, the activities of individuals, groups or political parties, either national or foreign, that had as their objective the alteration of the domestic peace of either of the two republics, and that in the future they would have recourse to direct negotiation and, when necessary, to the procedures of pacific settlement.[28]

On August 3, 1949 the Government of Cuba requested the good services of the Committee to find a solution to a controversy between it and the Government of Peru over asylum granted two Peruvian citizens by the Cuban Embassy in Lima on December 29, 1948. The Committee took no action, however, since on August 17 the Cuban Government advised it that the asylees had left the Embassy on August 14.

Also on August 3, 1949 the Committee met at the request of the Representative of the United States of America to consider the situation existing in the political areas of the Caribbean. As a result of its deliberations the Committee addressed a note to the representatives on the Council of the Organization to inform them of the situation that had arisen and request their respective governments for the information and suggestions they might have to offer that would contribute to a more accurate appraisal of the situation. In response to this request the Governments of Costa Rica, Cuba, the Dominican Republic, Guatemala, Haiti, Nicaragua, the United States of America and Venezuela sent the Committee observations and information. After careful study of the problem as well as the information and observations received from the governments, the Committee prepared a series of conclusions which were approved at a public meeting held on September 14, 1949. It is of interest to point out that those conclusions received the express support of the Council of the Organization, acting provisionally as Organ of Consultation, on April 8, 1950, when it declared that it supported the said conclusions with the understanding that they were applicable not only to the situation

---

[28] *Ibid.*, Appendix D. On February 16, 1949 the OAS Council took cognizance of a note from the Government of Haiti calling attention to the same dispute and requesting an immediate meeting of the Organ of Consultation. On February 25 the Council decided to refrain from convoking the meeting. See *Inter-American Treaty of Reciprocal Assistance, Applications*, vol. 1, pp. 69–76.

in the Caribbean area but also to all the American states without exception.[29]

On December 6, 1949 the Cuban Representative sent a note to the Chairman of the Committee in which he stated that his government "would be pleased to receive a visit from the Committee . . . so that it can determine for itself that there are no movements or preparations on Cuban territory" intended for the purpose of launching an aggression against the Dominican regime, as was alleged in news reports emanating from official agencies in the Dominican Republic. After taking into account all the factors in the case, the Committee decided not to take advantage of the Cuban Government's suggestion that it visit the scene of the alleged incidents.[30]

In the same month, December 1949, serious concern was expressed in the Committee with respect to the granting of special powers for the declaration of war, requested by the President of the Dominican Republic and later authorized by that nation's Congress. The Committee transmitted its concern to the Dominican Government, through its representative on the Council of the OAS.[31]

On November 26, 1951 the Government of Cuba again requested the services of the Committee to aid in solving a problem that had arisen between it and the Government of the Dominican Republic in connection with the seizure by Dominican authorities of five Cuban sailors off the vessel "Quetzal". The Committee informed the Dominican Government of this request and it, in turn, requested the Committee to suggest a method to solve the controversy referred to in the minutes of the Committee's meeting on September 9, 1948 and Resolution II.4 approved by the Council of the Organization acting provisionally as Organ of Consultation on April 8, 1950. After holding several meetings, including some with the Foreign Ministers of the two governments, the Committee terminated its activities in this case on December 25, 1951, when the parties signed the declaration that appears in the minutes of that meeting.[32]

On November 18, 1953 the Committee's services were requested in a note from the Minister of Foreign Affairs of Colombia to find a procedure that would lead to a solution of the dispute between that country and Peru, as a result of the asylum granted to Mr. Víctor Raúl Haya de la Torre in the Colombian Embassy in Lima. The Committee immediately transmitted a copy of the note to the Gov-

---

[29] Cf. Report of Peace Committee to the Tenth Inter-American Conference, op. cit., Appendix E; also, see the decisions of the provisional Organ of Consultation on April 8, 1950, on p. 125, infra.

[30] See the Inter-American Peace Committee's answer to the Cuban Representative, ibid., Appendix F.

[31] See the note addressed to the Representative of the Dominican Republic, ibid., Appendix G.

[32] See the minutes of the meeting on December 25, ibid., Appendix H.

ernment of Peru and offered its good services toward a solution of the dispute. The Peruvian Government declined to accept this offer, and invoked the reservation it attached to Resolution XIV of the Second Meeting of Consultation according to which "the Committee shall function only at the request of the interested parties," as well as Article 7 of the Committee's Statutes. Nevertheless, the Committee made a thorough study of the case and, on January 21, 1954, approved certain conclusions which it transmitted to the two parties. In its conclusions the Committee suggested that bilateral negotiations designed to put an end to the dispute be undertaken; that the said negotiations be carried out, with the promptness a case of this kind requires, in the American capital agreed on by the parties; and that the Committee be informed of the result of the procedure it had suggested.[33]

The next case handled by the Committee was the controversy involving Guatemala, Honduras and Nicaragua. On June 19, 1954 the Representative of Guatemala on the Council of the Organization delivered a note to the Chairman of the Committee in which he appealed to the Committee "to avert a violation of the peace of the American Continent." The note cited incidents that had occurred on May 22, June 7, 14, 15, 16, 17, and 19 which, in the opinion of the Guatemalan Government constituted "an outrage and acts of aggression" against Guatemala. Therefore, he requested him to convoke the Inter-American Peace Committee on an emergency basis so that it might proceed to adopt the necessary measures. The Committee met on June 19 and, as a first measure, transmitted a copy of the Guatemalan note to the Representatives of Honduras and Nicaragua, the countries that were specifically mentioned as instigators of the incidents denounced. That night the Chairman of the Committee received an urgent telephone call from the Guatemalan Foreign Minister confirming the seriousness of the facts denounced and requesting that the Committee leave for Guatemala as soon as possible. However, on June 20 the Committee suspended the trip it intended to make that same afternoon in view of the fact that the Chairman was informed by telephone by the Representative of Guatemala that he had new instructions to request the Committee to suspend its trip since his government had submitted the case to the Security Council of the United Nations on the same date as it had submitted it to the Committee, and the Security Council, meeting that day, had taken cognizance of the Guatemalan complaint. On Monday, June 21, this same representative again contacted the Chairman of the Committee to state that his government had decided to withdraw the request it had made to the Committee. On June 22

[33] See the Conclusions, *ibid.,* Appendix I.

and 23, the Representatives of Honduras and Nicaragua, respectively, requested the Committee to continue its action in the case in order to clear up the accusations made by the Guatemalan Government. Acceding to this request, the Committee met to hear the representatives of the two countries, both of whom proposed that it name a special subcommittee to visit the three countries involved as soon as possible and to obtain all the information it deemed necessary in order to clarify the facts. The Committee informed the Guatemalan Representative of this, to determine whether or not his government would accept a visit by the information subcommittee. On June 26 the Committee received the Guatemalan note of acceptance and therefore decided to constitute itself as a Subcommittee of Information and leave for Central America on Monday, June 28.

However, due to the changes that occurred in the Guatemalan Government on June 27, 28 and 29, the Committee inquired of that country's representative whether the new Guatemalan authorities were disposed to make available all necessary facilities for the performance of its mission. In view of the affirmative reply the Committee began its trip to Guatemala on Tuesday, June 29, but on its arrival in Mexico City that same night it discovered that, due to the course of events in Guatemala, the authorities had decided to request the Committee not to continue its trip. Upon obtaining confirmation of this decision by the new Guatemalan Government on June 30, the Committee decided to return to Washington and issued a press release in Mexico City, with the prior approval of the three interested parties, in which it stated, among other things, that the aforementioned countries had informed it that the controversy involving them which had occasioned the Committee's trip had ceased to exist.[34]

As will be seen below, this case also resulted in an application of the Inter-American Treaty of Reciprocal Assistance.[35] For the moment it is of interest only to point out that at the special meeting held on July 2, the Council of the Organization requested the Secretary General, upon transmitting to the Secretary General of the United Nations the text of the resolution postponing *sine die* the Meeting of Consultation of Ministers of Foreign Affairs that had been convoked for July 7, to inform him that the Inter-American Peace Committee, an autonomous agency of the OAS, would, in accordance with its Statutes, present a report on its activities directly to the Security Council.[36]

---

[34] For further details regarding this case see the Peace Committee Report to the Fifth Meeting of Consultation, *op. cit.*, Appendix D.

[35] See "Situation in Guatemala (1954)", p. 131, *infra*. Regarding the action of the U.N. Security Council as a result of the Guatemalan request in reference also see p. 184, *infra*.

[36] See *Applications*, vol. 1, pp. 159–163.

The Peace Committee did not act again until early 1956. On February 27 of that year the Representative of Cuba on the OAS Council addressed a note to the Chairman of the Committee requesting that he convoke the Committee so that it might take cognizance of the "conflict that, much to the regret of the Cuban Government, the Government of the Dominican Republic has unilaterally provoked, by the persistent activities that government has been carrying on for several months, which show all the characteristics of preparations for aggression and interference in the internal affairs of Cuba." He likewise requested that the Committee recommend "the procedure it deemed opportune for the solution of the existing conflict."

Following its normal procedure, the Committee informed the Dominican Government of this request and received a reply on March 7 stating, among other things, that there was no conflict whatsoever between the two governments deriving from preparations by the Dominican Government for aggression against Cuba and interference in its affairs, and that the Cuban Government had not exhausted the resources of direct diplomatic channels for the purpose of clarifying matters between itself and the Dominican Government. After receiving the pertinent information from both parties the Committee discussed the problem with their respective representatives, in an attempt, within the scope of its competence, to arrive at a clarification that would bring about an understanding between them. At a meeting held on April 20 the Committee approved a declaration, point V of which stated that, taking into account all the aspects of the matter and within the spirit of Article 7 of its Statutes, the Committee "hopes that, through regular diplomatic channels, the two governments concerned will be able to settle their difficulties, within a short time."[37]

16. *Activities of the Committee Since the Fifth Meeting of Consultation (1959)*

The last case summarized above concludes the activities of the Inter-American Peace Committee during the time it was governed by its first Statutes. During the period from May 9, 1956, the date on which the present Statutes approved by the Council of the Organization entered into force, to the Fifth Meeting of Consultation (August 1959)—since which time the Committee has carried out new activities in accordance with Resolution IV of that Meeting— no cases were presented for its consideration, most probably for the reasons the Committee itself stated in its report to the Fifth Meeting. During the period that began with the adoption of Resolution IV,

---

[37] For further details regarding this case see the Peace Committee Report to the Fifth Meeting, *op. cit.*, Appendix E.

on the other hand, the Committee's activities have been numerous, although only two of the cases were handled on the basis of its Statutes.

In chronological order, the Committee's first action in accordance with Resolution IV was brought about by the complaint lodged on August 15, 1959 by the Minister of Foreign Affairs of Haiti before the Fifth Meeting of Consultation, that his country had been invaded on August 13. On August 17 the Haitian Foreign Minister presented additional information to the Meeting, stating that the invading forces had sailed from a Cuban port and that the authorities of that country had said they had been unable to prevent their departure.[38] These events were brought to the attention of the Inter-American Peace Committee by note of August 31 addressed to the Chairman by the Representative of Haiti on the Council of the OAS, in which the Haitian Government, basing itself on the aforementioned Resolution IV, requested the Committee to make a thorough investigation of the events that had taken place. The Committee considered it advisable, within the scope of a work plan drawn up in order to carry out a study of international tensions in the Caribbean area, to visit several countries in that region; therefore, it appointed a Subcommittee which visited Haiti in October 1959.

According to the Haitian authorities interviewed by the Committee, the unsuccessful invasion was a typical case of intervention and a violation of the Convention on Duties and Rights of States in the Event of Civil Strife, signed in Havana in 1928. Although the Haitian Government did not present a formal accusation against the Government of Cuba, it expressed serious concern over the fact that that government had not taken the necessary measures to prevent the departure of the invaders, and emphasized what it considered to be improper activities carried out in the past by Cuban diplomats in Port-au-Prince which constituted acts of intervention in the internal affairs of Haiti. Finally the Government of Haiti requested the support and cooperation of the Organization so as to ensure that such acts of aggression would not be repeated and that its sovereignty and territorial integrity would be respected.

During its visit to Haiti, the Subcommittee interviewed five prisoners of Cuban nationality, sole survivors of the invasion force, who stated that they had sailed from the Cuban port of Puerto Padre under the orders of Major Henry Fuertes, alias "El Argelino", and that upon starting out they were unaware of their real destination. In its Report to the Seventh Meeting of Consultation, held in San José, Costa Rica a year later, the Committee pointed out that al-

---

[38] *Cf.* Quinta Reunión de Consulta de Ministros de Relaciones Exteriores, *Actas y Documentos,* OEA/Ser. F/III. 5, Washington, D.C., 1961, pp. 145–147.

though the Government of Haiti had expressed serious concern to the Subcommittee over the possibility of another invasion similar to the one that occurred in August 1959, this had not happened due, to a great extent, to the failure of the 1959 invasion and to the interest shown by the competent organs of the Organization in the appeal made to them by the Government of Haiti.[39]

The next action by the Committee took place toward the end of 1959, at the request of the Government of Venezuela. In a note addressed to the Chairman of the Committee by the Venezuelan Representative on November 25, he informed him that on the night of November 19 an aircraft of United States registry, manned by two Cuban citizens, had erroneously dropped leaflets over the island of Curaçao, inciting the army of Venezuela to rebel against the legally constituted authorities of that country. The intention had been to drop these leaflets over a Venezuelan city. Having carried out this operation, the crew of the aircraft had to make a forced landing on the island of Aruba, where they were arrested by the Dutch authorities. The aircraft had departed from Miami, making stops in Nassau and Ciudad Trujillo (now Santo Domingo).

The Committee obtained full information from the Governments of the United States of America, Venezuela and the Netherlands. On the basis of a study of the case and in the light of the statements made by the persons directly involved, the Committee concluded that the necessary arrangements for the flight from Ciudad Trujillo to Aruba, as well as the loading of the leaflets in Ciudad Trujillo, could not have been carried out without the connivance of the Dominican authorities.[40]

In the request presented to the Peace Committee by the Government of Ecuador in February 1960, the Dominican Government was once again involved. According to the Ecuadorian note, the Dominican Government not only refused to grant the Ecuadorian Embassy in Ciudad Trujillo the facilities it required for the performance of its duties, but had also "carried out repudiable acts, perpetrated with inimical intent, to *impede* the performance of those duties." On February 24 the Representative of Ecuador expanded upon his previous statement and again requested the Committee to "take urgent action, in accordance with the instruments that determine its competence, and particularly pursuant to the duties, powers, and attributes assigned to it in Resolution IV. . . ." At the Committee's initiative

---

[39] *Cf. Report of the Inter-American Peace Committee to the Seventh Meeting of Consultation of Ministers of Foreign Affairs,* OEA/Ser.F/II.7/Doc. 6, 5 August 1960, p. 3. The Spanish text, minus appendices, was also published in Séptima Reunión de Consulta de Ministros de Relaciones Exteriores, *Actas y Documentos,* OEA/Ser.F/III.7, Washington, D.C., 1961, pp. 419–431.

[40] *Ibid.,* p. 5.

discussions were begun with the Representative of the Dominican Republic on February 25. On March 8 the Dominican Representative stated orally that his government recognized the competence of the Committee in accordance with its Statutes and not on the basis of Resolution IV; also, that his government would accept the Committee's services only with respect to the problem of the situation of the Ecuadorian Embassy in Ciudad Trujillo and not with respect to the asylees, inasmuch as the Dominican Government had previously denounced the conventions on diplomatic asylum.

Regarding this matter, the Committee stated that it preferred not to express an opinion at that time as to which instrument governed its competence but that, in any event, it did not believe it feasible to separate the problem of the presence of Dominican nationals in the Ecuadorian Embassy in Ciudad Trujillo from that of the situation of the aforesaid diplomatic mission, inasmuch as it was convinced that the former matter was exercising a determining influence on the latter situation. After having held several additional discussions with the Dominican Representative, the Committee formally inquired of him whether his government would consent to its taking action in the matter. The reply was that the matter of the situation of the Ecuadorian Embassy could be dealt with directly by the two governments "without the mediation of an international organization being essential for this purpose." When this point of view was transmitted to the Representative of Ecuador, he indicated that inasmuch as the efforts made by his Embassy in Ciudad Trujillo had been fruitless, his government had reached the conclusion that it was useless to continue direct negotiations and therefore insisted that the Committee use every means at its disposal to achieve the settlement of the dispute.

After exploring the possibilities of finding a formula by which the two governments could resume their conversations, on March 30 the Committee transmitted to the two representatives a "basis of understanding" by virtue of which the departure of the asylees in the Ecuadorian Embassy to Ecuador would be permitted under certain conditions and conversations would be begun between the two governments for the purpose of normalizing the situation of that diplomatic mission. This basis was rejected by the Dominican Representative. The Ecuadorian Representative, for his part, after informing the Committee that his government accepted the basis, in turn rejected a formula proposed by the Dominican Representative, considering it to be wholly inadmissable, and reiterated his desire that the Committee continue its efforts to find a solution to the problems raised.

In view of these circumstances, in the report on this case presented to the OAS Council on April 12, the Committee stated, among other conclusions, that it regretted that its efforts had not been successful and that the Dominican Government had not accepted the offer of its services. In this connection, the Committee also expressed its concern over the fact that the Dominican Government had not collaborated with it in the search for the solution of a problem the continuation of which would evidently increase tensions among the member states of the Organization. At the same time, the Committee cherished the hope that the Dominican Government would not permit measures to be taken which might endanger the safety or well-being of the asylees in the Ecuadorian Embassy.[41]

The third case of the group in reference was brought about by yet another complaint against the Government of the Dominican Republic. This one was contained in a Venezuelan note of February 17, 1960, requesting the Committee to investigate "the flagrant violations of human rights by the Government of the Dominican Republic, which are aggravating the tensions in the Caribbean." In spite of the fact that this case was presented only a day later than the foregoing one, and the close relation between the cases in view of the subject matter, the Committee handled them, at least for the record, separately and distinctly.

Given the nature of the complaint lodged by Venezuela, the Committee believed that in order to carry out an investigation it was desirable to visit the Dominican Republic, and it therefore inquired of that government whether it would be willing for the Committee to make that visit. The Dominican Government, in the exercise of the option provided for in Resolution IV.2, answered in the negative. Nevertheless, the Committee decided to obtain, through the means available to it, all possible data and for that purpose it requested information from the other American governments, received testimony from Dominican exiles and from nationals of other countries who had recently been in the Dominican Republic, and examined extensive and reliable press material as well as valuable information provided it by certain other representatives of member states. On June 6 the Committee transmitted to the Council of the OAS a report on the case that contained, among others, the following observations:[42]

> On the basis of the evidence which it has been able to gather, the Committee has reached the conclusion that international tensions in the Caribbean region have been aggravated by flagrant and widespread violations of human rights which have been committed and continue to be committed in the Dominican Republic. Among these violations, mention must be made of the denial of free assembly and of free speech, arbitrary arrests, cruel and inhuman treatment of political prisoners, and the use of intimidation and terror as political weapons. Some of

---

41 See complete text of the Committee's report on this case, *ibid.,* Appendix C.
42 See complete text of the Committee's report on this case, *ibid.,* Appendix D.

the victims of these grave acts appeared before the Committee and made statements. These acts constitute the denial of fundamental rights set forth in the American Declaration of the Rights and Duties of Man, as well as of principles of the Charter of the Organization of American States.

. . . the Committee stresses the fact that international tensions in the Caribbean area, far from diminishing, have been increased and that, in its view, these tensions will continue to increase so long as the flagrant violations of human rights in the Dominican Republic persist.

The next action by the Inter-American Peace Committee took place as a result of a note addressed to its Chairman on July 2, 1961, by the Representative of Mexico on the OAS Council. In that note he transcribed a telegram received from the Minister of Foreign Affairs of Mexico, in which he made reference to a message which the Minister of Foreign Affairs of Guatemala had addressed to the Secretary General of the OAS, informing him of the fact that in Mexican territory, adjacent to the Guatemalan border "communist troops are being trained for an invasion into Guatemalan territory in the immediate future." The said message also stated that in recent days the Chief of the Cuban Armed Forces, Major Raúl Castro, had arrived in Mexico for the purpose of personally inspecting the condition of the invader troops and that ex-President Cárdenas had done the same. The Government of Guatemala provided this information, according to the message, in view of the fear that grave disorders might occur in the immediate future and cause it to invoke the Inter-American Treaty of Reciprocal Assistance, considering that "these movements are of extracontinental origin and have extracontinental support."

In his cable the Mexican Foreign Minister urgently requested the Inter-American Peace Committee to "proceed immediately to make as thorough an investigation in Mexican territory as it deems necessary in order to establish whether, as the Government of Mexico assures, the imputation is false." This request was based specifically on Resolution IV.1 (a) of the Fifth Meeting of Consultation. On the same day the Representative of Mexico requested the Chairman of the OAS Council to convoke a special meeting for the purpose of "informing that body concerning the steps my government has taken with regard to a series of totally unfounded assertions that have been made public by the Minister of Foreign Affairs of Guatemala." At the meeting, held that same afternoon, the Guatemalan Representative stated that the Guatemalan message had been sent to the Secretary General purely for purposes of information and that it contained no direct or implied accusation against the Government of the United Mexican States.

Immediately following the Council meeting, the Peace Committee met for the purpose of hearing the Representative of Mexico, who repeated his request that the Committee take action in the case, reiterating his government's invitation for the Committee to go to Mexico as soon as possible. The Committee decided affirmatively regarding its competence to take action on this matter pursuant to Resolution IV, and transmitted this decision to the Representative of Guatemala with a request that he supply, as soon as possible, the complementary data that might be useful and necessary in order to carry out the investigation requested by the Mexican Government. On June 5 the Guatemalan Representative replied that the position of his government concerning the matter raised by the Government of Mexico had been clearly established in the special meeting of the Council and that therefore his government did not consider that it should report any specific circumstance. In the report on this case presented to the Eighth Meeting of Consultation the Committee stated that it had "in view of the position assumed by the Government of Guatemala, and taking into account the statements made by its Representative in the abovementioned Council meeting, as well as the declarations of the Representative of Mexico, reached the conclusion, in a meeting held on June 5, 1961, that there was no doubt whatever 'concerning the manner in which the Government of Mexico is fulfilling its international obligations' and that, consequently, it was not necessary for the Committee to visit Mexican territory and make the requested investigation."[43]

Some of the most intense activities carried out by the Inter-American Peace Committee resulted from the case relative to the facts denounced by the Representative of Peru at the special meeting of the OAS Council on October 16, 1961. As will be noted when this application of the Inter-American Treaty of Reciprocal Assistance is examined later, the denunciation referred to the grave violations of essential rights being committed by the ruling regime in Cuba, to the action of international communism in the American countries and the incorporation of the Cuban Government in the Sino-Soviet bloc, and to communist infiltration by that government in the said countries. Basing itself on the decision taken by the Council on November 22 that the Committee "is an appropriate organ, in accordance with the terms of Resolution IV . . . to deal with the facts denounced . . ." the Representative of Peru presented a note to this effect to the Committee on November 24.[44] Following its normal procedure, the Committee invited the Representative of Cuba to appear before it to state the point of view of his government. In view of the fact that the Cuban Representative did not attend the meeting

---

[43] Cf. *Report of the Inter-American Peace Committee to the Eighth Meeting of Consultation of Ministers of Foreign Affairs 1962*, OEA/Ser. L/III/CIP/1/62, 14 January 1962, pp. 18-21.

[44] See "Exclusion of the Cuban Government and Partial Suspension of Trade with Cuba (1961–1962)", p. 157, *infra*.

to which he had been invited, the Committee addressed him by note to inquire whether his government would agree, in accordance with Resolution IV.2, to a visit by the Committee to the Republic of Cuba to carry out the investigations it considered necessary. This second request was also denied.

In its report to the Eighth Meeting of Consultation the Committee pointed out that despite the Cuban Government's refusal to give its consent for a visit to the territory of Cuba, it obtained as much information as possible with respect to the matter that was the subject of the Peruvian complaint, through the very publications of the Cuban Government, as well as plentiful documentation from numerous trustworthy sources and testimony from many persons who had recently left Cuba or had visited that country at various times. The Committee also stated that it had received valuable data from governments of various member states.

The Committee systematically examined the three categories of facts denounced by the Government of Peru in the light of all the evidence as well as the pertinent principles and objectives of the inter-American system, and as a result drew up the Final Considerations that follow:[45]

> 1. The identification of the Government of Cuba with the Marxist-Leninist ideology and socialism of the Soviet type, together with the rebuilding of the Cuban political organization on the basis of the one-party system of government that is in accordance with that ideology, presuppose positions that are basically antagonistic to the principle established in the Charter of the Organization of American States that
>> The solidarity of the American States and the high aims which are sought through it require the political organization of those States on the basis of the effective exercise of representative democracy. (Article 5, d)
>
> With regard to this point, it is well to recall, also, the Declaration of Santiago, Chile, which the present Government of Cuba signed jointly with the other American governments, in which there are enounced certain "principles and attributes of the democratic system in this hemisphere." In addition to the fact that other declarations of Inter-American Conferences and Meetings of Consultation of Ministers of Foreign Affairs have condemned the communist ideology and system, in the Declaration of San José, Costa Rica, the Seventh Meeting reaffirmed
>> . . . that the inter-American system is incompatible with any form of totalitarianism and that democracy will achieve the full scope of its objectives in the hemisphere only when all the American republics conduct themselves in accordance with the principles stated in the Declaration of Santiago, Chile, approved at the Fifth Meeting of Consultation of Ministers of Foreign Affairs, the observance of which it recommends as soon as possible.
>
> Along this line of thinking, the Committee feels that the present Government of Cuba, given the political ideology with which it has identi-

---

[45] See the complete text of the Committee's report on this case, *op. cit.,* pp. 22–48.

fied itself and the form in which it has organized itself, impedes the exercise of the right of self-determination, as it is conceived in the inter-American system, that is, as the right of each and all of the citizens to contribute with his vote, given in free elections, to the formation of the government that they may prefer to give themselves. In this sense, the Fifth Meeting of Consultation declared that "The governments of the American republics should be the result of free elections" and that "Perpetuation in power, or the exercise of power without a fixed term and with the manifest intent of perpetuation, is incompatible with the effective exercise of democracy."

2. The serious and systematic violation of human rights by the Government of Cuba not only constitutes one of the principal causes of the international tensions that now are affecting the peace of the Hemisphere but is in open contradiction to various instruments of the inter-American system, and particularly to the Charter of the Organization, Article 13 of which establishes that in the free development of its cultural, political, and economic life, "The State shall respect the rights of the individual. . . ."

3. The present connections of the Government of Cuba with the Sino-Soviet bloc of countries are evidently incompatible with the principles and standards that govern the regional system, and particularly with the collective security system established by the Charter of the Organization and the Inter-American Treaty of Reciprocal Assistance. The acceptance of the military aid offered by the Soviet Union was what motivated the Seventh Meeting of Consultation to declare that

. . . the acceptance of a threat of extracontinental intervention by any American state endangers American solidarity and security, and that this obliges the Organization of American States to disapprove it and reject it with equal vigor.

The same Declaration of San José

Proclaims that all member states of the regional organization are under obligation to submit to the discipline of the inter-American system, voluntarily and freely agreed upon, and that the soundest guarantee of their sovereignty and their political independence stems from compliance with the provisions of the Charter of the Organization of American States.

It is evident that the ties of the Cuban Government with the Sino-Soviet bloc will prevent the said Government from fulfilling the obligations stipulated in the Charter of the Organization and the Treaty of Reciprocal Assistance.

4. As regards the intense subversive activity in which the countries of the Sino-Soviet bloc are engaged in America and the activities of the Cuban Government that are pointed out in this report, it is evident that they would constitute acts that, within the system for the "political defense" of the Hemisphere, have been classed as acts of "political aggression" or "aggression of a nonmilitary character." Such acts represent attacks upon inter-American peace and security as well as on the sovereignty and political independence of the American states, and therefore a serious violation of fundamental principles of the inter-American system, as has been repeatedly and explicitly declared at previous Inter-American Conferences and Meetings of Consultation. By way of example, it is appropriate to recall that the Bogotá Conference in its Resolution XXXII, "The Preservation and Defense of Democracy in America," condemned "In the name of international law, interference

by any foreign power, or by any political organization serving the interests of a foreign power, in the public life of the nations of the American continent."

An examination of the application of the Inter-American Treaty of Reciprocal Assistance, to which reference has been made, leads to an appreciation of the decisive role played by the Peace Committee's considerations, as well as the information contained in other sections of its report, in the measures and resolutions adopted by the Meeting of Consultation held in January 1962 at Punta del Este, Uruguay.

In the two remaining cases, the Inter-American Peace Committee's activities were governed by its Statutes. The first of these is the Honduras-Nicaragua case, which at an earlier stage had been the object of an application of the Rio Treaty.[46] As can readily be seen, this was one of the most outstanding contributions by this peace instrument.

On February 16, 1961, the Representative of Nicaragua on the OAS Council requested the Inter-American Peace Committee to suggest methods and steps conducive to a solution of "the questions that have arisen about the execution of the judgment of the International Court of Justice on November 18, 1960, delivered in the dispute between Nicaragua and Honduras concerning the Arbitral Award made by His Majesty the King of Spain on December 23, 1906." The Arbital Award had decided the border dispute pending between the two countries since the last century, and in its judgment the Court had declared that the Award "is valid and binding and that Nicaragua is under an obligation to give effect to it."[47] As a result of discussions between the Chairman of the Committee and the representatives of both countries, the Government of Honduras consented to the Committee's action. Also in consultation with the two representatives, early in March the Committee prepared a Basis of Arrangement which was accepted by both governments and which stated as follows:

> 1. The Government of Nicaragua will immediately withdraw its authorities from the territory. ["Territory" was understood to mean the region which, according to the Arbitral Award of December 23, 1906, belonged to Honduras and was then occupied by Nicaraguan authorities.] The withdrawal of authorities from the zone of Teotecacinte will proceed in conformance with the results of the demarcation of the said zone, and according as this demarcation may be carried out.
> 2. There is hereby established the Honduras-Nicaragua Mixed Commission, which will be composed of the Chairman of the Inter-American Peace Committee, . . . , as Representative of Honduras, and . . . , as

---

[46] See "Border Dispute between Honduras and Nicaragua (1957)", p. 134, *infra.*

[47] *Cf.* International Court of Justice, Reports of Judgments, Advisory Opinions and Orders, *Judgment of 18 November 1960,* ICJ Reports 1960, p. 192.

Representative of Nicaragua. The Chairman of the Mixed Commission will be the Chairman of the Inter-American Peace Committee.

3. The Mixed Commission will begin its meetings in the place and at the time determined by the Chairman; it will go into the territory as soon as possible and will remain there for as long as may be necessary to complete its task. It is understood that a part of this task will consist of supervising the orderly departure of those persons who wish to move to Nicaragua, and in this undertaking the Commission will have the fullest cooperation of the two governments. During the time that the Mixed Commission is in the territory, the Chairman may be represented by the official of the Organization of American States whom the Secretary General thereof appoints for the purpose.

4. The powers of the Mixed Commission are:

a. To aid the two governments in their efforts to guarantee the inhabitants of the territory a choice between the two nationalities, and to permit those persons who may wish to do so to move to Nicaragua.

b. Under the terms of the Arbitral Award of December 23, 1906, to fix on the ground the boundary line from the juncture of the Bodega or Poteca River with the Guineo River as far as Portillo de Teotecacinte, as well as to verify the starting point of the natural boundary between the two countries at the mouth of the Coco River.

c. To supervise the setting of landmarks for the boundary line laid out according to the preceeding paragraph.

d. Any other powers that the two governments may confer upon it, at the suggestion of the Inter-American Peace Committee.

5. In exercising the powers set forth in paragraph 4 b., the Mixed Commission will avail itself of the Committee of Engineers already created by the two governments.

6. In the event of disagreement between the Representatives of Honduras and Nicaragua on the Mixed Commission, the Chairman will make the final decision. This power may not be delegated.

7. The Secretary General of the Organization of American States will provide the Mixed Commission with the technical staff and secretariat requested by the Chairman. The latter will appoint the officials he feels would be useful to remain at those places within the territory that the Mixed Commission itself may decide upon.

8. Under the terms of Article 1 of its Statutes, the Inter-American Peace Committee will suggest measures and steps conducive to a settlement of all questions that may arise between the two governments in carrying out the Arbitral Award of December 23, 1906, and that are not submitted to the Mixed Commission in accordance with this Basis. Acquired rights to private property in the territory will be respected, in conformance at all times with the constitution and laws of the Republic of Honduras.

In the middle of March 1961 the Committee traveled to the two countries to hold conversations with the respective Chiefs of State regarding the execution of the Basis of Arrangement and to set up the Honduras-Nicaragua Mixed Commission provided for therein. Taking advantage of the occasion the Committee visited part of the "territory" located in the border region of the Coco or Segovia River, and installed the Mixed Commission, in the town of Waspam on the Nicaragua side of the Coco River, where it immediately began its work.

When the Eighth Meeting of Consultation was held (January 1962), the Committee reported on the activities it had carried out up to that time, as well as those of the Mixed Commission in compliance with the Basis of Arrangement. In the first place, it pointed out that "the region from which the Nicaraguan authorities were to withdraw, since, in conformity with the Arbital Award, it belonged to Honduras, amounted to approximately 8,700 square kilometers." It also indicated that by the middle of May 1961 the transfer of all the persons who chose to live in Nicaraguan territory had been carried out and that they were approximately 4,000 in all. During this phase of the operation, various officials of the Pan American Union participated in the work of the Mixed Commission. Their principal mission was to witness the withdrawal of the Nicaraguan authorities and the arrival of the Honduran authorities, as well as to live with the inhabitants of the region during the brief period in which incidents might have occurred. For its part, the Mixed Commission, using a map prepared by the Honduran-Nicaraguan Committee of Engineers mentioned in paragraph 5 of the Basis of Arrangement, fixed the western and northern boundaries of the Sitio de Teotecacinte, up to a point called Murupuchí.[48]

In July 1962 the Mixed Commission received a report and aerial photo map from the Committee of Engineers with data on the starting point of the natural boundary at the mouth of the Coco River. In December of that year the Mixed Commission went to the mouth of the Coco River in order to make a survey of the area and an on-the-spot study of the aforementioned report and map. As a result of its inspection the Mixed Commission, on December 15, 1962, verified the location of the starting point of the natural boundary. Once this was done the Commission went to the Teotecacinte area to make the final inspection of the placement of boundary markers on the boundary line it had fixed in that area. The Committee of Engineers had been erecting these boundary markers since September 1961. In its report to the Council on all these activities, the Inter-American Peace Committee stated that with the activities described the Honduras-Nicaragua Mixed Commission fully complied with the duties with which it was charged under the Basis of Arrangement and the controversy between Honduras and Nicaragua concerning the Arbitral Award of December 23, 1906 was definitely settled.[49]

---

[48] See text of the Committee's report on this case, *op. cit.*, pp. 3–17.

[49] *Cf. Report of the Inter-American Peace Committee to the Council of the Organization of American States on the Termination of the Activities of the Honduras-Nicaragua Mixed Commission,* OEA/Ser. L/III/II.9, 16 July 1963.

The second and final action taken by the Inter-American Peace Committee in accordance with its present Statutes was occasioned by the controversy between Panama and the United States of America in January 1964. This same situation was also the object of an application of the Inter-American Treaty of Reciprocal Assistance, as will be seen later. The request for the Committee to take action was presented simultaneously by the representatives of both parties on January 10, 1964. That same night the Committee traveled to Panama where it remained until January 15, during which time it worked intensely, first of all to help both parties in their efforts to reestablish and maintain public order. For this purpose, at the Committee's initiative and with the consent of the two interested governments, a Mixed Committee on Cooperation was established, composed of one member of the Inter-American Peace Committee, who was its chairman, and one civilian and one military representative of each of the parties. The first objective was fully achieved soon after the work of the Mixed Committee began. Also, thanks to the mediating action of the Peace Committee, an immediate solution was found to the problems connected with the simultaneous raising of the flags of Panama and the United States at various places in the Canal Zone, as well as those having to do with the free transit of individuals and vehicles.

Once those initial aims were accomplished, the Committee devoted its efforts to helping both governments reach an agreement or understanding whereby they could solve the difficulties existing between them. As a result of these efforts the Committee issued the following press release in Panama City on January 15, 1964:

> The Inter-American Peace Committee, based on its Statutes which authorize it to offer its good offices to the States requesting them, has carried on conversations with Representatives of the Republic of Panama and the United States and notes with satisfaction the re-establishment of the peace which is an indispensable condition for understanding and negotiation between the parties.
>
> As a consequence, the Inter-American Peace Committee has invited the parties to re-establish their diplomatic relations as quickly as possible. The parties have agreed to accept this invitation and, as a consequence thereof, have agreed to begin formal discussions which will be initiated thirty (30) days after diplomatic relations are re-established, by means of representatives who will have sufficient powers to discuss without limitations all existing matters of any nature which may affect the relations between the United States and Panama.

The agreement outlined in the press release met with difficulties derived from the differences of interpretation by the interested parties regarding some of its terms, which led the Committee to renew its discussions with both parties in Washington, D. C. These discussions, which were held on a continuous basis until January 29, had no positive results and on that date the Representative of Panama informed the Committee that he would present the matter to the OAS Council and invoke the Inter-American Treaty of Reciprocal Assistance.[50] In view of this the Peace Committee considered its action terminated and on January 30 issued a press release which in part reads as follows:[51]

> After many discussions with the representatives of both parties, Messrs. Galileo Solís and Edwin Martin, the Committee gained their acceptance of the agreement dated January 15, which appears in Press Release N°3 of the Committee, by which the parties, after agreeing to reestablish diplomatic relations, decided that they would "begin formal discussions . . . by means of representatives who will have sufficient powers to discuss without limitations all existing matters of any nature which may affect the relations between the United States and Panama."
>
> The same day, authorized spokesmen of each party made known diverging interpretations of the document, without having requested the good offices of the Committee in resolving these differences of interpretation. In his press release of January 15, 1964, the Minister of Foreign Affairs of Panama said: "Notwithstanding the fact that the Inter-American Peace Committee suggested that the parties resume their diplomatic relations in order to begin negotiations on relations between the two countries, the Government of Panama will not resume those relations until it is assured by the Government of the United States that it will begin negotiations to conclude a new treaty to replace the existing ones."
>
> In view of these circumstances and the fact that the Committee had returned to Washington, the conversations were resumed on January 20 at its headquarters, with the express agreement of both parties. For several days without interruption, various formulas were proposed and studied, but no agreement was reached. In these conversations, the Government of the United States was represented by Ambassador Ellsworth Bunker and the Government of Panama by Ambassador Miguel J. Moreno. Finally, yesterday, the Representative of Panama said that since no formal promise had been obtained from the United States to begin negotiations to conclude a new treaty on the Panama Canal, Panama found it necessary to bring the matter before the Council of the Organization of American States and to ask for a meeting of the Organ of Consultation, in application of the Treaty of Reciprocal Assistance.
>
> Because of this fact, the Inter-American Peace Committee, basing itself on Article 2 of its Statutes, which establishes that it ". . . shall take up the case only with the prior consent of the Parties and when no other procedure for its pacific settlement is in progress," considered its action terminated and decided duly to present its report to the Council of the Organization of American States.

---

[50] See "Situation Between Panama and the United States of America (1964)", p. 146, *infra.*

[51] For further details regarding the Committee's action in this case see *Report of the Inter-American Peace Committee to the Second Special Inter-American Conference on the Activities of the Committee since the Tenth Inter-American Conference 1954–1965*, OEA/Ser. L/III/II.10, 31 March 1965, pp. 49-53.

Chapter VI

General Structure of the Collective Security System

Chapter V of the Charter of the Organization of American States deals with Collective Security and, as in the case of the chapter relative to the pacific settlement of disputes, the basic principles on which the inter-American system rests are laid down therein. The first article of Chapter V sets forth the principle of solidarity in the face of every act of aggression against the integrity or inviolability of the territory or against the sovereignty or political independence of an American state. Article 25, the second, points out the acts, facts or situations, as well as the circumstances, which justify the application of the collective security system, that is, the application of "the measures and procedures established in the special treaties on the subject." Notwithstanding other instruments that also govern the regional system, the only one that falls within the category of "special treaties" is the Inter-American Treaty of Reciprocal Assistance, which had already been concluded at the Inter-American Conference for the Maintenance of Continental Peace and Security, held at Rio de Janeiro in 1947.

Any study limited to the provisions of the treaty and of the OAS Charter (those of Chapter V as well as others on this subject) would fail to provide a complete picture of the inter-American collective security system in its present status. To this effect, the other instruments referred to above must be borne in mind, as well as certain applications of the Rio Treaty, by virtue of which the system has undergone an unparalleled development and strengthening during the last few years. As will be seen later, the regional system has been developed and strengthened particularly in the fields of security against subversion and self-defense. Within this same order of ideas, for the moment it will be sufficient to add that the system's historical antecedents have played a very important part in this interesting phenomenon.

17. *Historical Development*

The inter-American collective security system has its first historical antecedents in the efforts of the Latin American countries to preserve their independence in the face of the danger represented by the proposals and plans for reconquest by their former mother countries. It is of interest to point out that since 1826, when Simón Bolívar convoked the first Congress of Panama, the strongest motivating force in the creation, development, and strengthening of the regional system has been, and continues to be, the threats and acts of aggression by extracontinental powers.

As indicated in the Introduction, the Treaty of Perpetual Union, League, and Confederation signed at the Congress of Panama had as one of its main objectives the defense and consolidation of the liberty and independence of the new republics, to which end it contained provisions for the mutual guarantee of the integrity of their respective territories. The additional convention established the quota of troops to be provided by each republic in order to constitute and maintain a permanent army of 60,000 soldiers, and set forth the organization and direction of this army. The creation of an international armed force to ward off the threats of reconquest is also stipulated in the treaty concluded at the second Congress of Lima (1864-65), the last of the four Latin American congresses held after 1826 with the objective of organizing a confederation and establishing a collective mechanism to face the extracontinental danger.[1]

Due to the fact that by the end of the century that danger had disappeared, the First International American Conference (1889-90) was primarily concerned with the consideration of the methods for preventing war among the American countries as well as the pacific settlement of disputes, the increase of commercial traffic and of the methods of communication, etc. Nevertheless, it is of interest to point out the resolution by which the so-called "right of conquest" was outlawed.[2] No treaty directly related to collective security was signed until the Sixth Conference (Havana 1928). The Convention on Duties and Rights of States in the Event of Civil Strife, signed at that time, is another important antecedent in relation to an aspect of the system to be developed and perfected years later.[3] Also closely related with that system is the outlawing of the so-called "right to intervene" by Article 8 of the Convention on Rights and Duties of States, signed at the Seventh Conference (Montevideo 1933). Article 11 of that convention also stipulates "the precise obligation not to recognize territorial acquisitions or special advantages which have been obtained by force whether this consists in the employment of

---

[1] See p. iv, *supra*. For the corresponding provisions of these instruments see *International Conferences* (1889–1928), p. xxiv and Yepes, *op. cit.*, pp. 117, 129, and 255.

[2] Cf. *International Conferences* (1889–1928), p. 44.

[3] The complete text of this Convention as well as the Additional Protocol thereto appear in *Appendix 15*, p. 403, *infra*.

arms, in threatening diplomatic representations, or in any other effective coercive measure."[4]

At the Inter-American Conference for the Maintenance of Peace, held in Buenos Aires in 1936 at the initiative of President Roosevelt, the foundation was laid for a procedure which later became one of the characteristics of the present collective security system. Then, too, the fundamental principle upon which the said system rests was set forth, that is, "that every act susceptible of disturbing the peace of America affects each and every one of them [the American re publics], and justifies the initiation of the procedure of consultation provided for in the Convention for the Maintenance, Preservation and Reestablishment of Peace, signed at this Conference."[5] As indicated in the foregoing Chapter, this convention stipulated that in the event the peace of the American republics was menaced, their governments would consult together for the purpose of finding and adopting methods of peaceful cooperation. The procedure of consultation was also extended to cover the case of war or a virtual state of war between American countries.[6]

Two years later, at the Eighth International Conference of American States (Lima 1938) this declaration of solidarity was reiterated, along with the obligation to have recourse to the procedure of consultation, "in case the peace, security or territorial integrity of any American Republic is thus threatened by acts of any nature that may impair them."[7] The Second Meeting of Consultation of Ministers of Foreign Affairs (Havana 1940) extended the principle of solidarity to cover "any attempt on the part of a non-American State against the integrity or inviolability of the territory, the sovereignty or the political independence of an American State," and declared that such an attempt "shall be considered as an act of aggression against the States which sign this declaration."[8]

The principle of solidarity, as set forth in the foregoing declaration, was reaffirmed by the Third Meeting of Consultation (Rio de Janeiro 1942) in Resolution I on "Breaking of Diplomatic Relations". The same Meeting adopted other resolutions based on the Havana declaration, such as the one concerning the severance of commercial and financial relations with the nations signatory to the Tripartite Pact and the territories dominated by them (Res. V), and one relative to

---

[4] Cf. International Conferences, 1st Sup. (1933–1940), p. 121.

[5] See the complete text of the Declaration of Principles of Inter-American Solidarity and Co-operation, ibid., p. 160.

[6] See other aspects of the Convention on p. 75, supra.

[7] See the complete text of the Declaration of the Principles of the Solidarity of America or "Declaration of Lima" in International Conferences, 1st Sup. (1933–1940), p. 308.

[8] See the complete text of Resolution XV, Reciprocal Assistance and Co-operation for the Defense of the Nations of the Americas, ibid., p. 360.

the condemnation of Japanese aggression (Res. XXIV). For the moment it will be sufficient to call attention to the distinction made in the preamble of Resolution XVII, on "Subversive Activities", between "Acts of aggression of the nature contemplated in Resolution XV [of the Second Meeting of Consultation] . . . against the integrity and inviolability of the territory . . ." on the one hand and "Acts of aggression of a non-military character," which Resolution XVII considers to be "preliminary to and an integral part of a program of military aggression," on the other. Nevertheless, the resolution appears to make no distinction between these categories of acts of aggression as far as the decision of the American republics to maintain their integrity and solidarity is concerned, nor in relation to their decision to give their fullest cooperation in the enforcement of measures of continental defense.[9]

The Inter-American Conference on Problems of War and Peace (Mexico City 1945) reaffirmed and developed the foregoing principles as well as the methods and procedures of the collective security system. Regarding the former, it extended the principle by virtue of which an attack against the integrity or the inviolability of the territory or against the sovereignty or political independence of an American state would be considered an act of aggression against all the other American states, to cover attacks by any state, that is, attacks by extracontinental powers as well as by those within the Continent. In addition, the conference recommended that, for the purpose of meeting threats or acts of aggression against any American republic following the establishment of peace, the governments consider the conclusion of a treaty establishing procedures whereby such threats or acts may be met by the use, by all or some of the signatories of the said treaty, of any one or more of the following measures: recall of chiefs of diplomatic missions; breaking of diplomatic relations; breaking of consular relations; breaking of postal, telegraphic, telephonic, radio-telephonic relations; interruption of economic, commercial, and financial relations and use of armed force to prevent or repel aggression.[10] The instrument referred to was signed two years later at the Inter-American Conference for the Maintenance of Continental Peace and Security, and is known as the Inter-American Treaty of Reciprocal Assistance.

18. *Present Structure: Self-Defense and Collective Action*

In the Rio Treaty as in the OAS Charter, two types of action are established: self-defense and, properly speaking, collective action;

[9] *Cf. International Conferences,* 2nd Sup. (1942–1954), pp. 10, 19, 25, and 35. On Resolution XVII also see p. 114, *infra.*

[10] See the complete text of Resolution VII, Reciprocal Assistance and American Solidarity, in *International Conferences,* 2nd Sup. (1942–1954), p. 66.

that is, the action of one or several states in self-defense, and the action of the competent regional organ, which may, in turn, be an action of collective self-defense. In this sense, "reciprocal assistance" has two forms: the assistance which the states on their own initiative provide the injured state and the assistance which, collectively, it is agreed to provide via the competent organ. In general terms, the distinction between them corresponds to the distinction made by both instruments regarding the acts, facts, or situations they contemplate.

Thus, according to the Rio Treaty, in the event of an "armed attack" the assistance occurs "in the exercise of the inherent right of individual or collective self-defense recognized by Article 51 of the Charter of the United Nations." In this Article 3, as in Articles 5 and 7, the Rio Treaty refers to other aspects of the situation or conflict that occur as a result of the armed attack. However, when dealing with "an aggression which is not an armed attack," "an extra-continental or intra-continental conflict," or "any other fact or situation that might endanger the peace of America," Article 6 calls for an immediate meeting of the Organ of Consultation "in order to agree on the measures which must be taken in case of aggression to assist the victim of the aggression or, in any case, the measures which should be taken for the common defense and for the maintenance of the peace and security of the Continent." By virtue of the exception stipulated in Article 3.a, this mechanism is also applicable to an armed attack that takes place outside the area described in Article 4.

In Chapter V on Collective Security, the Charter contemplates these general categories of acts, facts, or situations, although it does not specify, as does the Rio Treaty, what type of action is to be taken in each case. It is of interest to note, in this connection, that when the Charter sets forth the principle of solidarity it refers to "Every act of aggression by a State against the territorial integrity or the inviolability of the territory or against the sovereignty or political independence of an American State" (Art. 24) and not only to "armed attack", as does the Rio Treaty, and that it does not limit the validity of "collective self-defense" to an aggression of that nature (Art. 25). This does not mean that the Bogotá Conference had the intention of extending the principle of self-defense to every kind of aggression, but it does permit one to see in this concept, the broadest and most flexible in the Charter, a basis for its later development.

The same is true regarding the "threat" of armed attack, also omitted from Article 3 of the Rio Treaty. Nevertheless, the threat of armed attack, or any other type of aggression, was explicitly mentioned in the Report of the Rapporteur of the Second Committee of the Conference of Rio de Janeiro, as a fact or situation of the kind foreseen in Article 6, to which the mechanism of consultation would be applicable in accordance with the provisions of that article.[11] It is also impossible to deny the significance of the fact that the preamble of the Rio Treaty speaks, in broad and flexible terms, of providing for "effective reciprocal assistance to meet armed attacks against any American State, and in order to deal with threats of aggression against any of them." All this explains why Resolution II. 3 of the Eighth Meeting of Consultation relates the institution of self-defense to the "threats" of aggression,[12] and why the action taken by the Organization of American States during the so-called "October crisis" was due, not to an armed attack but to a fact or situation that at any moment might have become "an active threat to the peace and security of the Continent."[13]

Of equal significance is the fact that Article 9 of the Rio Treaty authorizes the Organ of Consultation to "characterize as aggression" acts which are neither "armed attack" nor "invasion, by the armed forces of a State, of the territory of an American State." Although the purpose of the article appears to have been that of providing, by means of these two examples, the criteria on which to base the characterization of "aggression" (the genus of which "armed attack" and "invasion" are similar species), nothing prevents the characterization as acts of aggression, of certain acts, analogous to invasion or armed attack, which do not exactly possess the characteristics of the acts described in Article 9. In this regard, acts which have been compared to armed attack for purposes of self-defense or other reasons should be borne in mind, such as "aid to armed bands" as foreseen in the Act Relating to the Definition of Aggression (1932-33), including the state's tolerance of these activities, and material aid to "guerrillas" operating in the territory of a third state, which was the position assumed by certain governments in the course of the debates in the United Nations on the Greek question (1947). In brief, like the Charter, the Rio Treaty intrinsically appears to authorize a certain flexibility in interpreting the type of action that follows from the different hypotheses of aggression. As will be seen later, the interpretations and applications of the treaty during the latter years appear to bear out this opinion.

Without prejudice to a further examination, in the following section, of the acts and facts or situations to which the sphere of

---

[11] The complete text of this passage from the Report of the Rapporteur is quoted in *Background Memorandum on the Convocation of the Meeting* [Eighth Meeting of Consultation], Pan American Union, Department of Legal Affairs, OEA/Ser.F/II.8/Doc.2 Corr., 2 January 1962, p. 7. The Spanish text is also published in Octava Reunión de Consulta de Ministros de Relaciones Exteriores, *Actas y Documentos,* OEA/Ser. F/III.8, p. 5.

[12] See p. 117, *infra.*

[13] See p. 165, *infra.*

validity of the inter-American collective security system is presently extended, reference should now be made to the conditions to which each of the two types of action under consideration is subject. As far as self-defense is concerned, given its essentially provisional character, Article 3.2 of the Rio Treaty establishes that on the request of the state or states directly attacked, each of the others may determine the immediate measures which it may individually take "until the decision of the Organ of Consultation"; this Organ shall meet without delay for the purpose of examining those measures and agreeing upon the ones of a collective character that should be taken. On the other hand, the U.N. Charter authorizes the exercise of individual or collective self-defense "until the Security Council has taken measures necessary to maintain international peace and security."

As can be seen, the former guarantees the provisional nature of self-defense more effectively that the latter. In effect, although the U.N. Charter would permit the state or states acting in self-defense to argue that the measures taken by the Council are not the "necessary" ones, the Rio Treaty impedes the raising of any question regarding the efficacy of such measures since it only requires that the Organ of Consultation meet and take a decision. However, according to Article 3.4, "Measures of self-defense provided for under this Article may be taken until the Security Council of the United Nations has taken the measures necessary to maintain international peace and security." This appears to be an inconsistency on which the legislative history of the article casts no light. But it should rather be understood as an attempt to establish two conditions, one to be required by the Organ of Consultation and the other by the Security Council.

As regards the procedure and jurisdiction to take collective action in the event of armed attack or of a conflict such as those foreseen in Article 7 of the treaty, the meeting of the Organ of Consultation is automatic. On the other hand, in the case of the other acts, facts, or situations, the machinery of consultation must be set in motion by any of the states parties to the Rio Treaty and the Council of the Organization ("Governing Board of the Pan American Union" as it was known when the treaty was signed) will decide by an absolute majority of its members entitled to vote whether the meeting of the Organ of Consultation shall be held. The Council itself is authorized to "act provisionally as an organ of consultation until the meeting of the Organ of Consultation . . . takes place," that is, the Meeting of Consultation of Ministers of Foreign Affairs.[14] When it acts with

---

[14] As indicated previously, the Meeting of Consultation does not always serve as the Organ of Consultation. According to Article 39 of the Charter, it "shall be held in order to consider problems of an urgent nature and of common interest to the American States." In this regard see p. 10, *supra.*

this character, as it has frequently done, the Council has the same competence as the Organ of Consultation. Besides, as will be seen later, even when not acting as provisional organ of consultation the Council can exercise the jurisdiction in the field of collective security which has lately been conferred on it.

The jurisdiction of the Organ of Consultation is of special importance when examined in the light of the measures that may be applied within the regional system. The Charter as well as the Rio Treaty repeatedly refer to the applicable measures, but only in Article 8 of the latter is one of the categories specifically set down: "For the purposes of this Treaty, the measures on which the Organ of Consultation may agree will comprise one or more of the following: recall of chiefs of diplomatic missions; breaking of diplomatic relations; breaking of consular relations; partial or complete interruption of economic relations or of rail, sea, air, postal, telegraphic telephonic, and radiotelephonic or radiotelegraphic communications; and use of armed force." Given the terms of the article, the measures enumerated appear to be neither precise nor exclusive, and in practice the Organ of Consultation has not been prevented from taking similar measures which are not explicity spelled out therein.[15] In addition, the decisions which call for the application of the measures foreseen in Article 8 are obligatory for all states parties to the treaty, with the sole exception, also stipulated in Article 20, that no state is obligated to use armed force without its consent.

As far as the other measures of a collective nature are concerned neither of the two instruments permits a satisfactory classification. At most, one can distinguish between those contemplated for cases of armed attack and those to be agreed upon in the event of the acts, facts, or situations foreseen in Article 6 of the treaty, on the one hand, and the measures such as those enumerated in Article 8, apart from the circumstances in which they are applied (Articles 3 or 6) and those explicitly foreseen in Article 7, such as calling upon the contending states to suspend hostilities and solve the dispute by peaceful means, on the other. In the two following chapters the variety of the measures taken by the Organ of Consultation in practice will be seen.

Although once again the inter-American instruments are silent on the subject, it is interesting to inquire just which measures of self-defense the states are authorized to take until the Organ of Consultation meets and takes a decision. Naturally the problem only arises when the exercise of self-defense is allowed in cases of aggression which, strictly speaking, is not "armed attack". One of the principal motives—if not the main one—for the resistance of many govern-

---

[15] In this regard see "Exclusion of the Cuban Government and Partial Suspension of Trade with Cuba (1961-1962)", p. 157, *infra.*

ments and publicists to the widening of the sphere of validity of this institution lies precisely in the idea that measures of self-defense necessarily involve the resort to armed force. From the practical as well as the juridical view this is untrue. At least it is not true in the inter-American system where the institution has been extended to cover "aggression which is not an armed attack." Subject to the possibility of returning to this matter after examining the corresponding applications of the Rio Treaty, it is sufficient to add that neither the treaty nor the OAS Charter, intrinsically, impedes the development and strengthening of individual or collective self-defense, of the nature and scope in reference.

The Charter contains a provision which should not be overlooked when examining the measures that may be taken, either as collective action on the part of the competent organ or in the exercise of self-defense. Reference is made to Article 19, according to which "Measures adopted for the maintenance of peace and security in accordance with existing treaties do not constitute a violation of the principles set forth in Articles 15 and 17." Those articles consecrate the principles of nonintervention and of the inviolability of the territory of a state, respectively. This is a provision equivalent to Article 2.7 of the U.N. Charter, although in the latter case the exception to the principle of nonintervention only extends to the application of "enforcement measures."[16]

Finally, the inter-American collective security system is a regional system constructed on the provisions of the U.N. Charter on "Regional Arrangements" (Chapter VIII) and self-defense (Art. 51). Article 10 of the Rio Treaty also establishes that "None of the provisions of this Treaty shall be construed as impairing the rights and obligations of the High Contracting Parties under the Charter of the United Nations." Nevertheless, certain applications of the treaty have given rise to problems of interpretation in the Security Council which cannot be ignored. Chapter X of Part Two will deal with these cases.

19. *The System for "Political Defense": Security Against Subversion*

One of the most characteristic and noteworthy aspects of the development and strengthening of the inter-American collective security system lies in the fact that a system for the "political defense" of

---

[16] See the complete text of Articles 15 and 17 of the OAS Charter in *Appendix 1*, p. 331 *infra*. Paragraph 7 of Article 2 of the U.N. Charter reads: "Nothing contained in the present Charter shall authorize the United Nations to intervene in matters which are essentially within the domestic jurisdiction of any state or shall require the Members to submit such matters to settlement under the present Charter; but this principle shall not prejudice the application of enforcement measures under Chapter VII."

the Continent has been incorporated into it, that is, a system for security against subversion. As part of the effort to protect democratic institutions against subversive propaganda and other activities inspired by totalitarian ideologies, it is based on the principles of inter-American solidarity and cooperation in this matter, that made their first appearance at the Buenos Aires Conference (1936), which declared "the existence of a common democracy throughout America."[17] Later, in view of the growing danger posed by Nazi-Fascist ideologies and activities, the first three meetings of consultation adopted various resolutions directed toward counteracting the subversive propaganda and other activities of the Axis powers. Finding themselves once again threatened by the subversive action of the international communist movement, the American republics renewed their efforts to strengthen their internal security.[18]

The system for political defense or security against subversion, as originally conceived of and later developed, sprang from the idea that subversive activity directed, aided, or instigated by extracontinental powers and inspired by totalitarian ideologies incompatible with democracy, constituted "acts of political aggression" or "aggression of a non-military character." This qualification, which appears in Resolution XVII and attached Memorandum of the Third Meeting of Consultation (Rio de Janeiro 1942), included, according to this resolution and others adopted by the two prior meetings of consultation, acts such as propaganda, espionage, and sabotage, as well as the instigation of public disorder or any other activity designed to disturb the political life of the country.[19]

The Bogotá Conference (1948), referring now to the "political activity of international communism or any other totalitarian doctrine," pointed out its "interventionist tendency," and the Tenth Inter-American Conference (Caracas 1954) condemned in more explicit terms "The activities of the international communist movement as constituting intervention in American affairs."[20] More recently, the Inter-American Peace Committee, in its report to the Eighth Meeting of Consultation (1962) described the subversive activities of the Sino-Soviet bloc and the Cuban Government in America as acts of "political aggression" or "aggression of a non-military character";

[17] See the Declaration cited in Note 5, *supra*.

[18] The texts of these resolutions appear in *International Conferences,* 1st Sup. (1933–1940), pp. 333, 353, and 354, and 2nd Sup. (1942–1954), p. 25.

[19] See the complete text of Resolution XVII and the attached Memorandum, *International Conferences,* 2nd Sup. (1942–1954), p. 25.

[20] See the complete text of Resolution XXXII, The Preservation and Defense of Democracy in America, of the Bogotá Conference, and Resolution XCIII, Declaration of Solidarity for the Preservation of the Political Integrity of the American States Against the Intervention of International Communism, of the Tenth Conference, *ibid.,* pp. 270 and 433, respectively.

the Committee added that "Such acts represent attacks upon inter-American peace and security as well as on the sovereignty and political independence of the American states, and therefore a serious violation of fundamental principles of the inter-American system."[21] For this reason the Organ of Consultation decided to suspend immediately trade with Cuba in arms and implements of war of every kind.[22]

From the foregoing it becomes clear that subversive action directed, aided or abetted by extracontinental powers (and today also by American countries dominated by them) constitutes a special category of act, fact or situation of the type foreseen in the OAS Charter and the Rio Treaty, particularly "aggression which is not an armed attack." This opinion is corroborated by statements in the report of the Investigating Committee of the Organ of Consultation that studied the Venezuelan complaint against Cuba, as well as the resolution later adopted by the Ninth Meeting of Consultation (1964). The report points out that the "acts of intervention" carried out by Cuba and outlined therein "in particular, the shipment of arms, constitute a policy of aggression on the part of the present Government of Cuba against the territorial integrity, the political sovereignty, and the stability of the democratic institutions of Venezuela." And the resolution of the Organ of Consultation declared "that the acts verified by the Investigating Committee constitute an aggression and an intervention on the part of the Government of Cuba in the internal affairs of Venezuela, which affects all of the member states." The second paragraph of the same resolution condemns the said government "for its acts of aggression and of intervention against the territorial inviolability, the sovereignty, and the political independence of Venezuela."[23] Consequently, the Organ of Consultation, in unequivocal terms, has designated these subversive activities as acts of "aggression" covered by the pertinent provisions of the Rio Treaty.

The decisions of the Ninth Meeting of Consultation also reveal other aspects of the incorporation of the system of security against subversion into the inter-American system of collective security. Originally, the manner of counteracting subversive activities lay, solely, in the various measures for internal security recommended by the Meetings of Consultation and the Inter-American Conferences. Granted that "subversive action recognizes no boundaries" as affirmed

---

[21] See the Final Considerations of that report on p. 98, *supra*.

[22] See "Exclusion of the Cuban Government and Partial Suspension of Trade with Cuba (1961–1962)", p. 157, *infra*.

[23] See the pertinent passages from the Report of the Investigating Committee and the complete text of Resolution I of the Ninth Meeting of Consultation on pp. 167 and 168, *infra*.

by the Fourth Meeting of Consultation (Washington, D.C. 1951),[24] it was also recognized from the very beginning that in addition to internal measures it was necessary to attain a high degree of international cooperation among the American republics. In the early stages this cooperation consisted in an exchange of information regarding the subversive activities about which each country had knowledge and later in the establishment of inter-American agencies of a technical and consultative nature. The first of these was the Emergency Advisory Committee for Political Defense, created by the Third Meeting of Consultation to study and coordinate the measures recommended in Resolution XVII, which functioned in Montevideo from 1942 to 1948.[25] The Eighth Meeting of Consultation (1962) created the Special Consultative Committee on Security, whose purpose is to advise the member states that may desire and request such assistance, in that field, and it has been active since its establishment in 1962.[26]

In the same resolution that created this Committee, the Organ of Consultation requested the OAS Council "to maintain all necessary vigilance, for the purpose of warning against any acts of aggression, subversion, or other dangers to peace and security, or the preparation of such acts, resulting from the continued intervention of Sino-Soviet powers in this hemisphere, and to make recommendations to the governments of the member states with regard thereto." This attribution of authority, which conferred on a political organ the duty of maintaining vigilance over subversive activity, is a new step toward an intensified international cooperation in this field. The next stage began with the decision of the Organ of Consultation to apply measures regarding trade in arms with Cuba, to which reference has been made, and to authorize the OAS Council to study the feasibility and desirability of extending the suspension of trade to other items, and to discontinue the measure or measures adopted at such time as the Government of Cuba demonstrates its compatibility with the purposes and principles of the inter-American system.[27]

This new phase of international cooperation to counteract subver-

---

[24] See the complete text of Resolution VIII, Strengthening of Internal Security, of the Fourth Meeting in *International Conferences*, 2nd Sup. (1942–1954), p. 299.

[25] For information regarding the activities and publications of the Committee of Montevideo see the Report prepared by the Department of Legal Affairs at the request of the Fourth Meeting, entitled *Strengthening of Internal Security*, 1953, *passim.*

[26] See the complete text of Resolution II, which created the Committee, in *Final Act*, OEA/Ser.C/II.8 Corr. Pursuant to the request contained in paragraph 2.c of that resolution, in May 1962 the Committee submitted to the OAS Council its *Initial General Report*, OEA/Ser. L/X/II.1, Rev. 2.

[27] See the complete text of Resolution VIII on p. 161, *infra.*

sive activity definitively incorporates the original political defense system into the inter-American collective security system, as far as procedures and measures are concerned. With reference to the intense wave of terrorism, sabotage and other subversive activities unleashed by Castrocommunism in Venezuela and other Latin American countries after the so-called October crisis, the Special Consultative Committee on Security, in a study prepared at the request of the Committee of the OAS Council charged with the function of maintaining vigilance, stated that "The degree of development attained by the political-military apparatus that has been established in Cuba is rendering the system of security against subversion increasingly inadequate and ineffective, based solely on the isolated measures that each country might adopt." In the Committee's opinion these events "constitute a situation of such gravity and urgency that it can be adequately and effectively dealt with only by adopting the measures provided for in the Treaty," that is, the Rio Treaty.[28]

In line with this concept and the precedent already established by the Eighth Meeting of Consultation, the Organ of Consultation that studied the Venezuelan complaint, after having declared the subversive activities alleged against the Cuban Government to be "an aggression and an intervention" resolved "To apply, in accordance with the provisions of Article 6 and 8" of the Rio Treaty, the following measures: that the American states not maintain diplomatic or consular relations with the Cuban Government; the suspension of all trade, whether direct or indirect, except in foodstuffs, medicines, and medical equipment that may be sent to Cuba for humanitarian reasons; and the suspension of all sea transportation except such as may be necessary for reasons of a humanitarian nature.[29]

The process of integrating the inter-American security systems has also reached the institution of self-defense. In the first place, the Eighth Meeting of Consultation, in one of its aforementioned resolutions, urged "the member states to take those steps that they may consider appropriate for their individual or collective self-defense, and to cooperate, as may be necessary or desirable, to strengthen their capacity to counteract threats or acts of aggression, subversion, or other dangers to peace and security resulting from the continued intervention in this hemisphere of Sino-Soviet powers, in accordance with the obligations established in treaties and agreements such as the

---

[28] *Cf. Paper Prepared at the Request of the Council Committee,* etc., OEA/ Ser. L/X/II. 3, 8 February 1963, pp. 44–45. The Council Committee mentioned is the Special Committee to Study Resolutions II.1 and VIII of the Eighth Meeting of Consultation which, in turn, presented its report in July 1963, OEA/Ser. G/IV, C-i-605, Rev. 3.

[29] See the complete text of Resolution I of the Ninth Meeting of Consultation, p. 168, *infra.*

Charter of the Organization of American States and the Inter-American Treaty of Reciprocal Assistance."

This paragraph of Resolution II was the basis for a statement made by the Foreign Ministers of the Americas at the conclusion of the Informal Meeting held in Washington, D.C. on October 2-3, 1962. This was that "the Soviet Union's intervention in Cuba threatens the unity of the Americas and its democratic institutions, and that this intervention has special characteristics which, pursuant to paragraph 3 of Resolution II of the Eighth Meeting of Consultation of Ministers of Foreign Affairs, call for the adoption of special measures, both individual and collective."[30] It is evident, therefore, that for the Foreign Ministers of the Americas the special characteristics of Soviet action require and justify the resort to measures of individual and collective self-defense contemplated by Resolution II of Punta del Este, notwithstanding the fact that the action in question does not correspond to the only form of aggression specifically mentioned in Article 3 of the Rio Treaty.

The Ninth Meeting of Consultation continued and made a substantial contribution to this broadening of the sphere of validity of self-defense. In accordance with the aforementioned Resolution I.5 it resolved "To warn the Government of Cuba that if it should persist in carrying out acts that possess characteristics of aggression and intervention against one or more of the member states of the Organization, the member states shall preserve their essential rights as sovereign states by the use of self-defense in either individual or collective form, which could go so far as resort to armed force, until such time as the Organ of Consultation takes measures to guarantee the peace and security of the hemisphere." Comparison with Resolution II.3 of the Eighth Meeting, reveals that Resolution I, on defining the acts to which the application of individual or collective self-defense is extended, foresees the exercise of this right in response to the forms and techniques of "indirect aggression" employed by Castrocommunism. In the second place, in extending the sphere of validity of self-defense, Resolution I does so more directly and specifically than does Resolution II of the Eighth Meeting. Third, by omitting the reference to "obligations established in treaties and agreements" that appears in the latter, Resolution I requires, as its only limitation deriving from these instruments, that the use of self-defense be subject to the measures that may be taken by the Organ of Consultation to guarantee continental peace and security. In the fourth place, by referring explicitly to the "resort to armed force," Resolution I contemplates concrete measures of self-defense.

---

[30] See the complete text of the Final Communiqué issued by the Informal Meeting of Foreign Ministers in *The Department of State Bulletin,* vol. XLVII, No. 1217, 22 October 1962, p. 598.

20. *Regimen Applicable to Exiles and Political Refugees*

In a broad sense, the inter-American collective security system includes the regimen applicable to political exiles and refugees established by the Convention on Duties and Rights of States in the Event of Civil Strife (Havana 1928), the Protocol to this Convention opened for signature in 1957, and, to a degree, the Convention on Territorial Asylum (Caracas 1954).[31] Therefore, it is of interest to distinguish this regimen from the one that has been put into effect to counteract subversive action directed or instigated by extracontinental powers and inspired by totalitarian ideologies incompatible with democracy. Notwithstanding certain analogies or similarities, they are two basically different regimens, as will be immediately appreciated.

The three instruments in reference, as indicated by the General Secretariat of the OAS in the Memorandum prepared for the Eighth Meeting of Consultation,[32] only propose to establish and specify the measures to be taken by the American states to prevent activities intended to instigate civil strife in other countries from being prepared or carried on in their respective territories. In this sense, the activities dealt with by these instruments, even though intrinsically they may also be of a "subversive" character, are promoted and carried on by private individuals (political exiles or refugees), at times with a certain degree of connivance and even of participation on the part of some local authorities, although in the latter case, the activities are not necessarily imputable to the government itself. Precisely what the aforementioned instruments do is prescribe the standards that each government should observe with respect to such acts. The conditions that prevailed when the OAS Council, acting provisionally as Organ of Consultation, decided, on April 22, 1950, that the Havana Convention of 1928 on civil strife should be strengthened and perfected, clearly show the nature of the activities it was intended to prevent, as well as the type of conduct that could be imputed to the governments.[33]

The subversive activity dealt with by the system for political defense, on the other hand, differs in nature and objectives. It is a question of acts of the government themselves, prepared on their own territory and carried out on that of other countries through agents, who may be officials or private individuals, nationals or aliens. It is not, therefore, a case of activities merely tolerated by a government

---

[31] See the complete texts of these three instruments in *Appendices 15* and *7*, pp. 403 and 362, respectively.

[32] See p. 32 *et seq.* of the Memorandum cited in Note 11.

[33] In this regard see Resolution V of the Organ of Consultation on p. 129, *infra.*

or, in which there is a certain degree of connivance or participation by its authorities, but rather of subversive activities instigated, organized, and generally financed by extracontinental powers or that are part of a plan of action of an international character.

The foregoing does not rule out the possibility that one single case or situation may involve subversive activities of the different kinds that have just been described. For example, as the Inter-American Peace Committee pointed out in its report to the Seventh Meeting of Consultation (1960): "Finally, the nature of the international tensions in the Caribbean has been modified and the tensions themselves considerably heightened as a result of an increasing desire during recent months on the part of the Soviet Union and other extracontinental powers to intervene more actively in inter-American affairs. It is evident from statements made by the highest officials of these powers that they are seeking to exploit for their own purposes some of the aspects of the situation existing in the Caribbean. Recognition of this problem has been in large measure responsible for the decision of the American governments to convoke the Seventh Meeting of Consultation of Ministers of Foreign Affairs. The threat of extracontinental intervention has thus given to the problem of Caribbean tensions a new and serious aspect, which is a matter of concern to all the countries of the Americas."[34]

The facts pointed out in this report constitute the basis for the Declaration of San José, Costa Rica, adopted by the Seventh Meeting of Consultation, which reads as follows:[35]

> The Seventh Meeting of Consultation of Ministers of Foreign Affairs,
>
> 1. Condemns energetically the intervention or the threat of intervention, even when conditional, by an extracontinental power in the affairs of the American republics and declares that the acceptance of a threat of extracontinental intervention by any American state endangers American solidarity and security, and that this obliges the Organization of American States to disapprove it and reject it with equal vigor.
>
> 2. Rejects, also, the attempt of the Sino-Soviet powers to make use of the political, economic, or social situation of any American state, inasmuch as that attempt is capable of destroying hemispheric unity and endangering the peace and security of the hemisphere.
>
> 3. Reaffirms the principle of nonintervention by any American state in the internal or external affairs of the other American states, and reiterates that each state has the right to develop its cultural, political, and economic life freely and naturally, respecting the rights of the individual and the principles of universal morality, and as a consequence, no American state may intervene for the purpose of imposing upon another American state its ideologies or its political, economic, or social principles.

---

[35] Cf. *Final Act,* OEA/Ser. C/II.7, 29 August 1960.
[34] Cf. OEA/Ser. F/II.7, Doc. 6, 5 August 1960, p. 14.

4. Reaffirms that the inter-American system is incompatible with any form of totalitarianism and that democracy will achieve the full scope of its objectives in the hemisphere only when all the American republics conduct themselves in accordance with the principles stated in the Declaration of Santiago, Chile, approved at the Fifth Meeting of Consultation of Ministers of Foreign Affairs, the observance of which it recommends as soon as possible.

5. Proclaims that all member states of the regional organization are under obligation to submit to the discipline of the inter-American system, voluntarily and freely agreed upon, and that the soundest guarantee of their sovereignty and their political independence stems from compliance with the provisions of the Charter of the Organization of American States.

6. Declares that all controversies between member states should be resolved by the measures for peaceful solution that are contemplated in the inter-American system.

7. Reaffirms its faith in the regional system and its confidence in the Organization of American States, created to achieve an order of peace and justice that excludes any possible aggression, to promote solidarity among its members, to strengthen their collaboration, and to defend their sovereignty, their territorial integrity, and their political independence, since it is in this Organization that its members find the best guarantee for their evolution and development.

8. Resolves that this declaration shall be known as "The Declaration of San José, Costa Rica."

A reading of the foregoing declaration clearly reveals a recognition of the new tone the international tensions in the Caribbean area had assumed. It also reveals the regional organization's decision to disapprove and reject, as a danger to American solidarity and security, the acceptance by any American state of the intervention or threat of intervention by an extracontinental power in the affairs of the American republics. Finally, the Declaration of San José sets down the obligation of all member states to submit to the discipline of the inter-American system. Therefore, the Declaration is the starting point for the measures later taken by the Organ of Consultation in application of the Rio Treaty and other inter-American instruments.

Chapter VII

Applications of the Inter-American Treaty of Reciprocal Assistance (Rio Treaty)

To the date of publication, the Inter-American Treaty of Reciprocal Assistance (Rio Treaty) has been applied 13 times. In the majority of these cases the OAS Council has acted provisionally as Organ of Consultation pursuant to Article 12, either because it was considered unnecessary to hold a Meeting of Consultation of Ministers of Foreign Affairs or because the urgency of the situation did not allow it. The applications are presented in chronological order, except those dealing with the Cuban situation, which appear in the next Chapter. Also included at the end of this Chapter is a resumé of five requests which did not occasion applications of the treaty.

21. *Conflict Between Costa Rica and Nicaragua (1948-1949)*

On December 11, 1948 the Representative of Costa Rica informed the Chairman of the OAS Council that the night before "the territory of Costa Rica" had been "invaded by armed forces proceeding from Nicaragua." In his opinion, these facts "constitute a situation which, in letting loose an armed conflict in the territory of Costa Rica, endangers the peace of America." The said Representative pointed out that the case in question fell within those foreseen in Article 6 of the Rio Treaty. At the meeting held on December 14, the Council decided to convoke a meeting of consultation, constitute itself as provisional Organ of Consultation and appoint a committee to investigate on the spot the facts denounced and their antecedents.

On December 24 the Council acting provisionally as Organ of Consultation received the report of the Committee of Information and, at its suggestion, approved the resolution which read in part:

THE COUNCIL OF THE ORGANIZATION OF AMERICAN STATES, ACTING PROVISIONALLY AS ORGAN OF CONSULTATION,

RESOLVES:

I. To request the Governments of Costa Rica and Nicaragua, in compliance with the Inter-American Treaty of Reciprocal Assistance, to give full assurances to the Provisional Organ of Consultation that they will immediately abstain from any hostile act toward each other.

II. To make known, with due respect to the Government of Nicaragua, that, in the light of data gathered by the Committee of Information especially appointed for the purpose, that Government could and should have taken adequate measures at the proper time for the purpose of preventing: (a) the development, in Nicaraguan territory, of activities intended to overthrow the present regime in Costa Rica, and (b) the departure from Nicaraguan territory of revolutionary elements who crossed the frontier and today are prisoners or are still fighting against the Government of Costa Rica.

III. To make known, with due respect to the Government of Costa Rica, that it can and should take adequate measures to rid its territory of groups of nationals or foreigners, organized on a military basis with the deliberate purpose of conspiring against the security of Nicaragua and other sister republics, and of preparing to fight against their governments.

IV. To request very respectfully that both governments, by every available means, faithfully observe the principles and rules of nonintervention and solidarity contained in the various inter-American instruments signed by them.

V. To continue in consultation until positive assurances have been received from the Governments of Costa Rica and Nicaragua, that, as they are assuredly disposed to do, they will adhere strictly to the lofty principles and rules that constitute the juridical basis of American international life.

On that same date and in order to carry out the foregoing resolution, the Council named an Inter-American Commission of Military Experts, composed of five members, to also proceed to Costa Rica and Nicaragua. The Commission was to see that the measures in the foregoing resolution, which the Council had indicated to the parties as being necessary for the solution of the conflict, were carried out.

Later the possibility of a Pact of Amity to be signed by both parties was discussed, in order to put an end to the differences and reaffirm good relations between them. At its meeting on January 25 the Council appointed a new Committee, which included representatives of the parties, to draft the said instrument. This Committee's report was approved by the Council on January 28. At the same meeting it was decided that the Commission of Military Experts should continue to function for as long as necessary, and that it should be authorized, if it considered it necessary and with the consent of the parties, to establish mixed commissions to help the two states carry out faithfully the resolution approved on December 24. At a meeting held on February 17, the Council received the report of the Inter-American Commission of Military Experts and requested a Joint Committee, composed of the Committee that had prepared the draft Pact of Amity and the Committee of Information mentioned above, to prepare the final text of the Pact of Amity, in the light of the report of the Military Committee and of observations made during the meeting.

The Pact of Amity was signed on February 21, 1949. Pursuant to it, the Governments of Costa Rica and Nicaragua agreed to prevent the repetition in the future of events such as those under study by the provisional Organ of Consultation; to recognize their obligation to submit disputes to methods for pacific settlement, for which purpose they recognized as having full validity as to disputes between them, the American Treaty on Pacific Settlement (Pact of Bogotá); and likewise to reach agreement as to the best manner of putting into practice the provisions of the Convention on the Duties and Rights of States in the Event of Civil Strife, in cases contemplated by that Convention.[1]

22. *Situation in the Caribbean (1950)*

On January 3, 1950 the Government of Haiti, considering that certain incidents that had suddenly occurred between that country and the Dominican Republic constituted a situation that threatened the peace of the Continent, requested the immediate convocation of the Organ of Consultation for the purpose of adopting the security and defense measures provided for by Articles 6 and 8 of the Rio Treaty.[2] On January 6 the Government of the Dominican Republic presented a similar request so that the Organ of Consultation might "study and find a remedy for the abnormal conditions prevailing in the Caribbean area." In response to these two requests, the Council decided to issue the convocation, constitute itself provisionally as Organ of Consultation and appoint a Committee to make an on-the-spot investigation of the facts and their antecedents.

The Investigating Committee, composed of representatives of five countries, was authorized to receive evidence, hear statements, and use any other source of information necessary for the clarification of the facts and antecedents denounced. The Committee was to prepare one or more reports containing a recital of the facts, the documentary material considered pertinent, and the conclusions at which it might arrive as a result of its investigations. The Committee visited Haiti, the Dominican Republic, Cuba, Guatemala, as well as Mexico at the specific invitation of that government, and interviewed officials and private citizens in each of those countries.

The Committee left Washington on January 22 and returned on February 15 after which it prepared an extensive report which was submitted to the Council of the Organization acting as Provisional

---

[1] For documentation and further details regarding this conflict see *Inter-American Treaty of Reciprocal Assistance, Applications*, vol. 1 (1948-1959), p. 27 *et seq*. The complete text of the Havana Convention on Civil Strife is included in *Appendix 15*, p. 403, *infra*.

[2] See the request presented by the Government of Haiti in February of the previous year, on p. 86, *supra*.

Organ of Consultation on March 13. The report dealt with Case "A", the request of Haiti, and Case "B", the request of the Dominican Republic. The Committee also prepared certain general considerations since it considered "that it would not have fulfilled adequately its mission if, in addition to investigating the facts fully and carefully, it did not attempt to specify certain basic factors contributing to the irregularities occurring in the Caribbean area, with the objective of presenting to the Organ of Consultation conclusions as to the steps that can be taken to eliminate those factors and avoid the repetition of such irregularities."

The latter explains the breadth of the decisions taken by the Organ of Consultation on the basis of the five draft resolutions presented by the Investigating Committee. The said decisions, discussed at the meetings held on April 3, 4, 5, and 8 and approved at the final meeting, are as follows:

I

The Council of the Organization of American States, acting provisionally as Organ of Consultation,

Having seen the Report presented by the Committee which investigated the facts and antecedents to which the Note of the Haitian Government of January 3, 1950, refers; and

CONSIDERING: That the Organ of Consultation, convoked January 6, 1950, in conformity with Article 6 of the Inter-American Treaty of Reciprocal Assistance, should take the steps it considers most advisable for the maintenance of the peace and security of the Continent,

DECLARES:

1. That the facts verified by the Investigating Committee, from among those charged against the Government of the Dominican Republic, are contrary to norms contained in several inter-American instruments, such as the Convention on the Rights and Duties of States, signed at Montevideo in 1933; the Additional Protocol Relative to Non-Intervention, signed at Buenos Aires in 1936, the principle of which is also contained in Article 15 of the Charter of the Organization of American States, as well as in other provisions that govern the peaceful relations of the Members of the Organization.

2. That the danger to international peace that might arise from the events that have affected relations between Haiti and the Dominican Republic has fortunately been dispelled; but that, because of their gravity, those events might have very seriously disturbed American solidarity; and that, if repeated, they would give occasion for application of the procedures of the Inter-American Treaty of Reciprocal Assistance in order to protect the principle of non-intervention and to ensure the inviolability or the integrity of the territory or the sovereignty or the political independence of any American State against aggression on the part of any State or group of States;

3. That, on the other hand, the laws that have been passed in the Dominican Republic to repeal the war powers granted by its Congress to the Executive Power, and to prevent subversive activities on the part of political refugees in its territory, express a clear intention to

maintain peace, and show its disposition that, in the future, those events will not be repeated; and

RESOLVES:

1. To request the Government of the Dominican Republic to take immediate and effective measures to prevent government officials from tolerating, instigating, encouraging, aiding, or fomenting subversive or seditious movements against other Governments;

2. To request the Dominican Government to comply strictly with the Joint Declaration of June 9, 1949, the observance of which is equally the responsibility of the Haitian Government;

3. To point out to both Governments the advisability of strengthening their relations on the basis of a bilateral treaty inspired in the aims of the Havana Convention of 1928 on the Duties and Rights of States in the Event of Civil Strife, and also, taking into account the special geographical situation of Haiti and the Dominican Republic, the advisability of incorporating in the agreement or treaty that they sign special provisions to prevent the inhabitants, national or foreign, of each country, from taking part in activities of any kind capable of disturbing the internal order of the neighboring country;

4. To point out to the Governments of Haiti and the Dominican Republic the advisability of reaching a bilateral agreement to deal with the problems connected with the employment of Haitian workers in the Dominican Republic;

5. To request the Governments of Haiti and the Dominican Republic to make every effort, within the limits of their respective constitutional powers, to avoid the continuation of any systematic and hostile propaganda, expressed through any medium whatsoever, against each other, or against other American countries and their respective Governments;

6. Finally, inspired by the basic principle of American solidarity, to express its fervent hope that both sister Republics, once the present difficulties have been removed, will find means of reestablishing, as soon as possible, the good relations that should always exist among all the members of the American community.

II

The Council of the Organization of American States, acting provisionally as Organ of Consultation,

CONSIDERING: That the Report submitted by the Investigating Committee which was created by the Organ of Consultation in its Resolution of January 6, 1950, clearly establishes that in the past there did exist, and that in some respects there still persists, an abnormal situation constituting a threat to the established institutions of the nations in the Caribbean area and an obstacle to the maintenance of normal friendly relations among certain States located therein;

That the Organ of Consultation, having been convoked to study this situation, is therefore under an obligation, in accordance with Article 6 of the Inter-American Treaty of Reciprocal Assistance, to take steps which contribute to the maintenance of the peace and security of the Continent,

DECLARES:

1. That there existed within Cuba in 1947 and within Guatemala in

1949, armed groups of various nationalities, which were not part of the regular armed forces of those countries and which were animated by the unconcealed purpose of overthrowing the Government of the Dominican Republic by force;

2. That officials of the Governments of Cuba and Guatemala not only expressed openly their sympathy with these subversive organized movements, but in some cases lent them aid;

3. That the facts verified by the Investigating Committee, from among those charged against the Governments of Cuba and Guatemala, are contrary to principles set forth in various inter-American instruments, such as the Convention on Rights and Duties of States, signed at Montevideo in 1933, the Additional Protocol Relative to Non-Intervention signed at the Inter-American Conference for the Maintenance of Peace (Buenos Aires, 1936), the Convention on the Duties and Rights of States in the Event of Civil Strife, concluded at Havana in 1928, and the Charter of the Organization of American States;

4. That likewise there occurred on the part of the Dominican Republic acts which are set forth in the Report and Conclusions of the Investigating Committee and some examined in Resolution I of the Council acting provisionally as Organ of Consultation, which evidently are contrary to the standards of harmonious inter-American relations subscribed to by all the American Governments.

5. That, even though the said facts fortunately did not result in the violation of international peace, they did very seriously weaken American solidarity; and if they were to persist or recur, they would give occasion for the application of the procedures of the Inter-American Treaty of Reciprocal Assistance in order to protect the principle of non-intervention and to ensure the inviolability or the integrity of the territory or the sovereignty or the political independence of any American State against aggression on the part of any State or group of States;

6. That the declarations formulated by the Chief Executives, to which reference is made in the Report of the Committee, constitute a gurarantee against future recurrence of acts of this kind; and

RESOLVES:

1. To request the Governments of Cuba and Guatemala to adopt adequate measures so that they will not permit the existence in their territories of groups of nationals or foreigners organized on a military basis with the deliberate purpose of conspiring against the security of other countries; and to request also the Governments of Cuba, Guatemala, and the Dominican Republic to take adequate measures to ensure absolute respect for the principle of non-intervention, the observance of which is also, naturally, incumbent upon the Government of Haiti;

2. To request the Governments of Cuba and Guatemala to take effective measures to control war materials that may now be or may have been in the possession of the revolutionary groups, and to prevent illegal traffic in arms and possible use of the aforementioned war materials for purposes incompatible with inter-American juridical commitments;

3. To request the Governments of Cuba, Guatemala, Haiti, and the Dominican Republic to make every effort, within the limits of their respective constitutional powers, to avoid any systematic and hostile propaganda, expressed through any medium whatsoever, against one

another, or against other American countries and their respective governments;

4. To recommend, in view of the fact that the bilateral negotiations initiated in September 1948 under the auspices of the Inter-American Peace Committee have not yet produced any satisfactory result, that the Governments of Cuba and the Dominican Republic make an effort to arrive as speedily as possible at a settlement of their controversy and that, if such a settlement should not be achieved within six months, this controversy should be submitted to one of the methods of pacific settlement specified in the Pact of Bogotá;

5. To support the conclusions of the Inter-American Peace Committee, approved on September 14, 1949, relative to the situation existing in the Caribbean area, on the understanding that the said conclusions are applicable not merely to the aforesaid situation, but to all American States without exception;

6. Finally, inspired by the basic principles of American solidarity, to express its fervent hope that the said sister Republics, once the present difficulties have been removed, will find means of reestablishing, as soon as possible, the good relations that should always exist among all members of the American community.

III

The Council of the Organization of American States, acting provisionally as Organ of Consultation,

CONSIDERING: That it has approved Resolutions designed to eliminate the factors that have for some time disturbed relations among certain American countries, and that, to facilitate compliance with the said Resolutions, it is advisable to establish a Special Committee, provisional in character and having a clearly defined purpose,

RESOLVES:

To appoint a Committee, composed of five of its Members, which, always respecting the principle of non-intervention, will acquaint itself with the manner in which Resolutions I and II are being carried out and place itself at the service of the interested Parties to facilitate compliance with the said Resolutions, in a thoroughly conciliatory spirit. This Committee shall submit within three months, and likewise at the conclusion of its work, a Report thereon to the Governments, through the General Secretariat of the Organization of American States.

IV

The Council of the Organization of American States, acting provisionally as Organ of Consultation,

CONSIDERING: That both the principle of representative democracy and that of non-intervention are established in many inter-American instruments, and that both are basic principles of harmonious relations among the countries of America; and

That there exists some confusion of ideas as to the means of harmonizing the effective execution and application of the basic principle of non-intervention and that of the exercise of representative democracy,

RESOLVES:

1. To reaffirm the principles of representative democracy, in accord-

ance with Article 5(d) of the Charter of the Organization of American States, and of suffrage and participation in the government, set forth in Article XX of the American Declaration of the Rights and Duties of Man, as fundamental in the inter-American system, and to express the opinion that, consequently, agreement should be sought on legitimate means to make them completely effective;

2. To declare that the aforementioned principles do not in any way nor under any concept authorize any Government or group of Governments to violate inter-American commitments relative to the principle of non-intervention or to give the appearance of legitimacy to violations of the rules contained in Article 1 of the Havana Convention of 1928, on Duties and Rights of States in the Event of Civil Strife, the Protocol Relative to Non-Intervention (Buenos Aires 1936), and Article 15 of the Charter of the Organization of American States.

V

The Council of the Organization of American States, acting provisionally as Organ of Consultation,

CONSIDERING: That among the factors that have helped create a situation susceptible of disturbing peace and security in the Caribbean area are some so complex and far-reaching that they require a careful study designed to enable the competent organs of the Organization of American States to take adequate measures to bring about their definitive elimination;

That to this end and without prejudice to the measures that the Organ of Consultation may take in cases of conflicts between American States, in accordance with the Inter-American Treaty of Reciprocal Assistance, the facts ascertained by the Investigating Committee show that other steps are needed;

That among the problems pointed out by the Investigating Committee are: that of making the principle of representative democracy more effective; that of strengthening and supplementing the principles and standards that the Governments should observe with relation to activities aimed at fomenting civil strife in other countries; and that of considering the problem created by the presence, in various countries, of political refugees and exiles proceeding from other American nations,

RESOLVES:

1. To recommend to the Council of the Organization that, through its competent Organs, it undertake as promptly as possible the study of the following matters:

a) The possibilities of stimulating and developing, within the provisions of Articles 13, 15, and 19 of the Charter of the Organization of American States, and with due respect to the sovereignty of the States, the effective exercise of representative democracy, set forth in Article 5(d) of the Charter, as well as in Article XX of the American Declaration of the Rights and Duties of Man.

b) The strengthening and perfecting of the Havana Convention of 1928 on the Duties and Rights of States in the Event of Civil Strife, in order to determine the measures that Governments should employ to prevent, within the territory under their jurisdiction, the preparation of activities designed to foment civil strife in other countries. In this study there should be taken into account the suitability of coordinating the said Convention and other inter-American instruments on the subject with the Charter of the Organization of American States and the Inter-American Treaty of Reciprocal Assistance, seeking, furthermore, to make effective Article 15 of the Charter of the Organization of American States.

c) Regimen of political asylees, exiles, and refugees.

2. The study of the point relative to the Havana Convention shall be entrusted in the first instance to the Department of International Law and Organization of the Pan American Union, which should begin by drafting a questionnaire addressed to all the American Governments, with the request that they indicate the modifications, clarifications, or amplifications that in their opinion the clauses of the aforesaid Havana Convention require.

3. When the replies are received from the Governments, it shall be incumbent upon the Department of International Law and Organization to prepare a draft Additional Protocol, which, when it has been found acceptable by the Council of the Organization of American States shall be submitted at once to the Governments for approval and opened for signature by their plenipotentiaries.

4. The study of points (a) and (c) shall be entrusted to the Inter-American Council of Jurists or, if that body is in recess, to the Inter-American Juridical Committee.

5. When such study has been completed, the Inter-American Council of Jurists or the Inter-American Juridical Committee shall send to the Council of the Organization of American States a detailed Report, with the conclusions it has reached and the suggestions it considers advisable, so that the said topics may be included in the agenda of the Tenth Inter-American Conference or of an earlier competent meeting. In any event, the Council or the Committee shall report within six months to the Council of the Organization of American States, rendering an account of the status of the said study.

It will be noted that Resolution I, dealing with Case "A", and Resolution II, dealing with Case "B", refer to the imputability of the facts denounced in each case, to the juridical standards and principles involved, and to the future measures that should be taken by the governments responsible for these facts in order to avoid a repetition in the future. Resolution III ordered the appointment of a Committee that was to acquaint itself with the manner in which Resolutions I and II were being carried out and place itself at the service of the interested parties to facilitate their compliance. This Committee presented three reports, on June 30 and October 31, 1950, and finally on May 4, 1951. Resolution IV defined the relationship between the principle of representative democracy and that of suffrage and participation in government and the principle of nonintervention and the rules contained in Article 1 of the Havana Convention of 1928 on the Duties and Rights of States in the Event of Civil Strife, the Protocol Relative to Non-Intervention of Buenos Aires (1936) and Article 15 of the OAS Charter.

Resolution V contains the dispositions recommended by the Investigating Committee regarding the factors and problems that had helped create a situation susceptible of disturbing peace and security in the Caribbean area among which were the possibility of making more effective the principles of representative democracy; the establishment and implementation of the principles and standards which the governments should observe with relation to the activities aimed at instigating civil strife in other countries; and the consideration of the problem created by the presence, in various countries, of political refugees and exiles from other American nations. In this regard the Organ of Consultation recommended to the Council of the Organization the studies mentioned in subparagraphs a, b, and c of paragraph 1 of Resolution V. From these studies, carried out with the participation of the Inter-American Council of Jurists and its Permanent Committee, the Inter-American Juridical Committee, as well as the Department of Legal Affairs of the Pan American Union, came the Draft Protocol to the Havana Convention on civil strife, opened for signature in 1957, and the Conventions on Territorial Asylum and Diplomatic Asylum, approved by the Tenth Inter-American Conference (1954).[3]

23. *Situation in Guatemala (1954)*

According to Resolution XCIII of the Tenth Inter-American Conference (Caracas 1954) "the domination or control of the political institutions of any American State by the international communist movement, extending to this Hemisphere the political system of an extracontinental power, would constitute a threat to the sovereignty and political independence of the American States, endangering the peace of America, and would call for a Meeting of Consultation to consider the adoption of appropriate action in accordance with existing treaties."[4] A fact or situation of this nature was what motivated the next convocation of the Organ of Consultation in accordance with Article 6 of the Rio Treaty.

In a note to the Chairman of the Council, dated June 26, the representatives of ten member states stated: "Our Governments view with increasing concern the demonstrated intervention of the international communist movement in the Republic of Guatemala and the danger which this involves for the peace and security of the Continent. The recent outbursts of violence in the area intensify considerably this concern and pose an urgent need to hold a meeting of

---

[3] For documentation and further details regarding this application of the Rio Treaty see *Applications*, vol. 1, p. 79 *et seq.* The complete text of the three instruments mentioned appears in *Appendices 15,* 7 and 6, on pp. 403, 362, and 357, respectively.

[4] See the complete text of Resolution XCIII in *International Conferences,* 2nd Sup. (1942-1954), p. 433.

the Organ of Consultation. It is abundantly clear that the nations of this Continent are today faced with a situation which they believe endangers the peace of America and affects the sovereignty and political independence of the American states." At a special meeting on June 28 the Council convoked a Meeting of Ministers of Foreign Affairs to serve as Organ of Consultation "for the purpose of considering all aspects of the danger to the peace and security of the continent resulting from the penetration of the political institutions of Guatemala by the international communist movement, and the measures which it is desirable to take."

The Council held another special meeting on July 2 to consider the possibility of postponing the meeting of consultation, in view of the events that had taken place in Guatemala since the previous meeting. Considering that the change of government that had taken place had transformed the situation, the Council decided to postpone the meeting *sine die.*[5]

With regard to this application of the Rio Treaty the action of another regional agency, the Inter-American Peace Committee, should be recalled, as well as the fact that the Council had asked the Secretary General of the OAS not only to transmit to the U.N. Secretary General its decision to postpone the meeting of consultation *sine die,* but also to inform him that the said Committee would send a report on its activities directly to the Security Council.[6]

24. Conflict Between Costa Rica and Nicaragua (1955-1956)

This application of the Rio Treaty actually constitutes a second phase of the one that took place in 1948-1949 as a result of the conflict between the two countries. Once again, at the request of the Government of Costa Rica, the Council of the Organization resolved, at its meeting on January 11, 1955, to convoke a meeting of consultation and follow the usual procedure, that is, constitute itself and act provisionally as Organ of Consultation in accordance with Article 12 of the Rio Treaty and authorize its Chairman to appoint an Investigating Committee. Acceding to a new petition of the Costa Rican Representative, on January 12 the Council, acting provisionally as Organ of Consultation, decided to request the governments that were in a position to do so to place at the disposal of the Investigating Committee, which had left that same morning for Costa Rica, aircraft to make pacific observation flights over the

---

[5] For documentation and further details regarding this application of the Rio Treaty see *Applications,* vol. 1, p. 159 *et seq.*

[6] See the summary of this action by the Peace Committee on p. 89, *supra.* With respect to the action by the Security Council on the request presented by the Guatemalan Government prior to the convocation of the Organ of Consultation, that is on June 19, see p. 184, *infra.*

regions affected by the situation, in the name of the Committee and under its supervision. Taking into consideration the increasing seriousness of the situation which affected the integrity, the sovereignty and the political independence of Costa Rica, the Council met again on January 14 and resolved, among other things, "To condemn the acts of intervention of which Costa Rica is victim and call attention to the grave presumption that there exist violations of international treaties in force."

On January 16 the Council held two meetings, at which it resolved, respectively, to request the governments to expedite the orders for the purchase of aircraft that Costa Rica had placed with them, and to request the Investigating Committee that, in accordance with the wishes expressed by the Governments of Nicaragua and Costa Rica, it proceed with utmost urgency to prepare in consultation with them and put into effect a plan for effective surveillance of their common frontier. The plan for surveillance of the frontier entered into force at noon on January 20, the date on which the Council met again, this time at the request of the Nicaraguan Government. In the resolution approved at that meeting the Council requested the Investigating Committee to report, urgently, on the charge made by the Government of Nicaragua that two P-51 aircraft of the Costa Rican Government had crossed over the border between the two countries, as well as on the application of the plan for surveillance of that border.

Subsequent events contributed to a solution of the dispute, which is set forth in the resolutions adopted by the Council at the recommendation of the Investigating Committee. In Resolution II the Council called upon the parties to appoint their respective members of the Commission of Investigation and Conciliation that it was incumbent upon them to name according to Article XVII of the American Treaty of Pacific Settlement (Pact of Bogotá) and to sign the bilateral agreement mentioned in Article IV of the Pact of Amity which had put the said treaty into force between the two countries. Pursuant to Resolution III a Special Committee was created, composed of nine members of the Council, for the purpose of offering its cooperation to the parties in carrying out the pertinent provisions of Resolution II.

The Special Committee met several times in compliance with its mandate and on August 4 submitted an oral report to the Council acting provisionally as Organ of Consultation. That afternoon the Council resolved that the Special Committee should meet, as soon as its Chairman deemed it convenient, to draft a report covering the course of the bilateral negotiations between the parties for the purpose of preparing the Bilateral Agreement provided for in Resolutions II and III of February 24 and to express its opinion as to the advisability of canceling arrangements for the meeting of consultation. The report in question was later prepared and presented to the provisional Organ of Consultation at its meeting on September 8, at which it was decided to cancel the convocation of the meeting of consultation and to retain the Special Committee while the negotiations for the signing of the bilateral agreement were in progress. Finally, on January 18, 1956, the Committee presented to the Council its report on the agreements signed by the parties, with which it considered its mission concluded. For its part, the Council took note of the happy results of the bilateral negotiations and transmitted the report to the governments of the member states along with a copy of the agreements signed by the Governments of Costa Rica and Nicaragua at the Pan American Union on January 9, 1956.[7]

25. Border Dispute Between Honduras and Nicaragua (1957)

At the request, first, of the Government of Honduras and, later, of the Government of Nicaragua, the Council of the Organization resolved in May 1957 to convoke the Organ of Consultation, to set in due course the date and site of the meeting, and to constitute itself and act provisionally as such. It also authorized its Chairman to appoint a committee to investigate, on the spot, the pertinent facts and their antecedents. The Investigating Committee's first action was to obtain a cease-fire which was signed on May 5 by the two governments parties to the border dispute that had arisen regarding the Arbitral Award made by the King of Spain on December 23, 1906. The cease-fire agreement also contained a solemn pledge to refrain from any act or activity in any way susceptible of aggravating the situation. To carry it out, the Committee was authorized to present a plan for troop withdrawal to ensure that no further acts of force would take place. The Committee was assisted in carrying out its mission by military advisers of the countries represented on it. Meanwhile, each party prepared a complaint on violations of the agreement.

In its report to the Council, which was taken up at the meetings held on May 16 and 17, the Investigating Committee recommended that it support and maintain in effect all the measures of a practical nature adopted by the Committee; that it request the governments of the parties to maintain in effect the troop-withdrawal plan agreed upon until a final settlement of the dispute was obtained; that within the letter and the spirit of Article 7 of the Rio Treaty, it take the measures necessary to reestablish or maintain inter-American peace and security and to solve the dispute by peaceful means and, to that

---

[7] For documentation and further details regarding this application of the Rio Treaty see *Applications*, vol. 1, p. 167 *et seq.*

end, to entrust to an *ad hoc* committee the immediate study of the possibilities of a pacific and definitive settlement of the legal controversy that had given rise to the conflict. If no pacific means of settlement were found among those enumerated in the American Treaty on Pacific Settlement (Pact of Bogotá), which both states had ratified, and they did not wish to have recourse to the Inter-American Peace Committee, then the proper organ for settling the controversy was the International Court of Justice. On May 17 the Council decided to establish the committee recommended by the Investigating Committee, to cooperate with the Governments of Honduras and Nicaragua and at a later meeting, on May 24, the Council approved the other recommendations made by the Investigating Committee.

The *Ad Hoc* Committee collaborated actively with the parties during the 30-day period established by the Council. In its report, the Committee presented a draft resolution stating that in accordance with the spirit and letter of the Rio Treaty it should be used not only to eliminate any armed conflict but also to promote means of pacific settlement of the controversy that caused the situation. The draft resolution also called for resort to the International Court of Justice, under the terms which appear in the resolution approved by the Council on July 5, which is as follows:

THE COUNCIL OF THE ORGANIZATION OF AMERICAN STATES ACTING PROVISIONALLY AS ORGAN OF CONSULTATION,

HAVING SEEN

The report of the *Ad Hoc* Committee charged with collaborating with the governments of Honduras and Nicaragua in accordance with the resolutions approved on May 17 and May 24, 1957, by this Council, acting provisionally as Organ of Consultation; and

CONSIDERING:

That the regional system has demonstrated its effectiveness in carrying out its noble purpose of guaranteeing the sovereignty and independence of the American republics and fraternal relations between them;

That, in accordance with the letter and the spirit of the Inter-American Treaty of Reciprocal Assistance—the Rio Treaty—the application of this instrument should lead not only to the elimination of any armed conflict but also to the promotion of measures for the pacific settlement of the controversy that is considered to have given rise to such a situation;

That the American Treaty on Pacific Settlement—the Pact of Bogotá —which has been ratified by the governments of Honduras and Nicaragua, provides procedures that are applicable to the case under consideration; and

Pursuant to, and in execution of, the Rio Treaty,

RESOLVES:

1. To express its satisfaction at the voluntary and simultaneous

acceptance by the governments of Honduras and Nicaragua of the procedure of pacific settlement that, with the collaboration of the Ad Hoc Committee, was subscribed to by both parties, and the text of which is as follows:

THE HIGH CONTRACTING PARTIES,

FOLLOWING the recommendations of the Council of the Organization of American States, acting provisionally as Organ of Consultation, which were actuated by the provisions of the Inter-American Treaty of Reciprocal Assistance that are applicable to controversies between American states, which provisions urge such states to take the necessary measures to reestablish peace and settle their controversies by pacific means; and

DESIROUS of reestablishing as soon as possible the harmonious fraternal relations that are a traditional characteristic of relations between the American republics and particularly between countries that, like those of Central America, consider themselves to be linked by historic ties of solidarity,

AGREE to carry out, through the application of the American Treaty on Pacific Settlement—the Pact of Bogotá—and for the purpose of settling once and for all the difference that is separating them at this time, the judicial procedure outlined below:

(1) The Parties, having recognized and accepted in the Pact of Bogotá the jurisdiction of the International Court of Justice as *ipso facto* compulsory, shall submit thereto the disagreement existing between them with respect to the Arbitral Award handed down by His Majesty the King of Spain on December 23, 1906, with the understanding that each, within the framework of its sovereignty, shall present such facets of the matter in disagreement as it deems pertinent.

(2) The procedure to be followed by the Court shall be that established in its Statutes and Rules of Procedure.

(3) The decision, after having been duly pronounced and officially announced to the parties, shall decide the disagreement definitively and without right of appeal, and shall be carried out without delay.

(4) If one of the High Contracting Parties should fail to comply with the obligations imposed upon it by the decision of the International Court of Justice, the other, before having recourse to the United Nations Security Council, shall request a Meeting of Consultation of Ministers of Foreign Affairs of the American States to decide upon all the measures that it is appropriate to take to enable the decision of the Court to be carried out.

(5) If, as a result of the application of the aforementioned judicial procedure, all phases of the disagreement with respect to the Arbitral Award handed down by His Majesty the King of Spain on December 23, 1906, are not definitively settled, the High Parties shall, without delay, apply the arbitral procedure provided by the aforesaid Pact of Bogotá to settle definitively the new situation created between them, which shall be clearly defined in the additional agreement that the High Parties are to sign to this end within a period of three months from the date they are officially notified of the decision.

(6) In accepting the procedure set forth in this instrument and

the pertinent application of the Pact of Bogotá to the case here considered, the High Contracting Party that made a reservation to the aforesaid international agreement declares that the aforesaid reservation shall not take effect.

2. To express its appreciation to the governments concerned for the active and effective cooperation they gave to the Council, acting provisionally as Organ of Consultation, and the Ad Hoc Committee, to enable the procedural agreement whose text has been quoted in the preceding paragraph to be reached.

3. To request the governments of Honduras and Nicaragua to maintain the present status quo, without thereby altering any of the legitimate rights claimed by both Parties, until a definitive settlement of the controversy is achieved by the application of rules of law and without at any time disrupting the peace between the Parties.

4. To state that the Honduran-Nicaraguan Joint Military Committee is empowered to deal with any differences that might arise during the period mentioned in the preceding paragraph, with respect to the agreement referred to in its current regulations.

5. To transmit this document with each Party's note of acceptance to the Secretary-General of the United Nations and, through him, to the International Court of Justice.

6. To express its strong hope that the procedure set forth in the first paragraph of this resolution will settle, once and for all, the disagreement that has temporarily separated two countries like Honduras and Nicaragua, which are linked in a very special way by geographic and historic ties and called upon by destiny to maintain and strengthen their cordial relations in this important region of the Americas.

The definitive agreement between the parties was signed on July 21, in the presence of the members of the Council of the Organization acting provisionally as Organ of Consultation. It contains substantially the same stipulations as those in the foregoing text regarding the conditions under which the controversy would be submitted to the International Court of Justice.[8]

26. *Situation in Nicaragua (1959)*

The next application of the Rio Treaty that corresponds to this Chapter took place in June 1959 and was caused by further activities of political exiles and refugees in Central America. In a special meeting on June 4 the OAS Council took up a complaint by the Representative of Nicaragua that his country had been the victim of an armed invasion by individuals of various nationalities who had reached Nicaraguan territory by means of airplanes obtained in Costa Rica, and that another invasion by sea was expected, all of

[8] For documentation and further details regarding this application of the Rio Treaty see *ibid.,* p. 245 *et seq.* In the solution of the problems that arose with regard to the execution of the judgment handed down by the Court on November 18, 1960 the Inter-American Peace Committee played a very active part. Regarding its activities see p. 100, *supra.*

which endangered the peace of the Continent. The Council decided to convoke the Organ of Consultation, to set in due course the place and date of the meeting, and to constitute itself and act provisionally as such. It further authorized its Chairman to appoint a committee to gather the necessary additional information on the situation as a preliminary to any decision on measures to be taken.

After several meetings in Washington, D.C., the Committee traveled to Nicaragua and bordering countries on June 14, and on its return submitted a report to the provisional Organ of Consultation at the meetings held on June 26 and 28. Following is a summary that appears at the end of the aforesaid report, in which the Committee emphasizes the information it considers most significant:

1. According to the data gathered by the Honduran-Nicaraguan Joint Military Commission, there is in Honduras a force of approximately 70 men, of various nationalities, which possesses armaments and equipment of Dominican and United States manufacture, obtained from unknown sources. This group proposed to cross the frontier to promote civil strife in Nicaragua. The Government of Honduras has taken some of the members of this force prisoner and has announced its intention of taking the measures necessary for preventing it from entering Nicaragua.

2. The Honduran-Nicaraguan Joint Military Commission is carrying on intensive work to prevent situations like that referred to in the preceding paragraph, and in regard to which it has formulated truly useful recommendations. The Government of Nicaragua would like this agency to act more rapidly than it did in the case cited.

3. The group of 110 armed men, transported to Nicaragua on May 31 and June 1 by the same airplane belonging to a private Costa Rican airline, left from Punta Llorona, located in the southwest region of Costa Rica, on the Pacific Ocean. This group, made up of 107 Nicaraguans and three Costa Ricans, managed to evade the vigilance of the Costa Rican authorities. Some of the leaders of this movement solicited aid from the Government of Cuba, which was denied them. The arms they carried appear to have been bought directly in the black market in San José.

4. There is in Costa Rica a group of Nicaraguan exiles, members of the Nicaraguan Revolutionary Movement, which under the leadership of Dr. Enrique Lacayo Farfán, has the aim of achieving the fall of the Government of Nicaragua. It has the sympathy and aid of important Costa Rican elements.

5. The Governments of Costa Rica and Honduras, in accordance with the principle of non-intervention, have declared their neutrality with respect to the events in Nicaragua and have taken various measures to prevent the organization of armed forces that propose to penetrate that country for the purpose of promoting civil strife.

6. Around June 16, the Government of Costa Rica discovered in Punta Llorona a well-armed contingent apparently composed of approximately 160 men, gathered presumably for the purpose of going to Nicaragua to fight against the Government. When this group was discovered, the Government of Costa Rica offered to its members that, if

they surrendered their arms, it would permit the Costa Ricans to return to their homes and the foreigners to leave the country. Later the group appears to have begun to dissolve.

7. Until now the reports transmitted by the Government of Nicaragua to that of Costa Rica, to the effect that a group of armed men is concentrated in the northwest region of Costa Rica near the frontier, have been neither confirmed nor disproved. The Committee has telegraphed to the Government of Costa Rica, on June 24, requesting reports on this and other points.

8. There is a considerable clandestine traffic in arms in the Caribbean zone. Rebel groups have taken advantage of this situation to obtain arms from various sources, apparently without great difficulty.

9. There are various bilateral arrangements and agreements between the Government of Nicaragua and the bordering countries that relate to the problems involved in the situation denounced by the Government of Nicaragua before the Council of the Organization. For one reason or another, including the lack of ratification of some of them, the said agreements have not been so useful as could have been expected for preventing the development of incidents among those countries or in solving them.

On July 28 the Council decided to terminate the Committee's activities, cancel the convocation of the Meeting of Consultation of Ministers of Foreign Affairs and, consequently, terminate its provisional action as Organ of Consultation, recommending to the governments of the member states that they strengthen the measures designed to maintain peace, observing the principle of nonintervention.[9]

27. Application of Measures to the Dominican Republic (1960-1962)

At a special meeting on July 8, 1960, the Council of the Organization, at the request of the Venezuelan Government, convoked the Organ of Consultation, constituted itself provisionally as such and authorized its Chairman to appoint a committee to investigate the facts denounced by that government regarding "the acts of intervention and aggression by the Government of the Dominican Republic against the Government of Venezuela, which culminated in the attempt upon the life of the Venezuelan Chief of State." At another special meeting held on July 29, the Council decided to set the date and site for the Sixth Meeting of Consultation of Ministers of Foreign Affairs Serving as Organ of Consultation (August 16, San José, Costa Rica).

The Investigating Committee's report was submitted to the Council of the Organization, acting provisionally as Organ of Consultation, and after having been transmitted to the governments was considered

---

[9] For documentation and further details regarding this application of the Rio Treaty see *Applications*, vol. 1, p. 369 *et seq*.

by the Meeting of Consultation. In that report the Committee arrived at the following conclusions:

1. The attempt against the life of the President of Venezuela perpetrated on June 24, 1960, was part of a plot intended to overthrow the Government of that country.

2. The persons implicated in the aforementioned attempt and plot received moral support and material assistance from high officials of the Government of the Dominican Republic.

3. This assistance consisted principally of providing the persons implicated facilities to travel and to enter and reside in Dominican territory in connection with their subversive plans; of having facilitated the two flights of the plane of Venezuelan registry to and from the Military Air Base of San Isidro, Dominican Republic; of providing arms for use in the coup against the Government of Venezuela and the electronic device and the explosive which were used in the attempt; as well as of having instructed the person who caused the explosion in the operation of the electronic device of that explosive and of having demonstrated to him the destructive force of the same.

It will be noted that on this occasion the Investigating Committee limited itself to setting forth the facts for which it had found proof and refrained from characterizing them, contrary to the practice of former investigating committees. The Meeting of Consultation did characterize and condemn them, however, and agreed upon the measures that should be applied to the Dominican Republic. The complete text of Resolution I of that Meeting is as follows:

The Sixth Meeting of Consultation of Ministers of Foreign Affairs Serving as Organ of Consultation in Application of the Inter-American Treaty of Reciprocal Assistance,

HAVING SEEN the Report of the Investigating Committee appointed pursuant to the provisions of the third paragraph of the resolution approved by the Council of the Organization of American States on July 8, 1960, and

CONSIDERING:

That the Charter of the Organization of American States sets forth the principle that international order consists essentially of respect for the personality, sovereignty and independence of states, and the faithful fulfillment of obligations derived from treaties and other sources of international law;

That in connection with the incident denounced by the Government of Venezuela before the Inter-American Peace Committee on November 25, 1959, that organ of the inter-American system reached the conclusion that "the necessary arrangements to carry out the flight from Ciudad Trujillo to Aruba—planned for the purpose of dropping leaflets over a Venezuelan city—and to load these leaflets in Ciudad Trujillo, could not have been carried out without the connivance of the Dominican authorities";

That the Committee of the Council of the Organization of American States acting provisionally as Organ of Consultation that was entrusted with the investigation of the acts denounced by the Government of

Venezuela, reached the conclusion that the Government of the Dominican Republic issued diplomatic passports to be used by Venezuelans who participated in the military uprising that took place in April 1960 in San Cristóbal, Venezuela;

That the Committee of the Council of the Organization of American States acting provisionally as Organ of Consultation, which was charged with the investigation of the acts denounced by the Government of the Republic of Venezuela, also reached the conclusions that:

[The conclusions included here are those that appear in the report of the Investigating Committee and are transcribed above.]

That the aforementioned actions constitute acts of intervention and aggression against the Republic of Venezuela, which affect the sovereignty of that state and endanger the peace of America; and

That in the present case collective action is justified under the provisions of Article 19 of the Charter of the Organization of American States,

RESOLVES:

To condemn emphatically the participation of the Government of the Dominican Republic in the acts of aggression and intervention against the State of Venezuela that culminated in the attempt on the life of the President of that country, and, as a consequence, in accordance with the provisions of Articles 6 and 8 of the Inter-American Treaty of Reciprocal Assistance,

AGREES:

1. To apply the following measures:
   a. Breaking of diplomatic relations of all the member states with the Dominican Republic;
   b. Partial interruption of economic relations of all the member states with the Dominican Republic, beginning with the immediate suspension of trade in arms and implements of war of every kind. The Council of the Organization of American States, in accordance with the circumstances and with due consideration for the constitutional or legal limitations of each and every one of the member states, shall study the feasibility and desirability of extending the suspension of trade with the Dominican Republic to other articles.
2. To authorize the Council of the Organization of American States to discontinue, by a two-thirds affirmative vote of its members, the measures adopted in this resolution, at such time as the Government of the Dominican Republic should cease to constitute a danger to the peace and security of the hemisphere.
3. To authorize the Secretary General of the Organization of American States to transmit to the Security Council of the United Nations full information concerning the measures agreed upon in this resolution.

In order to comply with the mandate conferred upon it by the Sixth Meeting of Consultation, the Council named a Special Committee. In its first report, submitted to the Council on December 21, 1960, the Committee reached the conclusion that not only had there been no change in the attitude of the Dominican Government which would justify the suspension of the measures adopted but also that it was desirable to extend the suspension of trade to petroleum and petroleum products and trucks and spare parts. At its meeting on January 4, 1961 the Council resolved that it was feasible and desirable that the member states extend the suspension of their trade with the Dominican Republic to the export of those articles. Later the Special Committee appointed a Subcommittee which visited the Dominican Republic in June, September, and November of that year. In its third report the Subcommittee pointed out that having examined the latest situation in the Dominican Republic in all its meaning and significance, it believed that "it should be objectively recognized that the Government of the Dominican Republic is no longer a danger to the peace and security of the Americas," and that, consequently, the Council "should cancel the measures imposed upon the Dominican Government." The Committee shared these conclusions and submitted them to the Council for its consideration. At its meeting on January 4, 1962 the Council decided to cancel the measures agreed upon by the Sixth Meeting of Consultation as well as those agreed upon by the Council itself in compliance with its mandate.[10]

28. *Situation Between the Dominican Republic and Haiti (1963-1965)*

To a degree, the situation that occurred between these two countries in April 1963 was simply a new phase of a situation that has existed between them since 1949, in which the presence of political exiles and refugees of each in the territory of the other has played a principal role. The specific aspect which gave rise to this new application of the Rio Treaty, as denounced by the Representative of the Dominican Republic to the Council of the Organization at the special meeting on April 28, 1963, was that his government had knowledge that the Chancery of the Dominican Embassy in Port-au-Prince had been "broken into yesterday by members of the Haitian Public Force and that members of that Force are still there and have also entered the Embassy residence, grossly interfering with the freedom of movement in the latter."

At the April 28 meeting the Council acceded to the proposal by the Representative of Costa Rica that it convoke a meeting of consultation and constitute itself and act provisionally as Organ of Consultation. At another meeting held that same day, the Council acting provisionally as Organ of Consultation authorized its Chair-

---

[10] For documentation and further details regarding this application of the Rio Treaty see *Applications,* vol. 2, p. 3 *et seq.*

man to appoint a five-member committee to make an on-the-spot study of the events denounced by the Dominican Republic. During that same meeting, the Representative of Haiti read a cable addressed by his government to the Secretary General of the Organization requesting a special meeting of the Council to decide, in accordance with the terms of Articles 39 and 40 of the OAS Charter, to convoke immediately the Organ of Consultation "to take cognizance of the indescribable aggression that the Dominican Republic plans to undertake within twenty-four hours against the sovereignty and inalienable rights of the people and the Government of Haiti."

The Chairman of the Council cabled the Chiefs of State of the two countries requesting them to refrain from taking any steps that might hinder the negotiations to be undertaken by the Organ of Consultation "to bring about a peaceful solution of the conflict." Both Chiefs of State, in reply, stated that they were willing to cooperate with the Special Committee appointed by the Organ of Consultation. The latter, at the meeting held on May 8, took further measures, as can be seen from the text of the resolution approved on that date, which reads as follows:

THE COUNCIL OF THE ORGANIZATION OF AMERICAN STATES, ACTING PROVISIONALLY AS ORGAN OF CONSULTATION,

HAVING HEARD the information furnished at this meeting by the Chairman of the Council of the Organization acting provisionally as Organ of Consultation regarding the development of events in connection with the situation existing between Haiti and the Dominican Republic; and

CONSIDERING:

The progress that has been made to date toward diminishing the tensions existing between the two countries; and

The fact that, notwithstanding this progress, it is evident that conditions still persist that may affect the peace and security,

RESOLVES:

1. To make another friendly appeal to the governments of both countries that, within a generous spirit of hemispheric solidarity, they continue to give their valuable cooperation to the efforts being made by this Organ, and that they refrain from taking any action incompatible with the obligations established by the Charter of the Organization of American States not to resort to the threat or the use of force, except in the case of self-defense, and to submit all international disputes to the procedures for pacific settlement of the inter-American system.

2. To authorize the Committee created by this Organ, by the resolution adopted last April 28, to make an on-the-spot study of the situation existing between Haiti and the Dominican Republic and to offer the parties their services for the purpose of finding a prompt solution to the conflict and to ward off the threats to the peace and security of the area.

3. To authorize the Chairman of the Council of the Organization to increase the number of members on this committee, in the event that this should be necessary, for the mission called for in paragraph 2.

In the report submitted to the Council on July 16, the Special Committee related the investigations and interviews it had carried out and presented a study of the facts denounced by each of the parties to the dispute, and then formulated a series of conclusions that served as a basis for the resolution adopted by the provisional Organ of Consultation that day. That resolution reads as follows:

THE COUNCIL OF THE ORGANIZATION OF AMERICAN STATES, ACTING PROVISIONALLY AS ORGAN OF CONSULTATION,

HAVING SEEN the first and second reports of the Committee appointed in accordance with the resolution adopted on April 28, 1963,

RESOLVES:

1. To renew the plea to the Governments of the Dominican Republic and Haiti to refrain from performing any act incompatible with the obligations established by the Charter of the Organization not to resort to the threat or the use of force, except in the case of self-defense, and to submit all their international disputes to the procedures of pacific settlement, and that in this connection it express to the Dominican Government the concern caused by the mobilization and concentration of armed forces on the Dominican-Haitian border, as well as profound pleasure that it has withdrawn them.

2. To urge the Government of Haiti, in a spirit of inter-American cooperation and with adequate speed, to agree to grant the respective safeconducts to the asylees who are still in the premises of various diplomatic missions in Port-au-Prince, in accordance with the law in force in America.

3. To take note of the statements made by the Government of Haiti to the effect that it respects the inviolability of the residences and offices of the diplomatic missions in Port-au-Prince and the privileges and immunities of their personnel, and to urge that government to take the measures necessary in order to give full force to those principles.

4. To urge the Government of Haiti to observe the principle of respect for human rights consecrated in the Charter of the Organization of American States, inasmuch as compliance with that principle effectively contributes to the maintenance of peace and the diminution of international tensions, and in view of the statement made to the Committee by the Foreign Minister of Haiti to the effect that his government adheres to that principle.

5. To urge the Governments of Haiti and the Dominican Republic to observe, in their capacity as parties thereto, the obligations set forth in the 1954 Convention on Territorial Asylum and the Convention on the Rights and Duties of States in the Event of Civil Strife and the Additional Protocol thereto.

6. To suggest to the same governments that they continue to adopt measures aimed at avoiding acts of hostility toward the nationals of one state in the territory of the other state.

7. To continue acting provisionally as Organ of Consultation.

On August 6 the provisional Organ of Consultation met again, at the request of the Representative of Haiti, to consider certain facts denounced by that government relative to an armed invasion by a group of Haitian exiles carried out "from Dominican territory" during the night of August 4-5. After hearing a lengthy statement by the Representative of Haiti, as well as an answering statement by the Dominican Representative, the Organ of Consultation resolved to instruct the Special Committee, in compliance with the resolutions adopted on April 28 and May 8, to study, with the urgency the case required, the events denounced by the Government of Haiti and to report at the earliest opportunity.

On August 15 the Committee presented a preliminary report in which, among other things, it stated that in the situation then existing between Haiti and the Dominican Republic, the aspect pointed to in its second report, with reference to the subversive activities that Haitian exiles in the Dominican Republic might engage in against the Government of Haiti, was of particular significance, and that, in this connection, the provisions of Article IX of the Convention on Territorial Asylum could serve as a basis for a solution satisfactory to both parties.[11] At its meeting on August 15 the Council merely took note of that report as well as of the Committee's decision to travel to the region again to continue its study in compliance with its mandate.

After holding several interviews at its headquarters and traveling to the region, the Committee prepared its third report, dated October 24, in which it formulated the following conclusions and recommendations: That the invasions of Haitian territory on August 5 and 15 originated in Dominican territory, although it could not determine whether the authorities of the Dominican Government participated in any manner in the preparation and carrying out of those invasions; that the recommendations contained in its second report, which were nearly all adopted by the provisional Organ of Consultation in its resolution of July 16, constituted a broad framework within which all the problems that had recently existed between the two countries could be solved; and that it considered it pertinent to suggest that whenever possible the two governments undertake direct negotiations in order to reach a general agreement, with or without the auspices of the competent inter-American organs, on the various aspects that constitute the causes of the frequent friction between the two countries.

The provisional Organ of Consultation did not meet again until November 30, 1964. During this long period the Special Committee

---

[11] See the text of Article IX of the Convention in *Appendix 7*, p. 362, *infra.*

continued its efforts, with few interruptions, and direct negotiations were also carried out between the parties. At a meeting held on that date, the Council listened to a lengthy statement by the Chairman of the Committee as well as observations by some of its members.[12] The Council met again on December 2 and was informed by the Haitian Ambassador that his government had permitted all the persons who had taken asylum in the Embassies of Argentina and Colombia in Port-au-Prince to leave the country. After expressing its satisfaction over the progress made, the Council decided to request the Special Committee to continue its efforts in order to reach a definitive solution of the situation.[13]

Finally, in a declaration issued on December 15, the Special Committee set forth the conditions established by the parties that would make possible the initiation of a new phase in the analysis and solution of the causes of friction between them. These conditions referred to the procedure to be followed to resolve the problems related to the persons who had taken territorial asylum in each country. In that same declaration the Committee stated that the parties had agreed to begin formal negotiations on January 2, 1965, under the auspices of the Committee, at the headquarters of the Pan American Union.[14]

29. *Situation Between Panama and the United States of America (1964)*

The situation between Panama and the United States of America in January 1964 also gave rise to an application of the Rio Treaty.[15] On January 29 the Representative of Panama addressed the Chairman of the OAS Council to renew the request cabled by the Minister of Foreign Affairs of his country to the Chairman of the Council on January 9, the date on which the situation had arisen. In the Panamanian note in reference it was indicated that "Since the friendly intervention of the Inter-American Peace Committee has ceased, my government considers that, in conformity with Articles 9 and 6 of the Inter-American Treaty of Reciprocal Assistance, the convocation of the Organ of Consultation continues to be urgent and undeferable, in order that the aforesaid Organ may take cognizance of the acts of aggression against Panama and, in respect of them, may take all the

---

[12] See the verbatim minutes of the meeting, OEA/Ser.G/II, C-a-556.

[13] *Cf.* OEA/Ser.G/II, C-a-557.

[14] *Cf.* OEA/Ser.G/V, C-d-128. For documentation and further details regarding this application of the Rio Treaty, up to and including the presentation of the Third Report of the Special Committee, see *Applications,* vol. 2, p. 159 *et seq.*

[15] For the Inter-American Peace Committee's activities that preceded this application of the Rio Treaty, see p. 103, *supra.*

measures. . . ." The note also mentioned "measures designed to obtain compensation from the United States of America for the damage and injuries sustained by Panama as a result of the aggression."

The Council held a special meeting on January 31 and after listening to statements by the representatives of the parties decided to hold another meeting on February 4. At this second meeting it decided to convoke the Organ of Consultation and to constitute itself and act provisionally as such. On February 7, the Council acting provisionally as Organ of Consultation approved the following resolution:

WHEREAS:

Article 4 of the Charter of the Organization of American States proclaims the following as the first two essential purposes of the Organization: "To strengthen the peace and security of the continent" and "to prevent possible causes of difficulties and to ensure the pacific settlement of disputes that may arise among the member states";

The Inter-American Treaty of Reciprocal Assistance recognizes the preeminent position within the inter-American system of the procedures for the pacific settlement of controversies, and explicitly and especially mentions the principles set forth in the preamble and declarations of the Act of Chapultepec; and

At the special meetings of the Council held on January 31 and February 4, 1964, both the Representative of the Government of Panama and the Representative of the United States Government expressed a desire that the tragic events that occurred in Panama last January 9 and 10 be fully investigated,

THE COUNCIL OF THE ORGANIZATION OF AMERICAN
STATES ACTING PROVISIONALLY AS ORGAN
OF CONSULTATION,

RESOLVES:

1. To urge both governments to abstain from committing any act that might result in violating the peace in Panama.

2. To establish a general committee composed of all the members of the Council, acting provisionally as Organ of Consultation, with the exception of the Representatives of the parties in conflict.

3. The general committee shall:
   a. Investigate, fully and at once, the acts that occurred in Panama on January 9 and 10, and thereafter, and submit a report to the Organ of Consultation on the matter and on the efforts exerted by the Governments of the United States and Panama during subsequent days to find a solution to the dispute;
   b. Propose to the parties procedures intended to ensure that the peace will not be violated while an effort is being made to find a solution to the dispute between them;
   c. Bearing in mind the causes of the dispute, to assist the parties in their search for a fair solution thereof and to submit a report to the Organ of Consultation on this phase of the subject; and
   d. Create the special committees that it deems necessary for the fulfillment of its task.

4. To request the American governments and the Secretary General of the Organization to furnish full cooperation in order to facilitate the work of the general committee.

The General Committee established by this resolution met that same day and decided to send a five-man delegation to Panama to initiate the task conferred on it by paragraph 3 of the resolution. During its stay in Panama the Delegation directed its intense activities both toward an investigation of the facts as well as assisting the parties in finding a just solution of the controversy that existed between them. On its return to Washington the Delegation presented an oral report to the General Committee and continued its endeavors for several weeks until on March 15 it issued the following press release:

The Delegation of the General Committee of the Council of the Organization of American States acting provisionally as Organ of Consultation is pleased to announce that, on the 12th of March, 1964, the Governments of the United States of America and of the Republic of Panama, through their duly authorized representatives, communicated to the Delegation their acceptance of the text of a Joint Declaration which, in the English and Spanish languages, reads as follows:

English text

The Governments of the Republic of Panama and of the United States of America have agreed to re-establish diplomatic relations as soon as possible to seek the prompt elimination of the causes of conflict relative to the Panama Canal and to attempt to resolve other problems existing between them, without limitations or preconditions of any kind.

Consequently, within 30 days following re-establishment of diplomatic relations, both Governments will designate special ambassadors with sufficient powers to carry out discussions and negotiations with the objective of reaching a just and fair agreement which will eliminate the abovementioned causes of conflict and resolve the other problems referred to above. Any agreements that may result would be subject to the constitutional processes of each country.

Spanish text

Los Gobiernos de la República de Panamá y de los Estados Unidos de América han convenido en restablecer relaciones diplomáticas a la brevedad posible para procurar la pronta eliminación de las causas de conflicto relativas al Canal de Panamá y para tratar de resolver otros problemas existentes entre ellos, sin limitaciones o precondiciones de ninguna especie.

En consecuencia, dentro de los 30 días siguientes al restablecimiento de relaciones diplomáticas, ambos Gobiernos nombrarán Embajadores Especiales con poderes suficientes para llevar a cabo discusiones y negociaciones con el objeto de llegar a un convenio justo y equitativo que elimine las antedichas causas de conflicto y resuelva los damás problemas referidos. Cualesquiera convenios que resulten estarían sujetos a los procedimientos constitucionales de cada país.

The Delegation records that both texts are equally authentic and that the words "agreement" in the English version and "convenio" in the Spanish version are used in the broadest sense that they have in international law.

The Delegation, being convinced that the text of the Joint Declaration is clear and precise, calls upon the parties to begin immediately compliance with the agreement that they have concluded.

Lastly, the Delegation announces that it has requested a meeting of the General Committee on the 17th of this month for the purpose of receiving the Delegation's report on the manner in which it has carried out its mission.

Washington, D.C., March 15, 1964

The Joint Declaration did not enter into force between the parties due to circumstances that occurred shortly after its publication and that were related mainly to the interpretation of certain terms contained therein. When informed of this situation, the General Committee decided to request the Chairman of the Council of the Organization to enter into conversations with the parties in order to clarify certain points and attempt to reach a solution of the problem. On April 3 the Chairman informed the General Committee about his efforts and announced that the Governments of Panama and the United States of America had agreed on a new Joint Declaration. The new declaration was signed that same day by the Representatives of the two governments in the presence of the other members of the Council and is contained in the following press release:[16]

The Chairman of the General Committee of the Council of the Organization of American States acting provisionally as Organ of Consultation is pleased to announce that the duly authorized Representatives of the Governments of the Republic of Panama and of the United States of America have agreed, on behalf of their governments, to a Joint Declaration which in the English and Spanish languages reads as follows:

JOINT DECLARATION

In accordance with the friendly declarations of the Presidents of the United States of America and of the Republic of Panama of the 21st and 24th of March, 1964, respectively, annexed hereto, which are in agreement in a sincere desire to resolve favorably all the differences between the two countries;

Meeting under the Chairmanship of the President of the Council and recognizing the important cooperation offered by the Organization of American States through the Inter-American Peace Committee and the Delegation of the General Committee of the Organ of Consultation, the Representatives of both governments have agreed:

1. To re-establish diplomatic relations.

2. To designate without delay Special Ambassadors with sufficient powers to seek the prompt elimination of the causes of conflict between the two countries, without limitations or preconditions of any kind.

---

[16] For documentation and further details regarding this application of the Rio Treaty see *Applications,* vol. 2, p. 215 *et seq.*

3. That therefore, the Ambassadors designated will begin immediately the necessary procedures with the objective of reaching a
just and fair agreement which would be subject to the constitutional processes of each country.

Washington, D. C.
April 3, 1964.

DECLARACION CONJUNTA

De conformidad con las amistosas declaraciones de los Presidentes
de los Estados Unidos de América y de la República de Panamá del 21
y 24 de marzo de 1964, respectivamente, adjuntas a la presente, que
coinciden en un sincero deseo de resolver favorablemente todas las
diferencias de los dos países;

Reunidos bajo la Presidencia del señor Presidente del Consejo y
luego de reconocer la valiosa cooperación prestada por la Organización
de los Estados Americanos a través de la Comisión Interamericana de
Paz y de la Delegación de la Comisión General del Organo de Consulta,
los Representantes de ambos gobiernos han acordado:

1. Restablecer relaciones diplomáticas.

2. Designar sin demora Embajadores Especiales con poderes suficientes para procurar la pronta eliminación de las causas de
conflicto entre los dos países, sin limitaciones ni precondiciones
de ninguna clase.

3. En consecuencia, los Embajadores designados iniciarán de inme-
diato los procedimientos necesarios con el objeto de llegar a un
convenio justo y equitativo que estaría sujeto a los procedimientos
constitucionales de cada país.

Washington, D. C.
3 de abril de 1964

The Chairman of the General Committee of the Council of the
Organization of American States acting provisionally as Organ of
Consultation records that the parties agree that both texts are equally
authentic and that the words "agreement" in the English version and
"convenio" in the Spanish version cover all possible forms of international engagements.

During the course of this application of the Rio Treaty the Panamanian Government submitted the matter for consideration to the
Security Council of the United Nations. Although the world organization took no action in this regard, reference will be made later to
the procedure it followed.[17]

30. *Requests of the Governments of Haiti (1949), Ecuador (1955), the Dominican Republic (1959), Peru (1961), and Bolivia (1962)*

As was indicated in the introduction to this Chapter, of all the requests presented, five did not result in applications of the Rio Treaty.
The first of these, presented by the Government of Haiti on February

---

[17] See p. 187, *infra.*

16, 1949, was based on facts denounced by that country, consisting of activities carried out by Haitian exiles from the territory of the Dominican Republic, and that created "a situation susceptible of endangering the peace." At the meeting on February 25, considering that in the course of the statement made during that meeting and the one held on February 18 declarations had been made which led to the belief that the two governments could reach a friendly agreement, through recourse to the pacific procedures established in inter-American instruments, the Council decided to refrain from convoking the Organ of Consultation.[18]

The second of these requests was presented by the Representative of Ecuador on September 8, 1955, in connection with "a serious situation created by the Government of Peru that is affecting and placing in imminent danger the integrity of its territory, its sovereignty, and its political independence." At the special meeting held on that date, the Council of the Organization decided to take cognizance of the Ecuadorian note and the statement by the Representative of Peru as well as the declarations by the Representatives of Argentina, Brazil, Chile and the United States of America, guarantor states of the Protocol of Peace, Friendship and Boundaries signed by the Governments of Ecuador and Peru at Rio de Janeiro on January 29, 1942. The Council also expressed its satisfaction at the rapidity with which the governments of the guarantor states acted in considering the situation at that meeting and decided to request those governments to furnish information as soon as possible with respect to the development of the situation and the measures taken.[19]

The third of this group of requests was one presented on July 2, 1959 by the Representative of the Dominican Republic for the Council of the Organization to take cognizance of the international situation which had arisen in the Caribbean area and apply the Rio Treaty. The Dominican note, considered by the Council at a special meeting held that same afternoon, contained certain charges against Cuba and Venezuela in connection with the two invasions of the Dominican Republic in June of that same year. At the meeting on July 2 the Representatives of Cuba and Venezuela rejected those charges and declared themselves against the application of the Rio Treaty. As indicated below, at a later meeting the Council decided to convoke, not the Organ of Consultation, but a Meeting of Con-

---

[18] For óther aspects of the Haitian complaint see *Applications,* vol. 1, p. 69. It will be recalled that the application of the Rio Treaty in the "Situation in the Caribbean (1950)" began with a request by the Haitian Government. In this regard see p. 124, *supra.* For the Inter-American Peace Committee's activities in the Dominican-Haitian case (1949), see p. 86, *supra.*

[19] For further details of this request see *Applications,* vol. 1, p. 231 *et seq.*

sultation of Ministers of Foreign Affairs in accordance with Articles 39 and 40 of the OAS Charter.[20]

On October 12, 1961 the Representative of Peru on the OAS Council requested that as soon as possible it convoke a Meeting of Consultation of Ministers of Foreign Affairs in application of the Rio Treaty. It will be recalled that the Council decided to point out that the Inter-American Peace Committee was "an appropriate organ, in accordance with the terms of Resolution IV of the Fifth Meeting of Consultation of Ministers of Foreign Affairs, to deal with the facts denounced in the request presented by the Government of Peru."[21]

The last of the requests in reference was presented by the Government of Bolivia on April 18, 1962, and based on "an imminent threat of aggression against its territorial integrity on the part of the Government of Chile," motivated by the diversion of the waters of the Lauca River. After listening to statements made by the representatives of the two countries during several meetings, the Council approved the following resolution at a special meeting on May 24:

THE COUNCIL OF THE ORGANIZATION OF AMERICAN STATES,

CONSIDERING:

The request made by the Government of Bolivia on April 18 of this year and the statements of the Representatives of Bolivia and Chile at the special meetings held on April 20 and 26 and on May 3, 8, and 11, 1962;

That, according to their statements, the Governments of Bolivia and Chile, during the course of the negotiations regarding the Lauca River, have recognized the applicability of the provisions of Resolution LXXII of the Seventh International Conference of American States on industrial and agricultural use of international rivers;

That Article 22 of the Charter of the Organization of American States establishes that: "In the event that a dispute arises between two or more American States which, in the opinion of one of them, cannot be settled through the usual diplomatic channels, the Parties shall agree on some other peaceful procedure that will enable them to reach a solution"; and

That, therefore, as they have indicated that they would do in their statements, the Governments of Bolivia and Chile should avail themselves of the measures for peaceful settlement provided for in the inter-American system,

RESOLVES:

1. To express the hope that the Governments of Bolivia and Chile

---

[20] In connection with this meeting see p. 156, *infra*. For other aspects of the Dominican situation that motivated this request see *Applications*, vol. 1, p. 411 *et seq.*

[21] For further documents and details regarding this request see *Applications*, vol. 2, p. 61, as well as p. 158, *infra*. For the Inter-American Peace Committee's activities in connection with the Peruvian request see p. 97, *supra*. Also see the application of the Rio Treaty based on the Peace Committee's report on p. 157, *infra*.

restore normal diplomatic relations as soon as possible.

2. To make a friendly plea to the Government of Bolivia that, in accordance with the spirit of cooperation it has demonstrated in the consideration of this matter, it resort to one of the means for pacific settlement of disputes provided for in the inter-American system.

3. To make a friendly plea to the Government of Chile that it continue cooperating toward finding a pacific means that holds the best possibility of settling the dispute promptly.

4. To offer the Governments of Bolivia and Chile, under the terms of the American Treaty on Pacific Settlement (Pact of Bogotá), which both of them signed at the Ninth International Conference of American States, the services of the Council that are described in the Treaty, in connection with the procedures for pacific settlement.

The foregoing resolution led to an exchange of notes between the two governments and the Chairman of the Council of the Organization, and from August 1 on, various efforts in search of a solution to the controversy.[22]

---

[22] For documentation and further details regarding this request see *Applications*, vol. 2, p. 83 *et seq.*

Chapter VIII

Applications of the Rio Treaty Brought About by the "Cuban Situation"

Since 1959, the "Cuban situation" has been the cause of four of the 13 applications of the Inter-American Treaty of Reciprocal Assistance. As a result of the second (January 1962), the present Government of Cuba was excluded from participation in the inter-American system. The two applications that followed, therefore, had to do with a member state temporarily deprived of representation in the organs and agencies of that system. This circumstance, not present in any other applications of the treaty, does not appear to have had any consequences as far as the functioning of the regional mechanism of collective security is concerned.

31. First Incidents (1959)

The landing of a group of armed men, nearly all Cubans and bound from a Cuban port, near the Panamanian town of Nombre de Dios in April 1959 motivated the first of the four applications of the Rio Treaty in reference. On the basis that the invasion was a fact covered by Article 6 of the treaty and "without charges being made by one state against another," the Representative of Panama on the OAS Council, by note of April 27, requested the convocation of the Organ of Consultation. During special meetings held that same day and the 28th, the Council heard statements by the Representatives of Panama and Cuba, the latter denying all responsibility for the facts denounced, and decided to convoke the Organ of Consultation, constitute itself and act provisionally as such and authorize its Chairman to appoint an investigating committee. The same resolution also requested the governments to place airplanes at the disposal of the committee for making peaceful observation flights over the territory of Panama and recommended that they consider favorably any requests from the Panamanian Government for the arms necessary for its self-defense.

Based on the investigations carried out up to the night of April 29, the Committee informed the Council, in its first message, that it had concluded that "the invasion of Panamanian soil was organized abroad, that the vessel carrying the invaders sailed from a Cuban port, and that the invading force was composed almost entirely of foreigners." In the report it later submitted to the Council, the Committee stated that "82 of the imprisoned invaders were Cubans, one was from the United States and another was Panamanian." The Investigating Committee considered its labors finished once the invading forces had unconditionally surrendered to the Panamanian authorities and the threat of new landings had not materialized. As a result of its investigations, the Committee reached the following conclusions:

1. That the Republic of Panama was the victim of an invasion, organized abroad, that sailed from a Cuban port and was composed almost entirely of foreigners.
2. That this case is comprehended in the provisions of Article 6 of the Inter-American Treaty of Reciprocal Assistance, which establishes: "If the inviolability or the integrity of the territory or the sovereignty or political independence of any American State should be affected by an aggression which is not an armed attack or by an extra-continental or intra-continental conflict, or by any other fact or situation that might endanger the peace of America, the Organ of Consultation shall meet immediately in order to agree on the measures which must be taken in case of aggression to assist the victim of the aggression or, in any case, the measures which should be taken for the common defense and for the maintenance of the peace and security of the Continent."
3. That the effective and prompt action of the Organization of American States in accordance with the Inter-American Treaty of Reciprocal Assistance was a decisive factor in the happy solution of the case.
4. That this incident emphasizes the importance of effective and complete vigilance on the part of the Contracting States of the Convention on Duties and Rights of States in the Event of Civil Strife, to prevent the inhabitants of their territories, nationals and aliens, from crossing the frontier or embarking for the purpose of starting or promoting civil strife in another American republic.
5. That the situation that motivated the convocation of the Organ of Consultation on April 28, 1959, has ceased to exist, and that therefore the convocation should be canceled and the activities of the Council acting provisionally as Organ of Consultation should be terminated.

Using as a basis the conclusions arrived at by the Committee, on June 18, 1959 the Council of the Organization acting provisionally as Organ of Consultation resolved to recommend to the American governments "that they study and, if they deem it necessary, strengthen the measures that they are now applying in their respective territories to prevent situations like that which has affected the Republic of Panama." It further recommended "to those governments that have not yet become parties to the 1928 Convention of Havana on Duties and Rights of States in the Event of Civil Strife, or to the

1957 Protocol thereto, that they consider the advisability of doing so in the near future."[1]

The Cuban Government was also involved in the invasion of Nicaragua by armed individuals of various nationalities in June 1959, mentioned in the foregoing section. It will be recalled that the armed invaders reached Nicaraguan territory by aircraft obtained in Costa Rica. The Nicaraguan Government also immediately denounced before the OAS Council a threatened invasion by sea, which it considered could endanger the peace of the Continent. In an interview with the Committee appointed by the Chairman of the Council acting provisionally as Organ of Consultation on June 4, the Chief of State of Nicaragua stated that he had received reports that one of the three schooners that had left Cuba was sailing for Cozumel, Mexico, and the other two were headed for Puerto Cortés, Honduras. Although an armed force of some size, composed of individuals of various nationalities, was formed in Honduras, the situation eventually was resolved with the cooperation of the armed forces of the Central American countries. The Council had declared that its June 4 resolution did "not imply, in any way, prejudgment of the nature of the facts, nor intervention in the affairs of a member state." By its resolution of July 28 the Council terminated the activities of the Committee, canceled the convocation of the Meeting of Consultation and recommended to the governments of the member states of the OAS that they strengthen the measures designed to maintain peace, observing the principle of nonintervention.[2]

While this was going on, the Cuban Government was also involved in two armed invasions of the Dominican Republic in June 1959. In his complaint, the Representative of the Dominican Republic on the OAS Council alleged that the invasions had been organized on Cuban territory with the participation of the Government of Venezuela. The Council met on July 2 and again on July 6. During the latter meeting the Representatives of Haiti and Ecuador proposed that a meeting of consultation be held, not in application of the Rio Treaty but in accordance with Article 39 of the OAS Charter. A proposal was formally presented at the July 10 meeting by the Representatives of Brazil, Chile, Peru, and the United States of America to the effect that a meeting of consultation be convoked in accordance with Articles 39 and 40 of the Charter, to consider "the serious situation which exists in the Caribbean area." At a final meeting on July 13, this proposal was approved and the Fifth Meeting

---

[1] For documentation and further details regarding this application of the Rio Treaty see *Applications,* vol. 1, p. 325 *et seq.*

[2] For documentation and further details regarding this application of the Rio Treaty see *ibid.,* p. 369 *et seq.* See also the summary on p. 138, *supra.*

of Consultation of Ministers of Foreign Affairs was held in Santiago, Chile, from August 12 to 18, 1959.[3]

The last of the incidents in reference motivated the denunciation made by the Minister of Foreign Affairs of Haiti during the Fifth Meeting of Consultation. This complaint dealt with an armed expedition which had set out from a Cuban port and landed on Haitian territory, and with the fact that the Cuban Government had not taken the measures necessary to prevent the departure of the invaders. A few days after the close of the Fifth Meeting of Consultation the Haitian Government presented its complaint to the Inter-American Peace Committee and requested a complete investigation of the facts.[4]

32. Exclusion of the Cuban Government and Partial Suspension of Trade with Cuba (1961-1962)

The first specific and direct application of the Rio Treaty as a result of the Cuban situation originated in a request by the Government of Peru on October 16, 1961. The Peruvian Representative on the OAS Council, in notes of October 12 and 16, set forth the background and considerations for his government's complaint, which in brief attributed the following acts to the Cuban Government:

> 1. Acts of force, intrinsically illegal on the part of the ruling regime in Cuba, to the detriment of citizens of that nation and foreigners, such as executions, imprisonments, deportations, physical maltreatment, and confiscations of property.
>
> 2. Action of international communism in the countries of America and incorporation of the Cuban Government in the Sino-Soviet bloc.
>
> 3. Communist infiltration by the Government of Cuba in the other countries of America, making use of its diplomatic officers, official missions, and secret agents, for the purpose of instigating subversion and revolution against legitimately constituted governments and democratic institutions.

The Peruvian note of October 12 requested the immediate convocation of the meeting of consultation in accordance with the Rio Treaty. At a special meeting on October 25, the Council decided to transmit the Peruvian request to the General Committee for study.

---

[3] For further details regarding this application of the Rio Treaty see *Applications*, vol. 1, p. 411 *et seq*. The Fifth Meeting of Consultation adopted several resolutions aimed at promoting the respect for human rights and strengthening the principle of representative democracy, as well as a resolution which conferred new functions and powers on the Inter-American Peace Committee (Resolution IV), the text of which is included in *Appendix 14*, p. 402, *infra*. For the text of the other resolutions see the Final Act of the Fifth Meeting, OEA/Ser.C/II.5.

[4] Regarding the Peace Committee's action, and the complaint presented to the Fifth Meeting, see the summary of this case on p. 92, *supra*.

In its report to the Council the General Committee observed that "Without having gone into the substance of the statement made by the Government of Peru, the General Committee has been able to see that, formally, the facts denounced are closely related to each other, which leads to the conclusion that if they are to be studied and investigated it would be appropriate for a single agency to do so." And in this respect it suggested that, in accordance with Resolution IV of the Fifth Meeting of Consultation, the Inter-American Peace Committee could take charge of this task. At the suggestion of the General Committee, the Council resolved, at a special meeting on November 22, "To point out that the Inter-American Peace Committee is an appropriate organ, in accordance with the terms of Resolution IV of the Fifth Meeting of Consultation of Ministers of Foreign Affairs, to deal with the facts denounced in the request presented by the Government of Peru."

While the Inter-American Peace Committee proceeded with the study and investigation requested by the Peruvian Government,[5] the Government of Colombia requested, by note of November 14, the convocation of a meeting of consultation pursuant to Article 6 of the Rio Treaty "to consider the threats to the peace and to the political independence of the American states that might arise from the intervention of extracontinental powers directed toward breaking American solidarity, and particularly to: a. Point out the various types of threats to the peace or certain acts that, if they occur, justify the application of measures for the maintenance of the peace and security, pursuant to Chapter V of the Charter of the Organization of American States and the provisions of the Inter-American Treaty of Reciprocal Assistance; and b. Determine the measures that it is advisable to take for the maintenance of the peace and security of the hemisphere."

At a special meeting on December 4 the OAS Council approved the following resolution:

> THE COUNCIL OF THE ORGANIZATION OF AMERICAN STATES,
>
> CONSIDERING:
> The note presented by the Delegation of Colombia, dated November 9, 1961, in which it requests the convocation of a Meeting of Consultation of Ministers of Foreign Affairs, in accordance with Article 6 of the Inter-American Treaty of Reciprocal Assistance, to consider the threats to the peace and to the political independence of the American states that might arise from the intervention of extracontinental powers directed toward breaking American solidarity,
>
> RESOLVES:
> 1. To convoke a Meeting of Consultation of Ministers of Foreign

---

[5] See p. 97, *supra* regarding the Peace Committee's activities.

Affairs to serve as Organ of Consultation, in accordance with Article 6 and 11 of the Inter-American Treaty of Reciprocal Assistance, in order to consider the threats to the peace and to the political independence of the American states referred to in the preamble of this resolution, and particularly to point out the various types of threats to the peace or certain acts that, in the event they occur, justify the application of measures for the maintenance of the peace and security, pursuant to Chapter V of the Charter of the Organization of American States and the provisions of the Inter-American Treaty of Reciprocal Assistance, and to determine the measures that it is advisable to take for the maintenance of the peace and security of the Continent.

2. To set January 10, 1962, as the date of the inauguration of the Meeting.

3. To authorize the Chairman of the Council to present to the Council, at the appropriate time, after consultation with the representatives of the member states, a recommendation on the site of the Meeting of Consultation.

In accordance with a later resolution by the Council, the Eighth Meeting of Consultation was held at Punta del Este, Uruguay, from January 22 to 31, 1962. The Punta del Este meeting adopted several resolutions and decisions, besides those relative to the exclusion of the present Cuban Government from participation in the inter-American system and the partial suspension of trade with Cuba.[6] Resolution VI was based primarily on the concept—shared by 20 of the 21 governments represented at the meeting—of the incompatibility between the adherence of a member of the OAS to Marxism-Leninism and the inter-American system. Also of considerable influence in the decision was the Cuban Government's alignment with the communist bloc which was considered, again by 20 of the 21 governments, as a fact that "breaks the unity and solidarity of the hemisphere." In the following text the remaining considerations can be seen:

VI
EXCLUSION OF THE PRESENT GOVERNMENT OF CUBA FROM PARTICIPATION IN THE INTER-AMERICAN SYSTEM

WHEREAS:

The inter-American system is based on consistent adherence by its constituent states to certain objectives and principles of solidarity, set forth in the instruments that govern it;

Among these objectives and principles are those of respect for the freedom of man and preservation of his rights, the full exercise of representative democracy, nonintervention of one state in the internal or external affairs of another, and rejection of alliances and agreements

---

[6] See especially Resolution I, Communist Offensive in America, and Resolution II which created the Special Consultative Committee on Security referred to on p. 116, *supra*. The complete text of both resolutions appears in *Applications*, vol. 2, pp. 69-70, respectively.

that may lead to intervention in America by extracontinental powers;

The Seventh Meeting of Consultation of Ministers of Foreign Affairs, held in San José, Costa Rica, condemned the intervention or the threat of intervention of extracontinental communist powers in the hemisphere and reiterated the obligation of the American states to observe faithfully the principles of the regional organization;

The present Government of Cuba has identified itself with the principles of Marxist-Leninist ideology, has established a political, economic, and social system based on that doctrine, and accepts military assistance from extracontinental communist powers, including even the threat of military intervention in America on the part of the Soviet Union;

The Report of the Inter-American Peace Committee to the Eighth Meeting of Consultation of Ministers of Foreign Affairs establishes that:

The present connections of the Government of Cuba with the Sino-Soviet bloc of countries are evidently incompatible with the principles and standards that govern the regional system, and particularly with the collective security established by the Charter of the Organization of American States and the Inter-American Treaty of Reciprocal Assistance;

The abovementioned Report of the Inter-American Peace Committee also states that:

It is evident that the ties of the Cuban Government with the Sino-Soviet bloc will prevent the said government from fulfilling the obligations stipulated in the Charter of the Organization and the Treaty of Reciprocal Assistance;

Such a situation in an American state violates the obligations inherent in membership in the regional system and is incompatible with that system;

The attitude adopted by the present Government of Cuba and its acceptance of military assistance offered by extracontinental communist powers breaks down the effective defense of the inter-American system; and

No member state of the inter-American system can claim the rights and privileges pertaining thereto if it denies or fails to recognize the corresponding obligations,

The Eighth Meeting of Consultation of Ministers of Foreign Affairs, Serving as Organ of Consultation in Application of the Inter-American Treaty of Reciprocal Assistance,

DECLARES:

1. That, as a consequence of repeated acts, the present Government of Cuba has voluntarily placed itself outside the inter-American system.

2. That this situation demands unceasing vigilance on the part of the member states of the Organization of American States, which shall report to the Council any fact or situation that could endanger the peace and security of the hemisphere.

3. That the American states have a collective interest in strengthening the inter-American system and reuniting it on the basis of respect for human rights and the principles and objectives relative to the exercise of democracy set forth in the Charter of the Organization; and, therefore

RESOLVES:

1. That adherence by any member of the Organization of American States to Marxism-Leninism is incompatible with the inter-American system and the alignment of such a government with the communist bloc breaks the unity and solidarity of the hemisphere.

2. That the present Government of Cuba, which has officially identified itself as a Marxist-Leninist government, is incompatible with the principles and objectives of the inter-American system.

3. That this incompatibility excludes the present Government of Cuba from participation in the inter-American system.

4. That the Council of the Organization of American States and the other organs and organizations of the inter-American system adopt without delay the measures necessary to comply with this resolution.

The OAS Council took note of this resolution on February 14, 1962 and decided that, pursuant to paragraphs 3 and 4 of the operative part of the resolution, the present Cuban Government had been excluded from participation in the Council, its committees and its organs, as of the date of its adoption. At the same time, it requested the Secretary General to transmit the text of the Final Act of the Eighth Meeting of Consultation to the other organs and agencies of the inter-American system for their information and consequent purposes.

On April 26, 1961 the Inter-American Defense Board had decided that the participation of the Cuban regime in the preparation of defense plans was highly prejudicial to the Board's work and to hemisphere security. In Resolution VII, the Meeting of Consultation decided to immediately exclude the present Government of Cuba from the Board until the Council of the Organization determines by a vote of two thirds of its members that membership of the said government is not prejudicial to the work of the Board or to the security of the hemisphere.

The resolution relative to the partial suspension of trade with Cuba was based, for its part, on the intense subversive activity in which the countries of the Sino-Soviet bloc and the Cuban Government had been engaged, an activity that the Meeting of Consultation considered "a serious violation of fundamental principles of the inter-American system," thus sharing, once more, the opinion expressed by the Inter-American Peace Committee. The complete text of this resolution is as follows:

VIII
ECONOMIC RELATIONS

WHEREAS:

The Report of the Inter-American Peace Committee to the Eighth Meeting of Consultation of Ministers of Foreign Affairs states, with regard to the intense subversive activity in which the countries of the Sino-Soviet bloc and the Cuban Government are engaged in America, that such activity constitutes "a serious violation of fundamental principles of the inter-American system"; and,

During the past three years 13 American states have found it necessary to break diplomatic relations with the present Government of Cuba,

The Eighth Meeting of Consultation of Ministers of Foreign Affairs, Serving as Organ of Consultation in Application of the Inter-American Treaty of Reciprocal Assistance,

RESOLVES:

1. To suspend immediately trade with Cuba in arms and implements of war of every kind.

2. To charge the Council of the Organization of American States, in accordance with the circumstances and with due consideration for the constitutional or legal limitations of each and every one of the member states, with studying the feasibility and desirability of extending the suspension of trade to other items, with special attention to items of strategic importance.

3. To authorize the Council of the Organization of Amercian States to discontinue, by an affirmative vote of two thirds of its members, the measure or measures adopted pursuant to the preceding paragraphs, at such time as the Government of Cuba demonstrates its compatibility with the purposes and principles of the system.

As indicated elsewhere, in order to carry out the mandate contained in paragraph 2 of the foregoing resolution the OAS Council appointed a Special Committee, on which it also conferred the duty of maintaining vigilance, contained in Resolution II.1 of the same Meeting of Consultation.[7] As will be seen below, the mandate contained in Resolution VIII. 2 was automatically canceled by the adoption by the Ninth Meeting of Consultation of measures that included the suspension of all "trade, whether direct or indirect, with Cuba" and "all sea transportation", except for that of a humanitarian nature.[8]

33. Action by the Organ of Consultation During the "October Crisis" (1962)

The most dramatic and, for reasons set forth below, peculiar of all the applications of the Rio Treaty was the one brought about by the so-called "October crisis". On October 22, 1962 the Representative of the United States of America on the OAS Council addressed a note to the Chairman of the Council in which he stated that his government had "received conclusive evidence of the fact that the Government of Cuba has permitted its territory to be used for the establishment of offensive weapons with nuclear capability provided by extracontinental powers." In his opinion this new and serious

---

[7] See p. 198, infra.

[8] See p. 169, infra. For documentation and further details regarding this application of the Rio Treaty see Applications, vol. 2, p. 67 et seq.

development in Cuba constituted a situation which endangered the peace of America and affected the sovereignty and political independence of the American states. Because of these considerations he requested that pursuant to Article 6 of the Rio Treaty the Organ of Consultation be convoked immediately "in order to consider the action which should be taken in the light of this new situation for the common defense and for the maintenance of the peace and security of the Continent."

The OAS Council held two special meetings the next day, during the first of which the following resolution was unanimously approved:

WHEREAS:

The Government of the United States of America, in a note dated October 22, 1962, has requested convocation of the Organ of Consultation in order to consider, in accordance with Articles 6 and 8 of the Inter-American Treaty of Reciprocal Assistance, the action that should be taken, because of new and serious developments in Cuba, for the common defense and for the maintenance of the peace and security of the Continent;

The Council of the Organization of American States has heard the declaration presented by the Representative of the United States that the Government of Cuba has permitted the establishment by extracontinental powers on its territory of offensive weapons with nuclear capability; and

The establishment of such weapons provided by a communist power in the territory of an American State gravely endangers the common defense and the peace and security of the Continent,

THE COUNCIL OF THE ORGANIZATION OF AMERICAN STATES,

RESOLVES:

1. To convoke the Organ of Consultation in accordance with the provisions of the Inter-American Treaty of Reciprocal Assistance, to meet at a time and place to be decided later;

2. To constitute itself and to act provisionally as Organ of Consultation in accordance with Article 12 of the aforementioned Inter-American Treaty of Reciprocal Assistance.

At the second meeting, held the afternoon of the same day, October 23, the Council, now acting provisionally as Organ of Consultation, approved the following resolution, also unanimously:

WHEREAS:

The Inter-American Treaty of Reciprocal Assistance of 1947 (The Rio Treaty) recognizes the obligation of the American republics to "provide for effective reciprocal assistance to meet armed attacks against any American state, and in order to deal with threats of aggression against any of them";

Article 6 of the said Treaty states:

"If the inviolability or the integrity of the territory or the sovereignty or political independence of any American State should be affected by an aggression which is not an armed attack or by an extra-continental or intra-continental conflict, or by any other fact or situation that might endanger the peace of America, the Organ of Consultation shall meet immediately in order to agree on the measures which must be taken in case of aggression to assist the victim of the aggression or, in any case, the measures which should be taken for the common defense and for the maintenance of the peace and security of the Continent";

The Eighth Meeting of Consultation of Ministers of Foreign Affairs in Punta del Este in January, 1962, agreed in Resolution II "To urge the member states to take those steps that they may consider appropriate for their individual and collective self-defense, and to cooperate, as may be necessary or desirable, to strengthen their capacity to counteract threats or acts of aggression, subversion, or other dangers to peace and security resulting from the continued intervention in this hemisphere of Sino-Soviet powers, in accordance with the obligations established in treaties and agreements such as the Charter of the Organization of American States and the Inter-American Treaty of Reciprocal Assistance";

The Ministers of Foreign Affairs of the American Republics meeting informally in Washington, October 2 and 3, 1962, reasserted "the firm intention of the Governments represented and of the peoples of the American Republics to conduct themselves in accordance with the principles of the regional system, staunchly sustaining and consolidating the principles of the Charter of the Organization of American States, and affirmed the will to strengthen the security of the hemisphere against all aggression from within or outside the hemisphere and against all developments or situations capable of threatening the peace and security of the hemisphere through the application of the Inter-American Treaty of Reciprocal Assistance of Rio de Janeiro. It was the view of the Ministers that the existing organizations and bodies of the inter-American system should intensify the carrying out of their respective duties with special and urgent attention to the situation created by the communist regime in Cuba and that they should stand in readiness to consider the matter promptly if the situation requires measures beyond those already authorized";

The same meeting "recalled that the Soviet Union's intervention in Cuba threatens the unity of the Americas and its democratic institutions, and that this intervention has special characteristics which, pursuant to paragraph 3 of Resolution II of the Eighth Meeting of Consultation of Ministers of Foreign Affairs, call for the adoption of special measures, both individual and collective"; and

Incontrovertible evidence has appeared that the Government of Cuba, despite repeated warnings, has secretly endangered the peace of the Continent by permitting the Sino-Soviet powers to have intermediate and medium-range missiles on its territory capable of carrying nuclear warheads,

THE COUNCIL OF THE ORGANIZATION OF AMERICAN STATES, ACTING PROVISIONALLY AS ORGAN OF CONSULTATION,

RESOLVES:

1. To call for the immediate dismantling and withdrawal from Cuba of all missiles and other weapons with any offensive capability.

2. To recommend that the member states, in accordance with Articles

6 and 8 of the Inter-American Treaty of Reciprocal Assistance, take all measures, individually and collectively including the use of armed force, which they may deem necessary to ensure that the Government of Cuba cannot continue to receive from the Sino-Soviet powers military material and related supplies which may threaten the peace and security of the Continent and to prevent the missiles in Cuba with offensive capability from ever becoming an active threat to the peace and security of the Continent.

3. To inform the Security Council of the United Nations of this resolution in accordance with Article 54 of the Charter of the United Nations, and to express the hope that the Security Council will, in accordance with the draft resolution introduced by the United States, dispatch United Nations observers to Cuba at the earliest moment.

4. To continue to serve provisionally as Organ of Consultation and to request the member states to keep the Organ of Consultation duly informed of measures taken by them in accordance with paragraph 2 of this resolution.

In the operative part of the foregoing resolution the Organ of Consultation "recommended" to the member states that, in accordance with Articles 6 and 8 of the Rio Treaty, they take all measures, individually and collectively including the use of armed force, which they might deem necessary not only to ensure that the Government of Cuba could not continue to receive military material and related supplies but also to prevent the missiles in Cuba with offensive capability "from ever becoming an active threat to the peace and security of the Continent."

The express mention of Articles 6 and 8 might lead to the impression that this was a collective action, by the Organ of Consultation, that consisted in adopting measures such as those mentioned in the second of those articles. However, this was not the case. Rather, it was a *sui generis* way of exercising self-defense. This is amply corroborated by the mention made in the preamble of the resolution not only of Resolution II. 3 of the Eighth Meeting of Consultation of Ministers of Foreign Affairs, but also of certain passages from the press release issued by the Informal Meeting of Ministers of Foreign Affairs, held in Washington a few weeks earlier on October 2-3. Above all, it is corroborated by the fact that the Organ of Consultation limited itself to "recommending" the measures to be adopted by the member states; that is, it did not "agree" to apply measures in this case of self-defense, as it had in other cases. In reality the only collective action discernible in the October 23 resolution is the decision to recommend the exercise of self-defense.

Several American governments, acting in accordance with paragraph 2 of the resolution, informed the Council regarding the measures they had adopted or their willingness to cooperate in this matter. Among them were the governments of Panama, the United States of America, Argentina, Costa Rica, the Dominican Republic, Guatemala, Haiti, Honduras, and Colombia. The measure adopted by the United States, of which the Council was informed, consisted of the "Interdiction of the Delivery of Offensive Weapons to Cuba", issued by the President of the United States, that entered into force on October 24 at 2:00 p.m.

The October crisis ended when the missiles were withdrawn from Cuba in accordance with the understanding reached by the Governments of the United States and the Soviet Union. From the very beginning the matter had also been brought before the United Nations Security Council and for this reason the world organization was also active in this phase of the Cuban situation.[9]

34. *Measures Agreed on by the Ninth Meeting of Consultation (1963-1964)*

On the contrary from the foregoing case, this new application of the Rio Treaty in relation with the Cuban situation was brought about by the subversive action of Castrocommunism, dramatized by an intense wave of terrorism, sabotage, and other activities unleashed by agents of that movement as a result of the October crisis. This intense subversive action was mainly concentrated in Venezuela, which eventually caused the government of that country to request the convocation of the Organ of Consultation in accordance with Article 6 of the Rio Treaty "to consider the measures that should be taken to deal with the acts of intervention and aggression on the part of the Government of Cuba that affect the territorial integrity and the sovereignty of Venezuela, as well as the operation of its democratic institutions." This request, contained in a note from the Representative of Venezuela on the OAS Council dated November 29, 1963, was taken under consideration by that body at the special meeting on December 3.

Departing from its usual procedure, the Council limited itself at that time to convoking the Organ of Consultation and constituting itself provisionally to act as such. It immediately held its first meeting as provisional Organ of Consultation and appointed a committee to investigate the facts denounced by Venezuela. Upon its return from that country the Investigating Committee presented an extensive, well-documented report which the Organ of Consultation decided to transmit to the governments. At a later meeting on June 26, 1964, the Ninth Meeting of Consultation of Ministers of Foreign Affairs

---

[9] For documentation and further details regarding this application of the Rio Treaty, including the correspondence exchanged between the two governments mentioned and between the Cuban Government and the U.N. Secretary-General, see *ibid.*, p. 109 *et seq.*

was convoked and was held in Washington, D.C., at OAS headquarters, from July 21 to 26, 1964.

In the course of its activities the Investigating Committee deemed it advisable to afford the Cuban Government the opportunity to submit, in writing, if it so desired, the information and comments it considered necessary, so as to determine its responsibility in connection with certain points in the Venezuelan complaint. The Cuban Government cabled on February 3 that it "neither recognizes, admits, nor accepts the jurisdiction of the Organization of American States," and, without referring to the points mentioned—in the words of the Investigating Committee's report—it "expressed its ideas on matters that were outside the competence of the Committee and made statements that were injurious to the Organization and to its members. In view of this, the Committee decided unanimously to ignore the receipt of this communication." The Committee, with the aid of military experts, made an exhaustive examination of the facts denounced by the Government of Venezuela, and arrived at the following Conclusions:

A

In formulating its conclusions, the Committee considers it pertinent to make some general observations on the policy of intervention in the hemisphere of the present Government of Cuba, which has been substantiated in the investigation of the charges made by Venezuela:

1. The present Government of Cuba since its institution in 1959 has carried on, supported, and directed in various ways a policy of intervention in the hemisphere through propaganda methods, provision of funds, training in sabotage and guerrilla operations, and the supply of arms to support those movements that seek to subvert national institutions through force in order to install communist regimes.

2. This support of subversion, which generally takes the form of political aggression, has had positive application in the Republic of Venezuela, the primary objective in Cuba's policy of expansion and ideological penetration in the hemisphere. The vast natural resources of Venezuela, its strategic importance in the hemisphere, and its status as a democratic country were factors that motivated the present Government of Cuba to make use of the subversive action of organizations that employ force and violence to overthrow that democratic government.

B

1. The Republic of Venezuela has been the target of a series of actions sponsored and directed by the Government of Cuba, openly intended to subvert Venezuelan institutions and to overthrow the democratic Government of Venezuela through terrorism, sabotage, assault, and guerrilla warfare.

2. A characteristic manifestation of this policy of aggression has been the systematic and hostile propaganda campaign carried out through information organs that are under the control of the Government of Cuba and that are directed against Venezuelan institutions, the President of the Republic, and other high government officials, inciting the people

of Venezuela to rebellion and, in addition, giving direct support to subversive movements.

3. Other manifestations of this policy of aggression are found in the supply of funds and the indoctrination and training in Cuba of numerous Venezuelans who later returned to their country to participate in subversive movements.

4. An important element in this intervention in Venezuela, directed by the Government of Cuba, was the shipment of arms that was found on the Peninsula of Paraguaná in the State of Falcón on November 1, 1963, close to the date of the general elections. The shipment was made up of arms originating in Cuba that were surreptitiously landed at a solitary spot on the coast, for the purpose of being used in subversive operations to overthrow the constitutional Government of Venezuela.

With respect to this shipment, the following facts are noteworthy:

a. The perforations and obliterations that were made on the various weapons in places where the Cuban coat of arms and other identification marks had been stamped, in an effort to hide their well-known Cuban origin.

b. The conditioning and packing of the arms for immediate use, the quantity and quality of the arms, and the instructions for their use, which were found in the hands of communist groups. These arms were to be used to support subversive activities and guerrilla action by organizations disciplined and trained for such purposes.

c. The discovery, at the same spot where the shipment of arms was found, of a boat with an outboard motor, which motor was sent from Montreal, Canada, to Havana by air on October 1, 1963, for delivery to the National Institute of Agrarian Reform of Cuba, an official institution of that country.

5. The policy of aggression on the part of the Government of Cuba was confirmed by the discovery on November 4, 1963, by Venezuelan authorities, of a plan of operations, the "Caracas Plan", prepared for the subversive action of the so-called "Armed Forces of National Liberation". This plan anticipated the use of arms similar in type and numerical proportion to the shipment of arms mentioned in the preceding paragraph. The objective of the plan was to capture the city of Caracas, to prevent the holding of elections on December 1, 1963, and to seize control of the country.

6. Consequently, the acts of intervention that have been outlined, and, in particular, the shipment of arms, constitute a policy of aggression on the part of the present Government of Cuba against the territorial integrity, the political sovereignty, and the stability of the democratic institutions of Venezuela.

Resolution I of the Ninth Meeting of Consultation deals with the "Application of Measures to the Present Government of Cuba" and is based on the Investigating Committee's conclusions. It reads as follows:

The Ninth Meeting of Consultation of Ministers of Foreign Affairs, Serving as Organ of Consultation in Application of the Inter-American Treaty of Reciprocal Assistance,

HAVING SEEN the report of the Investigating Committee designated on December 3, 1963, by the Council of the Organization of

American States, acting provisionally as Organ of Consultation, and

CONSIDERING:

That the said report establishes among its conclusions that "the Republic of Venezuela has been the target of a series of actions sponsored and directed by the Government of Cuba, openly intended to subvert Venezuelan institutions and to overthrow the democratic Government of Venezuela through terrorism, sabotage, assault, and guerrilla warfare"; and

That the aforementioned acts, like all acts of intervention and aggression, conflict with the principles and aims of the inter-American system,

RESOLVES:

1. To declare that the acts verified by the Investigating Committee constitute an aggression and an intervention on the part of the Government of Cuba in the internal affairs of Venezuela, which affects all of the member states.

2. To condemn emphatically the present Government of Cuba for its acts of aggression and of intervention against the territorial inviolability, the sovereignty, and the political independence of Venezuela.

3. To apply, in accordance with the provisions of Articles 6 and 8 of the Inter-American Treaty of Reciprocal Assistance, the following measures:

    a. That the governments of the American states not maintain diplomatic or consular relations with the Government of Cuba;

    b. That the governments of the American states suspend all their trade, whether direct or indirect, with Cuba, except in foodstuffs, medicines, and medical equipment that may be sent to Cuba for humanitarian reasons; and

    c. That the governments of the American states suspend all sea transportation between their countries and Cuba, except for such transportation as may be necessary for reasons of a humanitarian nature.

4. To authorize the Council of the Organization of American States, by an affirmative vote of two thirds of its members, to discontinue the measures adopted in the present resolution at such time as the Government of Cuba shall have ceased to constitute a danger to the peace and security of the hemisphere.

5. To warn the Government of Cuba that if it should persist in carrying out acts that possess characteristics of aggression and intervention against one or more of the member states of the Organization, the member states shall preserve their essential rights as sovereign states by the use of self-defense in either individual or collective form, which could go so far as resort to armed force, until such time as the Organ of Consultation takes measures to guarantee the peace and security of the hemisphere.

6. To urge those states not members of the Organization of American States that are animated by the same ideals as the inter-American system to examine the possibility of effectively demonstrating their solidarity in achieving the purposes of this resolution.

7. To instruct the Secretary General of the Organization of American States to transmit to the United Nations Security Council the text of the

present resolution, in accordance with the provisions of Article 54 of the United Nations Charter.

The measures that the Organ of Consultation agreed to apply are of the nature of those established in Article 8 of the Rio Treaty. It will be noted, however, that the measure relative to diplomatic or consular relations is not phrased as an express and direct agreement on the breaking of relations. This was due to the fact that since only four countries maintained relations with Cuba at that time, the decision would have appeared to be directed to them alone, although when the measure was taken that was in fact the situation. It is also interesting to note the exceptions that were made in the economic measures for humanitarian reasons.

As far as the measures are concerned, it is equally interesting to point out the action contemplated in paragraph 5 of Resolution I, that is, the use of either individual or collective self-defense, including the resort to armed force, if the Cuban Government were to persist in carrying out acts such as those which motivated the application of measures by the Organ of Consultation.

Finally, the importance of Resolution II, the "Declaration to the People of Cuba", should not be ignored. In it the Ninth Meeting of Consultation expressed, among other things, "Its firm conviction that the emphatic condemnation of the policy of the present Cuban Government of aggression and intervention against Venezuela will be taken by the people of Cuba as a renewed stimulus for its hope there will come to prevail in that country a climate of freedom that will offer to man in Cuba a favorable environment for the development of his personality and the realization of his just aspirations." The special political significance of this declaration should be weighed not only in the light of the measures applied on this occasion, but also of the exclusion of the Cuban Government from the OAS at the Eighth Meeting of Consultation held in Punta del Este two years earlier.[10]

---

[10] For documentation and further details regarding this application of the Rio Treaty see *ibid.*, p. 181 *et seq.*

Chapter IX

Action by the OAS in the Dominican Situation (1965)

The recent action by the OAS in the Dominican Republic was brought about by events that occurred starting on April 24, 1965, the date on which the revolutionary movement against the existing government began. Without prejudice to a further examination in a later chapter of some of the more interesting political-juridical and institutional aspects of this new inter-American collective action,[1] following is a description of that action in broad terms.

The Inter-American Peace Committee was the first to be informed of the serious events occurring in Santo Domingo, capital city of the Dominican Republic, at a meeting called by its Chairman on April 27. The next day the Dominican Representative reported on those events to the OAS Council at a regular meeting of that body. On the morning of April 29 the Council held a special meeting, called by its Chairman, specifically to consider the situation prevailing in the light of new developments. At that time the Council decided to send a message, through the OAS Secretary General, to the Papal Nuncio, Dean of the Diplomatic Corps in the Dominican Republic, expressing its strong desire that all armed action or hostilities be suspended. In that message, which was also addressed to all the diplomatic representatives of the American republics in Santo Domingo, to the Dominican authorities, to the political parties of whatever tendency, and to the Dominican people, the Secretary General also asked to be informed regarding the situation in the country and the prospects for achieving an immediate cease-fire, for the purpose of informing the OAS Council, which intended to remain attentive to the development of events.[2]

At the request this time of the Representative of Chile, the Council met again during the night of April 29-30 to take up a request by the Government of Chile that the Meeting of Consultation of Ministers of Foreign Affairs be convoked on May 1, in accordance with the first part of Article 39 of the OAS Charter. In addition to agreeing to convoke that meeting and to setting May 1 as its starting

---

[1] See p. 205, *infra*.
[2] The complete text of that message appears in OEA/Ser. G/III/C-sa-569.

171

date, the Council approved another resolution again calling upon all authorities, political groupings, and opposing forces to pursue immediately all possible means by which a cease-fire might be established and all hostilities and military operations suspended, and urging them to permit the establishment of an "international neutral zone of refuge" encompassing the area immediately surrounding the embassies of foreign governments, the inviolability of which would be respected by all opposing forces.[3]

The Council met again in the afternoon of April 30 to receive a report on the efforts being made by the Papal Nuncio to achieve a cease-fire and agreed to authorize the Secretary General to go to the Dominican Republic in order "to communicate with the dean of the diplomatic corps and aid him in his peacemaking mission; to indicate the presence of the Organization of American States, which the serious Dominican situation requires; to report to the Meeting of Foreign Ministers from the scene of action, in order to plan the work of the Committee appointed by the Meeting; and to express the appreciation of the Council to the Papal Nuncio, dean of the diplomatic corps, and to all who have collaborated with him."[4] The Secretary General left for the Dominican Republic that same day, in order to undertake immediately the mission entrusted to him.

At its first plenary session on May 1, the Tenth Meeting of Consultation decided to name a Special Committee composed of the Representatives of Argentina, Brazil, Colombia, Guatemala, and Panama to go immediately to Santo Domingo, to do everything possible to obtain the reestablishment of peace and normal conditions, and give priority to the following two functions:[5]

> a. To offer its good offices to the Dominican armed groups and political groups and to diplomatic representatives for the purpose of obtaining urgently:
> i. A cease-fire; and
> ii. The orderly evacuation of persons who have taken asylum in diplomatic missions and of all foreign citizens who desire to leave the Dominican Republic; and
> b. To investigate all aspects of the current situation in the Dominican Republic that led to the convocation of this Meeting.

Upon its arrival in Santo Domingo the Special Committee immediately undertook negotiations to obtain a formal cease-fire and achieve the other purposes stipulated in the foregoing resolution. It was considered essential to reach a new agreement that would ratify and supplement the existing cease-fire, negotiated by the Papal Nuncio,

---

[3] *Ibid.*

[4] *Cf.* OEA/Ser. G/III/C-sa-570.

[5] See the complete text of the resolution in OEA/Ser.F/II.10, Doc. 78 Rev. 5.

and cover other vital questions such as the establishment and demarcation of a security zone to be respected by both sides; the extension of facilities for the distribution of food, medicines, and medical equipment; the guarantees required for evacuation of refugees in the diplomatic missions accredited in Santo Domingo and respect and protection for these missions and their personnel; and, finally, recognition of the full authority of the Committee, for the purposes of strict compliance with the obligations assumed by both sides under such an agreement. As a result of its negotiations the Committee secured, on May 5, the signature of the agreement contained in the "Act of Santo Domingo" as follows:[6]

ACT OF SANTO DOMINGO

The Parties signing below who declare that they represent, in the capacities mentioned, respectively, the Military Junta of Government and the "Constitutional Government" hereby place on record that they have reached the following agreement as a result of the discussions held with the two Parties by the Special Committee of the Tenth Meeting of Consultation of Ministers of Foreign Affairs, whose members also sign the present Act as a guaranty of its compliance and execution, functions that both Parties agree the Committee may carry out.

1. The Parties who sign the present Act ratify the cease-fire agreement signed on April 30 last.

2. The Parties accept the establishment of a safety zone in the city of Santo Domingo, demarcated within the boundaries indicated on the map attached to this document and signed by the same Parties who sign the present Act.

3. The Parties bind themselves especially to respect this safety zone, within which there is guaranteed, in the manner that the Organization of American States may deem appropriate, adequate protection and safety for all persons found within that zone of refuge.

4. The Parties undertake to give all necessary facilities to the International Red Cross or to the international agency that the Organization of American States may designate to carry out in any part of the City of Santo Domingo or of the Dominican Republic the distribution of food, medicine, and medical and hospital equipment that are being sent as a result of the appeal made by the Tenth Meeting of Consultation of Ministers of Foreign Affairs. They also undertake to provide all facilities required by the Organization of American States so that medical and sanitary personnel sent by the governments can be transported to any point in the City of Santo Domingo or Dominican territory, to perform their services.

5. The Parties undertake to provide all necessary safety measures for the evacuation of asylees in foreign embassies or diplomatic missions who so request of them.

6. The Parties undertake to respect the diplomatic missions and to offer all cooperation necessary to guarantee the safety of all

---

[6] *Cf.* OEA/Ser.F/II.10, Doc. 38 Rev. See also the First Report by the Special Committee, OEA/Ser.F/II.10, Doc. 47 Rev.

personnel of those missions and of asylees or refugees therein.

7. The Parties declare that they accept and recognize the full competence of the Special Committee appointed by the Tenth Meeting of Consultation of Ministers of Foreign Affairs, for purposes of the faithful observance of what is agreed to in this Agreement.

IN WITNESS WHEREOF the present document, which shall be known as the Act of Santo Domingo, is signed in four original copies, of which one shall be deposited in the General Secretariat of the Organization of American States, one shall be for each of the Parties, and one shall be for the files of the Committee.

The Secretary General of the Organization of American States shall transmit certified copies to each of the member states.

May 5, 1965

After making a direct report to the Meeting of Consultation, the Special Committee went to Santo Domingo again on May 11 and returned to Washington to submit its Second Report to the Meeting. In that report the Committee pointed out the many difficulties it had faced in carrying out its negotiations to achieve a climate of peace and normality that would permit a solution of the Dominican problem, and indicated that it had achieved the basic objectives for which it had been established, pursuant to the resolution of May 1. For these reasons the Committee considered its mandate to have been fulfilled and recommended, as an immediate measure, that a representative of the Tenth Meeting of Consultation be appointed to act in the Dominican Republic in accordance with the Meeting's instructions.[7]

As a result of the Special Committee's recommendations the Meeting of Consultation decided to appoint the OAS Secretary General, who was still in the Dominican Republic fulfilling the mission entrusted to him by the Council on April 30, to represent it in accordance with the following mandate:[8]

1. To reiterate the gratitude of the Meeting to the Special Committee for the outstanding service it has rendered.

2. To entrust the Secretary General of the Organization of American States with carrying out the following activities in the Dominican Republic, on behalf of the Meeting of Consultation:

a. To negotiate a strict cease-fire in accordance with the Act of Santo Domingo;

b. To offer his good offices to the parties in conflict, with a view to the establishment of a climate of peace and conciliation that will permit the functioning of democratic institutions in the Dominican Republic;

c. To coordinate, insofar as relevant, action leading to the attainment of the objectives set forth in this resolution, with that which the

---

[7] Cf. OEA/Ser.F/II.10, Doc. 81 Rev.

[8] See the complete text of the resolution in the document cited in Note 5.

Representative of the Secretary-General of the United Nations is undertaking; and

d. To keep the Meeting duly informed of the negotiations he undertakes and the results thereof.

On May 6 the Tenth Meeting of Consultation had agreed to request the governments of the member states that were willing and capable of doing so to make contingents of their land, naval, air, or police forces available to the OAS, within their capabilities and to the extent they could do so, to form an inter-American force that would operate under the authority of the Meeting. This force was to have "as its sole purpose, . . . that of cooperating in the restoration of normal conditions in the Dominican Republic, in maintaining the security of its inhabitants and the inviolability of human rights, and in the establishment of an atmosphere of peace and conciliation that will permit the functioning of democratic institutions." On May 22 the Meeting adopted another resolution concerning that force, which stipulated that the Secretary General should assume the functions referred to in paragraph 3 of the May 6 resolution, that is, to work out the technical measures necessary to establish a Unified Command of the OAS for the coordinated and effective action of that force. The same May 22 resolution requested the Government of Brazil to designate the Commander and the Government of the United States of America to designate the Deputy Commander of that force.

The next day the Secretary General and the chiefs of the national contingents already available to the OAS in Santo Domingo, signed the Act Establishing the "Inter-American Peace Force", as it was officially designated by a resolution of the Meeting of Consultation adopted on June 2.[9]

Also on June 2, 1965, the Meeting of Consulation, considering that the situation prevailing in the Dominican Republic continued to be a danger to peace, and that, consequently, the OAS should continue to exert efforts and to take the steps necessary for the prompt restoration of democratic order in that country, resolved to appoint an ad hoc committee made up of representatives of Brazil, El Salvador, and the United States of America, which would act on its behalf for the following purposes:[10]

a. To continue the task begun by the Special Committee and now being carried out by the Secretary General providing good offices to all the parties, for the purpose of achieving the establishment of a climate of peace and reconciliation that will permit the functioning of democratic institutions in the Dominican Republic and its economic and social recovery;

b. To provide the Inter-American Force, through its Commander and on

[9] Cf. Ibid., resolutions of May 22 and June 2, respectively.
[10] See the complete text of the resolution in ibid.

behalf of the Tenth Meeting of Consultation under whose authority it functions, the directives necessary for the effective accomplishment of that Force's sole purpose, as defined in paragraph 2 of the resolution adopted by this Meeting on May 6, 1965; and

c. To keep the Tenth Meeting of Consultation duly informed of its activities and the results thereof.

The Committee left for Santo Domingo on June 3 and, upon its arrival, initiated, together with the Secretary General, a series of exploratory conversations. As a result of these conversations and a careful study of the situation the Committee was convinced that the best way of achieving this objective was through free, democratic general elections. For this purpose, on June 18, 1965 the Ad Hoc Committee and the Secretary General presented for the consideration of the parties and of the Dominican people as a whole a plan of action containing, in essence, the following points:[11]

1. General elections for the President and Vice President of the Republic, members of the National Congress, and for municipal authorities to be held throughout the country, within a period of from six to nine months, the time required to make the necessary arrangements.

2. In order that such elections might be free and reflect the will of the Dominican people, the OAS would cooperate fully in the preparation and holding of the elections, through its competent organs, especially a technical advisory commission composed of jurists and experts from the member states which would be established, and the Inter-American Commission on Human Rights, which would remain in the country throughout the pre-electoral period.

Furthermore, the Inter-American Peace Force, reduced to the number strictly necessary to carry out its mission, would supplement the efforts of the Dominican authorities in the maintenance of peace during the electoral process.

3. Full amnesty would be granted to all who had participated in the civil strife, following surrender of the arms in possession of the irregular forces to the Organization of American States.

4. Establishment of a provisional government representing all sectors to carry the country to the elections, maintain law and order and insure respect for human rights, restore the normal functioning of public administration, and institute urgent and necessary programs for the rehabilitation and development of the economic and social life of the country.

5. OAS technical and economic assistance enabling the country to institute programs of national rehabilitation.

6. Preparation of an institutional act to serve as a provisional charter until the people decide the constitutional issue by means of a Constitutional Assembly.

The "Constitutional Government" and the "Government of National Reconstruction" submitted their replies to this proposal on June 23. On August 9, after frequent and active negotiation with the

---

[11] *Cf.* OEA/Ser.F/II.10, Doc. 180 Corr.

parties in conflict and a new, broad exchange of impressions with Dominican citizens from all representative sectors of the country, the Ad Hoc Committee presented the parties with a new proposal entitled "Act of Dominican Reconciliation", which contained the bases for a final agreement. One of these bases was the acceptance by both parties of a Provisional Government headed by Mr. Héctor García Godoy and of the "Institutional Act", pursuant to which the said Government would perform its functions and hold elections. On the same date the Committee made public its proposal and requested the Dominican people for support of the plan for national reconciliation.[12]

On August 31, 1965 the Act of Dominican Reconciliation and the Institutional Act were signed in Santo Domingo. The Act of Reconciliation was signed by the Constitutional Government with a reservation and, in the case of the Government of National Reconstruction, by the Armed Forces and National Police with a Declaration since the Government had resigned the day before. The Institutional Act was signed by the Constitutional Government and by the Provisional Government. The latter also signed the Act of Reconciliation, along with the Ad Hoc Committee. On September 3 Mr. García Godoy took possession as Provisional President.[13]

In its Second General Report to the Meeting of Consultation the Ad Hoc Committee stated that it considered that it had fulfilled one of the fundamental tasks entrusted to it, that is, "achieving the establishment of a climate of peace and reconciliation that will permit the functioning of democratic institutions in the Dominican Republic. . . ." Nevertheless, in view of the enormity of the problems faced by the Dominican Republic in order to achieve those objectives, the Committee indicated that the Provisional Government would need all the technical assistance the OAS and its members could provide. Consequently, it believed that during the months ahead it would be necessary to provide for the continuation or establishment, by the OAS, of activities such as: maintenance of elements of the Inter-American Peace Force in the Dominican Republic until the Tenth Meeting of Consultation, in agreement with the President of the Provisional Government, decides upon its withdrawal; the continuing presence of the Inter-American Commission on Human Rights, at the request of the Provisional Government; designation of an Electoral Committee to advise the Provisional Government on the organization and holding of elections, as provided for in Article 51 of the Institutional Act; and, establishment of a program of technical and economic assistance. Consequently, the Ad Hoc Committee sub-

---

[12] *Cf.* OEA/Ser.F/II.10, Doc. 280 Corr. 4.

[13] *Cf.* The complete text of the Act of Dominican Reconciliation and the Institutional Act appears in OEA/Ser.F/II.10, Doc. 363, 7 September 1965.

mitted the following recommendations to the Meeting of Consultation:[14]

1. That the Tenth Meeting of Consultation of Ministers of Foreign Affairs continue its work until the installation of the Constitutional Government that is chosen in the elections to be held in accordance with the Institutional Act.

2. That the Ad Hoc Committee of the Tenth Meeting of Consultation continue to function in order that it may give advice and guidance to the Inter-American Peace Force until its withdrawal from the Dominican Republic, as well as to continue reporting to the Tenth Meeting of Consultation on the situation in that country.

3. That in view of the difficult economic situation of the Dominican Republic as a result of the events that have taken place since April 24, 1965, the Tenth Meeting of Consultation recommend to the member states that they offer, through the OAS, technical and economic assistance to that country and that it request the assistance of the Inter-American Committee on the Alliance for Progress in the preparation and implementation of an economic recovery and development plan for the country.

4. That the Tenth Meeting of Consultation designate an outstanding personality of one of the member states as Special Representative of the OAS in the Dominican Republic, who would be appointed by the Secretary General of the Organization, in accordance with the Charter of the OAS, to supervise and coordinate all the technical and economic assistance activities that the OAS may carry out in the Dominican Republic during the term of the Provisional Government.

5. That the General Secretariat make a study of the claims Dominican citizens present to the OAS Office in Santo Domingo for damages and injuries suffered as a result of the armed action that began on April 24, 1965, to determine which of them could be compensated for by the OAS.

6. That, as was requested by the Ad Hoc Committee on August 20, 1965, the Tenth Meeting of Consultation adopt a resolution amending paragraph 5 of the resolution of May 6, 1965, to read that "the manner and date of withdrawal of the Inter-American Peace Force shall be determined jointly by the Provisional Government and the Tenth Meeting of Consultation of Ministers of Foreign Affairs, upon the initiative of the President of the Provisional Government, when he deems it advisable."

Before concluding this Chapter, reference should be made to one very important aspect of OAS action in the Dominican situation.

One of the primary tasks that the Special Committee appointed on May 1 undertook in the Dominican Republic was the provision of prompt assistance to the people of that country in order to alleviate their most immediate needs, especially for food and medicine, resulting from the fighting that was going on. For this reason, on May 3 the Committee sent a message to the Tenth Meeting of Consultation

[14] Cf. Second General Report by the Committee, OEA/Ser. F/II.10, Doc. 374 Rev. 3, 24 September 1965.

urgently requesting that, within a spirit of fraternal solidarity with the Dominican people, food, medicine, and medical personnel be sent there in order to improve the situation and avert the possible epidemics and other calamities which would make conditions even more difficult.

In reply to this humanitarian request by the Committee, the Tenth Meeting of Consultation that same day adopted a resolution in which it made an urgent appeal to all the member states of the Organization to place at the disposal of the General Secretariat, within the limits of their capabilities, food, medicines, medical supplies, and trained medical personnel to be sent immediately to the Dominican Republic for the humanitarian purpose of giving succor to the Dominican people without any distinctions whatsoever. In response, planes and ships loaded with food, medicine, and medical supplies and personnel arrived from various American countries. In order to handle the distribution of this material the OAS set up at its headquarters the Relief Operation Coordinating Center and the Secretary General immediately organized in Santo Domingo, with personnel from the Pan American Union especially recruited for the job, the OAS Emergency Aid Operation, which has been in charge of the distribution of several thousand tons of food and a large amount of medicines, in collaboration with the International Red Cross, the Dominican Red Cross, CARITAS and several other religious groups.[15]

The intense activities the Inter-American Commission on Human Rights has carried out in the Dominican Republic should also be pointed out and have been summarized in Chapter IV.

---

[15] At its June 9 meeting, the OAS Council approved a resolution by which a Special Fund was established to cover administrative expenses for the Emergency Aid Operation of the OAS to the Dominican Republic, and $197,000 was assigned to that Fund to cover the estimated costs for two months.

Chapter X

Ties and Relationships Between the Inter-American System of Peace and Security and That of the United Nations

The study of the inter-American system of peace and security would be incomplete if no reference were made to its ties and relationships with the peace and security system established by the United Nations Charter. These ties and relationships are explicitly or implicitly contained in various provisions of that instrument, especially in Chapter VIII regarding Regional Arrangements, which reads as follows:

Article 52

1. Nothing in the present Charter precludes the existence of regional arrangements or agencies for dealing with such matters relating to the maintenance of international peace and security as are appropriate for regional action, provided that such arrangements or agencies and their activities are consistent with the Purposes and Principles of the United Nations.

2. The Members of the United Nations entering into such arrangements or constituting such agencies shall make every effort to achieve pacific settlement of local disputes through such regional arrangements or by such regional agencies before referring them to the Security Council.

3. The Security Council shall encourage the development of pacific settlement of local disputes through such regional arrangements or by such regional agencies either on the initiative of the states concerned or by reference from the Security Council.

4. This Article in no way impairs the application of Articles 34 and 35.

Article 53

1. The Security Council shall, where appropriate, utilize such regional arrangements or agencies for enforcement action under its authority. But no enforcement action shall be taken under regional arrangements or by regional agencies without the authorization of the Security Council, with the exception of measures against any enemy state, as defined in paragraph 2 of this Article, provided for pursuant to Article 107 or in regional arrangements directed against renewal of aggressive policy on the part of any such state, until such time as the Organization may, on request of the Governments concerned, be

charged with the responsibility for preventing further aggression by such a state.

2. The term enemy state as used in paragraph 1 of this Article applies to any state which during the Second World War has been an enemy of any signatory of the present Charter.

Article 54

The Security Council shall at all times be kept fully informed of activities undertaken or in contemplation under regional arrangements or by regional agencies for the maintenance of international peace and security.

It will be noted that Article 52, paragraph 1, while authorizing regional arrangements and agencies and requiring that they and their activities be consistent with the purposes and principles of the United Nations, establishes that these are arrangements or agencies "for dealing with such matters relating to the maintenance of international peace and security as are appropriate for regional action." In this sense, like other provisions of the Charter, this paragraph takes into account regional action in the field of pacific settlement as well as regional action in the field of collective security. The same is also true of paragraph 4 of Article 52 and of Article 54. On the other hand, paragraphs 2 and 3 of Article 52 deal with the "pacific settlement of local disputes" and Article 53 provides for "enforcement action," and in each case the conditions or circumstances in which regional action may be taken are established.

The sphere of regional action, however, is not limited to the "pacific settlement of local disputes" nor to the taking of "enforcement action." Paragraph 1 of Article 52 mentions "activities" and Article 54 speaks of "activities undertaken or in contemplation," both of them in reference to activities relative to the maintenance of international peace and security. It is obvious that regional action may take the form of activities that do not exactly constitute the pacific settlement of a dispute or the application of measures such as those established in Article 53. In this respect, aside from the obligation to maintain the Security Council informed of all such activities and from the exception stipulated in Article 52, paragraph 4, the Charter contains no specific provisions relative to the conditions or circumstances in which the activities in reference are to be undertaken or contemplated. For its part, self-defense can take the form of a regional action, that is, of an action agreed upon by the competent regional organ. In this connection, it must be determined to what point the provisions contained in Article 54 are applicable, bearing in mind the specific provisions of Article 51 that govern the exercise of the right of self-defense, as well as the pertinent provisions of the regional instruments.

In the following sections the ties and relationships between the two systems of peace and security are examined in the light of the foregoing considerations. It will be seen that the provisions of the United Nations Charter and those of the inter-American instruments —and perhaps as a result the practice of these bodies—are not sufficiently consistent or harmonious to permit a precise definition of these ties and relationships. The examination of the deliberations and decisions of U.N. organs will necessarily be limited.

35. *Provisions and Practice Regarding Pacific Settlement*

On the subject of the pacific settlement of "any dispute, the continuance of which is likely to endanger the maintenance of international peace and security," the U.N. Charter indicates among the pacific means through which the parties shall "first of all" seek a solution to such disputes, the resort to regional agencies or arrangements (Art. 33.1). In specific reference to local disputes, Article 52.2 provides that the members of the United Nations who are parties to regional agreements or constitute such agencies "shall make every effort" to achieve pacific settlement of such disputes prior to referring them to the Security Council. Paragraph 3 of the same article also establishes that the Security Council shall encourage the development of pacific settlement of local disputes through such regional arrangements or by such regional agencies. When it deems it necessary, the Council shall also call upon the parties to settle their disputes by pacific means, including resort to regional agencies or arrangements (Art. 33.2).

As far as the inter-American instruments which also contemplate the connections and ties between the two systems of peace and security are concerned, in the American Treaty on Pacific Settlement (Pact of Bogotá) the American republics solemnly reaffirm "their commitments made in earlier international conventions and declarations, as well as in the Charter of the United Nations" and agree "to have recourse at all times to pacific procedures" (Art. I). For its part, the Inter-American Treaty of Reciprocal Assistance establishes that "the High Contracting Parties undertake to submit every controversy which may arise between them to methods of peaceful settlement and to endeavor to settle any such controversy among themselves by means of the procedures in force in the Inter-American System before referring it to the General Assembly or the Security Council of the United Nations" (Art. 2). This procedure, the significance of which is obvious, was modified the following year at the Bogotá Conference (1948) when the obligation to resort to regional procedures was limited. In effect, in the pertinent provisions of the OAS Charter (Art. 20) and the Pact of Bogotá (Arts. II and L) no mention is made of the U.N. General Assembly.

The scope of these stipulations must also be interpreted in the light of the general provision contained in Article 102 of the OAS Charter and Article 10 of the Rio Treaty to the effect that none of the provisions contained in these inter-American instruments shall be construed as impairing the rights and obligations of the American states under the Charter of the United Nations. It would appear that the purpose of these instruments is to oblige the parties to make every effort possible to reach a pacific settlement of their disputes before submitting them to the Security Council, as specified in Article 52.2 of the U.N. Charter, or to that organ or the General Assembly in accordance with the terms of Article 52.4.

An examination of the provisions of the U.N. Charter and inter-American instruments regarding "pacific settlement" might lead to interpretations at variance with the one contained in the preceding paragraphs but the differences between them would be in tone rather than in substance. Subject to further discussion of this point, for the moment what matters most is to discover the real nature of the "disputes" contemplated in the aforementioned provisions. Only by this means can their sphere of applicability be determined to some degree. Once again it must be stated that neither the U.N. Charter nor the inter-American instruments are sufficiently clear and precise. In fact, the only thing that seems evident is that the term "disputes" should be understood in the broad sense and that it comprehends, therefore, not only ordinary international disputes and differences but also those disputes which include armed conflict or which are likely to result in acts or situations capable of breaking the peace. Article 33 of the U.N. Charter, which contains the general provisions on this subject even mentions disputes, "the continuance of which is likely to endanger the maintenance of international peace and security."

From the point of view that interests us particularly here, the difficulty in arriving at exact interpretations is increased by the fact that while the U.N. Charter makes a distinction between "dispute" and "situation" as far as the jurisdiction of its organs and, above all, the procedure to be followed is concerned, this distinction does not appear in the provisions of Chapter VIII on regional arrangements. The inter-American instruments make no such distinction. The provisions contained in Chapter IV of the OAS Charter and in the Pact of Bogotá only refer to the pacific settlement of "disputes" and the provisions of Chapter V of the Charter and those of the Rio Treaty are limited to "acts", "facts", or "situations" that endanger peace.

The practice of these organizations, far from shedding light on this subject, has perhaps added to the confusion. As could be noted in the review of the activities of the Inter-American Peace Committee and the applications of the Rio Treaty, it is not always possible to distinguish exactly between a "dispute", or an "act", "fact", or "situation", above all when certain disputes have clearly been armed "conflicts" which have given rise to an application of the Rio Treaty. As far as U.N. practice is concerned, as will be seen below, the provisions generally applied are those contained in Article 52.2, in spite of the fact that the nature of the "disputes" has not always been the same. Apart from these considerations what is perhaps most important is to discover what the reactions of the United Nations have been when requests have been presented by a member state in connection with a case already under consideration by the regional agency. In this regard, the practice of the international organization does appear to have been quite consistent.

The "Situation in Guatemala (1954)" was the first time the Security Council became involved in a problem of relations between the world and regional organizations.[1] In its request for the urgent convocation of the Council the Guatemalan Government invoked Articles 34, 35, and 39 of the U.N. Charter so that it might take the measures necessary to prevent the disruption of peace and international security in Central America "and also to put a stop to the aggression in progress against Guatemala." According to the first draft resolution presented by Brazil and Colombia and amended by France, the Security Council would have made reference to the provisions of Chapter VIII of the U.N. Charter, transmitted "the complaint of the Government of Guatemala to the Organization of American States for urgent consideration," and requested the regional organization to inform the Council on the measures taken. This draft resolution received the affirmative vote of ten members of the Council but was vetoed by the Soviet Union. At a subsequent meeting, on June 20, 1954, the Security Council adopted a French draft resolution merely calling for the immediate termination of any action likely to cause bloodshed and requesting all members of the U.N. to abstain from giving assistance to any such action.[2]

The second case taken up by the Security Council was the denunciation presented on July 11, 1960 by the Government of Cuba against the United States of America "of repeated threats, reprisals and aggressive acts" alleged against the latter country. Argentina and Ecuador submitted a draft resolution in which, among other things, the Council took note of the fact that the situation was under study by the OAS. The majority of the Council members supported this draft on the grounds that in that phase the situation should be dealt

---

[1] See the action by the Inter-American Peace Committee and the application of the Rio Treaty, *supra*, pp. 90 and 131, respectively.

[2] *Cf. Yearbook of the United Nations 1954*, Columbia University Press, 1955, p. 94 *et seq.*

with by the regional organization, particularly in view of the fact that it was already under examination by that body.[3] The Soviet Union and Poland opposed the draft on the basis that the question was not the same one under study by the OAS. On July 19 the Council, by a vote of eight against, two in favor, and one abstention, rejected the amendments proposed by the Soviet Union and approved the Latin American draft resolution by which it decided to adjourn the consideration of the question pending the receipt of a report from the OAS; invited the members of the OAS to lend their assistance towards the achievement of a peaceful solution of the situation in accordance with the purposes and principles of the U.N. Charter; and urged all other states to refrain from any action which might increase the existing tensions between Cuba and the United States. The preamble of this resolution made mention not only of Articles 24, 33, 34, 35, 36, 52, and 113 of the U.N. Charter but also of Articles 20 and 102 of the Charter of the OAS.[4] In December of the same year the Cuban Government renewed its petition to the Security Council, charging that the United States Government was about to commit "direct military aggression" against Cuba. No decision was adopted by the Council on this charge.[5]

The next case was also brought about by an accusation made by the Cuban Government against the Government of the United States, this time in the form of a request that an item be placed on the agenda of the fifteenth session of the General Assembly. The request was originally presented on October 18, 1960 but was not discussed until April 15, 1961. The discussion continued until April 21 and coincided with the invasion of Cuba which occurred during that week. Mexico submitted a draft resolution according to which, among other things, the General Assembly would have made an urgent appeal to all states to ensure that their territories and resources were not used to promote a civil war in Cuba, asking them to cooperate in the search for a peaceful solution to the situation. In the course of the debate the Mexican Representative stated that his draft resolution, by mentioning Article 33 of the U.N. Charter, contemplated the use of the regional agency but that it was for the parties concerned to agree voluntarily to use inter-American procedures. Argentina, Chile, Colombia, Honduras, Panama, Uruguay, and Vene-

---

[3] The agency in reference was the Inter-American Peace Committee which was then making a study of international tensions in the Caribbean area. The Committee's report on this subject appears as doc. CIP-2-60, 14 April 1960, and also as an appendix to its report to the Seventh Meeting of Consultation of Ministers of Foreign Affairs, OEA/Ser. F/II.7, Doc. 6.

[4] See U.N. Security Council Official Documents, meetings 874–876, and S/4378, 4388, 4392, 4394, 4395.

[5] See *ibid.*, meetings 921–923, and S/4605, 4611, 4612.

zuela also submitted a draft resolution which, with certain amendments, was adopted by the General Assembly. In its resolution the General Assembly exhorted all member states to take such peaceful action as was open to them to remove existing tension, and in one of its paragraphs also recalled the last two paragraphs of the Security Council resolution of July 19, 1960, that is, the invitation to all OAS members to lend their assistance toward the achievement of a peaceful solution and the exhortation to all other states to refrain from any action which might increase the existing tensions between Cuba and the United States; it also recalled the peaceful means of settlement established at the Seventh Meeting of Consultation (August 1960).[6]

By a cable of May 5, 1963 the Government of Haiti requested a meeting of the Security Council to examine what it called "the grave situation caused by repeated threats of aggression and acts of interference on the part of the Dominican Republic, which infringed upon the sovereignty and territorial integrity of Haiti and endangered international peace and security." On April 28 and May 3 the Security Council had been informed that the OAS Council had decided to convoke the Organ of Consultation and that it had appointed an Investigating Committee.[7] The Security Council included the item on its agenda on May 8, 1963 and at a meeting held on the following day the President drew attention to the text of the May 8 resolution adopted by the OAS Council. The discussion centered mainly on the question of the relationship between the Security Council and the regional agencies, as defined in Article 52 of the Charter. Venezuela, the United States, Norway, the Philippines, China, the United Kingdom, and France maintained that while any member of the OAS had the right to bring a controversy before the Security Council, action should be taken by the Council only when efforts for a peaceful settlement at the regional level had failed. Brazil, Ghana, Morocco, and other members supported the view that the Security Council was competent to deal with the matter and a member state need not await action by the regional agency. The President noted that the majority of the members of the Council felt it preferable, for the moment, to leave the initiative to the re-

---

[6] Cf. United Nations General Assembly, 15th Session, First Committee (meetings 1100, 1106, 1107), Plenary (meetings 909, 910); documents A/4519, 4537, 4543, 4581, 4631, 4701, 4708, 4725; A/C.I/L.275, 276; A/4744. The "peaceful means of settlement" alluded to was the Ad Hoc Good Offices Committee created by Resolution II of the Seventh Meeting of Consultation and composed of high-level representatives of the Governments of Venezuela, Mexico, Brazil, Colombia, Chile, and Costa Rica. Cf. *Final Act of the Seventh Meeting of Consultation*, OEA/Ser. C/II.7, p. 5.

[7] See "Situation Between the Dominican Republic and Haiti (1963–1965)", p. 142, *supra.*

gional organization, which was trying to bring about an amicable settlement and that the two parties had indicated that they saw no objection to that procedure.

Subsequently, on May 14, the Haitian Government complained to the Security Council that Dominican troops were still deployed on the Dominican-Haitian border. On August 5 it reported that it had requested a meeting of the regional agency to consider an act of armed aggression originating from the Dominican Republic. On August 19 Haiti drew the attention of the U.N. Secretary-General to the increasingly tense situation between the two countries, stating that the Haitian Government did not consider that the OAS Organ of Consultation had discharged its responsibility in the matter since the Investigating Committee had still not visited Haiti, and requested the Secretary-General to use his good offices with U.N. organs to bring about the dispatch of military observers to the Haitian-Dominican frontier and to take the measures necessary for this purpose. On August 30 Haiti asked for an urgent meeting of the Security Council, on September 3 it withdrew the request, and on September 23 it informed the Security Council that early that morning armed bands had crossed the border and attacked a Haitian military district headquarters. During this period the Security Council had also been kept informed of the activities of the regional agency.

On July 4, 1964 Haiti once again addressed the Security Council to denounce acts of aggression by the Dominican Republic. The Council took no action however, nor was any specific action requested by Haiti.[8]

On January 10, 1964 the Permanent Representative of Panama requested the President of the Security Council to convoke that organ as soon as possible in order to consider urgent matters relative to the serious situation between his country and the United States. The Council met that same day and heard statements by the representatives of both parties as well as by other members. In the course of the debate the Representative of Brazil suggested that the Council President be authorized to call upon the two governments for an immediate cease-fire and an end to the bloodshed and to take the necessary measures to restrain the military forces under their control and protect the civilian population. In the opinion of the Brazilian Representative, in this way the Security Council would not be acting in a manner incompatible with the provisions of the OAS Charter and, on the contrary, would be strengthening any decision which the regional organization might take. The representatives of the parties

---

[8] *Cf.* U.N. Security Council Official Documents, meetings 1035, 1036; documents S/5301, 5307, 5302, 5304, 5309, 5306, 5311, 5315, 5373, 5383, 5387, 5374, 5391, 5398, 5399, 5404, 5411, 5413, 5416, 5430, 5431, 5433; A/5502.

were in agreement with the Brazilian suggestion and when the meeting closed at dawn of the following day the President of the Security Council announced that if there were no objections he would consider that suggestion as having been adopted. There were no objections and on January 11 the President addressed telegrams to the Minister of Foreign Affairs of Panama and to the Secretary of State of the United States in the foregoing terms.[9]

The final case that falls within this section is the "Dominican Situation" (1965). In accordance with Article 54 of the U.N. Charter, on April 30, 1964 the Secretary General of the OAS began informing the Security Council about the activities undertaken or in contemplation, first by the OAS Council and later by the Tenth Meeting of Consultation of Ministers of Foreign Affairs.[10] That same day the Secretary-General of the United Nations received a note from the Minister of Foreign Affairs of Cuba in which his government denounced "before the world, through the United Nations, this new and unheard-of aggression against the sovereignty and independence of another country which has been carried out with cynical imperialist insolence by the United States Government, and it draws attention to the threat to peace which this criminal action entails." On May 1 the Permanent Representative of the Soviet Union requested the President of the Security Council for an urgent meeting of the Council "to consider the question of the armed interference by the United States in the internal affairs of the Dominican Republic."[11]

After a lengthy discussion that began on May 3, on May 14 the Security Council approved, by the affirmative vote of 11 members, a draft resolution presented by the Representatives of the Ivory Coast, Jordan, and Malaysia. According to this resolution, based on an earlier draft presented by the Representative of Uruguay, the Council called for a strict cease-fire; invited the Secretary-General to send, as an urgent measure, a representative to the Dominican Republic for the purpose of reporting to the Council on the situation; and called upon all concerned in the Dominican Republic to cooperate with the representative of the Secretary-General in the carrying out of this task.[12]

Pursuant to this resolution the Secretary-General immediately sent

---

[9] Cf. Ibid., meeting 1086. The text of the telegrams appears in S/5519.

[10] See "Action by the OAS in the Dominican Situation (1965)", Chapter IX, supra. Regarding the communication by the OAS Secretary General see U.N. Doc. S/6313.

[11] Cf. U.N. Security Council, S/6314 and 6316, respectively.

[12] Cf. U.N. Security Council Official Documents, meetings 1196–1233; S/6346 (Uruguayan draft); 6355 (tripartite draft) and S/RES/203 (1965) (Council resolution).

his Military Adviser, Major General I. J. Rikhye, to Santo Domingo and a few days later sent Mr. José A. Mayobre there as his Representative. In connection with the mandate contained in the Security Council resolution, the Secretary-General later invoked a declaration by the President of the Council and "the unanimous desire of the members" of that body and instructed his Representative that "his urgent efforts should be devoted to an immediate securing of a suspension of hostilities so that the humanitarian work of the Red Cross to search for the dead and the wounded might be facilitated." In this way the original mandate of the Secretary-General's Representative was enlarged and, therefore, so too was the degree of participation by the world organization in the activities being carried out, including the negotiations with the contending parties in order to reestablish a state of normality in the Dominican Republic.[13]

36. *Application of Measures Agreed on by the Regional Agency*

The provisions and precedents mentioned above are not the only ones in which the basic ties and relationships between the two peace and security systems can be appreciated. With regard to the collective action set forth in Chapter VIII of the U.N. Charter (and transcribed earlier) it is of particular interest to determine the true significance of the expression "enforcement action" (*medidas coercitivas* in the Spanish text). This, in turn, will allow us to determine the scope of the prohibition against taking enforcement action "under regional arrangements or by regional agencies without the authorization of the Security Council," as established in Article 53.1.

There are two interpretations of this expression. One of them holds that it includes all the measures contemplated in Articles 41 and 42 of the U.N. Charter since they are taken against the will of the state. According to the other interpretation only the measures established in Article 42 fall within the category of enforcement action, if and when Article 41 does not include armed force. The text of the aforementioned articles is as follows:

Article 41

The Security Council may decide what measures not involving the use of armed force are to be employed to give effect to its decisions, and it may call upon the Members of the United Nations to apply such measures. These may include complete or partial interruption of economic relations and of rail, sea, air, postal, telegraphic, radio, and other means of communication, and the severance of diplomatic relations.

---

[13] In this regard see the Reports by the U.N. Secretary-General to the Security Council S/6371 and Add. 1 and 2; and 6353, 6358, 6365, 6369, 6378, 6380, 6386, 6408, 6420, 6432, 6447 and Add. 1, 6459, 6530 and Corr. 1, 6542, 6553, 6615, 6649 and Corr. 1.

Article 42

Should the Security Council consider that measures provided for in Article 41 would be inadequate or have proved to be inadequate, it may take such action by air, sea, or land forces as may be necessary to maintain or restore international peace and security. Such action may include demonstrations, blockade, and other operations by air, sea, or land forces of Members of the United Nations.

The second interpretation appears in the following passage from a well-known report by Dr. Alberto Lleras Camargo. Dr. Lleras, then Director General of the Pan American Union, chaired Committee 4 of Commission III, which dealt with "Regional Arrangements" at the San Francisco Conference.[14]

In the Charter of the United Nations there are two types of measures, closely coordinated with the procedure to be followed in the Security Council when faced with threats of aggression, with the refusal of the States to comply with the recommendations of the Council, or with a breach of the peace. The first type is that of Article 41, according to which the Security Council is empowered to decide what measures *not involving the use of armed force* are to be employed to give effect to its decisions, and it is empowered to call upon the Members of the United Nations to apply such measures. But if these measures are or have proved to be inadequate, coercive measures will next be applied, with the use of air, sea, or land forces. There is a clear distinction for the reader of the Charter between the measures of Article 41 (enforcement action) which are not coercive, in the sense that they lack the element of physical violence that is closely identified with military action, and those of Article 42. Enforcement action, with the use of physical force, is obviously the prerogative of the Security Council, with a single exception: individual or collective self-defense. But the other measures, those of Article 41, are not; it may even be said that it is within the power of any State—without necessarily violating the purposes, principles, or provisions of the Charter—to break diplomatic, consular, and economic relations or to interrupt its communications with another State. Thus the use of armed force by the American States is subject to two limitations: they may not use it except in self-defense, when there has been armed attack, or in other cases of aggression and threat of aggression, under the authority of the Security Council.

If the pertinent provisions of the U.N. Charter, particularly Article 52.1, are interpreted in the light of the real reason for authorizing regional action in matters relative to the maintenance of international peace and security, there appears to be no other logical interpretation than that the prohibition contained in Article 53 is only a relative, not an absolute, limitation on regional action. If the expression "enforcement action" were understood to apply

---

[14] *Cf.* Inter-American Conference for the Maintenance of Continental Peace and Security, *Report on the Results of the Conference.* Congress and Conference Series No. 53, Washington, D.C., Pan American Union, 1947, pp. 41–42.

to all the measures contemplated in the U.N. Charter, in what would regional action consist? In other words, why authorize regional arrangements or agencies to take up matters relative to the maintenance of international peace and security susceptible of regional action, if that action must be authorized by the Security Council? Furthermore, it should be noted that Article 54 contemplates regional "activities" undertaken or in contemplation for the maintenance of international peace and security—activities which can include the application of measures—regarding which the sole obligation is to keep the Security Council informed.

Apart from the objective validity of these interpretations, how has Article 53 been interpreted in practice in the cases where the Organ of Consultation has agreed to apply measures? This question arose after the Sixth Meeting of Consultation, the first occasion on which the Organ of Consultation decided to apply measures such as those established in Article 8 of the Rio Treaty. Since the measures agreed on were only of a diplomatic and economic or commercial nature, the Organ of Consultation limited itself to authorizing "the Secretary General of the Organization of American States to transmit to the Security Council of the United Nations full information concerning the measures agreed upon in this resolution."

When the question arose once again within the Security Council, the applicability of Article 54 of the U.N. Charter was reiterated. Upon receipt by the Security Council of a certified copy of the Final Act of the Sixth Meeting of Consultation, the First Deputy Minister for Foreign Affairs of the Soviet Union requested the Council President to immediately convoke a meeting of the Council to consider the decision taken by the Organ of Consultation in regard to the Dominican Republic, in order to approve this decision pursuant to Article 53 of the Charter. The Representatives of Argentina, Ecuador, and the United States presented another draft resolution by which the Security Council would merely "take note" of the information transmitted by the Secretary General of the OAS and especially of Resolution I of the Organ of Consultation. This second draft resolution was approved by nine votes in favor and two abstentions (Poland and the Soviet Union).[15]

The procedure was repeated on the occasion of the exclusion of the present Government of Cuba from the OAS and the partial suspension of trade and traffic in arms and war material with that country agreed on by the Eighth Meeting of Consultation. This time it was the Representative of the Cuban Government who requested the President of the Security Council to convoke an im-

---

[15] See U.N. Security Council Official Documents, meetings 893–895; S/4477 and 4481 (Soviet note and draft resolution, respectively); and S/4484 (draft by the three countries).

mediate meeting of that body. The Council met on February 27, 1962 and after a lengthy discussion of whether or not the Cuban note should be included on the agenda, especially since the question had been discussed and decided in 1960 in connection with similar measures adopted by the inter-American organ, the Council failed to include this topic on its agenda, by a vote of four in favor and seven abstentions.

The Representative of Cuba again addressed the President of the Security Council on March 8 to request another meeting of the Council, to ask the International Court of Justice to give an advisory opinion on the following legal questions:

1. Under the United Nations Charter, did the OAS have the right, as a regional agency, to take the enforcement action provided for in Article 53 of the United Nations Charter without the authorization of the Security Council?

2. Could the expression "enforcement action" in Article 53 of the United Nations Charter be considered to include the measures provided for in Article 41 of the United Nations Charter? Was the list of those measures in Article 41 exhaustive?

3. Did the OAS Charter provide for any procedure for expelling a state member of the organization, in particular because of its social system?

Later the Cuban Representative submitted a draft resolution regarding the presentation of this request to the Court, in the above terms, which was discussed during seven Council meetings held between March 14 and 23. At the last meeting the draft resolution was submitted to a vote, and at the request of the Representative of Ghana the paragraph that corresponded to point two above was voted separately. The paragraph was not adopted, by a vote of four in favor and seven abstentions. The vote on the remaining paragraphs was seven against, two in favor, and one abstention.[16]

In view of this oft-reiterated position by the Security Council, the question never even arose when the Ninth Meeting of Consultation agreed to apply new and more severe measures to Cuba and its Government. The Security Council was promptly informed of this decision by the Secretary General of the OAS, pursuant to Article 54 of the U.N. Charter.

37. *The Adoption of Measures for Self-Defense*

The situation is different when the measures in question are not those agreed on by the competent regional agency of the nature and purpose foreseen in Chapter VIII of the U.N. Charter, but

---

[16] See *ibid.*, meetings 991–998; S/5080, 5086, 5088, and 5095 (notes from the Cuban Representative and draft resolution presented by him).

rather measures adopted in exercise of the right of individual and collective self-defense, recognized by Article 51 of the U.N. Charter. According to Article 51:

> Nothing in the present Charter shall impair the inherent right of individual or collective self-defense if an armed attack occurs against a Member of the United Nations, until the Security Council has taken measures necessary to maintain international peace and security. Measures taken by Members in the exercise of this right of self-defense shall be immediately reported to the Security Council and shall not in any way affect the authority and responsibility of the Security Council under the present Charter to take at any time such action as it deems necessary in order to maintain or restore international peace and security.

In the first place, here there is no question about the intrinsic nature of the measures since Article 51, in contrast to Article 53, makes no distinction between "enforcement action" and other measures. In the second place, according to Article 51 the sole obligation is for members to inform the Security Council immediately of any measures taken in self-defense. Curiously, according to Article 5 of the Rio Treaty "The High Contracting Parties shall immediately send to the Security Council of the United Nations, in conformity with Articles 51 and 54 of the Charter of the United Nations, complete information concerning the activities undertaken or in contemplation in the exercise of the right of self-defense or for the purpose of maintaining inter-American peace and security." It would appear that the Rio Treaty extends the obligation of informing the Security Council, established by Article 51, by including not only the "activities undertaken" in the exercise of the right of self-defense but also those "in contemplation." In any event, what must remain perfectly clear is that self-defense measures, whether undertaken individually or by agreement of the competent regional agency, even including the use of armed force, do not require authorization by the United Nations Security Council.

In further reference to the obligation to report to the Security Council, it should be noted that paragraph 3 of the resolution adopted on October 23, 1962 by the Council of the OAS acting provisionally as Organ of Consultation, by which it was decided to inform the Security Council of the terms of the resolution, was in compliance with Article 5 of the Rio Treaty rather than with Article 54 of the U.N. Charter. This was true in view of the fact that in its resolution the provisional Organ of Consultation limited itself to "recommending" to the member states the taking of such individual and collective measures as they deemed necessary. What did have to be reported to the Security Council, as was done by the Secretary General from October 29 on, were the measures undertaken by the various American governments pursuant to the October 23 resolution.[17]

For the same reason, according to the pertinent provision of the U.N. Charter it was unnecessary for the Ninth Meeting of Consultation of Ministers of Foreign Affairs to instruct the Secretary General to transmit the complete text of Resolution I to the Security Council, in view of the fact that paragraph 5 of that resolution merely contemplated the eventual exercise of self-defense: that is, it dealt solely and exclusively with activities or measures that did not yet fulfill the requisites of Article 51. To be precise, in order for the obligation to report about eventual measures of self-defense to exist, such measures must be "in contemplation," specifically, as an action agreed on by the regional agency. The inapplicability of Article 54 appears evident since although paragraph 5 of Resolution I does not exclude this type of action, it does not specifically contemplate it.

---

[17] Given the nature of the Security Council's action in the October crisis, the question did not arise during the deliberations nor during the negotiations that took place simultaneously between the parties. For a summary of both see *Yearbook of the United Nations 1962,* p. 104 *et seq.* The texts of the messages exchanged between the Government of the United States of America and the Soviet Union, and between the Cuban Government and the Secretary-General of the U.N. appear in *Applications,* vol. 2, p. 109 *et seq.*

Chapter XI

Review and Evaluation of the Regional System

It is undeniable that an evaluation of the inter-American peace and security system as a whole, including its normative and institutional aspects as well as its practical achievements, produces notably positive results. In order to corroborate this statement it will be sufficient to point out not only the most noteworthy features of the development and strengthening the system has undergone, but also the shortcomings and deficiencies which have not yet been overcome. The development and strengthening of the system in the field of collective security has been made possible, primarily, by the following factors: first, the principle of solidarity against aggression, in the sense that, pursuant to Article 24 of the OAS Charter, "Every act of aggression by a State against the territorial integrity or the inviolability of the territory or against the sovereignty or political independence of an American State shall be considered an act of aggression against the other American States." And, second, the intrinsic flexibility of the instruments that govern the system, which has allowed them to be interpreted and applied according to the requirements of the circumstances, thus contributing more effectively to the purposes and objectives they pursue.

Logically, the development and strengthening of any collective security system, general or regional, requires a quite clear and precise idea of the acts, facts, or situations that justify its application. Thus, for example, at an early stage in the development of the consultation procedure mention was made only of "every act susceptible of disturbing the peace of America," or of a case in which "the peace, security or territorial integrity of any American Republic is thus threatened by acts of any nature that may impair them." Later the Charter and the Inter-American Treaty of Reciprocal Assistance with more precision specifically contemplated cases of "armed attack," "aggression which is not an armed attack," "extracontinental or intracontinental conflict," and "any other fact or situation that might endanger the peace of America." The Rio Treaty also authorized the Organ of Consultation to characterize as "aggression" other acts not included under Article 9, which has made possible the gradual definition of concrete categories of acts, facts, and situations of the nature of those contemplated by the Treaty and the Charter.

In this connection it is particularly interesting to point out two such categories. One is the "threat" of aggression, which the Rio Treaty only mentions in its preamble. The Eighth Meeting of Consultation, in Resolution II.3, expressly refers to it and that meeting had been convoked to consider "the threats to the peace and to the political independence of the American states." In a later application of the Rio Treaty there was an opportunity to refer to this category and to include it among those that specifically appear therein. In effect, the action taken by the Council of the Organization acting provisionally as Organ of Consultation during the so-called October crisis (1962) was the result, not of an armed attack, but of a fact or situation which might at any moment become an "active threat to the peace and security of the Continent."

The other category has to do with acts of "subversion." During the Second World War, in the face of the danger represented by the Nazi-Fascist activities of the Axis powers, what is known as the system for the "political defense" of the hemisphere was developed. Within this system the different forms adopted by subversive action directed, aided, or instigated by extracontinental powers were defined and characterized as "acts of political aggression" or "aggression of a non-military character." The Bogotá Conference (1948), the Fourth Meeting of Consultation (1951), and the Tenth Inter-American Conference (1954) once more confronted this problem of growing subversive action on the part of the international communist movement. In 1962 the Eighth Meeting of Consultation became aware of the urgent need to strengthen the system for "political defense" once the Foreign Ministers were able "to verify that the subversive offensive of communist governments, their agents and the organizations which they control, has increased in intensity." They also recognized that international communism employs extremely complex subversive techniques.

From the beginning the political defense system was conceived as a system for the protection of the democratic institutions of the hemisphere. Due to the close ties between subversive activity and military aggression carried out in other areas, "indirect aggression" does not yet appear as a separate concept in the inter-American system. Just as the Emergency Advisory Committee for Political Defense, which functioned in Montevideo from 1942 to 1948, pointed out, "in the Western Hemisphere, the program of political aggression of the members of the Tripartite Pact was completely incorporated in its vast political and military plan." This is not the case when the system for the political defense of the hemisphere, in its second phase, is applied to counteract the subversive action of international communism. The "act of political aggression" or the "aggression of a non-military character" is no longer considered as being necessarily connected with war or with a policy of armed aggression. Furthermore, it is primarily considered as a concept that describes acts which, in themselves, are new forms or techniques of aggression. This new focus coincides with the United Nations view of "indirect aggression." As far as their intrinsic nature is concerned, the acts which constitute such aggression have not changed substantially, as can be seen from their enumeration in the resolutions adopted by the American republics since the Bogotá Conference.

Subversive activity instigated, organized, and often financed by international communism, was carefully studied by the Department of Legal Affairs of the Pan American Union in 1952, at the request of the Fourth Meeting of Consultation, and later in a document prepared prior to the Eighth Meeting of Consultation. The latter document also points out the difference between subversive activity and the activities contemplated by the inter-American regimen applicable to political exiles and refugees. Finally, it should be recalled that in its report to the Eighth Meeting of Consultation the Inter-American Peace Committee, when referring to acts of "political aggression" or "aggression of a non-military character," expressed that "Such acts represent attacks upon inter-American peace and security as well as on the sovereignty and political independence of the American states." From this it can be deduced, as already indicated, that the subversive action directed, aided, or instigated by extra-continental powers (and today, also by American countries dominated by them) constitutes a special category of act, fact, or situation of the nature of those foreseen in the Charter of the Organization and the Rio Treaty, particularly of "aggression which is not an armed attack." Certain statements in the report of the Investigating Committee of the Organ of Consultation that studied the Venezuelan charges against Cuba, as well as the resolution adopted by the Ninth Meeting of Consultation (1964), amply corroborate this observation. In a word, the different forms of aggression to which the Rio Treaty is applicable have been considerably clarified, and thus many obstacles which still impede the United Nations from achieving a definition of aggression have been overcome.

The development and strengthening of the inter-American system of collective security is also evident in the competence of its organs. The Sixth Meeting of Consultation (1960) did not limit itself only to energetically condemning the participation of the Dominican Government in the "acts of intervention and aggression" against the Government of Venezuela, which culminated in an attempt against the life of the Venezuelan Chief of State, and to agreeing on the application of diplomatic and economic or commercial measures. It also requested the Council of the Organization to study the feasibility and desirability of extending the suspension of trade with the Dominican Republic to other articles. It also authorized the Council to discontinue, by a two-thirds affirmative vote of its members, the measures adopted once the Dominican Government should cease to constitute a danger to the peace and security of the hemisphere.

It is of great interest to point out the fact that in this application of the Rio Treaty the Organ of Consultation delegated such highly political functions and powers to the OAS Council. The Eighth Meeting of Consultation adopted the same position in the fight against the intense subversive action by the countries of the international communist movement when it conferred similar powers on the Council regarding the measures taken against Cuba and its Government; and the Ninth Meeting authorized it, for the third time, to discontinue the measures adopted at such time as the Cuban Government shall have ceased to constitute a danger to the peace and security of the hemisphere. The Eighth Meeting conferred yet another task on the Council when it created the Special Consultative Committee on Security, that is, the duty of maintaining all necessary vigilance for the purpose of warning against any acts of aggression, subversion, or other dangers to peace and security, or the preparation of such acts, resulting from the continued intervention of Sino-Soviet powers in this hemisphere, and to make recommendations to the governments of the member states with regard thereto.

The nature and scope of the measures applied by the Organ of Consultation reveal new aspects of the development and strengthening undergone by the inter-American collective security system. On the one hand, the flexibility of the terms in which these provisions are described permitted the Eighth Meeting of Consultation to take a measure not explicitly foreseen in the Rio Treaty. Its decision to exclude the present Government of Cuba from participation in the inter-American system, in effect, confirmed the fact that not only is the enumeration in Article 8 neither precise nor exclusive, but also that the terms of Article 6 are sufficiently broad and flexible to include any measures "which should be taken for the common defense and for the maintenance of the peace and security of the Continent," that is, to assure the maximum efficacy of the system. Aside from the standard of effectiveness, applied with increasing frequency in the interpretation of international treaties, the measure of exclusion is completely in accordance with the unanimous recognition by the other governments of the incompatibility of the conduct of the government so excluded with the inter-American system.

In another line of thought, it is interesting to point out that the measures enumerated in Article 8 of the Rio Treaty were applied to counteract subversive activities. This was the reason for the Eighth

Meeting's decision to partially suspend trade with Cuba and for the Ninth Meeting's resolve not to maintain diplomatic or consular relations with the Cuban Government and to suspend all trade and sea transportation with that country except for certain articles of a humanitarian nature. Prior to the latter decision the need to resort to measures of this kind became evident in the face of the continuing and increasing subversive action by Castro communism. It will be recalled that, with reference to the wave of terrorism, sabotage, and other subversive activities that movement had unleashed in some Latin American countries as a result of the October crisis, the Special Consultative Committee declared that "The degree of development attained by the political-military apparatus that has been established in Cuba is rendering the system of security against subversion increasingly inadequate and ineffective, basely solely on the isolated measures that each country might adopt."

These incidents, in fact, are part of a situation so urgent and serious that it can only be adequately and effectively dealt with through the application of the measures set forth in the Rio Treaty. This explains the decision taken by the Ninth Meeting of Consultation as well as its resolve regarding the possible use of individual and collective self-defense in the face of future "acts that possess characteristics of aggression and intervention." Thus, the process of integrating the two systems—that of collective security and that of security against subversion—has also reached the institution of self-defense.

Nevertheless, as far as the application of measures is concerned, the system has not yet been able to overcome an important breach in the Rio Treaty. Although the fact that "Decisions which require the application of the measures specified in Article 8" shall be binding is expressly consigned in the treaty, as well as the sole exception which exempts a state from compliance with those decisions, it does not specify what action shall be taken in the case of an unjustified failure to comply by one or more states. It is true that the U.N. Charter, Article 25 of which also declares that Security Council decisions are obligatory, is equally silent in this regard. But it is also true that a deficiency in the world system cannot excuse or justify deficiencies in the regional system. Therefore, it is to be hoped that eventually an inter-American conference or meeting of consultation will fill this serious breach in the Rio Treaty in the same way other aspects of the treaty have been gradually complemented and perfected according to the requirements of the circumstances and the lofty interests of collective security.

In a sense, the process of development and strengthening of the inter-American collective security system is of even greater significance with regard to self-defense. Prior to the aforementioned

decision by the Ninth Meeting of Consultation, the Eighth Meeting
had already urged the member states to take those steps that they
might consider appropriate for their individual or collective self-
defense to counteract the threats or acts of aggression, subversion,
or other dangers to peace and security resulting from the continued
intervention in this hemisphere of Sino-Soviet powers. This broadening of the sphere of validity of self-defense appears once again
in paragraph 5 of Resolution I of the Ninth Meeting, now however
considerably more definite and precise than in paragraph 3 of Resolution II of the Eighth Meeting. The importance of these two
resolutions, along with the one adopted during the October crisis,
can be appreciated completely only when one recalls the initiatives
and efforts that have been made in the United Nations, with little
positive result, to extend the sphere of application of self-defense
beyond the case of armed attack expressly set forth in the Charter
of that organization and in the Rio Treaty.

The action taken by the Council of the OAS acting provisionally
as Organ of Consultation during the so-called October crisis, as was
mentioned above, was due not to the existence of an armed attack
but to a fact or situation which might at any time become "an active
threat to the peace and security of the Continent." Aside from this,
it is interesting to note that the Organ of Consultation did not
"agree" to apply certain measures, which is what it does when it
acts, exclusively, in accordance with Article 8 of the treaty. This
time it resolved "To recommend to the member states" that they
take certain individual and collective measures, including armed force,
which they deemed necessary. This action by the Organ of Consultation falls more within the province of Article 6 which specifies
in general terms "the measures which should be taken for the common defense and for the maintenance of the peace and security of the
Continent."

The October 23 resolution, as well as Resolution I of the Ninth
Meeting, present other equally important aspects as far as the development and strengthening of the regional collective security
system is concerned. Although the use of the right of self-defense
need not be authorized by the international organ that has jurisdiction over the individual or collective measures taken in this regard,
nothing prevents that organ from examining the need for and advisability of the action in the face of a fact or situation which threatens
the peace or political independence of the member states, nor from
"recommending" to them the adoption of measures of self-defense.
In the case of regional agencies, this type of action may be the only
way to achieve the effective functioning of the collective security
system. Thus, for example, when faced with facts or situations that
might require the use of armed force, as occurred during the October

crisis or can occur in the supposition mentioned in paragraph 5 of Resolution I of the Ninth Meeting, the regional agency cannot use it or any other "enforcement action," as a collective action or measure, pursuant to Article 53 of the U.N. Charter, without authorization by the Security Council. Such authorization would naturally be subject to the unanimous consent of all the permanent members of that Council.

Therefore, the importance of the resolutions in reference is obvious since they have opened a new path which will surely make it possible to avert other acts, facts, or situations that result from the continued intervention of the international communist movement in America, just as effectively as the October 23 resolution did. Since World War II, armed attack is not the most common form of aggression and it is the different forms of so-called "indirect aggression" which constitute the most constant and serious danger to the security and preservation of the political institutions of the countries of the free world. For this reason the Organ of Consultation has believed that the resort to self-defense to avert that danger within the regional collective security system may be necessary and perfectly justifiable. Bear in mind the fact that neither the Rio Treaty nor the U.N. Charter created self-defense; they merely recognized this right, and in so doing they took into consideration what then appeared to be its only justification: armed attack. In contrast with reprisals, whose incompatibility with post-war instruments no one can seriously doubt when they involve the use of force, self-defense continues to be an institution of general international law, and in so recognizing it the said instruments have also regulated its use. This recognition is due to the fact that, even more than in regard to internal order, the international organization is not yet sufficiently effective to be able to guarantee the territorial integrity or political independence of a state that is the victim of aggression.

As a logical corrollary of the foregoing, it must also be admitted that the degree to which the use of self-defense is authorized must be in direct relation to the effectiveness of the collective security system. In effect, granted the function of self-defense within this system, it would be unreasonable to place restrictions on its use, even though they were formally specified in applicable instruments, if such restrictions were inconsistent with the essential purpose and *raison d'être* of the collective security system. To be precise, it would be sufficient to require the state or states in the exercise of self-defense to do so in a manner compatible with the provisions of the said instruments and with the rules of general international law that govern this institution.

Turning now to the pacific settlement of disputes, it is evident that the institutional development and strengthening the inter-

American system has undergone in the field of collective security is not appreciated. In contrast with the noteworthy labors of the Inter-American Peace Committee and those of the Organ of Consultation on the many occasions when it has achieved the pacific settlement of a dispute, the instruments and machinery of peace still suffer from certain gaps and deficiencies. This subject was included among the Nine Points regarding the Strengthening of the Inter-American System, which Dr. José A. Mora, Secretary General of the OAS, submitted for consideration by the Council of the Organization in October 1964, and covered more adequately in his report of April 14, 1965, to the Second Special Inter-American Conference. His premise is that despite the categorical manner in which the OAS Charter sets forth the obligation to submit all international controversies that arise between American states to the pacific procedures established therein, and the fact that at the same Bogotá Conference the "special treaty" was signed which established these procedures in order that "no dispute between American States shall fail of definitive settlement within a reasonable period," it is undeniable that, viewed in the light of a modern system of pacific settlement, the inter-American system is somewhat insufficient and ineffective and that this can and must be corrected.

In the Secretary General's opinion this can be seen, first of all, from the fact that the abovementioned "special treaty"—the American Treaty on Pacific Settlement (Pact of Bogotá)—has been ratified by only nine states. The lack of ratifications clearly indicates that the Pact of Bogotá is unacceptable to the majority of the member states, although not always for the same reasons. The attempts to revise it corroborate this fact and, furthermore, reveal that several states are willing to make the necessary effort to achieve a formula which will make the pact acceptable to all the non ratifying states. A renewal of these attempts would seem highly desirable since, at the present time, conditions are much more favorable for arriving at satisfactory results.

However, even though the Pact of Bogotá were to be fully in effect, the problem would not necessarily be completely resolved. There are certain types of controversy, or in a controversy certain special circumstances may exist, for which the pact may not provide the best solution. In effect this system of settlement only foresees the participation of the parties directly concerned and, therefore, reserves to them the power of setting in motion the methods and procedures established by this instrument. What is lacking is the machinery that will permit states not parties to a controversy but with special and justifiable interest in its solution because of their status as members of the regional community, or an inter-American organ charged with keeping vigilance over the maintenance of pacific relations between the states, to set in motion the method or procedure that will lead to a solution of the controversy.

To be exact, this is rather a defect of the present inter-American peace system, by reason of its not having developed in accordance with the essential purpose of the OAS Charter, particularly in regard to the second point, since competence of that kind has not been conferred on any of the organs of the inter-American system. In the U.N. Charter, on the other hand, there exists machinery which permits the international agency to urge the parties to settle their controversies by pacific means and even to recommend the procedures or methods of settlement it considers most appropriate, regardless of whether or not the interested parties request its assistance and whenever such controversies endanger international peace and security.

It cannot be denied, however, that the deficiency in the system of pacific settlement foreseen in the OAS Charter has been overcome in part. The Inter-American Treaty of Reciprocal Assistance not only attempts to provide reciprocal aid in the event of acts or threats of aggression but also "to assure peace, through adequate means." Some of the facts or situations contemplated by the Rio Treaty can constitute controversies that might be settled by recourse to one of the methods or procedures of pacific settlement. Therefore, in cases of facts or situations of this nature, the Organ of Consultation has had recourse to different methods or procedures. As an illustration, witness two of the most recent applications of the Rio Treaty. In one of these, the Dominican-Haitian case, the Organ of Consultation authorized the members of its Committee "to make an on-the-spot study of the situation . . . and to offer the parties their services for the purpose of finding a prompt solution to the conflict and to ward off the threats to the peace and security of the area." In the conflict between Panama and the United States, the Organ of Consultation created a General Committee on which it conferred the following attributes, among others: "to assist the parties in their search for a fair solution [of the conflict] and to submit a report to the Organ of Consultation." It will be noted that on occasion the competent organ in the field of collective security has taken the initiative in promoting the pacific settlement of certain controversies through the methods and procedures foreseen in the Charter and has even offered its services to this end. Nevertheless, if the inter-American system of pacific settlement were not deficient, as has been mentioned, surely the parties would have refrained from requesting the application of the Rio Treaty and the recourse to the machinery for collective security would have been avoided.

The Inter-American Peace Committee has also helped to overcome the deficiencies of the system of pacific settlement to a certain extent. In view of the fact that this committee was created to keep "constant vigilance to insure that States between which any dispute exists or may arise, of any nature whatsoever, may solve it as quickly as possible," its contribution would surely have been even more productive if its competence had not been subordinated to "the prior consent of the Parties" as was done in 1956 when the present Statutes were adopted. These Statutes also reserved to the states "directly concerned" in a dispute or controversy the power of requesting its action, in contrast to the original Statutes according to which the Committee could act at the request of any American state, whether or not it was a directly interested party or a member of the Committee. In this regard, the observations made by the Committee itself in its Report to the Fifth Meeting of Consultation should be recalled. These observations, expressly shared by several delegations at that meeting, showed a very justified concern over the return to that agency of the competence which had allowed it to perform such valuable work during the period when its activities were governed by its former Statutes.

This is, in fact, a fundamental question. How can the Committee be expected to keep constant vigilance to ensure that states between which any dispute or controversy exists or may arise shall solve it as quickly as possible, as both Resolution XIV of the Second Meeting of Consultation (1940) and the Statutes stipulate, when its activities are subject to the prior consent of the parties directly concerned? Furthermore, in view of the fact that the valuable and productive work of the Committee has been due not only to its permanent character but also, and more importantly, to the power to promote a pacific settlement which has permitted it to assist the parties to find adequate methods of settlement, how can the Committee be expected to continue this task when its competence is subject to that condition? In order to assure the effectiveness of the Committee, it is necessary to authorize it once again to act at the request of any American state, whether or not it is directly concerned in a dispute or controversy.

With further reference to these considerations, the Secretary General adds in his Report that it will also be important to link the Committee more closely and directly to the OAS Council, without this constituting a loss or limitation of its autonomy. In accordance with its present Statutes the Committee shall duly inform the Council of its activities and the results of its efforts. In fact, what would prevent the Council from utilizing the Committee when a controversy or matter susceptible of solution by methods or procedures of pacific settlement is brought before it, and when it considers the Committee an appropriate organ? The Council's lack of competence in the field of pacific settlement can easily be overcome. As in the case of the powers and attributes conferred on the Council by the Sixth, Eighth, and Ninth Meetings of Consultation in the field of collective security—a field in which the fundamental or political problem is considerably accentuated—it would be sufficient for the inter-American conference to modify the Statutes to this end.

In brief, the inter-American system of pacific settlement has not yet reached the degree of development required by the principle set forth in the Charter that "no dispute between American States shall fail of definitive settlement within a reasonable period." Therefore, this system cannot, in every case, be the proper vehicle through which every effort shall be made "to achieve pacific settlement of local disputes," in accordance with Article 52 of the U.N. Charter. Obviously, a revision of the system is necessary and cannot be postponed. Particularly for those controversies that by their very nature or by the circumstances in which they occur are susceptible of becoming conflicts or situations that affect peace or the good relations among American states, the strengthening of the present machinery would appear to be unavoidable. If this has been done with regard to the system of collective security, and obstacles of a political nature much greater than those now faced have been overcome, there is no way of justifying the failure to put forth this new effort.

In a report to the Second Special Inter-American Conference, the Inter-American Peace Committee itself once again draws attention to the need for reestablishing its competence to act at the request of the parties or of any American state and, furthermore, to report to the OAS Council regarding situations that can affect the peace of America. To this end, it proposes the corresponding modifications in the Statutes of 1956. The Committee, according to the report, "complements the Inter-American Treaty of Reciprocal Assistance in a very useful way. Strengthening it will avoid the anomaly of having available only one instrument of collective security and of its having to be utilized for the functions of good offices, mediation, and conciliation." The controversy over the use of the waters of the Lauca River should be pointed out as a prime example of this point since the Committee could have taken action in this case had its former Statutes still been in effect.

In order to complete this review and evaluation of the inter-American peace and security system it only remains to add a few observations regarding the more interesting political-juridical and institutional aspects of the recent action by the OAS in the Dominican situation. This, of course, refers to the collective action undertaken toward the end of April and later continued with the consent of the Provisional Government, and not to the unilateral action that preceded it, which cannot be justified in the light of the instruments that rule the inter-American system. In this connection it may still be thought that the close relationship between these two actions denatures the collective action in the sense that it converts it into an attempt to "legitimatize", so to speak, a unilateral action which is incompatible with the aforementioned instruments. Viewed from another angle, however, politically and even juridically speaking, the question arises as to what might have been the consequences of a unilateral action which was not replaced and surpassed by a subsequent collective action. In other words, in contrast to the idea of pure and simple "legitimization" is the concept of an action by an international organization putting an end to an action which is incompataible with the principles governing that organization in order that it can perform its functions and assure the achievement of its objectives. The brief observations which follow part from this second concept.

Above all, it must be emphasized that in its origin and initial phases the Dominican situation constituted a wholly internal civil struggle. This, then, is the first time inter-American organs have attempted to find a pacific solution for the type of conflict which has traditionally been barred to collective action. This makes even more significant the action taken by the OAS Council when the revolutionary movement occurred. With no mention of the old problem of its lack of competence to deal with matters of a political nature, the Council took the first measures to attain an immediate cease-fire and the eventual reestablishment of peace and normality. It also decided to inform the United Nations Security Council, in accordance with Article 54 of the U.N. Charter, of the initiatives it was taking.

The action by the Meeting of Consultation reveals even more interesting aspects of the general development and strengthening of the inter-American system. In the first place, without acting as Organ of Consultation the Tenth Meeting made and carried out decisions, particularly of a political and military nature, which imply an exercise of powers not explicitly granted it in Article 39 of the Charter. In accordance with a literal interpretation of Article 39 the Meeting would have had to limit itself to "considering" the situation as a problem "of an urgent nature and of common interest to the American States." Nor would it be sufficient to mention the fact, brought out in Chapter II, that the Meetings of Consultation have been exercising the same kind of competence that the Charter assigns to the "supreme organ", the Inter-American Conference. There is no explanation, therefore, other than that once again one of the principal political organs of the system has exercised functions and powers inherent to it, when faced with the need to assure the achievement of the essential objectives contained in the Charter of Bogotá.

The action by the OAS in the Dominican situation has also had important repercussions on the functions and attributes of the Secretary General. Article 83.*f* of the Charter, specifying among the functions of the Pan American Union those "entrusted to it by the Inter-American Conference, and the Meeting of Consultation of Ministers of Foreign Affairs," sets no limits. Thus, when in its resolution of May 20, 1965 the Tenth Meeting of Consultation named the Secretary General as its Representative, it conferred on him the authority previously granted to the Special Committee it had named on May 1, and ordered him specifically "To offer his good offices to the parties in conflict, with a view to the establishment of a climate of peace and conciliation that will permit the functioning of democratic institutions in the Dominican Republic." By resolution of May 22 the Tenth Meeting requested him to work out, with the military commanders of the Inter-American Peace Force just established, the technical measures necessary to establish a Unified Command of the OAS. In a June 2 resolution, creating an Ad Hoc Committee "To continue the task begun by the Special Committee and now being carried out by the Secretary General," the Tenth Meeting enlarged the mandate to include the "economic and social recovery" of the country.

This Chapter cannot be concluded without at least a brief reference to certain aspects of the ties and connections between the inter-American system of peace and security and that of the United Nations, revealed by the Dominican case. In the examination in Chapter X of the practice of the U.N. organs in the face of requests by member states to take up cases already under study by the competent regional organization, it was possible to observe the degree to which the Security Council in this case departed from what had until then been a fairly consistent practice. It is not a question of ignoring the functions and powers which the U.N. Charter confers on the said organs or the recognized right of every member state, whether or not it is a member of a regional organization, to have recourse to those organs even regarding matters susceptible of regional action. However, if Chapter VIII of the U.N. Charter, which authorizes and regulates regional action, has any meaning and objective it is precisely that of allowing the states members of regional agencies to comply with the obligation of making every possible effort to achieve the pacific settlement of local controversies through those agencies.

It is evident that nothing in the Dominican case justified the Security Council's intervention. On May 14, date on which that Council invited the Secretary-General to send a representative and called upon all concerned in the Dominican Republic to cooperate with that representative in the carrying out of this task, the inter-American mechanism had been set in motion and the Tenth Meeting had already named a Special Committee. This explains why the Special Committee, in its second report to the Meeting, expressed its concern over the terms of the Security Council resolution, "With all the more reason since this was the first time such an interference between the world agency of the United Nations and our regional Organization of American States had been recorded, at a time when the representation entrusted to the Special Committee was taking a most significant step toward the solution that America was waiting for." In marked contrast with this declaration is the statement made to the press by the United Nations Secretary-General some days later, to the effect that the peace action undertaken by the OAS might establish "an embarrassing precedent" since the League of Arab States or the Organization of African Unity might invoke similar rights.

Up to now the Security Council had observed the norm laid down in paragraph 3 of Article 52 of the Charter, according to which that organ "shall encourage the development of pacific settlement of local disputes through such regional arrangements or by such regional agencies either on the initiative of the states concerned or by reference from the Security Council." By its departure from this norm it is evident that the Council brought about the simultaneous action of two international organizations and with it a situation ostensibly unfavorable to the common objective of maintaining international peace and security. The Council might well, as it had repeatedly done in the past, have allowed time for the regional action to produce results, above all bearing in mind that some results had already been obtained and that, on the same date as its decision, the danger of this situation really affecting international peace and security had been averted. The provisions of the U.N. Charter, as well as those of inter-American instruments and of other regional instruments, establish a concurrent jurisdiction of the world organization and the regional agency, which should be exercised in accordance with the particular circumstances in each case. In order to avoid the potential inconvenience of simultaneous action, it is necessary for the United Nations organs to abstain from exercising their functions and powers when their intervention is premature and unjustifiable.

PART THREE

Economic and Social Cooperation

The promotion, "by cooperative action," of the economic, social, and cultural development of the American states is one of the purposes set forth in the OAS Charter. That Charter also establishes the principles and procedures that regulate inter-American cooperation in this field. The Alliance for Progress program formally agreed on at Punta del Este, however, considerably developed and strengthened both the principles and the institutional framework established by the Bogotá Conference. The following four chapters contain a description and general evaluation of this important sphere of activity of the inter-American system, including the process of economic integration taking place among the Latin American countries.

Chapter XII

The Alliance For Progress, New Concept of Inter-American Solidarity and Democracy

The Alliance for Progress is not just a current expression of inter-American solidarity in the economic and social fields; it also represents a new concept of democracy. These two concepts merged with each other after a relatively brief time lapse, which culminated in the Declaration and the Charter of Punta del Este. The purpose of this Chapter is to study the historic process preceding the Alliance.

38. *Operation Pan America (1958) and the Act of Bogotá (1960)*

The present action program for the economic and social development of Latin America is the inevitable result of a number of factors and powerful political and ideological forces, which sometimes differ from the forces and factors that determined the concept of development characteristic of the postwar period.

As has been shown in a recent document, from a purely economic standpoint, the problem of development in this region became evident during the middle of the 1950's. Latin America emerged from the Second World War virtually unscathed physically, with a much higher capacity for production than it had before the war, and with enormous international reserves. A rise in prices of imports after the war tended to reduce the purchasing power of accumulated international assets, but, on the other hand, the great demand for food and raw materials tended to raise export prices and income in foreign exchange. At the same time, the resumption of private investments helped to provide funds for increasing capital formation, production, income, and consumption. During the 1950-1955 period, the Latin American economies grew at an average annual rate of 4.8% which was higher than that of any other part of the world, except Western Europe, Japan, and the western part of Asia.

During the middle of the 1950's, Latin America's economic expansion came to a grinding halt. The decline of export prices and the deterioration of the terms of trade, along with the declining rate of savings and investments slowed economic growth, while population pressures continued unabated. These cracks in the economic foundations of Latin America's development revealed the existence of an antiquated, unhealthy social structure that was undermining material progress and presenting a constant hazard to social stability. In these circumstances, a radical transformation in the approach to Latin American development began to take shape, leading to the presentation of Operation Pan America in 1958 and the signing of the Act of Bogotá in 1960, and culminating in 1961 with the Charter of Punta del Este, which formally established the Alliance for Progress.[1]

The Alliance for Progress, therefore, is an action program agreed upon and put into effect only relatively recently. But although, in the words of the Charter of Punta del Este, it was conceived as "a great cooperative effort to accelerate the economic and social development of the participating countries of Latin America," it represents, in turn, the culmination of principles and commitments set forth in the Charter of the Organization of American States. Among these provisions, Article 26 states that: "The Member States agree to cooperate with one another, as far as their resources may permit and their laws may provide, in the broadest spirit of good neighborliness, in order to strengthen their economic structure, develop their agriculture and mining, promote their industry and increase their trade."[2]

The Alliance stems most directly from the aggregate of measures taken during the five-year period preceding the Charter of Punta del Este.[3] It was the process required, both to define the real objectives of inter-American cooperation in this field and to establish the machinery to make their attainment possible. To a certain extent, both aspects of the question were brought up at the Meeting of Ministers of Finance or of Economy, held in Quitandinha (Petropolis, Brazil 1954). At this meeting, it was formally stated that a massive investment of foreign capital was needed, with a goal of a billion dollars a year, most of which should come from international credit institu-

---

[1] Cf. *Report of the Secretary General of the Organization of American States to the Second Special Inter-American Conference,* OEA/Ser.E/XIII.1, Doc. 16, vol. II Rev., 14 April 1965, p. 4.

[2] It is interesting to recall that one of the objectives of the First Inter-American Conference (1889–1990) was "to preserve and promote the prosperity" of the American states. Cf. *International Conferences* (1889–1928), p. 5. Since then this desire and this purpose have constantly appeared in the inter-American conferences and meetings, often in the form of concrete recommendations and drafts. *Ibid.,* and 1st and 2nd Sups., *passim.*

[3] In spite of the declared purposes of the Economic Agreement of Bogotá (1948) its relation to the program of the Alliance is quite remote, not only chronologically but also from the point of view of the conception and goals of the development program. Also, the numerous and important reservations attached to the Agreement at the time of signature finally made it inoperative. The complete text of the Agreement appears in *International Conferences,* 2nd Sup. (1942–1954), p. 213.

tions.[4] No agreement was reached at this meeting, nor at the Economic Conference of Buenos Aires in 1957, where it was decided to continue studying the proposal.[5] The following year, the General Secretariat of the OAS published its study on financing the economic development of Latin America, emphasizing that for this purpose, it was necessary to establish a regional institution with a capital of 2 to 3.5 billion dollars.[6]

The establishment of the Inter-American Development Bank (IDB) was the result of this action. After it became known that the United States was willing to participate in negotiating an instrument to establish an inter-American financing institution, the IA-ECOSOC appointed a specialized committee, whose work was concluded on April 8, 1959 with the signing of the agreement establishing the IDB.[7] In December 1960, four Central American republics signed another agreement, with a view to establishing the Central American Bank for Economic Integration, which would have an authorized capital of 16 million dollars and would give preference to the financing of projects designed to promote economic integration, and would pay special attention to investments in infrastructure and regional industries.[8]

Paralleling these initiatives and accomplishments were others whose content and objectives were much more vast. In general, these objectives stem from "Operation Pan America", whose nature, characteristics, and basic aims are set forth in an *Aide-Memoire,* presented to the American governments by the Government of Brazil in August 1958. This document states that Operation Pan America, proposed by President Juscelino Kubitschek "is not an undertaking limited by time, with objectives to be attained in a short period; rather it is a reorientation of hemispheric policy, intended to place Latin America, by a process of full appraisement, in a position to participate more effectively in the defense of the West, with a growing sense of vitality and a greater development of its capacities. Thus,

---

[4] *Cf.* Resolutions Approved at the Meeting of Ministers of Finance or Economy as the IV Extraordinary Meeting of the Inter-American Economic and Social Council, November 22–December 2, 1954, Brazil, ESSE—Doc. 184/54, 2 December 1954.

[5] *Cf. Final Act* of the Economic Conference of the OAS, August 15–September 4, 1957, Conferences and Organizations Series No. 58, Washington, D.C., Pan American Union.

[6] *Cf. Financing of Economic Development in Latin America,* ES-Doc. 30/58, Washington, D.C., Pan American Union, 1958.

[7] Regarding the structure and functions of the IDB see Chapter XIII, 42, *infra.* The complete text of the Agreement Establishing the IDB appears in *Appendix 16,* p. 407, *infra.*

[8] Regarding this and other organs of the Central American Common Market see Chapter XV, 54, *infra.*

Operation Pan America is more than a mere program; it is an entire policy." From another standpoint, it "is conceived as involving the joint action of the twenty-one republics of the Western Hemisphere, the preservation of its strictly multilateral nature being indispensable. Bilateral matters will continue to be handled through the channels normally followed in such cases, without becoming part of the aforesaid Operation."

The basic objectives of Operation Pan America are listed as follows: 1. Reaffirmation of the principle of hemispheric solidarity; 2. Recognition of underdevelopment as a problem of common interest; 3. Adaptation of inter-American organs and agencies, if necessary, to the requirements of more dynamic action to carry on the struggle against underdevelopment; 4. Technical assistance for increased productivity; 5. Measures to stabilize the market for basic commodities; 6. Adaptation to present needs and expansion of the resources of international financial institutions; 7. Reaffirmation of private initiative in the struggle against underdevelopment; and 8. Revision by each country, where necessary, of its fiscal and economic policy, for the purpose of assuring means to promote economic development.[9]

The political aspects of development were carefully considered at the Fifth and Seventh Meetings of Consultation of Ministers of Foreign Affairs, held, respectively, in Santiago, Chile, in August 1959, and in San José, Costa Rica, in August 1960. At the first, it was stated that "the stability of democracy, the safeguarding of human rights, the security of the hemisphere, and its preservation from the dangers that threaten the liberty and the independence of the American republics make necessary an increase in economic cooperation among them, in order to raise the standard of living of a rapidly expanding population."[10] For its part, the Seventh Meeting declared that "the elimination of economic underdevelopment, a collective responsibility of the member states, is essential to the attainment of the political and social stability of the hemisphere" and that "it is necessary to intensify inter-American economic cooperation by a substantial increase of existing resources and the improvement and adaptation of the agencies devoted to the said cooperation, or the possible creation of new ones appropriate to the urgent problems of underdevelopment."[11] Both resolutions recommended that the American

[9] Cf. "Operation Pan America" and the Work of the Committee of 21, OEA/Ser. X/3.1.1, 15 August 1960, in which are included the three aide-memoire presented by the Government of Brazil.

[10] See the complete text of Resolution XI, Economic Underdevelopment and Preservation of Democracy, in Final Act of the Fifth Meeting of Consultation, OEA/Ser. C/II.5, p. 12.

[11] See the complete text of Resolution VII, Economic Underdevelopment and Political Instability, in Final Act of the Seventh Meeting of Consultation, OEA/Ser. C/II.7, p. 8.

governments promptly take steps to intensify inter-American co-operation in the struggle against underdevelopment.

To consider the objectives of Operation Pan America and the recommendations of the Meetings of Consultation referred to above, as well as the methods and instruments necessary to attain them, the OAS Council, at a meeting attended by the Ministers of Foreign Affairs of the 21 republics, resolved to establish a "Special Committee to Study the Formulation of New Measures for Economic Co-operation" ("Committee of 21"). The Committe held three meetings: in Washington (November-December 1958); Buenos Aires (April-May 1959); and Bogotá (September 1960), as a result of which the Council adopted 50 resolutions.[12] The most far-reaching of these is the "Act of Bogotá", which incorporated the proposal of the United States for establishing an inter-American program for social development.

Among the common objectives of the American peoples, the Act of Bogotá placed social progress at the fore. In this respect, it recognized that the impact of economic development programs on social welfare may be long delayed, and that, consequently, prompt measures should be taken to meet social needs. The Act, therefore, recommends the establishment of an "inter-American program for social development," oriented toward agrarian and fiscal or tax reforms, improvement of housing, community services, health, and education, and an increase in the mobilization of national resources.[13]

These events necessarily brought with them important changes in the mechanism of cooperative action. The Act of Bogotá itself recommended changes in the Inter-American Economic and Social Council (IA-ECOSOC) to strengthen the inter-American system in the field of economic and social cooperation. It also established a special fund for social development, which would contribute capital resources and technical assistance on flexible terms and conditions, as a means of supporting the efforts of the Latin American countries that planned to initiate or expand institutional improvements. To the fund the United States contributed 500 million dollars, of which 394 million would be administered by the IDB, 100 million would be used by the Agency for International Development, and 6 million would be placed at the disposal of the Pan American Union, the General Secretariat of the OAS.

The Secretary General of the OAS took various measures so that

---

[12] *Cf.* Document cited in Note 9, *passim.* See also the verbatim minutes of the special meeting of the OAS Council on July 8, 1959, OEA/Ser. G./II, C-a-331, p. 125, and the regular meeting on October 11, 1960, OEA/Ser. G/ II, C-a-387, p. 36.

[13] The complete text of the Act of Bogotá appears in *Appendix 17*, p. 437, *infra.*

the Organization would be in a position to perform the tasks with which it had been entrusted. One of those steps was the invitation to the directors of the specialized organizations to discuss coordinated action to fulfill the aims of the Act of Bogotá. Another was to appoint an advisory committee on economic and social affairs to determine the important problems of organization and administration that had to be solved in order to provide instruments and mechanisms for carrying out the inter-American program for economic and social cooperation. The report submitted by the committee was presented for consideration to the Special Meeting of Senior Government Representatives to Strengthen the IA-ECOSOC, which was held at the Pan American Union from November 28 to December 9, 1960. During this meeting, the Secretary General announced the establishment of a mechanism to assure coordination at the highest secretariat level between the OAS, the IDB, and the Economic Commission for Latin American (ECLA), that is, the Ad Hoc Committee on Cooperation. Finally, to strengthen the General Secretariat and to enable it to assume its new responsibilities, organizational changes were made in the Pan American Union, and the post of the Assistant Secretary for Economic and Social Affairs was established.

The next stage in the process being discussed came with the address delivered by the late President Kennedy on March 13, 1961, when he called upon all the peoples of the hemisphere to join in a new *Alliance for Progress,* "a vast cooperative effort, unparalleled in magnitude and nobility of purpose, to satisfy the basic needs of the American people for homes, work and land, health and schools." The plan would extend over a period of ten years and involve an investment of several billion dollars. A few weeks later, the United States made a formal proposal to the Council of the OAS that a Special Meeting of the IA-ECOSOC at the Ministerial Level be convoked. At its meeting of May 31, the Council adopted the agenda of the special meeting, which had been drawn up with the cooperation of experts appointed by the Secretary General, who were also responsible for preparing the documents and reports that served as a basis for the discussions. The meeting took place from August 5 to 17, in Punta del Este, Uruguay, where the Charter formally establishing the Alliance for Progress was adopted.

39. *The Declaration and Charter of Punta del Este (1961)*

At Punta del Este, besides the Charter formally establishing the Alliance for Progress, a "Declaration to the Peoples of America" was adopted.[14] This Declaration states: "This Alliance is established

---

[14] The complete text of both instruments appears in *Appendix 18,* p. 443, *infra.*

on the basic principle that free men working through the institution
of representative democracy can best satisfy man's aspirations, including those for work, home and land, health and schools. No system
can guarantee true progress unless it affirms the dignity of the individual which is the foundation of our civilization." Consequently, the
signatory countries bound themselves, on the one hand, "to improve
and strengthen democratic institutions through application of the
principle of self-determination by the people," and on the other, "to
accelerate economic and social development, thus rapidly bringing
about a substantial and steady increase in the average income in
order to narrow the gap between the standard of living in Latin
American countries and that enjoyed in the industrialized countries."
Within the same frame of reference, the Preamble of the Charter
declares: "We, the American Republics, hereby proclaim our decision to unite in a common effort to bring our people accelerated
economic progress and broader social justice within the framework
of personal dignity and political liberty."

On these bases, the Declaration of Punta del Este and, with more
detail and precision, the Charter formulate a ten-year program of
action for the economic and social development of Latin America.
In broad terms, the objectives of this program are as follows: to
achieve a rate of economic growth of no less than 2.5% per year
per capita and more equitable distribution of national income; to
diversify national economic structures, especially through industrialization; to increase considerably agricultural productivity and production through comprehensive agrarian reform and improved storage, transportation, and marketing services; to increase resources from
the external sector of the economics by maintaining stable prices for
basic export products, undertaking programs to avoid excessive fluctuations in the foreign exchange receipts from exports, and strengthening economic integration agreements, with a view to achieving a
Latin American common market; and to adopt a broad social welfare program in the fields of education, health, and housing.

In Title II, the Charter sets forth certain "basic requirements" for
accomplishing these ends. The first two of these are "that comprehensive and well-conceived national programs of economic and social
development, aimed at the achievement of self-sustaining growth,
be carried out in accordance with democratic principles" and that
these national programs or plans "be based on the principle of self-
help—as established in the Act of Bogotá—and on the maximum
use of domestic resources, taking into account the special conditions
of each country." National plans should be directed specifically toward improvement of human resources; the development of natural
resources; strengthening of the agricultural base; agrarian reform;
tax reform; the mobilization of domestic resources; promotion of the

flow of foreign investments; and improvement of marketing systems. The Charter also contemplates "immediate and short-term action measures" as a supplement to national programs, for the purpose of completing projects already under way, initiating others designed especially to meet the most pressing economic and social needs, and facilitating the preparation or undertaking of long-term programs. The Charter further states that in working toward economic integration and complementary economies, efforts should be made to achieve an appropriate coordination of national plans, or to engage in joint planning for various economies through the existing regional integration organizations.

Another of the basic requirements set forth in the Charter of Punta del Este is that of external assistance. In this respect, the Declaration states: "This declaration expresses the conviction of the nations of Latin America that these profound economic, social, and cultural changes can come about only through the self-help efforts of each country. Nonetheless, in order to achieve the goals which have been established with the necessary speed, domestic efforts must be reinforced by essential contributions of external assistance." The Charter is even more explicit on the matter: "The economic and social development of Latin America will require a large amount of additional public and private financial assistance on the part of capital-exporting countries, including the members of the Development Assistance Group and international lending agencies." Both the Declaration and the Charter are referring, in particular, to the financial and technical assistance of the United States. It is stipulated that that country will provide most of the financing, amounting to at least 20 billion dollars, principally in public funds, during the decade of the 60's. The aid will take the form of subsidies or loans, with flexible terms and conditions.

In the report referred to at the beginning of this chapter, the Secretary General of the OAS pointed out the principal elements or aspects of the new approach to development, according to the documents and instruments discussed. The first is that the development of Latin America must be a multilateral effort. This means that the inter-American system must be strengthened so that it may be a more effective means by which the member states that have abundant resources may add their cooperation to the efforts carried out by the poorer countries, in the struggle to overcome their condition of underdevelopment. This is what the Latin American countries were convinced of when they recognized in the Charter of Punta del Este that the significant economic, social, and cultural changes must be based on the efforts of each country itself. As long as there exist in the Western Hemisphere vast differences of wealth between countries, this cooperation can be achieved most effectively through the multilateral instrument of the inter-American system, which serves to safeguard the sovereignty and interests of all the members alike. This protection cannot be achieved exclusively through bilateral channels, or through the formation of opposing blocs within the hemisphere.

Another important element in the new approach is that economic development and social progress must occur simultaneously. Experience of the last two decades clearly shows that economic development is not merely a matter of the accumulation of physical and financial capital; basically, it is a problem of human resources and of people's attitudes. So long as antiquated social structures persist, reflected in unequitable systems of land tenure, taxation, educational and employment opportunities, and income distribution, the possibilities for absorbing new technology and capital will remain limited, personal initiative will continue to be stifled, and the chances for sustained development will be severely curtailed. An essential part of the Alliance for Progress is that, through inter-American financial, technical, and economic cooperation, economic and social advances can be achieved simultaneously so that they may mutually reinforce each other.

The third important principle underlying the new approach to Latin American economic development is that it must be based on the formulation of comprehensive plans and on the initiation of effective planning procedures. In the final analysis, planning means nothing more than governing well. With limited resources and virtually unlimited needs, it is necessary to establish priorities and to adopt policies to mobilize and channel those resources toward the desired objectives. In this respect, planning is not just the formulation of a plan; also, and perhaps more importantly, it means the establishment of an administrative organization to execute the plan and constantly adjust or adapt it to changing needs and circumstances.

One more important aspect of the new approach to Latin American development is the need to assure substantial amounts of external financial assistance, largely from public sources, to supplement national efforts. Just as it is now recognized that private foreign investments cannot be the major source of external financing, although they play a key role in the development process, it is also apparent that public financial aid can be fully effective only if it is complemented by the mobilization of national resources and energies. However great the external financial aid, it cannot make a lasting contribution to the development of a country unless there are also the human resources, the administrative mechanisms, the local sources of financing, and, above all, the firm national will and determination to work for the development of the country.

Finally, it is today recognized that Latin America's potential development in the coming decades will depend to a large extent on its ability to expand and diversify its exports, to gain freer access to foreign markets, and to integrate its compartmentalized economies into a common market. Solution of the first problem not only requires elimination of present restrictions and discriminations against Latin America's traditional exports, but also measures to stimulate the export of manufactures and semimanufactures. These may include not only domestic measures to render such exports more competitive but also temporary preferential tariff treatment. As to economic integration, the acceleration of this process does not depend necessarily upon the establishment of new agencies. Rather, it depends, upon political willingness to achieve integration and upon the adoption of economic and social measures at the national level to produce a dynamic advance of the national economies. Without the strengthening of the national economies, it is very difficult to achieve the elimination of tariff barriers and exposure of the national industries to intraregional competition, as the European experience amply illustrates.[15]

In summary, Operation Pan America, the Act of Bogotá, and the Declaration and Charter of Punta del Este represent some of the decisive stages in a relatively rapid process that has seen the development and culmination of a new concept of inter-American solidarity. They are stages in which a great collective undertaking was outlined for the economic development and social improvement of Latin America, within the framework of democracy. In this respect, the Alliance for Progress proposes to carry forward an economic and social revolution that will put an end to antiquated and unjust economic, social, and institutional structures and redistribute the land and other wealth to raise the living standards of the people. But all this is to be done within the framework of respect for law, human rights, and fundamental freedoms, as well as the effective exercise of representative democracy, which the OAS Charter consecrates as essential principles and fundamental duties of the state. It was for this reason that the Declaration to the Peoples of America could declare that "the inter-American community is now beginning a new era when it will supplement its institutional, legal, cultural and social accomplishments with immediate and concrete actions to secure a better life, under freedom and democracy, for the present and future generations."

---

[15] *Cf.* Report cited in Note 1, pp. 4–6.

Chapter XIII

Institutional Framework of the Alliance

By its very nature as a "common" or "cooperative" enterprise, as the Charter of Punta del Este states, the Alliance for Progress cannot be carried out only through national development plans. The internal effort, including even the execution of the said plans and the attainment of external technical and financial assistance, require suitable multilateral machinery. It will be seen that the inter-American system is the institutional framework adopted at Punta del Este. Even though the international organization did not offer all the means and procedures necessary for complete achievement of the vast objectives of the Alliance, the intrinsic flexibility of the OAS Charter and the willingness of the American governments have made possible the required structural and functional changes.

40. *The Machinery Created at Punta del Este*

The Inter-American Economic and Social Council (IA-ECOSOC) is the central organ of the machinery created at Punta del Este. To achieve this there was no need to depart from the OAS Charter, in view of the functions and responsibilities it entrusts to the IA-ECOSOC in the field of economic and social cooperation. Article 63 establishes that this organ of the Council "has for its principal purpose the promotion of the economic and social welfare of the American nations through effective cooperation for the better utilization of their natural resources, the development of their agriculture and industry and the raising of the standards of living of their peoples." To accomplish this purpose, Article 64 *b* states that the IA-ECOSOC shall "Act as coordinating agency for all official inter-American activities of an economic and social nature." From an institutional point of view, even more important is Article 27 which states "If the economy of an American State is affected by serious conditions that cannot be satisfactorily remedied by its own unaided effort, such State may place its economic problems before the Inter-American Economic and Social Council to seek through consultation the most appropriate solution for such problems."

The system of consultation, essential element of the machinery of the Alliance for Progress, was instituted even prior to the Bogotá

219

Conference (1948); Resolution CVII of the Eighth Conference (Lima 1938) extended the method of consultation to any economic, cultural, or other question which, by reason of its importance, justified it and in the examination and solution of which the American states had common interest.[1] Also prior to Punta del Este is the resolution adopted on July 8, 1959 by the OAS Council, based on a draft submitted by the Special Committee to Study the Formulation of New Measures for Economic Cooperation ("Committee of 21"), according to which "should an American state find itself in the situation envisaged in Article 27 of the Charter of the Organization of American States, but one that because of its urgency and importance requires immediate attention on a higher level, it will be appropriate for it to request a Meeting of Consultation of Ministers of Foreign Affairs, as provided in Chapter XI of the aforesaid Charter, to consider the problem and to seek solutions thereto through inter-American cooperative action."[2] Although nothing prohibits consultation in the economic and social field from being carried out through an inter-American conference or a meeting of any other organ created in the future in which the Foreign Ministers take part, within the machinery created at Punta del Este it is the IA-ECOSOC, with its new structure, through which inter-American cooperation is carried out.

As indicated in the foregoing chapter, Punta del Este saw the culmination of the process of restructuring and strengthening both the IA-ECOSOC, begun more than a decade before, and the General Secretariat of the OAS, as far as the field of economic and social activities was concerned. Specifically, the IA-ECOSOC Statutes, approved by the OAS Council in 1950, contemplated an "annual" special meeting and provided that "For the purpose of securing the widest participation of the national authorities responsible for the execution of the programs of economic and social cooperation, the member states may accredit one Delegate each for that Special Meeting, together with Alternate Delegates and technical advisers, especially appointed." The special meeting was held from March 20 to April 10, 1950, and large, select delegations from the 21 American republics attended, some headed by the respective Ministers of Finance or Economy, as well as observers from United Nations, ECLA, FAO, and five inter-American agencies. The Meeting of Ministers of Finance or Economy, referred to in 1950, was later convoked by the Tenth Inter-American Conference (Caracas 1954) specifically for the purpose of being "the Fourth Extraordinary Meeting of the Inter-American

---

[1] See the complete text of Resolution XVII, Improvement in the Procedure of Consultation, in *International Conferences,* 1st Sup. (1933–1940), p. 307.

[2] *Cf. Decisions Taken at the Meetings of the Council of the OAS,* Volume XII, January–December 1959, OEA/Ser. G/III, vol. XII. Also see the verbatim minutes of the special meeting held on July 8, 1959, C-a-331, p. 135.

Economic and Social Council," and was held in Brazil in 1954.[3]

Within this process, the recommendations and measures that resulted from the third meeting of the Committee of 21 and the Special Meeting of Senior Government Representatives to Strengthen the IA-ECOSOC, held in Washington toward the end of 1960, constituted the decisive stage. Part IV of the Act of Bogotá, adopted by the Committee of 21, stated that considering "the need for providing instruments and mechanisms for the implementation of the program of inter-American economic and social cooperation which would periodically review the progress made and propose measures for further mobilization of resources," the committee recommended that the IA-ECOSOC undertake to organize "annual consultative meetings" which "should begin with an examination by experts and terminate with a session at the ministerial level." In accordance with the mandate in the Act, the Special Meeting in turn presented several recommendations which were later approved by the OAS Council. Among them were those relative to the two consecutive short meetings of the IA-ECOSOC foreseen in the Act, and the strengthening of the secretariat. Regarding the latter the Secretary General was to present to the Council a plan for the reorganization and strengthening of the activities and services of the General Secretariat in the field of economic and social activities adequate for the new mechanism.[4]

With regard to the annual IA-ECOSOC meetings, the Charter of Punta del Este only provides that that organ shall "review annually the progress achieved in the formulation, national implementation, and international financing of development programs," and submit appropriate recommendations to the OAS Council. One of the resolutions annexed to the Charter establishes the vehicle by which the "annual review of economic and social progress" is to be carried out, that is, the Annual Meeting of the IA-ECOSOC at the Ministerial Level. This meeting, as stated above, is to be preceded by another IA-ECOSOC meeting at the expert level. According to that same resolution "The purpose of the annual review is to analyze and discuss the social and economic progress achieved by member countries and the problems encountered in each country, to exchange opinions on possible measures that might be adopted to intensify further social and economic progress, to prepare reports on the outlook for the future, and to make such recommendations as may be considered appropriate on policies and measures of a general nature to pro-

---

[3] See the complete text of Resolution LXVI, Meeting of Ministers of Finance or Economy, in *International Conferences*, 2nd Sup. (1942–1954), p. 409.

[4] The complete text of the Act of Bogotá appears in *Appendix 17*, p. 437, *infra*. Regarding the recommendations of the Special Meeting see the Final Report, OEA/Ser. G/V, C-d-888, 16 December 1960.

mote further economic and social development, in accordance with the Act of Bogotá and the Charter of Punta del Este." This "process of confrontation", as it is called, is based on the reports presented by each country as well as on other working documents of an analytical and statistical nature prepared by the General Secretariat. The results of each annual review are to be summed up in a report issued by the meeting, covering the principal accomplishments and problems of economic and social development in Latin America, the future tasks that need emphasis, and the outlook for the area as a whole.[5]

The machinery created at Punta del Este includes other institutions and procedures in response to the specific goals and objectives of the program of the Alliance. One of these, the OAS-IDB-ECLA Tripartite Committee on Cooperation already existed in December 1960, and in the Charter it was only necessary to define its functions within the said program. Principal among these is the provision of technical assistance for the formulation of national development plans, at the request of the governments. What is entirely new, on the other hand, is the evaluation of national plans and the establishment, to this end, of the Panel of Nine experts, elected by the IA-ECOSOC at the suggestion of the OAS-IDB-ECLA Tripartite Committee. The Panel of Nine is annexed to the IA-ECOSOC but enjoys complete technical autonomy.

The evaluation of national programs is not obligatory. Each government may present a development plan for consideration by an ad hoc committee, composed of three members of the Panel of Nine and an equal number of experts not on the panel. The committee will study the development program, exchange opinions with the interested government as to possible modifications and, with its consent, report its conclusions to the IDB and to other governments and institutions that may be prepared to extend external financial and technical assistance in connection with the execution of the program. In considering a development program presented to' it, the ad hoc committee will examine its consistency with the principles of the Act of Bogotá and the Charter of Punta del Este. The recommendations of the ad hoc committee will be of great importance in determining the distibution of public funds under the Alliance.

Pursuant to another of the annexed resolutions, the Punta del Este meeting recommended that the OAS Secretary General immediately establish "task forces to undertake investigations and studies" and, drawing on the experiences of the member states, to prepare reports and adopt conclusions of a general nature for Latin America in the

---

[5] *Cf.* Official Documents Emanating from the Special Meeting of the IA-ECOSOC at the Ministerial Level, Punta del Este, Uruguay, August 1961, OEA/Ser. H/XII.1, Resolution D.

fields of education, land reform and agricultural development, and public health, that may serve as a basis for the member states in preparing their national development programs. The same resolution foresees the collaboration that non-American entities may provide the task forces. Two additional resolutions recommended the appointment of a committee to negotiate the elimination of restrictions on coffee consumption and maintained the Committee on Basic Products of the IA-ECOSOC.[6]

This then, in general terms, is the institutional framework of the Alliance for Progress established by the Charter and other instruments emanating from Punta del Este. Nevertheless, the experience acquired during these four years suggested certain changes and innovations. In spite of the fact that at times these involve important structural and functional changes and innovations, it has not been necessary to amend formally the OAS Charter. Once again, the notable adaptability of the inter-American system and the governments' desire to perfect and strengthen the multilateral machinery as required by the needs of Latin American development have been sufficient.

41. *Structure and Procedures of the Present Machinery*

Notwithstanding the importance of the changes and innovations referred to above, during the first four years of the Alliance there has been no need to introduce any substantial modifications in the machinery created at Punta del Este. In some respects, the Inter-American Committee for the Alliance for Progress (CIAP), which was created mainly to fill a certain institutional void produced by the long intervals between the annual IA-ECOSOC meetings, is an exception. With this in mind at the first annual meeting (Mexico, October 1962), the IA-ECOSOC decided to create immediately six special committees to meet during those intervals, analyze the information available regarding the march of the Alliance in the fields assigned to each one and report to the IA-ECOSOC during its meeting at the expert level.[7]

The CIAP was created by another IA-ECOSOC resolution, adopted at that same meeting, and by a later decision by the OAS Council. Two outstanding Latin Americans were assigned to study the structure and activities of the organizations and agencies of the inter-American system with responsibilities in regard to the Alliance and to recommend, if they considered it necessary, the required structural and procedural changes in that system so that the Alliance "may take

---

[6] *Ibid.,* Resolutions A.4, C.3, and C.7, respectively.

[7] *Cf. Final Report* of the First Annual Meeting of the IA-ECOSOC at the Ministerial Level, OEA/Ser.H/XII.4, p. 21.

on the efficiency and the dynamic qualities called for by the Charter of Punta del Este." These two individuals enjoyed complete autonomy in their labors and presented a report to the governments and to the IA-ECOSOC in order that it and the OAS Council might adopt the measures indicated. The two individuals chosen by the Council were former Presidents Juscelino Kubitschek (Brazil) and Alberto Lleras Camargo (Colombia), who presented their reports to the Council on June 15, 1963.[8]

As a contribution to the task entrusted to the two former Presidents, the Secretary General of the OAS prepared a memorandum in which he carefully examined not only the institutional question but also the substantive problems facing the Alliance.[9] The studies they presented were not limited to the institutional problem either. Although other problems evaluated by these three documents will be dealt with in a later chapter, their proposals coincided essentially with the idea of providing the IA-ECOSOC with a body which would function during the lapse between its annual meetings and, among other functions, would above all promote the execution of the policies laid down by it. Certain differences could be noted between the proposals, however, particularly with reference to the composition and competence of the new body.

With regard to the first, former President Lleras proposed that the said body be headed by a Chairman who, as an independent international officer, occupying an outstanding position, would act as co-ordinator of the Alliance. In this way, the Chairman would exercise nearly all the functions and attributes to be conferred on the new body, which were primarily related to the distribution of funds under the Alliance. Since this was a matter regarding which even the IA-ECOSOC itself lacked competence, the Secretary General had suggested that the Chairman be given the power to make recommendations, based on the recommendations the IA-ECOSOC presented to him. The former Presidents, on the other hand, proposed that that body be given broader competence, although neither of them defined the actual nature and scope. This may have been due to the very complexity of the subject, with its technical aspects derived from the different sources of external assistance, as well as political aspects which cannot be overlooked.[10]

---

[8] The IA-ECOSOC resolution appears in the report cited in Note 7, p. 24 and the OAS Council resolution in the decision taken at the meeting on November 20, 1962, OEA/Ser. G/III, C-sa-468.

[9] *The Dynamics of the Alliance and the Inter-American System.* This memorandum was presented to former Presidents Kubitschek and Lleras on December 13, 1962 and distributed at the meeting of the OAS Council on June 18, 1963.

[10] The reports of former Presidents Kubitschek and Lleras appear in OEA/Ser.G/V, C-d-1102 and 1103, respectively, both of June 15, 1963.

The former Presidents' studies and proposals were considered at the Second Annual Meeting of the IA-ECOSOC, held at São Paulo, Brazil, in November 1963. To aid in the deliberations the Secretary General of the Organization prepared another memorandum in which, after making a comparative analysis of the similarities, special characteristics, and differences between them, he presented "bases for discussion" harmonizing the structural and procedural changes in the inter-American system proposed by the former Presidents. In harmonizing these changes it was necessary to take into consideration technical, financial, juridical, institutional, and political factors relating to the feasibility and advisability of the proposals. The Secretary General also felt it desirable to call attention to certain questions and needs of the development of Latin America at that stage, which could not be ignored at the time a restructuring of the machinery of the Alliance was under consideration.[11] The São Paulo meetings also took note of a report prepared by the Panel of Nine, whose conclusions and proposals differed substantially, in some respects, from those of the former Presidents and the bases of discussion prepared by the General Secretariat.[12]

This explains why this subject received such detailed consideration particularly during the meeting at the expert level. Nevertheless, the difficulties would have been much greater if the idea of creating a new inter-American agency, entirely independent from the OAS, to carry out the program of the Alliance had not lost force by then. In his first memorandum the Secretary General pointed out that the idea was obviously unrealistic in that, among other things, it involved the danger of promoting an international technocracy, completely divorced from the national or regional political forces that alone are able to give reality and substance to the objectives of the Alliance.[13] The two former Presidents, for their part, had agreed on the advisability of creating a new body within the present institutional framework and as a part of and subordinate to the IA-ECOSOC. In contrast to the European experience at the end of the war, when the Organization of European Economic Cooperation was established, which was used to justify the creation of a new inter-American agency, there existed the basic structure of the OAS to carry out socio-economic cooperation. And in view of the need for the machinery of the Alliance to have sufficient autonomy to be able to carry

11 Cf. New Mechanism on the Alliance for Progress, OEA/Ser.H/X.4, CIES/344, 24 September 1963. To this memorandum is appended a comparative analysis of the similarities, special characteristics, and differences found in the reports of the two former Presidents.

12 Cf. Segundo Informe de la Nómina de los Nueve al CIES, 1° octubre 1962 a 30 septiembre 1963, OEA/Ser. H/X. 4, CIES/370, 19 octubre 1963.

13 See the document cited in Note 9, pp. 9–13.

out its objectives, it was appropriate to point out the fact, more obvious each day, of the development and strengthening of the IA-ECOSOC and the increasing expansion of its powers.

The idea, quite closely related to the foregoing one, that the new body of the IA-ECOSOC should be invested with "executive" functions and attributes was the only one that posed a problem during the discussions. This idea appeared in the Report by the Panel of Nine, mentioned above, and the delegations from certain countries shared and defended it. As has been stated, the proposals of the former Presidents were somewhat ambiguous on this point. In any case the new body was created "for the purpose of representing multilaterally the Alliance for Progress and, in the same way, coordinating and promoting its implementation in accordance with the Charter of Punta del Este, and of carrying out the mandates of this resolution and those it receives from the Council of the Organization of American States or the Inter-American Economic and Social Council."[14] This decision demonstrated that as regards the general development program for Latin America, the American governments were not yet ready to confer on international agencies functions and attributes that require the exercise of supranational powers. It must be admitted, however, that a proposal such as this was even less acceptable in view of the fact that not all the governments would be represented in the agency in question.

The foregoing in no way implies that the agency created at São Paulo, the CIAP, does not have important functions and attributes. On the contrary, certain duties and functions conferred on it, which the CIAP exercises "in keeping with the general orientation and lines of policy established by the Inter-American Economic and Social Council in its meetings at the ministerial level," were not even possessed by the IA-ECOSOC itself in accordance with former instruments. Perhaps the most significant example is the distribution of funds under the Alliance. In this respect, the CIAP is to make an annual estimate of the financing actually needed for Latin American development and of the total funds that may be available from the various domestic and external sources in addition to a continuing review of national and regional plans, steps taken, and efforts made within the framework of the Alliance, and to make specific recommendations to the members of the Alliance and to the regional organizations in the hemisphere concerning those plans, steps and efforts. On the basis of these estimates and reviews the CIAP will prepare and present annual proposals on the amount and sort of domestic resources each country would have to utilize to achieve the

---

[14] See the complete text of the IA-ECOSOC resolution that created CIAP in *Appendix 19*, p. 459, *infra.*

objectives of the Alliance, as well as proposals for determining the distribution among several countries of public funds under the Alliance, which contribute to the external financing of the general plans and specific programs for development.

The CIAP also has other duties and functions in relation to the work carried out by the IA-ECOSOC during its annual meetings, such as cooperating with each country and with the IDB or other financial agents in their negotiations to obtain external assistance; to coordinate those efforts which require multilateral action, such as economic integration; to review the programs and budgets of the OAS relative to all areas of economic and social cooperation, including the special funds. In this regard, the CIAP and its chairman were assigned important responsibilities by the Statutes of the new Special Development Assistance Fund, approved by the Third Annual Meetings of the IA-ECOSOC (Lima, December 1964).

This Special Fund has filled another important institutional gap in the machinery of the Alliance. As a "multilateral fund for financing the activities of the Alliance for Progress," as stated by its Statutes,[15] it has replaced the former system of subsidies and contributions made by the Government of the United States of America to the OAS. The activities thus financed are, among others, those of organizing or carrying out studies of general or specific problems connected to planning and development; conducting meetings of experts on these problems; providing technical assistance to the countries, as well as technical services for the preparation of feasibility studies on specific investment projects; conducting informational activities and programs to promote the Alliance; conducting training and other activities related to the Program of Technical Cooperation of the OAS. The Special Fund is to be administered under the authority of the IA-ECOSOC, which shall establish the general policy for its activities and operations, accept the pledges of voluntary contributions from the member states and approve the annual Program-Budget of the Fund. The Fund shall likewise be financed by special contributions in cash, personnel, equipment, materials, and services made by the governments of the member states and by contributions in cash or kind, from nonmember governments and from other sources, both private or public.

The Statutes confer the following duties and functions, among others, on the CIAP or its Chairman: to provide the Secretary General of the OAS with guidelines covering activities to be included in the Annual Program-Budget of the Fund, as well as criteria covering priorities; to review the said Program-Budget and present to the IA-ECOSOC its conclusions and recommendations without which

---

[15] See the complete text of the Statutes in *Appendix 20*, p. 464, *infra*.

no project can be submitted for its approval; to review the Annual Report on the operation of the Fund and present to the IA-ECOSOC its evaluation of these activities and recommendations for improving it; to advise the General Secretariat in the preparation of projects to be carried out and approve those in excess of $50,000. On the other hand, the Statutes assign to the Secretary General the responsibility, before the IA-ECOSOC, of administering the Fund and executing its activities. To this end he shall receive the contributions from the member states and other sources; issue the internal regulations of the Fund after consultation with the Chairman of the IA-ECOSOC; approve agreements relative to the operation of the Fund and, after consulting the Chairman, the draft Annual Program-Budget. Finally, the Statutes confer on the Executive Secretary of the CIAP, who also performs that function for the IA-ECOSOC, certain tasks and powers which he is to exercise under the direction of the Secretary General.

In summary then it should be stated that, in line with one of the most outstanding characteristics of the inter-American system, the development and strengthening of the machinery of the Alliance for Progress continue their course. In the Analysis of the March of the Alliance at the ministerial meeting in Lima, the IA-ECOSOC observed that "The work accomplished by CIAP in the short time since it was established is the best proof of how well advised IA-ECOSOC was to decide upon its creation, for it has given the Alliance the Latin American image and the multilateral significance that it needed." Nevertheless, one of the resolutions adopted by that same meeting recommended to the CIAP that "if it considers it necessary to improve its present institutional structure in order to strengthen its activities, it prepare a report containing the proposals that it deems advisable to submit to the governments for consideration."[16] Later, in his Report to the Second Special Inter-American Conference, the Secretary General, after pointing out "that the flexibility of the juridical-institutional structure of the OAS has permitted the governments to develop and strengthen the machinery of inter-American cooperation in the economic and social fields in the manner and to the extent that have been required by the needs of development," added the following: "We need only add that in the future the rhythm of this process should not be interrupted when genuine imperatives of Latin American development require strengthening that machinery even more. As has happened up to now, the governments will surely be willing to take advantage of the vast resources that the constitutional order of the Organization provides them. Only

---

[16] *Cf. Final Report* of the Third Annual Meeting of the IA-ECOSOC at the Ministerial Level, OEA/Ser. H/XII. 9, pp. 37 and 16, respectively.

with the spirit of renovation and the energy that have characterized previous government decisions can the great objectives of the Charter of Punta del Este be attained."[17]

As far as the nature of the Alliance for Progress is concerned, it can be observed that from an institutional as well as a substantive point of view it was originally conceived by Operation Pan America and the Act of Bogotá as a basically multilateral enterprise. At its culmination at Punta del Este it was incorporated into the inter-American system as the most recent and daring expression of inter-American cooperation in this field. In reality, there have always been manifestations of traditional bilateralism, along with the cooperative action, which have not yet been completely overcome in practice. Therefore, the true significance of the process of development and strengthening of the Alliance lies rather in the fact that, through it, its multilateral character is being accentuated and perfected.

It is also appropriate here to transcribe the following passage from the aforementioned report of the Secretary General: "Now then, we may ask whether the full attainment of those great objectives can be reached with the participation of only the technical organs of the inter-American system. Development is not an exclusively economic and social phenomenon. Rather, in the expression used by the President of the European Economic Community, Walter Hallstein, referring to economic integration, it is, in practice, an 'eminently political phenomenon'. Hence it is necessary for certain steps and decisions to be taken by political organs. The work done by the Council of the Organization in the stages referred to above, clearly reveals to what extent the vigorous intervention of the political organs of the inter-American system may be necessary and useful. Article 58 of the Charter provides not only the powers that are reserved to the Council with respect to the decisions taken by its three organs in the exercise of their respective technical autonomy, but also the responsibilities of the former in 'the sphere of action of the Council'. From this it follows that the Council of the Organization should take an ever more active part in all the political, institutional, and budgetary aspects of development plans."[18] The same might be said of the other political organs—the Inter-American Conference and the Meeting of Consultation of Ministers of Foreign Affairs—whose functions and attributes permit them to take initiatives and decisions of much greater scope than the OAS Council. Without undermining the present powers of the IA-ECOSOC, or interrupting its development, those organs can take the initiatives and decisions at a political level which are sometimes required to accelerate the march of the Alliance for Progress.

---

[17] Cf. OEA/Ser. E/XIII. 1, Doc. 16, vol. I, p. 17.
[18] Ibid., pp. 17–18.

42. *The Inter-American Development Bank (1959)*

The Inter-American Development Bank (IDB) is a regional institution established by 20 American countries—19 from Latin America and the United States—to accelerate the development of its member nations, individually and collectively. The idea for the creation of a regional financial institution was first broached more than 75 years ago at the First International American Conference (Washington 1889-1890), which recommended that member states grant concessions conducive to the establishment of a regional American bank.

The desire of the American countries for such an institution was reiterated at several subsequent inter-American conferences, although its precise form varied as the economic and social problems of Latin America grew more complex, and as new techniques and procedures for channeling external financing into developing areas began to emerge.

Thus, when the IDB was established December 30, 1959, it was conceived as a development financing institution designed to help solve the basic economic and social problems facing Latin America, by helping the countries of the region to achieve faster development and higher living standards.

To accomplish its purpose, the Agreement Establishing the IDB gave it the following functions:[19] to promote the investment of public and private capital for development purposes; to utilize its own capital, funds raised by it in financial markets, and other available resources, for financing the development of the member countries, giving priority to those loans and guarantees that will contribute most effectively to their economic growth; to encourage private investment in projects, enterprises, and activities contributing to economic development and to supplement private investment when private capital is not available on reasonable terms and conditions; to cooperate with the member countries to orient their development policies toward a better utilization of their resources, in a manner consistent with the objectives of making their economies more complementary and of fostering the orderly growth of their foreign trade; and to provide technical assistance for the preparation, financing, and implementation of development plans and projects, including the study of priorities and the formulation of specific project proposals.

The basic authority of the IDB resides in its Board of Governors, which consists of one governor appointed by each one of its member countries. At the first meeting of the Board held in San Salvador,

---

[19] The complete text of the Agreement appears in *Appendix 16,* p. 407, *infra.*

El Salvador, in February 1960, the IDB was formally organized, its president, Dr. Felipe Herrera, was elected and its first Board of Executive Directors was chosen. The Board of Directors, which consists of seven members—six elected by the Latin American member countries and one appointed by the United States—is responsible for the conduct of the operations of the IDB.

The Bank began operations October 1, 1960, and authorized its first loan the following February. By September 30, 1965, it had authorized 298 loans totaling $1,335.4 million and disbursements on those loans by the same date totaled more than $525 million. (Dollar figures used in this chapter may include, as appropriate, U.S. dollars or the U.S. dollar equivalent of amounts in other currencies.)

The Bank's function of being a complementary source of financing for the domestic capital of its member countries is illustrated by the fact that the total cost of the economic and social development projects and programs partially financed by the Bank as of September 30, 1965 was some $3.6 billion.

This means that the loans approved by the IDB through that date helped to mobilize other funds, chiefly domestic Latin American resources, totaling $2,300 million, or close to 65% of the total cost of the projects.

The IDB carries out its functions with two separate funds of its own: the ordinary capital resources and the Fund for Special Operations. The ordinary capital resources are authorized at $2,150,000,000 of which $475,000,000 represents "paid-in" capital and $1,675,-000,000 "callable" capital. Of the "paid-in" portion, $381,580,000 has been subscribed by the 20 member countries (50% in dollars and 50% in the currencies of the respective member countries), and $93,420,000 is available for subscription partly by present members and partly by other countries which might join the IDB in the future. The $1,675,000,000 callable portion includes $903,405,000 subscribed by members; $484,835,000 subscribed or to be subscribed by the end of 1965, and $286,760,000 available for subscription by present or by future members. The subscribed callable capital, payable in gold or in the currencies needed to meet obligations constitutes, in effect, a guarantee of the IDB's securities and thus enables it to borrow funds in the world's capital markets. With its ordinary capital resources, the IDB authorizes directly reproductive loans, subject to current banking practices and repayable in the currencies lent. These loans are made chiefly for the acquisition of capital goods and, in certain cases, for technical services.

The authorized resources of the Fund for Special Operations currently are $1,123,158,000, which include $519,474,000 already contributed to the Bank; $600,000,000 still to be contributed, half by the end of 1965 and the other half by the end of 1966, and $3,-

684,000 still unassigned. More than 80% of the total contributions to this Fund are to be United States dollars and the remaining 20% are to be currencies of the Latin American member countries. The Fund for Special Operations is used to make loans on terms and conditions, including possible repayment in the borrower's currency, which make it possible to deal with special circumstances arising in specific countries or with regard to specific projects.

The IDB also administers the Social Progress Trust Fund which the United States Government established in 1961 to stimulate social development in Latin America as part of the Alliance for Progress program. As administrator of the Fund, it is authorized to make commitments totaling up to $525,000,000. The Trust Fund is used to make loans for land settlement and improved land use; housing for low-income groups; community water supply and sanitation facilities, and higher education and advanced training. As of September 30, 1965 virtually all of these resources had been committed. Under a resolution put into effect by the Board of Governors in March 1965, social development projects previously financed with the Trust Fund are now being financed with the resources of the Fund for Special Operations.

The three abovementioned sources of funds are maintained, utilized, and accounted for entirely separate from one another.

Carrying out one of the functions assigned to it by its Charter, the IDB is actively seeking to increase the flow of external resources to finance economic development in Latin America. Its progress in this undertaking indicates the confidence which private financial circles have in the development potential of the region as well as in the efficacy and soundness of the Bank. Funds have been obtained from the world's capital markets through three main techniques: the sale of bonds guaranteed by the IDB's callable capital, the sale of loan participations without the IDB's guarantee, and the administration of funds. External resources have also been mobilized through the parallel financing technique, in which credits extended by suppliers of equipment and capital goods concurrently supplement the IDB's loans.

As of September 30, 1965 the IDB had sold six bond issues totaling $272.6 million. Three of these, one 1962 issue for $75 million and two 1964 issues for $50 million and $100 million, respectively, were sold in the United States. Three others were sold in Europe: one for lire equivalent to $24.2 million in Italy in 1962, another for Deutsche marks equivalent to $15 million in Germany, and a third for pounds sterling equivalent to $8.4 million in the United Kingdom. By September 30, 1965 the IDB had sold a total of $22 million in participations in its ordinary capital loans to banks in the United States, Europe, and Canada and to the UN Special

Fund. The latter has also purchased participations totaling $1.6 million in loans extended from the Fund for Special Operations.

In December 1964 the IDB signed an agreement with the Canadian Government to administer a fund, which now totals 20 million Canadian dollars, to finance economic, technical, and educational assistance projects in Latin America. Loans from this fund may be granted free of interest, or at little interest, for periods of up to 50 years but such loans bear a service charge. Loan proceeds are used to purchase goods and services in Canada. In addition, in June 1965 Canada made available another 15 million Canadian dollars through its Export Credits Insurance Corporation to finance economic development projects in Latin America in cooperation with the IDB. These funds are utilized for loans of up to 20 years, including grace periods, are extended at commercial interest rates, and are used for the purchase of goods and services in Canada. Under a contract signed in March 1965, the Spanish Government made $20 million available for Latin American development: $12.5 million in the form of a direct loan to the IDB and $7.5 million in the form of a commitment to purchase participations in loans extended by the IDB from its own resources. Participations will be determined by the amount of goods and services placed in Spain under usual competitive procedures in the course of the IDB's ordinary operations. Finally, in September 1965 an agreement was signed with the Government of the Netherlands to channel 36 million guilders, equivalent to $10 million, into development projects in Latin America in cooperation with the IDB. Under the agreement, loans will be granted by The Netherlands Investment Bank for Developing Countries at terms of up to 25 years and at interest rates not higher than those charged in the IDB's ordinary operations. Up to 80% of these funds will be used to acquire goods and services in the Netherlands; the remaining 20% may be spent to cover local costs in the borrower country.

43. *Participation by Extracontinental Agencies and Governments*

At the end of Chapter II reference was made to the provisions of the OAS Charter regarding cooperative relations between the Organization and the inter-American specialized agencies and world agencies. In the Charter of Punta del Este international cooperation, including that of extracontinental governments, is conceived as part of the "external assistance" to economic and social development in Latin America, which explains its importance for the attainment of the objectives of the Alliance for Progress. The following chapter will show that this cooperation extends to two large areas—financial aid and technical assistance. In both spheres, extracontinental agencies and governments participate in the deliberations and labors of inter-

American agencies. For example, observers from numerous agencies and governments take part regularly in the annual IA-ECOSOC meetings and certain agencies, such as ECLA and FAO, participate in inter-American bodies like the Inter-American Committee for Agricultural Development (CIDA). The above shows the degree to which international cooperation has been institutionalized in line with the goals of the Alliance.

Another part of the process of institutionalization consists in agreements with the abovementioned agencies. To date, agreements have been concluded with four specialized agencies of the United Nations, the first three on authorization by the OAS Council and the fourth by the Pan American Health Organization:

i. *International Labour Organisation*
The agreement with the ILO was signed in Washington, D.C., by the Secretary General of the OAS on July 7, 1950. The Director General of the ILO signed it in Geneva on July 26, 1950. It entered into force on that date.
This agreement, like those signed with UNESCO and FAO, mentioned below, contains provisions for the purpose of coordinating the work of the two organizations, the regional and the United Nations, in order to attain common objectives and prevent the duplication of effort. In general the three agreements are similar, establishing the bases of cooperation, joint action, reciprocal consultation, exchange of information and documents, and reciprocity of representation.

ii. *United Nations Educational, Scientific, and Cultural Organization*
The agreement with UNESCO was signed in Havana on December 8, 1950, by the Secretary General of the OAS and the Director General of UNESCO. In June 1950 a subsidiary agreement entered into force, which expired at the end of 1954, on the training of personnel and the preparation of materials for fundamental education. This agreement was replaced by another signed on October 20, 1954.
This new agreement established procedures for cooperation in the field of fundamental education in Latin America and set up a Joint Advisory Committee which gives special attention to the activities of the Latin American Fundamental Education Center that functions in Pátzcuaro, Mexico, under the authority of UNESCO, and to the work of the Editorial Latinoamericana de Educación Fundamental [Latin American Fundamental Education Publishers], which is under the direction of the OAS in Washington. On July 24, 1962, an additional agreement was signed by the Secretary General of the OAS and the Director General of UNESCO, to facilitate coordination and joint action in the preparation and implementation of programs in fields of common interest. Furthermore, in 1951, through an exchange of notes, bases of cooperation and coordination were established between the Department of Legal Affairs of the Pan American Union and the Secretariat of UNESCO in the fields of copyright.

iii. *United Nations Food and Agriculture Organization*
This agreement was signed at the Pan American Union on May

2, 1952, by the Secretary General of the OAS and the Director General of FAO.

iv. *World Health Organization*
On May 24, 1949, the Pan American Health Organization, at that time known as the Pan American Sanitary Organization, signed an agreement in Washington, D.C., with the World Health Organization (WHO), on the basis of the latter's Constitution. Under the agreement the Conference of PAHO, through its Directing Council and its Bureau, serve, respectively, as the regional committee and regional office of WHO in the Western Hemisphere.

A second group of agreements includes the following:

i. *General Agreement on Tariffs and Trade (GATT)*
In 1959 an agreement was concluded between the Inter-American Economic and Social Council and the high contracting parties to the General Agreement on Tariffs and Trade. That agreement, which was entered into in agreement with the Council of the Organization, in accordance with Article 61 of the Charter of the OAS, entered into force on December 22, 1959. Cooperative relations were thereby established which include cooperation between the respective secretariats, the exchange of studies, documents, and information of common interest, and reciprocal invitations to be represented at meetings where matters of mutual interest are discussed. These bases of cooperation appear, in more or less similar terms, in all of the agreements concluded with this type of organization.

ii. *Intergovernmental Committee for European Migration*
The agreement with this Committee was also concluded by the Inter-American Economic and Social Council in agreement with the Council of the Organization, in accordance with Article 61 of the Charter of the OAS. It entered into effect August 4, 1959.

iii. *United International Bureaus for the Protection of Industrial and Intellectual Property*
The agreement between these Bureaus and the OAS was concluded by decision of the Council of the Organization through an exchange of notes between the Secretary General of the OAS and the Directors of the Bureaus. It entered into force August 31, 1959.

iv. *European Atomic Energy Community (EURATOM)*
This agreement was concluded between EURATOM and the Inter-American Nuclear Energy Commission (IANEC), on authorization by the Council of the Organization through an exchange of notes between the Secretary General of the OAS and the Director of Foreign Relations of the European Atomic Energy Community. It became effective in 1963.

v. *International Atomic Energy Agency*
The agreement with this agency was also concluded, upon authorization by the Council of the Organization, between the Inter-American Nuclear Energy Commission and the said Agency, in accordance with the provisions of Article 21 of the Statutes of the IANEC. It entered into force December 22, 1960.

vi. *Organization for Economic Cooperation and Development (OECD)*
This agreement, which was also concluded on the Council's authorization through an exchange of notes between the Secretary General of the OAS and the Secretary General of the OECD, entered into force on December 16, 1963.

vii. *International Telecommunication Union*
On October 31, 1963, notes were exchanged between the Secretary General of the OAS and the Secretary General of the International Telecommunication Union, under which the two secretariats agreed to consult with each other in relation to the technical aspects of telecommunications.

Mention should also be made here of two bodies, integral parts of the institutional machinery of the Alliance, through which international agencies lend their cooperation to it. One of these, the CIDA referred to above, is composed of the OAS, IDB, FAO, ECLA, and the Inter-American Institute of Agricultural Sciences. Created the same day the Charter of Punta del Este was approved, it seeks to coordinate the action of its member agencies with respect to agricultural planning and agrarian reform, and to make basic studies on the problems faced by the development of agriculture in Latin America. The OAS has given full support to this Committee, contributing technical personnel, covering its operating expenses in large part, and offering office space, equipment, and the use of its administrative services in the same way these are made available to its own offices.

The second body is the OAS-IDB-ECLA Tripartite Committee on Coordination, set up prior to the Charter of Punta del Este, at the suggestion of the Secretary General of the OAS in a note of November 29, 1960, addressed to the President of the IDB and the Assistant Secretary of the United Nations in charge of ECLA. It was established on a permanent basis in order to ensure coordination at the highest possible level among the three agencies with respect to general programs designed to fix the order of priority in the various phases of regional and national economic development, in the training of experts in development, and the periodic publication of studies on the region as a whole and on each country. The Charter of Punta del Este recommended the continuation and strengthening of the machinery of coordination. Subsequently the IA-ECOSOC broadened the functions of the Committee in regard to basic products. Among its major activities is the coordination of the tripartite planning missions, on which each of the three agencies is represented.

With reference to the working relations among the OAS, inter-American entities, and other international agencies, in his report to the Second Special Inter-American Conference the Secretary General stated that these cooperative relations could be further developed and made even closer, in which connection it would be proper to seek from non-American intergovernmental organizations an expansion of the contributions they are making to the programs and activities involved in Latin America's economic and social development. Beyond question, in his opinion, the time has come for these relations to enter upon a more advanced stage of international cooperation and the OAS should participate directly and actively in any kind of activities undertaken by those organizations in the regional community, in order that the collective will and interests of the American countries may always be represented therein.[20]

---

[20] *Cf.* Report of the OAS Secretary General cited in Note 17, p. 28 *et seq.*

Chapter XIV

The March of the Alliance

Four years have now gone by since a program of action for the Alliance for Progress was agreed on at Punta del Este and that program to carry forward the economic and social development of Latin America has embarked on its fifth year. During that time it has been possible to note important achievements along with some not altogether insignificant frustrations. Both of these have received mention at the three annual meetings of the IA-ECOSOC, at those of the CIAP and of the Subcommittees that carry out the "country reviews", as well as in the studies and reports by the General Secretariat of the OAS. With a basis in these sources, primarily, the principal aspects of the march of the Alliance are herein described and evaluated.

44. *The Internal Effort: National Development Programs and "Country Reviews"*

The execution of economic and social national development programs is, as will have been noted, one of the most important aspects of the internal effort foreseen in the Charter of Punta del Este. The procedure established in Title II, in spite of not being obligatory, has in practice given highly satisfactory results. In fact, the advisory groups on planning have made a valuable contribution to various countries in the preparation and formulation of their development plans, thus partially filling the gap created by the scarcity of technicians, which circumstance made difficult the formulation of well-founded economic and social development plans. Particularly in Central America, Paraguay, Uruguay, Peru, and the Dominican Republic, these groups have made or are now making their contribution in the stage of preparation of plans.

Latin American experience in the planning of development since the Punta del Este meeting is as yet very brief and incomplete. The technique applied in the preparation and execution of plans, naturally enough, is still in the process of revision and improvement. In the years immediately following the initiation of the Alliance for Progress, various circumstances that could only with great difficulty be modified in a short period—scarcity of technical experts, administrators, and entrepreneurs; insufficient knowledge about natural resources; the low level of statistics; and other economic, social, and political factors—all worked against any immediate evidence of the beneficial effects of planned development.

Nonetheless, the impulse given by the Alliance for Progress to the idea of putting the economic policy of the Latin American countries on an orderly basis through the preparation of development programs has already begun to show positive results in the economic, social, and institutional fields. The development plans of nine nations—Colombia, Chile, Bolivia, Venezuela, Mexico, Honduras, Ecuador, Panama, and Peru—were evaluated by ad hoc committees of the Panel of Experts, and the planning process in the other nations is now sufficiently advanced to make it possible to state that by the end of 1965 or in the course of the next year, almost all of Latin America will have programs that will have been duly evaluated and started on their way to execution. In fact, in some cases, the situation has already advanced to a second stage, where initial plans are being significantly corrected or new programs for the continuation of those now reaching their end are being prepared.[1]

The procedure established in the Charter was supplemented and strengthened at the Second Annual Meeting of the IA-ECOSOC. In fact, among the powers and attributes conferred on the CIAP is that of making "a continuing review of national and regional plans, steps taken, and efforts made within the framework of the Alliance, and to make specific recommendations to the members of the Alliance and to the regional organizations in the Hemisphere concerning those plans, steps and efforts."[2]

CIAP has been doing this via the so-called "country reviews", in accordance with the procedure adopted at its first meeting, held in Mexico in July 1964. At that same meeting it agreed to examine the plans of each Latin American country in the three subsequent months, for which task it appointed subcommittees.[3] The Chairman or a member of CIAP designated by him, presided over each session. Other CIAP members participated as well as members of the Panel of Nine and the Secretariat. An evaluation of the country's program, and of its financing needs during 1965 and 1966, was made by the Panel of Nine, the Secretariat, or by both groups acting in collaboration. The country program was presented by a senior official of the

---

[1] Cf. Report of the Secretary General of the Organization of American States to the Second Special Inter-American Conference, vol. II, "The Alliance for Progress to Date", OEA/Ser.E/XIII.1, Doc. 16, vol. II Rev., pp. 9, 16–17.

[2] See the resolution establishing the CIAP, II.3.d, in Appendix 19, p. 459, infra.

[3] The Alliance for Progress: Its Third Year 1963–1964, IA-ECOSOC, Washington, D.C., Pan American Union, 1965, p. 121.

government concerned, usually at the ministerial level. Representatives of the lending agencies were present and actively participated in discussions marked by candor, mutual understanding, and in general, by a high degree of consensus which reflected in the final reports.

During these meetings, as well as during its labors and those of CIAP during 1965, the subcommittees received evaluation reports from the Panel of Nine, basic documents prepared by the Executive Secretariat, and information provided by the governments. On this basis they have been able to examine in detail not only future programs and plans but also recent economic and social evolution, as well as the degree to which the development programs have been carried out during these first years of the Alliance.[4]

45. *Agrarian Reform and Other Structural Reforms*

In a sense, structural reforms are the highest expression of the "internal effort" the Latin American countries have obligated themselves to make within the Alliance for Progress. Agrarian reform is one of these. Without underestimating other factors that adversely affect agricultural development, the deficient, anachronistic structure of land tenure, and the political and institutional barriers to its change, constitute the principal obstacles to the more rapid development of agriculture and, in general, of the rural sector of the population of Latin America. An effective policy of agricultural development and agrarian reform not only represents an economic problem, centered around operation, adoption of modern techniques, and marketing; it also involves an institutional and political problem. This last arises from the need to change the legal status of existing properties in the legislation of most of the Latin American countries in order to permit expropriation, in such a way as to make it possible to change traditional agrarian structures and make proper use of this scarce and inextensible economic resource. In accordance with this evaluation, stress has insistently been laid on the need for carrying out agrarian reform, in the Latin American countries, based on changing the structure of land tenure so as to permit a better distribution of income derived from agriculture, supplemented by other measures such as agricultural credit, technical assistance, improved marketing, more effective taxation, etc.[5]

This explains the explicit and categorical terms in which the

---

[4] For more complete information on the country reviews, as far as national development programs are concerned, see the CIAP Report to the Third Annual Meeting of the IA-ECOSOC, in the document cited in Note 3, pp. 1-48. For more recent aspects see p. 277, *infra*.

[5] See the "CIAP Policy Statement. The State of the Alliance for Progress and Prospects for 1965", prepared by the IA-ECOSOC at its Third Annual Meeting at the Ministerial Level, in the document cited in Note 3, p. 1.

instruments of the Alliance speak of structural reforms. The Charter of Punta del Este, for example, referring to the objectives of the Alliance, includes that of encouraging, "in accordance with the characteristics of each country, programs of comprehensive agrarian reform leading to the effective transformation, where required, of unjust structures and systems of land tenure and use, with a view to replacing latifundia and dwarf holdings by an equitable system of land tenure so that, with the help of timely and adequate credit, technical assistance and facilities for the marketing and distribution of products, the land will become for the man who works it the basis of his economic stability, the foundation of his increasing welfare, and the guarantee of his freedom and dignity."

Since 1961, applying the principles set forth in the Charter, 12 countries of Latin America have enacted agrarian reform laws: Brazil, Chile, Colombia, Costa Rica, the Dominican Republic, Ecuador, Guatemala, Honduras, Nicaragua, Panama, and Paraguay. In Uruguay the National Economic and Social Development Plan, the National Agricultural Development Plan, and the Agricultural Promotion laws have all been submitted to the Congress. Chile is about ready to adopt a new law substantially modifying the previous one; Mexico, Bolivia, and Venezuela already had agrarian reform legislation that antedated the Charter of Punta del Este. Although obviously such legislation varies according to the countries, in line with each one's individual characteristics, it can be stated that certain basic principles have been accepted and incorporated in most of these laws. Among them one may mention the regionalization or zonification of the reform; deferred payment, by means of bonds, for expropriated land; introduction of various forms of land tenure; etc.[6]

The same is true of fiscal or tax reform. In the Declaration of Punta del Este, the Latin American countries agreed on the need "to reform tax laws, demanding more from those who have most, to punish tax evasion severely, and to redistribute the national income in order to benefit those who are most in need, while, at the same time, promoting savings and investment and reinvestment of capital." The Charter of Punta del Este, in turn, indicated the necessity of including in national development programs efforts and measures for "more effective, rational, and equitable mobilization and use of financial resources through the reform of tax structures. . . ."

At the Special Meeting at Punta del Este, Resolution A-3 was also adopted, pursuant to which the OAS-IDB-ECLA Joint Tax Program, initiated by these institutions in October 1960, was incorporated into the Alliance. Since that time, work under the program

---

[6] *Cf.* Report of the Secretary General cited in Note 1, pp. 20-22.

has been proceeding at a good pace, beginning with the meeting of the Conferences on Tax Administration (Buenos Aires, October 1961) and on Fiscal Policy (Santiago, Chile, December 1962). These conferences, as well as the meetings of Special Committee III of the IA-ECOSOC, Fiscal and Financial Policy and Administration, and the publications of the Program have served not only to pinpoint the technical aspects of the need for and projections of a tax reform, but also to create an interest in the countries in these objectives and a concern about attaining them. At the request of Paraguay and Peru, the Program also provided technical assistance in the planning and execution of reforms in those countries, and progress has been made in the preparation of the Model Fiscal Code for Latin America.

In this field the internal effort has been expressed by the following principal measures. With respect to the income tax, a system of a single tax on total income with graduated scales, instead of unrelated levies, has been adopted in Guatemala, the Dominican Republic, and Uruguay. New tax laws have been adopted and the tax structure substantially reformed in Brazil, Chile, Colombia, the Dominican Republic, Ecuador, El Salvador, Haiti, Honduras, Mexico, Panama, and Venezuela. Other reforms in the income tax itself have been adopted in Argentina, Costa Rica, Paraguay, and Peru. Property taxes have been introduced in Costa Rica, Guatemala, Nicaragua, Panama, and Uruguay, and the structure or administration of already existing property taxes has been improved in Chile, Colombia, Costa Rica, Ecuador, Honduras, Nicaragua, and Paraguay. Sales and excise taxes have been extended through their adoption in Argentina, Colombia, El Salvador, Honduras, Nicaragua, and Peru, and already existing indirect taxes have been reformed in Chile, Costa Rica, Ecuador, Guatemala, Nicaragua, Panama, Paraguay, and Peru. Finally, all the countries have adopted measures in regard to taxes on foreign trade and legislation on tax incentives.

There has still not been time for the result of these changes in the tax systems to become fully evident, but there has already been an appreciable increase in the fiscal revenues of the countries.[7]

As far as administrative reform is concerned, the present situation can be described, in general terms, as follows. A certain awareness has been created among government authorities, various sectors of public opinion, and the ordinary citizenry about the importance of introducing substantial improvements in the public administration, considering its strategic role in the entire process of development, especially in the phase of execution of the plans. Likewise a good number of countries of the hemisphere have understood that the

---

[7] *Ibid.,* pp. 18-20.

process of development is one of the most delicate and complex tasks that modern society has undertaken, and that present administrative structures do not have the qualities of dynamism and balance to do the job. Therefore, they have begun to make substantial reforms in the organizations of the public sector in order to adapt them to the social changes that are taking place and to enable them to serve as adequate instruments for speeding up those changes.

On the other hand, the people who must plan and carry out the development programs are of fundamental importance. Aware of this fact, a number of Latin American countries have made notable progress in improving their personnel administration. In this regard, it has been learned that a permanent qualified staff in government service is not all that is needed; it is also important to train and educate those employees, so that they may handle the development programs with growing efficiency and provide the best possible public service. To meet this need, schools of public administration at the university level have been organized, and other institutes have been created to train and prepare the technicians who will be called upon to carry forward the reform in public administration. It must be noted that the process of administrative reform for economic development presupposes social changes, and is therefore not accomplished automatically merely by the decision to effect the change. It requires intensive and prolonged national effort to overcome all of the administrative obstacles that impede the process of economic and social modernization. This effort is being made in the majority of the countries of Latin America.[8]

Administrative reform is another field covered by the CIAP's country reviews. The subcommittees suggested that it would be well if those systems—including relations with local governments, decentralized agencies, and nongovernmental organizations—were adapted to the duties that execution of the Alliance for Progress will entail, especially in relation to carrying out a planned development policy. On several occasions the subcommittees stressed the importance of administrative reform, and they had an opportunity to study, especially in the case of Chile, the reforms carried out in the area of tax administration. Many of the government representatives mentioned the programs that are being carried out in their countries, and the subcommittees could appreciate the efforts made; however, these have not yet, generally speaking, taken full effect, as can be seen in the shortcomings observed in the drafting of projects and in other fields of development policy.[9]

---

[8] *Ibid.*, pp. 22-23.
[9] *Cf.* Document cited in Note 3, pp. 90-91.

46. *Integration of National Markets*

The initiatives and measures being undertaken to integrate national markets are another important expression of the internal effort and are considered a logical complement to structural reforms. When examining in detail proposals for accelerating the Alliance for Progress through national economic integration, the CIAP considered "The need to improve and widen national markets . . . to be one of the most important means to accelerate this national economic integration and, at the same time, to reinforce the efforts under way for regional economic integration in Latin America, and to help develop conditions under which exports of Latin American agricultural products and manufactures could be expanded."

The symptoms of this problem of national markets, described in detail by the CIAP, are well known: substantial underutilization of existing industrial capacity, sluggishness in the growth of agricultural production and income, and an increased disparity between development levels of urban and rural areas. The importance of this pressing problem has long been recognized. Limited and poorly organized national markets are part of the underdevelopment problem itself. The CIAP expressed its firm conviction that it was time to make a fresh attack on this chronic problem and to stimulate a conscious strategy to improve and expand national markets in the Latin American countries. The essence of this strategy is to develop new initiatives and an experimental and imaginative approach on the part of individuals, private groups, and public bodies in Latin America leading to the launching of specific national or local projects.

The major focus would be on improvements in marketing conditions: to reduce distribution costs and improve techniques for the achievement of greater efficiency in the marketing of agricultural products in the urban centers; to improve marketing conditions in the rural areas for manufactured products; and to facilitate marketing of agricultural and manufactured products to the ports. This approach, which would necessarily involve the improvement and expansion of many existing policies and activities, required the adoption of measures in the agricultural sector as well as in the industrial sector. Such measures, together with land reform and other agricultural measures, would increase effective demand for manufactured products; and the availability in rural areas of efficiently marketed manufactured goods could serve as an incentive for the diversification of agricultural production. CIAP felt that a successful effort to expand national markets would have other important consequences. The diversification and improved efficiency of industrial and agricultural production and a successful organization and expansion of national markets would help to surmount the very similar problems faced in diversifying and expanding exports of agricultural products and manufactured goods. In the same manner, the broadened base of domestic industry would facilitate the expansion of intraregional trade and the success of the integration movements in Latin America. By providing more full and efficient use of industrial plants and the more effective exploitation of agriculture and fishery potential it will also assist the Latin American nations in their efforts to earn more foreign exchange. Raising agricultural incomes could also serve to ease the implementation of structural reforms in the agricultural sector.

In accordance with the action program adopted by the CIAP, it proposed that its Chairman undertake certain concrete measures to improve and expand national markets. Among these was that of encouraging active discussion by the National Committees for the Alliance for Progress, as well as other interested groups—e.g., industry, labor, agriculture, fisheries, research institutions, cooperatives, etc. —in order to apply this concept of the expansion of national markets to the unique problems of the various countries and to generate specific projects by interested groups in Latin America. The CIAP also proposed that representatives of the international and national agencies presently dealing with the many facets of the national market problem, such as industrial expansion, agricultural development, external financing, and technical assistance, be invited to form a working group.[10]

In the course of the country reviews, the CIAP subcommittees examined this sphere of action from different points of view, through projects relating to: a) agricultural marketing and credit—storage, transportation, distribution, and so on; b) marketing of animal products—slaughterhouses, meat-packing plants, and so on; c) improvement in the utilization of industrial capacity; d) marketing of fish; and e) transportation and communications systems. The subcommittees felt, in general, that this was one of the fields still neglected by development policy and one in which there were many possibilities for effective projects.[11]

47. Health, Housing, Social Participation, and Labor Policy

The Charter of Punta del Este establishes that one of the objectives of the Alliance for Progress is "To increase life expectancy at birth by a minimum of five years, and to increase the ability to learn and produce, by improving individual and public health. To attain this goal it will be necessary, among other measures, to provide adequate potable water supply and sewage disposal to not less than

[10] Cf. "Final Report of the First Meeting of the CIAP" in ibid., pp. 131-149.
[11] Ibid., p. 91.

70 per cent of the urban and 50 per cent of the rural population; to reduce the present mortality rate of children less than five years of age by at least one-half; to control the more serious communicable diseases, according to their importance as a cause of sickness, disability, and death; to eradicate those illnesses, especially malaria, for which effective techniques are known; to improve nutrition; to train medical and health personnel to meet at least minimum requirements; to improve basic health services at national and local levels; and to intensify scientific research and apply its results more fully and effectively to the prevention and cure of illness." Since then there have been increased efforts to solve public health problems in Latin America.

The functioning of health services, both curative and preventive, is a well-organized part of the social services of the public sector. In many countries these services, which are far from covering the more urgent needs in this field, account for 10 to 15% of the total national budget. Mention may be made of the important advance in improving the standard of living of wide sectors of the population, the improvement in the administrative systems for planning health programs, the expansion of welfare, medical, and hospital services, and the progress in eradicating certain types of disease. However, problems still persist, generally in relation to rural areas, that are difficult to reduce to figures. In short, vast regions of the hemisphere still do not have medical and health personnel, appropriate welfare services, drinking water and sewage disposal systems, and adequate systems for the prevention and cure of diseases.

Most of the countries have created planning units in their health ministries and their coordination with the national planning agencies is being worked out, although at a slow pace. Only two countries— Ecuador and Honduras—have succeeded in integrating their national health plans with their national economic and social development plans. In general, these activities are hampered by the lack of trained personnel. Attempts are being made to solve this problem through a progressive effort to train officials, assistance in this task being rendered by various international agencies. By the joint effort of the Latin American Institute of Economic and Social Planning, which operates in Santiago, Chile, and the Pan American Health Organization (PAHO), over 100 experts in planning in this field have been trained.

Likewise, a significant advance has been made in the organization of hospital centers and in the administration of existing ones, and in the effective work done by mobile services, all of which means a marked increase in the number of persons given care, although the relation between the number of hospital beds and the population has remained stationary or has even declined. Works of environmental sanitation, which consisted principally in the construction of water mains and sewers, have made considerable progress, although unequally as between urban and rural areas. The urban areas have absorbed almost all of the external funds made available for this purpose. Some countries (Bolivia, Costa Rica, the Dominican Republic, El Salvador, Honduras, Panama, and Paraguay) have established central semiautonomous agencies to administer and carry out water supply programs; these are in addition to those that already existed in other countries.

The PAHO has been carrying on important work in the control of yellow fever and eradication of *Aedes aegypti* (no cases of urban yellow fever have occurred in the hemisphere in the last ten years); the eradication of malaria, as part of the world-wide campaign (43 million persons are now living in regions in which the disease has been eradicated, or where its occurrence is sporadic, as a result of the campaign begun in 1956); the fight against other communicable diseases, such as smallpox (which has resulted in the reduction of cases of this disease from 30,000 per year in the period 1940-1950 to about 6,000 in 1963), tuberculosis, and leprosy. The PAHO has also helped to reduce infant mortality in the hemisphere, and has made notable advances in this field. Nevertheless, further effort is needed in this field, since according to present figures more than one of every seven children will die before reaching the age of five.

A basic program that was recently started is that designed to provide potable water to 50 million inhabitants of rural regions. This program is part of the Alliance for Progress, and is based primarily on the self-help efforts of the communities.

In accordance with the Charter of Punta del Este, the governments have been giving increasing importance to the formulation of health plans. The PAHO, in cooperation with the Latin American Institute of Economic and Social Planning, has organized courses in health planning for about 100 high officials of the various ministries of health. The Ministers of Health, in their meeting held in 1963 reached the conclusion that it is essential to integrate the objectives of the Ten-Year Public Health Program provided for in the Charter of Punta del Este in a rational manner with the national economic and social development plans, in order to be able to attain those objectives within the time set.[12]

As another of its principal objectives the Charter of Punta del Este calls for an increase in "the construction of low-cost houses for low-income families in order to replace inadequate and deficient housing and to reduce housing shortages; and to provide necessary public services to both urban and rural centers of population."

---

[12] *Cf*. Report of the Secretary General cited in Note 1, pp. 27-29.

In general terms, it may be noted that although good progress has been made since the signing of the Charter, the construction of new housing has not reached a level that will permit solution of the existing problem. The joint progress achieved in the administrative and functional structure of official housing agencies warrants special emphasis. A number of institutions were improved and national plans were prepared. The important role played by external aid must be stressed. Of the 450 million dollars in loans approved from 1961 to 1965 by the Social Progress Trust Fund of the Inter-American Development Bank, 200 million were for housing.

With respect to rural housing, in some cases activities were coordinated with government agrarian reform machinery. At the same time measures were taken to limit speculation in urban land suitable for building, to initiate or strengthen systems of domestic financing, and to promote savings and loan associations; and legal provisions were adopted for the purpose of channeling part of available national resources into the housing sector. The taking of housing censuses was continued, although it is still not possible to express the magnitude of the problem in terms of exact figures. The present deficit has been estimated at 15.5 million housing units in 19 countries of Latin America, a shortage that will worsen in the next few years if present levels of financing and construction remain static, even without taking into account the increase in population to be expected.

To compensate for the shortage of public funds, many countries have begun to try to attract the private sector toward the housing field. A majority of the countries have held to the policy of devoting most of their official action to the improvement of housing for low-income families, although certain pressure has been noted on the part of medium-income families seeking to obtain a larger share of the benefits, principally through the savings and loan associations and cooperatives. Both systems have taken on new impulse in a number of countries and are beginning to represent an appreciable contribution. Self-help construction systems have continued to be used to an increasing extent, with variations according to local or regional characteristics, and their expansion or introduction in various places is being studied.

The great concentration of population in the cities, above all in the capitals of the countries, has led to the focusing of official effort on the problem of urban housing. This has had a detrimental effect on rural housing which, although not totally neglected, has generally occupied second place in government attention. The problems of rural housing and of the sectors with the lowest incomes, consisting of families that lack the capacity to pay off the minimum debt under the various systems of financing, remain pending in all of the countries of Latin America, without exception.

As an example of national effort, the case of Mexico may be cited, where the public sector has constructed important multiple housing units through the effort of various government agencies and organizations. In addition to these directly effective accomplishments, mechanisms have been set up within the existing banking structure that will permit the generation of savings on a massive scale for the purpose of channeling them into the construction of low-cost housing; the General Law on Credit Institutions and Auxiliary Organizations was amended; and two trust funds were set up in the Bank of Mexico—the Operation and Bank Discount Fund for Low-Cost Housing (FOVI) and the Guaranty and Support Fund for Low-Cost Housing Loans (FOGA).

The General Secretariat of the OAS carries out, on a continuing basis, various activities involving advisory services and high-level training in this field. It likewise cooperates with the countries in improving their basic information in order to expedite the channeling of external resources toward this sector. Important instruments of the Secretariat in making these efforts are the Inter-American Housing and Planning Center in Bogotá, Colombia, and the Inter-American Program of Urban and Regional Planning in Lima, Peru. Both programs carry out training activities, research, and the preparation of documents in their respective fields.[13]

The need for participation by the great majorities in the efforts being made by the countries for their development is being met by both the steadily increasing action of the private sector and the coordination and encouragement carried on by the governments. By way of example, mention may be made of the People's Cooperation movement in Peru, which includes the work of various communities and groups in self-help endeavors. Peru was also the first country to apply for external aid for projects of social participation. An OAS-IDB mission completed its studies on this matter in April 1965. In Chile an agency has been set up at ministerial level to coordinate and promote efforts of the people. Guatemala organized a national office for community development called Joint Action, and early in 1965 it began to train the medium-level personnel needed for such work. The university associations of Costa Rica, Chile, and Peru have been working actively in community development, literacy, school construction, and public works programs. The cooperative movement, which extends into numerous fields in Latin America, has expanded and has enjoyed support at both the national and inter-American levels.

At the inter-American level, the Inter-American Conference of Ministers of Labor on the Alliance for Progress is outstanding be-

---

[13] *Ibid.*, pp. 24-26.

cause of the importance of its recommendations. This conference was convened by the Council of the Organization of American States and was held at Bogotá, Colombia, May 5-11, 1963. One of the points on the agenda was "the participation of the workers of Latin America in national plans for economic and social development." The principles and recommendations of this conference in general advocated the active participation by workers in the development of their countries, in order to attain the objectives of the Alliance with greater speed and effectiveness. For example, in Venezuela and Colombia, workers' banks are being actively organized, designed to provide workers with credit and investment agencies suited to their resources. Legislation was recently enacted in Venezuela making it possible for democratic organizations of workers to participate actively in most government-controlled enterprises.

The General Secretariat of the OAS works intensively in this field through the provision of training, information, and technical assistance. Among these activities are inter-American courses for the training of personnel in community development in Bolivia and Mexico; regional courses for the training of personnel in cooperatives; inter-American courses for the training of managers of labor union cooperatives, which have been given at the headquarters of the Inter-American Housing and Planning Center; and courses in the administration of social welfare programs, given in Buenos Aires, Argentina. The General Secretariat also engages in active and varied activities for the provision of information and technical assistance in response to the requests and needs of the countries in accordance with the principles of the Charter of Punta del Este calling for the effective participation of the whole of society in the development of the hemisphere.

Finally, the measures taken by certain governments to assure their workers salaries adequate for their needs should be mentioned. In El Salvador a minimum wage for agricultural workers has been established. Honduras is making progress in the establishment of a flexible system of minimum wages. Chile has begun applying a policy of salaries closely linked to national development as far as productivity, capacity, and production of goods and services are concerned. Similar efforts can be noted in other countries, such as Colombia, Nicaragua and the Dominican Republic, to face unemployment by improving or creating machinery that has a bearing on the labor market.[14]

48. *Education, Science, and Culture*

The Punta del Este Meeting adopted the general lines of a Ten-Year Education Program, the implementation of which would be

---

[14] *Ibid.*, pp. 29-30.

dependent on the magnitude of the effort made by the countries themselves and on the volume of external assistance available to them. This Program, presented as Resolution A-1, contains the express agreement that each country should adopt an overall education plan for the attainment of precisely defined goals within the next ten years, for the purpose of raising the cultural level of the peoples of Latin America and fitting them to participate constructively in economic and social development, and sets forth among others, the following goals to be attained within that period: at least six years of elementary education, free and compulsory, for the entire school-age population; carrying out of systematic adult-education campaigns, directed toward community development, training of manpower, cultural extension, and the eradication of illiteracy; reform and expansion of intermediate education so that a much higher proportion of the new generation may enjoy the opportunity to continue their general education and receive some type of high-quality vocational or professional training; carrying out of studies to determine the varied needs for qualified manpower in industrial, agricultural, and social development programs; reform, extension, and improvement of higher education so that a very much higher proportion of young people may have access to it; reorientation of the structure, content, and methods of education at all levels; and development and strengthening of national and regional centers for education and advanced training of teachers, professors, and specialists in the various aspects of planning and administration of the educational services.

A careful analysis of the goals agreed upon and the commitments undertaken reveals clearly the fundamental role education plays in the achievement of the objectives of the Alliance for Progress. Underdevelopment, with all its consequences, is based mainly on an illiterate and ignorant population. It must therefore be borne in mind that in the process of transformation on which the countries have embarked, the objectives of a fair distribution of income and an increase in its per capita level will only be attainable in those countries that have ensured for their peoples an adequate education. The correlation that exists between educational levels and annual per capita income levels has been clearly demonstrated.

The great and fundamental importance of educational development becomes even more manifest when it is recalled that the great objectives of the Charter of Punta del Este include the consolidation of liberty and of the institutions of representative democracy, the establishment and development of productive industries, the carrying out of agrarian reform, and the improvement of public health, to list only a few examples, since education is the only possible source of the trained and qualified personnel that is essential for their achievement. Education may therefore be described as the backbone of the Alliance for Progress.

Resolution A-1 recommended that the Conference on Education and Economic and Social Development in Latin America (held in Santiago, Chile 1962) and the Third Inter-American Meeting of Ministers of Education (held in Bogotá, Colombia 1963) devote special attention to determining in specific detail the broad goals of the Ten-Year Education Program. In compliance with this mandate, the two meetings proposed the broad lines of educational policy for the region, adopted criteria for the determination of priorities for national and inter-American efforts, and recommended specific measures to solve the problems and eliminate the obstacles that hamper educational development.

The Santiago Conference adopted a declaration recommending, among other things, "That each and every one of the States participating in the Conference take the necessary steps to devote to education the maximum economic resources compatible with its productive and financial capacity and with the balance of other social costs, so as to achieve in 1965 a situation in which Latin America as a whole can devote to education not less than 4 per cent of its gross product, it being understood that the countries that are now substantially below that level shall endeavour to increase the present proportion by at least 1 per cent by 1965 and a further 1 per cent by 1970." It also recommended that not less than 15% of the funds made available by the Alliance for Progress be allotted to educational programs.

For its part, the Meeting of Ministers of Education approved a Final Act laying down the guidelines of the policy that the Latin American countries propose to follow in order to bring to their peoples the benefits of education, science, and culture and thereby accelerate the rate of progress achieved in carrying out their economic and social development plans. Among these guidelines, special mention should be made of the fact that educational policy must provide not only for the progress of the students from the elementary school to higher education, but also create conditions, particularly in the cycles of study at the secondary level, that will make it possible for students who cannot or who do not wish to go on to more advanced studies to be able to perform useful functions within society.

The progress achieved by the Latin American countries in the economic and social fields, the change in attitude on the part of their peoples and governments towards the educational problem, and the desire of the governments to honor the commitments entered into at Punta del Este and to comply with the resolutions adopted at Santiago and Bogotá have all helped to stimulate considerably the development of education during the period 1961-1964.

In this regard, there has been a sharpening of awareness of development in Latin America and, as a natural consequence, a widening acceptance of the idea of promoting education and linking it more closely with the general development plans. All the countries have continued to make serious efforts to improve their educational planning machinery, and special services for this purpose have been set up in almost all of them. As far as elementary education is concerned, enrollment has increased by 5 million (from 24 million in 1960 to 29 million in 1963), which represents an average annual increase of 7%. The proportion of total elementary school-age population enrolled increased from 77% in 1960 to 86% in 1963. Substantial progress has also been made in the number of teachers granted certificates. In addition, a number of countries are acting to intensify their literacy and adult education programs. Efforts have been made in the majority of cases to orient these programs to meet the present needs of economic and social development. The use of modern teaching methods and audiovisual equipment has also been extended.

Enrollment in Latin American institutions of higher education rose substantially during the period 1960-1963, from 527,000 in 1960 to 653,000 in 1963, an average annual increase of 7%. This increase in enrollment was accompanied by an expansion of opportunity, through the establishment of schools or faculties to meet new needs, which has contributed to a change in the structure of this level of education and in its percentage composition by groups of specialities. Thus, for example, the percentage of students studying the educational sciences rose from 4% in 1960 to 9% in 1962, while the enrollment in the exact and natural sciences rose by 3 percentage points in the same period. A number of countries have established planning departments and boards or services for the planning of higher education and liaison with the ministry of education. Almost all the countries have made efforts to improve the quality and conditions of university teaching by sending teachers abroad, organizing study seminars, establishing full-time teaching staffs, and revising the regulations governing teachers.[15]

The Charter of Punta del Este establishes that the American republics shall work toward strengthening of "the capacity for basic and applied research; and to provide the competent personnel required in rapidly-growing societies," and that "National development shall incorporate self-help efforts directed toward . . . promoting the establishment and expansion of local institutions for basic and applied research." The Ten-Year Education Program, in turn, foresees "Encouragement of the teaching of the sciences and of scientific

---

[15] *Ibid.,* pp. 55-74.

and technological research, as well as intensification of the education and advanced training of scientists and science teachers."

Scientific and technological activities, therefore, constitute one of the basic elements of economic and social development. The fundamental role played by science and technology in the more developed countries is shown by the fact that they devote approximately 3% of their gross national product to scientific and technological research. In contrast, the scientific and technological effort carried out in the member countries of the OAS is in most cases insignificant, a fact that undoubtedly constitutes one of the major obstacles to development and to the achievement of the goals contained in the Charter of Punta del Este. The lack of a clearly defined policy for science and technology in the member states is one of the most serious problems that they must solve if they are to achieve a better utilization of their manpower and material resources and a more effective implementation of their development plans. This situation is reflected in the shortage of specialized personnel at the various levels, in the inadequacy of some curricula, and in the magnitude of the resources required for the modernization of education and of scientific and technological research.

The activities and efforts in Latin America relate to two major fields: education and research, and the application of science and technology to development, including the use of nuclear energy. In the field of scientific education and research, the majority of the countries are displaying interest in the promotion of science and of technological research. Some already have a governmental organization responsible for scientific and technological education. Reforms have been initiated in the science curricula at both the elementary and secondary levels. A number of countries have set up special institutions for the training of science teachers, while others have launched advanced training programs. This effort is, however, still insufficient. Although in a number of countries there is an official agency responsible for scientific and technological research, organized programs for the promotion of research and the training of research workers are almost nonexistent.

The activities in the field of technology have been concentrated in four main areas: a. manpower resources; b. industrial productivity; c. standardization for economic integration; and d. technological research. Regarding the first, Argentina, Brazil, Colombia, Chile, Costa Rica, Ecuador, El Salvador, Guatemala, Honduras, Mexico, Nicaragua, Peru, Uruguay, and Venezuela are participating in the Inter-American Manpower Program. To facilitate action at the national level, wide opportunities for a cooperative approach have been provided through meetings for the exchange of experiences between officials responsible for national programs (Washington 1961;

Buenos Aires 1962; Santiago 1964; and Washington 1965). A technical methodological analysis of the systems applicable in the Latin American countries has been organized with the collaboration of high-level international experts (Mexico 1963). As far as the need to accelerate the technical training of industrial leaders is concerned, the IA-ECOSOC and the CIAP have approved a Business Administration Program that is financed out of the Special Development Assistance Fund. Intensive courses for administrators and courses for teachers and instructors are being offered in the Inter-American Center for Business Administration, and national courses in various member countries, in close cooperation with the Latin American Association of Productivity Centers and the national centers.

The efforts to promote economic integration have been hampered by the lack of technical standards precisely identifying the products that are traded. The urgent need for such technical standards was pointed out on a number of occasions (Meeting of Experts on Standardization, Rio de Janeiro 1947 and the Annual Meetings of the IA-ECOSOC). A Regional Standardization Program is being carried out in close cooperation with the Pan American Standards Committee and the national institutes of standardization. The interest aroused in technical circles is demonstrated by the active participation of the standardization agencies of the United States and Latin American countries in the program, under which technical seminars have been held in Argentina, Brazil, Chile, Colombia, Guatemala, Mexico, and Peru.

Finally, the importance of the level of technological development to economic and social development, as measured by the degree of efficiency in the utilization of natural resources and by the extent of incorporation of equipment and processes adapted to local social and economic conditions has been the subject of study by the specialized organs of the OAS. Activities carried out under the program so far have facilitated technical meetings of special interest (Conference of Experts on Manufacturing Metallurgy, held in Buenos Aires in 1964, and Meeting of Experts on Technological Research, held in Bogotá in 1962) and a preliminary analysis of the capacity for technological research in the hemisphere (Preliminary Report of the Latin American Institutes of Technological Research).

The field of science and technology also embraces the activities of the Inter-American Nuclear Energy Commission (IANEC), a technical body that has been functioning since 1959. The IANEC has carried out valuable work in promoting the peaceful applications of nuclear energy, which is destined to play an important role in the very near future in the economic development of Latin America, in the fields of power generation, the desalinization of sea water, the excavation of canals, the increasing of agricultural productivity, food conservation, the improvement of industrial processes and output, and advances in basic research.[16]

The idea of progress in the absence of cultural values is inconceivable. There has never existed, does not now exist, and could not exist a society with an advanced level of material and technical development without a parallel flowering of cultural expression. It follows, therefore, that progress as an integral concept necessarily implies development and improvement of both material and spiritual human resources and possibilities. For this reason, the Alliance's Ten-Year Education Program specifically recommends "That each country adopt an over-all education plan for the attainment of precisely defined goals within the next ten years, for the purpose of raising the cultural level of the peoples of Latin America and fitting them to participate constructively in economic and social development." Aside from the guidelines laid down in its Charter, the policy of the OAS on the subject of culture has been guided by a series of resolutions and recommendations that have emanated from various organs of the system and that the General Secretariat has been progressively converting, as its resources have permitted, into work programs. After the Punta del Este meeting, the Special Meeting of the Inter-American Cultural Council at the Ministerial Level, held in Bogotá in 1963, was the most important event in this field of activity.

Study of the report presented by the General Secretariat to that meeting reveals that if anything may be said to characterize the present situation in Latin America it is the similarity of the problems and the disparity of the solutions. Moreover, no common frame of reference exists for the evaluation of cultural questions either by themselves or in relation to the rest of the needs of each country. It is obviously desirable to bring about in the field of culture, in order better to safeguard and secure its permanent values, the same benefits of planned state action that are being pursued in the field of public education. It is necessary also to make the same reservation: planning in the field of culture does not imply controlled or muzzled culture but, on the contrary, culture that is fostered and stimulated by the state, which provides it with suitable means for its free expression and the essential instruments for its flourishing. It is a well-known principle that inter-American action is dependent at all times on efforts at the national level, which it supplements and reinforces through direct technical assistance or other forms of international cooperation.

One of the most important resolutions of the Cultural Council in the field of culture itself is its recommendation that, in the light of

---

[16] *Ibid.*, pp. 75-82.

the benefits gained from the specialized technical meetings in the economic, social, educational, and scientific fields, this practice be extended to matters pertaining specifically to culture. The First Inter-American Meeting of Directors of Cultural Affairs was one of the earliest results of this recommendation.[17]

49. Basic Products and Trade Policy

As Chapter XII indicates, among the objectives of the Alliance for Progress is that of broadening economic resources through the maintenance of stable prices for basic export products. In this regard, at its first meeting the CIAP "felt that Latin America is interested basically in the reorganization of international trade to accelerate development and that financial resources of external origin constitute a true additional contribution to those economies and not simply a compensation for the relative decrease in export income."[18]

At the First Annual Meeting of the IA-ECOSOC at the Ministerial Level, special emphasis was placed on the problems of Latin America's basic export products and on the action that could be taken to defend them. This effort was directed in general toward specific representations to be undertaken by action groups comprised of the member countries most directly concerned. In many cases the terms of reference of these groups were related to the European Common Market and the threat to Latin America implicit in discriminatory policies against their traditional exports. That danger was enhanced by the prospective entry of Great Britain and the United States into the common market.

At the meeting in São Paulo, in view of the fact that those countries had not joined the common market, the interest of the IA-ECOSOC shifted to the United Nations Conference on Trade and Development. In recognition of the necessity of presenting a common position at that conference, the Special Committee on Latin American Coordination was convoked, which produced the Charter of Alta Gracia. Finally, following the conference in Lima, the IA-ECOSOC instructed the CIAP about the lines of action to be followed on trade and development.[19]

Latin America's strategy in regard to its foreign trade policy is in the process of transformation. This change began to take form about the end of 1961 when serious concern regarding the international trade situation and its effects on the economic development of the less-industrialized countries was voiced in United Nations circles. At that time it was suggested that a world conference to discuss trade

---

[17] *Ibid.*, pp. 82-87.
[18] Cf. Document cited in Note 3, p. 140.
[19] *Cf.* Report cited in Note 1, p. 31.

problems be called. This process of change has not developed into a definite course of action as yet and it may be some time before this occurs.

The principal direct causes for this political phenomenon, which has been occurring over the past 30 years or more, have been well identified.

Given the structure of the Latin American economies, exports constitute an extremely important and dynamic growth factor. However, beginning with the great world depression of the thirties, which caused an abrupt decrease in world trade, many of the countries of the area have been forced to resort to an accelerated replacement of exports, through industrialization, to compensate for the lack of vitality in their exports. In general, it can be affirmed that the exports from most of the countries of the area have continued to lag considerably in relation to their national economic development requirements, although it is evident that they have experienced certain periods of improvement. On the other hand, the process of replacing imports has advanced very rapidly in several countries of the area and is already quite complete in the case of those that have pursued this policy in the most intensive and determined manner. After a period of forced "inward" growth, during which important bottlenecks were created for the external sector, several countries of the area are feeling an acute need for the establishment of conditions, on an international level, that would permit the initiation of a new phase in which "outward" growth would again play a really dynamic role.

Unquestionably the concepts and techniques that have characterized the use of the classical instruments of foreign trade policies that are available to the Latin American countries, such as bilateral agreements, multilateral customs tariff agreements, the General Agreement on Tariffs and Trade (GATT), the agreements of a traditional sort to stabilize the prices of basic products and the regional cooperative machinery of the inter-American system, as well as those of world scope, have demonstrated, in general, but little efficacy in remedying the trends in international trade that are unfavorable to Latin America. Latin America, its hand forced by this combination of circumstances, has no choice but to emphasize again, within its economic policy, the dynamic role that exports should play and, in order to accomplish this, a substantial readjustment in the principles and practices of world trade is needed.

The process that shapes this policy has been formed by a long series of international events that give it content and expression, and it is appropriate to mention at least those of an inter-American character in order to have a clear idea of the variety of circumstances that affect it. Among them the following may be mentioned: the discussions on foreign trade problems that took place at the IA-ECOSOC meetings in Mexico City in 1962 and in São Paulo in 1963, mentioned previously, and the creation of the Special Committee on Latin American Coordination (CECLA) to agree, at the political level and in an exclusive meeting of the Latin American countries, upon the position that they should take at the UN Conference on Trade and Development held in Geneva in the spring of 1964; the preparatory work of ECLA and the Santiago and Brasília meetings at the technical level to identify the principal elements for establishing a position to be taken by Latin America at the abovementioned Geneva Conference; the CECLA meeting at Alta Gracia held under the auspices of the OAS, which was attended, as observers, by the United States of America and a group of developing countries of Asia and Africa, and in which Latin America's position for the Geneva Conference was agreed upon and set forth in the Charter of Alta Gracia; Resolution III on regional and international economic coordination, adopted at the Ninth Meeting of Consultation of Ministers of Foreign Affairs, of the OAS member countries in July 1964; the IA-ECOSOC meeting in Lima in December 1964, where the lines of action which emerged from the Geneva Conference were given approval and at the same time directives were sent to the CIAP to foster solutions in line with that policy; and the Declaration of Lima, in December 1964, which was formulated by the Latin American countries and by means of which a Latin American committee was created, outside of the IA-ECOSOC and similar to CECLA, to coordinate the Latin American positions on foreign trade and development.[20]

50. *External Financing*

The official long-term loans granted to Latin America have nearly doubled since Fiscal Year 1960-1961. The principal sources of this type of financing (various financial agencies of the United States Government, the group of institutions of the International Bank for Reconstruction and Development, and the various types of transactions by the Inter-American Bank) authorized in that year a total of US$890 million in long-term loans. In the year 1963-1964 the figure had reached US$1.585 billion and it is probable that in 1965 it will total between US$1.7 and US$2 billion. Of the sources mentioned above, those which have contributed most to this increase have been the agencies of the United States Government and, among these, the Agency for International Development (AID). The increase in the operations of the Food for Peace Program (activities carried out in accordance with Public Law 480) was also substantial. Actually these agencies have contributed more than two thirds of the

[20] *Ibid.*, pp. 48-50.

total amount of financing registered for the year 1963-1964 in spite of the considerable decrease in the financing effected by the Export-Import Bank (EXIMBANK).

The Inter-American Development Bank (IDB) has been another very important factor in the increase in loans. The IDB had just begun operations at the time of the signing of the Charter of Punta del Este, but in spite of this soon distinguished itself for both the number and the amount of its loans. As indicated earlier, as of September 30, 1965, the Bank had granted 298 loans totaling $1,335.4 million from its own resources and the Social Progress Trust Fund. These loans were distributed as follows.

(in thousands of dollars)

Country	Ordinary Capital Resources		Fund for Special Operations		Social Progress Trust Fund		Grand Total	
	No.	Amount	No.	Amount	No.	Amount	No.	Amount
Argentina	20	$118,076	4	$ 8,581	4	$ 43,500	28	$ 170,157
Bolivia			6	26,560	6	14,600	12	41,160
Brazil	21	154,640	7	37,115	10	62,060	38	253,815
Chile	13	68,535	4	11,683	13	33,938	30	114,156
Colombia	14	61,686	3	7,856	9	49,937	26	119,479
Costa Rica	4	11,502	2	6,200	6	12,640	12	30,342
Dominican Republic	1	6,000	1	5,000	5	10,285	7	21,285
Ecuador	2	8,343	3	8,462	9	27,783	14	44,588
El Salvador	4	6,959	1	183	6	22,040	11	29,182
Guatemala	4	8,438	2	535	4	14,320	10	23,293
Haiti			2	5,860			2	5,860
Honduras	2	510	5	19,540	5	7,635	12	27,685
Mexico	11	80,467	2	13,600	8	35,524	21	129,591
Nicaragua	4	12,230	3	16,700	4	13,135	11	42,065
Panama			3	4,200	3	12,862	6	17,062
Paraguay	2	2,750	7	23,260	3	7,800	12	33,810
Peru	9	24,772	1	475	10	45,250	20	70,497
Uruguay	5	22,043	3	5,240	2	10,500	10	37,783
Venezuela	4	30,744	1	2,700	8	73,000	13	106,444
Central America			2	14,204	1	2,925	3	17,129
	120	$617,695	62	$217,954	116	$499,734	298	$1,335,383

A salient feature of the IDB's lending has been the variety and scope of the fields covered, both in expanding the productive capacity of its member countries and in fostering their social development. In the field of economic development, one of its main concerns has been that of enlarging the volume of external funds available for agriculture and industry, with special emphasis on small- and medium-scale enterprises which lack access to international credit facilities. It has succeeded in doing this chiefly through loans to national development institutions which relend the proceeds to small and medium entities.

Since it began operations the IDB has also been aware of the pressure of social problems on its member countries and consequently has sought a harmonious balance between economic development and social progress. This need was foreseen in the Agreement Establishing the IDB in 1959 and was reinforced in the Act of Bogotá in 1960. The IDB's role in this field has been of a pioneering nature since social projects had previously been financed by international financial agencies only on a limited scale. In its lending operations, the IDB has endeavored to meet the needs of both the public and private sectors in its member countries. Of the $835.7 million in loans approved from its own resources, $431.6 million (52%) was for projects being executed by the public sector, and $404.1 million (48%) was for private sector projects.

The 298 loans extended by the IDB as of September 30, 1965, have been distributed by sectors in the following manner:

(in millions of dollars)

	IDB'S Own Resources	Social Progress Trust Fund	Total
Industry and Mining	$357.6	$	$357.6
Agriculture	223.8	90.4	314.2
Electric Power and Transport	165.6		165.6
Water Supply and Sewage Systems	76.6	161.7	238.3
Housing		215.5	215.5
Advanced Education		32.1	32.1
Export Financing	12.1		12.1
	$835.7	$499.7	$1,335.4

During its first year of operations, IDB loans were used primarily to finance specific projects, with special emphasis on fields not previously covered by external financing. Later, in line with the recommendations of the Charter of Punta del Este to strengthen economic and social development planning, the IDB began to support the execution of national development plans by financing individual projects contained in the overall plans.

As planning efforts advanced in member countries, the IDB also sought to channel loans and technical assistance into fields and projects deemed of high priority in the programs evaluated by the Panel of Nine. In addition, it has participated in various efforts to obtain the external financing required for the execution of national development plans. In June 1962, for example, the IDB entered into an agreement with the U.S. Agency for International Development (AID) to finance the first phase of Bolivia's ten-year development plan. The same year, the Bank joined in the Advisory Group organized by the World Bank to seek the external financing required to carry out Colombia's national development plan, which had previously been evaluated by the Panel of Nine. Since then, the IDB has financed several projects in the plan. In October 1963 the IDB was selected by Ecuador as financial agent for its ten-year development plan. The first meeting of the Consultative Group, organized by the IDB, was held at its headquarters in June 1965, and was attended by representatives of 19 nations. During the three-day meeting the Group considered projects calling for a total of $179 million in external financing and expressed interest in financing $173 million worth.

The Bank's concern with fostering the process of regional economic development stems from the mandate of its Agreement "to cooperate with the member countries to orient their development policies toward a better utilization of their resources, in a manner consistent with the objectives of making their economies more complementary and of fostering the orderly growth of their foreign trade." To foster integration the IDB evaluates loan applications in terms of the impact the project will have on the integration process in Latin America. This is one of the criteria of priorities that serves as a determining factor in its decisions. Accordingly, all loan applications are considered not only in the light of advantages to the economy of the applicant country, but also as they relate to prevailing conditions in other countries of the region.

Taking advantage of the potential of multinational markets, the IDB has granted several loans to expand exports from one member country to another in Latin America. It has also financed projects in Uruguay and Honduras, which, in addition to serving national areas, are improving communications with neighboring countries. In addition to financing projects at the national level, three loans have been extended for multinational programs. Two of these, aggregating $14 million, have been made to the Central American Bank for Economic Integration to help finance an economic development program. The third, for $3,000,000, was granted through the same institution to the national universities of the five Central American countries to finance an overall program for the improvement of instruction in the basic sciences in order to promote technological progress within the framework of regional integration.

One of the measures taken by the IDB to promote the economic integration of Latin America has been the establishment of a program to finance intraregional exports of capital goods. In accordance with a resolution adopted by the Fourth Meeting of the Board of Governors, the Board of Executive Directors of the Bank approved on September 30, 1963, the basic regulations governing the organization and operation of this program. At the same time, the IDB allocated an initial amount of $30,000,000 from its ordinary capital resources to finance it. In preparing these regulations, the following general criteria were applied: a) the basic objective of the program is to promote the development of Latin America's capital goods industry by increasing intraregional trade; b) the program should contribute to the mobilization of local and foreign resources; c) the program should afford maximum flexibility within the framework of a simple, adaptable operating mechanism.

The capital goods eligible for export financing under the program must originate in the Latin American member countries of the IDB. To be classified as such, the goods must be produced or manufactured with raw materials or parts originating in the exporting country or in any of its other Latin American member countries. Goods are also considered to originate in such a country when they include imported components not originating in the Latin American countries, provided that the final process conferring a new identity upon such goods has been carried out in the exporting country and that the c.i.f. value of the components imported from outside the region is less than 50% of the FOB price of the product.

It should be noted that the program permits the financing not only of finished capital goods, but also of components used in their manufacture. The program is therefore designed to promote a much greater flow of trade than is evidenced by the statistics on exports of finished capital goods. The IDB has so far extended five lines of credits totaling $12,000,000 under this program. These lines of credit include $3,000,000 each to Argentina, Brazil, and Mexico, $2,000,000 to Chile, and $1,000,000 to Peru.

In comparison with Calendar Year 1960, total disbursements have also increased during the subsequent years. However if one analyzes the changes occurring in this category during the period 1961-1964, it can be affirmed that rather than an increase in the flow of official funds for the development of the area, originating in the abovementioned sources, what has occurred is a change in their structure. We note, thus, that US$954 million was disbursed in 1961 while the total increased only to US$1,054 million (provisional figures) in 1964, that is, approximately 10%. A very significant portion of this amount—US$240 million—represents disbursements or deliveries of goods that were United States grants or donations. The proportion of donations was much smaller at the beginning of this period and has steadily grown until it represents approximately 24% of the total operations. The bulk of these donations covers the delivery of foodstuffs under Public Law 480 of the United States, and this activity has practically quadrupled. On the other hand, deliveries made in accordance with this law, that are not in the form of grants but represent local currency credits, have been reduced by half. The disbursements called "development credits" have fluctuated within a moderately rising range, reaching a total of US$722.5 million in 1963 and dropping slightly in 1964. The most dynamic factor involved in the increase in these disbursements was the beginning of IDB operations, since, in only three years, its disbursements have increased from US$6.6 million to US$198 million. There has been a very important change in the kind of loans corresponding to these disbursements and in the content of grants. Loans are presently classified as hard or conventional loans (that is, those that are granted at a rate of interest above $4\frac{1}{2}\%$, with grace periods not exceeding two years, and with amortization periods of up to 20 years) and soft loans (those granted under terms that are, generally speaking, very much more advantageous). It can be asserted, taking into account the change in the disbursement pattern by principal sources of financing, that while at the beginning of this period over two thirds of the financing consisted of conventional loans, in 1964 this proportion had been reduced to a little more than one third, almost inverting, therefore, the previous proportion.

Besides the development financing referred to in the preceding paragraphs, in order to have a more complete picture of all official financing, it is necessary to mention, even though very briefly, compensatory financing, that is, that which is effected by the International Monetary Fund and the United States Treasury to assist countries through short-term loans designed to overcome situations involving cyclic and sporadic disequilibrium in their international payments. This type of financial cooperation tends to fluctuate a great deal because of its compensatory character. While in some years it has amounted to a considerable share of total financing, in others its importance has diminished appreciably. In 1964, when the majority of the countries in this area experienced relatively favorable conditions with regard to their balances of payments, operations in this category totaled approximately US$160 million, increasing the total amount of official disbursements in all categories that year to US$1,216 million, a sum somewhat less than that for 1961. Taking all the contributions from official sources in the United States as a whole, i.e., including grants, development credits, and short-term compensatory credits, it can be stated that there was no definite upward trend since the annual average of the first two years of the period under study was some US$810 million and that of the last two years, US$820 million.

Another important aspect of the financing carried out is the use by sector or economic activity to which it is put. In disbursing long-term development loans a considerable increase in those allocated to agriculture is noted. A substantial increase in multisectoral loans is observed also, the greatest portion of which, it is presumed, are directed to agriculture and industry. This type of loan had accounted for 19% of total disbursements in 1963. A similar increase has occurred in connection with disbursements made for housing programs, potable water system, and education, which, in 1960, were insignificant but recently amounted to approximately 15% of the total. This change is due principally to the emergence of the IDB as one of the principal sources of disbursements in the area. There is a characteristic that merits attention, in regard to the structure of disbursements by use category, and this is that over half of the disbursements coming from the principal financing sources still are destined for infrastructure projects in the economic and social fields, where the increase in production tends to be on a long-term basis. A more immediate effect on production capacity could be obtained if disbursements in the industrial and agricultural fields were increased.

The disbursements in reference have been increased in practically all of the countries of the area in relation to those at the beginning of the period, except in Ecuador and Haiti. In over half of the countries the disbursements have more than tripled and in some, such as Bolivia, Chile, and the Dominican Republic, the increase has been really extraordinary. However, it should be pointed out that in some cases the initial level used for comparison, i.e., that of 1960, was quite low. The average annual per capita disbursement in Brazil, Haiti, and Guatemala has been, throughout the period, lower than the average for the area as a whole while in the case of Chile, Costa Rica, and Panama, it was markedly higher than the average.

Upon examining the present institutional framework of the Alliance for Progress in the previous chapter, mention was made of the duty conferred on the CIAP in the financing field, that is, of making "an annual estimate of the financing actually needed for Latin American development and of the total funds that may be available from the various domestic and external sources." On the basis of these estimates and the review of national and regional plans, steps taken, and efforts made, the CIAP is "(ii) To prepare and present annual proposals for determining the distribution among the several countries of public funds under the Alliance. . . ." In accordance with the procedure agreed on at its first meeting to carry out country reviews, bearing in mind the recommendations of its subcommittees, the CIAP is to make a global recommendation regarding Latin American requirements for external financing during 1965 and 1966, as well as preliminary estimates of its distribution by country on the basis of each one's internal efforts and use of its national resources.

In its policy statement on "The State of the Alliance for Progress and Prospects for 1965", the CIAP made the following preliminary estimate of Latin American requirements and availabilities for 1965:[21]

---

[21] *Ibid.,* pp. 42-46 and document cited in Note 3, pp. 12-16, 30-31, 19.

(In millions of dollars)

Requirements		Availabilities	
Deficit on Current Account	$1 078	Disbursements from already contracted loans	$1 300
Amortization of the public and monetary sector	1 899	Disbursements from possible additional development loans (IBRD, IDB, Ex-Im Bank, AID, PL 480, Europe, etc.)	400
Increase in international liquid-assets	262		
	$3 239		
LESS		New and extended suppliers credits, bank lending, and swap renewals	600
Net flow of private capital	131	Debt rescheduling, refunding, roll-overs for some countries, plus IMF and US Treasury loans	600
		Possible additional private long-term capital	200
	$3 108		$3 100

51. *Technical Cooperation and Assistance*

OAS programs and activities in the field of technical cooperation and assistance began long before the Punta del Este Meeting and so, since then it has only been necessary to adapt and enlarge them in accordance with the specific goals of the Alliance for Progress. The most important means used are: the Program of Technical Cooperation of the OAS, the Fellowship Program, the Professorship Program, the Extracontinental Training Program, the Program of Direct Technical Assistance, and the Technical Assistance Programs for the planning of the Alliance for Progress. At the present time the major part of the financial resources for these programs has been included in the Special Development Assistance Fund approved at the Third Annual Meeting of the IA-ECOSOC at the Ministerial Level.

The Program of Technical Cooperation is characterized (and in this respect it differs from the other programs) by the fact that it is a multilateral program sponsored jointly by the member states of the OAS, devoted to providing technical training on the professional level for the benefit of all, and financed by voluntary contributions of the member countries themselves. Its Bases, approved by the IA-ECOSOC in 1956, established a Technical Cooperation Board composed of representatives of the Pan American Union and the Inter-American Specialized Organizations, which had, among other duties, that of studying and submitting to the OAS Council the projects prepared by the cooperating agencies; rendering an opinion to the Council on the projects presented by the governments and each year presenting a complete draft of the program and budget for the following year. The same provision established the position of Executive Director of the Program of Technical Cooperation, responsible to the Council for compliance with the directives set forth in the Bases and those subsequently provided by the Council.

The new directions pointed out in the Act of Bogotá and the Charter of Punta del Este, together with the results of an evaluation of the entire Program made in 1962 by a group of experts, by decision of the IA-ECOSOC, advised that these Bases be revised because they were considered to be inadequate, although it was nevertheless recognized that the Program had accomplished magnificent work, in spite of its limited resources. As a result of this evaluation, the IA-ECOSOC approved the new Bases for the Program on October 26, 1962.

In 1963 the Program completed 13 years of continuous activity: Twenty-two projects, covering the most varied fields of specialization, were operated during this period. In spite of the variety in the fields of training, these projects may be grouped into five overall fields of activity: Social Sciences; Economic Development; Agriculture; Health, and Education. If the distribution of these projects by years is analyzed, it is seen that there was a growing rate of operation, in spite of the declines shown in 1957 and 1960, and that from a total of 6 to 7 active projects during the first years of the Program, it grew to 12 projects in 1962 and to 13 in 1963.

In 1963 the Program operated 13 projects, ten of which were carrying on training activities and three of which were in a reorganizational phase in order to adapt them to the new Bases, in accordance with IA-ECOSOC recommendations. These three were: No. 102, Inter-American Training Course on the Administration of Social Welfare Programs; No. 105, Inter-American Training Program in Business Administration; and No. 209, Training Center for Regional Economic Development. The main purpose of the projects is to provide advanced training to professional workers and specialists, to enable them to contribute more effectively to the economic and social development of the member states of the OAS. Altogether more than

12,000 students have been trained under the Program in the 13-year period from 1951 to 1963, inclusive. In 1963, a total of 1,275 students, coming from virtually all the member countries of the OAS, were trained. If the distribution of professional workers trained is analyzed by field of activity, it is seen that the largest number of students received training in fields related to agriculture, next in number were those trained in matters connected with economic development, the social sciences, education, and health.

In 1964, after the available funds had been verified, four new projects approved by the IA-ECOSOC on a priority basis were to be initiated. These are: Project No. 211, Inter-American Training Program in Transportation; No. 212, Inter-American Program for the Improvement of Science Teaching; No. 213, Inter-American Center for Land and Water Resources Development; and No. 214, Inter-American Training Center in Public Administration.

It may be said in conclusion that the impact of the Program of Technical Cooperation in the Latin American countries is evident in many aspects of the national life of these countries and in fields as different as those of statistical studies for economic development plans, agricultural extension work and the improvement of rural life, the control and eradication of foot-and-mouth disease, and the planning of community building or development. The Punta del Este recommendations gave a new orientation to the Program by indicating what should be given priority and diversifying its fields of training, so that they will be duly coordinated with those other programs of the General Secretariat that are connected with economic and social development.

The Fellowship Program, which began to function on July 1, 1958, as a regular, continuing, educational activity of the OAS, was seven years old in June 1965. The purpose of the Program, which originated in Recommendation No. 22 of the Inter-American Committee of the Presidential Representatives, is to contribute to the economic, social, scientific, and cultural progress of the member countries and to promote closer relations and understanding among them. The Program operates in coordination with and under a common administration with the Professorship Program. During the period shown above, the Program granted 3,158 fellowships of which 2,552 were new and 606 were extensions. The fellows were selected from a total of 10,004 applications received. In granting the fellowships, preference was given to the fields of specialization that the governments considered of greatest interest, and the high percentage that has gone to economic development is of note. As regards the distribution of the fellows by country of origin and country of study, it can be estimated that approximately the same proportion of students and research students came from or went to the United States (including Puerto Rico) as from or to Latin America.

The Professorship Program, like the Fellowship Program, is a regular and continuing activity of the OAS. Its purposes are to raise the academic level of training of the technical and scientific personnel of the member states so that these states will be able to increase their rate of economic, scientific, social, and cultural development, and to encourage exchange of knowledge and techniques. The Program therefore endeavors to contribute to the development and improvement of those national and regional American universities and centers of advanced studies and research that are capable of and have proper facilities for taking maximum advantage of the aid offered by the Program.

The Professorship Program was five years old in June 1965. In these five years it has granted 37 professorships. Nevertheless, the funds of the Program have been very limited in relation to its possibilities for action and the interest it has awakened in the study centers of the hemisphere.

Early in 1962, the General Secretariat of the OAS promoted various contacts designed to obtain the participation of non-American countries in the economic and social development plans of Latin American within the framework of the Alliance for Progress. As a result of these negotiations, several governments of Western Europe and that of Israel offered training opportunities and fellowships. At the same time, the General Secretariat was negotiating with the Agency for International Development (AID) of the United States Government for the purpose of obtaining the necessary funds for the transportation of the fellows. On September 28, 1962, an agreement was signed between the Pan American Union and AID under which the latter provided the sum of $240,000 to defray the costs of the international travel of the fellowship students. The same agreement authorized the expenditure of up to 10% of this amount for administrative expenses and a maximum of $100.00 per fellow as a contribution toward the cost of winter clothing and textbooks. Two months later the funds were available and it was then possible to commence the Extracontinental Training Program.

The Program has as its purpose to utilize to the maximum the opportunities for training outside the hemisphere for scientists, technical experts, and other professional persons of the member countries, with a view to assisting in the economic and social development of these countries. With this as its goal, it is endeavoring to meet the need for personnel for regional, national, and sectoral development plans, by training the specialists that these plans require. Thus, the preparation of training projects is subject to the priorities established in the Charter of Punta del Este and the Act of Bogotá; in the recommendations of the Council of the Organization, the IA-ECOSOC, and the Inter-American Cultural Council; as well as in the national, regional, and sectoral development plans. At the same time, the Program coordinates its training projects with the various programs and projects of the inter-American system, for the purpose of supplementing them and avoiding duplication.

The number of fellowships that have been offered up to this time by countries outside the hemisphere surpass in large measure the possibilities for international travel that are available with the funds at hand. The increased interest that the many governments outside the hemisphere have shown in the Program is the best indication of the advantages and guarantees that the Program offers to countries that are concerned about development problems. The fact that non-American governments are gradually showing preference for providing their technical assistance through the Pan American Union instead of the traditional ways of bilateral agreements leads to the supposition that the effectiveness of the Program is being clearly recognized. Among the countries with which contact is being maintained and which have made offers and entered into negotiations are the following, listed in alphabetical order: Belgium, Denmark, France, Israel, Italy, Japan, The Netherlands, Norway, Portugal, Spain, Sweden, Switzerland, the United Kingdom, and West Germany.

The Program of Direct Technical Assistance recommended by the Inter-American Committee of Presidential Representatives began its activities on July 1, 1958. On April 22, 1959 the Council of the Organization approved the General Standards governing this Program. Its main purpose is to contribute to the economic and social development of the American countries by means of advisory missions and services to the member states that request them. This Program is characterized by its great flexibility and the rapidity with which requests are met. The Program has received 253 requests since it was started and has completed 153 missions. In the period between January 1, 1963 and June 30, 1964, it received 61 requests and carried out 48 missions. Under the program of the Alliance for Progress, the Pan American Union, in compliance with the provisions of the Charter of Punta del Este and the Agreement between the Pan American Union and the United States Government signed on November 29, 1961, is responsible for: 1. general programming, which includes assistance in the establishment or strengthening of national planning machinery; 2. general programming, which refers to assistance in the formulation or improvement of national development programs; 3. preparation or improvement of national economic and social, sectoral, or geographical plans; 4. preparation of specific investment projects. Eight missions, with a total of 93 experts, have been working since this program was started.

In the specific case of the Program of Direct Technical Assistance, it was proposed at the last meeting of the IA-ECOSOC that the budget be gradually increased over the next four years and that certain changes be made in the present policy of the Program such as: that the missions remain for a longer period and that greater emphasis be placed on encouraging economic and social development. Unfortunately, the IA-ECOSOC was not in a position at that time to take a definitive decision on the new standards proposed, although it stated that it was in favor of extending the duration of the missions and of the Program's paying the per diem expenses of the experts. The General Secretariat likewise proposed, at the aforementioned meeting, that a multilateral fund be established for the purpose of continuing with the previously described assistance programs and with other assistance activities that are now being carried on by the OAS under the Alliance for Progress. This proposal was accepted in principle at the meeting of the IA-ECOSOC in São Paulo and, after being studied by the CIAP, was accepted at the Third Annual Meeting of the IA-ECOSOC when the Special Development Assistance Fund was approved.[22]

Serious handicaps to the formulation and execution of development plans and programs in the Latin American countries are the shortage of specialized technical personnel and the lack of efficient operating agencies. Failure to overcome these handicaps has weakened the effectiveness of foreign financial assistance and limited the capacity of these countries to absorb capital. For this reason, the Inter-American Development Bank (IDB), exercising one of the powers granted by its Agreement, has used technical assistance as an indispensable supplement to its financial activities in overcoming these problems. Its technical assistance activities have been especially designed to expand the capacity of the member countries to absorb foreign capital and to use investment funds more effectively.

Up to September 30, 1965, the IDB had authorized $47 million for nearly 400 separate technical assistance projects. Technical assistance extended from its own funds has generally been related to the field of economic development; that financed from the Social Progress Trust Fund has been connected with social progress projects in fields spelled out in the Trust Fund Agreement: improved land use, potable water and sanitation, housing, advanced education, and the mobilization of domestic resources. General planning, feasi-

---

[22] Cf. *Report of the Secretary General 1963-June 30, 1964*, OEA/Ser.D/ III.15, p. 97 *et seq.*

bility studies, and preinvestment projects absorbed close to 50% of all resources allocated for technical assistance. An additional 13% has gone for technical assistance connected with improved land use. Remaining technical assistance authorizations were devoted to projects related to the strengthening of national development institutions, to the IDB's training programs and to operations in the fields of housing and sanitation. Approximately $1.3 million worth of the IDB's technical assistance has helped establish or reorganize development institutions in several Latin American countries and thus improved their capacity to effectively use domestic and external resources. In cooperation with the United Nations Special Fund, the IDB used its technical assistance to help establish the Latin American Institute of Economic and Social Planning. Technical assistance is also being provided for joint missions to several member countries to help them prepare national economic and social development plans. The IDB is also cooperating with the OAS and ECLA on a program of studies in the tax and fiscal fields in Latin America.

Integration is a complex process, requiring a large volume of technical assistance, and the IDB is making important contributions in this field. The principal purpose of its technical assistance program is to promote development projects involving two or more countries, which will lead to an expansion of trade and economic complementarity in Latin America. At the same time, the program seeks to strengthen relatively less-developed countries in order to bring about more balanced growth of its members.

Noteworthy in this connection is the overall program for the development of border zones undertaken by the Governments of Colombia and Venezuela, for which the IDB has granted technical assistance. At the request of the two governments and with the participation of their respective planning agencies, an IDB study mission was sent to explore means of bringing about the integrated development of their border areas. The mission's report, submitted to two governments in mid-1964, suggested several infrastructure projects that could be undertaken jointly and made several recommendations on matters pertaining to commercial relations and programming. A similar study is being undertaken with the IDB's assistance, for the joint development of border areas between Ecuador and Colombia. Technical assistance has also been provided to the Governments of Bolivia, Peru, Ecuador, and Colombia for a study of the possibility of building a highway linking the Amazon regions of those countries.

Another important undertaking to encourage the integration movement was the establishment of the Institute for Latin American Integration as a unit of the IDB in Buenos Aires. Inaugurated August 24, 1965, the Institute is the first study center in Latin America devoted exclusively to the analysis of the process of regional integration in all its economic, technical, legal, and institutional aspects, and to the training of the personnel required by that process. The Institute's specific activities will include the training of officials, the offering of instruction at the postgraduate level, research work, the provision of advisory services, and the dissemination of research results and studies.

A major contribution to the march of the Alliance has been the encouraging interest and participation of agencies and nations from outside the Western Hemisphere or outside the framework of the inter-American system. Likewise, the bilateral programs of the Government of the United States continued at a high level in both the financial and the technical assistance spheres. A recent report of the Development Assistance Committee (DAC) of the Organization for Economic Cooperation and Development (OECD) indicates a substantial rise in the amount of technical assistance and training provided by DAC member countries (including the United States) to Latin America. The information indicates an increase in total cost of this assistance from US$45 million in 1962 to US$80 million in 1963, with a further increase estimated for 1964. Of these totals, the Government of the United States provided approximately half. However, the share of countries other than the United States has been rising continuously and "several countries have in addition continued to make important technical assistance contributions to dependencies or former dependencies with which they have special links in the Western Hemisphere." The OECD report notes, however, that in proportion to its size Latin America would appear to receive somewhat less than its proportionate share of technical assistance except insofar as training grants are concerned. In expenditures, technical assistance to Latin America accounted for about 10% of DAC countries' bilateral technical assistance expenditures.

Aside from technical assistance, the greater portion of DAC assistance to Latin America has been in the form of loans (except for the United States). In 1963 DAC technical cooperation grants to the member states of the OAS totaled US$80 million of which US$68 million was provided by the United States. The latter country also provided US$129 million in other forms of assistance. Total DAC loans to Latin America were US$472.6 million, of which US$122 million came from countries other than the United States. In the technical assistance category, the DAC countries in 1963 provided 1,248 advisory experts and 492 teachers to Latin America. The United States provided about 75% of the advisory services. Europe has in the last three years become an important center of training for Latin American students. In 1963, 6,419 fellowships were awarded for study in the DAC countries. Of these 3,270 were awarded by the United States, and 3,149 by other DAC countries. Of the total fellowships, 1,188 were in the field of education; 408 in agriculture; 1,631 in industry, technology, and trade; 352 in health and sanitation; 1,102 in public administration, economics, finance, and social services; and 1,738 in miscellaneous fields.

Finally, the United Nations Expanded Program of Technical Assistance and its Regular Program plus the Special Fund carried out operations in Latin America in 1963 to a total value of US$20 million compared to about $16 million in the previous year. About 1,100 experts from the United Nations worked in Latin America in 1963 and about 1,000 fellowships were granted to Latin America. These figures represent about one fifth of U.N. aid to developing countries. In regard to the Special Fund, up to early 1964, of a total of 375 projects involving US$335 million approved since creation of the Fund, 102 projects involving $88 million had been allocated to Latin America.[23]

52. *General Evaluation of the March of the Alliance*

The goal of this final section of the chapter is not to evaluate the march of the Alliance for Progress by means of the multiple aspects and complex problems presently presented by the program for the economic and social development of Latin America. It is merely an effort to call attention to the most outstanding points revealed by the program in its first four years, particularly in those aspects and problems related to the "internal effort" the Latin American countries have obligated themselves to make.

The process of planning, new to most of the countries of the region, necessarily was affected at first by deficiencies that only the passage of time can correct. Without attempting to exhaust the list of such defects, among the more outstanding are the following: the lack of skill in projecting financial variables, which has resulted in inability, in some cases, to meet the programmed goals because of the shortage of domestic or external resources; the lack of adequate definition of the plans themselves and of the policies needed to attain their objectives, and the slowness with which some of these measures have been adopted; insufficient participation in the planning process by important groups and institutions; scarcity of projects that have been sufficiently studied and adequately prepared; formulation of the plan in terms unsuited to later verification of its execution; and the absence of any systematic effort for a continuing review of the plan for the purpose of making any necessary periodic adjustments,

---

[23] Regarding extracontinental assistance see the Report of the Secretary General cited in Note 1, pp. 47-48.

in order to make the plan at all times an adequate instrument for the coordination of the economic and social policy.

Despite the difficulties encountered in the preparation and execution of the plans, it may be noted that the planning of development in Latin America has helped, in varying degrees and in accordance with the situation in the individual countries, to: determine the most appropriate objectives of the development policies and the means required to attain them, thereby contributing toward the adoption of more rational governmental decisions in economic and social matters; emphasize the necessity of increasing exports and accelerating the economic integration of Latin America; emphasize the necessity of increasing the volume of investments to the level required to reach the proposed growth goal, and indicate the sectoral composition of the level of investment required for a process of balanced development; determine to what extent resources for financing investment must be increased and identify the internal and external sources of such resources; adequately prepare the policy of industrial and agricultural development, which will make it possible to provide more precise guidelines to private enterprise; increase investment in infrastructure and step up its rationalization; identify the economy's bottlenecks and help to solve them through greater coordination in the policy adopted in the various fields and sectors; and arouse an interest in the whole society in the problem of development, thereby helping to bring all social groups into the effort to reach the goals set at Punta del Este.[24]

The foregoing explains why the CIAP, in its First Report to the IA-ECOSOC, should decide to reaffirm the need for economic and social development planning as one of the essential elements of the Alliance and one of the most important indications of domestic effort. The CIAP would not be able to fulfill its responsibilities unless the countries prepared their development plans within a reasonable period. For the CIAP, planning is a continuous process which starts with the formulation of projects and the elaboration of the plan and is completed with its orderly execution, efficient administration, and evaluation of the final results. Consequently, it recommended to the countries that the agencies responsible for this process be strengthened, without neglecting the improvement of basic statistics, which must be adapted to the requirements of the planning process; and it urged the countries which have not yet presented development plans to proceed with their preparation, and the countries with plans to initiate or continue the preparation of long-term plans.

---

[24] *Ibid.,* pp. 16-17.

For its part, the IA-ECOSOC, in its most recent analysis of the Alliance for Progress to date, expressed that the experience acquired during the first months of operation of CIAP indicated that that body's efficiency in discharging its duties will rise in proportion to the existence of suitably prepared and evaluated plans. The system of country reviews, far from relegating long-term planning to a secondary position, emphasizes even more how much it is needed in order to increase efficiency of internal policy and to establish firmer foundations for international financial cooperation. Plan preparation and evaluation, carried out in the terms of the Charter of Punta del Este, will continue to represent in the future, as they have up to now, an important contribution to the success of the mission conferred on CIAP.

With further reference to the need for planning, the IA-ECOSOC pointed out that the plans that have been prepared have served up to now as a basis for estimating the external financial resources necessary to support the expenditures and investments which will permit the reaching of a set goal of economic development, but in some cases they have not taken sufficiently into account that programs should be, above all, ways of reorganizing and encouraging internal effort and expressions of basic governmental policy aimed at ensuring the best use of national resources. In addition, the elements of economic development have not yet been adequately coordinated with those of social progress. The evident advantages attained by the Latin American countries in adopting the principle of development planning have been partially counteracted by adverse circumstances which the governments have not been in a position to overcome rapidly. But the countries of Latin America remain firm in their decision to continue forward in the fields of economic development and social progress, in an effort to overcome the structural deficiencies which in the past have impeded the reaching of higher levels of well-being. To that end, they now declare their intention of planning development properly, overcoming existing obstacles and correcting the very serious defects still found in the preparation and execution of development programs.

Regarding the latter, experience in Latin American planning points to the advisability of setting up preinvestment systems, by means of which basic statistics can be improved, a more complete knowledge of human and natural resources can be gained, viable and financially feasible investment programs and projects can be prepared, and the administrative structure can be improved in order to make it an effective instrument for formulating, executing, and directing development programs. Furthermore, in the preparation stage of the plan, it is necessary to have executive officers at the different levels of government participate more actively in formulating overall strategy and presenting the different sectoral programs; it is also necessary that the business, labor, and cultural sectors participate to the extent needed and that an effort be made to keep the public well informed of the plan's objectives and of the means which will be used to achieve them.

The same analysis goes on to state that the very content of the plans should be improved in order to attain the following main objectives: to avoid the usual excessively broad goals and projections and give greater importance to the sectoral analysis of programs. In the preparation of development programs, greater emphasis should be given to the formulation of regional plans, incorporated into the national program and leading to the attainment of greater efficiency and coordination in government action at the regional level. The many defects still in the plans of the social sectors, especially in education and health, must be overcome. Moreover, in the preparation of general programs, greater attention should be given to income redistribution as one of the basic objectives of these programs. Also, priority should be assigned to the planning of agrarian policy in general, and to its coordination with the agrarian reform program. Equally important is financial programming in both the public and the private sectors. In order to further Latin American economic integration, an effort should be made to coordinate national development plans.[25]

As the CIAP indicates in the Report of its Fourth Meeting (April 1965), the first series of country reviews, made in 1964, has proved to be a happy step towards perfecting a truly multilateral instrument in the implementation of the Alliance for Progress. However, both CIAP and the IA-ECOSOC are clearly aware that in order for the country reviews to become completely effective, for the member countries and for the financing institutions, a more profound and penetrating investigation must be made into both future plans and progress achieved in carrying out past plans and policies. The aim of CIAP was to make a transitional experiment out of the 1964 country reviews that would present an overall picture of the system, plans, and prospects of each Latin American nation. The reviews made it possible to identify the critical tasks that must be undertaken by the countries themselves, by the credit institutions, and, more frequently, by the nations and credit institutions working in close cooperation. They helped to establish a basis of financing for the coordination of teamwork between all of the interested credit institutions, and to speed the development effort of Latin America as a whole, and as among these institutions, CIAP, and the countries themselves.

---

[25] *Cf.* Document cited in Note 3, pp. 134, 32-34.

Nevertheless, the process must go further in order to enable CIAP to determine more precisely the specific measures taken by the countries since the 1964 review to carry out the specific reforms that are necessary and to adopt financial, economic, and social policies conducive to achieving the objectives of the Charter of Punta del Este. It is equally important that CIAP examine, in the light of the foregoing, the extent to which requirements of external resources are met. In this connection, it is well to recall the orientation to be followed by the 1965 country reviews, provided by the IA-ECOSOC at its Third Annual Meeting at the Ministerial Level (Lima 1964).[26]

On that occasion the IA-ECOSOC believed that the process of country reviews should constitute the principal activity of CIAP and should be continued and intensified. Results of the first year of effort by CIAP reflect the crucial importance of efficient country reviews and indicate that in the future these reviews can be substantially improved in order to serve as a guide, not only for the governments of Latin America, but also to international financing institutions. In its opinion, intensification of these reviews can be achieved by means of: a) improvement of the statistical basis; and b) a closer analysis of operating and sectorial problems, for example: i) evaluation of programs in the field of structural reform; transformation of the agrarian structure; and educational, tax, and administrative reforms; ii) attention to certain key problems in the development effort. Special importance should be given, among these, to progress in social programs and to fiscal problems represented by inflation and deficit spending. It would also be well to look into certain aspects that demonstrate the effort made to eliminate the limitations of underdevelopment itself, such as results of the policy of export diversification.

In addition, the members of CIAP and of the Panel of Experts should conduct on-the-spot analyses and examinations of development efforts. The countries under study should make every possible effort to contribute to the success of the reviews by contributing better information. The Secretariat, for its part, has a vital role to play in this process.

In brief, the country reviews highlighted the need to strengthen planning in the Latin American countries both to rationalize the internal development effort and to provide a better basis for multilateral cooperation. In the light of the country reviews carried out, the analysis of planning summarized in the CIAP final report of its Mexico Meeting was confirmed. The review process was performed with much greater ease and thoroughness in countries that have

---

[26] Cf. *The Alliance for Progress in 1965. An Interim Report.* OEA/Ser.H/ XIII, CIAP/219 Rev., 11 May 1965, pp. 27-29.

planned their development because more reliance could be attached to their estimates, a clearer picture of their strategy could be observed, and their specific needs for international cooperation could be better evaluated. Realistic country plans are needed so that the individual development projects fit together into a coherent whole and can be implemented with a minimum of costs and a maximum of leverage. More realistic country plans and more effective project preparation and execution are basically two sides of the same coin.

The country reviews underline particularly the important role of planning in identifying the characteristics of the institutional reforms required by the economic and social structure of each Latin American country and the essential function that the plan fulfills in the coordination of the execution of those reforms and of the economic and social development policies. Moreover, at this stage of the process of planning in some Latin American countries the issue of proper execution of programs emerges. This is the beginning of a critical phase in the planning effort: the time when the discipline of the programs must be observed in order to keep the development efforts within the framework of the Alliance for Progress.

In an evaluation of the Alliance, the efforts and achievements in the field of structural reform are exceptionally important. These, as stated above, are the most perfect manifestation of the internal effort made by the Latin American countries pursuant to the program agreed on at Punta del Este. As far as fiscal or tax reform is concerned, in the course of their country reviews the IA-ECOSOC subcommittees observed that, in general, since the beginning of the Alliance, all the countries had made efforts to introduce structural reforms in their tax systems and to strengthen the administration of taxes. This is probably one of the fields in which the greatest domestic effort has been made, notwithstanding the political problems that any reform of this nature entails. In spite of those efforts, in view of the increase in expenditures, the increase in current revenues has not always reached the rate of growth required for it to be the fundamental basis for the formation of public savings, upon which the efficient execution of investment programs in development plans depends.[27]

Agrarian reform, on the other hand, is quite another matter; so much so that the IA-ECOSOC was moved to declare explicitly, at its Third Annual Meeting at the Ministerial Level, that the internal effort in this field was still insufficient, in the following words: ". . . because, in general, efforts made to date have been insufficient to achieve the objectives of agrarian reform, and because agricultural and livestock production has lagged behind population growth, there

---

[27] Cf. Document cited in Note 3, p. 86.

has been no noticeable improvement in living conditions for the vast majority of farm people, and this is a serious obstacle to economic development and to the strengthening of democratic institutions." At that time, the IA-ECOSOC also declared that the structural changes implied by agrarian reform are a fundamental requisite for development of the countries of the area, and that, to be effective, agrarian reform must: produce a change in the structure of land tenure that will permit of increasing the income of the farmer and achieve the best possible combination of factors for agricultural production; give the land its social function, preventing land and the income it generates from becoming instruments of speculation and economic domination; modernize rural life by incorporating the farmer into the national economy and facilitating the growth of demand for products of other sectors; and improve the power structure by giving the farmer a real voice in decisions and a share in political, economic, and social opportunities. It further stated that, since the relationship between the anachronistic structure of land tenure and the situation described is undeniable, the solution of land-tenure problems must be squarely faced by carrying out substantial reforms on a significant scale, in order to replace latifundia and minifundia by an equitable system of ownership; and that simultaneously, with a view to promoting agriculture and livestock, agricultural-credit and technical assistance programs must be strengthened, as must programs for expanding farming areas through settlement of new lands wherever the ratio of land to man is unsatisfactory.

In this respect, the IA-ECOSOC considered that expansion of agricultural production and colonization are not acceptable substitutes for agrarian reform. As the Charter of Punta del Este declares, reform must be directed toward the effective transformation of structures, eliminating unjust systems of ownership and exploitation of land.

With regard to another aspect of the same problem it pointed out that, according to the accepted view in the Americas, agrarian reform should be integral, which means that solution of the land-tenure problem should be accompanied by the provision of technical, economic, and social assistance, and of appropriate facilities for marketing agricultural products, assuring just prices, so that the land will become for the man who works it the basis of his economic stability, the foundation of his increasing welfare, and the guarantee of his freedom and dignity. Moreover, agrarian reform must be integrated; or, in other words, its planning and execution must be consistent with planned development in all other sectors of the economy. Agrarian reform programming should be implemented by utilizing available resources, avoiding delays for the sake of perfectionism, in order that it may be carried out as rapidly as possible.

Finally, according to the IA-ECOSOC, because of the urgent nature of agrarian problems, the governments should quickly overcome legal, financial, administrative, and political obstacles that are delaying proper fulfillment of the commitments made in the Charter of Punta del Este, particularly those that refer to the change in the pattern of land tenure and to the legal means for obtaining land.[28]

A more careful examination of these and other aspects of the march of the Alliance for Progress would require considerably more space than is available here. However, one general observation must be made, based on the following passage from one of the Punta del Este instruments, the Declaration to the Peoples of America: "This declaration expresses the conviction of the nations of Latin America that these profound economic, social, and cultural changes can come about only through the self-help efforts of each country. Nonetheless, in order to achieve the goals which have been established with the necessary speed, domestic efforts must be reinforced by essential contributions of external assistance." By means of a continuing review of factors which may have been holding back the march of the Alliance, the General Secretariat of the OAS has become aware of the exaggerated emphasis sometimes placed on the insufficiency or sluggishness of external assistance or on the supposed defects of the multilateral machinery. In their reports to the OAS Council on the structural and procedural changes the inter-American system should undergo in order for the Alliance to acquire the "efficiency and the dynamic qualities called for by the Charter of Punta del Este," former Presidents Kubitschek and Lleras were in substantial agreement with this position, which is indisputable. Since this action program calls for a profound transformation of the socio-economic and juridico-institutional structures of the Latin American countries, the primary responsibility for the effective achievement of the goals of the Alliance for Progress lies, and will remain, in the willingness and ability of the respective governments to introduce the necessary internal changes, with the vigor and firmness such development requires.

---

[28] Cf. *Final Report* of the Third Annual Meeting of the IA-ECOSOC at the Ministerial Level, OEA/Ser.H/XII.9, pp. 13-14.

Chapter XV

Latin American Economic Integration

The Declaration and Charter of Punta del Este consider Latin American economic integration one of the essential objectives of the Alliance for Progress. The basic instruments of the two current Latin American integration processes also stem from the idea that integration is fundamental to the economic and social development of the region. This explains the close relationship, both substantive and institutional, between the respective regional programs and the general program of the Alliance—a relationship that is doubly justified if one bears in mind that the goal is "the ultimate fulfillment of aspirations for a Latin American common market." It is on this basis, which in no way affects the essentially autonomous nature of the phenomenon of Latin American integration, that the following discussion rests.

53. *The Latin American Integration Process*

Latin American economic integration is the result, primarily, of conditions peculiar to the region and, therefore, should be carried out at its own pace and conditioned by the development problems it is attempting to resolve. To the internal requirements are added certain external stimuli, such as the forming of large international economic units (e.g., European Common Market), which reinforce the tendency toward integration on the part of the countries in the area so as to create a condition of internal growth vis-à-vis a possible decrease in the demand for their traditional export products. As long as international trade is dominated by large economic blocs, the Latin American countries will become increasingly aware that their isolated individual efforts are totally insufficient to solve the problems this situation creates. In this way, economic integration appears to be a self-defense measure on the part of these countries, when viewed from three perspectives, whose juridical and political consequences will require further study. These are: 1. recognition of a common interest on the part of the Latin American nations; 2. the articulation and manifestation of this common interest by means of adequate institutions; and 3. the harmonization of national interests with those of the group, which must find expression in the very planning of the industrial development to which all the countries aspire.

Furthermore, from a world political perspective in the present context, the fact that Latin America will have 600 million inhabitants at the end of this century in continuous population growth gives extraordinary dimensions to the problem of its economic and social development. If the area with the most rapid rate of growth in the world—whose juridical and political principles are rooted in the system of values of western civilization—is incapable of achieving an industrial growth-rate sufficient to absorb the work force and create adequate living conditions, its population growth obviously will bring with it a negative factor. But if, on the other hand, by means of a coordinated internal effort as well as international cooperation Latin America can make definite progress in the process of civilization under the rule of law, its population explosion will be an advantage.

The importance of the establishment of a Latin American common market, therefore, cannot and should not be ignored. At the same time, however, there are enormous obstacles, of a geographic nature (lack of communications, distance between the participating countries), an economic nature (scarcity of trade between countries in the zone, dependence of national economies on a few export products), a political nature (attempts to reach a national, community solution at a time of nationalistic fervor, failure to explain to the people the need for integration), and a legal nature (insufficient legal teaching and research into the techniques and principles of supranational action; need to explain the legal nature of the integration process and its relation to the problem of sovereignty, etc.). Nevertheless, the peoples' will to progress, the multilateral programs of cooperation such as the Alliance for Progress, and, above all, the desire for political renewal as well as economic development and social improvement expressed by the more wholesome elements, create the conditions for a grand enterprise that presents a challenge to the ability and creative imagination of the Latin spirit. In that spirit can be found the basis for the optimism with which Latin American integration should be viewed.

The two existing nuclei of integration are the Central American Common Market and the Latin American Free Trade Association (LAFTA). The first is regulated by a central system of standards, the General Treaty for Central American Economic Integration, signed at Managua, Nicaragua on December 13, 1960. Around the Treaty, forming an organic whole, are grouped the earlier and later instruments that regulate the integration process.[1] The General Treaty provides for the free trade of all products originating in the

---

[1] The complete text of the treaty appears in *Appendix 21*, p. 470, *infra*.

zone within five years, with the sole limitations that are the subject of special treatment. The parties also agreed to adopt a uniform tariff policy, within that same period, for import products originating outside the zone. The establishment of a uniform tariff is based on the terms of an earlier document, the Central American Agreement on the Equalization of Import Duties and Charges (1959). The process has already been applied to more than 97% of the items in the Standard Central American Tariff Nomenclature (NAUCA). The Central American countries not only aspire to free trade but also to an integrated industrial development. To this end, by means of a protocol they have created a Regimen for Integration Industries, as well as a Special System for the Promotion of Productive Activities. In addition, they also concluded a Central American Convention on Fiscal Incentives for Industrial Development.

The treaty establishing the LAFTA, signed in Montevideo, Uruguay on February 18, 1960, establishes, as its immediate objective, a Free Trade Area in which, through a gradual reciprocal reduction of all duties, charges, and restrictions on trade, free trade will be established among the signatory countries within a 12-year period.[2] With this in mind the treaty provides for annual meetings for the corresponding negotiations. Also, the parties shall reciprocally grant each other the unconditional and unlimited most-favored-nation treatment, with exception of the preferential treatment established for lesser developed countries.

Aside from its immediate trade purpose, the treaty is conceived as the initial instrument in a broader process, that is, the formation of a future Latin American common market with specific socio-economic goals. This larger objective arises from the *comunis intentio* of the parties as expressed in the preamble and in Article 54 and in the reiteration of its objectives that appears in Resolution No. 100 of the IV Meeting of the Conference of the said Parties (1964): "The fundamental objective of the Montevideo Treaty is to promote the economic and social development of the Contracting Parties by means of the gradual establishment of complementary economies and economic integration." The same concept appears in the preamble of the Treaty of Managua which reaffirms that its purpose is "to unify the economies of the four countries and jointly to promote the development of Central America in order to improve the living conditions of their people." In this respect, in the Charter of Punta del Este these same countries, parties to the aforementioned treaties, together with the remaining members of the inter-American system, conceived of these instruments of integration as effective measures for the achieve-

---

[2] The complete text of the treaty appears in *Appendix 23*, p. 485, *infra.*

ment of that objective, to which end they agreed to carry forward the "cooperative effort to accelerate . . . development."

54. *The Alliance and Economic Integration*

As indicated above, both the Declaration and the Charter of Punta del Este take up and develop the concept from which spring the Latin American integration instruments.[3] The former agrees "To accelerate the integration of Latin America so as to stimulate the economic and social development . . ." and the latter states that "The American republics consider that the broadening of present national markets in Latin America is essential to accelerate the process of economic development in the Hemisphere. It is also an appropriate means for obtaining greater productivity through specialized and complementary industrial production which will, in turn, facilitate the attainment of greater social benefits for the inhabitants of the various regions of Latin America. The broadening of markets will also make possible the better use of resources under the Alliance for Progress." Therefore, it is evident that both give the economic integration of Latin America a primary role in the task of advancing the economic and social development of the region.

This can be easily explained. When, at Punta del Este, integration was conceived as essential to national development, at the same time national growth was conceived as a part of the growth of the whole region. Thus, at Punta del Este Latin American economic integration received decisive political support by being incorporated into the program of the Alliance. The integration process within the framework of the Alliance for Progress, in turn, invigorates the inter-American system by joining it more organically to the "rising expectations" of the Latin American masses. In this way, the social and economic content of the system, which began to assume a more concrete form after the Act of Bogotá, finds a new and vital expression in the Latin American economic integration process.

As a logical consequence, the Charter specifically establishes that "In working toward economic integration and complementary economies, efforts should be made to achieve an appropriate coordination of national plans, or to engage in joint planning for various economies through the existing regional integration organizations. Efforts

---

[3] In this respect it should be recalled that in one of the resolutions it approved on July 8, 1959 the OAS Council declared "That the creation of the Latin American regional market is a basic objective for the acceleration of the development of the Latin American economies". See the complete text of Resolution XIV, Latin American Regional Market, in the *Decisions Taken at the Meetings of the Council of the OAS*, volume XII, January-December 1959, OEA/Ser.G/III, Vol. XII, p. 100.

should also be made to promote an investment policy directed to the progressive elimination of unequal growth rates in the different geographic areas, particularly in the case of countries which are relatively less developed." In its most recent analysis of the march of the Alliance, the IA-ECOSOC indicated, as one of the principal objectives that would be achieved with the improvement of the content of national plans, that "In the preparation of development programs, greater emphasis should be given to the formulation of regional plans, incorporated into the national program and leading to the attainment of greater efficiency and coordination in government action at the regional level."[4] At its earlier Meeting at the Expert Level, the IA-ECOSOC pointed out the "interest in coordinating the various economic development plans and in overcoming obstacles to the achievement of this end" and that "An example of the usefulness that such coordination of national plans can have already exists in Central America."[5]

This close relationship between the Latin American integration process and the economic and social development of the region explains, in turn, why Title III of the Charter of Punta del Este repeatedly provides for cooperation and assistance in integration programs. The institutional aspect will be examined in the following section. For the moment it will be enough to point out the fields in which the Alliance provides that cooperation and assistance.

The General Secretariat of the OAS as well as the IDB, along with other extracontinental governments and entities that cooperate with the program of the Alliance, constantly provide advice and other kinds of technical assistance to the integration organs, as was seen in Chapter XIV. In Central America the assistance missions also take part in the programming referred to above. With regard to financial cooperation, the aid has consisted in promoting the financing of multinational projects, for which the CIAP has created a permanent committee, or in designating part of its resources to finance the said projects, as the IDB does. For its part the IA-ECOSOC, ever since its First Annual Meetings, has been promoting cooperation and assistance in both fields, in favor of integration programs. In the most recent of these initiatives, in Lima (December 1964), the IA-ECOSOC recommended to the CIAP and the IDB "that they make available maximum technical and financial support to facilitate and expedite the

---

[4] Cf. *The Alliance for Progress: Its Third Year 1963-1964*, IA-ECOSOC, Pan American Union, 1965, p. 34.

[5] See the complete text of Resolution A-3/E63, Preparation of Studies on the Bases for, and Possibilities of, Planning at the Regional Integration Level, Second Annual Meeting of the IA-ECOSOC at the Expert Level, *Final Report*, OEA/Ser.H/XII.5, pp. 12-13.

Latin American integration process, in accordance with the principles of the Charter of Punta del Este."[6]

Nor can it be ignored that the economic integration foreseen in the Charter of Punta del Este is integration "in Latin America," for which it is considered advisable to establish adequate relationships between the two present processes and between these and any Latin American country. In the preamble to the IA-ECOSOC resolution referred to above it is stated very explicitly that the treaties of Montevideo and Managua "constitute the basic existing instruments for the attainment of the ultimate objective: the economic integration of Latin America." This is easily explained in the light of the Alliance's objective of strengthening "existing agreements on economic integration, with a view to the ultimate fulfillment of aspirations for a Latin American common market that will expand and diversify trade among the Latin American countries and thus contribute to the economic growth of the region."

What has happened since Punta del Este, as far as the achievement of this objective is concerned? The institutional aspects of the matter will be seen in the following section. For the moment only the recent initiatives and proposals designed to encourage the general economic integration of the region will be taken up.

These proposals were contained in a document sent to the Latin American Chiefs of State on April 12, 1965, prepared on "their own and exclusive responsibility" by Messrs. Raúl Prebisch, Director General of the Latin American Institute for Economic and Social Planning; José A. Mayobre, Executive Director of the ECLA; Felipe Herrera, President of the IDB; and Carlos Sanz de Santamaría, Chairman of the CIAP. The proposals constituted their reply to a letter addressed to them on January 6 by Eduardo Frei, the President of Chile, expressing his concern regarding the Latin American integration process which, in his opinion, has been "slow and difficult."

The document generally agrees on the need to move forward with the integration process. After analyzing the available instruments, especially the Montevideo Treaty, the functions of the IDB, CIAP, and the Panel of Nine, it concludes that "the machinery already available must be fully utilized." But they also considered that "Other important steps are also indispensable. Agreements to supplement the Montevideo Treaty are necessary: Instruments are required for the programming and promotion of investments at the regional level; a compensatory payments and reciprocal credit system is lacking; it is necessary to define more precisely, in the light of experience, the principle of reciprocity, special treatment for the relatively less de-

---

[6] See the complete text of Resolution 10-M/64, Economic Integration of Latin America, *Final Report* of the Third Annual Meeting of the IA-ECOSOC at the Ministerial Level, OEA/Ser.H/XII.9, pp. 17-18.

veloped countries, procedures to correct the dislocations that could emerge from the liberation of intra-regional trade, and the fundamental role of the Latin American entrepreneur in the over-all context of the common market."

The specific proposals made by Messrs. Prebisch, Mayobre, Herrera, and Sanz de Santamaría to intensify the integration process are: a) Establishment of quantitative targets for the desired maximum level of customs duties—including restrictions of equivalent effect—to be attained and to adopt a gradual and automatic mechanism for the application of such a system; b) Gradual elimination of the application of quantitative and other nontariff restrictions on intraregional trade; c) Establishment of a common tariff *vis-à-vis* the rest of the world; and d) Establishment of a system of reciprocal preferences for member countries to enjoy in their intraregional trade pending the establishment of the definitive preferences in the common tariff. These "four closely interrelated commitments [should be] fulfilled within a period of ten years."[7]

A few weeks earlier the ECLA had published a document entitled "Contribution to Economic Integration Policy in Latin America", in which it also urged the Latin American governments to undertake new commitments. These new commitments would include: a progressive and automatic system of tariff reduction for intraarea trade, covering all products and based on an annual linear reduction; gradual abolition, during a ten-year period, of the quantitative and other restrictions not equivalent to customs duties now in force, "so that at the end of this period the restrictions on reciprocal trade would consist solely of customs duties within the maximum limit indicated above" (not exceeding 20% of the c.i.f. value of each item); a common external tariff to be drawn up and approved, within five years, and gradually put into effect in the subsequent years; minimum preference margins to be negotiated and established for the products of the member countries "where those resulting from the tariff reduction process prove inadequate" and until the common external tariff is negotiated. These various undertakings would be supplemented by escape clauses to permit countries to take emergency measures in cases where the fulfillment of such agreements would result in serious harm to national products or in major balance-of-payments difficulties. Furthermore, special sectoral agreements may be concluded regarding basic industries or others that are part of the general process of industrialization.[8]

---

[7] Cf. *Proposals for the Creation of the Latin American Common Market* (IDB). President Frei's letter was published separately in IDB document GN-19, 25 January 1965.

[8] Cf. *A Contribution to Economic Integration Policy in Latin America*, United Nations, E/CN.12/728, 20 April 1965, *passim*.

55. *Institutional Structure of Integration*

In order to examine adequately the institutional framework within which the process of Latin American economic integration is taking place the following two major aspects must be set forth: the structure and competence of the integration organs themselves (those of the Central American Common Market and of LAFTA), and the ties and relationships between each of these and the inter-American system (and the other extracontinental governments and entities that collaborate in the Alliance for Progress program). The recent initiatives and proposals to encourage integration and strengthen its institutional framework must also be examined in the light of these two aspects. The characteristics of Latin American integration studied in the foregoing section lead, of necessity, to this approach to the question. The examination of the march of the Alliance, in turn, made it possible to appreciate to a degree the impact made on the functioning and activities of the organs of integration and on inter-American organs by the existing interaction between the integration process and the general program for the development of Latin America.

The institutional structure of the Central American Common Market is infinitely more complex than that of LAFTA. Although basically it continues to be the same as was established by the General Treaty signed in Managua in 1960, the new "Charter of San Salvador" (1962), a substitute for the one which originally created the Organization of Central American States (ODECA) and which entered into force in 1965, introduced certain important structural changes.[9] The treaty establishes three organs: the Central American Economic Council, the Executive Council, and the Permanent Secretariat (SIECA), with headquarters in Guatemala City. The first of the three is composed of the Ministers of Economy of each of the five countries and among its powers and attributes are those of directing the integration of the Central American economies and coordinating the economic policy of the said countries. The Executive Council, among its many functions, is given the task of applying and administering the treaty and of laying down the measures necessary to ensure the fulfillment of the undertakings entered into pursuant to the treaty. According to Article XXII of that instrument, it also has the functions formerly entrusted to the Central American Trade Commission and the Central American Commission for Industrial Integration. SIECA, in addition to serving as the secretariat of both councils, is charged with watching over the correct application of the treaty and of other integration instruments.

---

[9] The complete text of these two instruments appears in *Appendices 21* and *22,* on pp. 470 and 480, respectively, *infra.*

The Central American Bank for Economic Integration is the financial organ of the Common Market and it is regulated by a convention signed on July 4, 1960. It functions with capital provided by the member states, contributions from the Government of the United States and loans obtained from international agencies. It is also the means by which the other Alliance for Progress funds are made available to the zone. Other important agencies and institutions are the former Committee for Economic Cooperation in the Central American Isthmus, made up of the five Ministers of Economy under the sponsorship of ECLA, which has been the guiding agency in the formulation and execution of the integration program; the Central American Institute for Industrial Research and Technology (ICAITI); the Advanced School of Public Administration of Central America (ESAPAC); and the Central American Chamber of Compensation.

The new Charter of the ODECA, on the other hand, in Article 1 (Purposes) states that the five countries of the area "are an economic-political community which aspires to the integration of Central America," and it establishes new organs: a) the Meeting of Heads of State, which is the Supreme Organ of the Organization; b) the Conference of Ministers of Foreign Affairs, which is the Principal Organ; c) the Executive Council, which is the Permanent Organ; d) The Legislative Council, composed of three representatives from each of the Legislative Powers of the Member States; e) the Central American Court of Justice, composed of the Presidents of the Judicial Powers of each of the five states; f) the Central American Economic Council, composed of the Ministers of Economy; g) the Cultural and Educational Council, composed of the Ministers of Education or their representatives; and h) the Defense Council, composed of the Ministers of Defense or of the heads of equivalent departments. ODECA headquarters remain in San Salvador, where both the Executive Council and the General Secretariat of the Organization are also located.[10]

The Montevideo Treaty establishes, as organs of LAFTA, the Conference of the Contracting Parties and the Standing Executive Committee. The first is the supreme organ of the Association and, among its functions and duties, it is to take the necessary steps to carry out

---

[10] It will be noted that two of the organs—the Executive Council and the Central American Economic Council—are also provided for in the Treaty of Managua. Nevertheless, this coincidence does not extend to the functions and powers conferred on the respective organs by the two instruments. In this regard, attention should be drawn to the declaration of the Central American Foreign Ministers, issued at an Informal Meeting held in Managua in February 1965, to the effect that the Economic Council and the Executive Council provided for in the treaty, as well as the SIECA, would retain all the characteristics conferred on them by the said treaty, in their structure and functioning, when the restructuring of the ODECA takes place.

the treaty and to study the results of its implementation and to promote the negotiations provided for in Article 4 and to assess the results thereof. The Committee is the permanent organ and is responsible for supervising the implementation of the treaty, along with other responsibilities such as undertaking studies, suggesting measures, and submitting such recommendations to the Conference as it deems appropriate for the effective implementation of the treaty. The Committee consists of a Permanent Representative of each Contracting Party and has a secretariat which also has its headquarters in Montevideo. Pursuant to Article 43 of the treaty, the Committee has created the following Advisory Commission: on Statistics (CAE), Transportation (CAT), Nomenclature (CAN), Origin (CAO), Customs Matters (CAAA), Monetary Matters (CAAM), and Industrial Development (CADI).[11]

Pursuant to the recommendation made by the Charter of Punta del Este, mentioned in the foregoing section—relative to the establishment of effective relationships between the two integration processes —the respective secretariats have kept up an exchange of informational material. The goal however is "to facilitate economic integration in Latin America," and at its First Annual Meeting at the Ministerial Level the IA-ECOSOC, when expressing its satisfaction for the step taken in this regard, again urged "the two groups to strengthen their ties, with a view to more rapid integration of Latin America."[12] Nevertheless, and aside from other factors which are not of concern here, given its present structure and powers, none of the organs of these groups has the juridical personality necessary to deal and act in the name and representation of the member states that make them up. In an effort to overcome this and other obstacles and faults in the present institutional framework of Latin American integration, the foregoing initiatives and proposals have been made.

In his letter to Messrs. Presbisch, Mayobre, Herrera, and Sanz de Santamaría, President Frei stated that "It is obvious that those [institutional mechanisms] of Montevideo have proved inadequate. Experience with other, similar processes demonstrates the need for introducing certain supranational elements into our regional organizations. As evidence of our determination to attain these objectives, I have sent to the National Congress within the past few days a con-

---

[11] The complete text of the treaty appears in *Appendix 23*, p. 485, *infra.*

[12] This relationship between the two integration processes was later broadened by the Agreement between the two secretariats which entered into force by means of an exchange of notes on July 1, 1965, in order to systematize the relations of reciprocal collaboration and consultation in order to join forces for the attainment of their common purpose, the promotion of a higher degree of development through the respective processes of economic integration. Carta Informativa de la SIECA, No. 47, 12 September 1965.

stitutional reform bill which would legalize our participation in the establishment of Latin American entities with supranational authority."[13] In the document the four abovementioned individuals prepared, they admitted it was "necessary to set up institutional machinery which will make use of the various agencies and facilities already in operation and will thus make it possible to co-ordinate all action taken in connexion with the objectives and general criteria stated above." The most noteworthy characteristics of that machinery would be the following: There would be a Council of Ministers, with the "supreme power of decision," which would have the help of advisory committees composed of high-level technical officials from the member countries, and that of a committee composed of representatives of the workers, entrepreneurs, universities, and technical and professional organizations. With regard to its mode of operation it "would be desirable that the right to veto the Council's decisions should be restricted from the outset." The "executive authority" would vest in a Board, composed of a Chairman and a limited number of members who would represent not the governments appointing them but the community itself. Among the Board's functions would be those of ensuring that the objectives of the integration policy were attained and that the general criteria of that policy, including the principle of reciprocity and the necessary tariff-adjustment and preferential measures, were applied; proposing to the Council measures designed to accelerate that process; promoting the negotiation of sectoral complementarity agreements; and acting as a court of first instance in disputes on interpretation. A third organ would be the Latin American Parliament, composed of representatives of the region's parliaments, and which would be a regional forum in which the major currents of public opinion would converge to elucidate the most important problems of integration, thus creating a climate of opinion favorable to the political decisions integration will require. It is also suggested that the Board reach an agreement with the IDB on the establishment of an instrument which would actively promote the preparation of studies and projects designed to promote investments in the regional market. Finally, to solve conflicts of interpretation, an *ad hoc* conciliation committee should be established, to act as a supreme court; its members would be drawn by lot from a list of persons designated for the purpose by the member countries beforehand. This experiment might lead to the establishment of a regional court of justice.[14]

In the ECLA document referred to above it is also stated that the establishment of community institutions that are effective and ade-

---

[13] *Cf.* IDB document GN-19, 25 January 1965.
[14] *Cf.* Document cited in Note 7, pp. 26-29.

quate to the task is an important condition of the integration process, along with these institutions' capacity to watch over the obligations entailed by integration, to search for a common trade policy, to formulate and put into practice a regional investment policy and co-ordinate financial and monetary policies. The institutional structure contemplated is essentially the same as the one proposed by Messrs. Prebisch, Mayobre, *et al.* except that the functions and powers of each organ are set forth in greater detail. The decisions of the Council of Ministers should be adopted unanimously but could be reached by a simple majority in some cases, such as in decisions on requests for exception to the rules in force and in dealing with disputes arising out of the application of the agreements. The Board, whose jurisdiction would extend to many fields, "would not be a supranational authority, since it would not impose any new obligations on the Parties." As far as the judicial organ is concerned, *ad hoc* arbitration tribunals would be established when necessary, competent to deal with complaints relating to non-compliance by one of the Parties with agreements or obligations entered into under the treaty or other instruments deriving from the treaty. The tribunal could serve as the legal advisory body to the other community institutions.[15]

In the institutional structure proposed in both documents, two outstanding characteristics should be pointed out. One refers to the internal order of Latin American integration and has particular interest because of the competence granted the organs. Despite the fact that the establishment of an economic community is contemplated, none of the organs appears to have sufficient juridical personality to act in representation of the community nor to contract obligations in its name; nor would any of the organs be vested, for the time being, with the minimum of supranational competence inherent to the very concept of an "economic community," or at any rate, with the sufficient amount to give the process of economic integration of the region the energy and vigor required. This timidity or lack of boldness on the part of the proposals contrasts sharply with the fact that the countries who would be required to make the delegation of sovereignty that supranationality supposes, have already demonstrated their willingness to participate in international and inter-American agencies vested with supranational powers in other fields.[16]

---

15 *Cf.* Document cited in Note 8, p. 171 *et seq.*

16 Reference should be made here to the document prepared by the OAS General Secretariat for the Economic Conference held in Buenos Aires in 1957, entitled "Liberalization of Inter-Latin American Trade" (Doc. 3, May 1957), which urged the creation of supranational institutions in the following terms: "Nations must give up pursuing their national economic interests in favor of promoting regional interests. The successful operation of a customs union may require the unification or complete coordination of the monetary, fiscal and

The second characteristic has to do with the external order and consists of the scarce and somewhat sporadic attention the proposals give to the ties and relationships between the institutional machinery of integration and the inter-American system (as well as the international entities that cooperate with the Alliance for Progress program). And this, in turn, contrasts with the observation made at the beginning of this section with regard to the institutional impact of the existing interaction between the integration process and the general program of development in Latin America.

Since its First Annual Meeting at the Ministerial Level, the IA-ECOSOC was of the opinion that "for most effective annual review of the development of the two integration movements, it would be most desirable that they be invited to present reports on their activities to the IA-ECOSOC, so that the Annual Meeting at the Ministerial Level may have the most exact information on the subject, without prejudice to the studies and documents that the Executive Secretariat of the IA-ECOSOC may consider it appropriate to present on its own initiative." Even though Resolution D of Punta del Este made no specific mention of economic integration among the matters to be included in the annual review, the IA-ECOSOC has been doing so ever since its First Annual Meeting, in the same way and for the same reason that it has examined the other aspects of the march of the Alliance.[17] At the meeting in São Paulo (1963) these ties and relationships were developed and strengthened. In fact, among the duties and functions conferred on CIAP was that of coordinating "those efforts within the Alliance which require multilateral action, such as economic integration, . . ." for which it was authorized to seek the technical advice of LAFTA and SIECA.[18] It is for this reason that the "Advances of economic integration . . ." have been included in the CIAP's annual country reviews, as indicated in the preceding chapter. Reference should also be made, once again, to the close institutional ties and relationships required by the continuous and growing cooperation and assistance, both technical and financial, that inter-American agencies provide to Latin American organs, in order to make more viable or facilitate integration programs.

Such ties and relationships do not, nor will their eventual development and strengthening, constitute an institutional situation incompatible with the autonomy which the organs of Latin American integration must necessarily enjoy—both those presently existing and

---

other functions of member governments, perhaps even including a common currency and exchange control authority. This probably goes beyond what can be accomplished by 'coordination' of the activities of sovereign states."

[17] Cf. *Final Report*, OEA/Ser.H/XII.4, p. 30.

[18] See the resolution by which the IA-ECOSOC created the CIAP in *Appendix 19*, p. 459, *infra*.

those that may be created in the future. There neither can nor must be any doubt on this point. On the contrary, it is a question of maintaining and intensifying, as far as convenient and justifiable, the ties and relationships between the institutional machinery for Latin American integration and the inter-American system (and the other entities that cooperate in the Alliance for Progress program). On this subject, a recent document has this to say: "While regional economic integration is essential for achieving sustained development, its realization depends in its initial phases on the reform of the antiquated structures of the national economies and their overcoming their present state of economic stagnation. Thus, while Latin American economic integration is a Latin American responsibility, its success depends on inter-American cooperation within the framework of the Alliance for Progress."[19]

---

[19] Cf. *Report of the Secretary General of the OAS to the Second Special Inter-American Conference*, OEA/Ser.E/XIII.1, Doc. 16, 14 April 1965, vol. II, p. 5.

Postscript

This study was already being printed when three important meeting were held: the Second Special Inter-American Conference, the meeting of the Special Committee to Prepare a Draft Proposal on Amendments to the OAS Charter, and a Meeting of the Ministers of Foreign Affairs of the member countries of the Latin American Free Trade Association (LAFTA). The first was convoked as indicated in the Introduction, to consider "various matters of fundamental importance in strengthening the inter-American system," and it convoked the meeting of the Special Committee. The last, in turn, was held "with the primary objective of adopting the political solutions necessary for stimulating the process of economic integration and complementary economies of the member countries." Although it will be impossible to study in detail the results of these three meetings, a brief summary of the decisions taken by them will, at least, aid in making a general evaluation in the light of the common purpose for which they were convoked.

A. *The Second Special Inter-American Conference* *(Rio de Janeiro, November 17-30, 1965)*

The Conference at Rio de Janeiro considered nearly all the aspects and problems connected with the structure and functioning of the inter-American system. Although it took certain decisions that immediately affect the present structure and functioning, its most outstanding decisions are those which lead to the amendment of the OAS Charter in accordance with the procedure provided in its Article 111. In convoking still another Special Inter-American Conference, it also agreed on preparatory work to be completed prior to it.

Nature and Extent of the Amendments Foreseen

Resolution I of the Rio Conference convokes the Third Special Inter-American Conference. The resolution also entrusts to a Special Committee the preparation of a preliminary draft proposal on amendments, which the Council of the Organization shall refer to the governments together with its observations, if any, 60 days prior to the Third Inter-American Conference. That conference is to open in July 1966 and the Special Committee is set to meet on February 25. The complete text of Resolution I follows:

I
"THE ACT OF RIO DE JANEIRO"
AMENDMENTS OF THE CHARTER OF BOGOTÁ

WHEREAS:

The inter-American system is the most expressive manifestation of the will of the American states in that which relates to firm guarantees of peace and security in the hemisphere, to the rule of the principles of law, both internally and in their foreign relations, and to the economic and social development of the people of the hemisphere;

The experience gained since the Charter of the Organization of American States came into effect indicates the need for strengthening the structure and more effectively coordinating the activities of the organs of the system, to attain fully the objectives set forth in the preceding paragraph, and

The inter-American system should be empowered, in accordance with the purposes and principles of the Charter of the OAS, to resolve more effectively the various problems of the hemisphere,

THE SECOND SPECIAL INTER-AMERICAN CONFERENCE REAFFIRMS:

The principles and standards in effect that are embodied in Part One of the Charter of the Organization of American States;

DECLARES:

1. That is is essential to forge a new dynamism for the inter-American system and to avoid duplication of efforts and conflicts of jurisdiction among its organs, in order to facilitate cooperation between the American states and obtain a more rational utilization of the resources of the Organization;

2. That it is essential to modify the working structure of the Organization of American States as defined in the Charter; and

RESOLVES

1. To convoke, in accordance with Articles 36 and 111 of the OAS Charter, the Third Special Inter-American Conference, to be held in the city of Buenos Aires. The Council of the Organization in agreement with the host country, shall set a day in July 1966 for the opening of the conference.

2. To entrust to a Special Committee, composed of representatives of each of the member states, the preparation of a preliminary draft proposal on amendments to the Charter of the Organization. The Council of the Organization of American States shall convoke the aforesaid Committee to meet in Panama and shall receive its conclusions. The Council shall refer these to the governments together with its observations, if any, at least 60 days before the Inter-American Conference to be convoked in accordance with paragraph 1 is held.

3. The preliminary draft of these amendments shall include additional standards for inter-American cooperation in the economic, social, and cultural fields.

4. The Special Committee shall use the following guidelines for the amendment of the Charter of the Organization:

    a. An inter-American conference, as the highest body of the Organization of American States, shall be convened annually at a different location and on a fixed date, for the purposes set forth in Article 33 of the Charter and to approve the program and budget of the Organization, to determine the quotas of the member states, and to coordinate the activities of the organs and agencies of the inter-American system.

b. The Meeting of Consultation of Ministers of Foreign Affairs shall be retained in the form established in Article 39 of the Charter.

c. There shall be three Councils, directly responsible to the Inter-American Conference, as follows:

   1) The present Council of the Organization, which shall be permanent in nature and, in addition to the pertinent powers that may be assigned to it in the Charter of the Organization and inter-American treaties and agreements such as those relative to the maintenance of peace and the peaceful settlement of disputes, shall be the executive body for the decisions the Inter-American Conference or the Meeting of Consultation does not entrust to the Inter-American Economic and Social Council, to the Inter-American Educational, Scientific and Cultural Council, or to other organs;

   2) The Inter-American Economic and Social Council, which shall meet at least once a year and shall have a permanent executive committee with a structure similar to those of CIAP; CIAP shall act as the executive committee of the IA-ECOSOC so long as the Alliance for Progress is in force; and

   3) The Inter-American Educational, Scientific, and Cultural Council, which shall meet when convoked by the Inter-American Conference and shall have as its duties, in addition to promoting education, science, and culture, those assigned to the present Inter-American Cultural Council in Articles 73 and 74 of the OAS Charter, with the exception of the last part of subparagraph (h) of Article 74, where reference is made to the Council of the Organization. The Inter-American Educational, Scientific and Cultural Council shall have a permanent committee, and its activities in the fields of education and training should be closely coordinated, whenever pertinent, with those of the IA-ECOSOC.

d. The Pan American Union shall continue to function as the central and permanent organ of the Organization of American States and the General Secretariat of the Organization, adapting its functions to the needs of the inter-American system.

e. The Secretary General and the Assistant Secretary General of the Organization shall hold office for five years.

f. The present Inter-American Juridical Committee of Rio de Janeiro shall be maintained as an advisory organ with the structure and functions deemed desirable by the Special Committee, and the situation of the Inter-American Council of Jurists shall be studied.

g. A study shall be made of the advisability of locating the permanent headquarters of all the Councils in one place or having them geographically decentralized, as well as a study of the feasibility of proceeding similarly in the case of the other OAS organs and agencies. In both cases all reasons and circumstances for and against one or the other of these solutions shall be considered.

h. The provisions of the Act of Washington, signed at the First Special Inter-American Conference on December 18, 1964, regulating the admission of new members shall be included; and

DECIDES:

That this resolution shall be known as "The Act of Rio de Janeiro."

In accordance with the mandate entrusted to the Special Committee, the proposed amendments to the OAS Charter will affect some of its substantive principles and standards as well as the structure and functioning of the Organization. In the preamble and the declaration of Resolution I the purpose and character of these amendments are set forth explicitly: that is, to strengthen the structure and more effectively coordinate the activities of the organs of the inter-American system, to empower it to resolve more effectively the various problems of the hemisphere, forging a new dynamism for the system and avoiding duplication of efforts and conflicts of jurisdiction among its organs. In brief, the Rio de Janeiro Conference reaffirmed the purpose contained in the resolution convoking it: that of strengthening the inter-American system by introducing into the Charter the amendments or changes necessary for that end.

What, however, is the real nature and extent of the proposed amendments? Or, to put it another way, will these amendments or changes in substance and in structure really lead to the effective strengthening of the inter-American system? As has been seen from this study, during the last five years the inter-American system has undergone, in both substance and form, a process of development and strengthening unparalleled by any other international system or organization. It is undeniable that this process cannot and should not be interrupted and that in some fields the system still has serious gaps and defects which must be overcome, as has also been pointed out in this study. Therefore, what is of real importance and significance in the proposed amendments is the degree to which they can further develop and strengthen the system, forging for it a new and genuine dynamism and, above all, overcoming the gaps and defects still evident in it.

From the point of view of substance or dogma, the conference only agreed to include additional standards of inter-American cooperation in the economic, social and cultural fields. As will be seen later, the amendments to the OAS Charter in these fields will be made in accordance with the "guidelines" set forth in Chapters I through V of Resolution II of the Rio Conference. The conference also limited itself to a reaffirmation of the principles and standards embodied in Part One of the Charter, among which are those of an economic, social and cultural character. This total reaffirmation, which conformed with the intention often expressed during the discussions, that the amendments should not affect the principles and standards embodied in the first three chapters of that Part of the Charter, constitutes a decision which may hinder the work of re-building the inter-American system and forging for it a new and genuine dynamism. In fact, the strengthening of the institutional framework of an international organization may well require the revising of principles which have governed it since its founding, particularly those which define the fundamental rights and duties of the member states and those which have to do with the powers of the organization itself.

When Resolution I is analyzed in the light of the discussions at the Rio Conference, some doubts are also raised as to whether the proposed structural amendments are appropriate to achieve the in-dicated objective, at least to the extent that will allow an appre-ciable degree of development and strengthening of the system. Thus, for example, in spite of the fact that the Inter-American Conference is the "supreme organ" of the OAS, it is to be given no new powers and duties of any importance. True, its meeting annually—instead of every five years as at present—will provide an opportunity to deal more frequently at a high political level with the matters and problems of interest to the system. However, this had been occur-ring in practice, with increasing frequency, through the Meetings of Consultation of Ministers of Foreign Affairs, the Special Inter-American Conferences foreseen in Article 36 of the Charter and the Annual Meeting of the Inter-American Economic and Social Coun-cil at the Ministerial Level to review the Alliance for Progress.

By retaining the Meeting of Consultation "in the form established in Article 39 of the Charter," Resolution I once again reveals the rather conservative spirit that dominated the Rio de Janeiro Confer-ence. In this regard it should be pointed out, furthermore, that the Meeting of Consultation is one of the organs that has acted most dynamically and contributed, perhaps more than any other, to the development and strengthening of the inter-American system, often exercising powers not specifically conferred on it by Article 39. Therefore, what is to prevent introducing into that Article the nec-essary changes so that when a future Meeting of Consultation is con-voked "to consider a problem of an urgent nature and of common interest to the American States", it will at least have the powers it has in fact exercised in the past? In summary, the changes foreseen for these two outstanding political organs of the system are noth-ing more than the more frequent meeting of one of them. Without prejudice to the practical advantages which will logically result, from the point of view of the more direct coordination the Inter-American Conference will exercise over the three councils, the scope of action and the nature of the powers of the "supreme organ" will continue to be substantially the same as those established by Article 33 and other provisions of the present Charter.

Up to this point the "guidelines" to be used by the Special Committee in planning the structural amendments are quite clear and precise. But this is not true with regard to the proposed reorganization of the councils. In addition, Resolution I leaves to the Special Committee the study and decision regarding other amendments on which there was no agreement at Rio de Janeiro. The manner and degree in which the three councils shall be "directly responsible to the Inter-American Conference" is an example of the former. It is evident that this is a "direct" relationship and that, consequently, the present relationship, by virtue of which the so-called technical councils are organs of the Council of the Organization, is to be changed. It might be asked here, among other things, whether the new relationship of responsibility will be greater or lesser than the present one and, concretely, whether it will in any way affect the technical autonomy presently enjoyed by these councils. The question today as much more complex due to the institutional and political development and strengthening acquired by the two technical councils mentioned in Resolution I. In this sense, how will the proposed relationship of direct responsibility be reconciled with the ministerial level at which these councils have been meeting?

Resolution I raises many other questions, some of which the Special Committee entrusted with the preparation of the preliminary draft proposal on amendments may be unable to answer. By way of illustration the following may be mentioned. What position will the Council of the Organization occupy within the new structure, particularly with respect to the many duties it has under the present structure regarding the activities of the other organs and the functioning of the Organization in general? With regard to CIAP, what is meant by describing this permanent committee of the I-A ECOSOC as "executive" considering that at Rio de Janeiro no such competence was intended to be conferred on that body? When the "permanent headquarters" of the councils and of the other OAS organs and agencies are spoken of, does this refer to the place where their meetings are held or where their respective secretariats are located? How does this tie in with the proposal that the Pan American Union shall continue to function as the central and permanent organ of the OAS and the General Secretariat of the Organization, "adapting its functions to the needs of the inter-American system?"

Other Decisions by the Conference and General Evaluation of its Results

The Rio Conference took other decisions relating to the rebuilding of the inter-American system. Some of these are also of interest from the viewpoint of the amendments to the OAS Charter. A brief summary of these decisions will provide new evidence for evaluating the results of the conference in the light of the purpose for which it was convoked.

Additional Standards in the Economic and Social Field

The mandate entrusted to the Special Committee, by which it is to draw up a preliminary draft proposal on amendments, specifies that additional standards in the economic, social and cultural fields are to be included. These standards will be prepared in accordance with the "guidelines" set forth in Resolution II of the Rio Conference. Chapter I of that resolution begins by linking political security and development, by stating that "The principles of solidarity that inspire the activities of inter-American cooperation in the political field and in that of mutual security must, of necessity, be applicable also to the economic and social field, inasmuch as the American Republics have resolved to unite in a common effort to enable their peoples to attain the greater social justice and more rapid and balanced economic progress essential to the security of the hemisphere." This parallel between security and development—as between underdevelopment and internal political instability—had already been drawn in the inter-American system, although in terms less explicit and categorical than those used by the Rio Conference.

The next chapter of Resolution II deals with the national social and economic effort. Here the Conference stated that "The economic and social progress of the countries depends fundamentally on mobilizing their national, human, and material resources," and that for the improvement of health, education, housing and the system of land tenure, etc., it is essential "among other things, to generate national resources and establish an adequate domestic institutional structure." It will be recalled that the Alliance for Progress was conceived, from the beginning, as a declaration that "expresses the conviction of the nations of Latin America that these profound economic, social, and cultural changes can come about only through the self-help efforts of each country." Although at that time it was admitted that "Nonetheless, in order to achieve the goals which have been established with the necessary speed, domestic efforts must be reinforced by essential contributions of external assistance," it seems evident that now the intention is for the primary responsibility for the progress of the Alliance to rest, more than ever, on the internal effort. Perhaps this is only a fine distinction, but it is certain that this new and more categorical reaffirmation of national responsibility is of great interest in relation to the amendments proposed for the OAS Charter.

A similar situation is planted by Chapter III of Resolution II on "Mutual and External Economic and Social Assistance". The new concept in this field appears in the following paragraph: "The member states accept the obligation, within the framework of their constitutional processes and to the extent their resources permit, to help one another and to provide assistance, in the order of need to the less-developed countries of the system, with a view to achieving, on a national and regional level, the social and economic objectives set forth in this Act, for the purpose of putting the countries of the hemisphere in a situation of development as soon as possible." In the Charter of Punta del Este "The participating Latin American countries recognize that each has in varying degree a capacity to assist fellow republics by providing technical and financial assistance. They recognize that this capacity will increase as their economies grow. They therefore affirm their intention to assist fellow republics increasingly as their individual circumstances permit." It is true that the Rio resolution speaks of mutual assistance as the "obligation" of all the member states, but at the same time compliance with that obligation is immediately subject to conditions which should not be overlooked. In any event, it is interesting to point out this express recognition of the priority established for assisting the relatively less-developed countries. Chapter III is also very explicit in setting forth the requirements, conditions and procedures for mutual and external assistance, conceived in such a way as to make that assistance more just and effective.

The next chapter of Resolution II refers to foreign trade and begins by recognizing that "The close interdependence of international trade and economic and social developments compels the member states to join forces in order to ensure the undertaking of both collective and individual action," aimed at achieving a series of objective ennumerated in the chapter. Outstanding among these objectives are first, that no country should follow a trade policy incompatible with the interests of other member states and, second, that the needs of the comparatively less economically-developed countries should receive preferential attention. Some of the objectives already appear in the Charter of Punta del Este, particularly those relative to the basic export commodities, but the Rio resolution treats them in terms which may lead to their more effective achievement when the pertinent amendments are introduced into the OAS Charter.

The final chapter of Resolution II deals with the economic integration of Latin America. The Rio Conference expressly recognized that the integration of the Latin American nations is not only an essential instrument for their economic and social development but also "one of the basic objectives of the inter-American system and, for that reason, [the American States] will orient their efforts and take the measures that are necessary to accelerate the process of integration." The resolution then lists the efforts and measures thought necessary to strengthen and accelerate integration in all its aspects, which are in essence the efforts and measures that are being taken, above all in the last few years, with regard to the Central American Common Market and the Latin American Free Trade Association (LAFTA). Emphasis is placed on the continued provision of technical and financial assistance in the preparation and execution of multinational projects and to the organizations for regional integration. The idea of "mutual assistance" to facilitate the participation of the comparatively less-developed countries in Latin American programs of international economic cooperation is also emphasized.

Annual Meetings of Ministers of Foreign Affairs

The Rio Conference decided that until the proposed amendments to the OAS Charter are approved and enter into force, these annual meetings will be held "to consider common problems and activities of the inter-American system (Resolution III). Generally speaking, these annual meetings are the equivalent of the proposed annual meeting of the Inter-American Conference; that is, they are to serve the same purpose; the periodic and frequent holding of a high-level political meeting. The decision to have the Ministers of Foreign Affairs meet does not necessarily mean convoking the Meeting of Consultation established in Article 39 of the Charter. The Council of the Organization is to convoke each meeting "in accordance with the provisions of the Charter that, according to circumstances, may be pertinent." Logically, this can and should be understood to mean that the Council is authorized to convoke the meeting either in accordance with Article 39 or with Article 36, which calls for a special Inter-American Conference. In view of the flexibility that was given this provisional arrangement, two other possibilities should not be overlooked. Not established in the Charter but with precedents in practice are the meeting of the Council of the Organization at the ministerial level and the informal meeting of Ministers of Foreign Affairs. The only fact not left in doubt was the Rio Conference's explicit and decisive intention that the Ministers of Foreign Affairs themselves should meet annually.

Turning once more to the reason for holding these annual meetings, although the operative part of Resolution III is couched in somewhat vague and general terms, the same is not true of certain whereas clauses. In the last two clauses the following is stated:

> The American states have linked the maintenance of peace, the collective security of the hemisphere, the defense of representative democracy, and economic, social, and cultural development, to the institutions of the inter-American system; and
>
> It is likewise advisable to provide coordination among the organs and bodies of the inter-American system, and this necessity becomes increasingly urgent with the emergence of new forms of economic, social, and cultural integration and cooperation of common interest to the Continent.

As can be clearly seen from these two whereas clauses of Resolution III, the Rio Conference reaffirmed the close relationship between the maintenance of peace and the collective security of the Continent, the defense of democratic institutions and the economic, social, and cultural development of the countries of the Americas. In line with this concept, it pointed out the advisability of coordinating the activities of the organs and agencies of the inter-American system, above all now that this coordination becomes increasingly more urgent with the emergence of new forms of economic, social, and cultural integration and cooperation of common interest to the Continent. In summary, the Conference attempted to assure the periodic and frequent coordination and direction, at a high political level, of the activities being carried out in these various fields.

Peaceful Settlement of Disputes

The Conference at Rio de Janeiro was unable to reach an agreement on this subject. The Governments of Brazil and Ecuador had each presented a draft treaty on peaceful settlement and it was decided to transmit them to the Inter-American Juridical Committee for it to study them and prepare the pertinent observations (Resolution XII). In Resolution XIII the Conference requested the Special Committee, "in drawing up the preliminary draft amendments to the Charter, to strengthen the capacity of the Organization to give the member states effective aid in the peaceful settlement of their disputes, assigning the necessary powers to the Council of the Organization of American States." A third resolution transmitted to the Special Committee the minutes and documents of Committee III regarding this subject, "for its information and consideration in preparing the preliminary draft proposal on amendment of the Charter" (Resolution XIV). Furthermore, the Conference resolved to appeal to the governments that had not yet ratified the American Treaty on Pacific Settlement (Pact of Bogotá), to consider the advisability of doing so, as soon as possible (Resolution XV).

While none of these resolutions indicates a decision or agreement to introduce specific changes in the present inter-American peace system, the apparent intention of Resolution XIII, approved on the basis of a draft presented by the Government of the United States of America during Committee III's discussions, should be pointed out. The Special Committee is not only requested to include this subject in its draft amendments to the Charter but also, in so doing, "to strengthen the capacity of the Organization" in the field of peaceful settlement and, even more specifically, to assign the necessary powers to the Council of the Organization. If they are to comply with this mandate, the Special Committee and later the Inter-American Conference, convoked to amend the Charter, must introduce the necessary amendments so that the Council of the Organization can fill the great gap that exists in the inter-American system; that is, the lack of an organ and a procedure for promoting the pacific settlement of disputes, when the directly interested parties are unable to reach an agreement in this regard.

Human Rights and Representative Democracy

In a sense, certain decisions by the Rio Conference regarding the promotion of human rights constitute its most far-reaching immediate achievement. First of all, it was agreed that the Inter-American Commission on Human Rights "should be strengthened by broadening its responsibilities in an effort to promote greater respect for human rights in the hemisphere"; and that, without prejudice to the continuing work by the Commission, "it would be desirable to have an annual review at the ministerial level, of progress in the protection of human rights." To this end the Commission was authorized "to examine communications submitted to it and any other available information, so that it may address to the government of any American state a request for information deemed pertinent by the Commission, and so that it may make recommendations, when it deems this appropriate, with the objective of bringing about more effective observance of fundamental human rights." The Commission was also requested to submit a report annually to the Inter-American Conference or Meeting of Consultation, including a statement of progress achieved in the realization of the goals set forth in the American Declaration of the Rights and Duties of Man. The report should indicate the areas in which further steps are needed to give effect to the human rights set forth in the American Declaration, as well as such observations as the Commission may deem appropriate on matters covered in the communications submitted to it and in other information available to it (Resolution XXII).

With regard to the Commission's new powers—which are similar to those it has in fact exercised during the last few years—some concern should be aroused by the practical consequences that may result from the Commission's being required, in the exercise of those new functions, to "ascertain whether the domestic legal procedures and remedies of a member state have been duly pursued and exhausted." True, this requirement, to which international claims for damages caused to the person or property of a foreigner have traditionally been subjected, was incorporated into the European Convention for the Protection of Human Rights and Fundamental Freedoms. But are the violations of human rights for which this Convention was conceived always of the same nature, or surrounded by the same circumstances, as the cases or situations usually brought before the Inter-American Commission? Certainly not. In certain individual cases the Commission has often observed the principle of exhaustion of local remedies and has even taken into account information provided it by the government concerned. But in the case of massive violations, in addition to which life, personal security and other essential rights are involved, what is the sense of even inquiring whether "the domestic legal procedures and remedies of a member state have been duly pursued and exhausted?" For this reason, it would surely have been better for the Conference to have permitted the Commission to continue using its discretion and good judgment in this regard, instead of requiring it specifically to comply with a prerequisite which may hinder, or even completely frustrate its functions.

With regard to the principle of representative democracy, the Conference adopted an "Informal Procedure on the Recognition of De Facto Governments" which also signifies an important step in the development and strengthening of the inter-American system. That procedure is as follows:

1. To recommend to the member states that, immediately after the overthrow of a government and its replacement by a de facto government, they begin an exchange of views on the situation, giving due consideration to whether or not the overthrow of the government took place with the complicity and aid of one or more foreign governments, or of their respective officers or agents.

2. To recommend that the governments member states, in the exchange of views provided for in the preceding article, consider the following circumstances:

   a. Whether the de facto government proposes to take the necessary measures for the holding of elections within a reasonable period, giving its people the opportunity freely to participate in the consequent electoral process; and

   b. Whether the de facto government agrees to fulfill the international obligations assumed previously by its country, to respect the human rights expressed in the American Declaration of the Rights and Duties of Man, and to comply with the commitments assumed by the signatories of the Declaration of the Peoples of the Americas and the general principles of the Charter of Punta del Este.

3. To recommend that, once opinions have been exchanged, each government decide whether it will maintain diplomatic relations with the de facto government.

As can be seen, the significance of the foregoing decision lies not so much in its procedural aspect, since the mechanism established for exchanging views will not always be as effective as it might have been if the system of consultation established in the Charter had been adopted. Its significance lies rather in the fact that the recognition of de facto governments is looked upon as subject to conditions which for many years were deemed inadmissible, since they were considered to constitute an intervention in the domestic affairs of the state.

General Evaluation of the Results of the Conference

Considering that certain resolutions on the proposed amendment of the OAS Charter leave a margin for discretion and later decision, first to the Special Committee entrusted with drawing up the draft proposal and later to the Inter-American Conference convoked to carry out the amendment, it would appear somewhat premature to make a thorough evaluation of the results of the Conference at Rio de Janeiro. What can be judged is the degree to which the Conference, as an initial but guiding step in a process of reform which it has itself set in motion, was consistent with the purpose of strengthening the inter-American system.

In the foregoing pages certain explicit or implicit observations have already been made. In review, it might be added that the nature and extent of the reforms foreseen do not correspond to the marked emphasis placed by the Rio Conference on the need for amending the OAS Charter in order to empower the inter-American system "to resolve more effectively the various problems of the hemisphere" and to forge for it a "new dynamism". In order to completely achieve such a goal, particularly during a historic stage in which the system has demonstrated its ability to develop and strengthen itself when the circumstances have so required, it is obvious that the amendments could and should be more bold. An international system is not strengthened by a mere internal reorganization nor only by the improved coordination of the activities of its organs. It is truly strengthened when, in addition, new and greater powers are conferred on those organs that are responsible for ensuring the complete achievement of the essential objectives of the system in question. The latter is not reflected in the Rio resolutions. What they do reflect, instead, is the lack of a firm determination to enlarge and strengthen the present powers and attributes of the organs of the inter-American system.

Nor did the Conference show a firm and decided attitude with regard to the amendment of the substantive or dogmatic principles of the OAS Charter. Although there was unwillingness to formally confer new and greater powers on the organs of the system, circumstances have required and justified in the past that some of them exercise certain powers not expressly provided for in the Charter. The exercise of such powers can at times be hindered by certain substantive standards and principles established in that instrument, which reflect and hallow postulates and dogmas left over from an era that has for the most part been superseded. With regard to additional standards for inter-American cooperation in the economic, social, and cultural fields, in reiterating the observations above, it should be added that the efficacy of the amendment of the corresponding chapters of the Charter will depend, basically, on the terms in which the new provisions are conceived and expressed. The Rio resolution establishes objectives that are newer and bolder than the ones contained in the instruments that at present govern the Alliance for Progress. Nevertheless, their efficacy will depend less on the simple fact of such objectives being incorporated into an instrument with the legal standing of the Charter, than on the degree of clarity and precision given to the stipulations that it is agreed to introduce into the constitutional instrument of the inter-American system.

B. The Draft Proposal on Amendments Prepared By the Special Committee (Panama, February 25-April 1, 1966)

As stated at the beginning of this *Postscript,* the Rio de Janeiro Conference entrusted to a Special Committee the preparation of a preliminary draft proposal on amendments to the OAS Charter which the Council of the Organization is to refer to the governments, along with its observations, if any, 60 days prior to the Third Special Inter-American Conference that has been convoked in accordance with the provisions of Article 111 of the present Charter. The Special Committee met at the place and date indicated above and prepared a draft proposal in line with the general directives and guidelines laid down by the Rio Conference. For reasons of brevity, the following comments will be limited to the principal reforms that affect the structure and functioning of the Organization.

These amendments appear in Part Two, Chapter X, of the draft proposal, which corresponds to the same part and chapter (The Organs) of the present Charter. To begin with, the name of the

Inter-American Conference is changed to "General Assembly"; mention is made of "The Councils" instead of the Council; the Inter-American Juridical Committee is included, and the term "Pan American Union" is replaced by "General Secretariat" since it was decided that the two would no longer be used as synonyms. The new article further authorizes the establishment, "in addition to those provided for in this Charter and in accordance with the provisions thereof," of "such subsidiary organs, agencies, and other entities as are considered necessary." It should be pointed out here that the Bogotá Charter appears, from a strictly legal point of view, to reserve this faculty to the Inter-American Conference as the "supreme organ" of the Organization. In practice, however, this power, foreseen in Article 33, has more frequently been exercised by the Meeting of Consultation of Ministers of Foreign Affairs, the Council of the Organization and the Inter-American Economic and Social Council. In deference apparently to these important precedents, the draft proposal later includes among the powers common to the three new Councils, that of establishing entities such as those in reference. Although the draft proposal states that the Council "shall report" to the General Assembly on their use of this power, the Report of the Rapporteur of Subcommittee I of the Special Committee states that the existence of such subsidiary entities shall be subject to the "express or tacit approval" of the Assembly—a condition that constitutes a potential limitation on the extent of this power.

The General Assembly

In amending the provisions of the Charter with regard to the Inter-American Conference the Special Committee limited itself, with two exceptions to be explained later, to a repetition in more explicit terms of the general directives and guidelines laid down in Resolution I of Rio de Janeiro and the remaining provisions of the present Charter. Thus, new Chapter XI of the draft proposal includes, among the "principal powers" of the General Assembly, that of deciding the general action and policy of the Organization, determining the structure and functions of its organs, etc.; establishing measures for coordinating the activities of the organs, etc.; strengthening and coordinating cooperation with the United Nations and its specialized agencies; promoting collaboration with other international bodies whose purposes are similar to those of the OAS; approving the program-budget of the Organization and determining the quotas of the member states, etc. In brief, the General Assembly is endowed with functions and powers that correspond to the present Inter-American Conference and to the present Councils, especially the Council of the Organization. This transfer of functions and powers occurs again in the draft proposal in relation to other matters.

With further reference to the question of competence, the following passage from the Report of the Rapporteur of Subcommittee I is of interest: "It is understood that, except for the cases especially referred to in the Charter, the General Assembly or the Meeting of Consultation [which remained unchanged, as in Chapter XI of the present Charter] may not delegate the authority that the Charter itself expressly vests in them to any other agency or agencies." It should be clarified here that what is contemplated is a delegation of "authority" in the strict sense of the word, not the tasks or mandates which one organ frequently receives from another and which the draft proposal takes up in other provisions.

To fully appreciate the scope of this prohibition one need only recall the important part in the development and strengthening of the inter-American system during recent years played by the delegation of authority by organs that meet occasionally in favor of those in permanent session, or by permanent organs on those with specialized competence. While it is true that the draft proposal calls for the annual meeting of one of the abovementioned organs—the General Assembly—that meeting will last only two weeks during the year and there are functions and decisions, as has been repeatedly proved by recent experience, which cannot remain pending during a whole year or until a Meeting of Consultation can be held. It is to be hoped, therefore, that this restrictive criterion will not prevail during the Third Special Inter-American Conference and that, on the contrary, these organs and the Councils will be able to continue delegating their respective powers as they have in the past, under the circumstances and to the extent required and justified by the effective achievement of the basic purposes of the Charter.

To the principal powers of the General Assembly the Special Committee added that of adopting "the general standards to govern the operations of the General Secretariat." Since this provision does not represent the mere transfer of attributes that formerly belonged to the Council of the Organization, given the existence of other provisions in the draft proposal which have a bearing on this subject, it will be preferable to examine the question as a whole when the chapter dealing with the Secretariat is taken up.

The second of the two exceptions mentioned above is the establishment of a Preparatory Committee, composed of representatives of all the member states, which shall prepare the draft agenda of the meetings of the General Assembly; review the proposed program-budget and the draft resolution on quotas, and present a report thereon containing appropriate recommendations; and carry out such other functions as the General Assembly may assign to it. During the Panama meeting it was insisted that these attributes should be retained for the Council of the Organization, or at least that it should act as the Preparatory Committee. Without prejudice to a later mention of this matter, for the moment it will suffice to note that the basic idea which appears to have inspired the establishment of the new organ was to have a mechanism which, while it carries out the preparatory work required by the annual meetings of the General Assembly, will at the same time be consistent with the principle of the equal status of the three Councils introduced at the Rio de Janeiro Conference.

Provisions Common to the Councils

Chapter XIII of the draft proposal contains the provisions common to the three Councils. It will be recalled that, in accordance with the guidelines laid down by the Rio Conference, those organs are to be "directly responsible to the Inter-American Conference." How, then, did the Special Committee define this relationship of direct responsibility? According to the first provision the three Councils "are directly responsible to the General Assembly and each has the authority granted to it in this Charter and other inter-American instruments, as well as the functions assigned to it by the General Assembly and the Meeting of Consultation of Ministers of Foreign Affairs." The other provisions establish that "The Councils may, within the limits of this Charter and other inter-American instruments, make recommendations on matters within their authority." They may also present to the General Assembly studies and proposals, drafts of international instruments, and proposals on the holding of specialized conferences, on the creation, modification, or elimination of specialized organizations and other inter-American agencies, as well as on the coordination of their activities.

It is no simple matter, therefore, to determine with even relative accuracy the extent of the powers enjoyed by the Councils within the framework of their hierarchical relationship *vis-à-vis* the General Assembly. While it is true that these common provisions give the impression that the action of the Councils will be reduced to the adoption of recommendations and the presentation of studies and proposals, the value of which depends on subsequent approval by the General Assembly, the draft proposal contains other provisions, along with certain considerations, which give a different impression. For example, would the action undertaken by the new "Permanent Council of the Organization", as the present Council of the Organization is called in the draft proposal, in the field of peaceful settlement of disputes always be subject to subsequent action by the Assembly? Obviously not. Also, would all the decisions or resolutions approved by the Inter-American Economic and Social Council (IA-ECOSOC) pursuant to the provisions of the draft proposal relative to its competence, or of the Charter of Punta del Este and other basic instruments governing the Alliance for Progress, also be subject to approval by the Assembly? The reply to this second question, as well as to other similar ones in the same vein, would also be negative.

This is not merely an attempt to avoid an interpretation which might lead to an unrealistic approach to the new structure and functioning which the Special Committee has conceived for the OAS. Rather, it is an effort to interpret these common provisions of the draft proposal in the light of certain factors and considerations which could not have been overlooked at Panama. In the first place it should be pointed out, for example, that two of the provisions in reference contain the phrase "and other inter-American instruments" (as distinguished from that which provides the Permanent Council with the power to act "Within the limits of this Charter and of inter-American treaties and agreements, . . .") which appreciably broadens the sphere of action and of competence they establish. Furthermore, it should be noted that in the Rapporteur's Report it was specifically stated that "the Councils should all be able to make recommendations to the member states, thereby following existing practice." This amounts to an admission of the compatibility between a relationship of direct responsibility on the part of the Councils vis-à-vis the supreme organ and the Councils' power to continue making recommendations directly to the governments on matters within their competence. The only exception to this freedom of action would be the power to present studies, proposals, and projects, given the explicit terms in which this provision is couched. Even here, it should be pointed out, a subsequent provision authorizes the IA-ECOSOC to convoke, in urgent cases, specialized conferences with no requirement other than that of prior consultation with the member states.

Finally, it is equally interesting to point out that the draft proposal omits the principle contained in Article 58 of the present Charter, pursuant to which the three Councils or organs of the present Council of the Organization "shall have technical autonomy within the limits of this Charter; but their decisions shall not encroach upon the sphere of action of the Council of the Organization." The omission of this principle reaffirms the appreciably greater degree of autonomy granted to the three Councils within the new hierarchical relationship between each of them and the General Assembly. In the course of this study it can repeatedly be noted that the said principle has in fact been rendered meaningless by the institutional development and strengthening of one of those Councils, the IA-ECOSOC, whose annual meetings were raised to the ministerial level so that they might be consistent with the importance of the multilateral action program under its responsibility. As will be seen later, the Special Committee also included in the draft proposal provisions that foresee representation "of high rank" on the new Inter-American Council for Education, Science, and Culture and on IA-ECOSOC, as well as the annual meeting of the latter at the ministerial level.

The Permanent Council of the Organization

The next three chapters of the draft proposal deal with each of the Councils in order. In addition to the Permanent Council's competence to take cognizance, within the limits indicated above, of any matter referred to it by the General Assembly or the Meeting of Consultation, it is also to be "the executive body" for any decisions not entrusted by those two organs to the IA-ECOSOC, the Inter-American Council for Education, Science and Culture or to other bodies. Up to this point the guidelines established by Resolution I of the Rio Conference were followed. To these functions and powers were added others, related to the functioning of the General Secretariat and the mandate entrusted to the Preparatory Committee of the General Assembly, as will be seen later. First, the responsibility assigned to the Permanent Council in the field of peaceful settlement of disputes, which was the object of intense and detailed discussion at the Panama meeting, should be examined. During this discussion the various not only opposed but also differing positions that continue to exist in the hemisphere were expressed, and the result was a formula that made it possible to comply, at least to some degree, with the mandate contained in Resolution XIII of the Rio Conference to strengthen the capacity of the Organization in this field, assigning "the necessary powers" to that Council. That formula, in general terms, is as follows.

The draft proposal begins by stating that "The Permanent Council shall keep vigilance over the maintenance of friendly relations among the member states, and for that purpose shall effectively assist them in the peaceful settlement of their disputes," in accordance with the following provisions. To assist the Permanent Council in the exercise of these powers a committee shall be established, which shall be an organ of the Council. It remains to be decided whether this organ might be the Inter-American Peace Committee, with its present structure or in modified form, or a new committee. The parties to a dispute may resort to the Permanent Council to obtain its "good offices", in which case it shall have authority to assist the parties and to recommend the procedures it considers suitable for the peaceful settlement of the dispute, and, furthermore, through the Committee or by any other means, to "ascertain the facts in the dispute." Should the parties not have agreed to resort to the Council, the draft proposal contemplates a second procedure by which any party to a dispute in which none of the peaceful procedures set forth in Article 21 of the Charter is being followed may appeal to the Permanent Council to take cognizance of the dispute. In that case the Council shall immediately refer the request to the Committee, which shall consider whether or not the matter is within its competence and, if it deems it appropriate, shall offer its good offices to the other party or parties. If the other party or parties accept the offer of good offices, the same procedure described above would then follow. Should that offer be refused the Committee, in addition to informing the Council, may take steps to restore relations between the parties, if they were interrupted, or to reestablish harmony between them. Furthermore, once it has received the Committee's report the Permanent Council may make suggestions for bringing the parties together and, if it considers it necessary, it may urge them to avoid any action that might aggravate the dispute. Finally, if one of the parties should continue to refuse the good offices of the Committee or the Council, the latter shall limit itself to submitting a report to the General Assembly.

The IA-ECOSOC and the Inter-American Council for Education, Science, and Culture

In the reorganization of the remaining two Councils the draft proposal took into account the general directives and guidelines contained in the Rio de Janeiro resolutions and, at least in essential aspects, the institutional development and strengthening these two organs have undergone during the last few years. This was noted in the comment regarding the common provisions of the three Councils. It remains now to refer to other aspects worthy of mention with regard to the provisions of Chapters XV (IA-ECOSOC) and XVI (Inter-American Council for Education, Science, and Culture) of the draft proposal.

The former retains for IA-ECOSOC the responsibility of promoting cooperation among the American countries in order to attain accelerated economic and social development, in accordance with the new standards on this matter added to the Charter pursuant to Resolution II (Economic and Social Act of Rio de Janeiro) of the Rio Conference. To this end, it recognizes IA-ECOSOC's power, already widely exercised, to recommend programs and courses of action and periodically study and evaluate the efforts undertaken by the member states; it reiterates that of coordinating all economic and social activities of the Organization; it authorizes IA-ECOSOC, without its being subject, as at present, to the authority of another organ, to establish cooperative relations with the corresponding organs of the United Nations and with other national and international agencies, especially with regard to coordination of inter-American technical assistance programs, etc. As distinguished from the present Charter, the draft proposal foresees a Permanent Executive Committee which, like others also established by it, will represent all the member states of the Organization. Pursuant to a transitory provision the Inter-American Committee on the Alliance for Progress (CIAP) shall act as the permanent executive committee as long as the Alliance is in operation.

The reorganization of the Inter-American Council for Education, Science, and Culture in the draft proposal is somewhat similar to that of IA-ECOSOC. It, too, is empowered to recommend or adopt programs and measures in the various fields of its competence, and to promote and coordinate the educational, scientific, and cultural activities of the Organization, to establish cooperative relations with the corresponding organs of the United Nations and other national and international bodies, etc. Where a lack of equality or parity with IA-ECOSOC may be noted is in the nature and mechanics of its meetings. Although the draft proposal here, too, foresees representatives "of high rank", it does not contemplate meetings at the ministerial level and, again contrary to IA-ECOSOC, its regular annual meeting is to be convoked by the General Assembly.

The Inter-American Juridical Committee and the Inter-American Commission on Human Rights

The following chapter of the draft proposal deals with the Inter-American Juridical Committee, another of the organs established in the amendment of Article 32 of the Charter. The elimination of the Inter-American Council of Jurists (the third of the present organs of the Council of the Organization), already forecast at Rio, together with the strengthening of the Committee's structure and functions that occurred at Panama, lead to its being elevated in the draft proposal to the rank of principal organ. In effect, the Committee will assume the functions which Article 67 at present assigns to the Council of Jurists—plus the new one of studying "the juridical problems related to the integration of the American countries"—and will continue to undertake the studies and preparatory work assigned to it by the General Assembly, the Meeting of Consultation and the Councils, as well as those it considers advisable on its own initiative. The draft proposal, furthermore, authorizes the Committee to suggest the holding of specialized juridical conferences. For greater efficiency the Committee has been reorganized along the lines of the International Law Commission of the United Nations. It will be composed of nine jurists, elected by the General Assembly for a period of four years from panels of candidates presented by the member states. This is an attempt to insure that the Committee will operate in the future with maximum independence from the states whose nationals are on it. This is fundamental if, as stipulated in the draft proposal, the Committee is genuinely to represent "all of the member states of the Organization" and if it is, in truth, to "have the broadest possible technical autonomy."

Another chapter of the draft proposal deals with the Inter-American Commission on Human Rights which, among other functions, shall promote the observance and protection of human rights and serve as a consultative organ of the Organization in this matter. It also foresees that an inter-American convention on human rights shall determine the structure, competence, and operation of the said Commission, as well as those of other organs responsible for these matters. Although a draft convention was drawn up by the Inter-American Council of Jurists in 1959 and the Rio de Janeiro Conference resolved to convoke, at a relatively early date, a specialized conference to consider that draft, the adoption of the convention and, above all, its entry into force constitute proceedings and expectations that are subject to circumstances that will not be easily overcome, at least in the near future. It is for this reason, surely, that a transitory article of the draft proposal provides that, until the inter-American convention on human rights enters into force, "the present Inter-American Commission on Human Rights shall keep vigilance over the observance of human rights." By means of this wise provision it was possible not only to establish in the constitution of the OAS an inter-American mechanism designed to promote the observance and protection of human rights but also to reaffirm, in the same instrument, the existence of the present Commission which, for more than five years, has been carrying out its high function to the extent it has been possible.

The General Secretariat

In accordance with the mandate of the Rio Conference, in the draft proposal the General Secretariat retains its character of "central and permanent organ of the Organization." As such it shall not only perform the functions assigned to it in the Charter and other inter-American treaties and agreements, as established in Article 78 of the present Charter, but also those conferred upon it by the General Assembly. The importance of this potential third source of functions or powers for the General Secretariat should not be overlooked. In Chapter II of this study it is stated that given the role of the General Secretariat within the machinery and functioning of a modern international organization it is almost indispensable that there be a certain parallel between its role and the development and strengthening of the political organs. Therefore, in order for the central and permanent organ of the OAS to function effectively it is no longer sufficient to assign it functions, mandates or affairs sporadically, as occurred in the past; rather it must be given those permanent powers required and justified by the institutional development and strengthening of the Organization.

Aside from the provision that the Secretary General and Assistant Secretary General are to be elected by the General Assembly (for five-year terms) and not by the Council of the Organization, as at present, two other provisions in the draft proposal are consistent with this favorable attitude toward the strengthening of the General Secretariat's position as the central and permanent organ of the OAS. The first of them deals with the function of promoting economic, social, legal, scientific, and cultural relations among the member states. As distinguished from the corresponding provision in the present Charter, pursuant to which the Pan American Union or General Secretariat performs this function "under the direction" of the Council of the Organization, according to the draft proposal these relations must be promoted merely "in keeping with the actions and policies decided upon by the General Assembly and with the pertinent decisions of the Councils." Obviously, under the new provision the General Secretariat would enjoy much greater freedom of action. The second provision authorizes the General Secretariat to establish relations of cooperation, in accordance with decisions reached by the General Assembly or the Councils, with the Specialized Organizations as well as other national and international organizations. This is a new function, which the present Charter reserves to the Council of the Organization and its three organs "in agreement with the Council." There appears to be little doubt about the extent of the initiative authorized here. The General Secretariat is not required to use this power "in agreement with" any one organ but only "in accordance with decisions" reached either by the General Assembly or any of the Councils.

There is every reason to assume that the General Secretariat's role as central and permanent organ of the Organization will be strengthened, too, by the amendment the draft proposal makes to Article 83.c of the Charter, pursuant to which the Secretariat should "Place, to the extent of its ability, at the disposal of the Government of the country where a conference is to be held, the technical aid and personnel which such Government may request." The terms in which this function, common to every international secretariat, is couched allow the host government of the Inter-American Conference or the meetings of other organs to assume authority and take control of the secretariat services by appointing a "Secretary General" of the Conference or meeting. A considerable portion of the personnel of the General Secretariat of the Organization is thus subject to that authority and control. By virtue of the amendment in reference, the

General Secretariat would "Provide secretariat services for the General Assembly and, to the extent of its ability, for the other meetings of the Organization." In this way the Assembly or the meeting of the organ in question would be the recipient of the secretariat services, rather than the host government. Since these are international conferences and meetings, not convoked at the initiative and under the responsibility of individual governments, there is no way of justifying that the Organization, not merely the General Secretariat, continue to be deprived of a function that is inherent in its right to convoke meetings of its organs.

In open contrast to the orientation shown by the foregoing provisions the Special Committee included in its draft proposal a provision which seriously undermines the General Secretariat's jurisdiction in a field which, by definition, is exclusively its responsibility. This provision stipulates that the Secretary General shall appoint two Assistant Secretaries, one for economic and social affairs and the other for education, science, and culture (who shall also perform the functions of Secretaries of the IA-ECOSOC and the Inter-American Council for Education, Science and Culture, respectively), "with the prior approval of the respective Councils." It is not difficult to discern that this proposed amendment to the Charter not only has substantial bearing on the most elementary and essential attribute of the central and permanent organ of the Organization but also is manifestly incompatible with other provisions of the Charter which the Special Committee has included verbatim in its draft proposal. One of these provides that "The Secretary General shall direct the General Secretariat. . . ." Is it conceivable, in theory and in practice, that this authority be exercised over officials whose appointment is subject to the consent of a third party? Furthermore, it must be borne in mind that each of these Assistant Secretaries, in turn, has under his immediate jurisdiction and control various Departments, Offices and other sections, with all the consequences that this implies, including psychological ones, as far as respect for the authority of the Secretary General on the part of the personnel is concerned.

The situation is even more serious when considered from the point of view of those provisions that establish the basic principle on which the institution of an international secretariat is founded. These provisions stipulate that "the Secretary General and the personnel of the Secretariat shall not seek or receive instructions from any government . . .," and that "Every member of the Organization of American States pledges itself to respect the exclusively international character of the responsibilities of the Secretary General and the personnel, and not to seek to influence them in the discharge of their duties." Viewed from a strictly legal standpoint—as one example—is the appointment of members of the personnel, regardless of their positions or duties, subject to the approval of organs composed of government representatives compatible with these provisions and with the principle they embody?

The Secretariat's Responsibility to the other Organs

The Special Committee also included certain other provisions which are in marked contrast to the orientation revealed by those examined earlier and which do not conform to the pertinent directives issued by the Rio de Janeiro Conference or to the new responsibilities foreseen for the General Secretariat as a result of the proposed changes in the structure and functioning of the OAS. It will be recalled that the draft proposal transfers to the General Assembly the function, previously belonging to the Council of the Organization, of adopting the general standards to govern the operations of the Secretariat. The Council's action was based not only on Article 51 of the Charter, which establishes that "The Council shall be responsible for the proper discharge by the Pan American Union of the duties assigned to it," but on the fact that the Bogotá Charter does not specifically confer on the supreme organ, as the draft proposal now does, the power of adopting those general standards. The Council's authority over the Secretariat also stems from the fact that Article 53.f empowers it to adopt the resolutions that will enable the Secretary General to perform the duties envisaged in Article 84, which are "To establish, with the approval of the Council, such technical and administrative offices . . ." and "To determine the number of department heads, officers and employees . . . in accordance with the general standards established by the Council."

Besides transferring to the Assembly the duty of adopting the general standards to govern the operations of the Secretariat, the draft proposal further establishes that the Secretary General is "responsible to the General Assembly for the proper fulfillment of the obligations and functions of the General Secretariat"; a third provision, referring to the attributes now contained in Article 84, states that "The Secretary General shall exercise this authority in accordance with such general standards and budgetary provisions as may be established by the General Assembly." Given the apparently unequivocal content and purpose of these substantive amendments to the present system, how can the draft proposal include, simultaneously, the provisions contained in Article 51, to the effect of assigning, once more, to the Permanent Council the duty to "Supervise the observance of the standards governing the operation of the General Secretariat and, when the General Assembly is not in session, adopt provisions of a regulatory nature that enable the General Secretariat to carry out its administrative functions?" And, furthermore, how can the draft proposal establish that the Secretary General is "responsible to the General Assembly . . ." and at the same time state that this is true "notwithstanding" the powers of the Permanent Council outlined above?

In an apparent effort to avoid any conflicts that might arise over this clause, agreement was reached to have the Rapporteur's Report contain "a clarification . . . to the effect that the text proposed does not in any way imply that the General Secretariat has no responsibility to the General Assembly, since it will always be answerable to that organ for the way in which it performs the duties assigned to it." This clarification may or may not achieve its objective but it would be preferable to eliminate the phrase in question when the amendments are finally approved in the forthcoming Inter-American Conference. The real problem, however, does not lie in the maintenance or disappearance of this one phrase. It lies rather in the retention of the provisions contained in Articles 51 and 53f of the present Charter, that is, in the foregoing provision of the draft proposal which places the General Secretariat under the jurisdiction and authority of one of the three Councils, a move that is obviously of great importance. Is this provision compatible with the principle, issued by the Rio de Janeiro Conference and observed by the Special Committee in other sections of the draft proposal, of the parity and equal standing of those organs? Evidently not. In practice the situation may become even more serious from the point of view of the General Secretariat. For example, what would the Secretariat do if in the exercise of its jurisdiction the Permanent Council were to take measures that prevented the Secretariat from complying with its responsibilities for carrying out programs assigned by the other two Councils?

The exceptional importance of this question justifies a further look at these and other provisions contained in the draft proposal, in an effort to make a more detailed study of the advisability of the amendments to the Charter. Above all, it should be pointed out that one of the transitory provisions stipulates that "The Permanent Council shall serve as the Preparatory Committee unless the General Assembly decides otherwise." This new stipulation, which is not consistent with the basic idea that appears to have inspired the establishment of the Preparatory Committee, is also not compatible with the principle of the equal standing of the three Councils. In this regard, among the functions assigned to the Committee is that of examining the program-budget of the Organization and presenting a report to the Assembly with appropriate recommendations. Other provisions make the General Secretariat responsible for preparing the program-budget "on the basis of programs adopted by the Councils, agencies, and entities whose expenses are included in the program and budget, after consultation with the Councils or their permanent committees, and [submitting] it to the General Assembly and its preparatory committee." It can be seen that in what is perhaps the most important aspect for the effective operation of the Councils, the process of preparing the budget for their respective programs, once again the draft proposal departs from the principle of equality and does so precisely in that phase of the process prior to final approval by the Assembly.

This repeated inclination on the part of the Special Committee to retain the attributes which have traditionally belonged to an organ and which the Bogotá Charter made even more sacred when it consolidated the basic structure and functioning of the inter-American system, would not appear to conform to one of the essential objectives of Resolution I of Rio de Janeiro. It is stated there "That it is essential to forge a new dynamism for the inter-American system and to avoid duplication of efforts and conflicts of jurisdiction among its organs, in order to facilitate cooperation between the American states and obtain a more rational utilization of the resources of the Organization." What is more, that inclination is also inconsistent with certain changes that have taken place long before there was even any idea of amending the Charter. For example, since its establishment in 1950 the OAS Program of Technical Cooperation has been approved annually by the IA-ECOSOC. Furthermore, the direction and coordination of the Program, by decision of IA-ECOSOC, have been entrusted to a Coordinating Committee composed of the OAS Secretary General and the Directors of cooperating agencies. More recently, when the Special Development Assistance Fund was established, it was agreed that "The Secretary General shall be responsible to the IA-ECOSOC for the administration of the Fund and the execution of its activities" (Article 6, Statutes of the Fund). Like other special funds, it is established by the Secretary General and is excepted from approval by the Council of the Organization pursuant to Article 85 of the Regulations of the Pan American Union, approved by that Council in 1952.

In summary, once the dependence of IA-ECOSOC and the Inter-American Council for Education, Science, and Culture on the Council of the Organization has been eliminated and their activities and responsibilities in the field of inter-American cooperation have been completely removed from the Council's sphere of competence, would it be justifiable for the new Permanent Council to continue exercising attributes similar to those assigned it in the present Charter regarding the said activities and responsibilities? Furthermore, considering that it was the Council of the Organization itself, when faced with the growing importance of the functions assigned to IA-ECOSOC, that consented to delegate to it some of its attributes, why insist now on maintaining, and in a sense, reclaiming those attributes in the precise moment when the parity and equality of the Councils is being established so that each one may effectively, and not only apparently, enjoy the autonomy which that principle implies?

This question naturally was a source of concern during the Fourth Annual Meetings of IA-ECOSOC held in Buenos Aires during the final weeks of the meeting of the Special Committee in Panama. The Meeting at the Ministerial Level approved a resolution containing IA-ECOSOC's recommendations regarding the reorganization of the organs of the inter-American system. The first one is general in nature and refers to the same status for the three Councils; the remainder pertain to IA-ECOSOC. One of them states that this organ should enjoy complete autonomy within its sphere of competence and be subordinate only to the highest organ of the system. IA-ECOSOC should have adequate participation in the budget of the Organization to enable it to carry out its work program effectively. The resolution also adds that it should participate effectively in the preparation, prior approval and execution of its budget, which would be incorporated in a single budget to be considered by the General Assembly within the system of decentralized administration that is consistent with the autonomy and equal standing of the three Councils.

General Evaluation of the Process of Reform

To conclude this brief and incomplete analysis of the amendments to the OAS Charter it only remains to make a general comment on the aspect which is of major interest from the point of view of the purpose and objective of the Rio de Janeiro Conference. Here the same question should be asked as at the beginning of this *Postscript*, that is, will the amendments drawn up by the Special Committee really lead to the effective strengthening of the inter-American system? In order to strengthen the institutional framework of an international organization, according to the same philosophy which appears to have inspired Resolution I of Rio de Janeiro, it will not be enough merely to coordinate more effectively "the activities of the organs" and "to avoid duplication of efforts and conflicts of jurisdiction" among them; it will also be necessary to forge a "new dynamism" for the organization and empower it "to resolve more effectively the various problems" with which it is concerned.

As far as the former is concerned, in contrast to the various amendments agreed on at Panama which undoubtedly will improve and strengthen the present structure and functioning of the inter-American system are those which, as has been indicated, constitute a source of potential duplication and conflicts of jurisdiction among the organs which are precisely the focal point around which nearly all the major activity of the system takes place.

With regard to the latter, except for the new function assigned to the Permanent Council, the amendments prepared by the Special Committee contemplate no competence in addition to that which the Bogotá Charter confers on the various organs, which will in truth lead to an effective institutional strengthening of the system. An exception to this is found in the field of peaceful settlement, considering that it is here that the major gaps and deficiencies of the inter-American system lie. It can therefore be considered progress to have authorized the Council to promote the peaceful settlement of disputes at the request of only one of the parties. Although the procedure to be followed is not as effective as might have been hoped, there is no doubt but that it may serve as a basis so that, in favorable circumstances, the Council's action may to a greater or lesser degree overcome the serious limitations imposed by the amendments, just as in the past has occurred with the other organs, including the Council, despite the repeated objection of several countries that it lacks "political functions."

In summary, an objective evaluation of the amendments drawn up by the Special Committee reveals the limited way in which the purpose, stated in Resolution I of the Rio Conference, of strengthening the institutional framework of the inter-American system was achieved. When reference was made in the *Introduction* to this study to the convocation of that conference, it was also pointed out that the major changes in structure and functioning which have taken place in the inter-American system since the Bogotá Charter was adopted were not the result of meetings convoked for that specific purpose and that they had not always issued from meetings of the organs of higher political hierarchy. As has been shown, they were the result of specific needs to reorient the system and make it institutionally adequate. Since Bogotá, it has been on these occasions, sometimes in very dramatic circumstances, that the American governments have shown their genuine and firm determination to make the regional organization more dynamic.

Along this line of thought one might ask whether the experience of the Bogotá Conference might be repeated if there were really a favorable attitude toward reform. It should not be overlooked that that conference would probably have been unable to achieve even the consolidation and formalization in the Charter of the transformations undergone by the inter-American system up to that time without the assiduous preparatory work that preceded the conference and, furthermore, if those transformations had not been such that they could be incorporated into an instrument of that kind. Therefore, and above all given the extent and implications of some of the changes that have taken place especially during the last five years, and the fact that the process of change is continuing, is this a propitious moment to undertake the formal revision of the Bogotá Charter and, consequently, is it realistic to think that all the legal and political obstacles such an undertaking entails can be overcome? In this sense, is there not a serious risk that, in view of the need to overcome those obstacles, the reform will be less audacious than it must be in order for the spontaneous process of transformation and strengthening to continue its march?

C. *The Meeting of Ministers of Foreign affairs of LAFTA (Montevideo, November 3-6, 1965)*

With a view toward the primary objective for which it was held —that "of adopting the political solutions necessary for stimulating the process of economic integration and complementary economies of the member countries"—the Montevideo meeting took some important decisions, both with reference to certain substantive aspects of the integration process and the institutional framework of LAFTA. Outstanding among the former are its directives to the Conference of the Contracting Parties, which was to hold its Fifth Session immediately thereafter, and to the Standing Executive Committee of the Association, in order to improve the Free Trade Program.

These directives would, in effect, make it possible to overcome many defects in the present Program. For example, the need was recognized to establish an automatic mechanism to assure a more rapid rate of tariff reduction and elimination of all other restrictions that affect intraregional trade. This new mechanism, which may provide for different rates of tariff reduction in accordance with varying levels of economic development in the member countries or the nature of the productive sectors, will overcome all those difficulties that derive from the present principle of negotiated tariff reduction. This lengthy and incomplete process was adequate for LAFTA at the outset but has proved to be deficient at the present stage now that the rate of Latin American trade is on the rise and complementary economies extend to considerable productive sectors. This mechanism for automatic tariff reduction opens up vast perspectives for dynamic new Latin American trade activity. Furthermore, the Montevideo meeting was also involved in the attempt to achieve a correct application of the principle of reciprocity and of the protective clauses, which play a decisive role in this dynamic trade activity.

With regard to the rebuilding and strengthening of the institutional framework of LAFTA, the action taken by the Ministers of Foreign Affairs was consistent with the guidelines laid down in the preparatory work and, in particular, with the document prepared by the Executive Committee that served as a basis for discussion at the Montevideo meeting. Thus, for example, in its decision regarding the creation and immediate establishment of the Council of Ministers of Foreign Affairs, the meeting stated that the development of the integration process would be stimulated if the Ministers met periodically to take decisions regarding the political direction of the Association.

The meeting also recognized the advisability of establishing a mechanism for the solution of disputes that exist or may arise among the LAFTA member states, with respect to the application and execution of the Montevideo Treaty, and decided to request the Executive Committee to prepare a draft protocol to be considered by the Ministers at their next meeting. In the preparation of this draft, certain general bases are to be kept in mind such as compulsory conciliation with intervention by the Committee, arbitration, and the possibility that the parties may recognize the compulsory jurisdiction of ad hoc tribunals and accept a system of sanctions that will guarantee their decisions. The Executive Committee was also entrusted with the study of the possibility of adopting provisional mechanisms, within the powers provided by the Montevideo Treaty and other legal instruments in force, for the solution of existing disputes or those that may arise prior to the entry into force of the system that will be incorporated into the draft protocol.

Pursuant to another resolution it was agreed to involve the national legislatures in the work of LAFTA, in order to obtain the points of view of the sectors of public opinion represented and to create favorable conditions for the harmonization of law regarding LAFTA matters. To this end, the meeting recommended the establishment of permanent groups or committees in the national legislatures to study and consider LAFTA matters, and requested the Standing Executive Committee to invite the chairmen of such groups or committees to meet at least once a year, in order to examine and promote the Latin American integration process.

From the point of view of the institutional strengthening of that process, the Ministers' decision to create a Technical Committee is of considerably greater significance. This Committee would be established by the Fifth Session of the Conference and would be composed of four individuals, nationals of LAFTA member states, to be named by the Conference, with the Executive Secretary as coordinator. The members named would, according to the resolution, act only in a private and individual capacity. This Committee would carry out studies, make proposals and present projects to accelerate the process of economic and social integration within the directives provided by the Montevideo Treaty, by the resolutions already adopted by the Conference and those which the organs of LAFTA may provide in the future. These proposals and projects would be presented to the Executive Committee and if not approved or if no decision were taken regarding them for lack of competence, they would be brought before the Conference or Council of Ministers.

The Fifth Session of the Conference of the Contracting Parties was held immediately after the Montevideo meeting. As can be seen, the implementation of some of the decisions and directives adopted by the meeting remains to the Conference or to the Standing Executive Committee, which explains the important responsibility that rests on these two organs of LAFTA in carrying out the objective for which the Meeting of Ministers was held.

Appendices

1. CHARTER OF THE ORGANIZATION OF AMERICAN STATES

IN THE NAME OF THEIR PEOPLES, THE STATES REPRESENTED AT THE NINTH INTERNATIONAL CONFERENCE OF AMERICAN STATES,

Convinced that the historic mission of America is to offer to man a land of liberty, and a favorable environment for the development of his personality and the realization of his just aspirations;

Conscious that that mission has already inspired numerous agreements, whose essential value lies in the desire of the American peoples to live together in peace, and, through their mutual understanding and respect for the sovereignty of each one, to provide for the betterment of all, in independence, in equality and under law;

Confident that the true significance of American solidarity and good neighborliness can only mean the consolidation on this continent, within the framework of democratic institutions, of a system of individual liberty and social justice based on respect for the essential rights of man;

Persuaded that their welfare and their contribution to the progress and the civilization of the world will increasingly require intensive continental cooperation;

Resolved to persevere in the noble undertaking that humanity has conferred upon the United Nations, whose principles and purposes they solemnly reaffirm;

Convinced that juridical organization is a necessary condition for security and peace founded on moral order and on justice; and

In accordance with Resolution IX of the Inter-American Conference on Problems of War and Peace, held at Mexico City,

HAVE AGREED

upon the following

CHARTER
OF THE ORGANIZATION OF
AMERICAN STATES

PART ONE

CHAPTER I

NATURE AND PURPOSES

ARTICLE 1

The American States establish by this Charter the international organization that they have developed to achieve an order of peace and justice, to promote their solidarity, to strengthen their collaboration, and to defend their sovereignty, their territorial integrity and their independence. Within the United Nations, the Organization of American States is a regional agency.

ARTICLE 2

All American States that ratify the present Charter are Members of the Organization.

ARTICLE 3

Any new political entity that arises from the union of several Member States and that, as such, ratifies the present Charter, shall become a Member of the Organization. The entry of the new political entity into the Organization shall result in the loss of membership of each one of the States which constitute it.

ARTICLE 4

The Organization of American States, in order to put into practice the principles on which it is founded and to fulfill its regional obligations under the Charter of the United Nations, proclaims the following essential purposes:

a) To strengthen the peace and security of the continent;

b) To prevent possible causes of difficulties and to ensure the pacific settlement of disputes that may arise among the Member States;

c) To provide for common action on the part of those States in the event of aggression;

d) To seek the solution of political, juridical and economic problems that may arise among them; and

e) To promote, by cooperative action, their economic, social and cultural development.

CHAPTER II

PRINCIPLES

ARTICLE 5

The American States reaffirm the following principles:

a) International law is the standard of conduct of States in their reciprocal relations;

b) International order consists essentially of respect for the personality, sovereignty and independence of States, and the faithful fulfillment of obligations derived from treaties and other sources of international law;

c) Good faith shall govern the relations between States;

d) The solidarity of the American States and the high aims which are sought through it require the political organization of those States on the basis of the effective exercise of representative democracy;

e) The American States condemn war of aggression: victory does not give rights;

f) An act of aggression against one American State is an act of aggression against all the other American States;

g) Controversies of an international character arising between two or more American States shall be settled by peaceful procedures;

h) Social justice and social security are bases of lasting peace;

i) Economic cooperation is essential to the common welfare and prosperity of the peoples of the continent;

j) The American States proclaim the fundamental rights of the individual without distinction as to race, nationality, creed or sex;

k) The spiritual unity of the continent is based on respect for the cultural values of the American countries and requires their close cooperation for the high purposes of civilization;

1) The education of peoples should be directed toward justice, freedom and peace.

CHAPTER III
FUNDAMENTAL RIGHTS AND DUTIES OF STATES
ARTICLE 6
States are juridically equal, enjoy equal rights and equal capacity to exercise these rights, and have equal duties. The rights of each State depend not upon its power to ensure the exercise thereof, but upon the mere fact of its existence as a person under international law.

ARTICLE 7
Every American State has the duty to respect the rights enjoyed by every other State in accordance with international law.

ARTICLE 8
The fundamental rights of States may not be impaired in any manner whatsoever.

ARTICLE 9
The political existence of the State is independent of recognition by other States. Even before being recognized, the State has the right to defend its integrity and independence, to provide for its preservation and prosperity, and consequently to organize itself as it sees fit, to legislate concerning its interests, to administer its services, and to determine the jurisdiction and competence of its courts. The exercise of these rights is limited only by the exercise of the rights of other States in accordance with international law.

ARTICLE 10
Recognition implies that the State granting it accepts the personality of the new State, with all the rights and duties that international law prescribes for the two States.

ARTICLE 11
The right of each State to protect itself and to live its own life does not authorize it to commit unjust acts against another State.

ARTICLE 12
The jurisdiction of States within the limits of their national territory is exercised equally over all the inhabitants, whether nationals or aliens.

ARTICLE 13
Each State has the right to develop its cultural, political and economic life freely and naturally. In this free development, the State shall respect the rights of the individual and the principles of universal morality.

ARTICLE 14
Respect for and the faithful observance of treaties constitute standards for the development of peaceful relations among States. International treaties and agreements should be public.

ARTICLE 15
No State or group of States has the right to intervene, directly or indirectly, for any reason whatever, in the internal or external affairs of any other State. The foregoing principle prohibits not only armed force but also any other form of interference or attempted threat against the personality of the State or against its political, economic and cultural elements.

ARTICLE 16

No State may use or encourage the use of coercive measures of an economic or political character in order to force the sovereign will of another State and obtain from it advantages of any kind.

ARTICLE 17

The territory of a State is inviolable; it may not be the object, even temporarily, of military occupation or of other measures of force taken by another State, directly or indirectly, on any grounds whatever. No territorial acquisitions or special advantages obtained either by force or by other means of coercion shall be recognized.

ARTICLE 18

The American States bind themselves in their international relations not to have recourse to the use of force, except in the case of self-defense in accordance with existing treaties or in fulfillment thereof.

ARTICLE 19

Measures adopted for the maintenance of peace and security in accordance with existing treaties do not constitute a violation of the principles set forth in Articles 15 and 17.

CHAPTER IV

PACIFIC SETTLEMENT OF DISPUTES

ARTICLE 20

All international disputes that may arise between American States shall be submitted to the peaceful procedures set forth in this Charter, before being referred to the Security Council of the United Nations.

ARTICLE 21

The following are peaceful procedures: direct negotiation, good offices, mediation, investigation and conciliation, judicial settlement, arbitration, and those which the parties to the dispute may especially agree upon at any time.

ARTICLE 22

In the event that a dispute arises between two or more American States which, in the opinion of one of them, cannot be settled through the usual diplomatic channels, the Parties shall agree on some other peaceful procedure that will enable them to reach a solution.

ARTICLE 23

A special treaty will establish adequate procedures for the pacific settlement of disputes and will determine the appropriate means for their application, so that no dispute between American States shall fail of definitive settlement within a reasonable period.

CHAPTER V

COLLECTIVE SECURITY

ARTICLE 24

Every act of aggression by a State against the territorial integrity or the inviolability of the territory or against the sovereignty or political independence of an American State shall be considered an act of aggression against the other American States.

ARTICLE 25

If the inviolability or the integrity of the territory or the sovereignty or political independence of any American State should be affected by an armed attack or by an act of aggression that is not an armed attack, or by an extra-continental conflict, or by a conflict between two or more American States, or by any other fact or situation that might endanger the peace of America, the American States, in furtherance of the principles of continental solidarity or collective self-defense, shall apply the measures and procedures established in the special treaties on the subject.

CHAPTER VI
ECONOMIC STANDARDS
ARTICLE 26

The Member States agree to cooperate with one another, as far as their resources may permit and their laws may provide, in the broadest spirit of good neighborliness, in order to strengthen their economic structure, develop their agriculture and mining, promote their industry and increase their trade.

ARTICLE 27

If the economy of an American State is affected by serious conditions that cannot be satisfactorily remedied by its own unaided effort, such State may place its economic problems before the Inter-American Economic and Social Council to seek through consultation the most appropriate solution for such problems.

CHAPTER VII
SOCIAL STANDARDS
ARTICLE 28

The Member States agree to cooperate with one another to achieve just and decent living conditions for their entire populations.

ARTICLE 29

The Member States agree upon the desirability of developing their social legislation on the following bases:

a) All human beings, without distinction as to race, nationality, sex, creed or social condition, have the right to attain material well-being and spiritual growth under circumstances of liberty, dignity, equality of opportunity, and economic security;

b) Work is a right and a social duty; it shall not be considered as an article of commerce; it demands respect for freedom of association and for the dignity of the worker; and it is to be performed under conditions that ensure life, health and a decent standard of living, both during the working years and during old age, or when any circumstance deprives the individual of the possibility of working.

CHAPTER VIII
CULTURAL STANDARDS
ARTICLE 30

The Member States agree to promote, in accordance with their constitutional provisions and their material resources, the exercise of the right to education, on the following bases:

a) Elementary education shall be compulsory and, when provided by the State, shall be without cost;

b) Higher education shall be available to all, without distinction as to race, nationality, sex, language, creed or social condition.

ARTICLE 31

With due consideration for the national character of each State, the Member States undertake to facilitate free cultural interchange by every medium of expression.

PART TWO

CHAPTER IX

THE ORGANS

ARTICLE 32

The Organization of American States accomplishes its purposes by means of:

a) The Inter-American Conference;

b) The Meeting of Consultation of Ministers of Foreign Affairs;

c) The Council;

d) The Pan American Union;

e) The Specialized Conferences; and

f) The Specialized Organizations.

CHAPTER X

THE INTER-AMERICAN CONFERENCE

ARTICLE 33

The Inter-American Conference is the supreme organ of the Organization of American States. It decides the general action and policy of the Organization and determines the structure and functions of its Organs, and has the authority to consider any matter relating to friendly relations among the American States. These functions shall be carried out in accordance with the provisions of this Charter and of other inter-American treaties.

ARTICLE 34

All Member States have the right to be represented at the Inter-American Conference. Each State has the right to one vote.

ARTICLE 35

The Conference shall convene every five years at the time fixed by the Council of the Organization, after consultation with the government of the country where the Conference is to be held.

ARTICLE 36

In special circumstances and with the approval of two-thirds of the American Governments, a special Inter-American Conference may be held, or the date of the next regular Conference may be changed.

ARTICLE 37

Each Inter-American Conference shall designate the place of meeting of the next Conference. If for any unforeseen reason the Conference cannot be held at the place designated, the Council of the Organization shall designate a new place.

ARTICLE 38

The program and regulations of the Inter-American Conference shall be prepared by the Council of the Organization and submitted to the Member States for consideration.

CHAPTER XI

THE MEETING OF CONSULTATION OF MINISTERS OF FOREIGN AFFAIRS

ARTICLE 39

The Meeting of Consultation of Ministers of Foreign Affairs shall be held in order to consider problems of an urgent nature and of common interest to the American States, and to serve as the Organ of Consultation.

ARTICLE 40

Any Member State may request that a Meeting of Consultation be called. The request shall be addressed to the Council of the Organization, which shall decide by an absolute majority whether a meeting should be held.

ARTICLE 41

The program and regulations of the Meeting of Consultation shall be prepared by the Council of the Organization and submitted to the Member States for consideration.

ARTICLE 42

If, for exceptional reasons, a Minister of Foreign Affairs is unable to attend the meeting, he shall be represented by a special delegate.

ARTICLE 43

In case of an armed attack within the territory of an American State or within the region of security delimited by treaties in force, a Meeting of Consultation shall be held without delay. Such Meeting shall be called immediately by the Chairman of the Council of the Organization, who shall at the same time call a meeting of the Council itself.

ARTICLE 44

An Advisory Defense Committee shall be established to advise the Organ of Consultation on problems of military cooperation that may arise in connection with the application of existing special treaties on collective security.

ARTICLE 45

The Advisory Defense Committee shall be composed of the highest military authorities of the American States participating in the Meeting of Consultation. Under exceptional circumstances the Governments may appoint substitutes. Each State shall be entitled to one vote.

ARTICLE 46

The Advisory Defense Committee shall be convoked under the same conditions as the Organ of Consultation, when the latter deals with matters relating to defense against aggression.

ARTICLE 47

The Committee shall also meet when the Conference or the Meeting of Consultation or the Governments, by a two-thirds majority of the Member States, assign to it technical studies or reports on specific subjects.

CHAPTER XII

THE COUNCIL

ARTICLE 48

The Council of the Organization of American States is composed of one Representative of each Member State of the Organization, especially appointed by the respective Government, with the rank of Ambassador. The appointment may be given to the diplomatic representative accredited to the Government of the country in which the Council has its seat. During the absence of the titular Representative, the Government may appoint an interim Representative.

ARTICLE 49

The Council shall elect a Chairman and a Vice Chairman, who shall serve for one year and shall not be eligible for election to either of those positions for the term immediately following.

ARTICLE 50

The Council takes cognizance, within the limits of the present Charter and of inter-American treaties and agreements, of any matter referred to it by the Inter-American Conference or the Meeting of Consultation of Ministers of Foreign Affairs.

ARTICLE 51

The Council shall be responsible for the proper discharge by the Pan American Union of the duties assigned to it.

ARTICLE 52

The Council shall serve provisionally as the Organ of Consultation when the circumstances contemplated in Article 43 of this Charter arise.

ARTICLE 53

It is also the duty of the Council:

a) To draft and submit to the Governments and to the Inter-American Conference proposals for the creation of new Specialized Organizations or for the combination, adaptation or elimination of existing ones, including matters relating to the financing and support thereof;

b) To draft recommendations to the Governments, the Inter-American Conference, the Specialized Conferences or the Specialized Organizations, for the coordination of the activities and programs of such organizations, after consultation with them;

c) To conclude agreements with the Inter-American Specialized Organizations to determine the relations that shall exist between the respective agency and the Organization;

d) To conclude agreements or special arrangements for cooperation with other American organizations of recognized international standing;

e) To promote and facilitate collaboration between the Organization of American States and the United Nations, as well as between Inter-American Specialized Organizations and similar international agencies;

f) To adopt resolutions that will enable the Secretary General to perform the duties envisaged in Article 84;

g) To perform the other duties assigned to it by the present Charter.

ARTICLE 54

The Council shall establish the bases for fixing the quota that each Government is to contribute to the maintenance of the Pan American Union, taking into account the ability to pay of the respective countries and their determination to contribute in an equitable manner. The budget, after approval by the Council, shall be transmitted to the Governments at least six months before the first day of the fiscal year, with a statement of the annual quota of each country. Decisions on budgetary matters require the approval of two-thirds of the members of the Council.

ARTICLE 55

The Council shall formulate its own regulations.

ARTICLE 56

The Council shall function at the seat of the Pan American Union.

ARTICLE 57

The following are organs of the Council of the Organization of American States:

a) The Inter-American Economic and Social Council;
b) The Inter-American Council of Jurists; and
c) The Inter-American Cultural Council.

ARTICLE 58

The organs referred to in the preceding article shall have technical autonomy within the limits of this Charter; but their decisions shall not encroach upon the sphere of action of the Council of the Organization.

ARTICLE 59

The organs of the Council of the Organization are composed of representatives of all the Member States of the Organization.

ARTICLE 60

The organs of the Council of the Organization shall, as far as possible, render to the Governments such technical services as the latter may request; and they shall advise the Council of the Organization on matters within their jurisdiction.

ARTICLE 61

The organs of the Council of the Organization shall, in agreement with the Council, establish cooperative relations with the corresponding organs of the United Nations and with the national or international agencies that function within their respective spheres of action.

ARTICLE 62

The Council of the Organization, with the advice of the appropriate bodies and after consultation with the Governments, shall formulate the statutes of its organs in accordance with and in the execution of the provisions of this Charter. The organs shall formulate their own regulations.

A) *The Inter-American Economic and Social Council*

ARTICLE 63

The Inter-American Economic and Social Council has for its principal purpose the promotion of the economic and social welfare of the American nations through effective cooperation for the better utilization of their natural resources, the development of their agriculture and industry and the raising of the standards of living of their peoples.

ARTICLE 64

To accomplish this purpose the Council shall:

a) Propose the means by which the American nations may give each other technical assistance in making studies and formulating and executing plans to carry out the purposes referred to in Article 26 and to develop and improve their social services;

b) Act as coordinating agency for all official inter-American activities of an economic and social nature;

c) Undertake studies on its own initiative or at the request of any Member State;

d) Assemble and prepare reports on economic and social matters for the use of the Member States;

e) Suggest to the Council of the Organization the advisability of holding specialized conferences on economic and social matters;

f) Carry on such other activities as may be assigned to it by the Inter-American Conference, the Meeting of Consultation of Ministers of Foreign Affairs, or the Council of the Organization.

ARTICLE 65

The Inter-American Economic and Social Council, composed of technical delegates appointed by each Member State, shall meet on its own initiative or on that of the Council of the Organization.

ARTICLE 66

The Inter-American Economic and Social Council shall function at the seat of the Pan American Union, but it may hold meetings in any American city by a majority decision of the Member States.

B) *The Inter-American Council of Jurists*

ARTICLE 67

The purpose of the Inter-American Council of Jurists is to serve as an advisory body on juridical matters; to promote the development and codification of public and private international law; and to study the possibility of attaining uniformity in the legislation of the various American countries, insofar as it may appear desirable.

ARTICLE 68

The Inter-American Juridical Committee of Rio de Janeiro shall be the permanent committee of the Inter-American Council of Jurists.

ARTICLE 69

The Juridical Committee shall be composed of jurists of the nine countries selected by the Inter-American Conference. The selection of the jurists shall be made by the Inter-American Council of Jurists from a panel submitted by each country chosen by the Conference. The Members of the Juridical Committee represent all Member States of the Organization. The Council of the Organization is empowered to fill any vacancies that occur during the intervals between Inter-American Conferences and between meetings of the Inter-American Council of Jurists.

ARTICLE 70

The Juridical Committee shall undertake such studies and preparatory work as are assigned to it by the Inter-American Council of Jurists, the Inter-American Conference, the Meeting of Consultation of Ministers of Foreign Affairs, or the Council of the Organization. It may also undertake those studies and projects which, on its own initiative, it considers advisable.

ARTICLE 71

The Inter-American Council of Jurists and the Juridical Committee should seek the cooperation of national committees for the codification of international law, of institutes of international and comparative law, and of other specialized agencies.

ARTICLE 72

The Inter-American Council of Jurists shall meet when convened by the Council of the Organization, at the place determined by the Council of Jurists at its previous meeting.

C) *The Inter-American Cultural Council*

ARTICLE 73

The purpose of the Inter-American Cultural Council is to promote friendly relations and mutual understanding among the American peoples, in order to strengthen the peaceful sentiments that have characterized the evolution of America, through the promotion of educational, scientific and cultural exchange.

ARTICLE 74

To this end the principal functions of the Council shall be:

a) To sponsor inter-American cultural activities;

b) To collect and supply information on cultural activities carried on in and among the American States by private and official agencies both national and international in character;

c) To promote the adoption of basic educational programs adapted to the needs of all population groups in the American countries;

d) To promote, in addition, the adoption of special programs of training, education and culture for the indigenous groups of the American countries;

e) To cooperate in the protection, preservation and increase of the cultural heritage of the continent;

f) To promote cooperation among the American nations in the fields of education, science and culture, by means of the exchange of materials for research and study, as well as the exchange of teachers, students, specialists and, in general, such other persons and materials as are useful for the realization of these ends;

g) To encourage the education of the peoples for harmonious international relations;

h) To carry on such other activities as may be assigned to it by the Inter-American Conference, the Meeting of Consultation of Ministers of Foreign Affairs, or the Council of the Organization.

ARTICLE 75

The Inter-American Cultural Council shall determine the place of its next meeting and shall be convened by the Council of the Organization on the date chosen by the latter in agreement with the Government of the country selected as the seat of the meeting.

ARTICLE 76

There shall be a Committee for Cultural Action of which five States, chosen at each Inter-American Conference, shall be members. The individuals composing the Committee for Cultural Action shall be selected by the Inter-

American Cultural Council from a panel submitted by each country chosen by the Conference, and they shall be specialists in education or cultural matters. When the Inter-American Cultural Council and the Inter-American Conference are not in session, the Council of the Organization may fill vacancies that arise and replace those countries that find it necessary to discontinue their cooperation.

ARTICLE 77

The Committee for Cultural Action shall function as the permanent committee of the Inter-American Cultural Council, for the purpose of preparing any studies that the latter may assign to it. With respect to these studies the Council shall have the final decision.

CHAPTER XIII
THE PAN AMERICAN UNION
ARTICLE 78

The Pan American Union is the central and permanent organ of the Organization of American States and the General Secretariat of the Organization. It shall perform the duties assigned to it in this Charter and such other duties as may be assigned to it in other inter-American treaties and agreements.

ARTICLE 79

There shall be a Secretary General of the Organization, who shall be elected by the Council for a ten-year term and who may not be reelected or be succeeded by a person of the same nationality. In the event of a vacancy in the office of Secretary General, the Council shall, within the next ninety days, elect a successor to fill the office for the remainder of the term, who may be reelected if the vacancy occurs during the second half of the term.

ARTICLE 80

The Secretary General shall direct the Pan American Union and be the legal representative thereof.

ARTICLE 81

The Secretary General shall participate with voice, but without vote, in the deliberations of the Inter-American Conference, the Meeting of Consultation of Ministers of Foreign Affairs, the Specialized Conferences, and the Council and its organs.

ARTICLE 82

The Pan American Union, through its technical and information offices, shall, under the direction of the Council, promote economic, social, juridical and cultural relations among all the Member States of the Organization.

ARTICLE 83

The Pan American Union shall also perform the following functions:

a) Transmit *ex officio* to Member States the convocation to the Inter-American Conference, the Meeting of Consultation of Ministers of Foreign Affairs, and the Specialized Conferences;

b) Advise the Council and its organs in the preparation of programs and regulations of the Inter-American Conference, the Meeting of Consultation of Ministers of Foreign Affairs, and the Specialized Conferences;

c) Place, to the extent of its ability, at the disposal of the Government of the country where a conference is to be held, the technical aid and personnel which such Government may request;

d) Serve as custodian of the documents and archives of the Inter-American Conference, of the Meeting of Consultation of Ministers of Foreign Affairs, and, insofar as possible, of the Specialized Conferences;

e) Serve as depository of the instruments of ratification of inter-American agreements;

f) Perform the functions entrusted to it by the Inter-American Conference, and the Meeting of Consultation of Ministers of Foreign Affairs;

g) Submit to the Council an annual report on the activities of the Organization;

h) Submit to the Inter-American Conference a report on the work accomplished by the Organs of the Organization since the previous Conference.

ARTICLE 84

It is the duty of the Secretary General:

a) To establish, with the approval of the Council, such technical and administrative offices of the Pan American Union as are necessary to accomplish its purposes;

b) To determine the number of department heads, officers and employees of the Pan American Union; to appoint them, regulate their powers and duties, and fix their compensation, in accordance with general standards established by the Council.

ARTICLE 85

There shall be an Assistant Secretary General, elected by the Council for a term of ten years and eligible for reelection. In the event of a vacancy in the office of Assistant Secretary General, the Council shall, within the next ninety days, elect a successor to fill such office for the remainder of the term.

ARTICLE 86

The Assistant Secretary General shall be the Secretary of the Council. He shall perform the duties of the Secretary General during the temporary absence or disability of the latter, or during the ninety-day vacancy referred to in Article 79. He shall also serve as advisory officer to the Secretary General, with the power to act as his delegate in all matters that the Secretary General may entrust to him.

ARTICLE 87

The Council, by a two-thirds vote of its members, may remove the Secretary General or the Assistant Secretary General whenever the proper functioning of the Organization so demands.

ARTICLE 88

The heads of the respective departments of the Pan American Union, appointed by the Secretary General, shall be the Executive Secretaries of the Inter-American Economic and Social Council, the Council of Jurists and the Cultural Council.

ARTICLE 89

In the performance of their duties the personnel shall not seek or receive instructions from any government or from any other authority outside the Pan American Union. They shall refrain from any action that might reflect upon their position as international officials responsible only to the Union.

ARTICLE 90

Every Member of the Organization of American States pledges itself to respect the exclusively international character of the responsibilities of the Secretary General and the personnel, and not to seek to influence them in the discharge of their duties.

ARTICLE 91

In selecting its personnel the Pan American Union shall give first consideration to efficiency, competence and integrity; but at the same time importance shall be given to the necessity of recruiting personnel on as broad a geographical basis as possible.

ARTICLE 92

The seat of the Pan American Union is the city of Washington.

CHAPTER XIV

THE SPECIALIZED CONFERENCES

ARTICLE 93

The Specialized Conferences shall meet to deal with special technical matters or to develop specific aspects of inter-American cooperation, when it is so decided by the Inter-American Conference or the Meeting of Consultation of Ministers of Foreign Affairs; when inter-American agreements so provide; or when the Council of the Organization considers it necessary, either on its own initiative or at the request of one of its organs or of one of the Specialized Organizations.

ARTICLE 94

The program and regulations of the Specialized Conferences shall be prepared by the organs of the Council of the Organization or by the Specialized Organizations concerned; they shall be submitted to the Member Governments for consideration and transmitted to the Council for its information.

CHAPTER XV

THE SPECIALIZED ORGANIZATIONS

ARTICLE 95

For the purposes of the present Charter, Inter-American Specialized Organizations are the intergovernmental organizations established by multilateral agreements and having specific functions with respect to technical matters of common interest to the American States.

ARTICLE 96

The Council shall, for the purposes stated in Article 53, maintain a register of the Organizations that fulfill the conditions set forth in the foregoing Article.

ARTICLE 97

The Specialized Organizations shall enjoy the fullest technical autonomy and shall take into account the recommendations of the Council, in conformity with the provisions of the present Charter.

ARTICLE 98

The Specialized Organizations shall submit to the Council periodic reports on the progress of their work and on their annual budgets and expenses.

ARTICLE 99

Agreements between the Council and the Specialized Organizations contemplated in paragraph c) of Article 53 may provide that such Organizations transmit their budgets to the Council for approval. Arrangements may also be made for the Pan American Union to receive the quotas of the contributing countries and distribute them in accordance with the said agreements.

ARTICLE 100

The Specialized Organizations shall establish cooperative relations with world agencies of the same character in order to coordinate their activities. In concluding agreements with international agencies of a world-wide character, the Inter-American Specialized Organizations shall preserve their identity and their status as integral parts of the Organization of American States, even when they perform regional functions of international agencies.

ARTICLE 101

In determining the geographic location of the Specialized Organizations the interests of all the American States shall be taken into account.

PART THREE

CHAPTER XVI

THE UNITED NATIONS

ARTICLE 102

None of the provisions of this Charter shall be construed as impairing the rights and obligations of the Member States under the Charter of the United Nations.

CHAPTER XVII

MISCELLANEOUS PROVISIONS

ARTICLE 103

The Organization of American States shall enjoy in the territory of each Member such legal capacity, privileges and immunities as are necessary for the exercise of its functions and the accomplishment of its purposes.

ARTICLE 104

The Representatives of the Governments on the Council of the Organization, the representatives on the organs of the Council, the personnel of their delegations, as well as the Secretary General and the Assistant Secretary General of the Organization, shall enjoy the privileges and immunities necessary for the independent performance of their duties.

ARTICLE 105

The juridical status of the Inter-American Specialized Organizations and the privileges and immunities that should be granted to them and to their personnel, as well as to the officials of the Pan American Union, shall be determined in each case through agreements between the respective organizations and the Governments concerned.

ARTICLE 106

Correspondence of the Organization of American States, including printed matter and parcels, bearing the frank thereof, shall be carried free of charge in the mails of the Member States.

ARTICLE 107

The Organization of American States does not recognize any restriction on the eligibility of men and women to participate in the activities of the various Organs and to hold positions therein.

CHAPTER XVIII

RATIFICATION AND ENTRY INTO FORCE

ARTICLE 108

The present Charter shall remain open for signature by the American States and shall be ratified in accordance with their respective constitutional procedures. The original instrument, the Spanish, English, Portuguese and French texts of which are equally authentic, shall be deposited with the Pan American Union, which shall transmit certified copies thereof to the Governments for purposes of ratification. The instruments of ratification shall be deposited with the Pan American Union, which shall notify the signatory States of such deposit.

ARTICLE 109

The present Charter shall enter into force among the ratifying States when two-thirds of the signatory States have deposited their ratifications. It shall enter into force with respect to the remaining States in the order in which they deposit their ratifications.

ARTICLE 110

The present Charter shall be registered with the Secretariat of the United Nations through the Pan American Union.

ARTICLE 111

Amendments to the present Charter may be adopted only at an Inter-American Conference convened for that purpose. Amendments shall enter into force in accordance with the terms and the procedure set forth in Article 109.

ARTICLE 112

The present Charter shall remain in force indefinitely, but may be denounced by any Member State upon written notification to the Pan American Union, which shall communicate to all the others each notice of denunciation received. After two years from the date on which the Pan American Union receives a notice of denunciation, the present Charter shall cease to be in force with respect to the denouncing State, which shall cease to belong to the Organization after it has fulfilled the obligations arising from the present Charter.

IN WITNESS WHEREOF the undersigned Plenipotentiaries, whose full powers have been presented and found to be in good and due form, sign the present Charter at the city of Bogotá, Colombia, on the dates that appear opposite their respective signatures.

RESERVATIONS MADE AT THE TIME OF RATIFYING

Guatemala

None of the stipulations of the present Charter of the Organization of American States may be considered as an impediment to Guatemala's assertion of its rights over the territory of Belize by such means as at any time it may deem advisable.[1]

Peru

With the reservation that the principles of inter-American solidarity and cooperation and essentially those set forth in the preamble and declarations of the Act of Chapultepec constitute standards for the mutual relations between the American States and juridical bases of the inter-American system.

United States

That the Senate give its advice and consent to ratification of the Charter with the reservation that none of its provisions shall be considered as enlarging the powers of the Federal Government of the United States or limiting the powers of the several states of the Federal Union with respect to any matters recognized under the Constitution as being within the reserved powers of the several states.

STATUS OF THE
CHARTER OF THE ORGANIZATION OF AMERICAN STATES
Signed at Bogotá, April 30, 1948, at the
Ninth International Conference of American States

SIGNATORY COUNTRIES	DATE OF INSTRUMENT OF RATIFICATION	DATE OF DEPOSIT OF THE INSTRUMENT OF RATIFICATION
Argentina	January 19, 1956	April 10, 1956
Bolivia	September 25, 1950	October 18, 1950
Brazil	February 11, 1950	March 13, 1950
Colombia	December 7, 1951	December 13, 1951
Costa Rica	October 30, 1948	November 16, 1948
Cuba	July 8, 1952	July 16, 1952
Chile	May 5, 1953	June 5, 1953
Dominican Republic	April 11, 1949	April 22, 1949
Ecuador	December 21, 1950	December 28, 1950
El Salvador	August 15, 1950	September 11, 1950
Guatemala	March 18, 1955*	April 6, 1955*
Haiti	August 21, 1950	March 28, 1951
Honduras	January 13, 1950	February 7, 1950
Mexico	November 23, 1948	November 23, 1948
Nicaragua	June 21, 1950	July 26, 1950
Panama	March 16, 1951	March 22, 1951
Paraguay	March 30, 1950	May 3, 1950
Peru	May 15, 1952*	February 12. 1954*
United States	June 15, 1951*	June 19, 1951*
Uruguay	August 17, 1955	September 1, 1955
Venezuela	December 21, 1951	December 29, 1951

* With a reservation.

1 With respect to this reservation, the Pan American Union consulted the signatory governments, in accordance with the procedure established by paragraph 2 of Resolution XXIX of the Eighth International Conference of American States, to ascertain

The Charter entered into effect December 13, 1951, when the 14th ratification was deposited by Colombia. It was registered with the General Secretariat of the United Nations on January 16, 1952.

---

whether they found it acceptable or not. At the request of the Government of Guatemala, this consultation was accompanied by a formal declaration of that Government to the effect that its reservation did not imply any alteration in the Charter of the Organization of American States, and that Guatemala is ready to act at all times within the bounds of international agreements to which it is a party. In view of this declaration, the States that previously did not find the reservation acceptable expressed their acceptance.

2. ORGANOGRAM OF THE ORGANIZATION OF AMERICAN STATES

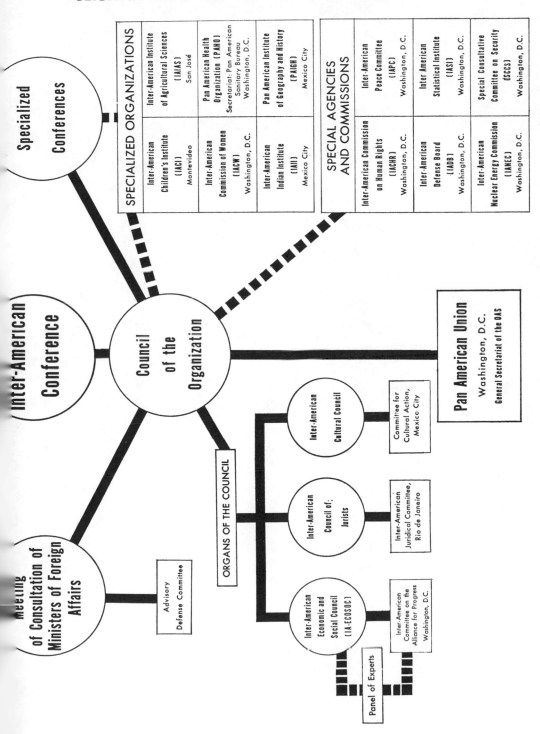

3. ACT OF WASHINGTON ON THE PROCEDURE FOR THE ADMISSION OF NEW MEMBERS (1964)

WHEREAS:

The common purposes pursued by the Organization of American States are to consolidate the ties of solidarity among the peoples of this hemisphere, to bring about closer cooperation among them, to obtain an order of peace and justice, and to defend their sovereignty, their territorial integrity, and their independence;

In establishing their mutual relations on bases of concord and friendship the member states have sought to eliminate from the Americas: in the political sphere, the doctrines and systems that, by impairing the personality of the individual, are a danger to peace; and in the economic sphere, the preferential systems that are prejudicial to cooperation and their development;

It is the will of the member states of the Organization of American States to permit the independent American states that so desire and that are willing to comply with the obligations of the Charter to participate in the benefits of their organization;

The inter-American system, as established in numerous resolutions of Inter-American Conferences and in provisions of the Charter itself, is founded upon respect for the sovereignty, territorial integrity, the independence of the states, and their equality before the law;

Resolution XCVI.3 and Resolution XCVII.2 of the Tenth Inter-American Conference, clearly establish a special situation with respect to the occupied territories that are the subject of litigation or claim between extracontinental countries and some American states;

Articles 2 and 108 of the Charter of the Organization of American States indicate that any state that wishes to be a member of the Organization must meet the following requirements:

a. That it be an independent state,
b. That it be located within the Western Hemisphere, and
c. That it sign and ratify the Charter of the Organization of American States;

Articles 24 and 25 of the Charter establish obligations for all the American states with respect to collective security of the hemisphere;

In accordance with those articles, the American states shall apply the measures and procedures established in the Inter-American Treaty of Reciprocal Assistance, for the purpose of fulfilling all the obligations arising from their condition as members of the Organization;

Article 33 of the Charter stipulates that the Inter-American Conference is the supreme organ of the Organization and that it decides the general action and policy of the Organization and determines the structure and functions of its Organs and has authority to consider any matter relating to friendly relations among the American states;

Article 50 authorizes the Council of the Organization to take cognizance, within the limits of the Charter and of inter-American treaties and agreements, of any matter referred to it by the Inter-American Conference or the Meeting of Consultation of Ministers of Foreign Affairs;

Pursuant to Article 51 of the Charter, the Council shall be responsible for the proper discharge by the Pan American Union of the duties assigned to it; and

It is necessary to establish a procedure for the admission of new members,

The First Special Inter-American Conference

RESOLVES:

1. That any independent American state that desires to become a member of the Organization should so indicate by means of a note addressed to the Secretary General, in which it declares that it is willing to sign and ratify the Charter of the Organization of American States and to accept all the obligations inherent in the condition of membership in the Organization, especially those relating to collective security expressly set forth in articles 24 and 25 of the Charter of the Organization.

2. That, once it is informed of the matter by the Secretary General, the Council of the Organization, in accordance with articles 108, 50, and 51 of the Charter, shall determine by the vote of two thirds of the member states whether it is appropriate that the Secretary General be authorized to permit the applicant state to sign the Charter of the Organization and to accept the deposit of the corresponding instrument of ratification.

3. That the Council of the Organization shall not take any decision with respect to a request for admission on the part of a political entity whose territory, in whole or in part, is subject, prior to the date of this resolution, to litigation or claim between an extracontinental country and one or more member states of the Organization of American States, until the dispute has been ended by some peaceful procedure.

4. That this instrument shall be known as the "Act of Washington."

4. CONVENTION ON ASYLUM
(Havana, 1928)

The Governments of the States of America, being desirous of fixing the rules they must observe for the granting of asylum, in their mutual relations have agreed to establish them in a Convention and to that end have appointed as Plenipotentiaries:

Who, after exchanging their respective full powers, found to be in good and due form, have agreed on the following:

ARTICLE 1.

It is not permissible for States to grant asylum in legations, warships, military camps or military aircraft, to persons accused or condemned for common crimes, or to deserters from the army or navy.

Persons accused of or condemned for common crimes taking refuge in any of the places mentioned in the preceding paragraph, shall be surrendered upon request of the local government.

Should said persons take refuge in foreign territory, surrender shall be brought about through extradition, but only in such cases and in the form established by the respective treaties and conventions or by the constitution and laws of the country of refuge.

ARTICLE 2

Asylum granted to political offenders in legations, warships, military camps or military aircraft, shall be respected to the extent in which allowed, as a right or through humanitarian toleration, by the usages, the conventions or the laws of the country in which granted and in accordance with the following provisions:

First: Asylum may not be granted except in urgent cases and for the period of time strictly indispensable for the person who has sought asylum to ensure in some other way his safety.

Second: Immediately upon granting asylum, the diplomatic agent, commander of a warship, or military camp or aircraft, shall report the fact to the Minister of Foreign Relations of the State of the person who has secured asylum, or to the local administrative authority, if the act occurred outside the capital.

Third: The Government of the State may require that the refugee be sent out of the national territory within the shortest time possible; and the diplomatic agent of the country who has granted asylum may in turn require the guaranties necessary for the departure of the refugee with due regard to the inviolability of his person, from the country.

Fourth: Refugees shall not be landed in any point of the national territory nor in any place too near thereto.

Fifth: While enjoying asylum, refugees shall not be allowed to perform acts contrary to the public peace.

Sixth: States are under no obligation to defray expenses incurred by one granting asylum.

ARTICLE 3

The present Convention does not affect obligations previously undertaken by the contracting parties through international agreements.

ARTICLE 4

After being signed, the present Convention shall be submitted to the ratification of the signatory States. The Government of Cuba is charged with transmitting authentic certified copies to the Governments for the aforementioned purpose of ratification. The instrument of ratification shall be deposited in the archives of the Pan American Union in Washington, the Union to notify the signatory governments of said deposit. Such notification shall be considered as an exchange of ratifications. This Convention shall remain open to the adherence of non-signatory States.

In witness whereof, the aforenamed Plenipotentiaries sign the present Convention in Spanish, English, French and Portuguese, in the city of Habana, the 20th day of February, 1928.

RESERVATION OF THE DELEGATION OF THE UNITED STATES OF AMERICA

The Delegation of the United States of America, in signing the present Convention, establishes an explicit reservation, placing on record that the United States does not recognize or subscribe to as part of international law, the so called doctrine of asylum.

5. CONVENTION ON POLITICAL ASYLUM
(Montevideo, 1933)

The Governments represented in the Seventh International Conference of American States:

Wishing to conclude a Convention on Political Asylum, to define the terms of the one signed at Habana, have appointed the following Plenipotentiaries:

Who, after having exhibited their Full Powers, which were found in good and due form, have agreed upon the following:

ARTICLE 1

In place of Article 1 of the Convention of Habana on Right of Asylum, of February 20, 1928, the following is substituted: "It shall not be lawful for the States to grant asylum in legations, warships, military camps, or airships to those accused of common offenses who may have been duly prosecuted or who may have been sentenced by ordinary courts of justice, nor to deserters of land or sea forces.

"The persons referred to in the preceding paragraph who find refuge in some of the above-mentioned places shall be surrendered as soon as requested by the local government."

ARTICLE 2

The judgment of political delinquency concerns the State which offers asylum.

ARTICLE 3

Political asylum, as an institution of humanitarian character, is not subject to reciprocity. Any man may resort to its protection, whatever his nationality, without prejudice to the obligations accepted by the State to which he belongs; however, the States that do not recognize political asylum, except with limitations and peculiarities, can exercise it in foreign countries only in the manner and within the limits recognized by said countries.

ARTICLE 4

When the withdrawal of a diplomatic agent is requested because of the discussions that may have arisen in some case of political asylum, the diplomatic agent shall be replaced by his government, and his withdrawal shall not determine a breach of diplomatic relations between the two States.

ARTICLE 5

The present Convention shall not affect obligations previously entered into by the High Contracting Parties by virtue of international agreements.

ARTICLE 6

The present Convention shall be ratified by the High Contracting Parties in conformity with their respective constitutional procedures. The Minister of Foreign Affairs of the Republic of Uruguay shall transmit authentic certified copies to the governments for the aforementioned purpose of ratification. The instrument of ratification shall be deposited in the archives of the Pan American Union in Washington, which shall notify the signatory governments of said deposit. Such notification shall be considered as an exchange of ratifications.

ARTICLE 7

The present Convention will enter into force between the High Contracting Parties in the order in which they deposit their respective ratifications.

ARTICLE 8

The present Convention shall remain in force indefinitely but may be denounced by means of one year's notice given to the Pan American Union, which shall transmit it to the other signatory governments. After the expiration of this period the Convention shall cease in its effects as regards the party which denounces but shall remain in effect for the remaining High Contracting Parties.

ARTICLE 9

The present Convention shall be open for the adherence and accession of the States which are not signatories. The corresponding instruments shall be deposited in the archives of the Pan American Union which shall communicate them to the other High Contracting Parties.

In witness whereof, the following Plenipotentiaries have signed this Convention in Spanish, English, Portuguese and French and hereunto affix their respective seals in the city of Montevideo, Republic of Uruguay, this 26th day of December, 1933.

DECLARATION

Since the United States of America does not recognize or subscribe to, as part of international law, the doctrine of asylum, the delegation of the United States of America refrains from signing the present Convention on Political Asylum.

6. CONVENTION ON DIPLOMATIC ASYLUM
(Caracas, 1954)

The governments of the Member States of the Organization of American States, desirous of concluding a Convention on Diplomatic Asylum, have agreed to the following articles:

ARTICLE I

Asylum granted in legations, war vessels, and military camps or aircraft, to persons being sought for political reasons or for political offenses shall be respected by the territorial State in accordance with the provisions of this Convention.

For the purposes of this Convention, a legation is any seat of a regular diplomatic mission, the residence of chiefs of mission, and the premises provided by them for the dwelling places of asylees when the number of the latter exceeds the normal capacity of the buildings.

War vessels or military aircraft that may be temporarily in shipyards, arsenals, or shops for repair may not constitute a place of asylum.

ARTICLE II

Every State has the right to grant asylum; but it is not obligated to do so or to state its reasons for refusing it.

ARTICLE III

It is not lawful to grant asylum to persons who, at the time of requesting it, are under indictment or on trial for common offenses or have been convicted by competent regular courts and have not served the respective sentence, nor to deserters from land, sea, and air forces, save when the acts giving rise to the request for asylum, whatever the case may be, are clearly of a political nature.

Persons included in the foregoing paragraph who *de facto* enter a place that is suitable as an asylum shall be invited to leave or, as the case may be, shall be surrendered to the local authorities, who may not try them for political offenses committed prior to the time of the surrender.

ARTICLE IV

It shall rest with the State granting asylum to determine the nature of the offense or the motives for the persecution.

ARTICLE V

Asylum may not be granted except in urgent cases and for the period of time strictly necessary for the asylee to depart from the country with the guarantees granted by the Government of the territorial State, to the end that his life, liberty, or personal integrity may not be endangered, or that the asylee's safety is ensured in some other way.

ARTICLE VI

Urgent cases are understood to be those, among others, in which the individual is being sought by persons or mobs over whom the authorities have lost control, or by the authorities themselves, and is in danger of being deprived of his life or liberty because of political persecution and cannot, without risk, ensure his safety in any other way.

ARTICLE VII

If a case of urgency is involved, it shall rest with the State granting asylum to determine the degree of urgency of the case.

ARTICLE VIII

The diplomatic representative, commander of a warship, military camp, or military airship, shall, as soon as possible after asylum has been granted, report the fact to the Minister of Foreign Affairs of the territorial State, or to the local administrative authority if the case arose outside the Capital.

ARTICLE IX

The official furnishing asylum shall take into account the information furnished to him by the territorial government in forming his judgment as to the nature of the offense or the existence of related common crimes; but this decision to continue the asylum or to demand a safe-conduct for the asylee shall be respected.

ARTICLE X

The fact that the Government of the territorial State is not recognized by the State granting asylum shall not prejudice the application of the present Convention, and no act carried out by virtue of this Convention shall imply recognition.

ARTICLE XI

The government of the territorial State may, at any time, demand that the asylee be withdrawn from the country, for which purpose the said State shall grant a safe-conduct and the guarantees stipulated in Article V.

ARTICLE XII

Once asylum has been granted, the State granting asylum may request that the asylee be allowed to depart for foreign territory, and the territorial State is under obligation to grant immediately, except in case of force majeure, the necessary guarantees, referred to in Article V, as well as the corresponding safe-conduct.

ARTICLE XIII

In the cases referred to in the preceding articles the State granting asylum may require that the guarantees be given in writing, and may take into account, in determining the rapidity of the journey, the actual conditions of danger involved in the departure of the asylee.

The State granting asylum has the right to transfer the asylee out of the country. The territorial State may point out the preferable route for the departure of the asylee, but this does not imply determining the country of destination.

If the asylum is granted on board a warship or military airship, departure may be made therein, but complying with the previous requisite of obtaining the appropriate safe-conduct.

ARTICLE XIV

The State granting asylum cannot be held responsible for the prolongation of asylum caused by the need for obtaining the information required to determine whether or not the said asylum is proper, or whether there are circumstances that might endanger the safety of the asylee during the journey to a foreign country.

ARTICLE XV

When, in order to transfer an asylee to another country it may be necessary to traverse the territory of a State that is a party to this Convention, transit shall be authorized by the latter, the only requisite being the presentation, through diplomatic channels, of a safe-conduct, duly countersigned and bearing a notation of his status as asylee by the diplomatic mission that granted asylum.

En route, the asylee shall be considered under the protection of the State granting asylum.

ARTICLE XVI

Asylees may not be landed at any point in the territorial State or at any place near thereto, except for exigencies of transportation.

ARTICLE XVII

Once the departure of the asylee has been carried out, the State granting asylum is not bound to settle him in its territory; but it may not return him to his country of origin, unless this is the express wish of the asylee.

If the territorial State informs the official granting asylum of its intention to request the subsequent extradition of the asylee, this shall not prejudice the application of any provision of the present Convention. In that event, the asylee shall remain in the territory of the State granting asylum until such time as the formal request for extradition is received, in accordance with the juridical principles governing that institution in the State granting asylum. Preventive surveillance over the asylee may not exceed thirty days.

Payment of the expenses incurred by such transfer and of preventive control shall devolve upon the requesting State.

ARTICLE XVIII

The official furnishing asylum may not allow the asylee to perform acts contrary to the public peace or to interfere in the internal politics of the territorial State.

ARTICLE XIX

If as a consequence of a rupture of diplomatic relations the diplomatic representative who granted asylum must leave the territorial State, he shall abandon it with the asylees.

If this is not possible for reasons independent of the wish of the asylee or the diplomatic representative, he must surrender them to the diplomatic mission of a third State, which is a party to this Convention, under the guarantees established in the Convention.

If this is also not possible, he shall surrender them to a State that is not a party to this Convention and that agrees to maintain the asylum. The territorial State is to respect the said asylum.

ARTICLE XX

Diplomatic asylum shall not be subject to reciprocity.

Every person is under its protection, whatever his nationality.

ARTICLE XXI

The present Convention shall be open for signature by the Member States of the Organization of American States and shall be ratified by the signatory States in accordance with their respective constitutional procedures.

ARTICLE XXII

The original instrument, whose texts in the English, French, Spanish, and Portuguese languages are equally authentic, shall be deposited in the Pan American Union, which shall send certified copies to the governments for the purpose of ratification. The instruments of ratification shall be deposited in the Pan American Union, and the said organization shall notify the signatory governments of the said deposit.

ARTICLE XXIII

The present Convention shall enter into force among the States that ratify it in the order in which their respective ratifications are deposited.

ARTICLE XXIV

The present Convention shall remain in force indefinitely, but may be denounced by any of the signatory States by giving advance notice of one year, at the end of which period it shall cease to have effect for the denouncing State, remaining in force, however, among the remaining signatory States. The denunciation shall be transmitted to the Pan American Union, which shall inform the other signatory States thereof.

RESERVATIONS

Guatemala

We make an express reservation to Article II wherein it declares that the States are not obligated to grant asylum; because we uphold a broad, firm concept of the right to asylum.

Likewise, we make an express reservation to the final paragraph of Article XX (Twenty), because we maintain that any person, without any discrimination whatsoever, has the right to the protection of asylum.

Uruguay

The government of Uruguay makes a reservation to Article II, in the part that stipulates that the authority granting asylum, is, in no case, obligated to grant asylum nor to state its reasons for refusing it. It likewise makes a reservation to that part of Article XV that stipulates: "the only requisite being the presentation, through diplomatic channels, of a safe-conduct, duly countersigned and bearing a notation of his status as asylee by the diplomatic mission that granted asylum. En route, the asylee shall be considered under the protection of the State granting asylum". Finally, it makes a reservation to the second paragraph of Article XX, since the government of Uruguay understands that all persons have the right to asylum, whatever their sex, nationality, belief, or religion.

Dominican Republic

The Dominican Republic subscribes to the above Convention with the following reservations:

First: The Dominican Republic does not agree to the provisions contained in Article VII and those following with respect to the unilateral determination of the urgency by the State granting asylum; and

Second: The provisions of this Convention shall not be applicable, consequently, insofar as the Dominican Republic is concerned, to any controversies that may arise between the territorial State and the State granting asylum, that refer specifically to the absence of a serious situation or the non-existence of a true act of persecution against the asylee by the local authorities.

Honduras

The delegation of Honduras subscribes to the Convention on Diplomatic Asylum with reservations with respect to those articles that are in violation of the Constitution and laws in force in the Republic of Honduras.

IN WITNESS WHEREOF, the undersigned Plenipotentiaries, having presented their plenary powers, which have been found in good and due form, sign this Convention, in the name of their respective Governments, in the city of Caracas, this twenty-eighth day of March, one thousand nine hundred and fifty-four.

7. CONVENTION ON TERRITORIAL ASYLUM
(Caracas, 1954)

The governments of the Member States of the Organization of American States, desirous of concluding a Convention regarding Territorial Asylum, have agreed to the following articles:

ARTICLE I

Every State has the right, in the exercise of its sovereignty, to admit into its territory such persons as it deems advisable, without, through the exercise of this right, giving rise to complaint by any other State.

ARTICLE II

The respect which, according to international law, is due the jurisdictional right of each State over the inhabitants in its territory, is equally due, without any restriction whatsoever, to that which it has over persons who enter it proceeding from a State in which they are persecuted for their beliefs, opinions, or political affiliations, or for acts which may be considered as political offenses.

Any violation of sovereignty that consists of acts committed by a government or its agents in another State against the life or security of an individual, carried out on the territory of another State, may not be considered attenuated because the persecution began outside its boundaries or is due to political considerations or reasons of state.

ARTICLE III

No State is under the obligation to surrender to another State, or to expel from its own territory, persons persecuted for political reasons or offenses.

ARTICLE IV

The right of extradition is not applicable in connection with persons who, in accordance with the qualifications of the solicited State, are sought for political offenses, or for common offenses committed for political ends, or when extradition is solicited for predominantly political motives.

ARTICLE V

The fact that a person has entered into the territorial jurisdiction of a State surreptitiously or irregularly does not affect the provisions of this Convention.

ARTICLE VI

Without prejudice to the provisions of the following articles, no State is under the obligation to establish any distinction in its legislation, or in its regulations or administrative acts applicable to aliens, solely because of the fact that they are political asylees or refugees.

ARTICLE VII

Freedom of expression of thought, recognized by domestic law for all inhabitants of a State, may not be ground of complaint by a third State on the basis of opinions expressed publicly against it or its government by asylees or refugees, except when these concepts constitute systematic propaganda through which they incite to the use of force or violence against the government of the complaining State.

ARTICLE VIII

No State has the right to request that another State restrict for the political asylees or refugees the freedom of assembly or association which the latter State's internal legislation grants to all aliens within its territory, unless such assembly or association has as its purpose fomenting the use of force or violence against the government of the soliciting State.

ARTICLE IX

At the request of the interested State, the State that has granted refuge or asylum shall take steps to keep watch over, or to intern at a reasonable distance from its border, those political refugees or asylees who are notorious leaders of a subversive movement, as well as those against whom there is evidence that they are disposed to join it.

Determination of the reasonable distance from the border, for the purpose of internment, shall depend upon the judgment of the authorities of the State of refuge.

All expenses incurred as a result of the internment of political asylees and refugees shall be chargeable to the State that makes the request.

ARTICLE X

The political internees referred to in the preceding article shall advise the government of the host State whenever they wish to leave its territory. Departure therefrom will be granted, under the condition that they are not to go to the country from which they came; and the interested government is to be notified.

ARTICLE XI

In all cases in which a complaint or request is permissible in accordance with this Convention, the admissibility of evidence presented by the demanding State shall depend on the judgment of the solicited State.

ARTICLE XII

This Convention remains open to the signature of the Member States of the Organization of American States, and shall be ratified by the signatory States in accordance with their respective constitutional procedures.

ARTICLE XIII

The original instrument, whose texts in the English, French, Portuguese, and Spanish languages are equally authentic, shall be deposited in the Pan American Union, which shall send certified copies to the governments for the purpose of ratification. The instruments of ratification shall be deposited in the Pan American Union; this organization shall notify the signatory governments of said deposit.

ARTICLE XIV

This Convention shall take effect among the States that ratify it in the order in which their respective ratifications are deposited.

ARTICLE XV

This Convention shall remain effective indefinitely, but may be denounced by any of the signatory States by giving advance notice of one year, at the end of which period it shall cease to have effect for the denouncing State, remaining, however, in force among the remaining signatory States. The denunciation shall be forwarded to the Pan American Union which shall notify the other signatory States thereof.

RESERVATIONS

Guatemala

We make express reservation to Article III (three) wherein it refers to the surrender of persons persecuted for political reasons or offenses; because according to the provisions of our Political Constitution, we maintain that such surrender of persons persecuted for political reasons may never be carried out.

We affirm, likewise, that the term "internment" in Article IX means merely location at a distance from the border.

Dominican Republic

The delegation of the Dominican Republic subscribes to the Convention on Territorial Asylum, with the following reservations:

Article I. The Dominican Republic accepts the general principle embodied in that article in the sense that, "Every State has the right to admit into its territory such persons as it deems advisable," but it does not renounce the right to make diplomatic representation to any other State, if for considerations of national security it deems this advisable.

Article II. It accepts the second paragraph of this article with the understanding that the latter does not affect the regulations of the frontier police.

Article X. The Dominican Republic does not renounce the right to resort to the procedures for pacific settlement of international disputes that may arise from the exercise of territorial asylum.

Mexico

The delegation of Mexico makes express reservation to Articles IX and X of the Convention regarding territorial asylum because they are contrary to the individual guarantees enjoyed by all the inhabitants of the Republic in accordance with the Political Constitution of Mexico.

Peru

The delegation of Peru makes reservation to the text of Article VII of the Convention regarding Territorial Asylum, insofar as it differs from Article VI of the draft proposal of the Inter-American Council of Jurists, with which the delegation concurs.

Honduras

The delegation of Honduras gives its approval to the Convention regarding Territorial Asylum with reservations with respect to those articles opposed to the Constitution and to the laws in force in the republic of Honduras.

Argentina

The delegation of Argentina has voted in favor of the Convention regarding Territorial Asylum, but makes express reservations in regard to Article VII, as it believes that the latter does not duly consider nor satisfactorily resolve the problem arising from the exercise, on the part of political asylees, of the right of freedom of expression of thought.

IN WITNESS WHEREOF, the undersigned Plenipotentiaries, having presented their plenary powers which have been found in good and satisfactory form, sign this Convention, in the name of their respective Governments, in the city of Caracas, this twenty-eighth day of March, one thousand nine hundred and fifty-four.

8. AMERICAN DECLARATION OF THE RIGHTS AND DUTIES OF MAN
(Bogotá, 1948)

WHEREAS:

The American peoples have acknowledged the dignity of the individual, and their national constitutions recognize that juridical and political institutions, which regulate life in human society, have as their principal aim the protection of the essential rights of man and the creation of circumstances that will permit him to achieve spiritual and material progress and attain happiness;

The American states have on repeated occasions recognized that the essential rights of man are not derived from the fact that he is a national of a certain state, but are based upon attributes of his human personality;

The international protection of the rights of man should be the principal guide of an evolving American law;

The affirmation of essential human rights by the American states together with the guarantees given by the internal regimes of the states establish the initial system of protection considered by the American states as being suited to the present social and juridicial conditions, not without a recognition on their part that they should increasingly strengthen that system in the international field as conditions become more favorable,

The Ninth International Conference of American States

AGREES:

To adopt the following

AMERICAN DECLARATION OF THE RIGHTS AND DUTIES OF MAN

PREAMBLE

All men are born free and equal, in dignity and in rights, and, being endowed by nature with reason and conscience, they should conduct themselves as brothers one to another.

The fulfillment of duty by each individual is a prerequisite to the rights of all. Rights and duties are interrelated in every social and political activity of man. While rights exalt individual liberty, duties express the dignity of that liberty.

Duties of a juridical nature presuppose others of a moral nature which support them in principle and constitute their basis.

Inasmuch as spiritual development is the supreme end of human existence and the highest expression thereof, it is the duty of man to serve that end with all his strength and resources.

Since culture is the highest social and historical expression of that spiritual development, it is the duty of man to preserve, practice and foster culture by every means within his power.

And, since moral conduct constitutes the noblest flowering of culture, it is the duty of every man always to hold it in high respect.

CHAPTER ONE

RIGHTS

Article I. Every human being has the right to life, liberty and the security of his person.

Right to life, liberty and personal security.

Article II. All persons are equal before the law and have the rights and duties established in this Declaration, without distinction as to race, sex, language, creed or any other factor.

Right to equality before the law.

Article III. Every person has the right freely to profess a religious faith, and to manifest and practice it both in public and in private.

Right to religious freedom and worship.

Article IV. Every person has the right to freedom of investigation, of opinion, and of the expression and dissemination of ideas, by any medium whatsoever.

Right to freedom of investigation, opinion, expression and dissemination.

Article V. Every person has the right to the protection of the law against abusive attacks upon his honor, his reputation, and his private and family life.

Right to protection of honor, personal reputation, and private and family life.

Article VI. Every person has the right to establish a family, the basic element of society, and to receive protection therefor.

Right to a family and to the protection thereof.

Article VII. All women, during pregnancy and the nursing period, and all children have the right to special protection, care and aid.

Right to protection for mothers and children.

Article VIII. Every person has the right to fix his residence within the territory of the state of which he is a national, to move about freely within such territory, and not to leave it except by his own will.

Right to residence and movement.

Article IX. Every person has the right to the inviolability of his home.

Right to inviolability of the home.

Article X. Every person has the right to the inviolability and transmission of his correspondence.

Right to the inviolability and transmission of correspondence.

Article XI. Every person has the right to the preservation of his health through sanitary and social measures relating to food, clothing, housing and medical care, to the extent permitted by public and community resources.

Right to the preservation of health and to well-being.

Article XII. Every person has the right to an education, which should be based on the principles of liberty, morality and human solidarity.

Right to education.

Likewise every person has the right to an education that will prepare him to attain a decent life, to raise his standard of living, and to be a useful member of society.

The right to an education includes the right to equality of opportunity in every case, in accordance with natural talents, merit and the desire to utilize the resources that the state or the community is in a position to provide.

Every person has the right to receive, free, at least a primary education.

Article XIII. Every person has the right to take part in the cultural life of the community, to enjoy the arts, and to participate in the benefits that result from intellectual progress, especially scientific discoveries.

Right to the benefits of culture.

He likewise has the right to the protection of his moral and material interests as regards his inventions or any literary, scientific or artistic works of which he is the author.

Article XIV. Every person has the right to work, under proper conditions, and to follow his vocation freely, in so far as existing conditions of employment permit.

Right to work and to fair remuneration.

Every person who works has the right to receive such remuneration as will, in proportion to his capacity and skill, assure him a standard of living suitable for himself and for his family.

Article XV. Every person has the right to leisure time, to wholesome recreation, and to the opportunity for advantageous use of his free time to his spiritual, cultural and physical benefit.

Right to leisure time and to the use thereof.

Article XVI. Every person has the right to social security which will protect him from the consequences of unemployment, old age, and any disabilities arising from causes beyond his control that make it physically or mentally impossible for him to earn a living.

Right to social security.

Article XVII. Every person has the right to be recognized everywhere as a person having rights and obligations, and to enjoy the basic civil rights.

Right to recognition of juridical personality and of civil rights.

Article XVIII. Every person may resort to the courts to ensure respect for his legal rights. There should likewise be available to him a simple, brief procedure whereby the courts will protect him from acts of authority that, to his prejudice, violate any fundamental constitutional rights.

Right to a fair trial.

Article XIX. Every person has the right to the nationality to which he is entitled by law and to change it, if he so wishes, for the nationality of any other country that is willing to grant it to him.

Right to nationality.

Article XX. Every person having legal capacity is entitled to participate in the government of his country, directly or through his representatives, and to take part in popular elections, which shall be by secret ballot, and shall be honest, periodic and free.

Right to vote and to participate in government.

Article XXI. Every person has the right to assemble peaceably with others in a formal public meeting or an informal gathering, in connection with matters of common interest of any nature.

Right of assembly.

Article XXII. Every person has the right to associate with others to promote, exercise and protect his legitimate interests of a political, economic, religious, social, cultural, professional, labor union or other nature.

Right of association.

Article XXIII. Every person has a right to own such private property as meets the essential needs of decent living and helps to maintain the dignity of the individual and of the home.

Right to property.

Article XXIV. Every person has the right to submit respectful petitions to any competent authority, for reasons of either general or private interest, and the right to obtain a prompt decision thereon.

Right of petition.

Article XXV. No person may be deprived of his liberty except in the cases and according to the procedures established by pre-existing law.

No person may be deprived of liberty for nonfulfillment of obligations of a purely civil character.

Every individual who has been deprived of his liberty has the right to have the legality of his detention ascertained without delay by a court, and the right to be tried without undue delay or, otherwise, to be released. He also has the right to humane treatment during the time he is in custody.

Right of protection from arbitrary arrest.

Article XXVI. Every accused person is presumed to be innocent until proved guilty.

Every person accused of an offense has the right to be given an impartial and public hearing, and to be tried by courts previously established in accordance with pre-existing laws, and not to receive cruel, infamous or unusual punishment.

Right to due process of law.

Article XXVII. Every person has the right, in case of pursuit not resulting from ordinary crimes, to seek and receive asylum in foreign territory, in accordance with the laws of each country and with international agreements.

Right of asylum.

Article XXVIII. The rights of man are limited by the rights of others, by the security of all, and by the just demands of the general welfare and the advancement of democracy.

Scope of the rights of man.

CHAPTER TWO
DUTIES

Article XXIX. It is the duty of the individual so to conduct himself in relation to others that each and every one may fully form and develop his personality.

Duties to society.

Article XXX. It is the duty of every person to aid, support, educate and protect his minor children, and it is the duty of children to honor their parents always and to aid, support and protect them when they need it.

Duties toward children and parents.

Article XXXI. It is the duty of every person to acquire at least an elementary education.

Duty to receive instruction.

Article XXXII. It is the duty of every person to vote in the popular elections of the country of which he is a national, when he is legally capable of doing so.

Duty to vote.

Article XXXIII. It is the duty of every person to obey the law and other legitimate commands of the authorities of his country and those of the country in which he may be.

Duty to obey the law.

Article XXXIV. It is the duty of every able-bodied person to render whatever civil and military service his country may require for its defense and preservation, and, in case of public disaster, to render such services as may be in his power.

It is likewise his duty to hold any public office to which he may be elected by popular vote in the state of which is is a national.

Duty to serve the community and the nation.

Article XXXV. It is the duty of every person to cooperate with the state and the community with respect to social security and welfare, in accordance with his ability and with existing circumstances.

Duties with respect to social security and welfare.

Article XXXVI. It is the duty of every person to pay the taxes established by law for the support of public services.

Duty to pay taxes.

Article XXXVII. It is the duty of every person to work, as far as his capacity and possibilities permit, in order to obtain the means of livelihood or to benefit his community.

Duty to work.

Article XXXVIII. It is the duty of every person to refrain from taking part in political activities that, according to law, are reserved exclusively to the citizens of the state in which he is an alien.

Duty to refrain from political activities in a foreign country.

9. THE DECLARATION OF SANTIAGO, CHILE ON REPRESENTATIVE DEMOCRACY (1959)

The Fifth Meeting of Consultation of Ministers of Foreign Affairs,

EXPRESSING the general aspiration of the American peoples to live in peace under the protection of democratic institutions, free from all intervention and all totalitarian influence; and

WHEREAS:

The faith of the peoples of America in the effective exercise of representative democracy is the best vehicle for the promotion of their social and political progress (Resolution XCV of the Tenth Inter-American Conference), while well-planned and intensive development of the economies of the American countries and improvement in the standard of living of their peoples represent the best and firmest foundation on which the practical exercise of democracy and the stabilization of their institutions can be established (Resolutions of the Special Committee to Study the Formulation of New Measures for Economic Cooperation);

In Resolution XXXII, the Ninth International Conference of American States, for the purpose of safeguarding peace and maintaining mutual respect among states, resolved, among other things, to reaffirm their decision to maintain and further an effective social and economic policy for the purpose of raising the standard of living of their peoples, and their conviction that only under a system founded upon a guarantee of the essential freedoms and rights of the individual is it possible to attain this goal; and to condemn the methods of every system tending to suppress political and civil rights and liberties, and in particular the action of international communism or any other totalitarian doctrine;

In Resolution XCV, the Tenth Inter-American Conference resolved to unite the efforts of all the American States to apply, develop, and perfect the principles of the inter-American system, so that they would form the basis of firm and solidary action designed to attain, within a short time, the effective realization of the representative democratic system, the rule of social justice and security, and the economic and cultural cooperation essential to the mutual well-being and prosperity of the peoples of the Continent;

Harmony among the American republics can be effective only insofar as human rights and fundamental freedoms and the exercise of representative democracy are a reality within each one of them, since experience has demonstrated that the lack of respect for such principles is a source of widespread disturbance and gives rise to emigrations that cause frequent and grave political tensions between the state that they leave and the states that receive them;

The existence of anti-democratic regimes constitutes a violation of the principles on which the Organization of American States is founded, and a danger to united and peaceful relationships in the hemisphere; and

It is advisable to state, with no attempt to be complete, some of the principles and attributes of the democratic system in this hemisphere, so as to permit national and international public opinion to gauge the degree of identification of political regimes and governments with that system, thus contributing to the eradication of forms of dictatorship, despotism, or tyranny, without weakening respect for the right of peoples freely to choose their own form of government,

DECLARES:

1. The principle of the rule of law should be assured by the separation of powers, and by the control of the legality of governmental acts by competent organs of the state.

2. The governments of the American republics should be the result of free elections.

3. Perpetuation in power, or the exercise of power without a fixed term and with the manifest intent of perpetuation, is incompatible with the effective exercise of democracy.

4. The governments of the American states should maintain a system of freedom for the individual and of social justice based on respect for fundamental human rights.

5. The human rights incorporated into the legislation of the American states should be protected by effective judicial procedures.

6. The systematic use of political proscription is contrary to American democratic order.

7. Freedom of the press, radio, and television, and, in general, freedom of information and expression, are essential conditions for the existence of a democratic regime.

8. The American states, in order to strengthen democratic institutions, should cooperate among themselves within the limits of their resources and the framework of their laws so as to strengthen and develop their economic structure, and achieve just and humane living conditions for their peoples; and

RESOLVES:

That this declaration shall be known as "The Declaration of Santiago, Chile."

10. STATUTE OF THE INTER-AMERICAN COMMISSION ON HUMAN RIGHTS (1960)

I

NATURE AND PURPOSES

ARTICLE 1

The Inter-American Commission on Human Rights, created by the Fifth Meeting of Consultation of Ministers of Foreign Affairs, is an autonomous entity of the Organization of American States, the function of which is to promote respect for human rights.

ARTICLE 2

For the purpose of this Statute, human rights are understood to be those set forth in the American Declaration of the Rights and Duties of Man.

II

MEMBERSHIP

ARTICLE 3

a. The Inter-American Commission on Human Rights shall be composed of seven members, nationals of the member states of the Organization, who shall be persons of high moral character and recognized competence in the field of human rights.

b. The members of the Commission shall represent all the member countries of the Organization of American States and act in its name.

ARTICLE 4

a. The members of the Commission shall be elected in their personal capacity by the Council of the Organization of American States from a list made up of panels of three persons proposed for the purpose by the governments of the member states of the Organization.

b. Each of the said governments shall propose a panel of three persons, on which it may include not only its own nationals but also those of the other member states of the Organization. The proponent governments shall submit with their panels biographical data for each candidate.

c. The vote of the Council of the Organization for election of the members of the Commission shall be taken by secret ballot, and the candidates who obtain the greatest number of votes and an absolute majority of the votes of the representatives of the member states shall be declared elected. If, in order to elect all the members of the Commission, it should become necessary to take several votes, the candidates receiving the smaller number of votes shall be eliminated successively in such manner as the Council determines.

d. Only one national of any one state may be elected a member of the Commission.

e. Members of the Commission may be re-elected in the same manner as that prescribed for their election.

ARTICLE 5

a. Except in the case of the first election of members of the Commission and elections that should be held to fill vacancies announced pursuant to Article 9, the Secretary General of the Organization of American States shall address the member states of the Organization in writing, through their representatives on the Council, at least six months prior to the date of the election, inviting them to submit their panels of three candidates within a period of three months.

b. The Secretary General shall prepare an alphabetical list of the candidates thus nominated and transmit it to the Council of the Organization.

c. The Council of the Organization shall set the date for the election of the members of the Commission and it shall elect them, in the manner prescribed by this Statute, from among the candidates whose names appear on the list referred to in the preceding paragraph.

ARTICLE 6

a. The members of the Commission shall be elected for four years.

b. Elections of members of the Commission that are held at the expiration of terms of office shall be conducted pursuant to the provisions of the preceding articles.

c. The Chairman of the Commission shall be elected by an absolute majority of the votes of its members; he shall hold office for two years; and he may be re-elected.

d. The Vice Chairman of the Commission shall be elected in the same manner and for the same term as the Chairman. The Vice Chairman shall replace the Chairman when the latter is temporarily prevented from performing his duties. In case of the death or the resignation of the Chairman, the Vice Chairman shall become Chairman, and at its next meeting the Commission shall elect a new Vice Chairman.

ARTICLE 7

a. In case of the death or the resignation of a member of the Commission, the Chairman shall immediately notify the Secretary General of the Organization of American States, who in turn shall inform the member states of the Organization.

b. In order to fill vacancies on the Commission when they occur, each government may propose a candidate within a period of one month, the nomination to be accompanied by the pertinent biographical data.

c. The Secretary General shall prepare an alphabetical list of the candidates thus nominated and transmit it to the Council of the Organization.

d. When the term of office is due to expire within six months following a vacancy, the vacancy shall not be filled.

ARTICLE 8

During their terms of office, the Chairman and the members of the Commission shall receive the emoluments and travel expenses provided for in the budget of the Pan American Union, under such terms and conditions as the Council of the Organization determines, with due regard to the importance of the Commission's tasks.

III

COMPETENCE AND PROCEDURE

ARTICLE 9

In carrying out its assignment of promoting respect for human rights, the Commission shall have the following functions and powers:

a. To develop an awareness of human rights among the peoples of America;

b. To make recommendations to the Governments of the member states in general, if it considers such action advisable, for the adoption of progressive measures in favor of human rights within the framework of their domestic legislation and, in accordance with their constitutional precepts, appropriate measures to further the faithful observance of those rights;

c. To prepare such studies or reports as it considers advisable in the performance of its duties;

d. To urge the Governments of the member states to supply it with information on the measures adopted by them in matters of human rights;

e. To serve the Organization of American States as an advisory body in respect of human rights.

ARTICLE 10

In performing its assignment, the Commission shall act in accordance with the pertinent provisions of the Charter of the Organization and bear in mind particularly that, in conformity with the American Declaration of the Rights and Duties of Man, the rights of each man are limited by the rights of others, by the security of all, and by the just demands of the general welfare and the advancement of democracy.

IV
SEAT AND MEETINGS
ARTICLE 11

a. The Secretary General of the Organization shall convoke the first meeting of the Commission.

b. After its first meeting, the Commission shall meet:
   i. For a maximum of eight weeks a year, in one or two regular meetings, as decided by the Commission itself;
   ii. In special meetings when so convoked by the Chairman or at the request of a majority of its members.

c. The permanent seat of the Commission shall be at the Pan American Union. The Commission may move to the territory of any American state when it so decides by an absolute majority of votes and with the consent of the government concerned.

V
QUORUM AND VOTING
ARTICLE 12

An absolute majority of the members of the Commission shall constitute a quorum.

ARTICLE 13

Decisions shall be taken by an absolute majority vote of the members of the Commission, except in the case of procedural matters, when decisions shall be taken by a simple majority.

VI
SECRETARIAT
ARTICLE 14

The Secretary General of the Organization of American States shall appoint the necessary technical and administrative personnel to serve as the Secretariat of the Commission. The Secretariat shall form part of the personnel of the Pan American Union and its expenses shall be included in the budget of the Pan American Union.

VII
REGULATIONS AND AMENDMENTS TO THE STATUTE
ARTICLE 15

The Commission shall prepare and adopt its own Rules and Regulations, in accordance with the provisions of this Statute.

ARTICLE 16

This Statute may be amended by the Council of the Organization.

11. INTER-AMERICAN TREATY OF RECIPROCAL ASSISTANCE
(Rio de Janeiro, 1947)

In the name of their Peoples, the Governments represented at the Inter-American Conference for the Maintenance of Continental Peace and Security, desirous of consolidating and strengthening their relations of friendship and good neighborliness, and

CONSIDERING: That Resolution VIII of the Inter-American Conference on Problems of War and Peace, which met in Mexico City, recommended the conclusion of a treaty to prevent and repel threats and acts of aggression against any of the countries of America;

That the High Contracting Parties reiterate their will to remain united in an inter-American system consistent with the purposes and principles of the United Nations, and reaffirm the existence of the agreement which they have concluded concerning those matters relating to the maintenance of international peace and security which are appropriate for regional action;

That the High Contracting Parties reaffirm their adherence to the principles of inter-American solidarity and cooperation, and especially to those set forth in the preamble and declarations of the Act of Chapultepec, all of which should be understood to be accepted as standards of their mutual relations and as the juridical basis of the Inter-American System;

That the American States propose, in order to improve the procedures for the pacific settlement of their controversies, to conclude the treaty concerning the "Inter-American Peace System" envisaged in Resolution IX and XXXIX of the Inter-American Conference on Problems of War and Peace;

That the obligation of mutual assistance and common defense of the American Republics is essentially related to their democratic ideals and to their will to cooperate permanently in the fulfillment of the principles and purposes of a policy of peace;

That the American regional community affirms as a manifest truth that juridical organization is a necessary prerequisite of security and peace, and that peace is founded on justice and moral order and, consequently, on the international recognition and protection of human rights and freedoms, on the indispensable well-being of the people, and on the effectiveness of democracy for the international realization of justice and security,

Have resolved, in conformity with the objectives stated above, to conclude the following Treaty, in order to assure peace, through adequate means, to provide for effective reciprocal assistance to meet armed attacks against any American State, and in order to deal with threats of aggression against any of them:

ARTICLE 1

The High Contracting Parties formally condemn war and undertake in their international relations not to resort to the threat or the use of force in any manner inconsistent with the provisions of the Charter of the United Nations or of this Treaty.

ARTICLE 2

As a consequence of the principle set forth in the preceding Article, the High Contracting Parties undertake to submit every controversy which may arise between them to methods of peaceful settlement and to endeavor to settle any such controversy among themselves by means of the procedures in force in the Inter-American System before referring it to the General Assembly or the Security Council of the United Nations.

ARTICLE 3

1. The High Contracting Parties agree that an armed attack by any State against an American State shall be considered as an attack against all the American States and, consequently, each one of the said Contracting Parties undertakes to assist in meeting the attack in the exercise of the inherent right of individual or collective self-defense recognized by Article 51 of the Charter of the United Nations.

2. On the request of the State or States directly attacked and until the decision of the Organ of Consultation of the Inter-American System, each one of the Contracting Parties may determine the immediate measures which it may individually take in fulfillment of the obligation contained in the preceding paragraph and in accordance with the principle of continental solidarity. The Organ of Consultation shall meet without delay for the purpose of examining those measures and agreeing upon the measures of a collective character that should be taken.

3. The provisions of this Article shall be applied in case of any armed attack which takes place within the region described in Article 4 or within the territory of an American State. When the attack takes place outside of the said areas, the provisions of Article 6 shall be applied.

4. Measures of self-defense provided for under this Article may be taken until the Security Council of the United Nations has taken the measures necessary to maintain international peace and security.

ARTICLE 4

The region to which this Treaty refers is bounded as follows: beginning at the North Pole; thence due south to a point 74 degrees north latitude, 10 degrees west longitude; thence by a rhumb line to a point 47 degrees 30 minutes north latitude, 50 degrees west longitude; thence by a rhumb line to a point 35 degrees north latitude, 60 degrees west longitude; thence due south to a point in 20 degrees north latitude; thence by a rhumb line to a point 5 degrees north latitude, 24 degrees west longitude; thence due south to the South Pole; thence due north to a point 30 degrees south latitude, 90 degrees west longitude; thence by a rhumb line to a point on the Equator at 97 degrees west longitude; thence by a rhumb line to a point 15 degrees north latitude, 120 degrees west longitude; thence by a rhumb line to a point 50 degrees north latitude, 170 degrees east longitude; thence due north to a point in 54 degrees north latitude; thence by a rhumb line to a point 65 degrees 30 minutes north latitude, 168 degrees 58 minutes 5 seconds west longitude; thence due north to the North Pole.

ARTICLE 5

The High Contracting Parties shall immediately send to the Security Council of the United Nations, in conformity with Articles 51 and 54 of the Charter of the United Nations, complete information concerning the activities undertaken or in contemplation in the exercise of the right of self-defense or for the purpose of maintaining inter-American peace and security.

ARTICLE 6

If the inviolability or the integrity of the territory or the sovereignty or political independence of any American State should be affected by an aggression which is not an armed attack or by an extra-continental or intra-continental conflict, or by any other fact or situation that might endanger the peace of America, the Organ of Consultation shall meet immediately in order to agree on the measures which must be taken in case of aggression to assist the victim of the aggression or, in any case, the measures which should be taken for the common defense and for the maintenance of the peace and security of the Continent.

ARTICLE 7

In the case of a conflict between two or more American States, without prejudice to the right of self-defense in conformity with Article 51 of the Charter of the United Nations, the High Contracting Parties, meeting in consultation shall call upon the contending States to suspend hostilities and restore matters to the *statu quo ante bellum,* and shall take in addition all other necessary measures to reestablish or maintain inter-American peace and security and for the solution of the conflict by peaceful means. The rejection of the pacifying action will be considered in the determination of the aggressor and in the application of the measures which the consultative meeting may agree upon.

ARTICLE 8

For the purposes of this Treaty, the measures on which the Organ of Consultation may agree will comprise one or more of the following: recall of chiefs of diplomatic missions; breaking of diplomatic relations; breaking of consular relations; partial or complete interruption of economic relations or of rail, sea, air, postal, telegraphic, telephonic, and radiotelephonic or radiotelegraphic communications; and use of armed force.

ARTICLE 9

In addition to other acts which the Organ of Consultation may characterize as aggression, the following shall be considered as such:

a. Unprovoked armed attack by a State against the territory, the people or the land, sea or air forces of another State;

b. Invasion, by the armed forces of a State, of the territory of an American State, through the trespassing of boundaries demarcated in accordance with a treaty, judicial decision, or arbitral award, or, in the absence of frontiers thus demarcated, invasion affecting a region which is under the effective jurisdiction of another State.

ARTICLE 10

None of the provisions of this Treaty shall be construed as impairing the rights and obligations of the High Contracting Parties under the Charter of the United Nations.

ARTICLE 11

The consultations to which this Treaty refers shall be carried out by means of the Meetings of Ministers of Foreign Affairs of the American Republics which have ratified the Treaty, or in the manner or by the organ which in the future may be agreed upon.

ARTICLE 12

The Governing Board of the Pan American Union may act provisionally as an organ of consultation until the meeting of the Organ of Consultation referred to in the preceding Article takes place.

ARTICLE 13

The consultations shall be initiated at the request addressed to the Governing Board of the Pan American Union by any of the Signatory States which has ratified the Treaty.

ARTICLE 14

In the voting referred to in this Treaty only the representatives of the Signatory States which have ratified the Treaty may take part.

ARTICLE 15

The Governing Board of the Pan American Union shall act in all matters concerning this Treaty as an organ of liaison among the Signatory States which have ratified this Treaty and between these States and the United Nations.

ARTICLE 16

The decisions of the Governing Board of the Pan American Union referred to in Articles 13 and 15 above shall be taken by an absolute majority of the Members entitled to vote.

ARTICLE 17

The Organ of Consultation shall take its decisions by a vote of two-thirds of the Signatory States which have ratified the Treaty.

ARTICLE 18

In the case of a situation or dispute between American States, the parties directly interested shall be excluded from the voting referred to in the two preceding Articles.

ARTICLE 19

To constitute a quorum in all the meetings referred to in the previous Articles, it shall be necessary that the number of States represented shall be at least equal to the number of votes necessary for the taking of the decision.

ARTICLE 20

Decisions which require the application of the measures specified in Article 8 shall be binding upon all the Signatory States which have ratified this Treaty, with the sole exception that no State shall be required to use armed force without its consent.

ARTICLE 21

The measures agreed upon by the Organ of Consultation shall be executed through the procedures and agencies now existing or those which may in the future be established.

ARTICLE 22

This Treaty shall come into effect between the States which ratify it as soon as the ratifications of two-thirds of the Signatory States have been deposited.

ARTICLE 23

This Treaty is open for signature by the American States at the city of Rio de Janeiro, and shall be ratified by the Signatory States as soon as possible in accordance with their respective constitutional processes. The ratifications shall be deposited with the Pan American Union, which shall notify the Signatory States of each deposit. Such notification shall be considered as an exchange of ratifications.

ARTICLE 24

The present Treaty shall be registered with the Secretariat of the United Nations through the Pan American Union, when two-thirds of the Signatory States have deposited their ratifications.

ARTICLE 25

This Treaty shall remain in force indefinitely, but may be denounced by any High Contracting Party by a notification in writing to the Pan American Union, which shall inform all the other High Contracting Parties of each notification of denunciation received. After the expiration of two years from the date of the receipt by the Pan American Union of a notification of denunciation by any High Contracting Party, the present Treaty shall cease to be in force with respect to such State, but shall remain in full force and effect with respect to all the other High Contracting Parties.

ARTICLE 26

The principles and fundamental provisions of this Treaty shall be incorporated in the Organic Pact of the Inter-American System.

IN WITNESS WHEREOF, the undersigned Plenipotentiaries, having deposited their full powers found to be in due and proper form, sign this Treaty on behalf of their respective Governments, on the dates appearing opposite their signatures.

Done in the city of Rio de Janeiro, in four texts respectively in the English, French, Portuguese and Spanish languages, on the second of September nineteen hundred forty-seven.

RESERVATIONS MADE AT THE TIME OF SIGNING

Honduras

The Delegation of Honduras, in signing the present Treaty and in connection with Article 9, section (b), does so with the reservation that the boundary between Honduras and Nicaragua is definitively demarcated by the Joint Boundary Commission of nineteen hundred and nineteen hundred and one, starting from a point in the Gulf of Fonseca, in the Pacific Ocean, to Portillo de Teotecacinte and, from this point to the Atlantic, by the line that His Majesty the King of Spain's arbitral award established on the twenty-third of December of nineteen hundred and six.

Nicaragua

The Delegate of Nicaragua, in signing the present Treaty, and with respect to the reservation made by the Delegation of Honduras on signing it and to the provisions of Article 9 (b), does so with the reservation that the boundary between Nicaragua and Honduras from the point known by the name of Portillo de Teotecacinte to the Atlantic Ocean has not been definitively drawn, by virtue of the fact that the royal Award rendered by His Majesty the King of Spain on December twenty-third, nineteen hundred six, has been impugned and protested by Nicaragua as nonexistent, null, and void. Consequently, the signing of this Treaty by Nicaragua may not be alleged as acceptance of arbitral awards that Nicaragua has impugned or whose validity is not definite.

STATEMENT MADE ON SIGNING THE TREATY

Ecuador

The Republic of Ecuador signs the present Inter-American Treaty of Reciprocal Assistance without reservations, because it understands that other instruments and the principles of international law do not bar the revision of treaties, either by agreement between the Parties or by the other pacific means consecrated by international law itself.

RESERVATIONS MADE AT THE TIME OF RATIFYING

Guatemala

The present Treaty poses no impediment whatever to Guatemala's assertion of its rights over the Guatemalan territory of Belize by whatever means it considers most appropriate; a Treaty that may at any time be invoked by the Republic with respect to the aforesaid territory.[1]

Honduras

With the reservation made at the time of signing.

Nicaragua

With the reservation made at the time of signing.

Ecuador

With the statement made on signing the Treaty.

---

[1] With respect to this reservation, the Pan American Union consulted the signatory governments, in accordance with the procedure established by paragraph 2 of Resolution XXIX of the Eighth International Conference of American States, to ascertain whether they found it acceptable or not. A number of replies being unfavorable, a second consultation was made accompanied, at the request of the Government of Guatemala, by a formal declaration of that Government to the effect that its reservation did not imply any alteration in the Inter-American Treaty of Reciprocal Assistance, and that Guatemala was ready to act at all times within the bounds of international agreements to which it was a party. In view of this declaration, the States that previously had not found the reservation acceptable now expressed their acceptance.

INTER-AMERICAN TREATY OF RECIPROCAL ASSISTANCE

Signed at the Inter-American Conference for the
Maintenance of Continental Peace and Security, held
in Rio de Janeiro from August 15 to September 2, 1947

SIGNATORY COUNTRIES	DATE OF INSTRUMENT OF RATIFICATION	DATE OF DEPOSIT OF THE INSTRUMENT OF RATIFICATION
Argentina	July 19, 1950	August 21, 1950
Bolivia	September 18, 1950	September 26, 1950
Brazil	March 5, 1948	March 25, 1948
Colombia	January 10, 1948	February 3, 1948
Costa Rica	November 20, 1948	December 3, 1948
Cuba	December 4, 1948	December 9, 1948
Chile	January 28, 1949	February 9, 1949
Dominican Republic	November 7, 1947	November 21, 1947
Ecuador	October 30, 1950	November 7, 1950
El Salvador	February 19, 1948	March 15, 1948
Guatemala	March 18, 1955*	April 6, 1955*
Haiti	October 30, 1947	March 25, 1948
Honduras	January 15, 1948*	February 5, 1948*
Mexico	November 23, 1948	November 23, 1948
Nicaragua	November 1, 1948*	November 12, 1948*
Panama	December 31, 1947	January 12, 1948
Paraguay	July 7, 1948	July 28, 1948
Peru	October 9, 1950	October 25, 1950
United States	December 12, 1947	December 30, 1947
Uruguay	September 7, 1948	September 28, 1948
Venezuela	September 9, 1948	October 4, 1948

* With a reservation.

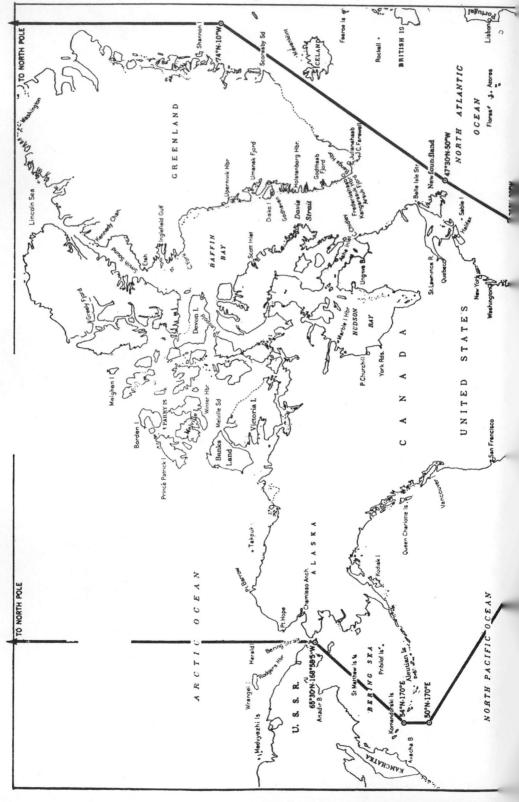

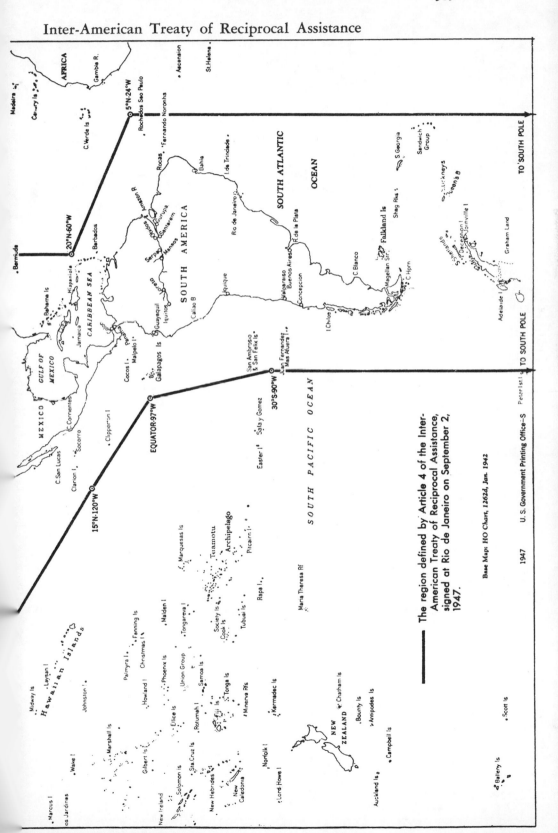

The region defined by Article 4 of the Inter-American Treaty of Reciprocal Assistance, signed at Rio de Janeiro on September 2, 1947.

Base Map: HO Chart, 12624, Jan. 1942

1947   U. S. Government Printing Office—S

12. AMERICAN TREATY ON PACIFIC SETTLEMENT
"Pact of Bogotá" (Bogotá, 1948)

In the name of their peoples, the Governments represented at the Ninth International Conference of American States have resolved, in fulfillment of Article XXIII of the Charter of the Organization of American States, to conclude the following Treaty:

CHAPTER ONE
GENERAL OBLIGATION TO SETTLE DISPUTES BY PACIFIC MEANS

ARTICLE I

The High Contracting Parties, solemnly reaffirming their commitments made in earlier international conventions and declarations, as well as in the Charter of the United Nations, agree to refrain from the threat or the use of force, or from any other means of coercion for the settlement of their controversies, and to have recourse at all times to pacific procedures.

ARTICLE II

The High Contracting Parties recognize the obligation to settle international controversies by regional pacific procedures before referring them to the Security Council of the United Nations.

Consequently, in the event that a controversy arises between two or more signatory states which, in the opinion of the parties, cannot be settled by direct negotiations through the usual diplomatic channels, the parties bind themselves to use the procedures established in the present Treaty, in the manner and under the conditions provided for in the following articles, or, alternatively, such special procedures as, in their opinion, will permit them to arrive at a solution.

ARTICLE III

The order of the pacific procedures established in the present Treaty does not signify that the parties may not have recourse to the procedure which they consider most appropriate in each case, or that they should use all these procedures, or that any of them have preference over others except as expressly provided.

ARTICLE IV

Once any pacific procedure has been initiated, whether by agreement between the parties or in fulfillment of the present Treaty or a previous pact, no other procedure may be commenced until that procedure is concluded.

ARTICLE V

The aforesaid procedures may not be applied to matters which, by their nature, are within the domestic jurisdiction of the state. If the parties are not in agreement as to whether the controversy concerns a matter of domestic jurisdiction, this preliminary question shall be submitted to decision by the International Court of Justice, at the request of any of the parties.

ARTICLE VI

The aforesaid procedures, furthermore, may not be applied to matters already settled by arrangements between the parties, or by arbitral award or by decision of an international court, or which are governed by agreements or treaties in force on the date of the conclusion of the present Treaty.

ARTICLE VII

The High Contracting Parties bind themselves not to make diplomatic representations in order to protect their nationals, or to refer a controversy to a court of international jurisdiction for that purpose, when the said nationals have had available the means to place their case before competent domestic courts of the respective state.

ARTICLE VIII

Neither recourse to pacific means for the solution of controversies, nor the recommendation of their use, shall, in the case of an armed attack, be ground for delaying the exercise of the right of individual or collective self-defense, as provided for in the Charter of the United Nations.

CHAPTER TWO
PROCEDURES OF GOOD OFFICES AND MEDIATION

ARTICLE IX

The procedure of good offices consists in the attempt by one or more American Governments not parties to the controversy, or by one or more eminent citizens of any American State which is not a party to the controversy, to bring the parties together, so as to make it possible for them to reach an adequate solution between themselves.

ARTICLE X

Once the parties have been brought together and have resumed direct negotiations, no further action is to be taken by the states or citizens that have offered their good offices or have accepted an invitation to offer them; they may, however, by agreement between the parties, be present at the negotiations.

ARTICLE XI

The procedure of mediation consists in the submission of the controversy to one or more American Governments not parties to the controversy, or to one or more eminent citizens of any American State not a party to the controversy. In either case the mediator or mediators shall be chosen by mutual agreement between the parties.

ARTICLE XII

The functions of the mediator or mediators shall be to assist the parties in the settlement of controversies in the simplest and most direct manner, avoiding formalities and seeking an acceptable solution. No report shall be made by the mediator and, so far as he is concerned, the proceedings shall be wholly confidential.

ARTICLE XIII

In the event that the High Contracting Parties have agreed to the procedure of mediation but are unable to reach an agreement within two months on the selection of the. mediator or mediators, or no solution to the controversy has been reached within five months after mediation has begun, the parties shall have recourse without delay to any one of the other procedures of peaceful settlement established in the present Treaty.

ARTICLE XIV

The High Contracting Parties may offer their mediation, either individually or jointly, but they agree not to do so while the controversy is in process of settlement by any of the other procedures established in the present Treaty.

CHAPTER THREE
PROCEDURE OF INVESTIGATION AND CONCILIATION
ARTICLE XV

The procedure of investigation and conciliation consists in the submission of the controversy to a Commission of Investigation and Conciliation, which shall be established in accordance with the provisions established in subsequent articles of the present Treaty, and which shall function within the limitations prescribed therein.

ARTICLE XVI

The party initiating the procedure of investigation and conciliation shall request the Council of the Organization of American States to convoke the Commission of Investigation and Conciliation. The Council for its part shall take immediate steps to convoke it.

Once the request to convoke the Commission has been received, the controversy between the parties shall immediately be suspended, and the parties shall refrain from any act that might make conciliation more difficult. To that end, at the request of one of the parties, the Council of the Organization of American States may, pending the convocation of the Commission, make appropriate recommendations to the parties.

ARTICLE XVII

Each of the High Contracting Parties may appoint, by means of a bilateral agreement consisting of a simple exchange of notes with each of the other signatories, two members of the Commission of Investigation and Conciliation, only one of whom may be of its own nationality. The fifth member, who shall perform the functions of chairman, shall be selected immediately by common agreement of the members thus appointed.

Any one of the contracting parties may remove members whom it has appointed, whether nationals or aliens; at the same time it shall appoint the successor. If this is not done, the removal shall be considered as not having been made. The appointments and substitutions shall be registered with the Pan American Union, which shall endeavor to ensure that the commissions maintain their full complement of five members.

ARTICLE XVIII

Without prejudice to the provisions of the foregoing article, the Pan American Union shall draw up a permanent panel of American conciliators, to be made up as follows:

a) Each of the High Contracting Parties shall appoint, for three-year periods, two of their nationals who enjoy the highest reputation for fairness, competence and integrity;

b) The Pan American Union shall request of the candidates notice of their formal acceptance, and it shall place on the panel of conciliators the names of the persons who so notify it;

c) The governments may, at any time, fill vacancies occurring among their appointees; and they may reappoint their members.

ARTICLE XIX

In the event that a controversy should arise between two or more American States that have not appointed the Commission referred to in Article XVII, the following procedure shall be observed:

a) Each party shall designate two members from the permanent panel of American conciliators, who are not of the same nationality as the appointing party.

b) These four members shall in turn choose a fifth member, from the permanent panel, not of the nationality of either party.

c) If, within a period of thirty days following the notification of their selection, the four members are unable to agree upon a fifth member, they shall each separately list the conciliators composing the permanent panel, in order of their preference, and upon comparison of the lists so prepared, the one who first receives a majority of votes shall be declared elected. The person so elected shall perform the duties of chairman of the Commission.

ARTICLE XX

In convening the Commission of Investigation and Conciliation, the Council of the Organization of American States shall determine the place where the Commission shall meet. Thereafter, the Commission may determine the place or places in which it is to function, taking into account the best facilities for the performance of its work.

ARTICLE XXI

When more than two states are involved in the same controversy, the states that hold similar points of view shall be considered as a single party. If they have different interests they shall be entitled to increase the number of conciliators in order that all parties may have equal representation. The chairman shall be elected in the manner set forth in Article XIX.

ARTICLE XXII

It shall be the duty of the Commission of Investigation and Conciliation to clarify the points in dispute between the parties and to endeavor to bring about an agreement between them upon mutually acceptable terms. The Commission shall institute such investigations of the facts involved in the controversy as it may deem necessary for the purpose of proposing acceptable bases of settlement.

ARTICLE XXIII

It shall be the duty of the parties to facilitate the work of the Commission and to supply it, to the fullest extent possible, with all useful documents and information, and also to use the means at their disposal to enable the Commission to summon and hear witnesses or experts and perform other tasks in the territories of the parties, in conformity with their laws.

ARTICLE XXIV

During the proceedings before the Commission, the parties shall be represented by plenipotentiary delegates or by agents, who shall serve as intermediaries between them and the Commission. The parties and the Commission may use the services of technical advisers and experts.

ARTICLE XXV

The Commission shall conclude its work within a period of six months from the date of its installation; but the parties may, by mutual agreement, extend the period.

ARTICLE XXVI

If, in the opinion of the parties, the controversy relates exclusively to questions of fact, the Commission shall limit itself to investigating such questions, and shall conclude its activities with an appropriate report.

ARTICLE XXVII

If an agreement is reached by conciliation, the final report of the Commission shall be limited to the text of the agreement and shall be published after its transmittal to the parties, unless the parties decide otherwise. If no agreement is reached, the final report shall contain a summary of the work of the Commission; it shall be delivered to the parties, and shall be published after the expiration of six months unless the parties decide otherwise. In both cases, the final report shall be adopted by a majority vote.

ARTICLE XXVIII

The reports and conclusions of the Commission of Investigation and Conciliation shall not be binding upon the parties, either with respect to the statement of facts or in regard to questions of law, and they shall have no other character than that of recommendations submitted for the consideration of the parties in order to facilitate a friendly settlement of the controversy.

ARTICLE XXIX

The Commission of Investigation and Conciliation shall transmit to each of the parties, as well as to the Pan American Union, certified copies of the minutes of its proceedings. These minutes shall not be published unless the parties so decide.

ARTICLE XXX

Each member of the Commission shall receive financial remuneration, the amount of which shall be fixed by agreement between the parties. If the parties do not agree thereon, the Council of the Organization shall determine the remuneration. Each government shall pay its own expenses and an equal share of the common expenses of the Commission, including the aforementioned remunerations.

CHAPTER FOUR

JUDICIAL PROCEDURE

ARTICLE XXXI

In conformity with Article 36, paragraph 2, of the Statute of the International Court of Justice, the High Contracting Parties declare that they recognize, in relation to any other American State, the jurisdiction of the Court as compulsory *ipso facto*, without the necessity of any special agreement so long as the present Treaty is in force, in all disputes of a juridical nature that arise among them concerning:

    a) The interpretation of a treaty;

    b) Any question of international law;

    c) The existence of any fact which, if established, would constitute the breach of an international obligation;

    d) The nature or extent of the reparation to be made for the breach of an international obligation.

ARTICLE XXXII

When the conciliation procedure previously established in the present Treaty or by agreement of the parties does not lead to a solution, and the said parties have not agreed upon an arbitral procedure, either of them shall be entitled to have recourse to the International Court of Justice in the manner prescribed in Article 40 of the Statute thereof. The Court shall have compulsory jurisdiction in accordance with Article 36, paragraph 1, of the said Statute.

ARTICLE XXXIII

If the parties fail to agree as to whether the Court has jurisdiction over the controversy, the Court itself shall first decide that question.

ARTICLE XXXIV

If the Court, for the reasons set forth in Articles V, VI and VII of this Treaty, declares itself to be without jurisdiction to hear the controversy, such controversy shall be declared ended.

ARTICLE XXXV

If the Court for any other reason declares itself to be without jurisdiction to hear and adjudge the controversy, the High Contracting Parties obligate themselves to submit it to arbitration, in accordance with the provisions of Chapter Five of this Treaty.

ARTICLE XXXVI

In the case of controversies submitted to the judicial procedure to which this Treaty refers, the decision shall devolve upon the full Court, or, if the parties so request, upon a special chamber in conformity with Article 26 of the Statute of the Court. The parties may agree, moreover, to have the controversy decided *ex aequo et bono*.

ARTICLE XXXVII

The procedure to be followed by the Court shall be that established in the Statute thereof.

CHAPTER FIVE

PROCEDURE OF ARBITRATION

ARTICLE XXXVIII

Notwithstanding the provisions of Chapter Four of this Treaty, the High Contracting Parties may, if they so agree, submit to arbitration differences of any kind, whether juridical or not, that have arisen or may arise in the future between them.

ARTICLE XXXIX

The Arbitral Tribunal to which a controversy is to be submitted shall, in the cases contemplated in Articles XXXV and XXXVIII of the present Treaty, be constituted in the following manner, unless there exists an agreement to the contrary.

ARTICLE XL

(1) Within a period of two months after notification of the decision of the Court in the case provided for in Article XXXV, each party shall name one arbiter of recognized competence in questions of international law and of the highest integrity, and shall transmit the designation to the Council of the Organization. At the same time, each party shall present to the Council a list of ten jurists chosen from among those on the general panel of members of the Permanent Court of Arbitration of The Hague who do not belong to its national group and who are willing to be members of the Arbitral Tribunal.

(2) The Council of the Organization shall, within the month following the presentation of the lists, proceed to establish the Arbitral Tribunal in the following manner:

    a) If the lists presented by the parties contain three names in common, such persons, together with the two directly named by the parties, shall constitute the Arbitral Tribunal;

b) In case these lists contain more than three names in common, the three arbiters needed to complete the Tribunal shall be selected by lot;

c) In the circumstances envisaged in the two preceding clauses, the five arbiters designated shall choose one of their number as presiding officer;

d) If the lists contain only two names in common, such candidates and the two arbiters directly selected by the parties shall by common agreement choose the fifth arbiter, who shall preside over the Tribunal. The choice shall devolve upon a jurist on the aforesaid general panel of the Permanent Court of Arbitration of The Hague who has not been included in the lists drawn up by the parties;

e) If the lists contain only one name in common, that person shall be a member of the Tribunal, and another name shall be chosen by lot from among the eighteen jurists remaining on the above-mentioned lists. The presiding officer shall be elected in accordance with the procedure established in the preceding clause;

f) If the lists contain no names in common, one arbiter shall be chosen by lot from each of the lists; and the fifth arbiter, who shall act as presiding officer, shall be chosen in the manner previously indicated;

g) If the four arbiters cannot agree upon a fifth arbiter within one month after the Council of the Organization has notified them of their appointment, each of them shall separately arrange the list of jurists in the order of their preference and, after comparison of the lists so formed, the person who first obtains a majority vote shall be declared elected.

Article XLI

The parties may by mutual agreement establish the Tribunal in the manner they deem most appropriate; they may even select a single arbiter, designating in such case a chief of state, an eminent jurist, or any court of justice in which the parties have mutual confidence.

Article XLII

When more than two states are involved in the same controversy, the states defending the same interests shall be considered as a single party. If they have opposing interests they shall have the right to increase the number of arbiters so that all parties may have equal representation. The presiding officer shall be selected by the method established in Article XL.

Article XLIII

The parties shall in each case draw up a special agreement clearly defining the specific matter that is the subject of the controversy, the seat of the Tribunal, the rules of procedure to be observed, the period within which the award is to be handed down, and such other conditions as they may agree upon among themselves.

If the special agreement cannot be drawn up within three months after the date of the installation of the Tribunal, it shall be drawn up by the International Court of Justice through summary procedure, and shall be binding upon the parties.

Article XLIV

The parties may be represented before the Arbitral Tribunal by such persons as they may designate.

ARTICLE XLV

If one of the parties fails to designate its arbiter and present its list of candidates within the period provided for in Article XL, the other party shall have the right to request the Council of the Organization to establish the Arbitral Tribunal. The Council shall immediately urge the delinquent party to fulfill its obligations within an additional period of fifteen days, after which time the Council itself shall establish the Tribunal in the following manner:

a) It shall select a name by lot from the list presented by the petitioning party.

b) It shall choose, by absolute majority vote, two jurists from the general panel of the Permanent Court of Arbitration of The Hague who do not belong to the national group of any of the parties.

c) The three persons so designated, together with the one directly chosen by the petitioning party, shall select the fifth arbiter, who shall act as presiding officer, in the manner provided for in Article XL.

d) Once the Tribunal is installed, the procedure established in Article XLIII shall be followed.

ARTICLE XLVI

The award shall be accompanied by a supporting opinion, shall be adopted by a majority vote, and shall be published after notification thereof has been given to the parties. The dissenting arbiter or arbiters shall have the right to state the grounds for their dissent.

The award, once it is duly handed down and made known to the parties, shall settle the controversy definitively, shall not be subject to appeal, and shall be carried out immediately.

ARTICLE XLVII

Any differences that arise in regard to the interpretation or execution of the award shall be submitted to the decision of the Arbitral Tribunal that rendered the award.

ARTICLE XLVIII

Within a year after notification thereof, the award shall be subject to review by the same Tribunal at the request of one of the parties, provided a previously existing fact is discovered unknown to the Tribunal and to the party requesting the review, and provided the Tribunal is of the opinion that such fact might have a decisive influence on the award.

ARTICLE XLIX

Every member of the Tribunal shall receive financial remuneration, the amount of which shall be fixed by agreement between the parties. If the parties do not agree on the amount, the Council of the Organization shall determine the remuneration. Each Government shall pay its own expenses and an equal share of the common expenses of the Tribunal, including the aforementioned remunerations.

CHAPTER SIX
FULFILLMENT OF DECISIONS
ARTICLE L

If one of the High Contracting Parties should fail to carry out the obligations imposed upon it by a decision of the International Court of Justice or by an arbitral award, the other party or parties concerned shall, before resorting to the Security Council of the United Nations, propose a Meeting of Consultation of Ministers of Foreign Affairs to agree upon appropriate measures to ensure the fulfillment of the judicial decision or arbitral award.

CHAPTER SEVEN

ADVISORY OPINIONS

ARTICLE LI

The parties concerned in the solution of a controversy may, by agreement, petition the General Assembly or the Security Council of the United Nations to request an advisory opinion of the International Court of Justice on any juridical question.

The petition shall be made through the Council of the Organization of American States.

CHAPTER EIGHT

FINAL PROVISIONS

ARTICLE LII

The present Treaty shall be ratified by the High Contracting Parties in accordance with their constitutional procedures. The original instrument shall be deposited in the Pan American Union, which shall transmit an authentic certified copy to each Government for the purpose of ratification. The instruments of ratification shall be deposited in the archives of the Pan American Union, which shall notify the signatory governments of the deposit. Such notification shall be considered as an exchange of ratifications.

ARTICLE LIII

This Treaty shall come into effect between the High Contracting Parties in the order in which they deposit their respective ratifications.

ARTICLE LIV

Any American State which is not a signatory to the present Treaty, or which has made reservations thereto, may adhere to it, or may withdraw its reservations in whole or in part, by transmitting an official instrument to the Pan American Union, which shall notify the other High Contracting Parties in the manner herein established.

ARTICLE LV

Should any of the High Contracting Parties make reservations concerning the present Treaty, such reservations shall, with respect to the state that makes them, apply to all signatory states on the basis of reciprocity.

ARTICLE LVI

The present Treaty shall remain in force indefinitely, but may be denounced upon one year's notice, at the end of which period it shall cease to be in force with respect to the state denouncing it, but shall continue in force for the remaining signatories. The denunciation shall be addressed to the Pan American Union, which shall transmit it to the other Contracting Parties.

The denunciation shall have no effect with respect to pending procedures initiated prior to the transmission of the particular notification.

ARTICLE LVII

The present Treaty shall be registered with the Secretariat of the United Nations through the Pan American Union.

ARTICLE LVIII

As this Treaty comes into effect through the successive ratifications of the High Contracting Parties, the following treaties, conventions and protocols shall cease to be in force with respect to such parties:

Treaty to Avoid or Prevent Conflicts between the American States, of May 3, 1923;

General Convention of Inter-American Conciliation, of January 5, 1929;

General Treaty of Inter-American Arbitration and Additional Protocol of Progressive Arbitration, of January 5, 1929;

Additional Protocol to the General Convention of Inter-American Conciliation, of December 26, 1933;

Anti-War Treaty of Non-Aggression and Conciliation, of October 10, 1933;

Convention to Coordinate, Extend and Assure the Fulfillment of the Existing Treaties between the American States, of December 23, 1936;

Inter-American Treaty on Good Offices and Mediation, of December 23, 1936;

Treaty on the Prevention of Controversies, of December 23, 1936.

ARTICLE LIX

The provisions of the foregoing Article shall not apply to procedures already initiated or agreed upon in accordance with any of the above-mentioned international instruments.

ARTICLE LX

The present Treaty shall be called the "PACT OF BOGOTÁ."

IN WITNESS WHEREOF, the undersigned Plenipotentiaries, having deposited their full powers, found to be in good and due form, sign the present Treaty, in the name of their respective Governments, on the dates appearing below their signatures.

Done at the City of Bogotá, in four texts, in the English, French, Portuguese and Spanish languages respectively, on the thirtieth day of April, nineteen hundred forty-eight.

RESERVATIONS

Argentina

"The Delegation of the Argentine Republic, on signing the American Treaty on Pacific Settlement (Pact of Bogotá), makes reservations in regard to the following articles, to which it does not adhere:

1) VII, concerning the protection of aliens;

2) Chapter Four (Articles XXXI to XXXVII), Judicial Procedure;

3) Chapter Five (Articles XXXVIII to XLIX), Procedure of Arbitration;

4) Chapter Six (Article L), Fulfillment of Decisions.

Arbitration and judicial procedure have, as institutions, the firm adherence of the Argentine Republic, but the Delegation cannot accept the form in which the procedures for their application have been regulated, since, in its opinion, they should have been established only for controversies arising in the future and not originating in or having any relation to causes, situations or facts existing before the signing of this instrument. The compulsory execution of arbitral or judicial decisions and the limitation which prevents the states from judging for themselves in regard to matters that pertain to their domestic jurisdiction in accordance with Article V are contrary to Argentine tradition. The protection of aliens, who in the Argentine Republic are protected by its Supreme Law to the same extent as the nationals, is also contrary to that tradition."

Bolivia

"The Delegation of Bolivia makes a reservation with regard to Article VI, inasmuch as it considers that pacific procedures may also be applied to controversies arising from matters settled by arrangement between the Parties, when the said arrangement affects the vital interests of a state."

Ecuador

"The Delegation of Ecuador, upon signing this Pact, makes an express reservation with regard to Article VI and also every provision that contradicts or is not in harmony with the principles proclaimed by or the stipulations contained in the Charter of the United Nations, the Charter of the Organization of American States, or the Constitution of the Republic of Ecuador."

United States of America

"1. The United States does not undertake as the complainant State to submit to the International Court of Justice any controversy which is not considered to be properly within the jurisdiction of the Court.

2. The submission on the part of the United States of any controversy to arbitration, as distinguished from judicial settlement, shall be dependent upon the conclusion of a special agreement between the parties to the case.

3. The acceptance by the United States of the jurisdiction of the International Court of Justice as compulsory *ipso facto* and without special agreement, as provided in this Treaty, is limited by any jurisdictional or other limitations contained in any Declaration deposited by the United States under Article 36, paragraph 4, of the Statute of the Court, and in force at the time of the submission of any case.

4. The Government of the United States cannot accept Article VII relating to diplomatic protection and the exhaustion of remedies. For its part, the Government of the United States maintains the rules of diplomatic protection, including the rule of exhaustion of local remedies by aliens, as provided by international law."

Paraguay

"The Delegation of Paraguay makes the following reservation:

Paraguay stipulates the prior agreement of the parties as a prerequisite to the arbitration procedure established in this Treaty for every question of a non-juridical nature affecting national sovereignty and not specifically agreed upon in treaties now in force."

Peru

"The Delegation of Peru makes the following reservations:

1. Reservation with regard to the second part of Article V, because it considers that domestic jurisdiction should be defined by the state itself.

2. Reservation with regard to Article XXXIII and the pertinent part of Article XXXIV, inasmuch as it considers that the exceptions of *res judicata,* resolved by settlement between the parties or governed by agreements and

treaties in force, determine, in virtue of their objective and peremptory nature, the exclusion of these cases from the application of every procedure.

3. Reservation with regard to Article XXXV, in the sense that, before arbitration is resorted to, there may be, at the request of one of the parties, a meeting of the Organ of Consultation, as established in the Charter of the Organization of American States.

4. Reservation with regard to Article LXV, because it believes that arbitration set up without the participation of one of the parties is in contradiction with its constitutional provisions."

Nicaragua

"The Nicaraguan Delegation, on giving its approval to the American Treaty on Pacific Settlement (Pact of Bogotá) wishes to record expressly that no provisions contained in the said Treaty may prejudice any position assumed by the Government of Nicaragua with respect to arbitral decisions the validity of which it has contested on the basis of the principles of international law, which clearly permit arbitral decisions to be attacked when they are adjudged to be null or invalidated. Consequently, the signature of the Nicaraguan Delegation to the Treaty in question cannot be alleged as an acceptance of any arbitral decisions that Nicaragua has contested and the validity of which is not certain.

Hence the Nicaraguan Delegation reiterates the statement made on the 28th of the current month on approving the text of the abovementioned Treaty in Committee III."

13. STATUTES OF THE INTER-AMERICAN PEACE COMMITTEE (1956)

I. COMPETENCE

ARTICLE 1

The Inter-American Peace Committee shall keep constant vigilance, within the scope of its authority, to ensure that states between which any dispute or controversy exists will solve it as quickly as possible, to which end it shall suggest measures and steps conducive to a settlement, and it shall at all times respect the methods or procedures agreed upon by the Parties.

ARTICLE 2

Any state directly concerned in a dispute or controversy with another American state may request the Committee to take action, but the Committee, once the provisions of Articles 15 and 16 of these Statutes have been complied with, shall take up the case only with the prior consent of the Parties and when no other procedure for its pacific settlement is in progress.

II. MEMBERSHIP

ARTICLE 3

The Committee is composed of five member states designated by the governments, through the Council of the Organization of American States, to serve for a five-year period.

ARTICLE 4

No member state may be re-elected to membership on the Committee at the conclusion of its term, nor shall it be permitted to serve again until at least one year has elapsed.

ARTICLE 5

One member state of the Committee shall be replaced each year. To this end, the governments shall each year designate, through the Council of the Organization of American States, the state that is to replace the outgoing member.

ARTICLE 6

If the term of a member of the Committee expires while the Committee is acting on a specific case, the term of that member shall be automatically extended, but only insofar as that particular case is concerned, and shall terminate upon the completion of the aforesaid case, without prejudice to the procedure set forth in the preceding article.

ARTICLE 7

The representatives of the member states of the Committee shall be designated by their respective governments and may be the same representatives that are accredited to the Council of the Organization of American States.

ARTICLE 8

The respective governments shall designate an alternate representative to replace the representative in the absence of the latter or when he is otherwise prevented from serving.

ARTICLE 9

The Committee shall be notified through the Secretary General of the Organization of American States, of the appointments mentioned in the two preceding articles.

ARTICLE 10

No state that is a member of the Committee may act in that capacity when it is an interested party in a dispute or controversy in which the Committee has been requested to take action.

ARTICLE 11

In cases of the kind mentioned in the preceding article, the Committee shall, without prejudice to its taking action with a legal quorum, request the Council of the Organization of American States to designate as soon as possible, as a substitute, another state whose representative shall act exclusively in connection with the aforesaid dispute or controversy.

III. CHAIRMANSHIP

ARTICLE 12

The chairmanship of the Committee shall rotate and a new Chairman shall be elected each year.

ARTICLE 13

In the absence of the Chairman, his functions shall be exercised temporarily by the representative with the longest period of service on the Committee.

IV. SEAT

ARTICLE 14

The Committee shall have its seat in the city of Washington, but may meet outside that city when it deems it necessary.

V. PROCEDURE

ARTICLE 15

When a state that is directly concerned in a dispute or controversy requests the Committee to take action, the Committee shall first consult the other Party or Parties thereto as to whether they consent to the Committee's taking action in the case.

ARTICLE 16

In the consultation referred to in the preceding article, the Committee shall offer its services, pursuant to its mandate and in accordance with the nature of its functions.

ARTICLE 17

If the replies received are in the affirmative, the Committee shall take up the case immediately. If the replies are in the negative, it shall refrain from doing so, confining itself to carrying out the provisions of Articles 18 and 22 of these Statutes.

ARTICLE 18

Both the communications mentioned in the three preceding articles and the replies received by the Committee shall be transmitted to the governments of the member states of the Organization of American States, through their respective representatives on the Council.

ARTICLE 19

When the Parties appear before the Committee, they shall be represented by delegates especially accredited for that purpose, who may be accompanied by advisers.

ARTICLE 20

For the Committee to hold a meeting, at least three of its members must be present.

ARTICLE 21

Likewise, decisions of the Committee shall be taken by a vote of at least three of its members.

ARTICLE 22

In each case the Committee shall duly inform the Council of the Organization of American States, the Meeting of Consultation of Ministers of Foreign Affairs, and the Inter-American Conference of its activities and the result of its efforts. In accordance with Article 54 of the Charter of the United Nations, the Committee shall also keep the Security Council of the United Nations informed of its activities.

VI. SECRETARIAT AND EXPENSES

ARTICLE 23

The General Secretariat of the Organization of American States shall provide the secretariat services and working facilities required for the functioning of the Committee.

ARTICLE 24

Any expenses incurred by the Committee as the result of its activities in a dispute or controversy shall be defrayed by the Parties thereto. The Pan American Union shall, whenever necessary, advance the funds required to meet such expenses.

ARTICLE 25

Any member state of the Organization of American States, or the Inter-American Peace Committee itself, may propose amendments to these Statutes for consideration by the Inter-American Conference.

TRANSITORY ARTICLE

To determine the initial membership of the Committee on the basis of these Statutes and to permit the change in membership provided for in Article 5, the governments shall designate, through the Council of the Organization of American States, five states to serve for terms of one, two, three, four, and five years, respectively. This designation shall be made within 90 days from the time these Statutes are approved by the Council. The term to be served by each state shall be decided by lot in the Council of the Organization of American States. The present members shall continue to serve until the new members of the Committee are designated.

14. RESOLUTION IV OF THE
FIFTH MEETING OF CONSULTATION (1959)

INTER-AMERICAN PEACE COMMITTEE

The Fifth Meeting of Consultation of Ministers of Foreign Affairs,

CONSIDERING:

The purposes for which this Meeting of Consultation has been convoked; and

That the Inter-American Peace Committee is a permanent entity and an appropriate one for assisting in the realization of the aforesaid purposes, in the manner established in this resolution,

RESOLVES:

1. To entrust to the Inter-American Peace Committee the study of the questions that were the subject of the convocation of this Meeting, without prejudice to the specific competency of other agencies, and to this end it shall examine:

   a. Methods and procedures to prevent any activities from abroad designed to overthrow established governments or provoke instances of intervention or aggression as contemplated in instruments such as the Convention on Duties and Rights of States in the Event of Civil Strife, without impairment to: (i) the rights and liberties of political exiles recognized in the Convention on Territorial Asylum; (ii) the American Declaration of the Rights and Duties of Man; and (iii) the national constitutions of the American states;

   b. The relationship between violations of human rights or the non-exercise of representative democracy, on the one hand, and the political tensions that affect the peace of the hemisphere, on the other; and

   c. The relationship between economic underdevelopment and political instability.

2. In the performance of its duties the Committee may, at the request of governments or on its own initiative, take action in regard to the subject matter referred to in paragraph 1, its action in either case being subject to the express consent of the states to investigations that are to be made in their respective territories.

3. The Committee shall immediately initiate broad studies on the questions to which paragraph 1 of this resolution refers, except in those situations governed by other international instruments, and it shall prepare a preliminary report so that the American governments may formulate their observations. This report shall be followed by a definitive report, which shall be presented at the Eleventh Inter-American Conference or, if so indicated, to the Meeting of Consultation of Ministers of Foreign Affairs, so that any pertinent decisions may be made.

4. The new powers that this resolution grants temporarily to the Inter-American Peace Committee shall be effective until the close of the Eleventh Inter-American Conference, which shall make the decision as to their definitive inclusion in the statutes of the said Committee.

15. CONVENTION ON DUTIES AND RIGHTS OF STATES IN THE EVENT OF CIVIL STRIFE

Signed at Havana, February 20, 1928, at the Sixth International Conference of American States

The Governments of the Republics represented at the Sixth International Conference of American States, held in the city of Habana, Republic of Cuba, in the year 1928, desirous of reaching an agreement as to the duties and rights of States in the event of civil strife, have appointed the following Plenipotentiaries:

(Here follow the names of the Plenipotentiaries.)

Who, after exchanging their respective full powers, which were found to be in good and due form, have agreed upon the following:

ARTICLE 1

The contracting States bind themselves to observe the following rules with regard to civil strife in another one of them:

First: To use all means at their disposal to prevent the inhabitants of their territory, nationals or aliens, from participating in, gathering elements, crossing the boundary or sailing from their territory for the purpose of starting or promoting civil strife.

Second: To disarm and intern every rebel force crossing their boundaries, the expenses of internment to be borne by the State where public order may have been disturbed. The arms found in the hands of the rebels may be seized and withdrawn by the Government of the country granting asylum, to be returned, once the struggle has ended, to the State in civil strife.

Third: To forbid the traffic in arms and war material, except when intended for the Government, while the belligerency of the rebels has not been recognized, in which latter case the rules of neutrality shall be applied.

Fourth: To prevent that within their jurisdiction there be equipped, armed or adapted for warlike purposes any vessel intended to operate in favor of the rebellion.

ARTICLE 2

The declaration of piracy against vessels which have risen in arms, emanating from a Government, is not binding upon the other States.

The state that may be injured by depredations originating from insurgent vessels is entitled to adopt the following punitive measures against them: Should the authors of the damages be warships, it may capture and return them to the Government of the State to which they belong, for their trial; should the damage originate with merchantmen, the injured State may capture and subject them to the appropriate penal laws.

The insurgent vessel, whether a warship or a merchantman, which flies the flag of a foreign country to shield its actions, may also be captured and tried by the State of said flag.

ARTICLE 3

The insurgent vessel, whether a warship or a merchantman, equipped by the rebels, which arrives at a foreign country or seeks refuge therein, shall be delivered by the Government of the latter to the constituted Government of the State in civil strife, and the members of the crew shall be considered as political refugees.

ARTICLE 4

The present Convention does not affect obligations previously undertaken by the contracting parties through international agreements.

ARTICLE 5

After being signed, the present Convention shall be submitted to the ratification of the signatory States. The Government of Cuba is charged with transmitting authentic certified copies to the Governments for the aforementioned purpose of ratification. The instrument of ratification shall be deposited in the archives of the Pan American Union in Washington, the Union to notify the signatory governments of said deposit. Such notification shall be considered as an exchange of ratifications. This Convention shall remain open to the adherence of non-signatory States.

IN WITNESS WHEREOF the aforenamed Plenipotentiaries sign the present Convention in Spanish, English, French and Portuguese, in the city of Habana, the 20th day of February, 1928.

RESERVATION MADE AT THE TIME
OF RATIFICATION

United States of America

Subject to the understanding that the provisions of Article 3 of the convention shall not apply where a state of belligerency has been recognized.

PROTOCOL TO THE CONVENTION ON DUTIES AND RIGHTS OF STATES IN THE EVENT OF CIVIL STRIFE

The High Contracting Parties, desirous of clarifying, supplementing, and strengthening the principles and rules stipulated in the Convention on Duties and Rights of States in the Event of Civil Strife, signed at Havana on February 20, 1928,

Have resolved, in order to carry out those purposes, to conclude the following Protocol:

ARTICLE 1

Each Contracting State shall, in areas subject to its jurisdiction:

a) Keep under surveillance the traffic in arms and war material that it has reason to believe is intended for starting, promoting, or supporting civil strife in another American State;

b) Suspend the exportation or importation of any shipment of arms and war material during the period of its investigation of the circumstances relating to the shipment, when it has reason to believe that such arms and war material may be intended for starting, promoting, or supporting civil strife in another American State; and

c) Prohibit the exportation or importation of any shipment of arms and war material intended for starting, promoting, or supporting civil strife in another American State.

ARTICLE 2

The provisions of Article 1 shall cease to be applicable for a Contracting State only when it has recognized the belligerency of the rebels, in which event the rules of neutrality shall be applied.

ARTICLE 3

The term "traffic in arms and war material", which appears in the third paragraph of Article 1 of the Convention on Duties and Rights of States in the Event of Civil Strife as well as in this Protocol, includes land vehicles, vessels, and aircraft of all types, whether civil or military.

ARTICLE 4

The provisions of the Convention on Duties and Rights of States in the Event of Civil Strife with respect to "vessels" are equally applicable to aircraft of all types, whether civil or military.

ARTICLE 5

Each Contracting State shall, in areas subject to its jurisdiction and within the powers granted by its Constitution, use all appropriate means to prevent any person, national or alien, from deliberately participating in the preparation, organization, or carrying out of a military enterprise that has as its purpose the starting, promoting or supporting of civil strife in another Contracting State, whether or not the government of the latter has been recognized.

For the purposes of this article, participation in the preparation, organization, or carrying out of a military enterprise includes, among other acts:

a) The contribution, supply or provision of arms and war material;

b) The equipment, training, collection, or transportation of members of a military expedition; or

c) The provision or receipt of money, by any method, intended for the military enterprise.

ARTICLE 6

The present Protocol does not affect obligations previously undertaken by the Contracting States through international agreements.

ARTICLE 7

This Protocol shall remain open in the Pan American Union for signature by the American States, and shall be ratified in conformity with their respective constitutional procedures.

ARTICLE 8

This Protocol may be ratified only by the States that have ratified or ratify the Convention on the Duties and Rights of States in the Event of Civil Strife. This Protocol shall enter into force between the States that ratify it, in the order in which they deposit their respective instruments of ratification.

ARTICLE 9

The original instrument of this Protocol, the English, French, Portuguese, and Spanish texts of which are equally authentic, shall be deposited with the Pan American Union, which shall transmit certified copies thereof to the Governments for purposes of ratification. The instruments of ratification shall be deposited with the Pan American Union, which shall notify the signatory States of such deposit. A certified copy of this Protocol shall be transmitted by the Pan American Union to the General Secretariat of the United Nations for registration.

ARTICLE 10

This Protocol shall remain in force indefinitely between the Contracting States. It may be denounced by any of them upon one year's notice. Such denunciation shall be addressed to the Pan American Union, which shall notify the other signatory States thereof.

ARTICLE 11

Each Contracting State shall refrain from denouncing the Convention on Duties and Rights of States in the Event of Civil Strife while this Protocol remains in force for that State.

IN WITNESS WHEREOF, the undersigned Plenipotentiaries, whose full powers have been presented and found to be in good and due form, sign this Protocol on the dates that appear opposite their respective signatures.

16. AGREEMENT ESTABLISHING THE INTER-AMERICAN DEVELOPMENT BANK (1959)

The countries on whose behalf this Agreement is signed agree to create the Inter-American Development Bank, which shall operate in accordance with the following provisions:

ARTICLE I

PURPOSE AND FUNCTIONS

Section 1. *Purpose*

The purpose of the Bank shall be to contribute to the acceleration of the process of economic development of the member countries, individually and collectively.

Section 2. *Functions*

(a) To implement its purpose, the Bank shall have the following functions:

    (i) to promote the investment of public and private capital for development purposes;

    (ii) to utilize its own capital, funds raised by it in financial markets, and other available resources, for financing the development of the member countries, giving priority to those loans and guarantees that will contribute most effectively to their economic growth;

    (iii) to encourage private investment in projects, enterprises, and activities contributing to economic development and to supplement private investment when private capital is not available on reasonable terms and conditions;

    (iv) to cooperate with the member countries to orient their development policies toward a better utilization of their resources, in a manner consistent with the objectives of making their economies more complementary and of fostering the orderly growth of their foreign trade; and

    (v) to provide technical assistance for the preparation, financing, and implementation of development plans and projects, including the study of priorities and the formulation of specific project proposals.

(b) In carrying out its functions, the Bank shall cooperate as far as possible with national and international institutions and with private sources supplying investment capital.

ARTICLE II

MEMBERSHIP IN AND CAPITAL OF THE BANK

Section 1. *Membership*

(a) The original members of the Bank shall be those members of the Organization of American States which, by the date specified in Article XV, Section 1 (a), shall accept membership in the Bank.

(b) Membership shall be open to other members of the Organization of American States at such times and in accordance with such terms as the Bank may determine.

Section 2. *Authorized Capital*

(a) The authorized capital stock of the Bank, together with the initial resources of the Fund for Special Operations established in Article IV (hereinafter called the Fund), shall total one billion dollars ($1,000,000,000) in terms of United States dollars of the weight and fineness in effect on January 1, 1959. Of this sum, eight hundred fifty million dollars ($850,000,000)[1] shall constitute the authorized capital stock of the Bank and shall be divided into 85,000[2] shares having a par value of $10,000 each, which shall be available for subscription by members in accordance with Section 3 of this article.

(b) The authorized capital stock shall be divided into paid-in shares and callable shares. The equivalent of four hundred million dollars ($400,000,000)[3] shall be paid in, and four hundred fifty million dollars ($450,000,000)[4] shall be callable for the purposes specified in Section 4 (a) (ii) of this article.

(c) The capital stock indicated in (a) of this section shall be increased by five hundred million dollars ($500,000,000) in terms of United States dollars of the weight and fineness existing on January 1, 1959, provided that:

(i) the date for payment of all subscriptions established in accordance with Section 4 of this article shall have passed; and

(ii) a regular or special meeting of the Board of Governors, held as soon as possible after the date referred to in subparagraph (i) of this paragraph, shall have approved the above-mentioned increase of five hundred million dollars ($500,000,000) by a three-fourths majority of the total voting power of the member countries.

(d) The increase in capital stock provided for in the preceding paragraph shall be in the form of callable capital.

(e) Notwithstanding the provisions of paragraphs (c) and (d) of this section, the authorized capital stock may be increased when the Board of Governors deems it advisable and in a manner agreed upon by a two-thirds majority of the total number of governors representing not less than three-fourths of the total voting power of the member countries.

Section 3. *Subscription of Shares*

(a) Each member shall subscribe to shares of the capital stock of the Bank. The number of shares to be subscribed by the original members shall be those set forth in Annex A of this Agreement, which specifies the obligation of each member as to both paid-in and callable capital. The number of shares to be subscribed by other members shall be determined by the Bank.

(b) In case of an increase in capital pursuant to Section 2, paragraph (c) or (e) of this article, each member shall have a right to subscribe, under such

---

[1] On January 28, 1964, the Board of Governors increased this amount to two billion one hundred and fifty million dollars ($2,150,000,000).

[2] The number of shares was increased by the Board of Governors on January 28, 1964, to 215,000 of which 30,000 shares are reserved for subscription by possible new members.

[3] This amount was increased by the Board of Governors on January 28, 1964, to four hundred and seventy-five million dollars ($475,000,000) of which seventy-five million dollars ($75,000,000) are reserved for possible new members.

[4] This amount was increased by the Board of Governors on January 28, 1964, to one billion six hundred and seventy-five million dollars ($1,675,000,000) of which two hundred and twenty-five million dollars ($225,000,000) are reserved for possible new members.

conditions as the Bank shall decide, to a proportion of the increase of stock equivalent to the proportion which its stock theretofore subscribed bears to the total capital stock of the Bank. No member, however, shall be obligated to subscribe to any part of such increased capital.

(c) Shares of stock initially subscribed by original members shall be issued at par. Other shares shall be issued at par unless the Bank decides in special circumstances to issue them on other terms.

(d) The liability of the member countries on shares shall be limited to the unpaid portion of their issue price.

(e) Shares of stock shall not be pledged or encumbered in any manner, and they shall be transferable only to the Bank.

Section 4. *Payment of Subscriptions*

(a) Payment of the subscriptions to the capital stock of the Bank as set forth in Annex A shall be made as follows:

(i) Payment of the amount subscribed by each country to the paid-in capital stock of the Bank shall be made in three installments, the first of which shall be 20 per cent, and the second and third each 40 per cent, of such amount. The first installment shall be paid by each country at any time on or after the date on which this Agreement is signed, and the instrument of acceptance or ratification deposited, on its behalf in accordance with Article XV, Section 1, but not later than September 30, 1960. The remaining two installments shall be paid on such dates as are determined by the Bank, but not sooner than September 30, 1961, and September 30, 1962, respectively.

Of each installment, 50 per cent shall be paid in gold and/or dollars and 50 per cent in the currency of the member.

(ii) The callable portion of the subscription for capital shares of the Bank shall be subject to call only when required to meet the obligations of the Bank created under Article III, Section 4 (ii) and (iii) on borrowings of funds for inclusion in the Bank's ordinary capital resources or guarantees chargeable to such resources. In the event of such a call, payment may be made at the option of the member either in gold, in United States dollars, or in the currency required to discharge the obligations of the Bank for the purpose for which the call is made.

Calls on unpaid subscriptions shall be uniform in percentage on all shares.

(b) Each payment of a member in its own currency under paragraph (a) (i) of this section shall be in such amount as, in the opinion of the Bank, is equivalent to the full value in terms of United States dollars of the weight and fineness in effect on January 1, 1959, of the portion of the subscription being paid. The initial payment shall be in such amount as the member considers appropriate hereunder but shall be subject to such adjustment, to be effected within 60 days of the date on which the payment was due, as the Bank shall determine to be necessary to constitute the full dollar value equivalent as provided in this paragraph.

(c) Unless otherwise determined by the Board of Governors by a three-fourths majority of the total voting power of the member countries, the liability of members for payment of the second and third installments of the paid-in portion of their subscriptions to the capital stock shall be conditional upon payment of not less than 90 per cent of the total obligations of the members due for:

> (i) the first and second installments, respectively, of the paid-in portion of the subscriptions; and
>
> (ii) the initial payment and all prior calls on the subscription quotas to the Fund.

Section 5. *Ordinary Capital Resources*

As used in this Agreement, the term "ordinary capital resources" of the Bank shall be deemed to include the following:

> (i) authorized capital, including both paid-in and callable shares, subscribed pursuant to Section 2 and 3 of this article;
>
> (ii) all funds raised by borrowings under the authority of Article VII, Section 1 (i) to which the commitment set forth in Section 4 (a) (ii) of this article is applicable;
>
> (iii) all funds received in repayment of loans made with the resources indicated in (i) and (ii) of this section; and
>
> (iv) all income derived from loans made from the afore-mentioned funds or from guarantees to which the commitment set forth in Section 4 (a) (ii) of this article is applicable.

ARTICLE III
OPERATIONS

Section 1. *Use of Resources*

The resources and facilities of the Bank shall be used exclusively to implement the purpose and functions enumerated in Article I of this Agreement.

Section 2. *Ordinary and Special Operations*

(a) The operations of the Bank shall be divided into ordinary operations and special operations.

(b) The ordinary operations shall be those financed from the Bank's ordinary capital resources, as defined in Article II, Section 5, and shall relate exclusively to loans made, participated in, or guaranteed by the Bank which are repayable only in the respective currency or currencies in which the loans were made. Such operations shall be subject to the terms and conditions that the Bank deems advisable, consistent with the provisions of this Agreement.

(c) The special operations shall be those financed from the resources of the Fund in accordance with the provisions of Article IV.

Section 3. *Basic Principle of Separation*

(a) The ordinary capital resources of the Bank as defined in Article II, Section 5, shall at all times and in all respects be held, used, obligated, invested, or otherwise disposed of entirely separate from the resources of the Fund, as defined in Article IV, Section 3 (h).

The financial statements of the Bank shall show the ordinary operations of the Bank and the operations of the Fund separately, and the Bank shall establish such other administrative rules as may be necessary to ensure the effective separation of the two types of operations.

The ordinary capital resources of the Bank shall under no circumstances be charged with, or used to discharge, losses or liabilities arising out of operations for which the resources of the Fund were originally used or committed.

(b) Expenses pertaining directly to ordinary operations shall be charged to the ordinary capital resources of the Bank. Expenses pertaining directly to special operations shall be charged to the resources of the Fund. Other expenses shall be charged as the Bank determines.

Section 4. *Methods of Making or Guaranteeing Loans*

Subject to the conditions stipulated in this article, the Bank may make or guarantee loans to any member, or any agency or political subdivision thereof, and to any enterprise in the territory of a member, in any of the following ways:

(i) by making or participating in direct loans with funds corresponding to the unimpaired paid-in capital and, except as provided in Section 13 of this article, to its reserves and undistributed surplus; or with the unimpaired resources of the Fund;

(ii) by making or participating in direct loans with funds raised by the Bank in capital markets, or borrowed or acquired in any other manner for inclusion in the ordinary capital resources of the Bank or the resources of the Fund, and

(iii) by guaranteeing in whole or in part loans made, except in special cases, by private investors.

Section 5. *Limitations on Ordinary Operations*

(a) The total amount outstanding of loans and guarantees made by the Bank in its ordinary operations shall not at any time exceed the total amount of the unimpaired subscribed capital of the Bank, plus the unimpaired reserves and surplus included in the ordinary capital resources of the Bank, as defined in Article II, Section 5, exclusive of income assigned to the special reserve established pursuant to Section 13 of this article and other income assigned by decision of the Board of Governors to reserves not available for loans or guarantees.

(b) In the case of loans made out of funds borrowed by the Bank to which the obligations provided for in Article II, Section 4 (a) (ii) are applicable, the total amount of principal outstanding and payable to the Bank in a specific currency shall at no time exceed the total amount of principal of the outstanding borrowings by the Bank that are payable in the same currency.

Section 6. *Direct Loan Financing*

In making direct loans or participating in them, the Bank may provide financing in any of the following ways:

(a) By furnishing the borrower currencies of members, other than the currency of the member in whose territory the project is to be carried out, that are necessary to meet the foreign exchange costs of the project.

(b) By providing financing to meet expenses related to the purposes of the loan in the territories of the member in which the project is to be carried out. Only in special cases, particularly when the project indirectly gives rise to an increase in the demand for foreign exchange in that country, shall the financing granted by the Bank to meet local expenses be provided in gold or in currencies other than that of such member; in such cases, the amount of the financing granted by the Bank for this purpose shall not exceed a reasonable portion of the local expenses incurred by the borrower.

Section 7. *Rules and Conditions for Making or Guaranteeing Loans*

(a) The Bank may make or guarantee loans subject to the following rules and conditions:

(i) the applicant for the loan shall have submitted a detailed proposal and the staff of the Bank shall have presented a written report recommending the proposal after a study of its merits. In special circumstances, the Board of Executive Directors, by a majority of the total voting power of the member countries, may require that a proposal be submitted to the Board for decision in the absence of such a report;

(ii) in considering a request for a loan or a guarantee, the Bank shall take into account the ability of the borrower to obtain the loan from private sources of financing on terms which, in the opinion of the Bank, are reasonable for the borrower, taking into account all pertinent factors;

(iii) in making or guaranteeing a loan, the Bank shall pay due regard to prospects that the borrower and its guarantor, if any, will be in a position to meet their obligations under the loan contract;

(iv) in the opinion of the Bank, the rate of interest, other charges and the schedule for repayment of principal are appropriate for the project in question;

(v) in guaranteeing a loan made by other investors, the Bank shall receive suitable compensation for its risk, and

(vi) loans made or guaranteed by the Bank shall be principally for financing specific projects, including those forming part of a national or regional development program. However, the Bank may make or guarantee over-all loans to development institutions or similar agencies of the members in order that the latter may facilitate the financing of specific development projects whose individual financing requirements are not, in the opinion of the Bank, large enough to warrant the direct supervision of the Bank.

(b) The Bank shall not finance any undertaking in the territory of a member if that member objects to such financing.

Section 8. *Optional Conditions for Making or Guaranteeing Loans*

(a) In the case of loans or guarantees of loans to nongovernmental entities, the Bank may, when it deems it advisable, require that the member in whose territory the project is to be carried out, or a public institution or a similar agency of the member acceptable to the Bank, guarantee the repayment of the principal and the payment of interest and other charges on the loan.

(b) The Bank may attach such other conditions to the making of loans or guarantees as it deems appropriate, taking into account both the interests of the members directly involved in the particular loan or guarantee proposal and the interests of the members as a whole.

Section 9. *Use of Loans Made or Guaranteed by the Bank*

(a) Except as provided in Article V, Section 1, the Bank shall impose no condition that the proceeds of a loan shall be spent in the territory of any particular country nor that such proceeds shall not be spent in the territories of any particular member or members.

(b) The Bank shall take the necessary measures to ensure that the proceeds of any loan made, guaranteed, or participated in by the Bank are used only for the purposes for which the loan was granted, with due attention to considerations of economy and efficiency.

Section 10. *Payment Provisions for Direct Loans*

Direct loan contracts made by the Bank in conformity with Section 4 (i) or (ii) of this article shall establish:

(a) All the terms and conditions of each loan, including among others, provision for payment of principal, interest and other charges, maturities, and dates of payment; and

(b) The currency or currencies in which payments shall be made to the Bank.

Section 11. *Guarantees*

(a) In guaranteeing a loan the Bank shall charge a guarantee fee, at a rate determined by the Bank, payable periodically on the amount of the loan outstanding.

(b) Guarantee contracts concluded by the Bank shall provide that the Bank may terminate its liability with respect to interest if, upon default by the borrower and by the guarantor, if any, the Bank offers to purchase, at par and interest accrued to a date designated in the offer, the bonds or other obligations guaranteed.

(c) In issuing guarantees, the Bank shall have power to determine any other terms and conditions.

Section 12. *Special Commission*

On all loans, participations, or guarantees made out of or by commitment of the ordinary capital resources of the Bank, the latter shall charge a special commission. The special commission, payable periodically, shall be computed on the amount outstanding on each loan, participation, or guarantee and shall be at the rate of one per cent per annum, unless the Bank, by a two-thirds majority of the total voting power of the member countries, decides to reduce the rate of commission.

Section 13. *Special Reserve*

The amount of commissions received by the Bank under Section 12 of this article shall be set aside as a special reserve, which shall be kept for meeting liabilities of the Bank in accordance with Article VII, Section 3 (b) (i). The special reserve shall be held in such liquid form, permitted under this Agreement, as the Board of Executive Directors may decide.

ARTICLE IV

FUND FOR SPECIAL OPERATIONS

Section 1. *Establishment, Purpose, and Functions*

A Fund for Special Operations is established for the making of loans on terms and conditions appropriate for dealing with special circumstances arising in specific countries or with respect to specific projects.

The Fund, whose administration shall be entrusted to the Bank, shall have the purpose and functions set forth in Article I of this Agreement.

Section 2. *Applicable Provisions*

The Fund shall be governed by the provisions of the present article and all other provisions of this Agreement, excepting those inconsistent with the provisions of the present article and those expressly applying only to the ordinary operations of the Bank.

Section 3. *Resources*

(a) The original members of the Bank shall contribute to the resources of the Fund in accordance with the provisions of this section.

(b) Members of the Organization of American States that join the Bank after the date specified in Article XV, Section 1 (a) shall contribute to the Fund with such quotas, and under such terms, as may be determined by the Bank.

(c) The Fund shall be established with initial resources in the amount of one hundred fifty million dollars (150,000,000)[1] in terms of United States dollars of the weight and fineness in effect on January 1, 1959, which shall be contributed by the original members of the Bank in accordance with the quotas specified in Annex B.

(d) Payment of the quotas shall be made as follows:

(i) Fifty per cent of its quota shall be paid by each member at any time on or after the date on which this Agreement is signed, and the instrument of acceptance or ratification deposited, on its behalf in accordance with Article XV, Section 1, but not later than September 30, 1960.

(ii) The remaining 50 per cent shall be paid at any time subsequent to one year after the Bank has begun operations, in such amounts and at such times as are determined by the Bank; provided, however, that the total amount of all quotas shall be made due and payable not later than the date fixed for payment of the third installment of the subscriptions to the paid-in capital stock of the Bank.

(iii) The payments required under this section shall be distributed among the members in proportion to their quotas and shall be made one half in gold and/or United States dollars, and one half in the currency of the contributing member.

(e) Each payment of a member in its own currency under the preceding paragraph shall be in such amount as, in the opinion of the Bank, is equivalent to the full value, in terms of United States dollars of the weight and fineness in effect on January 1, 1959, of the portion of the quota being paid. The initial payment shall be in such amount as the member considers appropriate hereunder but shall be subject to such adjustment, to be effected within 60 days of the date on which payment was due, as the Bank shall determine to be

---

[1] On January 28, 1964, the Board of Governors increased the authorized resources of the Fund for Special Operations to two-hundred and twenty-three million, one hundred and fifty-eight thousand dollars ($223,158,000), and on March 31, 1965, the Board increased the resources of the Fund further to one billion one hundred and twenty-three million, one hundred and fifty-eight thousand dollars ($1,123,158,000).

necessary to constitute the full dollar value equivalent as provided in this paragraph.

(f) Unless otherwise determined by the Board of Governors by a three-fourths majority of the total voting power of the member countries, the liability of members for payment of any call on the unpaid portion of their subscription quotas to the Fund shall be conditional upon payment of not less than 90 per cent of the total obligations of the members for:

    (i) the initial payment and all prior calls on such quota subscriptions to the Fund; and

    (ii) any installments due on the paid-in portion of the subscriptions to the capital stock of the Bank.

(g) The resources of the Fund shall be increased through additional contributions by the members when the Board of Governors considers it advisable by a three-fourths majority of the total voting power of the member countries. The provisions of Article II, Section 3 (b), shall apply to such increases, in terms of the proportion between the quota in effect for each member and the total amount of the resources of the Fund contributed by members.

(h) As used in this Agreement, the terms "resources of the Fund" shall be deemed to include the following:

    (i) contributions by members pursuant to paragraphs (c) and (g) of this section;

    (ii) all funds raised by borrowing to which the commitment stipulated in Article II, Section 4 (a) (ii) is not applicable, i.e., those that are specifically chargeable to the resources of the Fund;

    (iii) all funds received in repayment of loans made from the resources mentioned above;

    (iv) all income derived from operations using or commiting any of the resources mentioned above; and

    (v) any other resources at the disposal of the Fund.

Section 4. *Operations*

(a) The operations of the Fund shall be those financed from its own resources, as defined in Section 3 (h) of the present article.

(b) Loans made with resources of the Fund may be partially or wholly repayable in the currency of the member in whose territory the project being financed will be carried out. The part of the loan not repayable in the currency of the member shall be paid in the currency or currencies in which the loan was made.

Section 5. *Limitation on Liability*

In the operations of the Fund, the financial liability of the Bank shall be limited to the resources and reserves of the Fund, and the liability of members shall be limited to the unpaid portion of their respective quotas that has become due and payable.

Section 6. *Limitation on Disposition of Quotas*

The rights of members of the Bank resulting from their contributions to the Fund may not be transferred or encumbered, and members shall have no right of reimbursement of such contributions except in cases of loss of the status of membership or of termination of the operations of the Fund.

Section 7. *Discharge of Fund Liabilities on Borrowings*

Payments in satisfaction of any liability on borrowings of funds for inclusion in the resources of the Fund shall be charged:

(i) first, against any reserve established for this purpose; and

(ii) then, against any other funds available in the resources of the Fund.

Section 8. *Administration*

(a) Subject to the provisions of this Agreement, the authorities of the Bank shall have full powers to administer the Fund.

(b) There shall be a Vice President of the Bank in charge of the Fund. The Vice President shall participate in the meetings of the Board of Executive Directors of the Bank, without vote, whenever matters relating to the Fund are discussed.

(c) In the operations of the Fund the Bank shall utilize to the fullest extent possible the same personnel, experts, installations, offices, equipment, and services as it uses for its ordinary operations.

(d) The Bank shall publish a separate annual report showing the results of the Fund's financial operations, including profits or losses. At the annual meeting of the Board of Governors there shall be at least one session devoted to consideration of this report. In addition, the Bank shall transmit to the members a quarterly summary of the Fund's operations.

Section 9. *Voting*

(a) In making decisions concerning operations of the Fund, each member country of the Bank shall have the voting power in the Board of Governors accorded to it pursuant to Article VIII, Section 4 (a) and (b), and each Director shall have the voting power in the Board of Executive Directors accorded to him pursuant to Article VIII, Section 4 (a) and (c).

(b) All decisions of the Bank concerning the operations of the Fund shall be adopted by a two-thirds majority of the total voting power of the member countries, unless otherwise provided in this article.

Section 10. *Distribution of Net Profits*

The Board of Governors of the Bank shall determine what portion of the net profits of the Fund shall be distributed among the members after making provision for reserves. Such net profits shall be shared in proportion to the quotas of the members.

Section 11. *Withdrawal of Contributions*

(a) No country may withdraw its contribution and terminate its relations with the Fund while it is still a member of the Bank.

(b) The provisions of Article IX, Section 3, with respect to the settlement of accounts with countries that terminate their membership in the Bank also shall apply to the Fund.

Section 12. *Suspension and Termination*

The provisions of Article X also shall apply to the Fund with substitution of terms relating to the Fund and its resources and respective creditors for those relating to the Bank and its ordinary capital resources and respective creditors.

ARTICLE V
CURRENCIES

Section 1. *Use of Currencies*

(a) The currency of any member held by the Bank, either in its ordinary capital resources or in the resources of the Fund, however acquired, may be used by the Bank and by any recipient from the Bank, without restriction by the member, to make payments for goods and services produced in the territory of such member.

(b) Members may not maintain or impose restrictions of any kind upon the use by the Bank or by any recipient from the Bank, for payments in any country, of the following:

    (i) gold and dollars received by the Bank in payment of the 50 per cent portion of each member's subscription to shares of the Bank's capital and of the 50 per cent portion of each member's quota for contribution to the Fund, pursuant to the provisions of Article II and Article IV, respectively;

    (ii) currencies of members purchased with the gold and dollar funds referred to in (i) of this paragraph;

    (iii) currencies obtained by borrowings, pursuant to the provisions of Article VII, Section 1 (i), for inclusion in the ordinary capital resources of the Bank;

    (iv) gold and dollars received by the Bank in payment on account of principal, interest, and other charges, of loans made from the gold and dollar funds referred to in (i) of this paragraph; currencies received in payment of principal, interest, and other charges, of loans made from currencies referred to in (ii) and (iii) of this paragraph; and currencies received in payment of commissions and fees on all guarantees made by the Bank; and

    (v) currencies, other than the member's own currency, received from the Bank pursuant to Article VII, Section 4 (c) and Article IV, Section 10, in distribution of net profits.

(c) A member's currency held by the Bank, either in its ordinary capital resources or in the resources of the Fund, not covered by paragraph (b) of this section, also may be used by the Bank or any recipient from the Bank for payments in any country without restriction of any kind, unless the member notifies the Bank of its desire that such currency or a portion thereof be restricted to the uses specified in paragraph (a) of this section.

(d) Members may not place any restrictions on the holding and use by the Bank, for making amortization payments or anticipating payment of, or repurchasing part or all of, the Bank's own obligations, of currencies received by the Bank in repayment of direct loans made from borrowed funds included in the ordinary capital resources of the Bank.

(e) Gold or currency held by the Bank in its ordinary capital resources or in the resources of the Fund shall not be used by the Bank to purchase other currencies unless authorized by a two-thirds majority of the total voting power of the member countries.

Section 2. *Valuation of Currencies*

Whenever it shall become necessary under this Agreement to value any currency in terms of another currency, or in terms of gold, such valuation shall be determined by the Bank after consultation with the International Monetary Fund.

Section 3. *Maintenance of Value of the Currency Holdings of the Bank*

(a) Whenever the par value in the International Monetary Fund of a member's currency is reduced or the foreign exchange value of a member's currency has, in the opinion of the Bank, depreciated to a significant extent, the member shall pay to the Bank within a reasonable time an additional amount of its own currency sufficient to maintain the value of all the currency of the member held by the Bank in its ordinary capital resources, or in the resources of the Fund, excepting currency derived from borrowings by the Bank. The standard of value for this purpose shall be the United States dollar of the weight and fineness in effect on January 1, 1959.

(b) Whenever the par value in the International Monetary Fund of a member's currency is increased or the foreign exchange of such member's currency has, in the opinion of the Bank, appreciated to a significant extent, the Bank shall return to such member within a reasonable time an amount of that member's currency equal to the increase in the value of the amount of such currency which is held by the Bank in its ordinary capital resources or in the resources of the Fund, excepting currency derived from borrowings by the Bank. The standard of value for this purpose shall be the same as that established in the preceding paragraph.

(c) The provisions of this section may be waived by the Bank when a uniform proportionate change in the par value of the currencies of all the Bank's members is made by the International Monetary Fund.

Section 4. *Methods of Conserving Currencies*

The Bank shall accept from any member promissory notes or similar securities issued by the government of the member, or by the depository designated by each member, in lieu of any part of the currency of the member representing the 50 per cent portion of its subscription to the Bank's authorized capital and the 50 per cent portion of its subscription to the resources of the Fund, which, pursuant to the provisions of Article II and Article IV, respectively, are payable by each member in its national currency, provided such currency is not required by the Bank for the conduct of its operations. Such promissory notes or securities shall be non-negotiable, non-interest-bearing, and payable to the Bank at their par value on demand.

ARTICLE VI

TECHNICAL ASSISTANCE

Section 1. *Provision of Technical Advice and Assistance*

The Bank may, at the request of any member or members, or of private firms that may obtain loans from it, provide technical advice and assistance in its field of activity, particularly on:

(i) the preparation, financing, and execution of development plans and projects, including the consideration of priorities, and the formulation of loan proposals on specific national or regional development projects; and

(ii) the development and advanced training, through seminars and other forms of instruction, of personnel specializing in the formulation and implementation of development plans and projects.

Section 2. *Cooperative Agreements on Technical Assistance*

In order to accomplish the purposes of this article, the Bank may enter into agreements on technical assistance with other national or international institutions, either public or private.

Section 3. *Expenses*

(a) The Bank may arrange with member countries or firms receiving technical assistance, for reimbursement of the expenses of furnishing such assistance on terms which the Bank deems appropriate.

(b) The expenses of providing technical assistance not paid by the recipients shall be met from the net income of the Bank or of the Fund. However, during the first three years of the Bank's operations, up to three per cent, in total, of the initial resources of the Fund may be used to meet such expenses.

ARTICLE VII

MISCELLANEOUS POWERS AND DISTRIBUTION OF PROFITS

Section 1. *Miscellaneous Powers of the Bank*

In addition to the powers specified elsewhere in this Agreement, the Bank shall have the power to:

(i) borrow funds and in that connection to furnish such collateral or other security therefor as the Bank shall determine, provided that, before making a sale of its obligations in the markets of a country, the Bank shall have obtained the approval of that country and of the member in whose currency the obligations are denominated. In addition, in the case of borrowings of funds to be included in the Bank's ordinary capital resources, the Bank shall obtain agreement of such countries that the proceeds may be exchanged for the currency of any other country without restriction;

(ii) buy and sell securities it has issued or guaranteed or in which it has invested, provided that the Bank shall obtain the approval of the country in whose territories the securities are to be bought or sold;

(iii) with the approval of a two-thirds majority of the total voting power of the member countries, invest funds not needed in its operations in such obligations as it may determine;

(iv) guarantee securities in its portfolio for the purpose of facilitating their sale; and

(v) exercise such other powers as shall be necessary or desirable in furtherance of its purpose and functions, consistent with the provisions of this Agreement.

Section 2. *Warning to be Placed on Securities*

Every security issued or guaranteed by the Bank shall bear on its face a conspicuous statement to the effect that it is not an obligation of any government, unless it is in fact the obligation of a particular government, in which case it shall so state.

Section 3. *Methods of Meeting Liabilities of the Bank in Case of Defaults*

(a) The Bank, in the event of actual or threatened default on loans made or guaranteed by the Bank using its ordinary capital resources, shall take such action as it deems appropriate with respect to modifying the terms of the loan, other than the currency of repayment.

(b) The payments in discharge of the Bank's liabilities on borrowings or guarantees under Article III, Section 4 (ii) and (iii) chargeable against the ordinary capital resources of the Bank shall be charged:

(i) first, against the special reserve provided for in Article III, Section 13; and

(ii) then, to the extent necessary and at the discretion of the Bank, against the other reserves, surplus, and funds corresponding to the capital paid in for shares.

(c) Whenever necessary to meet contractual payments of interest, other charges, or amortization on the Bank's borrowings, or to meet the Bank's liabilities with respect to similar payments on loans guaranteed by it chargeable to its ordinary capital resources, the Bank may call upon the members to pay an appropriate amount of their callable capital subscriptions, in accordance with Article II, Section 4 (a) (ii). Moreover, if the Bank believes that a default may be of long duration, it may call an additional part of such subscriptions not to exceed in any one year one per cent of the total subscriptions of the members, for the following purposes:

(i) to redeem prior to maturity, or otherwise discharge its liability on, all or part of the outstanding principal of any loan guaranteed by it in respect of which the debtor is in default; and

(ii) to repurchase, or otherwise discharge its liability on, all or part of its own outstanding obligations.

Section 4. *Distribution of Net Profits and Surplus*

(a) The Board of Governors may determine periodically what part of the net profits and of the surplus shall be distributed. Such distributions may be made only when the reserves have reached a level which the Board of Governors considers adequate.

(b) The distributions referred to in the preceding paragraph shall be made in proportion to the number of shares held by each member.

(c) Payments shall be made in such manner and in such currency or currencies as the Board of Governors shall determine. If such payments are made to a member in currencies other than its own, the transfer of such currencies and their use by the receiving country shall be without restriction by any member.

ARTICLE VIII

ORGANIZATION AND MANAGEMENT

Section 1. *Structure of the Bank*

The Bank shall have a Board of Governors, a Board of Executive Directors, a President, an Executive Vice President, a Vice President in charge of the Fund, and such other officers and staff as may be considered necessary.

Section 2. *Board of Governors*

(a) All the powers of the Bank shall be vested in the Board of Governors. Each member shall appoint one governor and one alternate, who shall serve for five years, subject to termination of appointment at any time, or to reappointment, at the pleasure of the appointing member. No alternate may vote except in the absence of his principal. The Board shall select one of the governors as Chairman, who shall hold office until the next regular meeting of the Board.

(b) The Board of Governors may delegate to the Board of Executive Directors all its powers except power to:

  (i) admit new members and determine the conditions of their admission;

 (ii) increase or decrease the authorized capital stock of the Bank and contributions to the Fund;

(iii) elect the President of the Bank and determine his remuneration;

 (iv) suspend a member, pursuant to Article IX, Section 2;

  (v) determine the remuneration of the executive directors and their alternates;

 (vi) hear and decide any appeals from interpretations of this Agreement given by the Board of Executive Directors;

(vii) authorize the conclusion of general agreements for cooperation with other international organizations;

(viii) approve, after reviewing the auditors' report, the general balance sheet and the statement of profit and loss of the institution;

 (ix) determine the reserves and the distribution of the net profits of the Bank and of the Fund;

  (x) select outside auditors to certify to the general balance sheet and the statement of profit and loss of the institution;

 (xi) amend this Agreement; and

(xii) decide to terminate the operations of the Bank and to distribute its assets.

(c) The Board of Governors shall retain full power to exercise authority over any matter delegated to the Board of Executive Directors under paragraph (b) above.

(d) The Board of Governors shall, as a general rule, hold a meeting annually. Other meetings may be held when the Board of Governors so provides or when called by the Board of Executive Directors. Meetings of the Board of Governors also shall be called by the Board of Executive Directors whenever requested by five members of the Bank or by members having one fourth of the total voting power of the member countries.

(e) A quorum for any meeting of the Board of Governors shall be an absolute majority of the total number of governors, representing not less than two thirds of the total voting power of the member countries.

(f) The Board of Governors may establish a procedure whereby the Board of Executive Directors, when it deems such action appropriate, may submit a specific question to a vote of the governors without calling a meeting of the Board of Governors.

(g) The Board of Governors, and the Board of Executive Directors to the extent authorized, may adopt such rules and regulations as may be necessary or appropriate to conduct the business of the Bank.

(h) Governors and alternates shall serve as such without compensation from the Bank, but the Bank may pay them reasonable expenses incurred in attending meetings of the Board of Governors.

Section 3. *Board of Executive Directors*

(a) The Board of Executive Directors shall be responsible for the conduct of the operations of the Bank, and for this purpose may exercise all the powers delegated to it by the Board of Governors.

(b) There shall be seven executive directors, who shall not be governors, and of whom:

> (i) one shall be appointed by the member having the largest number of shares in the Bank;
>
> (ii) six shall be elected by the governors of the remaining members pursuant to the provisions of Annex C of this Agreement.

Executive directors shall be appointed or elected for terms of three years and may be reappointed or re-elected for successive terms. They shall be persons of recognized competence and wide experience in economic and financial matters.

(c) Each executive director shall appoint an alternate who shall have full power to act for him when he is not present. Directors and alternates shall be citizens of the member countries. None of the elected directors and their alternates may be of the same citizenship. Alternates may participate in meetings but may vote only when they are acting in place of their principals.

(d) Directors shall continue in office until their successors are appointed or elected. If the office of an elected director becomes vacant more than 180 days before the end of his term, a successor shall be elected for the remainder of the term by the governors who elected the former director. An absolute majority of the votes cast shall be required for election. While the office remains vacant, the alternate shall have all the powers of the former director except the power to appoint an alternate.

(e) The Board of Executive Directors shall function in continuous session at the principal office of the Bank and shall meet as often as the business of the Bank may require.

(f) A quorum for any meeting of the Board of Executive Directors shall be an absolute majority of the total number of directors representing not less than two thirds of the total voting power of the member countries.

(g) A member of the Bank may send a representative to attend any meeting of the Board of Executive Directors when a matter especially affecting that member is under consideration. Such right of representation shall be regulated by the Board of Governors.

(h) The Board of Executive Directors may appoint such committees as it deems advisable. Membership of such committees need not be limited to governors, directors, or alternates.

(i) The Board of Executive Directors shall determine the basic organization of the Bank, including the number and general responsibilities of the chief administrative and professional positions of the staff, and shall approve the budget of the Bank.

(j) Upon the admission to the Bank of new members, having votes totaling not less than 22,000, the Board of Governors may, by a two-thirds majority of the total number of governors representing not less than three-fourths of the total voting power of the member countries, increase by one the number of Executive Directors to be elected.[1]

Section 4. *Voting*

(a) Each member country shall have 135 votes plus one vote for each share of capital stock of the Bank held by that country.

(b) In voting in the Board of Governors, each governor shall be entitled to cast the votes of the member country which he represents. Except as otherwise specifically provided in this Agreement, all matters before the Board of Governors shall be decided by a majority of the total voting power of the member countries.

(c) In voting in the Board of Executive Directors:

    (i) the appointed director shall be entitled to cast the number of votes of the member country which appointed him;

    (ii) each elected director shall be entitled to cast the number of votes that counted toward his election, which votes shall be cast as a unit; and

    (iii) except as otherwise specifically provided in this Agreement, all matters before the Board of Executive Directors shall be decided by a majority of the total voting power of the member countries.

Section 5. *President, Executive Vice President, and Staff*

(a) The Board of Governors, by an absolute majority of the total number of governors representing not less than a majority of the total voting power of the member countries, shall elect a President of the Bank who, while holding office, shall not be a governor or an executive director or alternate for either.

Under the direction of the Board of Executive Directors, the President of the Bank shall conduct the ordinary business of the Bank and shall be chief of its staff. He also shall be the presiding officer at meetings of the Board of Executive Directors, but shall have no vote, except that it shall be his duty to cast a deciding vote when necessary to break a tie.

The President of the Bank shall be the legal representative of the Bank. The term of office of the President of the Bank shall be five years, and he may be reelected to successive terms. He shall cease to hold office when the Board of Governors so decides by a majority of the total voting power of the member countries.

(b) The Executive Vice President shall be appointed by the Board of Executive Directors on the recommendation of the President of the Bank. Under the direction of the Board of Executive Directors and the President of the Bank, the Executive Vice President shall exercise such authority and perform such functions in the administration of the Bank as may be determined by the Board of Executive Directors. In the absence or incapacity of the President of the Bank, the Executive Vice President shall exercise the authority and perform the functions of the President.

The Executive Vice President shall participate in meetings of the Board of Executive Directors but shall have no vote at such meetings, except that he

---

[1] This subsection was added by action of the Board of Governors on January 28, 1964.

shall cast the deciding vote, as provided in paragraph (a) of this section, when he is acting in place of the President of the Bank.

(c) In addition to the Vice President referred to in Article IV, Section 8 (b), the Board of Executive Directors may, on recommendation of the President of the Bank, appoint other Vice Presidents who shall exercise such authority and perform such functions as the Board of Executive Directors may determine.

(d) The President, officers, and staff of the Bank, in the discharge of their offices, owe their duty entirely to the Bank and shall recognize no other authority. Each member of the Bank shall respect the international character of this duty.

(e) The paramount consideration in the employment of the staff and in the determination of the conditions of service shall be the necessity of securing the highest standards of efficiency, competence, and integrity. Due regard shall be paid to the importance of recruiting the staff on as wide a geographical basis as possible.

(f) The Bank, its officers and employees shall not interfere in the political affairs of any member, nor shall they be influenced in their decisions by the political character of the member or members concerned. Only economic considerations shall be relevant to their decisions, and these considerations shall be weighed impartially in order to achieve the purpose and functions stated in Article I.

Section 6. *Publication of Reports and Provision of Information*

(a) The Bank shall publish an annual report containing an audited statement of the accounts. It shall also transmit quarterly to the members a summary statement of the financial position and a profit-and-loss statement showing the results of its ordinary operations.

(b) The Bank may also publish such other reports as it deems desirable to carry out its purpose and functions.

ARTICLE IX

WITHDRAWAL AND SUSPENSION OF MEMBERS

Section 1. *Right to Withdraw*

Any member may withdraw from the Bank by delivering to the Bank at its principal office written notice of its intention to do so. Such withdrawal shall become finally effective on the date specified in the notice but in no event less than six months after the notice is delivered to the Bank. However, at any time before the withdrawal becomes finally effective, the member may notify the Bank in writing of the cancellation of its notice of intention to withdraw.

After withdrawing, a member shall remain liable for all direct and contingent obligations to the Bank to which it was subject at the date of delivery of the withdrawal notice, including those specified in Section 3 of this article. However, if the withdrawal becomes finally effective, the member shall not incur any liability for obligations resulting from operations of the Bank effected after the date on which the withdrawal notice was received by the Bank.

Section 2. *Suspension of Membership*

If a member fails to fulfill any of its obligations to the Bank, the Bank may suspend its membership by decision of the Board of Governors by a two-thirds majority of the total number of governors representing not less than three fourths of the total voting power of the member countries.

The member so suspended shall automatically cease to be a member of the Bank one year from the date of its suspension unless the Board of Governors decides by the same majority to terminate the suspension.

While under suspension, a member shall not be entitled to exercise any rights under this Agreement, except the right of withdrawal, but shall remain subject to all its obligations.

Section 3. *Settlement of Accounts*

(a) After a country ceases to be a member, it no longer shall share in the profits or losses of the Bank, nor shall it incur any liability with respect to loans and guarantees entered into by the Bank thereafter. However, it shall remain liable for all amounts it owes the Bank and for its contingent liabilities to the Bank so long as any part of the loans or guarantees contracted by the Bank before the date on which the country ceased to be a member remains outstanding.

(b) When a country ceases to be a member, the Bank shall arrange for the repurchase of such country's capital stock as a part of the settlement of accounts pursuant to the provisions of this section; but the country shall have no other rights under this Agreement except as provided in this section and in Article XIII, Section 2.

(c) The Bank and the country ceasing to be a member may agree on the repurchase of the capital stock on such terms as are deemed appropriate in the circumstances, without regard to the provisions of the following paragraph. Such agreement may provide, among other things, for a final settlement of all obligations of the country to the Bank.

(d) If the agreement referred to in the preceding paragraph has not been consummated within six months after the country ceases to be a member or such other time as the Bank and such country may agree upon, the repurchase price of such country's capital stock shall be its book value, according to the books of the Bank, on the date when the country ceased to be a member. Such repurchase shall be subject to the following conditions:

(i) As a prerequisite for payment, the country ceasing to be a member shall surrender its stock certificates, and such payment may be made in such installments, at such times and in such available currencies as the Bank determines, taking into account the financial position of the Bank.

(ii) Any amount which the Bank owes the country for the repurchase of its capital stock shall be withheld to the extent that the country or any of its subdivisions or agencies remains liable to the Bank as a result of loan or guarantee operations. The amount withheld may, at the option of the Bank, be applied on any such liability as it matures. However, no amount shall be withheld on account of the country's contingent liability for future calls on its subscription pursuant to Article II, Section 4 (a) (ii).

(iii) If the Bank sustains net losses on any loans or participations, or as a result of any guarantees, outstanding on the date the country ceased to be a member, and the amount of such losses exceeds the amount of the reserves provided therefor on such date, such country shall repay on demand the amount by which the repurchase price of its shares would have been reduced, if the losses had been taken into account when the book value of the shares, according to the books of the Bank, was determined. In addition, the former member shall remain liable on any call pursuant to Article II, Section 4 (a) (ii), to the extent that it would have been required to respond if the impairment of capital had occurred and the call had been made at the time the repurchase price of its shares had been determined.

(e) In no event shall any amount due to a country for its shares under this section be paid until six months after the date upon which the country ceases to be a member. If within that period the Bank terminates operations all rights of such country shall be determined by the provisions of Article X, and such country shall be considered still a member of the Bank for the purposes of such article except that it shall have no voting rights.

ARTICLE X

SUSPENSION AND TERMINATION OF OPERATIONS

Section 1. *Suspension of Operations*

In an emergency the Board of Executive Directors may suspend operations in respect of new loans and guarantees until such time as the Board of Governors may have an opportunity to consider the situation and take pertinent measures.

Section 2. *Termination of Operations*

The Bank may terminate its operations by a decision of the Board of Governors by a two-thirds majority of the total number of governors representing not less than three fourths of the total voting power of the member countries. After such termination of operations the Bank shall forthwith cease all activities, except those incident to the conservation, preservation, and realization of its assets and settlement of its obligations.

Section 3. *Liability of Members and Payment of Claims*

(a) The liability of all members arising from the subscriptions to the capital stock of the Bank and in respect to the depreciation of their currencies shall continue until all direct and contingent obligations shall have been discharged.

(b) All creditors holding direct claims shall be paid out of the assets of the Bank and then out of payments to the Bank on unpaid or callable subscriptions. Before making any payments to creditors holding direct claims, the Board of Executive Directors shall make such arrangements as are necessary, in its judgment, to ensure a pro rata distribution among holders of direct and contingent claims.

Section 4. *Distribution of Assets*

(a) No distribution of assets shall be made to members on account of their subscriptions to the capital stock of the Bank until all liabilities to creditors shall have been discharged or provided for. Moreover, such distribution must be approved by a decision of the Board of Governors by a two-thirds majority of the total number of governors representing not less than three fourths of the total voting power of the member countries.

(b) Any distribution of the assets of the Bank to the members shall be in proportion to capital stock held by each member and shall be effected at such times and under such conditions as the Bank shall deem fair and equitable. The shares of assets distributed need not be uniform as to type of assets. No member shall be entitled to receive its share in such a distribution of assets until it has settled all of its obligations to the Bank.

(c) Any member receiving assets distributed pursuant to this article shall enjoy the same rights with respect to such assets as the Bank enjoyed prior to their distribution.

ARTICLE XI

STATUS, IMMUNITIES AND PRIVILEGES

Section 1. *Scope of Article*
To enable the Bank to fulfill its purpose and the functions with which it is entrusted, the status, immunities, and privileges set forth in this article shall be accorded to the Bank in the territories of each member.

Section 2. *Legal Status*
The Bank shall possess juridical personality and, in particular, full capacity:
(a) to contract;
(b) to acquire and dispose of immovable and movable property; and
(c) to institute legal proceedings.

Section 3. *Judicial Proceedings*
Actions may be brought against the Bank only in a court of competent jurisdiction in the territories of a member in which the Bank has an office, has appointed an agent for the purpose of accepting service or notice of process, or has issued or guaranteed securities.

No action shall be brought against the Bank by members or persons acting for or deriving claims from members. However, member countries shall have recourse to such special procedures to settle controversies between the Bank and its members as may be prescribed in this Agreement, in the by-laws and regulations of the Bank or in contracts entered into with the Bank.

Property and assets of the Bank shall, wheresoever located and by whomsoever held, be immune from all forms of seizure, attachment or execution before the delivery of final judgment against the Bank.

Section 4. *Immunity of Assets*
Property and assets of the Bank, wheresoever located and by whomsoever held, shall be considered public international property and shall be immune from search, requisition, confiscation, expropriation or any other form of taking or foreclosure by executive or legislative action.

Section 5. *Inviolability of Archives*
The archives of the Bank shall be inviolable.

Section 6. *Freedom of Assets from Restrictions*

To the extent necessary to carry out the purpose and functions of the Bank and to conduct its operations in accordance with this Agreement, all property and other assets of the Bank shall be free from restrictions, regulations, controls and moratoria of any nature, except as may otherwise be provided in this Agreement.

Section 7. *Privilege for Communications*

The official communications of the Bank shall be accorded by each member the same treatment that it accords to the official communications of other members.

Section 8. *Personal Immunities and Privileges*

All governors, executive directors, alternates, officers and employees of the Bank shall have the following privileges and immunities:

(a) Immunity from legal process with respect to acts performed by them in their official capacity, except when the Bank waives this immunity.

(b) When not local nationals, the same immunities from immigration restrictions, alien registration requirements and national service obligations and the same facilities as regards exchange provisions as are accorded by members to the representatives, officials, and employees of comparable rank of other members.

(c) The same privileges in respect of traveling facilities as are accorded by members to representatives, officials, and employees of comparable rank of other members.

Section 9. *Immunities from Taxation*

(a) The Bank, its property, other assets, income, and the operations and transactions it carries out pursuant to this Agreement, shall be immune from all taxation and from all customs duties. The Bank shall also be immune from any obligation relating to the payment, withholding or collection of any tax, or duty.

(b) No tax shall be levied on or in respect of salaries and emoluments paid by the Bank to executive directors, alternates, officials or employees of the Bank who are not local citizens or other local nationals.

(c) No tax of any kind shall be levied on any obligation or security issued by the Bank, including any dividend or interest thereon, by whomsoever held:

(i) which discriminates against such obligation or security solely because it is issued by the Bank; or

(ii) if the sole jurisdictional basis for such taxation is the place or currency in which it is issued, made payable or paid, or the location of any office or place of business maintained by the Bank.

(d) No tax of any kind shall be levied on any obligation or security guaranteed by the Bank, including any dividend or interest thereon, by whomsoever held:

(i) which discriminates against such obligation or security solely because it is guaranteed by the Bank; or

(ii) if the sole jurisdictional basis for such taxation is the location of any office or place of business maintained by the Bank.

Section 10. *Implementation*

Each member, in accordance with its juridical system, shall take such action as is necessary to make effective in its own territories the principles set forth in this article, and shall inform the Bank of the action which it has taken on the matter.

ARTICLE XII

AMENDMENTS

(a) This Agreement may be amended only by decision of the Board of Governors by a two-thirds majority of the total number of governors representing not less than three fourths of the total voting power of the member countries.

(b) Notwithstanding the provisions of the preceding paragraph, the unanimous agreement of the Board of Governors shall be required for the approval of any amendment modifying:

   (i) the right to withdraw from the Bank as provided in Article IX, Section 1;

  (ii) the right to purchase capital stock of the Bank and to contribute to the Fund as provided in Article II, Section 3 (b) and in Article IV, Section 3 (g), respectively; and

 (iii) the limitation on liability as provided in Article II, Section 3 (d) and Article IV, Section 5.

(c) Any proposal to amend this Agreement, whether emanating from a member or the Board of Executive Directors, shall be communicated to the Chairman of the Board of Governors, who shall bring the proposal before the Board of Governors. When an amendment has been adopted, the Bank shall so certify in an official communication addressed to all members. Amendments shall enter into force for all members three months after the date of the official communication unless the Board of Governors shall specify a different period.

ARTICLE XIII

INTERPRETATION AND ARBITRATION

Section 1. *Interpretation*

(a) Any question of interpretation of the provisions of this Agreement arising between any member and the Bank or between any members of the Bank shall be submitted to the Board of Executive Directors for decision.

Members especially affected by the question under consideration shall be entitled to direct representation before the Board of Executive Directors as provided in Article VIII, Section 3 (g).

(b) In any case where the Board of Executive Directors has given a decision under (a) above, any member may require that the question be submitted to the Board of Governors, whose decision shall be final. Pending the decision of the Board of Governors, the Bank may, so far as it deems it necessary, act on the basis of the decision of the Board of Executive Directors.

Section 2. *Arbitration*

If a disagreement should arise between the Bank and a country which has ceased to be a member, or between the Bank and any member after adoption of a decision to terminate the operation of the Bank, such disagreement shall be submitted to arbitration by a tribunal of three arbitrators. One of the arbitrators shall be appointed by the Bank, another by the country concerned, and the third, unless the parties otherwise agree, by the Secretary General of the Organization of American States. If all efforts to reach a unanimous agreement fail, decisions shall be made by a majority vote of the three arbitrators. The third arbitrator shall be empowered to settle all questions of procedure in any case where the parties are in disagreement with respect thereto.

ARTICLE XIV
GENERAL PROVISIONS

Section 1. *Principal Office*

The principal office of the Bank shall be located in Washington, District of Columbia, United States of America.

Section 2. *Relations with other Organizations*

The Bank may enter into arrangements with other organizations with respect to the exchange of information or for other purposes consistent with this Agreement.

Section 3. *Channel of Communication*

Each member shall designate an official entity for purposes of communication with the Bank on matters connected with this Agreement.

Section 4. *Depositories*

Each member shall designate its central bank as a depository in which the Bank may keep its holdings of such member's currency and other assets of the Bank. If a member has no central bank, it shall, in agreement with the Bank, designate another institution for such purpose.

ARTICLE XV
FINAL PROVISIONS

Section 1. *Signature and Acceptance*

(a) This Agreement shall be deposited with the General Secretariat of the Organization of American States, where it shall remain open until December 31, 1959, for signature by the representatives of the countries listed in Annex A. Each signatory country shall deposit with the General Secretariat of the Organization of American States an instrument setting forth that it has accepted or ratified this Agreement in accordance with its own laws and has taken the steps necessary to enable it to fulfill all of its obligations under this Agreement.

(b) The General Secretariat of the Organization of American States shall send certified copies of this Agreement to the members of the Organization and duly notify them of each signature and deposit of the instrument of acceptance or ratification made pursuant to the foregoing paragraph, as well as the date thereof.

(c) At the time the instrument of acceptance or ratification is deposited on its behalf, each country shall deliver to the General Secretariat of the Organization of American States, for the purpose of meeting administrative expenses of the Bank, gold or United States dollars equivalent to one tenth of one per cent of the purchase price of the shares of the Bank subscribed by it and of its quota in the Fund. This payment shall be credited to the member on account of its subscription and quota prescribed pursuant to Articles II, Section 3 (a) (i), and IV, Section 3 (d) (i). At any time on or after the date on which its instrument of acceptance or ratification is deposited, any member may make additional payments to be credited to the member on account of its subscription and quota prescribed pursuant to Articles II and IV. The General Secretariat of the Organization of American States shall hold all funds paid under this paragraph in a special deposit account or accounts and shall make such funds available to the Bank not later than the time of the first meeting of the Board of Governors held pursuant to Section 3 of this article. If this Agreement has not come into force by December 31, 1959, the General Secretariat of the Organization of American States shall return such funds to the countries that delivered them.

(d) On or after the date on which the Bank commences operations, the General Secretariat of the Organization of American States may receive the signature and the instrument of acceptance or ratification of this Agreement from any country whose membership has been approved in accordance with Article II, Section 1 (b).

Section 2. *Entry into Force*

(a) This Agreement shall enter into force when it has been signed and instruments of acceptance or ratification have been deposited, in accordance with Section 1 (a) of this article, by representatives of countries whose subscriptions comprise not less than 85 per cent of the total subscriptions set forth in Annex A.

(b) Countries whose instruments of acceptance or ratification were deposited prior to the date on which the agreement entered into force shall become members on that date. Other countries shall become members on the dates on which their instruments of acceptance or ratification are deposited.

Section 3. *Commencement of Operations*

(a) The Secretary General of the Organization of American States shall call the first meeting of the Board of Governors as soon as this Agreement enters into force under Section 2 of this article.

(b) At the first meeting of the Board of Governors arrangements shall be made for the selection of the executive directors and their alternates in accordance with the provisions of Article VIII, Section 3, and for the determination of the date on which the Bank shall commence operations. Notwithstanding the provisions of Article VIII, Section 3, the governors, if they deem it desirable, may provide that the first term to be served by such directors may be less than three years.

DONE at the city of Washington, District of Columbia, United States of America, in a single original, dated April 8, 1959, whose English, French, Portuguese, and Spanish texts are equally authentic.

ANNEX A

SUBSCRIPTIONS TO AUTHORIZED CAPITAL STOCK
OF THE BANK
(In shares of US$10,000 each)

Country	Paid-in Capital Shares	Callable Shares	Total Sub-scription
Argentina	5,157	5,157	10,314
Bolivia	414	414	828
Brazil	5,157	5,157	10,314
Chile	1,416	1,416	2,832
Colombia	1,415	1,415	2,830
Costa Rica	207	207	414
Cuba	1,842	1,842	3,684
Dominican Republic	276	276	552
Ecuador	276	276	552
El Salvador	207	207	414
Guatemala	276	276	552
Haiti	207	207	414
Honduras	207	207	414
Mexico	3,315	3,315	6,630
Nicaragua	207	207	414
Panama	207	207	414
Paraguay	207	207	414
Peru	691	691	1,382
United States of America	15,000	20,000	35,000
Uruguay	553	553	1,106
Venezuela	2,763	2,763	5,526
Total	40,000	45,000	85,000

ADDENDUM
AUTHORIZED CAPITAL STOCK OF THE BANK
As of January 28, 1964
(In shares of US$10,000 each)

Country	Paid-in Capital Shares	Callable Shares	Total
Argentina	5,157	17,291	22,448
Bolivia	414	1,388	1,802
Brazil	5,157	17,291	22,448
Chile	1,416	4,748	6,164
Colombia	1,415	4,744	6,159
Costa Rica	207	694	901
Dominican Republic	276	926	1,202
Ecuador	276	926	1,202
El Salvador	207	694	901
Guatemala	276	926	1,202
Haiti	207	694	901
Honduras	207	694	901
Mexico	3,315	11,115	14,430
Nicaragua	207	694	901
Panama	207	694	901
Paraguay	207	694	901
Peru	691	2,317	3,008
United States of America	15,000	61,176	76,176
Uruguay	553	1,854	2,407
Venezuela	2,763	9,264	12,027
Unassigned[1]	9,342	28,676	38,018
Total	47,500	167,500	215,000

[1] Available for subscription by present or by future members.

ANNEX B
CONTRIBUTION QUOTAS FOR THE FUND FOR
SPECIAL OPERATIONS
(In thousands of US$)

Country	Quota
Argentina	10,314
Bolivia	828
Brazil	10,314
Chile	2,832
Colombia	2,830
Costa Rica	414
Cuba	3,684
Dominican Republic	552
Ecuador	552
El Salvador	414
Guatemala	552
Haiti	414
Honduras	414
Mexico	6,630
Nicaragua	414
Panama	414
Paraguay	414
Peru	1,382
United States of America	100,000
Uruguay	1,106
Venezuela	5,526
Total	150,000

ADDENDUM
CONTRIBUTION QUOTAS FOR THE FUND FOR
SPECIAL OPERATIONS
As of March 31, 1965
(In thousands of US$)

Country	Quota
Argentina	48,873
Bolivia	3,924
Brazil	48,873
Chile	13,419
Colombia	13,410
Costa Rica	1,962
Dominican Republic	2,616
Ecuador	2,616
El Salvador	1,962
Guatemala	2,616
Haiti	1,962
Honduras	1,962
Mexico	31,419
Nicaragua	1,962
Panama	1,962
Paraguay	1,962
Peru	6,546
United States of America	900,000
Uruguay	5,241
Venezuela	26,187
Unassigned	3,684
Total	1,123,158

ANNEX C

ELECTION OF EXECUTIVE DIRECTORS

(a) The six executive directors referred to in Article VIII, Section 3 (b) (ii) shall be elected by the governors eligible to vote for that purpose.

(b) Each governor shall cast in favor of a single person all the votes to which the member he represents is entitled under Article VIII, Section 4.

(c) In the first place, as many ballots as are necessary shall be taken until each of four candidates receives a number of votes that represents a percentage not less than the sum of the percentages appertaining to the country with the greatest voting power and to the country with the least voting power. For the purposes of this paragraph, the total voting power of the countries entitled to participate in the voting provided for under this annex shall be counted as 100 per cent.

(d) In the second place, governors whose votes have not been cast in favor of any of the directors elected under paragraph (c) of this annex shall elect the other two directors on the basis of one vote for each governor. The two candidates who each receive a greater number of votes than any other candidate, on the same ballot, shall be elected executive directors, and the balloting shall be repeated until this occurs. After the balloting has been completed, each governor who did not vote for either of the candidates elected shall assign his vote to one of them.

The number of votes under Article VIII, Section 4, of each governor who has voted for or assigned his vote to a candidate elected hereunder shall be deemed for the purposes of Article VIII, Section 4 (c) (ii) to have counted toward the election of such candidate.

(e) Whenever the Board of Governors increases the number of Executive Directors in accordance with Article VIII, Section 3 (i), the additional Executive Director shall be elected at the next regular election of Executive Directors in accordance with sub-paragraph (c) of this Annex.[1]

---

[1] This subsection was added by action of the Board of Governors on January 28, 1964.

17. ACT OF BOGOTA (1960)
Measures For Social Improvement and Economic Development Within the Framework of Operation Pan America

The Special Committee to Study the Formulation of New Measures for Economic Cooperation,

RECOGNIZING that the preservation and strengthening of free and democratic institutions in the American republics requires the acceleration of social and economic progress in Latin America adequate to meet the legitimate aspirations of the peoples of the Americas for a better life and to provide them the fullest opportunity to improve their status;

RECOGNIZING that the interests of the American republics are so interrelated that sound social and economic progress in each is of importance to all and that lack of it in any American republic may have serious repercussions in others;

COGNIZANT of the steps already taken by many American republics to cope with the serious economic and social problems confronting them, but convinced that the magnitude of these problems calls for redoubled efforts by governments and for a new and vigorous program of inter-American cooperation;

RECOGNIZING that economic development programs, which should be urgently strengthened and expanded, may have a delayed effect on social welfare, and that accordingly early measures are needed to cope with social needs;

RECOGNIZING that the success of a cooperative program of economic and social progress will require maximum self-help efforts on the part of the American republics and, in many cases, the improvement of existing institutions and practices, particularly in the fields of taxation, the ownership and use of land, education and training, health and housing;

BELIEVING it opportune to give further practical expression to the spirit of Operation Pan America by immediately enlarging the opportunities of the people of Latin America for social progress, thus strengthening their hopes for the future;

CONSIDERING it advisable to launch a program for social development, in which emphasis should be given to those measures that meet social needs and also promote increases in productivity and strengthen economic development,

RECOMMENDS to the Council of the Organization of American States:

I

MEASURES FOR SOCIAL IMPROVEMENTS

An inter-American program for social development should be established which should be directed to the carrying out of the following measures of social improvement in Latin America, as considered appropriate in each country:

A. *Measures for the improvement of conditions of rural living and land use*
   1. The examination of existing legal and institutional systems with respect to:
      a. land tenure legislation and facilities with a view to ensuring a wider and more equitable distribution of the ownership of land, in a manner consistent with the objectives of employment, productivity and economic growth;
      b. agricultural credit institutions with a view to providing adequate financing to individual farmers or groups of farmers;
      c. tax systems and procedures and fiscal policies with a view to assuring equity of taxation and encouraging improved use of land, especially of privately-owned land which is idle.
   2. The initiation or acceleration of appropriate programs to modernize and improve the existing legal and institutional framework to ensure better conditions of land tenure, extend more adequate credit facilities and provide increased incentives in the land tax structure.
   3. The acceleration of the preparation of projects and programs for:
      a. land reclamation and land settlement, with a view to promoting more widespread ownership, and efficient use of land, particularly of unutilized or under-utilized land;
      b. the increase of the productivity of land already in use; and
      c. the construction of farm-to-market and access roads.
   4. The adoption or acceleration of other government service programs designed particularly to assist the small farmer, such as new or improved marketing organizations; extension services; research and basic surveys; and demonstration, education, and training facilities.

B. *Measures for the improvement of housing and community facilities*
   1. The examination of existing policies in the field of housing and community facilities, including urban and regional planning, with a view to improving such policies, strengthening public institutions and promoting private initiative and participation in programs in these fields. Special consideration should be given to encouraging financial institutions to invest in low-cost housing on a long-term basis and in building and construction industries.
   2. The strengthening of the existing legal and institutional framework for mobilizing financial resources to provide better housing and related facilities for the people and to create new institutions for this purpose when necessary. Special consideration should be given to legislation and measures which would encourage the establishment and growth of:
      a. private financing institutions, such as building and loan associations;
      b. institutions to insure sound housing loans against loss;
      c. institutions to serve as a secondary market for home mortgages;
      d. institutions to provide financial assistance to local communities for the development of facilities such as water supply, sanitation and other public works.
   Existing national institutions should be utilized, wherever practical and appropriate, in the application of external resources to further the development of housing and community facilities.

3. The expansion of home building industries through such measures as the training of craftsmen and other personnel, research, the introduction of new techniques, and the development of construction standards for low and medium-cost housing.

4. The lending of encouragement and assistance to programs, on a pilot basis, for aided self-help housing, for the acquisition and subdivision of land for low-cost housing developments, and for industrial housing projects.

C. *Measures for the improvement of educational systems and training facilities*

1. The re-examination of educational systems, giving particular attention to:

   a. the development of modern methods of mass education for the eradication of illiteracy;

   b. the adequacy of training in the industrial arts and sciences with due emphasis on laboratory and work experience and on the practical application of knowledge for the solution of social and economic problems;

   c. the need to provide instruction in rural schools not only in basic subjects but also in agriculture, health, sanitation, nutrition, and in methods of home and community improvement;

   d. the broadening of courses of study in secondary schools to provide the training necessary for clerical and executive personnel in industry, commerce, public administration, and community service;

   e. specialized trade and industrial education related to the commercial and industrial needs of the community;

   f. vocational agricultural instruction;

   g. advanced education of administrators, engineers, economists, and other professional personnel of key importance to economic development.

D. *Measures for the improvement of public health*

1. The re-examination of programs and policies of public health, giving particular attention to:

   a. strengthening the expansion of national and local health services, especially those directed to the reduction of infant mortality;

   b. the progressive development of health insurance systems, including those providing for maternity, accident and disability insurance, in urban and rural areas;

   c. the provision of hospital and health service in areas located away from main centers of population;

   d. the extension of public medical services to areas of exceptional need;

   e. the strengthening of campaigns for the control or elimination of communicable diseases with special attention to the eradication of malaria;

   f. the provision of water supply facilities for purposes of health and economic development;

   g. the training of public health officials and technicians;

   h. the strengthening of programs of nutrition for low-income groups.

E. *Measures for the mobilization of domestic resources*
1. This program shall be carried out within the framework of the maximum creation of domestic savings and of the improvement of fiscal and financial practices;
2. The equity and effectiveness of existing tax schedules, assessment practices and collection procedures shall be examined with a view to providing additional revenue for the purpose of this program;
3. The allocation of tax revenues shall be reviewed, having in mind an adequate provision of such revenues to the areas of social development mentioned in the foregoing paragraphs.

II

CREATION OF A SPECIAL FUND FOR SOCIAL DEVELOPMENT

1. The delegations of the governments of the Latin American republics welcome the decision of the Government of the United States to establish a special inter-American fund for social development, with the Inter-American Development Bank to become the primary mechanism for the administration of the fund.

2. It is understood that the purpose of the special fund would be to contribute capital resources and technical assistance on flexible terms and conditions, including repayment in local currency and the relending of repaid funds, in accordance with appropriate and selective criteria in the light of the resources available, to support the efforts of the Latin American countries that are prepared to initiate or expand effective institutional improvements and to adopt measures to employ efficiently their own resources with a view to achieving greater social progress and more balanced economic growth.

III

MEASURES FOR ECONOMIC DEVELOPMENT

The Special Committee,

HAVING IN VIEW Resolution VII adopted at the Seventh Meeting of Consultation of Ministers of Foreign Affairs expressing the need for the maximum contribution of member countries in hemisphere cooperation in the struggle against underdevelopment, in pursuance of the objectives of Operation Pan America,

EXPRESSES ITS CONVICTION

1. That within the framework of Operation Pan America the economic development of Latin America requires prompt action of exceptional breadth in the field of international cooperation and domestic effort comprising:
   a. additional public and private financial assistance on the part of capital exporting countries of America, Western Europe, and international lending agencies within the framework of their charters, with special attention to:
      i. the need for loans on flexible terms and conditions, including, whenever advisable in the light of the balance of payments situa-

tion of individual countries, the possibility of repayment in local currency,

    ii. the desirability of the adequate preparation and implementation of development projects and plans, within the framework of the monetary, fiscal and exchange policies necessary for their effectiveness, utilizing as appropriate the technical assistance of inter-American and international agencies,

    iii. the advisability, in special cases, of extending foreign financing for the coverage of local expenditures;

  b. mobilization of additional domestic capital, both public and private;

  c. technical assistance by the appropriate international agencies in the preparation and implementation of national and regional Latin American development projects and plans;

  d. the necessity for developing and strengthening credit facilities for small and medium private business, agriculture and industry.

RECOMMENDS:

1. That special attention be given to an expansion of long-term lending, particularly in view of the instability of exchange earnings of countries exporting primary products and of the unfavorable effect of the excessive accumulation of short- and medium-term debt on continuing and orderly economic development.

2. That urgent attention be given to the search for effective and practical ways, appropriate to each commodity, to deal with the problem of the instability of exchange earnings of countries heavily dependent upon the exportation of primary products.

IV

MULTILATERAL COOPERATION
FOR SOCIAL AND ECONOMIC PROGRESS

The Special Committee,

CONSIDERING the need for providing instruments and mechanisms for the implementation of the program of inter-American economic and social cooperation which would periodically review the progress made and propose measures for further mobilization of resources,

RECOMMENDS:

1. That the Inter-American Economic and Social Council undertake to organize annual consultative meetings to review the social and economic progress of member countries, to analyze and discuss the progress achieved and the problems encountered in each country, to exchange opinions on possible measures that might be adopted to intensify further social and economic progress, within the framework of Operation Pan America, and to prepare reports on the outlook for the future. Such annual meetings should begin with an examination by experts and terminate with a session at the ministerial level.

2. That the Council of the Organization of American States convene within 60 days of the date of this Act a special meeting of senior government repre-

sentatives to find ways of strengthening and improving the ability of the Inter-American Economic and Social Council to render effective assistance to governments with a view to achieving the objectives enumerated below, taking into account the proposal submitted by the Delegation of the Republic of Argentina in Document CECE/III-13:

    a. To further the economic and social development of Latin American countries;

    b. To promote trade between the countries of the Western Hemisphere as well as between them and extra-continental countries;

    c. To facilitate the flow of capital and the extension of credits to the countries of Latin America both from the Western Hemisphere and from extra-continental sources.

3. The special meeting shall:

    a. Examine the existing structure of the Inter-American Economic and Social Council, and of the units of the Secretariat of the Organization of American States working in the economic and social fields, with a view to strengthening and improving the Inter-American Economic and Social Council;

    d. Determine the means of strengthening inter-American economic and social cooperation by an administrative reform of the Secretariat, which should be given sufficient technical, administrative and financial flexibility for the adequate fulfillment of its tasks;

    c. Formulate recommendations designed to assure effective coordination between the Inter-American Economic and Social Council, the Economic Commission for Latin America, the Inter-American Development Bank, the United Nations and its Specialized Agencies, and other agencies offering technical advice and services in the Western Hemisphere;

    d. Propose procedures designed to establish effective liaison of the Inter-American Economic and Social Council and other regional American organizations with other international organizations for the purpose of study, discussion and consultation in the fields of international trade and financial and technical assistance;

    e. And formulate appropriate recommendations to the Council of the Organization of American States.

In approving the Act of Bogota the Delegations to the Special Committee, convinced that the people of the Americas can achieve a better life only within the democratic system, renew their faith in the essential values which lie at the base of Western civilization, and re-affirm their determination to assure the fullest measure of well-being to the people of the Americas under conditions of freedom and respect for the supreme dignity of the individual.

18. DECLARATION AND CHARTER OF PUNTA DEL ESTE (1961)

Declaration to the Peoples of America

Assembled in Punta del Este, inspired by the principles consecrated in the Charter of the Organization of American States, in Operation Pan America and in the Act of Bogotá, the representatives of the American Republics hereby agree to establish an Alliance for Progress: a vast effort to bring a better life to all the peoples of the Continent.

This Alliance is established on the basic principle that free men working through the institution of representative democracy can best satisfy man's aspirations, including those for work, home and land, health and schools. No system can guarantee true progress unless it affirms the dignity of the individual which is the foundation of our civilization.

Therefore the countries signing this declaration in the exercise of their sovereignty have agreed to work toward the following goals during the coming years:

To improve and strengthen democratic institutions through application of the principle of self-determination by the people.

To accelerate economic and social development, thus rapidly bringing about a substantial and steady increase in the average income in order to narrow the gap between the standard of living in Latin American countries and that enjoyed in the industrialized countries.

To carry out urban and rural housing programs to provide decent homes for all our people.

To encourage, in accordance with the characteristics of each country, programs of comprehensive agrarian reform, leading to the effective transformation, where required, of unjust structures and systems of land tenure and use; with a view to replacing latifundia and dwarf holdings by an equitable system of property so that, supplemented by timely and adequate credit, technical assistance and improved marketing arrangements, the land will become for the man who works it the basis of his economic stability, the foundation of his increasing welfare, and the guarantee of his freedom and dignity.

To assure fair wages and satisfactory working conditions to all our workers; to establish effective systems of labor-management relations and procedures for consultation and cooperation among government authorities, employers' associations, and trade unions in the interests of social and economic development.

To wipe out illiteracy; to extend, as quickly as possible, the benefits of primary education to all Latin Americans; and to provide broader facilities, on a vast scale, for secondary and technical training and for higher education.

To press forward with programs of health and sanitation in order to prevent sickness, combat contagious disease, and strengthen our human potential.

To reform tax laws, demanding more from those who have most, to punish tax evasion severely, and to redistribute the national income in order to benefit those who are most in need, while, at the same time, promoting savings and investment and reinvestment of capital.

To maintain monetary and fiscal policies which, while avoiding the disastrous effects of inflation or deflation, will protect the purchasing power of the many, guarantee the greatest possible price stability, and form an adequate basis for economic development.

To stimulate private enterprise in order to encourage the development of Latin American countries at a rate which will help them to provide jobs for their growing populations, to eliminate unemployment, and to take their place among the modern industrialized nations of the world.

To find a quick and lasting solution to the grave problem created by excessive price fluctuations in the basic exports of Latin American countries on which their prosperity so heavily depends.

To accelerate the integration of Latin America so as to stimulate the economic and social development of the Continent. This process has already begun through the General Treaty of Economic Integration of Central America and, in other countries, through the Latin American Free Trade Association.

This declaration expresses the conviction of the nations of Latin America that these profound economic, social, and cultural changes can come about only through the self-help efforts of each country. Nonetheless, in order to achieve the goals which have been established with the necessary speed, domestic efforts must be reinforced by essential contributions of external assistance.

The United States, for its part, pledges its efforts to supply financial and technical cooperation in order to achieve the aims of the Alliance for Progress. To this end, the United States will provide a major part of the minimum of twenty billion dollars, principally in public funds, which Latin America will require over the next ten years from all external sources in order to supplement its own efforts.

The United States will provide from public funds, as an immediate contribution to the economic and social progress of Latin America, more than one billion dollars during the twelve months which began on March 13, 1961, when the Alliance for Progress was announced.

The United States intends to furnish development loans on a long-term basis, where appropriate running up to fifty years and in general at very low or zero rates of interest.

For their part, the countries of Latin America agree to devote a steadily increasing share of their own resources to economic and social development, and to make the reforms necessary to assure that all share fully in the fruits of the Alliance for Progress.

Further, as a contribution to the Alliance for Progress, each of the countries of Latin America will formulate a comprehensive and well-conceived national program for the development of its own economy.

Independent and highly qualified experts will be made available to Latin American countries in order to assist in formulating and examining national development plans.

Conscious of the overriding importance of this declaration, the signatory countries declare that the inter-American community is now beginning a new era when it will supplement its institutional, legal, cultural and social accomplishments with immediate and concrete actions to secure a better life, under freedom and democracy, for the present and future generations.

THE CHARTER OF PUNTA DEL ESTE

Establishing an Alliance for Progress Within the Framework
of Operation Pan America

PREAMBLE

We, the American Republics, hereby proclaim our decision to unite in
a common effort to bring our people accelerated economic progress and
broader social justice within the framework of personal dignity and political
liberty.

Almost two hundred years ago we began in this Hemisphere the long struggle for freedom which now inspires people in all parts of the world. Today,
in ancient lands, men moved to hope by the revolutions of our young nations
search for liberty. Now we must give a new meaning to that revolutionary
heritage. For America stands at a turning point in history. The men and
women of our Hemisphere are reaching for the better life which today's
skills have placed within their grasp. They are determined for themselves and
their children to have decent and ever more abundant lives, to gain access
to knowledge and equal opportunity for all, to end those conditions which
benefit the few at the expense of the needs and dignity of the many. It is our
inescapable task to fulfill these just desires—to demonstrate to the poor and
forsaken of our countries, and of all lands, that the creative powers of free
men hold the key to their progress and to the progress of future generations.
And our certainty of ultimate success rests not alone on our faith in our-
selves and in our nations but on the indomitable spirit of free man which
has been the heritage of American civilization.

Inspired by these principles, and by the principles of Operation Pan
America and the Act of Bogotá, the American Republics hereby resolve to
adopt the following program of action to establish and carry forward an
Alliance for Progress.

TITLE I

OBJECTIVES OF THE ALLIANCE FOR PROGRESS

It is the purpose of the Alliance for Progress to enlist the full energies of
the peoples and governments of the American republics in a great cooperative effort to accelerate the economic and social development of the participating countries of Latin America, so that they may achieve maximum levels of
well-being, with equal opportunities for all, in democratic societies adapted
to their own needs and desires.

The American republics hereby agree to work toward the achievement of
the following fundamental goals in the present decade:

1. To achieve in the participating Latin American countries a substantial
and sustained growth of per capita income at a rate designed to attain, at the
earliest possible date, levels of income capable of assuring self-sustaining
development, and sufficient to make Latin American income levels constantly
larger in relation to the levels of the more industrialized nations. In this way
the gap between the living standards of Latin America and those of the more
developed countries can be narrowed. Similarly, presently existing differences
in income levels among the Latin American countries will be reduced by ac-

celerating the development of the relatively less developed countries and granting them maximum priority in the distribution of resources and in international cooperation in general. In evaluating the degree of relative development, account will be taken not only of average levels of real income and gross product per capita, but also of indices of infant mortality, illiteracy, and per capita daily caloric intake.

It is recognized that, in order to reach these objectives within a reasonable time, the rate of economic growth in any country of Latin America should be not less than 2.5 per cent per capita per year, and that each participating country should determine its own growth target in the light of its stage of social and economic evolution, resource endowment, and ability to mobilize national efforts for development.

2. To make the benefits of economic progress available to all citizens of all economic and social groups through a more equitable distribution of national income, raising more rapidly the income and standard of living of the needier sectors of the population, at the same time that a higher proportion of the national product is devoted to investment.

3. To achieve balanced diversification in national economic structures, both regional and functional, making them increasingly free from dependence on the export of a limited number of primary products and the importation of capital goods while attaining stability in the prices of exports or in income derived from exports.

4. To accelerate the process of rational industrialization so as to increase the productivity of the economy as a whole, taking full advantage of the talents and energies of both the private and public sectors, utilizing the natural resources of the country and providing productive and remunerative employment for unemployed or part-time workers. Within this process of industrialization, special attention should be given to the establishment and development of capital-goods industries.

5. To raise greatly the level of agricultural productivity and output and to improve related storage, transportation, and marketing services.

6. To encourage, in accordance with the characteristics of each country, programs of comprehensive agrarian reform leading to the effective transformation, where required, of unjust structures and systems of land tenure and use, with a view to replacing latifundia and dwarf holdings by an equitable system of land tenure so that, with the help of timely and adequate credit, technical assistance and facilities for the marketing and distribution of products, the land will become for the man who works it the basis of his economic stability, the foundation of his increasing welfare, and the guarantee of his freedom and dignity.

7. To eliminate adult illiteracy and by 1970 to assure, as a minimum, access to six years of primary education for each school-age child in Latin America; to modernize and expand vocational, technical, secondary and higher educational and training facilities, to strengthen the capacity for basic and applied research; and to provide the competent personnel required in rapidly-growing societies.

8. To increase life expectancy at birth by a minimum of five years, and to increase the ability to learn and produce, by improving individual and public health. To attain this goal it will be necessary, among other measures, to provide adequate potable water supply and sewage disposal to not less than 70

per cent of the urban and 50 per cent of the rural population; to reduce the present mortality rate of children less than five years of age by at least one-half; to control the more serious communicable diseases, according to their importance as a cause of sickness, disability, and death; to eradicate those illnesses, especially malaria, for which effective techniques are known; to improve nutrition; to train medical and health personnel to meet at least minimum requirements; to improve basic health services at national and local levels; and to intensify scientific research and apply its results more fully and effectively to the prevention and cure of illness.

9. To increase the construction of low-cost houses for low-income families in order to replace inadequate and deficient housing and to reduce housing shortages; and to provide necessary public services to both urban and rural centers of population.

10. To maintain stable price levels, avoiding inflation or deflation and the consequent social hardships and maldistribution of resources, always bearing in mind the necessity of maintaining an adequate rate of economic growth.

11. To strengthen existing agreements on economic integration, with a view to the ultimate fulfillment of aspirations for a Latin American common market that will expand and diversify trade among the Latin American countries and thus contribute to the economic growth of the region.

12. To develop cooperative programs designed to prevent the harmful effects of excessive fluctuations in the foreign exchange earnings derived from exports of primary products, which are of vital importance to economic and social development; and to adopt the measures necessary to facilitate the access of Latin American exports to international markets.

TITLE II

ECONOMIC AND SOCIAL DEVELOPMENT

Chapter I. Basic Requirements for Economic and Social Development

The American republics recognize that to achieve the foregoing goals it will be necessary:

1. That comprehensive and well-conceived national programs of economic and social development, aimed at the achievement of self-sustaining growth, be carried out in accordance with democratic principles.

2. That national programs of economic and social development be based on the principle of self-help—as established in the Act of Bogotá—and on the maximum use of domestic resources, taking into account the special conditions of each country.

3. That in the preparation and execution of plans for economic and social development, women should be placed on an equal footing with men.

4. That the Latin American countries obtain sufficient external financial assistance, a substantial portion of which should be extended on flexible conditions with respect to periods and terms of repayment and forms of utilization, in order to supplement domestic capital formation and reinforce their import capacity; and that, in support of well-conceived programs, which include the necessary structural reforms and measures for the mobilization of internal resources, a supply of capital from all external sources during the

e. Promotion through appropriate measures, including the signing of agreements for the purpose of reducing or eliminating double taxation, of conditions that will encourage the flow of foreign investments and help to increase the capital resources of participating countries in need of capital.

f. Improvement of systems of distribution and sales in order to make markets more competitive and prevent monopolistic practices.

Chapter III. Immediate and Short-Term Action Measures

1. Recognizing that a number of Latin American countries, despite their best efforts, may require emergency financial assistance, the United States will provide assistance from the funds which are or may be established for such purposes. The United States stands ready to take prompt action on applications for such assistance. Applications relating to existing situations should be submitted within the next 60 days.

2. Participating Latin American countries should, in addition to creating or strengthening machinery for long-term development programming, immediately increase their efforts to accelerate their development by giving special emphasis to the following objectives:

   a. The completion of projects already under way and the initiation of projects for which the basic studies have been made, in order to accelerate their financing and execution.

   b. The implementation of new projects which are designed:

      (1) To meet the most pressing economic and social needs and benefit directly the greatest number of people;

      (2) To concentrate efforts within each country in the less developed and more depressed areas in which particularly serious social problems exist;

      (3) To utilize idle capacity or resources, particularly under-employed manpower; and

      (4) To survey and assess natural resources.

   c. The facilitation of the preparation and execution of long-term programs through measures designed:

      (1) To train teachers, technicians, and specialists;

      (2) To provide accelerated training to workers and farmers;

      (3) To improve basic statistics;

      (4) To establish needed credit and marketing facilities; and

      (5) To improve services and administration.

3. The United States will assist in carrying out these short-term measures with a view to achieving concrete results from the Alliance for Progress at the earliest possible moment. In connection with the measures set forth above, and in accordance with the statement of President Kennedy, the United States will provide assistance under the Alliance, including assistance for the financing of short-term measures, totalling more than one billion dollars in the year ending March 1962.

Chapter IV. External Assistance in Support of National Development Programs

1. The economic and social development of Latin America will require a large amount of additional public and private financial assistance on the part of capital-exporting countries, including the members of the Development

coming ten years of at least 20 billion dollars be made available to the Latin American countries, with priority to the relatively less developed countries. The greater part of this sum should be in public funds.

5. That institutions in both the public and private sectors, including labor organizations, cooperatives, and commercial, industrial, and financial institutions, be strengthened and improved for the increasing and effective use of domestic resources, and that the social reforms necessary to permit a fair distribution of the fruits of economic and social progress be carried out.

Chapter II. National Development Programs

1. Participating Latin American countries agree to introduce or strengthen systems for the preparation, execution, and periodic revision of national programs for economic and social development consistent with the principles, objectives, and requirements contained in this document. Participating Latin American countries should formulate, if possible within the next eighteen months, long-term development programs. Such programs should embrace, according to the characteristics of each country, the elements outlined in the Appendix.

2. National development programs should incorporate self-help efforts directed toward:

a. Improvement of human resources and widening of opportunities by raising general standards of education and health; improving and extending technical education and professional training with emphasis on science and technology; providing adequate remuneration for work performed, encouraging the talents of managers, entrepreneurs, and wage earners; providing more productive employment for under-employed manpower; establishing effective systems of labor relations, and procedures for consultation and collaboration among public authorities, employer associations, and labor organizations; promoting the establishment and expansion of local institutions for basic and applied research; and improving the standards of public administration.

b. Wider development and more efficient use of natural resources, especially those which are now idle or under-utilized, including measures for the processing of raw materials.

c. The strengthening of the agricultural base, progressively extending the benefits of the land to those who work it, and ensuring in countries with Indian populations the integration of these populations into the economic, social, and cultural processes of modern life. To carry out these aims, measures should be adopted, among others, to establish or improve, as the case may be, the following services: extension, credit, technical assistance, agricultural research and mechanization; health and education; storage and distribution; cooperatives and farmers' associations; and community development.

d. More effective, rational and equitable mobilization and use of financial resources through the reform of tax structures, including fair and adequate taxation of large incomes and real estate, and the strict application of measures to improve fiscal administration. Development programs should include the adaptation of budget expenditures to development needs, measures for the maintenance of price stability, the creation of essential credit facilities at reasonable rates of interest, and the encouragement of private savings.

Assistance Group and international lending agencies. The measures provided for in the Act of Bogotá and the new measures provided for in this Charter, are designed to create a framework within which such additional assistance can be provided and effectively utilized.

2. The United States will assist those participating countries whose development programs establish self-help measures and economic and social policies and programs consistent with the goals and principles of this Charter. To supplement the domestic efforts of such countries, the United States is prepared to allocate resources which, along with those anticipated from other external sources, will be of a scope and magnitude adequate to realize the goals envisaged in this Charter. Such assistance will be allocated to both social and economic development and, where appropriate, will take the form of grants or loans on flexible terms and conditions. The participating countries will request the support of other capital-exporting countries and appropriate institutions so that they may provide assistance for the attainment of these objectives.

3. The United States will help in the financing of technical assistance projects proposed by a participating country or by the General Secretariat of the Organization of American States for the purpose of:

    a. Providing experts contracted in agreement with the governments to work under their direction and to assist them in the preparation of specific investment projects and the strengthening of national mechanisms for preparing projects, using specialized engineering firms where appropriate;

    b. Carrying out, pursuant to existing agreements for cooperation among the General Secretariat of the Organization of American States, the Economic Commission for Latin America, and the Inter-American Development Bank, field investigations and studies, including those relating to development problems, the organization of national agencies for the preparation of development programs, agrarian reform and rural development, health, cooperatives, housing, education and professional training, and taxation and tax administration; and

    c. Convening meetings of experts and officials on development and related problems.

The governments or abovementioned organizations should, when appropriate, seek the cooperation of the United Nations and its specialized agencies in the execution of these activities.

4. The participating Latin American countries recognize that each has in varying degree a capacity to assist fellow republics by providing technical and financial assistance. They recognize that this capacity will increase as their economies grow. They therefore affirm their intention to assist fellow republics increasingly as their individual circumstances permit.

Chapter V. Organization and Procedures

1. In order to provide technical assistance for the formulation of development programs, as may be requested by participating nations, the Organization of American States, the Economic Commission for Latin America, and the Inter-American Development Bank will continue and strengthen their agreements for coordination in this field, in order to have available a group of programming experts whose service can be used to facilitate the imple-

mentation of this Charter. The participating countries will also seek an intensification of technical assistance from the specialized agencies of the United Nations for the same purpose.

2. The Inter-American Economic and Social Council, on the joint nomination of the Secretary General of the Organization of American States, the Chairman of the Inter-American Committee on the Alliance for Progress, the President of the Inter-American Development Bank, and the Executive Secretary of the United Nations Economic Commission for Latin America, will appoint a panel of nine high-level experts, exclusively on the basis of their experience, technical ability, and competence in the various aspects of economic and social development. The experts may be of any nationality, though if of Latin American origin an appropriate geographical distribution will be sought. They will be attached to the Inter-American Economic and Social Council, but will nevertheless enjoy complete autonomy in the performance of their assigned duties. For administrative purposes and the purposes of better organization of its work, the Panel shall elect from among themselves a Coordinator. The Secretary General of the Organization of American States and the Coordinator shall conclude the agreements of a technical or administrative nature necessary for operations.

Four, at most, of the nine members may hold other remunerative positions that in the judgment of the officials who propose them, do not conflict with their responsibilities as independent experts. The Coordinator may not hold any other remunerative position. When not serving as members of ad hoc committees, the experts may be requested by the Coordinator to perform high-level tasks in connection with planning; the evaluation of plans; and execution of such plans. The Panel may also be requested to perform other high-level, specific tasks in its advisory capacity to the Inter-American Committee on the Alliance for Progress by the Chairman of that Committee, through the Coordinator of the Panel, provided such tasks are not incompatible with the functions set forth in paragraph 4. In the performance of such tasks the experts shall enjoy unquestioned autonomy in judgments, evaluations and recommendations that they may make.

The experts who perform their duties during only part of the year shall do so for a minimum of 110 days per year and shall receive a standard lump-sum payment in proportion to the annual remuneration, emoluments, and benefits of the other members of the Panel.

That proportion shall be set by the Secretary General within the authorizations provided in the budget of the OAS.

Each time the coordinator requires the services of the members of the Panel, they shall begin to provide them within a reasonable period.

The appointment of the members of the Panel will be for a period of at least one and not more than three years, and may be renewed.

3. Each government, if it so wishes, may present its program for economic and social development for consideration by an ad hoc committee, composed of no more than three members drawn from the Panel of Experts referred to in the preceding paragraph together with one or more experts not on the Panel, if the interested government so desires, provided that the number of such experts shall not exceed the number of those drawn from the Panel. The experts who compose the ad hoc committee will be appointed by the

Secretary General of the Organization of American States at the request of the interested government and with its consent. The Chairman of such ad hoc committee shall be one of the members of the Panel of Experts.

4. The Committee will study the development program, exchange opinions with the interested government as to possible modifications and, with the consent of the government, report its conclusions to the Inter-American Committee on the Alliance for Progress, to the Inter-American Development Bank, and to other governments and institutions that may be prepared to extend external financial and technical assistance in connection with the execution of the program. At the request of the interested government, the Panel will also reevaluate the development program.

5. In considering a development program presented to it, the ad hoc committee will examine the consistency of the program with the principles of the Act of Bogotá and of this Charter, taking into account the elements in the Appendix.

6. The General Secretariat of the Organization of American States will provide the technical and administrative services needed by the experts referred to in paragraphs 2 and 3 of this chapter in order to fulfill their tasks, in accordance with the agreements provided for in Point 2. The personnel for these services may be employed specifically for this purpose or may be made available from the permanent staffs of the Organization of American States, the Economic Commission for Latin America, and the Inter-American Development Bank, in accordance with the present liaison arrangements between the three organizations. The General Secretariat of the Organization of American States may seek arrangements with the United Nations Secretariat, its specialized agencies, and the Inter-American Specialized Organizations for the temporary assignment of necessary personnel.

7. A government whose development program has been the object of recommendations made by the ad hoc committee with respect to external financing requirements may submit the program to the Inter-American Development Bank so that the Bank may undertake the negotiations required to obtain such financing, including the organization of a consortium of credit institutions and governments disposed to contribute to the continuing and systematic financing, on appropriate terms, of the development program. However, the government will have full freedom to resort through any other channels to all sources of financing, for the purpose of obtaining, in full or in part, the required resources.

The ad hoc committee shall not interfere with the right of each government to formulate its own goals, priorities, and reforms in its national development programs.

The recommendations of the ad hoc committee will be of great importance in determining the distribution of public funds under the Alliance for Progress which contribute to the external financing of such programs. These recommendations shall give special consideration to Title I.1.

The participating governments and the Inter-American Committee on the Alliance for Progress will also use their good offices to the end that these recommendations may be accepted as a factor of great importance in the decisions taken, for the same purpose, by inter-American credit institutions, other international credit agencies, and other friendly governments which may be potential sources of capital.

8. The Inter-American Economic and Social Council will review annually the progress achieved in the formulation, national implementation, and international financing of development programs; and will submit to the Council of the Organization of American States such recommendations as it deems pertinent.

APPENDIX

ELEMENTS OF NATIONAL DEVELOPMENT PROGRAMS

1. The establishment of mutually consistent targets to be aimed at over the program period in expanding productive capacity in industry, agriculture, mining, transport, power and communications, and in improving conditions of urban and rural life, including better housing, education, and health.

2. The assignment of priorities and the description of methods to achieve the targets, including specific measures and major projects. Specific development projects should be justified in terms of their relative costs and benefits, including their contribution to social productivity.

3. The measures which will be adopted to direct the operations of the public sector and to encourage private action in support of the development program.

4. The estimated cost, in national and foreign currency, of major projects and of the development program as a whole, year by year over the program period.

5. The internal resources, public and private, estimated to become available for the execution of the programs.

6. The direct and indirect effects of the program on the balance of payments, and the external financing, public and private, estimated to be required for the execution of the program.

7. The basic fiscal and monetary policies to be followed in order to permit implementation of the program within a framework of price stability.

8. The machinery of public administration—including relationships with local governments, decentralized agencies and nongovernmental organizations, such as labor organizations, cooperatives, business and industrial organizations—to be used in carrying out the program, adapting it to changing circumstances and evaluating the progress made.

TITLE III

ECONOMIC INTEGRATION OF LATIN AMERICA

The American republics consider that the broadening of present national markets in Latin America is essential to accelerate the process of economic development in the Hemisphere. It is also an appropriate means for obtaining greater productivity through specialized and complementary industrial production which will, in turn, facilitate the attainment of greater social benefits for the inhabitants of the various regions of Latin America. The broadening of markets will also make possible the better use of resources under the Alliance for Progress. Consequently, the American republics recognize that:

1. The Montevideo Treaty (because of its flexibility and because it is open to the adherence of all of the Latin American nations) and the Central American Treaty on Economic Integration are appropriate instruments for

the attainment of these objectives, as was recognized in Resolution No. 11 (III) of the Ninth Session of the Economic Commission for Latin America.

2. The integration process can be intensified and accelerated not only by the specialization resulting from the broadening of markets through the liberalization of trade but also through the use of such instruments as the agreements for complementary production within economic sectors provided for in the Montevideo Treaty.

3. In order to insure the balanced and complementary economic expansion of all of the countries involved, the integration process should take into account, on a flexible basis, the condition of countries at a relatively less advanced stage of economic development, permitting them to be granted special, fair, and equitable treatment.

4. In order to facilitate economic integration in Latin America, it is advisable to establish effective relationships between the Latin American Free Trade Association and the group of countries adhering to the Central American Economic Integration Treaty, as well as between either of these groups and other Latin American countries. These arrangements should be established within the limits determined by these instruments.

5. The Latin American countries should coordinate their actions to meet the unfavorable treatment accorded to their foreign trade in world markets, particularly that resulting from certain restrictive and discriminatory policies of extracontinental countries and economic groups.

6. In the application of resources under the Alliance for Progress, special attention should be given not only to investments for multinational projects that will contribute to strengthening the integration process in all its aspects, but also to the necessary financing of industrial production, and to the growing expansion of trade in industrial products within Latin America.

7. In order to facilitate the participation of countries at a relatively low stage of economic development in multinational Latin American economic cooperation programs, and in order to promote the balanced and harmonious development of the Latin American integration process, special attention should be given to the needs of these countries in the administration of financial resources provided under the Alliance for Progress, particularly in connection with infrastructure programs and the promotion of new lines of production.

8. The economic integration process implies a need for additional investment in various fields of economic activity and funds provided under the Alliance for Progress should cover these needs as well as those required for the financing of national development programs.

9. When groups of Latin American countries have their own institutions for financing economic integration, the financing referred to in the preceding paragraph should preferably be channeled through these institutions. With respect to regional financing designed to further the purposes of existing regional integration instruments, the cooperation of the Inter-American Development Bank should be sought in channeling extra-regional contributions which may be granted for these purposes.

10. One of the possible means for making effective a policy for the financing of Latin American integration would be to approach the International Monetary Fund and other financial sources with a view to providing a means

for solving temporary balance-of-payments problems that may occur in countries participating in economic integration arrangements.

11. The promotion and coordination of transportation and communications systems is an effective way to accelerate the integration process. In order to counteract abusive practices in relation to freight rates and tariffs, it is advisable to encourage the establishment of multinational transport and communication enterprises in the Latin American countries, or to find other appropriate solutions.

12. In working toward economic integration and complementary economies, efforts should be made to achieve an appropriate coordination of national plans, or to engage in joint planning for various economies through the existing regional integration organizations. Efforts should also be made to promote an investment policy directed to the progressive elimination of unequal growth rates in the different geographic areas, particularly in the case of countries which are relatively less developed.

13. It is necessary to promote the development of national Latin American enterprises, in order that they may compete on an equal footing with foreign enterprises.

14. The active participation of the private sector is essential to economic integration and development, and except in those countries in which free enterprise does not exist, development planning by the pertinent national public agencies, far from hindering such participation, can facilitate and guide it, thus opening new perspectives for the benefit of the community.

15. As the countries of the Hemisphere still under colonial domination achieve their independence, they should be invited to participate in Latin American economic integration programs.

TITLE IV

BASIC EXPORT COMMODITIES

The American republics recognize that the economic development of Latin America requires expansion of its trade, a simultaneous and corresponding increase in foreign exchange incomes received from exports, a lessening of cyclical or seasonal fluctuations in the incomes of those countries that still depend heavily on the export of raw materials, and the correction of the secular deterioration in their terms of trade.

They therefore agree that the following measures should be taken:

Chapter I. National Measures
National measures affecting commerce in primary products should be directed and applied in order to:

1. Avoid undue obstacles to the expansion of trade in these products;
2. Avoid market instability;
3. Improve the efficiency of international plans and mechanisms for stabilization; and
4. Increase their present markets and expand their area of trade at a rate compatible with rapid development.

Therefore:

A. Importing member countries should reduce and if possible eliminate, as soon as feasible, all restrictions and discriminatory practices affecting the consumption and importation of primary products, including those with the highest possible degree of processing in the country of origin, except when these restrictions are imposed temporarily for purposes of economic diversification, to hasten the economic development of less developed nations, or to establish basic national reserves. Importing countries should also be ready to support, by adequate regulations, stabilization programs for primary products that may be agreed upon with producing countries.

B. Industrialized countries should give special attention to the need for hastening economic development of less developed countries. There-fore, they should make maximum efforts to create conditions, com-patible with their international obligations, through which they may extend advantages to less developed countries so as to permit the rapid expansion of their markets. In view of the great need for this rapid development, industrialized countries should also study ways in which to modify, wherever possible, international commitments which prevent the achievement of this objective.

C. Producing member countries should formulate their plans for produc-tion and export, taking account of their effect on world markets and of the necessity of supporting and improving the effectiveness of inter-national stabilization programs and mechanisms. Similarly they should try to avoid increasing the uneconomic production of goods which can be obtained under better conditions in the less developed countries of the Continent, in which the production of these goods is an important source of employment.

D. Member countries should adopt all necessary measures to direct techno-logical studies toward finding new uses and by-products of those primary commodities that are most important to their economies.

E. Member countries should try to reduce, and, if possible, eliminate within a reasonable time export subsidies and other measures which cause instability in the markets for basic commodities and excessive fluctuations in prices and income.

Chapter II. International Cooperation Measures
  1. Member countries should make coordinated, and if possible, joint efforts designed:
    a. To eliminate as soon as possible undue protection of the produc-tion of basic products;
    b. To eliminate taxes and reduce excessive domestic prices which discourage the consumption of imported basic products;
    c. To seek to end preferential agreements and other measures which limit world consumption of Latin American basic products and their access to international markets, especially the markets of Western European countries in process of economic integration, and of countries with centrally planned economies; and
    d. To adopt the necessary consultation mechanisms so that their marketing policies will not have damaging effects on the stability of the markets for basic commodities.
  2. Industrialized countries should give maximum cooperation to less

developed countries so that their raw material exports will have undergone the greatest degree of processing that is economic.

3. Through their representation in international financial organizations, member countries should suggest that these organizations, when considering loans for the promotion of production for export, take into account the effect of such loans on products which are in surplus in world markets.

4. Member countries should support the efforts being made by international commodity study groups and by the Commission on International Commodity Trade of the United Nations. In this connection, it should be considered that producing and consuming nations bear a joint responsibility for taking national and international steps to reduce market instability.

5. The Secretary General of the Organization of American States shall convene a group of experts appointed by their respective governments to meet before November 30, 1961 and to report, not later than March 31, 1962 on measures to provide an adequate and effective means of offsetting the effects of fluctuations in the volume and prices of exports of basic products. The experts shall:

   a. Consider the questions regarding compensatory financing raised during the present meeting;

   b. Analyze the proposal for establishing an international fund for the stabilization of export receipts contained in the Report of the Group of Experts to the Special Meeting of the Inter-American Economic and Social Council, as well as any other alternative proposals;

   c. Prepare a draft plan for the creation of mechanisms for compensatory financing. This draft plan should be circulated among the member Governments and their opinions obtained well in advance of the next meeting of the Commission on International Commodity Trade.

6. Member countries should support the efforts under way to improve and strengthen international commodity agreements and should be prepared to cooperate in the solution of specific commodity problems. Furthermore, they should endeavor to adopt adequate solutions for the short- and long-term problems affecting markets for such commodities so that the economic interests of producers and consumers are equally safeguarded.

7. Member countries should request other producer and consumer countries to cooperate in stabilization programs, bearing in mind that the raw materials of the Western Hemisphere are also produced and consumed in other parts of the world.

8. Member countries recognize that the disposal of accumulated reserves and surpluses can be a means of achieving the goals outlined in the first chapter of this Title, provided that, along with the generation of local resources, the consumption of essential products in the receiving countries is immediately increased. The disposal of surpluses and reserves should be carried out in an orderly manner, in order to:

    a. Avoid disturbing existing commercial markets in member countries, and

    b. Encourage expansion of the sale of their products to other markets.

However, it is recognized that:

    a. The disposal of surpluses should not displace commercial sales of identical products traditionally carried out by other countries; and

    b. Such disposal cannot substitute for large scale financial and technical assistance programs.

IN WITNESS WHEREOF this Charter is signed, in Punta del Este, Uruguay, on the seventeenth day of August, nineteen hundred sixty-one.

The original texts shall be deposited in the archives of the Pan American Union, through the Secretary General of the Special Meeting, in order that certified copies may be sent to the Governments of the Member States of the Organization of American States.

19. RESOLUTION ON THE CREATION OF THE INTER-AMERICAN COMMITTEE ON THE ALLIANCE FOR PROGRESS (CIAP) (1963)

WHEREAS:

The First Annual Meeting of the Inter-American Economic and Social Council adopted Resolution A-8, calling for a study of the inter-American system in order to ascertain whether its present structure meets the requirements of the Alliance for Progress program;

Resolution A-8 begins by recognizing "that the inter-American system as presently constituted, was in the main established prior to the Alliance for Progress, and, in consequence, may not possess a type of structure permitting of achievement of the objectives of the Charter of Punta del Este in the dynamic and efficient way called for";

That resolution charged two outstanding Latin Americans with studying the structure and activities of those organizations and agencies of the inter-American system that have responsibilities in regard to the Alliance, and empowered them to make, if necessary, recommendations regarding those structural and procedural changes that are required in the system and in its various organs in order that the Alliance for Progress may take on the efficiency and the dynamic qualities called for by the Charter of Punta del Este;

The Council of the Organization, after approving Resolution A-8, entrusted the former presidents of Brazil and Colombia, Juscelino Kubitschek and Alberto Lleras, with the preparation of a report and conclusions, to be brought to the attention of the governments of the member states and submitted to the Inter-American Economic and Social Council for consideration, if need be, at a special meeting;

Former presidents Kubitschek and Lleras accepted and carried out the mandate of the Inter-American Economic and Social Council, and rendered their conclusions in separate reports presented to the Council of the Organization, for transmittal to the governments at the Special Meeting held on June 15, 1963;

The reports of former presidents Kubitschek and Lleras, which have been presented to the Second Annual Meetings of the Inter-American Economic and Social Council for consideration, are in agreement regarding the need to create a permanent, multilateral body representing the Alliance for Progress, and for this purpose proposed the creation of an inter-American development committee;

The recommendations of the former presidents, which have been examined by the Inter-American Economic and Social Council, suggest ways of organizing the proposed new body so that the Alliance for Progress may have multilateral representations and possess functional mechanisms and sufficient authority to permit it to discharge its responsibilities with the dynamic qualities and efficiency required; and

Consideration has been given to the views expressed in this regard in the Memorandum of the General Secretariat of the Organization of American States (Doc. OEA/Ser.H/X.4, CIES/344), the Report of the Panel of Experts (Doc. OEA/Ser.H/X.4, CIES/370), and the Observations of the Board of Executive Directors of the Inter-American Development Bank,

The Second Annual Meeting of the Inter-American Economic and Social Council at the Ministerial Level,

RESOLVES:

To create an Inter-American Committee on the Alliance for Progress (CIAP), in accordance with the following provisions:

I. NATURE AND PURPOSE

1. The Inter-American Committee on the Alliance for Progress (CIAP) shall be a special, permanent committee of the Inter-American Economic and Social Council for the purpose of representing multilaterally the Alliance for Progress and, in the same way, coordinating and promoting its implementation in accordance with the Charter of Punta del Este, and of carrying out the mandate of this resolution and those it receives from the Council of the Organization of American States or the Inter-American Economic and Social Council.

II. DUTIES AND FUNCTIONS

2. The Inter-American Committee on the Alliance for Progress shall carry out its duties and functions in keeping with the general orientation and lines of policy established by the Inter-American Economic and Social Council in its meetings at the ministerial level.

3. To fulfill the purpose set forth in the preceding chapter, the Inter-American Committee on the Alliance for Progress shall have the following duties and functions:

   a. To study the problems that may arise in connection with the Alliance for Progress and to resolve them or suggest solutions to the competent authority in each case, in accordance with the standards and policies established therefor.
   b. To promote continuing improvements in the process of giving the Alliance a more multilateral character.
   c. To make an annual estimate of the financing actually needed for Latin American development and of the total funds that may be available from the various domestic and external sources.
   d. To make a continuing review of national and regional plans, steps taken, and efforts made within the framework of the Alliance, and to make specific recommendations to the members of the Alliance and to the regional organizations in the Hemisphere concerning those plans, steps and efforts. In discharging this duty, consideration shall be given to the evaluation reports of the ad hoc committees set up under the Charter of Punta del Este or those deriving from steps taken pursuant to paragraph 9 of this resolution.
   e. On the basis of the estimates referred to in paragraph 3.c and the review and the recommendations referred to in paragraph 3.d:
      i. To prepare and present proposals on the amount and sort of domestic resources each country would have to utilize to achieve the objectives of the Alliance, and

ii. To prepare and present annual proposals for determining the distribution among the several countries of public funds under the Alliance for Progress, referred to in Chapter V.7 of Title II of the Charter of Punta del Este, which contribute to the external financing of general plans and specific programs for the development of the Latin American countries, giving special consideration to the progress which, in line with its basic characteristics, each country makes toward reaching the objectives of the Charter of Punta del Este, and being especially mindful of Title I.1 of the Charter.

f. To cooperate with each country and with the Inter-American Development Bank or other financial agents which the country may designate, in their negotiations with governments and with any other source of financing for the purpose of obtaining the external assistance required to finance their development programs and plans.

g. To coordinate those efforts within the Alliance which require multilateral action, such as economic integration, foreign trade policies of the area, and, in general, those activities which are related to the economic and social development of Latin America and which are not specifically assigned to any other body.

h. To obtain information on the progress made in multilateral investment programs for integration purposes and, upon request by the countries concerned, to help in obtaining financing for such investments; in accordance with established criteria and procedures.

i. To coordinate the work of the special committees of the Inter-American Economic and Social Council and to decide upon the necessity for their meetings, which shall be convoked by the Chairman of the Inter-American Committee on the Alliance for Progress.

j. To review the budget of the Pan American Union for the Alliance for Progress, the budget of the Program of Technical Cooperation, and that of any other specific multilateral fund, as prepared by the General Secretariat for approval by the Inter-American Economic and Social Council.

k. To review the program and budget prepared by the Secretary General with respect to the regular operations of the Secretriat within the purview of the Inter-American Economic and Social Council—including the items for permanent professional and administrative personnel; for the operation of the Inter-American Economic and Social Council, the Inter-American Committee on the Alliance for Progress, and the Panel of Experts and for overhead directly related to these operations—for approval by the Inter-American Economic and Social Council, in accordance with Article 19.f of its Statutes.

l. To establish its Regulations and the rules of procedure it considers advisable for the performance of its functions.

4. The member states agree that, when providing financial and technical assistance through their own agencies and when instructing their representatives in the various international organizations that provide such assistance, they shall give special consideration to the recommendations of the Inter-American Committee on the Alliance for Progress, in accordance with paragraph 3.e (ii), regarding the distribution of external public funds under the Alliance for Progress.

III. MEMBERSHIP AND OPERATION

5. The Inter-American Committee on the Alliance for Progress shall be composed of a chairman and seven representatives of the member states of the Organization of American States. Each representative shall be entitled to one vote.

The chairman shall be elected for a three-year period and shall be eligible for re-election for one term only.

The representatives of the countries, proposed thereby, shall be appointed by the Inter-American Economic and Social Council for a two-year period, on the basis of the same distribution agreed upon for electing the Executive Directors of the Inter-American Development Bank (IDB) at the election immediately prior to each period. Such distribution shall not apply to the five countries of Central America, which, as a group, shall propose one representative.

At the time of the first appointment, three of the six members who represent the Latin American countries shall be selected by lot to serve for one year.

A member of the Inter-American Committee on the Alliance for Progress may be re-elected only in the event that the countries which proposed their appointment indicate to the Inter-American Economic and Social Council that this be done.

When in the exercise of its functions the Inter-American Committee on the Alliance for Progress is to consider matters specifically concerning a given country, it shall invite that country to appoint an ad hoc representative.

6. The Secretary General of the Organization of American States (OAS), the President of the Inter-American Development Bank (IDB), the Coordinator of the Panel of Experts, and the Principal Director of the Economic Commission for Latin America (ECLA) shall serve as permanent advisors to the Inter-American Committee on the Alliance for Progress and in that capacity may attend its meetings.

7. The Panel of Experts shall be the technical arm of the Inter-American Committee on the Alliance for Progress in carrying out its functions of evaluating development plans and programs, in the spirit of the provisions of Title II, Chapter V.3 of the Charter of Punta del Este, and, in general, it may be consulted by the Inter-American Committee on the Alliance for Progress in relation to other matters relating to its functions. The Inter-American Development Bank shall be the technical arm of the Committee in matters concerning the financing of Latin American development.

The Inter-American Committee on the Alliance for Progress may request the technical advice of the Latin American Free Trade Association (LAFTA) and the Permanent Secretariat of the General Treaty on Central American Economic Integration (SIECA) on matters of economic integration.

8. In conformity with existing provisions, the Inter-American Committee on the Alliance for Progress may invite representatives of governmental and non-governmental agencies, who are recognized international authorities and who may have a particular interest in matters to be taken up at given meetings, to attend these meetings as observers. The Organization for Economic Cooperation and Development (OECD) and the European Economic Community (EEC) shall be among the entities to be so invited.

9. Those countries which have only sectoral programs and those which have national development plans but do not request the formation of an ad hoc committee may come to an agreement with the Inter-American Committee on the Alliance for Progress as to the best way of evaluating their programs or plans in consonance with the aims of the Charter of Punta del Este.

10. In order to ensure more frequent information on the progress of the activities of the Inter-American Committee on the Alliance for Progress, the Chairman of the Inter-American Economic and Social Council, pursuant to Article 20 of its Statutes, shall convoke special meetings of the Inter-American Economic and Social Council at the ministerial level, when such shall be considered necessary.

11. The Inter-American Committee on the Alliance for Progress shall submit to the Inter-American Economic and Social Council for consideration an annual report on the fulfillment of its mandate and the draft resolutions that it may agree upon.

IV. CHAIRMAN

12. The Inter-American Economic and Social Council at the Ministerial Level shall elect an outstanding personality of the nationality of one of its members to be chairman of the Inter-American Committee on the Alliance for Progress. In addition to the functions and powers normal to the position, and to those which may be entrusted to him by the Inter-American Economic and Social Council and, on occasion by the Council of the Organization of American States, the Chairman shall be the permanent representative of the Inter-American Committee on the Alliance for Progress in actions required for rapid and effective execution of its decisions.

In the discharge of his duties, the Chairman shall be responsible only to the Inter-American Committee on the Alliance for Progress and the Inter-American Economic and Social Council.

The Chairman shall take office at a special ceremony in the presence of the Council of the Organization of American States.

V. SECRETARIAT AND HEADQUARTERS

13. The Executive Secretary of the Inter-American Economic and Social Council shall be the Secretary of the Inter-American Committee on the Alliance for Progress. Secretariat services shall be provided by the General Secretariat. Whenever the Chairman of the Inter-American Committee on the Alliance for Progress considers it indispensable to enlist the services of additional personnel in order to carry out the functions of the Committee more efficiently, he may request the Secretary General of the Organization of American States to take the necessary steps to appoint suitable persons.

14. The Inter-American Committee on the Alliance for Progress shall have its headquarters in Washington, D.C., United States of America, but it may hold meetings in any other city in the member states of the Organization of American States.

20. STATUTES OF THE
SPECIAL DEVELOPMENT ASSISTANCE FUND
(1964)

WHEREAS:

The Inter-American Committee on the Alliance for Progress has presented draft statutes for the establishment of the Special Development Assistance Fund,

The Third Annual Meeting of the Inter-American Economic and Social Council at the Ministerial Level
RESOLVES:

1. To approve the text of the Statutes of the Special Development Assistance Fund appended to this resolution.

2. To request the Inter-American Committee on the Alliance for Progress to study, in consultation with its permanent advisers, the operation of the Special Fund on a continuing basis and, if necessary, to present amendments to the Statutes to the Fourth Meeting of the Inter-American Economic and Social Council to facilitate achievement of the purposes of the Special Development Assistance Fund in the most effective and economical way possible.

APPENDIX

STATUTES OF THE SPECIAL DEVELOPMENT ASSISTANCE FUND
OBJECTIVES AND ACTIVITIES

ARTICLE 1

The Special Development Assistance Fund is established as a multilateral fund for financing the activities of the Alliance for Progress specified in Article 2. Such activities should not duplicate or replace those that are included in the regular program and budget of the General Secretariat or in programs of other agencies.

ARTICLE 2

The activities referred to in the preceding article shall be as follows:

a. To organize or carry out studies in the member states of the Organization of American States on general or specific problems related to planning and development, in coordination with the other agencies working in the same field;

b. To hold meetings of experts or governmental officials to consider the problems specified in (a) above, or to take cognizance of the results of the studies carried out;

c. To provide for the establishment and functioning of ad hoc committees for evaluating national development plans, at the request of the countries, and for other related activities;

Note: In the text certain shortened designations have been used. These terms, with their equivalents, are as follows:

Fund: Special Development Assistance Fund
IA-ECOSOC: Inter-American Economic and Social Council
CIAP: Inter-American Committee on the Alliance for Progress
Chairman: Chairman of CIAP

Secretary General: Secretary General of the Organization of American
    States
General Secretariat: General Secretariat of the Organization of American
    States
Executive Secretary: Executive Secretary of the Inter-American Economic
    and Social Council (Executive Secretary of CIAP)

d. To provide technical assistance, at the request of the countries, in coordination with other agencies working in the same field;

e. To provide technical services, at the request of the countries, in coordination with other agencies working in the same field, for the preparation
of feasibility studies on specific investment projects, the cost of which
must be reimbursed if financing for the projects is obtained;

f. To conduct informational activities and programs to promote the
Alliance for Progress, under the general policies approved by the Inter-
American Economic and Social Council (IA-ECOSOC) and the Inter-
American Committee on the Alliance for Progress (CIAP);

g. To conduct training and other activities related to the Program of
Technical Cooperation of the Organization of American States;

h. To promote training programs, within and without the Hemisphere, in
subjects related to economic and social progress; and

i. To provide for execution of such other programs or activities as
IA-ECOSOC may approve.

ORGANIZATION

ARTICLE 3

The Fund shall be organized and financed by the IA-ECOSOC and shall
be administered under its authority.

ARTICLE 4

IA-ECOSOC shall establish the general policy for the activities and operations of the Fund; accept the pledges of voluntary contributions from the
member states; approve the annual Program-Budget of the Fund; and
review the annual report, including that of the external auditors, on the
activities of the Fund. IA-ECOSOC shall, likewise, review the projections of
the program for the ensuing two years and make such comments and recommendations thereon as it deems appropriate.

ARTICLE 5

In its capacity as a special, permanent committee of IA-ECOSOC, with
functions of coordinating the implementation of the Alliance for Progress,
CIAP or its Chairman shall:

a. Provide the Secretary General with guidelines covering activities to be
included in the annual Program-Budget of the Fund and criteria covering priorities to be observed in formulating such program-budgets,
within the framework of general policies set by IA-ECOSOC;

b. Review the annual Program-Budget prepared by the Secretary General,
with the advice of the Chairman, in the light of established criteria, and
present to IA-ECOSOC its conclusions and recommendations thereon;

c. Review the annual report on the operation of the Fund, and present to
IA-ECOSOC its evaluation of the activities carried out and its recommendations for improving the performance of the Fund;

d. Present to the Secretary General such recommendations as it deems advisable for inclusion in, or amendment of, the Regulations of the Fund;

e. Advise the Secretary General in the preparation of the Regulations and the projects to be carried out with resources of the Fund and approve those in excess of $50,000; and

f. Advise the General Secretariat, through the Executive Secretary of CIAP, regarding the operations and activities of the Fund, presenting the recommendations that it deems advisable.

ARTICLE 6

The Secretary General shall be responsible to the IA-ECOSOC for the administration of the Fund and the execution of its activities. To this end he shall receive the contributions from the member states and other sources; issue the Regulations of the Fund, after consulting with the Chairman; approve agreements relative to the operation of the Fund; and approve, after consulting the Chairman, the draft annual Program-Budget of the Fund.

ARTICLE 7

Under the direction of the Secretary General, the Executive Secretary shall:

a. Have over-all authority and responsibility for the planning, coordination, and execution of the activities of the Fund, in accordance with these Statutes;

b. Work out agreements regarding contributions to the Fund, and present them to the Secretary General for his approval, along with any recommendations he deems pertinent;

c. Prepare an annual estimate of the sums expected to be available for financing the program of the Fund;

d. Prepare the draft annual Program-Budget of the Fund, with the assistance of appropriate units of the General Secretariat, and present it to the Secretary General together with his proposals regarding priorities and levels of financing; and, after it has been approved by the Secretary General, present the proposed annual Program-Budget to CIAP for review and to IA-ECOSOC at its annual meeting for final approval;

e. Prepare the Annual Report on the activities of the Fund for presentation to IA-ECOSOC, and periodic reports thereon for presentation to the Secretary General and to the Chairman;

f. Propose to the Secretary General such amendments to the Regulations as may be required to facilitate execution of the activities of the Fund; and

g. Coordinate the recruitment of professional personnel and make recommendations to the Secretary General regarding their appointment or engagement by contract.

FINANCING

ARTICLE 8

The activities of the Fund shall be financed with the following contributions:

a. Voluntary contributions, which shall be pledged annually by member states of the Organization of American States, preferably at the Annual Meeting of the Inter-American Economic and Social Council at the

Ministerial Level, and which may not be earmarked in whole or in part for particular activities;

b. Special contributions in cash, personnel, equipment, materials, and services made by the governments of the member states to assist in covering the local costs for specific projects. Such contributions shall not be considered part of the pledges made under (a) above; and

c. Contributions in cash or kind, from non-member governments and from other sources, both private or public.

The Fund will also receive the income derived from interest on its bank balances and other liquid assets, from sale of publications financed by the Fund, and from repayments for refundable activities, such as the preparation of projects for which financing has been obtained. These miscellaneous items of income will accrue to the reserve account.

ARTICLE 9

Pledges for voluntary contributions shall be made in U.S. dollars, but the member states may make payments in other currencies, provided the Secretary General determines that such currencies equal the contribution promised and are usable by the Fund.

ARTICLE 10

Up to 10 percent of the amount of the budget approved for the current annual Program-Budget shall be set aside in a reserve account, primarily for the purpose of ensuring the normal and continuous functioning of the program.

Notwithstanding the provision of Article 11, this reserve may also be used to take care of unexpected increases in the approved budgets and for costs connected with unforeseen activities; however, in no case may the withdrawal for any approved projects exceed 10 percent of the budget approved for such project, nor the total of withdrawals exceed 5 percent of the total annual Program-Budget. Costs connected with unforeseen activities shall not exceed $10,000 per project.

The reserve account shall not exceed 25 percent of the annual Program-Budget. After the reserve has reached 25 percent of the annual Program-Budget, the budget shall include for this purpose those amounts necessary to maintain the reserve at that level.

Withdrawals of funds from the reserve shall be approved by the Secretary General after consulting the Chairman. Such withdrawals shall be reported to IA-ECOSOC at its Annual Meeting.

ARTICLE 11

Funds may be allocated only for the purposes and within the amounts approved by IA-ECOSOC in the annual Program-Budget. IA-ECOSOC shall each year establish the percentage that can be transferred between projects in the approved budget.

The accounts of the Fund shall be kept separately from other accounts of the Pan American Union. Its assets may not be transferred to other funds.

ARTICLE 12

The Program-Budget of the Fund shall cover a twelve-month period. No fixed time limit is established for specific projects.

Projects included in the annual Program-Budget may be accompanied by a proposed plan of operations of up to three years in order to provide IA-ECOSOC with a basis for judging the implications of such projects.

ARTICLE 13

Any project forming part of the annual Program-Budget must have been favorably recommended by CIAP in order to be submitted to IA-ECOSOC for approval. Prior recommendation of CIAP is also required for any expansion or extension of projects included in the Program-Budgets of previous years, if such expansions or extensions were not provided for by IA-ECOSOC in adopting the project in its original form.

In the event that contributions to the Fund are not sufficient to cover the cost of projects included in the annual Program-Budget, CIAP shall determine which projects shall be carried out with the funds available. Apart from other criteria that may be taken into that determination, CIAP should endeavor to make certain, in the first place, that existing projects be fully implemented in the manner provided for when they were approved initially by IA-ECOSOC.

AUDITING AND EVALUATION

ARTICLE 14

IA-ECOSOC shall appoint external auditors of international reputation, who shall be engaged by the Secretary General to examine the accounts of the Fund. Their contract may be terminated only by decision of IA-ECOSOC. The auditors shall make their examination in accordance with the directives of IA-ECOSOC and standards of the General Secretariat.

ARTICLE 15

CIAP shall take the necessary measures for the conduct of periodic evaluations of the effectiveness of the Program of the Fund as a whole and of its component projects.

Evaluations shall be submitted to the Executive Secretary and by him to the Secretary General with any recommendations deemed pertinent. These evaluations shall be considered by CIAP in its annual review of the activities of the Fund.

REGULATIONS

ARTICLE 16

All activities of the Fund shall be carried out in accordance with these Statutes and the decisions of IA-ECOSOC. The Secretary General, in consultation with the Chairman, shall issue, within three months following the approval of these Statutes, Regulations, which shall include provisions on personnel and other administrative procedures, preparation of the budget, accounting, and evaluation, and such other provisions as may be necessary to attain the objectives of the Fund.

AMENDMENTS

ARTICLE 17

Amendments to these Statutes shall be proposed and adopted by IA-ECOSOC at its Annual Meeting at the Ministerial Level and may also be submitted by CIAP, by its Chairman on his own initiative, or by the Secretary General.

TRANSITORY ARTICLES

ARTICLE 1

The Fund shall commence operations on January 1, 1965.

ARTICLE 2

During the first year of operation of the Fund, the Program of Technical Cooperation shall be administered in conformity with its Bases as approved by IA-ECOSOC, except insofar as they are modified by, or may be incompatible with, the provisions of these Statutes. The Secretary General shall present to the next annual meeting of IA-ECOSOC such proposed amendments to the Bases as may be necessary to bring them into agreement with these Statutes.

ARTICLE 3

During the first year of operation those member states wishing to do so may make separate pledges to the Program of Technical Cooperation.

ARTICLE 4

During the first year, CIAP shall fix the percentage, provided for in Article 11, that may be transferred from one project to another in the approved budget, and shall appoint the external auditors referred to in Article 14.

21. GENERAL TREATY FOR CENTRAL AMERICAN ECONOMIC INTEGRATION (1960)

CHAPTER I

CENTRAL AMERICAN COMMON MARKET

ARTICLE I

The Contracting States agree to set up among themselves a common market which should be fully established in not more than five years from the date of the entry into force of this Treaty. They also undertake to set up a customs union among their territories.

ARTICE II

For the purposes of the previous Article, the Contracting Parties shall undertake to complete the establishment of a Central American free trade area within a period of five years and to adopt a uniform Central American tariff in accordance with the terms of the Central American Agreement on the Equalization of Import Duties and Charges.

CHAPTER II

TRADE REGIME

ARTICLE III

The signatory States shall grant free trade rights for all products originating in their respective territories, with the sole limitations included in the special regimes referred to in Annex A of this Treaty.

Accordingly, the natural products of the Contracting Countries and products manufactured in them shall be exempt from import and export duties, including consular fees, and all other taxes, surcharges and imposts levied on such imports and exports or on the occasion of their importation and exportation, whether such duties, fees, taxes, surcharges and imposts are national, municipal or of any other nature.

The exemptions provided for in this Article shall not include taxes or charges for lighterage, docking, warehousing and handling of goods or any other charges which may be legitimately levied by port, warehouse and transport services; nor shall they include exchange differentials resulting from the existence of two or more rates of exchange or from any other exchange measures adopted in any of the Contracting Countries.

Goods originating in the territory of the Contracting States shall be accorded national treatment in all of them and shall be exempt from any restrictions or measures of a quantitative nature, apart from control measures which are legally applicable in the territories of the Contracting States for reasons of a public health, security or police character.

ARTICLE IV

The Contracting Parties shall establish for given products special transitional arrangements excluding them from the direct free trade rights mentioned in Article III of this Treaty. Such products shall be automatically incorporated in the free trade regime not later than the end of the fifth year after the entry into force of this Treaty, except where specifically provided to the contrary in Annex A.

Annex A shall include products subject to special arrangements, trade in which shall comply with the conditions and requirements laid down therein. The said conditions and requirements may only be amended following multilateral negotiations in the Executive Council. Annex A shall form an integral part of this Treaty.

The signatory States shall agree that the Protocol to the Central American Agreement on the Equalization of Import Duties and Charges, concerning a Central American Preferential Tariff, shall not be applicable to trade in products subject to the special arrangements mentioned in this Article.

ARTICLE V

Goods which are accorded the advantages laid down in this Treaty must be covered by a customs form signed by the exporter which shall include a declaration of origin and shall be submitted for the visa of the customs officers of the countries of shipment and of destination, in accordance with the provisions laid down in Annex B of this Treaty.

When there is doubt regarding the origin of a product and the problem has not been settled by bilateral negotiations, either of the parties affected may ask the Executive Council to intervene in order to verify the origin of the said product. The Council shall not consider as originating in one of the Contracting Countries, those products which have come from or have been manufactured in a third country and have been merely assembled, packaged, bottled, cut up or diluted in the exporting country.

In the cases referred to in the previous paragraph, import of the goods concerned shall not be prevented, always provided that a guarantee is given to the importing country for the payment of the tariffs or other charges associated with the import. This guarantee shall become effective or shall be cancelled, as the case may be, when the problem has finally been settled.

The Executive Council shall establish, by means of regulations, the procedure to be followed in order to determine the origin of the goods.

ARTICLE VI

When the products in which trade is carried on are subject to charges, excise taxes or other internal duties of any kind, levied on production, sale, distribution or consumption in one of the Signatory Countries, the latter may impose an equal duty on goods of the same nature which it imports from another Contracting State, in which case it shall impose a duty of at least the same amount and under the same conditions, on imports coming from third countries.

The Contracting Parties agree that internal duties on consumption shall be established in accordance with the following conditions:

a) Such duties may be established for the amount deemed necessary when the article in question is produced nationally or when the said article is not produced in any of the Signatory States;

b) When an article is not produced in one of the Contracting Countries but is produced in another, the former may not levy duties on the consumption of the said article, except following a favorable decision by the Executive Council;

c) When one of the Parties has established an internal tax on consumption and production of the article thus taxed subsequently commences in one of the other Contracting Countries, although such production does not exist in the country imposing the tax, the Executive Council shall, if requested by the Party concerned, consider the case and report whether the existence of the tax is compatible with free trade. The States shall undertake to abolish, in conformity with their legal procedures, such taxes on consumption on receiving a notification calling for this from the Executive Council.

ARTICLE VII

None of the Signatory States shall establish or maintain regulations on the distribution or sale of goods originating in another Signatory State when such regulations tend to place or do in fact place the said goods in an unfavorable position *vis-à-vis* similar goods either of domestic origin or imported from any other country.

ARTICLE VIII

Articles which because of the internal arrangements of the Contracting Parties constitute state or other monopolies on the date of entry into force of this Treaty, shall remain subject to the relevant legal provisions in each country and, where applicable, to the conditions laid down in Annex A of this Treaty.

In the event of new monopolies being created or the regime governing existing ones being modified, consultations shall take place among the Parties with the aim of providing special rules for Central American trade in the corresponding articles.

CHAPTER III

EXPORT SUBSIDIES AND UNFAIR BUSINESS PRACTICES

ARTICLE IX

The governments of the Signatory States shall not grant exemptions or reductions in customs tariffs to imports coming from outside Central America when the articles concerned are produced in the Contracting States under satisfactory conditions.

When a Signatory State considers it is affected by the granting of customs exemption for imports, or by government imports which are not intended for the use of the government itself or of its institutions, it may submit the problem to the Executive Council, which shall consider it and come to a decision in the matter.

ARTICLE X

The Central Banks of the Signatory States shall closely cooperate in order to prevent currency speculations which might affect the exchange rates and so as to maintain the convertibility of the currencies of the respective countries on a basis which, under normal conditions, guarantees freedom, uniformity, and stability of exchange.

In the event of one of the Signatory States establishing quantitative restrictions on international monetary transfers, it shall adopt the necessary measures to ensure that such restrictions will not affect the other States in a discriminatory manner.

In the event of serious balance-of-payments difficulties which affect or might affect the monetary payment relations between the Signatory States, the Executive Council either *ex officio,* or at the request of one of the Parties, shall immediately study the problem in collaboration with the Central Banks, for the purpose of recommending to the Signatory Governments a satisfactory solution compatible with the maintenance of the multilateral free trade system.

ARTICLE XI

No Contracting State shall grant, directly or indirectly, any subsidy in favor of the export of goods intended for the territories of the other States, or establish or maintain any system resulting in the sale of a given commodity for export to another Contracting State at a price lower than the established price for the sale of the said commodity on the domestic market, making due allowance for differences in the conditions of sale and taxation, as well as for other factors affecting price comparability.

Any fixing of prices or price discrimination in one of the Signatory States shall be regarded as an indirect export subsidy if it results in the establishment of a sales price for a given commodity in the other Contracting States which is lower than that which would result from normal competition in the market of the exporting country.

When the import of products made in a Contracting State with raw materials acquired under monopoly conditions at artificially low prices might threaten the existing production in another Signatory State, the party which considers itself affected shall submit the problem for consideration by the Executive Council so that the latter can decide whether an unfair trade practice is actually involved. Within the five days following receipt of the request, the Executive Council shall issue a decision in the matter or authorize temporary suspension of free trade, while permitting trade subject to the provision of a guarantee for the amount of the customs dues. The said suspension shall be authorized for a period of 30 days, and the Council must issue a final decision before the expiry of this period. If no decision is reached within the five days laid down, the party affected may request a guarantee pending a final decision by the Executive Council. Tax exemptions of a general character granted by a Contracting State with a view to encouraging production shall, however, not be deemed to constitute an export subsidy.

Likewise, exemption from internal taxes on production, sales or consumption levied in the exporting country on goods exported to the territory of another State, shall not be deemed to constitute an export subsidy. Normally, the differences resulting from the sale of foreign exchange on the free market at a rate of exchange higher than the official rate shall not be deemed to be an export subsidy; but in case of doubt on the part of one of the Contracting States, the matter shall be submitted to the Executive Council for its consideration and opinion.

ARTICLE XII

Since it would be a practice contrary to the aims of this Treaty, each contracting State shall, through the legal means at its disposal, prevent the exportation of goods from its territory to that of the other States at a price lower than their normal value, if this would jeopardize or threaten to jeopardize production in the other countries or retard the establishment of a domestic or Central American industry.

A commodity shall be considered to be exported at a lower price than its normal value if the price of the said commodity is less than:

a) the comparable price, under normal trade conditions, for a similar commodity when intended for consumption in the domestic market of the exporting country; or

b) the highest comparable price for a similar commodity exported to a third country under normal trade conditions; or

c) the cost of production of the commodity in the country of origin plus a reasonable addition in respect of the sales cost and profit.

In each case, due allowance shall be made for differences in conditions of sale, differences in taxation and other differences affecting price comparability.

ARTICLE XIII

If one of the Contracting Parties considers that unfair business practices exist not included in Article XI, then it may not prevent trade by a unilateral decision, but shall submit the problem for consideration by the Executive Council in order that the latter may report whether such practices are in fact occurring. The Council shall render its decision within not more than 60 days from the date of receipt of the communication concerned.

When one of the Parties considers that there is evidence of unfair business practice, it shall ask the Executive Council for authorization to request a guarantee for the amount of the import duties involved.

If the Executive Council does not come to a decision within 8 days, the Party affected may request the guarantee pending a final decision by the Executive Council.

ARTICLE XIV

Once the Executive Council has come to a decision on unfair business practices, it shall inform the Contracting Parties whether or not protective measures against the said practices may be applied, pursuant to this Treaty.

CHAPTER IV

TRANSIT AND TRANSPORT

ARTICLE XV

Each of the Contracting States shall maintain full freedom of transit through its territory for goods proceeding to or from any of the other Signatory States, as well as for the vehicles transporting the said goods.

Such transit shall not be subject to deductions, discrimination or quantitative restrictions. Should there be traffic congestion or any other form of *force majeure,* each Signatory State shall give equitable attention both to the forwarding of goods intended for its own population and to that of goods in transit to the other States.

Transit operations shall be carried out by the routes prescribed by law for that purpose and be subject to the customs and transit laws and regulations applicable in the transit territory.

Goods in transit shall be exempt from all duties, taxes and other fiscal charges of a municipal or other character levied in connection with such transit, whatever the destination of the goods may be, but may remain subject to payment of the charges normally applicable for services rendered, which may in no case exceed the cost of the latter so that they constitute import taxes or duties.

CHAPTER V

CONSTRUCTION FIRMS

ARTICLE XVI

The Contracting States shall grant equality of treatment as compared with domestic firms to concerns of other Signatory States engaged in the construction of highways, bridges, dams, irrigation and electrification systems, housing and other works tending to promote the development of the Central American economic infra-structure.

CHAPTER VI

INDUSTRIAL INTEGRATION

ARTICLE XVII

The Contracting Parties adopt in this Treaty all the provisions of the Agreement Concerning the Rules Applicable to the Integrated Industries of Central America, and so as to put the said provisions into effect as soon as possible, they shall adopt, within not more than six months from the date of the entry into force of this Treaty, additional protocols in which shall be stipulated the industrial plants to be covered initially by the said Agreement, the free trade regime applicable to their products and the other conditions provided for in Article III of the said Agreement.

CHAPTER VII

CENTRAL AMERICAN BANK FOR ECONOMIC INTEGRATION

ARTICLE XVIII

The Signatory States agree to establish the Central American Bank for Economic Integration which shall have the legal status of a corporate body. The Bank shall act as an instrument for the financing and promotion of integrated economic growth, on the basis of balanced regional development. To this end, the Contracting States shall sign the Agreement setting up the said institution, which Agreement shall remain open for the signature or adhesion of any other Central American State which may wish to become a member of the Bank.

It shall be laid down, however, that members of the Bank may not obtain guarantees or loans from the said institution if they have not previously deposited the instruments of ratification of the following international agreements:

The present Treaty;

The Multilateral Treaty of Free Trade and Central American Economic Integration, signed on 10 June 1958;

The Agreement Concerning the Rules Applicable to the Integrated Industries of Central America, signed on 10 June 1958; and

The Central American Agreement on the Equalization of Import Charges, signed on 10 September 1959, and its Protocol, signed on the same date as the present Treaty.

CHAPTER VIII

FISCAL INCENTIVES TO INDUSTRIAL DEVELOPMENT

ARTICLE XIX

The Contracting States, with the aim of providing uniform fiscal incentives to industrial development, shall agree to bring about as soon as possible a reasonable standardization of the laws and provisions in force in this connection. To this end, they shall sign within six months from the date of the entry into force of this Treaty, a special protocol in which shall be stipulated the amount and kind of exemption, the limiting dates of the latter, the conditions under which they shall be granted, the systems of industrial classification and the rules and procedures for their application. Coordination of the application of these fiscal incentives to industrial development shall be the responsibility of the Executive Council.

CHAPTER IX

ORGANS

ARTICLE XX

To direct integration of the Central American economies and to coordinate the policy of the Contracting States in economic matters there shall be set up a Central American Economic Council, consisting of the Ministers of Economy of each of the Contracting Parties.

The Central American Economic Council shall meet whenever necessary or at the request of any of the Contracting Parties; it shall consider the work of the Executive Council and take whatever decisions it may deem appropriate. The Central American Economic Council shall be the body responsible for expediting the implementation of the resolutions of the Economic Cooperation Committee of the Central American Isthmus relating to economic integration. It may call on Central American or international technical organizations for their advice.

ARTICLE XXI

For the purpose of applying and administering the present Treaty, as well as of carrying on all negotiations and activities having as their aim the economic union of Central America, an Executive Council shall be set up consisting of one permanent member and one alternate designated by each of the Contracting Parties.

The Executive Council shall meet whenever necessary, at the request of any of the Contracting Parties, or when convened by the Permanent Secretariat, and its resolutions shall be adopted by a majority vote of all the members of the Council. In the event of agreement not being reached, the matter shall be referred to the Central American Economic Council so that the latter can come to a final decision concerning it.

Before coming to a decision, the Economic Council shall decide unanimously whether the matter shall be settled by the concurring votes of all its members or by a majority vote.

ARTICLE XXII

The Executive Council shall lay down the measures necessary to ensure the fulfillment of the undertakings entered into pursuant to this Treaty and to solve any problems which may arise in regard to the application of its provisions. Furthermore, the Council may suggest to governments the conclusion of additional multilateral agreements required to achieve the aims of economic integration of Central America, including a customs union between their territories.

The Executive Council shall assume on behalf of the Contracting Parties, the functions entrusted to the Central American Trade Commission in the Multilateral Treaty of Free Trade and Central American Economic Integration and in the Central American Agreement on the Equalization of Import Charges, as well as those entrusted to the Central American Commission for Industrial Integration in the Agreement Concerning the Rules Applicable to the Integrated Industries of Central America, and the functions and duties of the joint commissions of the bilateral treaties in force between the Contracting Parties.

Article XXIII

A Permanent Secretariat shall be set up, with the legal status of a corporate body, which shall be the Secretariat for both the Central American Economic Council and the Executive Council created under this Treaty.

The headquarters of the Secretariat shall be in Guatemala City, the capital of the Republic of Guatemala, and it shall be directed by a Secretary General appointed for a period of three years by the Central American Economic Council. The Secretariat shall establish whatever departments and sections may be necessary for carrying out its functions. Its expenses shall be in accordance with a general budget approved annually by the Central American Economic Council, and each of the Contracting Parties shall contribute to its maintenance an annual minimum sum equivalent to fifty thousand United States dollars (US $50,000), payable in the respective currencies of the Signatory Countries.

The officials of the Secretariat shall enjoy diplomatic immunity. Other diplomatic privileges shall be granted solely to the Secretariat and to the Secretary General.

Article XXIV

The Secretariat shall watch over the correct application as between the Contracting Parties, of this Treaty, of the Multilateral Treaty of Free Trade and Central American Economic Integration, of the Agreement Concerning the Rules Applicable to the Integrated Industries of Central America, of the Central American Agreement on the Equalization of Import Charges, of bilateral or multilateral free trade and economic integration treaties in force between any of the Contracting Parties, and of all other Agreements concluded or which may be concluded with the aim of Central American economic integration and whose interpretation is not specifically entrusted to any other body.

The Secretariat shall see that the resolutions of the Central American Economic Council and of the Executive Council set up under this Treaty are implemented and shall also exercise the functions delegated to it by the Executive Council. The regulations governing its functions shall be approved by the Economic Council.

The Secretariat shall also be responsible for carrying out the activities and studies assigned to it by the Executive Council and the Central American Economic Council. In executing these functions, it shall make use of studies and work already carried out by other Central American and international bodies and shall secure their cooperation as appropriate.

CHAPTER X

GENERAL PROVISIONS

ARTICLE XXV

The Signatory States agree not to sign unilaterally with non-Central American countries, new treaties affecting the principles of Central American economic integration. They shall also agree to maintain the "Central American exception clause" in any trade agreements they may conclude on the basis of most-favored-nation treatment with countries other than the Contracting Parties.

ARTICLE XXVI

The Signatory States agree to settle amicably, in conformity with the spirit of this Treaty, and through the Executive Council or the Central American Economic Council, any differences which may arise regarding the interpretation or application of any provision of this Treaty. If agreement cannot be reached, they shall submit the matter to arbitration. For the purpose of constituting the Arbitration Tribunal, each Contracting Party shall nominate to the General Secretariat of the Organization of Central American States, three judges from their respective Supreme Courts of Justice. The Secretary-General of the Organization of Central American States and the government representatives attached to that body shall select, by drawing lots, one arbitrator for each of the Contracting Parties, whereby all the arbitrators must be of different nationality. The award of the Arbitration Tribunal shall require the concurring votes of not less than three members and shall have the force of *res judicata* for all the Contracting Parties in respect of any ruling concerning the interpretation or application of the provisions of this Treaty.

ARTICLE XXVII

The present Treaty shall take precedence, among the Contracting Parties, over the Multilateral Treaty of Free Trade and Central American Economic Integration and over other bilateral or multilateral instruments of free trade concluded between the contracting parties; however, notwithstanding this, the said agreement shall continue to remain in force.

Among the respective Signatory States, the provisions of the trade and economic integration agreements referred to in the previous paragraph shall be applied in matters not considered in the present Treaty.

During such time as any of the Contracting Parties have not ratified the present Treaty or in the event of its denunciation by any of them, the trade relations of the States concerned with the remaining Signatory States shall be governed by previous commitments under the instruments in force referred to in the preamble to this Treaty.

ARTICLE XXVIII

The Contracting Parties agree to consult the Executive Council prior to concluding with one another new treaties which may affect free trade.

The Executive Council shall consider the matter and determine what effect the conclusion of the said agreements might have on the free trade regime established under the present Treaty. On the basis of the study made by the Executive Council, the party which considers itself affected by the conclusion of these new treaties may adopt the measures recommended by the Council with the aim of safeguarding its interests.

ARTICLE XXIX

For the purposes of customs regulations connected with free trade, the transit of goods and the application of the Uniform Central American Import Tariff, the Contracting Parties shall adopt within a period of not more than one year from the entry into force of this Treaty, special protocols providing for a Uniform Central American Customs Code and the necessary transport regulations.

CHAPTER XI

FINAL PROVISIONS

ARTICLE XXX

This Treaty shall be submitted for ratification by each State, in conformity with its constitutional or legal procedures.

The instruments of ratification shall be deposited with the General Secretariat of the Organization of Central American States.

The Treaty shall come into force, in the case of the first three States to ratify it, eight days after the date of deposit of the third instrument of ratification, and for the remaining State, on the date of deposit of the corresponding instrument.

ARTICLE XXXI

The duration of this Treaty shall be 20 years from the initial date of its entry into force and it may be renewed indefinitely.

On expiration of the period of 20 years mentioned in the previous paragraph, the Treaty may be denounced by any of the Contracting Parties. Denunciation shall become effective, for the denouncing State, five years after notice of it has been given and the Treaty shall continue to remain in force between the remaining Contracting States so long as at least two States continue to be parties to it.

ARTICLE XXXII

The General Secretariat of the Organization of Central American States shall act as depository of this Treaty, of which it shall send a certified copy to the Chancellery of each of the Contracting States. The said Chancelleries shall also be immediately notified of the deposit of each of the instruments of ratification, as well as of any denunciation which may occur. Upon the entry into force of the Treaty, the General Secretariat shall also send a certified copy to the Secretary-General of the United Nations for registration, in compliance with Article 102 of the United Nations Charter.

ARTICLE XXXIII

Adherence to the present Treaty shall remain open to any Central American State not among the original Signatories.

TRANSITIONAL ARTICLE

As soon as the Government of the Republic of Costa Rica formally adheres to the provisions of this Treaty, the bodies set up by the same shall form part of the Organization of Central American States following an incorporation agreement and the remodeling of the OCAS so as to enable the bodies created under this Treaty to retain all their characteristics as regards structure and functions.

IN WITNESS WHEREOF the respective plenipotentiaries have signed this Treaty in the City of Managua, capital of the Republic of Nicaragua, this thirteenth day of December 1960.

22. CHARTER OF THE ORGANIZATION OF CENTRAL AMERICAN STATES (ODECA) (1962)

WHEREAS:

It is necessary to provide the five States with a more effective instrument by establishing organs which assure their economic and social progress, eliminate the barriers which divide them, improve constantly the living conditions of their peoples, guarantee the stability and expansion of industry, and strengthen Central American solidarity,

THEREFORE:

The Governments of Costa Rica, Nicaragua, Honduras, El Salvador and Guatemala decide to replace the Charter signed on October 14, 1951, in San Salvador, Republic of El Salvador, by the following CHARTER OF THE ORGANIZATION OF CENTRAL AMERICAN STATES:

PURPOSES

ARTICLE 1

Costa Rica, Nicaragua, Honduras, El Salvador and Guatemala are an economic-political community which aspires to the integration of Central America. For this purpose the Organization of Central American States (ODECA) has been established.

ORGANS

ARTICLE 2

To achieve the purposes of the Organization of Central American States, the following Organs are established:
- a) The Meeting of Heads of State;
- b) The Conference of Ministers of Foreign Affairs;
- c) The Executive Council;
- d) The Legislative Council;
- e) The Central American Court of Justice;
- f) The Central American Economic Council;
- g) The Cultural and Educational Council; and
- h) The Council for Central American Defense.

ARTICLE 3

The Meeting of Heads of State is the Supreme Organ of the Organization. The Conference of Ministers of Foreign Affairs is the Principal Organ.

The Executive Council is the Permanent Organ of the Organization. Its seat shall be in the city of San Salvador.

PRINCIPAL ORGAN

ARTICLE 4

The Conference of Ministers of Foreign Affairs shall meet ordinarily once each year, and extraordinarily whenever at least three of them deem it necessary.

ARTICLE 5

At the Conference of Ministers of Foreign Affairs each Member State shall have only one vote.

Decisions on substantive questions must be adopted unanimously. If there is doubt as to whether a decision is substantive or procedural, it shall be resolved by unanimous vote.

ARTICLE 6

The Conference of Ministers of Foreign Affairs may create the subsidiary organs which it considers appropriate for the study of the different problems.

The seat of the different subsidiary organs shall be designated in accordance with an equitable geographic distribution and with the needs that determined their creation.

EXECUTIVE COUNCIL

ARTICLE 7

The Executive Council shall be composed of the Ministers of Foreign Affairs or their specially accredited representatives. It shall be the legal representative of the Organization.

ARTICLE 8

The Executive Council shall be presided over by one of its members. The Presidency shall rotate annually among the States Members of the Organization. The Council shall meet ordinarily once a week and extraordinarily when convoked by its President.

ARTICLE 9

The function of the Executive Council is to direct and coordinate the policy of the Organization for the fulfillment of its objectives. For the proper functioning of the offices charged with executing administrative tasks, the Council shall designate a Secretary and the necessary personnel. For this purpose it shall adopt the respective regulations to determine their obligations.

The Council shall be the means of communication between the Organs and the Member States.

LEGISLATIVE COUNCIL

ARTICLE 10

The Legislative Council is composed of three representatives from each of the Legislative Powers of the Member States.

This Council shall act as advisor and organ of consultation in legislative matters. Likewise, it shall study the possibilities of unifying the legislation of the Central American States.

ARTICLE 11

The Council shall establish the working Committees which it deems convenient, in accordance with its own regulations.

ARTICLE 12

The Legislative Council shall meet ordinarily once each year starting September 15, and extraordinarily whenever the Executive Council convokes it at the request of at least two governments of Member States.

ARTICLE 13

For the adoption of the resolutions and recommendations of the Council, a favorable vote of the majority of its members shall be required.

CENTRAL AMERICAN COURT OF JUSTICE

ARTICLE 14

The Central American Court of Justice is composed of the Presidents of the Judicial Powers of each of the Member States.

ARTICLE 15

The functions of the Central American Court of Justice are:

a) To decide the conflicts of a legal nature which arise among the Member States and which the latter agree to submit to it;

b) To prepare and render opinions on projects for the unification of Central American legislation, when so requested by the Conference of Ministers of Foreign Affairs or the Executive Council.

ARTICLE 16

The Central American Court of Justice shall meet whenever it deems it necessary or it is convoked by the Executive Council.

CENTRAL AMERICAN ECONOMIC COUNCIL

ARTICLE 17

The Central American Economic Council is composed of the Ministers of Economy of each of the Member States and shall be charged with the planning, coordination and execution of the Central American economic integration.

All the agencies of Central American economic integration shall form part of the Council.

ARTICLE 18

The Economic Council shall make annually a full report of its activities to the Executive Council, for the information of the Comference of Ministers of Foreign Affairs, based on the reports of the various agencies connected with the Program of Central American Economic Integration.

CULTURAL AND EDUCATIONAL COUNCIL

ARTICLE 19

The Cultural and Educational Council shall be composed of the Ministers of Education of the Member States or their representatives.

ARTICLE 20

The functions of the Cultural and Educational Council are:

a) To promote educational, scientific and cultural interchange between the Member States;

b) To undertake studies concerning the status of education, science and culture in the region;

c) To coordinate the efforts to achieve the uniformity of the educational systems in Central America;

d) To render a report of its activities to the Conference of Ministers of Foreign Affairs through the Executive Council of the Organization.

DEFENSE COUNCIL

ARTICLE 21

The Defense Council is composed of the Ministers of Defense or of the heads of equivalent departments, corresponding to them in rank or functions in the respective Member States.

ARTICLE 22

The Defense Council shall act as Organ of Consultation in matters of regional defense and shall watch over the collective security of the Member States. It shall report on its activities to the Conference of Ministers of Foreign Affairs through the Executive Council.

GENERAL PROVISIONS
ARTICLE 23

Any Member State may propose, through the Executive Council, a meeting of the Organs or of Ministers of other departments to deal with matters of Central American interest.

ARTICLE 24

The operation of the Organization shall not interfere with the internal regime of the States and none of the provisions of the present Charter shall affect the respect for and fulfillment of the constitutional norms of each of them, nor may it be interpreted in such a way as to impair the rights and obligations of the Central American States as members of the United Nations and of the Organization of American States, nor the particular positions which any of them may have assumed through specific reservations in treaties or agreements in force.

ARTICLE 25

The present Charter shall be ratified by the Central American States in the shortest possible time in accordance with their respective constitutional procedures.

It shall be registered with the (General) Secretariat of the United Nations in compliance with Article 102 of its Charter.

ARTICLE 26

Each of the Organs originating in the present Charter shall prepare its own regulations.

ARTICLE 27

The Organs shall meet at the seat of the Organization unless they decide otherwise.

ARTICLE 28

The original of the present Charter shall be deposited in the Office of the Organization, with shall forward a true certified copy to the Ministers of Foreign Affairs of the Member States.

The instruments of ratification shall be deposited in the Office of the Organization, which shall notify the Chancelleries of the Member States of the deposit of each of said instruments.

ARTICLE 29

The present Charter shall enter into force the day on which the instruments of ratification of the five Member States are deposited.

ARTICLE 30

This Agreement on the Organization of Central American States shall maintain the name of "Charter of San Salvador."

TRANSITIONAL PROVISIONS
ARTICLE 1

The present Agreement remains open to the Republic of Panama so that it may adhere at any time to this Charter and form part of the Organization of Central American States.

ARTICLE 2

Until the Republic of Panama adheres to this Charter and forms part of the Organization of Central American States, it may join any of the subsidiary agencies already established or which may be established in the future, signing for this purpose the Protocol or Protocols which may be necessary.

ARTICLE 3

The financial resources for the functioning of the Organization shall be the object of a special protocol between the Member States, and for this purpose the Central American Economic Council is entrusted with carrying out the corresponding studies.

Until the plan for financing ODECA goes into effect in definitive form and the necessary funds for this purpose can be counted upon, the Member States shall continue to contribute to the budget of the Organization with quotas proportional to the coefficients established in the distribution of quotas of the United Nations.

In case said coefficients should be modified, the Executive Council shall adjust the quotas of the Member States in accordance with these modifications.

ARTICLE 4

Within thirty days after the date of the deposit of the last instrument of ratification of the present Charter, the Ambassadors of the Member States accredited to ODECA shall form an *ad hoc* Committee to receive by inventory the assets of the Organization as well as the rendering of accounts by the General Secretariat.

ARTICLE 5

When the present Charter enters into force and the Executive Council is constituted, the latter shall elect its first President by drawing lots.

IN WITNESS WHEREOF:

The Ministers of Foreign Affairs of the Central American Republics sign this document in Panama City, Republic of Panama, on the twelfth day of December, Nineteen Hundred and Sixty-two,

23. TREATY ESTABLISHING A FREE TRADE AREA AND INSTITUTING THE LATIN AMERICAN FREE TRADE ASSOCIATION (MONTEVIDEO TREATY) INCLUDING THE RELEVANT PROTOCOLS AND RESOLUTIONS (1960)

The Governments represented at the Inter-Governmental Conference for the Establishment of a Free Trade Area among Latin American countries,

Persuaded that the expansion of present national markets, through the gradual elimination of barriers to intra-regional trade, is a prerequisite if the Latin American countries are to accelerate their economic development process in such a way as to ensure a higher level of living for their peoples,

Aware that economic development should be attained through the maximum utilization of available production factors and the more effective coordination of the development programs of the different production sectors in accordance with norms which take due account of the interests of each and all and which make proper compensation, by means of appropriate measures, for the special situation of countries which are at a relatively less advanced stage of economic development,

Convinced that the strengthening of national economies will contribute to the expansion of trade within Latin America and with the rest of the world.

Sure that, by the adoption of suitable formulas, conditions can be created that will be conducive to the gradual and smooth adaptation of existing productive activities to new patterns of reciprocal trade, and that further incentives will thereby be provided for the improvement and expansion of such trade,

Certain that any action to achieve such ends must take into account the commitments arising out of the international instruments which govern their trade,

Determined to persevere in their efforts to establish, gradually and progressively, a Latin American common market and, hence, to continue collaborating with the Latin American Governments as a whole in the work already initiated for this purpose, and

Motivated by the desire to pool their efforts to achieve gradually complementary and integrated national economics on the basis of an effective reciprocity of benefits, decide to establish a Free Trade Area and, to that end, to conclude a Treaty instituting the Latin American Free Trade Association; and have, for this purpose, appointed their plenipotentiaries who have agreed as follows:

CHAPTER I

NAME AND PURPOSE

ARTICLE 1

By this Treaty the Contracting Parties establish a Free Trade Area and institute the Latin American Free Trade Association (hereinafter referred to as "the Association"), with headquarters in the city of Montevideo (Eastern Republic of Uruguay).

The term "Area", when used in this Treaty, means the combined territories of the Contracting Parties.

CHAPTER II

PROGRAM FOR TRADE LIBERALIZATION

ARTICLE 2

The Free Trade Area, established under the terms of the present Treaty, shall be brought into full operation within not more than twelve (12) years from the date of the Treaty's entry into force.

ARTICLE 3

During the period indicated in article 2, the Contracting Parties shall gradually eliminate, in respect of substantially all their reciprocal trade, such duties, charges and restrictions as may be applied to imports of goods originating in the territory of any Contracting Party.

For the purposes of the present Treaty the term "duties and charges" means customs duties and any other charges of equivalent effect—whether fiscal, monetary or exchange—that are levied on imports.

The provisions of the present article do not apply to fees and similar charges in respect of services rendered.

ARTICLE 4

The purpose set forth in article 3 shall be achieved through negotiations to be held from time to time among the Contracting Parties with a view to drawing up:

(a) National Schedules specifying the annual reductions in duties, charges and other restrictions which each Contracting Party grants to the other Contracting Parties in accordance with the provisions of article 5; and

(b) A Common Schedule listing the products on which the Contracting Parties collectively agree to eliminate duties, charges and other restrictions completely, so far as intra-Area trade is concerned, within the period mentioned in article 2, by complying with the minimum percentages set out in article 7 and through the gradual reduction provided for in article 5.

ARTICLE 5

With a view to the preparation of the National Schedules referred to in article 4, sub-paragraph (a), each Contracting Party shall annually grant to the other Contracting Parties reductions in duties and charges equivalent to not less than eight (8) per cent of the weighted average applicable to third countries, until they are eliminated in respect of substantially all of its imports from the Area, in accordance with the definitions, methods of calculation, rules and procedures laid down in the Protocol.

For this purpose, duties and charges for third parties shall be deemed to be those in force on 31 December prior to each negotiation.

When the import regime of a Contracting Party contains restrictions of such a kind that the requisite equivalence with the reductions in duties and charges granted by another Contracting Party or other Contracting Parties is unobtainable, the counterpart of these reductions shall be complemented by means of the elimination or relaxation of those restrictions.

ARTICLE 6

The National Schedules shall enter into force on 1 January of each year, except that those deriving from the initial negotiations shall enter into force on the date fixed by the Contracting Parties.

ARTICLE 7

The Common Schedule shall consist of products which, in terms of the aggregate value of the trade among the Contracting Parties, shall constitute not less than the following percentages, calculated in accordance with the provisions of the Protocol:

Twenty-five (25) per cent during the first three-year period;

Fifty (50) per cent during the second three-year period;

Seventy-five (75) per cent during the third three-year period;

Substantially all of such trade during the fourth three-year period.

ARTICLE 8

The inclusion of products in the Common Schedule shall be final and the concessions granted in respect thereof irrevocable.

Concessions granted in respect of products which appear only in the National Schedules may be withdrawn by negotiation among the Contracting Parties and on a basis of adequate compensation.

ARTICLE 9

The percentages referred to in articles 5 and 7 shall be calculated on the basis of the average annual value of trade during the three years preceding the year in which each negotiation is effected.

ARTICLE 10

The purpose of the negotiations—based on reciprocity of concessions—referred to in article 4 shall be to expand and diversify trade and to promote gradually complementary economies for the countries in the Area.

In these negotiations the situation of those Contracting Parties whose levels of duties, charges and restrictions differ substantially from those of the other Contracting Parties shall be considered with due fairness.

ARTICLE 11

If, as a result of the concessions granted, significant and persistent disadvantages are created in respect of trade between one Contracting Party and the others as a whole in the products included in the liberalization program, the Contracting Parties shall, at the request of the Contracting Party affected, consider steps to remedy these disadvantages with a view to the adoption of suitable, non-restrictive measures designed to promote trade at the highest possible levels.

ARTICLE 12

If, as a result of circumstances other than those referred to in article 11, significant and persistent disadvantages are created in respect of trade in the products included in the liberalization program, the Contracting Parties shall, at the request of the Contracting Party concerned, make every effort within their power to remedy these disadvantages.

ARTICLE 13

The reciprocity mentioned in article 10 refers to the expected growth in the flow of trade between each Contracting Party and the others as a whole, in the products included in the liberalization program and those which may subsequently be added.

CHAPTER III

EXPANSION OF TRADE AND COMPLEMENTARY ECONOMIES

ARTICLE 14

In order to ensure the continued expansion and diversification of reciprocal trade, the Contracting Parties shall take steps:

(a) To grant one another, while observing the principle of reciprocity, concessions which will ensure that, in the first negotiation, treatment not less favorable than that which existed before the date of entry into force of the present Treaty is accorded to imports from within the Area;

(b) To include in the National Schedules the largest possible number of products in which trade is carried on among the Contracting Parties; and

(c) To add to these Schedules an increasing number of products which are not yet included in reciprocal trade.

ARTICLE 15

In order to ensure fair competitive conditions among the Contracting Parties and to facilitate increasing economic integration and complementary economies, particularly with regard to industrial production, the Contracting Parties shall make every effort—in keeping with the liberalization objectives of the present Treaty—to reconcile their import and export regimes, as well as the treatment they accord to capital, goods and services from outside the Area.

ARTICLE 16

With a view to expediting the process of integration and complementary economies referred to in article 15, the Contracting Parties:

(a) Shall endeavor to promote progressively closer coordination of the corresponding industrialization policies, and shall sponsor for this purpose agreements among representatives of the economic sectors concerned; and

(b) May negotiate mutual agreements on complementary economies by industrial sectors.

ARTICLE 17

The complementary economy agreements referred to in article 16, sub-paragraph (b), shall set forth the liberalization program to be applied to products of the sector concerned and may contain, *inter alia,* clauses designed to reconcile the treatment accorded to raw materials and other components used in the manufacture of these products.

Any Contracting Party concerned with the complementary economy programs shall be free to participate in the negotiation of these agreements.

The results of these negotiations shall, in every case, be embodied in protocols which shall enter into force after the Contracting Parties have decided that they are consistent with the general principles and purposes of the present Treaty.

CHAPTER IV

MOST-FAVORED-NATION TREATMENT

ARTICLE 18

Any advantage, benefit, franchise, immunity or privilege applied by a Contracting Party in respect of a product originating in or intended for consignment to any other country shall be immediately and unconditionally extended to the similar product originating in or intended for consignment to the territory of the other Contracting Parties.

ARTICLE 19

The most-favored-nation treatment referred to in article 18 shall not be applicable to the advantages, benefits, franchises, immunities and privileges already granted or which may be granted by virtue of agreements among Contracting Parties or between Contracting Parties and third countries with a view to facilitating border trade.

ARTICLE 20

Capital originating in the Area shall enjoy, in the territory of each Contracting Party, treatment not less favorable than that granted to capital originating in any other country.

CHAPTER V

TREATMENT IN RESPECT OF INTERNAL TAXATION

ARTICLE 21

With respect to taxes, rates and other internal duties and charges, products originating in the territory of a Contracting Party shall enjoy, in the territory of another Contracting Party, treatment no less favorable than that accorded to similar national products.

ARTICLE 22

Each Contracting Party shall endeavor to ensure that the charges or other domestic measures applied to products included in the liberalization program which are not produced, or are produced only in small quantities, in its territory, do not nullify or reduce any concession or advantage obtained by any Contracting Party during the negotiations.

If a Contracting Party considers itself injured by virtue of the measures mentioned in the previous paragraph, it may appeal to the competent organs of the Association with a view to having the matter examined and appropriate recommendations made.

CHAPTER VI

SAVING CLAUSES

ARTICLE 23

The Contracting Parties may, as a provisional measure and providing that the customary level of consumption in the importer country is not thereby lowered, authorize a Contracting Party to impose non-discriminatory restrictions upon imports of products included in the liberalization program which originate in the Area, if these products are imported in such quantities or under such conditions that they have, or are liable to have, serious repercussions on specific productive activities of vital importance to the national economy.

ARTICLE 24

The Contracting Parties may likewise authorize a Contracting Party which has adopted measures to correct its unfavorable overall balance of payments to extend these measures, provisionally and without discrimination, to intra-Area trade in the products included in the liberalization program.

The Contracting Parties shall endeavour to ensure that the imposition of restrictions deriving from the balance-of-payments situation does not affect trade, within the Area, in the products included in the liberalization program.

ARTICLE 25

If the situations referred to in articles 23 and 24 call for immediate action, the Contracting Party concerned may, as an emergency arrangement to be referred to the Contracting Parties, apply the measures provided for in the said articles. The measures adopted must immediately be communicated to the Committee mentioned in article 33, which, if it deems necessary, shall convene a special session of the Conference.

ARTICLE 26

Should the measures envisaged in this chapter be prolonged for more than one year, the Committee shall propose to the Conference, referred to in article 33, either *ex officio* or at the request of any of the Contracting Parties, the immediate initiation of negotiations with a view to eliminating the restrictions adopted.

The present article does not affect the provisions of article 8.

CHAPTER VII
SPECIAL PROVISIONS CONCERNING AGRICULTURE

ARTICLE 27

The Contracting Parties shall seek to coordinate their agricultural development and agricultural commodity trade policies, with a view to securing the most efficient utilization of their natural resources, raising the standard of living of the rural population, and guaranteeing normal supplies to consumers, without disorganizing the regular productive activities of each Contracting Party.

ARTICLE 28

Providing that no lowering of its customary consumption or increase in anti-economic production is involved, a Contracting Party may apply, within the period mentioned in article 2, and in respect of trade in agricultural commodities of substantial importance to its economy that are included in the liberalization program, appropriate non-discriminatory measures designed to:

(a) Limit imports to the amount required to meet the deficit in internal production; and

(b) Equalize the prices of the imported and domestic product.

The Contracting Party which decides to apply these measures shall inform the other Contracting Parties before it puts them into effect.

ARTICLE 29

During the period prescribed in article 2 an attempt shall be made to expand intra-Area trade in agricultural commodities by such means as agreements among the Contracting Parties designed to cover deficits in domestic production.

For this purpose, the Contracting Parties shall give priority, under normal competitive conditions, to products originating in the territories of the other Contracting Parties, due consideration being given to the traditional flows of intra-Area trade.

Should such agreements be concluded among two or more Contracting Parties, the other Contracting Parties shall be notified before the agreements enter into force.

ARTICLE 30

The measures provided for in this chapter shall not be applied for the purpose of incorporating, in the production of agricultural commodities, resources which imply a reduction in the average level of productivity existing on the date on which the present Treaty enters into force.

ARTICLE 31

If a Contracting Party considers itself injured by a reduction of its exports attributable to the lowering of the usual consumption level of the importer country as a result of measures referred to in article 28 and/or an anti-economic increase in the production referred to in the previous article, it may appeal to the competent organs of the Association to study the situation and, if necessary, to make recommendations for the adoption of appropriate measures to be applied in accordance with article 12.

CHAPTER VIII

MEASURES IN FAVOR OF COUNTRIES AT A RELATIVELY LESS ADVANCED STAGE OF ECONOMIC DEVELOPMENT

ARTICLE 32

The Contracting Parties, recognizing that fulfillment of the purposes of the present Treaty will be facilitated by the economic growth of the countries in the Area that are at a relatively less advanced stage of economic development, shall take steps to create conditions conducive to such growth.

To this end, the Contracting Parties may:

(a) Authorize a Contracting Party to grant to another Contracting Party which is at a relatively less advanced stage of economic development within the Area, as long as necessary and as a temporary measure, for the purposes set out in the present article, advantages not extended to the other Contracting Parties, in order to encourage the introduction or expansion of specific productive activities;

(b) Authorize a Contracting Party at a relatively less advanced stage of economic development within the Area to implement the program for the reduction of duties, charges and other restrictions under more favorable conditions, specially agreed upon;

(c) Authorize a Contracting Party at a relatively less advanced stage of economic development within the Area to adopt appropriate measures to correct an unfavorable balance of payments, if the case arises;

(d) Authorize a Contracting Party at a relatively less advanced stage of economic development within the Area to apply, if necessary and as a temporary measure, and providing that this does not entail a decrease in its customary consumption, appropriate non-discriminatory measures designed to protect the domestic output of products included in the liberalization program which are of vital importance to its economic development;

(e) Make collective arrangements in favor of a Contracting Party at a relatively less advanced stage of economic development within the Area with respect to the support and promotion, both inside and outside the Area, of financial or technical measures designed to bring about the expansion of existing productive activities or to encourage new activities, particularly those intended for the industrialization of its raw materials; and

(f) Promote or support, as the case may be, special technical assistance programs for one or more Contracting Parties, intended to raise, in countries at a relatively less advanced stage of economic development within the Area, productivity levels in specific production sectors.

CHAPTER IX

ORGANS OF THE ASSOCIATION

ARTICLE 33

The organs of the Association are the Conference of the Contracting Parties (referred to in this Treaty as "the Conference") and the Standing Executive Committee (referred to in this Treaty as "the Committee").

ARTICLE 34

The Conference is the supreme organ of the Association. It shall adopt all decisions in matters requiring joint action on the part of the Contracting Parties, and it shall be empowered, *inter alia*:

(a) To take the necessary steps to carry out the present Treaty and to study the results of its implementation;

(b) To promote the negotiations provided for in article 4 and to assess the results thereof;

(c) To approve the Committee's annual budget and to fix the contributions of each Contracting Party;

(d) To lay down its own rules of procedure and to approve the Committee's rules of procedure;

(e) To elect a Chairman and two Vice-Chairmen for each session;

(f) To appoint the Executive Secretary of the Committee; and

(g) To deal with other business of common interest.

ARTICLE 35

The Conference shall be composed of duly accredited representatives of the Contracting Parties. Each delegation shall have one vote.

ARTICLE 36

The Conference shall hold: (a) a regular session once a year; and (b) special sessions when convened by the Committee.

At each session the Conference shall decide the place and date of the following regular session.

ARTICLE 37

The Conference may not take decisions unless at least two-thirds (2/3) of the Contracting Parties are present.

ARTICLE 38

During the first two years in which the present Treaty is in force, decisions of the Conference shall be adopted when affirmative votes are cast by at least two-thirds (2/3) of the Contracting Parties and providing that no negative vote is cast.

The Contracting Parties shall likewise determine the voting system to be adopted after this two-year period.

The affirmative vote of two-thirds (2/3) of the Contracting Parties shall be required:

(a) To approve the Committee's annual budget;

(b) To elect the Chairman and Vice-Chairman of the Conference, as well as the Executive Secretary; and

(c) To fix the time and place of the sessions of the Conference.

ARTICLE 39

The Committee is the permanent organ of the Association responsible for supervising the implementation of the provisions of the present Treaty. Its duties and responsibilities shall be, *inter alia:*

(a) To convene the Conference;

(b) To submit for the approval of the Conference an annual work program and the Committee's annual budget estimates;

(c) To represent the Association in dealings with third countries and international organs and entities for the purpose of considering matters of common interest. It shall also represent the Association in contracts and other instruments of public and private law;

(d) To undertake studies, to suggest measures and to submit to the Conference such recommendations as it deems appropriate for the effective implementation of the Treaty;

(e) To submit to the Conference at its regular sessions an annual report on its activities and on the results of the implementation of the present Treaty;

(f) To request the technical advice and the cooperation of individuals and of national and international organizations;

(g) To take such decisions as may be delegated to it by the Conference; and

(h) To undertake the work assigned to it by the Conference.

ARTICLE 40

The Committee shall consist of a Permanent Representative of each Contracting Party, who shall have a single vote.

Each Representative shall have an Alternate.

ARTICLE 41

The Committee shall have a secretariat headed by an Executive Secretary and comprising technical and administrative personnel.

The Executive Secretary, elected by the Conference for a three-year term and eligible for reelection, shall attend the plenary meetings of the Committee without the right to vote.

The Executive Secretary shall be the General Secretary of the Conference. His duties shall be, *inter alia:*

(a) To organize the work of the Conference and of the Committee;

(b) To prepare the Committee's annual budget estimates; and

(c) To recruit and engage the technical and administrative staff in accordance with the Committee's rules of procedure.

ARTICLE 42

In the performance of their duties, the Executive Secretary and the secretariat staff shall not seek or receive instructions from any Government or from any other national or international entity. They shall refrain from any action which might reflect on their position as international civil servants.

The Contracting Parties undertake to respect the international character of the responsibilities of the Executive Secretary and of the secretariat staff and shall refrain from influencing them in any way in the discharge of their responsibilities.

ARTICLE 43

In order to facilitate the study of specific problems, the Committee may set up Advisory Commissions composed of representatives of the various sectors of economic activity of each of the Contracting Parties.

ARTICLE 44

The Committee shall request, for the organs of the Association, the technical advice of the secretariat of the United Nations Economic Commission for Latin America (ECLA) and of the Inter-American Economic and Social Council (IA-ECOSOC) of the Organization of American States.

ARTICLE 45

The Committee shall be constituted sixty days from the entry into force of the present Treaty and shall have its headquarters in the city of Montevideo.

CHAPTER X

JURIDICAL PERSONALITY—IMMUNITIES AND PRIVILEGES

ARTICLE 46

The Latin American Free Trade Association shall possess complete juridical personality and shall, in particular, have the power:

(a) To contract;

(b) To acquire and dispose of the movable and immovable property it needs for the achievement of its objectives;

(c) To institute legal proceedings; and

(d) To hold funds in any currency and to transfer them as necessary.

ARTICLE 47

The representatives of the Contracting Parties and the international staff and advisers of the Association shall enjoy in the Area such diplomatic and other immunities and privileges as are necessary for the exercise of their functions.

The Contracting Parties undertake to conclude, as soon as possible, an Agreement regulating the provisions of the previous paragraph in which the aforesaid privileges and immunities shall be defined.

The Association shall conclude with the Government of the Eastern Republic of Uruguay an Agreement for the purpose of specifying the privileges and immunities which the Association, its organs and its international staff and advisers shall enjoy.

CHAPTER XI

MISCELLANEOUS PROVISIONS

ARTICLE 48

No change introduced by a Contracting Party in its regime of import duties and charges shall imply a level of duties and charges less favorable than that in force before the change for any commodity in respect of which concessions are granted to the other Contracting Parties.

The requirement set out in the previous paragraph shall not apply to the conversion to present worth of the official base value (*aforo*) in respect of customs duties and charges, providing that such conversion corresponds exclusively to the real value of the goods. In such cases, the value shall not include the customs duties and charges levied on the goods.

ARTICLE 49

In order to facilitate the implementation of the provisions of the present Treaty, the Contracting Parties shall, as soon as possible:

(a) Determine the criteria to be adopted for the purpose of establishing the origin of goods and for classifying them as raw materials, semi-manu-factured goods or finished products;

(b) Simplify and standardize procedures and formalities relating to reciprocal trade;

(c) Prepare a tariff nomenclature to serve as a common basis for the presentation of statistics and for carrying out the negotiations provided for in the present Treaty;

(d) Determine what shall be deemed to constitute border trade within the meaning of article 19;

(e) Determine the criteria for the purpose of defining "dumping" and other unfair trade practices and the procedures relating thereto.

ARTICLE 50

The products imported from the Area by a Contracting Party may not be re-exported save by agreement between the Contracting Parties concerned.

A product shall not be deemed to be a re-export if it has been subjected in the importer country to industrial processing or manufacture, the degree of which shall be determined by the Committee.

ARTICLE 51

Products imported or exported by a Contracting Party shall enjoy freedom of transit within the Area and shall only be subject to the payment of the normal rates for services rendered.

ARTICLE 52

No Contracting Party shall promote its exports by means of subsidies or other measures likely to disrupt normal competitive conditions in the Area.

An export shall not be deemed to have been subsidized if it is exempted from duties and charges levied on the product or its components when destined for internal consumption, or if it is subject to drawback.

ARTICLE 53

No provision of the present Treaty shall be so construed as to constitute an impediment to the adoption and execution of measures relating to:

(a) The protection of public morality;

(b) The application of security laws and regulations;

(c) The control of imports or exports of arms, ammunition and other war equipment and, in exceptional circumstances, of all other military items, in so far as this is compatible with the terms of article 51 and of the treaties on the unrestricted freedom of transit in force among the Contracting Parties;

(d) The protection of human, animal and plant life and health;

(e) Imports and exports of gold and silver bullion;

(f) The protection of the nation's heritage of artistic, historical and archaeological value; and

(g) The export, use and consumption of nuclear materials, radioactive products or any other material that may be used in the development or exploitation of nuclear energy.

ARTICLE 54

The Contracting Parties shall make every effort to direct their policies with a view to creating conditions favorable to the establishment of a Latin American common market. To that end, the Committee shall undertake studies and consider projects and plans designed to achieve this purpose, and shall endeavor to coordinate its work with that of other international organizations.

CHAPTER XII

FINAL PROVISIONS

ARTICLE 55

The present Treaty may not be signed with reservations nor shall reservations be admitted at the time of ratification or accession.

ARTICLE 56

The present Treaty shall be ratified by the signatory States at the earliest opportunity.

The instruments of ratification shall be deposited with the Government of the Eastern Republic of Uruguay, which shall communicate the date of deposit to the Governments of the signatory and successively acceding States.

ARTICLE 57

The present Treaty shall enter into force for the first three ratifying States thirty days after the third instrument of ratification has been deposited; and, for the other signatories, thirty days after the respective instrument of ratification has been deposited, and in the order in which the ratifications are deposited.

The Government of the Eastern Republic of Uruguay shall communicate the date of the entry into force of the present Treaty to the Government of each of the signatory States.

ARTICLE 58

Following its entry into force, the present Treaty shall remain open to accession by the other Latin American States, which for this purpose shall deposit the relevant instrument of accession with the Government of the Eastern Republic of Uruguay. The Treaty shall enter into force for the acceding State thirty days after the deposit of the corresponding instrument.

Acceding States shall enter into the negotiations referred to in article 4 at the session of the Conference immediately following the date of deposit of the instrument of accession.

ARTICLE 59

Each Contracting Party shall begin to benefit from the concessions already granted to one another by the other Contracting Parties as from the date of entry into force of the reductions in duties and charges and other restrictions negotiated by them on a basis of reciprocity, and after the minimum obligations referred to in article 5, accumulated during the period which has elapsed since the entry into force of the present Treaty, have been carried out.

ARTICLE 60

The Contracting Parties may present amendments to the present Treaty, which shall be set out in protocols that shall enter into force upon their ratification by all the Contracting Parties and after the corresponding instruments have been deposited.

Article 61

On the expiration of the twelve-year term starting on the date of entry into force of the present Treaty, the Contracting Parties shall proceed to study the results of the Treaty's implementation and shall initiate the necessary collective negotiations with a view to fulfilling more effectively the purposes of the Treaty and, if desirable, to adapting it to a new stage of economic integration.

Article 62

The provisions of the present Treaty shall not affect the rights and obligations deriving from agreements signed by any of the Contracting Parties prior to the entry into force of the present Treaty.

However, each Contracting Party shall take the necessary steps to reconcile the provisions of existing agreements with the purposes of the present Treaty.

Article 63

The present Treaty shall be of unlimited duration.

Article 64

A Contracting Party wishing to withdraw from the present Treaty shall inform the other Contracting Parties of its intention at a regular session of the Conference, and shall formally submit the instrument of denunciation at the following regular session.

When the formalities of denunciation have been completed, those rights and obligations of the denouncing Government which derive from its status as a Contracting Party shall cease automatically, with the exception of those relating to reductions in duties and charges and other restrictions, received or granted under the liberalization program, which shall remain in force for a period of five years from the date on which the denunciation becomes formally effective.

The period specified in the preceding paragraph may be shortened if there is sufficient justification, with the consent of the Conference and at the request of the Contracting Party concerned.

Article 65

The present Treaty shall be called the Montevideo Treaty.

IN WITNESS WHEREOF the undersigned Plenipotentiaries, having desposited their full powers, found in good and due form, have signed the present Treaty on behalf of their respective Governments.

DONE in the City of Montevideo, on the eighteenth day of the month of February in the year One Thousand Nine Hundred and Sixty, in one original in the Spanish and one in the Portuguese language, both texts being equally authentic. The Government of the Eastern Republic of Uruguay shall be the depositary of the present Treaty and shall transmit duly certified copies thereof to the Governments of the other signatory and acceding States.

PROTOCOL NO. 1

ON NORMS AND PROCEDURES FOR NEGOTIATIONS

On the occasion of the signing of the Treaty establishing a Free Trade Area and instituting the Latin American Free Trade Association (Montevideo Treaty), the signatories, thereunto duly authorized by their Governments, hereby agree upon the following Protocol:

Title I

Calculation of weighted averages

1. For the purposes of article 5 of the Montevideo Treaty, it shall be understood that, as a result of the negotiations for the establishment of the National Schedules, the difference between the weighted average of duties and charges in force for third countries and that which shall be applicable to imports from within the area shall be not less than the product of eight per cent (8%) of the weighted average of duties and charges in force for third countries multiplied by the number of years that have elapsed since the Treaty became effective.

2. The reduction mechanism shall therefore be based on two weighted averages: one corresponding to the average of the duties and charges in force for third countries; and the other to the average of the duties and charges which shall be applicable to imports within the Area.

3. In order to calculate each of these weighted averages, the total amount that would be represented by the duties and charges on aggregate imports of the goods under consideration shall be divided by the total value of these imports.

4. This calculation will give a percentage (or *ad valorem* figure) for each weighted average. It is the difference between the two averages that shall be not less than the product of the factor 0.08 (or eight per cent) multiplied by the number of years elapsed.

5. The foregoing formula is expressed as follows:

$$t \leqslant T(1—0.08n)$$

in which t = weighted average of the duties and charges that shall be applicable to imports from within the area; T = weighted average of duties and charges in force for third countries; n = number of years since the Treaty entered into force.

6. In calculating the weighted averages for each of the Contracting Parties, the following shall be taken into account:

(a) Products originating in the territory of the other Contracting Parties and imported from the Area during the preceding three-year period and further products included in the National Schedule concerned as a result of negotiations;

(b) The total value of imports, irrespective of origin, of each of the products referred to in sub-paragraph (a), during the three-year period preceding each negotiation; and

(c) The duties and charges on imports from third countries in force as on 31 December prior to the negotiations, and the duties and charges applicable to imports from within the Area entering into force on 1 January following the negotiations.

7. The Contracting Parties shall be entitled to exclude products of little value from the group referred to in sub-paragraph (a), provided that their aggregate value does not exceed five per cent (5%) of the value of imports from within the Area.

TITLE II

Exchange of information

8. The Contracting Parties shall provide one another, through the Standing Executive Committee, with information as complete as possible on:

(a) National statistics in respect of total imports and exports (value in dollars and volume, by countries both of origin and of destination), production and consumption;

(b) Customs legislation and regulations;

(c) Exchange, monetary, fiscal and administrative legislation, regulations and practices bearing on exports and imports;

(d) International trade treaties and agreements whose provisions relate to the Treaty;

(e) Systems of direct or indirect subsidies on production or exports including minimum price systems; and

(f) State trading systems.

9. So far as possible, these data shall be permanently available to the Contracting Parties. They shall be specially brought up to date sufficiently in advance of the opening of the annual negotiations.

TITLE III

Negotiation of National Schedules

10. Before 30 June of each year, the Contracting Parties shall make available to one another, through the Standing Executive Committee, the list of products in respect of which they are applying for concessions and, before 15 August of each year (with the exception of the first year, when the corresponding final date shall be 1 October), the preliminary list of items in favor of which they are prepared to grant concessions.

11. On 1 September of each year (with the exception of the first year, when the corresponding date shall be 1 November), the Contracting Parties shall initiate the negotiation of the concessions to be accorded by each to the others as a whole. The concessions shall be assessed multilaterally, although this shall not preclude the conduct of negotiations by pairs or groups of countries, in accordance with the interest attaching to specific products.

12. Upon the conclusion of this phase of the negotiations, the Standing Executive Committee shall make the calculations referred to in title I of this Protocol and shall inform each Contracting Party, at the earliest possible opportunity, of the percentage whereby its individual concessions reduce the weighted average of the duties and charges in force for imports from within the Area, in relation to the weighted average of duties and charges applicable in the case of third countries.

13. When the concessions negotiated fall short of the corresponding minimum commitment, the negotiations among the Contracting Parties shall be continued, so that the list of reductions of duties and charges and other restrictions to enter into force as from the following 1 January may be simultaneously published by each of the Contracting Parties not later than 1 November of each year.

TITLE IV

Negotiation of the Common Schedule

14. During each three-year period and not later than on 31 May of the third, sixth, ninth and twelfth years from the time of the Treaty's entry into force, the Standing Executive Committee shall supply the Contracting Parties with statistical data on the value and volume of the products traded in the Area during the preceding three-year period, indicating the proportion of aggregate trade which each individually represented.

15. Before 30 June of the third, sixth and ninth years from the time of the Treaty's entry into force, the Contracting Parties shall exchange the lists of products whose inclusion in the Common Schedule they wish to negotiate.

16. The Contracting Parties shall conduct multilateral negotiation to establish, before 30 November of the third, sixth, ninth and twelfth years, a Common Schedule comprising goods whose value meets the minimum commitments referred to in article 7 of the Treaty.

TITLE V

Special and temporary provisions

17. In the negotiations to which this Protocol refers, consideration shall be given to those cases in which varying levels of duties and charges on certain products create conditions such that producers in the Area are not competing on equitable terms.

18. To this end, steps shall be taken to ensure prior equalization of tariffs or to secure by any other suitable procedure the highest possible degree of effective reciprocity.

IN WITNESS WHEREOF the respective representatives have signed the Protocol.

DONE in the City of Montevideo, this eighteenth day of the month of February in the year One Thousand Nine Hundred and Sixty, in one original in the Spanish and one in the Portuguese language, both texts being equally authentic.

The Government of the Eastern Republic of Uruguay shall act as depositary of the present Protocol and shall send certified true copies thereof to the Governments of the other signatory and acceding countries.

PROTOCOL NO. 2

ON THE ESTABLISHMENT OF A PROVISIONAL COMMITTEE

On the occasion of the signing of the Treaty establishing a Free Trade Area and instituting the Latin American Free Trade Association (Montevideo Treaty), the signatories, thereunto duly authorized by their Governments, taking into consideration the need to adopt and coordinate measures to facilitate the entry into force of the Treaty, hereby agree as follows:

1. A Provisional Committee shall be set up, composed of one representative of each signatory State. Each representative shall have an alternate.

At its first meeting the Provisional Committee shall elect from among its members one Chairman and two Vice-Chairmen.

2. The terms of reference of the Provisional Committee shall be as follows:

(a) To draw up its rules of procedure;

(b) To prepare, within sixty days from the date of its inauguration, its work program and to establish its budget of expenditures and the contributions to be made by each country;

(c) To adopt the measures and prepare the documents necessary for the presentation of the Treaty to the Contracting Parties of the General Agreement on Tariffs and Trade (GATT);

(d) To convene and prepare for the first Conference of Contracting Parties;

(e) To assemble and prepare the data and statistics required for the first series of negotiations connected with the implementation of the liberalization program provided for in the Treaty;

(f) To carry out or promote studies and research, and to adopt whatsoever measures may be necessary in the common interest during its period of office; and

(g) To prepare a preliminary draft agreement on the privileges and immunities referred to in article 47 of the Treaty.

3. In technical matters, the Provisional Committee shall be assisted in an advisory capacity by the United Nations Economic Commission for Latin America (ECLA) and the Inter-American Economic and Social Council (IA-ECOSOC), of the Organization of American States, in accordance with the relevant Protocol.

4. The Provisional Committee shall appoint an Administrative Secretary and other requisite staff.

5. The Provisional Committee shall be inaugurated on 1 April 1960, and its quorum shall be constituted by not less than four members. Up to that date, the Offices of the Inter-Governmental Conference for the Establishment of a Free Trade Area among Latin American Countries shall continue to discharge their functions, for the sole purpose of establishing the Provisional Committee.

6. The Provisional Committee shall remain in office until the Standing Executive Committee, provided for in article 33 of the Treaty, has been set up.

7. The Provisional Committee shall have its headquarters in the City of Montevideo.

8. The Officers of the abovementioned Conference are recommended to request the Government of the Eastern Republic of Uruguay to advance the necessary sums to cover the payment of staff salaries and the installation and operational expenses of the Provisional Committee during the first ninety days. These sums shall be subsequently reimbursed by the States signatories of the present Treaty.

9. The Provisional Committee shall approach the signatory Governments with a view to obtaining for the members of its constituent delegations, as well as for its international staff and advisers, such immunities and privileges as may be needful for the performance of their duties.

IN WITNESS WHEREOF the respective representatives have signed the present Protocol.

DONE in the City of Montevideo, this eighteenth day of the month of February in the year One Thousand Nine Hundred and Sixty, in one original in the Spanish and one in the Portuguese language, both texts being equally authentic. The Government of the Eastern Republic of Uruguay shall act as the depositary of the present Protocol and shall send certified true copies thereof to the Governments of the other signatory and acceding countries.

PROTOCOL NO. 3

ON THE COLLABORATION OF THE UNITED NATIONS ECONOMIC COMMISSION FOR LATIN AMERICA (ECLA) AND OF THE INTER-AMERICAN ECONOMIC AND SOCIAL COUNCIL (IA-ECOSOC) OF THE ORGANIZATION OF AMERICAN STATES

On the occasion of the signing of the Treaty establishing a Free Trade Area and instituting the Latin American Free Trade Association (Montevideo Treaty), the signatories, thereunto duly authorized by their Governments, hereby agree as follows:

1. With reference to the provisions of article 44 of the Treaty and in view of the fact that the secretariats of ECLA and of IA-ECOSOC have agreed to assist the organs of the Latin American Free Trade Association with advice on technical matters, a representative of each of the secretariats in question shall attend the meetings of the Standing Executive Committee of the abovementioned Association when the business to be discussed is, in the Committee's opinion, of a technical nature.

2. The appointment of the representatives referred to shall be subject to the prior approval of the members of the said Committee.

IN WITNESS WHEREOF the respective representatives have signed the present Protocol.

DONE at the City of Montevideo, this eighteenth day of the month of February in the year One Thousand Nine Hundred and Sixty, in one original in the Spanish and one in the Portuguese language, both texts being equally authentic. The Government of the Eastern Republic of Uruguay shall act as the depositary of the present Protocol and shall send certified true copies thereof to the Governments of the other signatory and acceding countries.

PROTOCOL NO. 4

ON COMMITMENTS TO PURCHASE OR SELL PETROLEUM AND PETROLEUM DERIVATIVES

On the occasion of the signing of the Treaty establishing a Free Trade Area and instituting the Latin American Free Trade Association (Montevideo Treaty), the signatories, thereunto duly authorized by their Governments, hereby agree:

To declare that the provisions of the Montevideo Treaty, signed on 18 February 1960, are not applicable to commitments to purchase or sell petroleum and petroleum derivatives resulting from agreements concluded by the signatories of the present Protocol prior to the date of signature of the abovementioned Treaty.

IN WITNESS WHEREOF the respective representatives have signed the present Protocol.

DONE at the City of Montevideo, this eighteenth day of the month of February in the year One Thousand Nine Hundred and Sixty, in one original in the Spanish and one in the Portuguese language, both texts being equally authentic.

The Government of the Eastern Republic of Uruguay shall act as depositary of the present Protocol and shall send certified true copies thereof to the Governments of the other signatory and acceding countries.

PROTOCOL NO. 5

ON SPECIAL TREATMENT IN FAVOR OF BOLIVIA AND PARAGUAY

On the occasion of the signing of the Treaty establishing a Free Trade Area and instituting the Latin American Free Trade Association (Montevideo Treaty), the signatories, thereunto duly authorized by their Governments, hereby agree:

To declare that Bolivia and Paraguay are at present in a position to invoke in their favor the provisions in the Treaty concerning special treatment for countries at a relatively less advanced stage of economic development within the Free Trade Area.

IN WITNESS WHEREOF the respective representatives have signed the present Protocol.

DONE in the City of Montevideo, this eighteenth day of the month of February in the year One Thousand Nine Hundred and Sixty, in one original in the Spanish and one in the Portuguese language, both texts being equally authentic.

The Government of the Eastern Republic of Uruguay shall act as depositary of the present Protocol and shall send certified true copies thereof to the Governments of the other signatory and acceding countries.

24. LIST AND STATUS OF INTER-AMERICAN TREATIES AND CONVENTIONS

This appendix contains three charts that list the treaties, conventions, and other instruments signed at Inter-American Conferences (Chart A), Special Conferences (Chart B), and those opened for signature at the Pan American Union (Chart C). Each chart shows the actions taken by country, on the respective treaties.

Only inter-American instruments are included. The status of other multilateral agreements is shown in two publications of the Pan American Union—Treaty Series No. 5, a chart revised annually; and Treaty Series No. 9 which presents similar data in more detail.

SYMBOLS

A	— Adherence subject to ratification
Ad	— Adherence deposited
Ar	— Adherence with reservations
AR	— Adherence ratified
ARd	— Adherence ratified and deposited
ARdr	— Adherence ratified and deposited with reservations
ARr	— Adherence ratified with reservations
D	— Denounced
R	— Ratified
Rd	— Ratification deposited
Rdr	— Ratification deposited with reservations
Rr	— Ratified with reservations
S	— Signatory
Sr	— Signed with reservations

CHART "A"

TREATIES AND CONVENTIONS SIGNED AT INTER-AMERICAN CONFERENCES

First Conference
Washington, 1889-1890
(No Treaties or conventions were signed)

Second Conference
Mexico, 1901-1902

A-1. Treaty of arbitration for pecuniary claims
A-2. Treaty for the extradition of criminals and for protection against anarchism
A-3. Convention on the practice of learned professions
A-4. Convention for the formation of codes on public and private international law
A-5. Convention on literary and artistic copyrights
A-6. Convention relative to the exchange of official, scientific, literary and industrial publications
A-7. Treaty on patents of invention, industrial drawings and models and trade-marks
A-8. Convention relative to the rights of aliens
A-9. Treaty on compulsory arbitration

Third Conference
Rio de Janeiro, 1906

A-10. Convention establishing the status of naturalized citizens who again take up their residence in the country of their origin
A-11. Convention on pecuniary claims
A-12. Convention on patents of invention, drawings and industrial models, trade-marks, and literary and artistic property
A-13. Convention on international law

Fourth Conference
Buenos Aires, 1910

A-14. Convention on inventions, patents, designs and industrial models
A-15. Convention on the protection of trade marks
A-16. Convention on literary and artistic copyright
A-17. Convention on pecuniary claims

Fifth Conference
Santiago de Chile, 1923

A-18. Treaty to avoid or prevent conflicts between the American States (Gondra Treaty)
A-19. Convention on publicity of customs documents
A-20. Convention for the protection of commercial, industrial, and agricultural trade marks and commercial names
A-21. Convention on uniformity of nomenclature for the classification of merchandise

Sixth Conference
Havana, 1928

A-22. Convention on status of aliens
A-23. Convention on asylum
A-24. Convention on consular agents
A-25. Convention on diplomatic officers
A-26. Convention on maritime neutrality
A-27. Convention on duties and rights of states in the event of civil strife
A-28. Convention on treaties
A-29. Convention on commercial aviation
A-30. Revision of the Convention of Buenos Aires on the protection of literary and artistic copyright
A-31. Convention on private international law (Bustamante Code)
A-32. Convention on the Pan American Union

Seventh Conference
Montevideo, 1933

A-33. Convention on the nationality of women
A-34. Convention on nationality
A-35. Convention on extradition
A-36. Optional clause annexed to the convention on extradition
A-37. Convention on political asylum
A-38. Convention on the teaching of history

A-39. Additional protocol to the general convention of inter-American conciliation of 1929
A-40. Convention on rights and duties of States

Eighth Conference
Lima, 1938
(No treaties or conventions were signed)

Ninth Conference
Bogotá, 1948

A-41. Charter of the Organization of American States
A-42. American treaty on pacific settlement (Pact of Bogotá)
A-43. Economic agreement of Bogotá
A-44. Inter-American convention on the granting of political rights to women
A-45. Inter-American convention on the granting of civil rights to women

Tenth Conference
Caracas, 1954

A-46. Convention on diplomatic asylum
A-47. Convention on territorial asylum
A-48. Convention for the promotion of inter-American cultural relations

	A-1 Pecuniary Claims	A-2 Anarchism	A-3 Learned Professions	A-4 Formation of Codes	A-5 Copyright	A-6 Exchange of Publications	A-7 Patents, etc.	A-8 Rights of Aliens	A-9 Compulsory Arbitration
				SECOND CONFERENCE MEXICO, 1901-02					
ARGENTINA	S	S	S	S	S	S	'S	S	S
BOLIVIA	S	S	Rd	Rd	S	S	S	Rd	S
BRAZIL									
CHILE	S	S	Rd	Rd	S	S	Rd	R	
COLOMBIA	Rd	S	S	S	S	Rd	S	R	
COSTA RICA	Rd	Rdr	Rd	Rd	Rd	Rd	Rd	R	
CUBA					ARd	ARd			
DOMINICAN REP.	Rd	R	D	Rd	Rd	Rd	Rd	Rd	Rd
ECUADOR	R	Rr	S	R	R	R	R	R	
El SALVADOR	Rd	Rd	Rd	R	Rd	Rd	Rd	Rd	Rd
GUATEMALA	Rd	Rd	Rd	R	Rd	Rd	Rd	Rd	Rd
HAITI	S	S	S	S	S	S	S		
HONDURAS	Rd	Sr	Rd	R	Rd	Rd	Rd	Rd	
MEXICO	Rd	Rd	S	S	S	Rd	S	S	Rd
NICARAGUA	S	Rr	Rd	S	Rd	Rd	Rd	R	
PANAMA									
PARAGUAY	S	S	S	S	S	S	S	S	S
PERU	Rd	S	Rd	S	S	S	S	S	Rd
UNITED STATES	Rd	S	S	S	Rd	Rd			
URUGUAY	S	S	S	S	S	S	S	S	Rd
VENEZUELA									

A-10 Status of Citizens	A-11 Pecuniary Claims	A-12 Patents, Literary Property	A-13 International Law	A-14 Patents, etc.	A-15 Trade Marks	A-16 Copyright	A-17 Pecuniary Claims	A-18 Gondra Treaty	A-19 Customs Documents	A-20 Trade Marks	A-21 Classification of Merchandise
THIRD CONFERENCE RIO DE JAN., 1906				FOURTH CONFERENCE BUENOS AIRES, 1910				FIFTH CONFERENCE SANTIAGO, 1923			
Rd	S	S	Rd	S	S	Rd	S	S	S	S	S
S	S	S	S	Ad	Ad	Ad	Ad	ARd			
D	S	Rd	Rd	Rd	Rd	Rd	Rd	Rd	Rd	Rd	Rd
Rd	Rd	Rd	Rd	S	S	Rd	S	Rd	Rd	S	Rd
Rd	Rd	S	Rd	S	S	Rd	S	Rd	S	S	S
Rd	Rd	Rd	Rd	Rd	D	Rd	Rd	ARd	Rd	S	Rd
S	Rd	S	S	Rd	Rd	S	S	Rd	Rd	Rd	Rd
	S	S	Rd	Rd	Rd	Rd	Rd	Rd	Rd	Rd	Rd
Rd	Rd	Rd	Rd	Rd	Rd	Rd	Rd	Rd	S	S	S
Rd	Rd	Rd	Rd	S	S	S	S	ARd	Rd	S	Rd
D	Rd	Rd	Rd	Rd	D	Rd	Rd	Rd	S	S	R
				Rd	Rd	Rd	S	Rd	Rd	Rd	Rd
Rd	Rd	Rd	Rd	Rd	D	Rd	Rd	Rd	S	S	S
S	Rd	S	Rd	S	S	Rd	S	ARd			
Rd	Rd	Rd	Rd	Rd	D	Rd	Rd	Rd	S	S	S
Rd	Rd	Rd	Rd	Rd	Rd	Rd	Rd	Rd	Rd	S	Rd
S	S	S	Rd	Rd	Rd	Rd	Rd	Rd	Rd	Rd	Rd
S	S	S	Rd	S	Rd	Rd	S	ARdr			
Rd	Rd	S	Rd	Rd	Rd	Rd	Rd	Rd	Rd	Rdr	D
S	S	S	Rd	Rd	Rd	Rd	Rd	Rdr	Rd	Rd	Rd
				S	S	S	S	Rd	S	S	S

A. TREATIES AND CONVENTIONS SIGNED

SIXTH CONFERENCE HAVANA, 1928

	A-22 Status of Aliens	A-23 Asylum	A-24 Consular Agents	A-25 Diplomatic Officers	A-26 Maritime Neutrality	A-27 Duties & Rights of States	A-28 Treaties	A-29 Commercial Aviation	A-30 Copyright	A-31 Bustamante Code	A-32 Pan American Union
ARGENTINA	Rd	S	S	S	S	Rd	S	S	S	Sr	S
BOLIVIA	S	S	S	S	Rd	Rd	Sr	S	S	Rdr	Rd
BRAZIL	Rd	Rd	Rd	Rd	S	Rd	Rd	S	S	Rdr	Rd
CHILE	Rd	S	S	Rdr	Sr	S	S	D	Sr	Rdr	Rd
COLOMBIA	Rd	Rd	Rd	Rd	Rd	Rd	S	S	R	Sr	S
COSTA RICA	Rd	Rd	S	Rd	S	Rd	S	Rdr	Rd	Rdr	Rd
CUBA	S	Rd	Rd	Rd	Sr	Rd	S	S	S	Rd	Rd
DOMINICAN REP.	Rd	D	Rdr	Rdr	Rd	Rd	Rd	D	S	Rdr	Rd
ECUADOR	Rd	Rd	Rd	Rd	Rd	Rd	Rd	Rd	Rd	Rdr	Rd
El SALVADOR	S	Rd	Rd	Rd	S	Rd		S	S	Rdr	S
GUATEMALA	Rd	Rd	S	S	S	S	S	D	Rd	Rd	Rd
HAITI	Rd	Rd	Rd	Rd	Rd	Rd	Rd	Rd	S	Rdr	Rd
HONDURAS	S	Rd	S	S	S	Rd	Rd	Rd	S	Rd	S
MEXICO	Rdr	Rd	Rd	Rd	S	Rd	Sr	D	S	S	Rd
NICARAGUA	Rd	Rd	Rd	Rd	Rd	Rd	Rd	Rd	Rd	Rd	Rd
PANAMA	Rd	Rd	Rd	Rd	Rd	Rd	Rd	Rd	Rd	Rd	Rd
PARAGUAY	S	Rd	S	S	S	Rd	S	S	S	Sr	S
PERU	Rd	Rd	Rd	Rd	S	Rd	Rd	S	S	Rd	Rd
UNITED STATES	Rdr	Sr	Rd	S	Rdr	Rdr	S	D	S		Rd
URUGUAY	Rd	Rd	Rd	Rd	S	Rd	S	S	S	Sr	Rd
VENEZUELA	S	S	Sr	Rd	S	S	S	S		Rdr	Rd

AT INTER-AMERICAN CONFERENCES

	A-33 Nationality of Women	A-34 Nationality	A-35 Extradition	A-36 Optional Clause, Extradition	A-37 Political Asylum	A-38 Teaching of History	A-39 Inter-American Conciliation	A-40 Rights and Duties of States	A-41 Charter of the OAS	A-42 Pact of Bogota	A-43 Economic Agreement	A-44 Political Rights to Women	A-45 Civil Rights to Women	A-46 Diplomatic Asylum	A-47 Territorial Asylum	A-48 Cultural Relations
	SEVENTH CONFERENCE MONTEVIDEO, 1933								NINTH CONFERENCE BOGOTA, 1948					TENTH CONFERENCE CARACAS, 1954		
	Rd		Rd	S	S	S		S	Rd	Sr	Sr	Rd	Rd	S	Sr	S
	S				S				Rd	Sr	S		S	S	S	S
	Rd	D	S		Rd	S		Rdr	Rd	Rd	S	Rd	Rd	Rd	Rd	Rd
	Rd	Rd	Rdr		Rd·	S	Rd	Rd	Rd	S	Sr	S	S	S	S	S
	Rd		Rd		Rd	Rd	ARd	Rd	Rd	S	Sr	Rd	Rd	S	S	S
	ARd				ARd			ARd	Rd	Rd	Rd	Rd	Rd	Rd	Rd	Rd
	Rd		S		Rd	S		Rd	Rd	S	Sr	Rd	Rd	S	S	S
	S		Rd		D	Rd	ARd	Rd	Rd	Rd	Sr	Rd	Rd	Rd	Sr	S
	Rd	Rd	Rdr		Rd	Rd	R	Rd	Rd	Sr	Sr	Rd	Rd	Rd	Rd	Rd
	Sr		Rdr		Rd	S		Rd	Rd	Rd	S	ARd	Rd	Rd	Rd	S
	Rd		Rd		Rd	Rd	ARd	Rd	Rdr	S	Sr	Rr	Rd	Sr	Sr	S
	S		S		Rd	S		Rd	Rd	Rd	S	Rd	S	Rd	Rd	Rd
	Rdr	ARdr	Rdr		Rd	Rd	ARd	Rd	Rd.	Rd	Rdr	ARd	Rd	Sr	Sr	S
	Rdr	Rdr	Rdr		Rd	Rd	ARd	Rd	Rd	Rd	Sr		Rd	Rd	Sr	S
	Rd		Rd		Rd	R	AR	Rd	Rd	Rdr	S	Rd	Rd	S	S	S
	Rd	ARd	Rd		Rd	Rd	A	Rd	Rd	Rd	Rd	Rd	Rd	Rd	Rd	Rd
	S		S		Rd	S	ARd	S	Rd	Sr	S	Rd	Rd	Rd	Rd	Rd
	S·		S		Rd	S		Sr	Rdr	Sr	S	Rd	S	Rd	Sr	S
	Rdr		Rdr				Rd	Rdr	Rdr	Sr	Sr	S				Rd
	S	Sr	S	S	S	S	S	S	Rd	Rd	Sr	S	S	Sr	S	S
							ARdr	Rd	Rd	S	Sr	S	S	Rd	Rd	Rd

CHART "B"

TREATIES AND CONVENTIONS SIGNED AT
SPECIAL CONFERENCES

B-1.   Inter-American convention on electrical communications
B-2.   The Pan American sanitary code
B-3(1). Additional protocol to the Pan American sanitary code
B-3(2). Additional protocol to the Pan American sanitary code
B-4.   General convention of inter-American conciliation
B-5.   General treaty of inter-American arbitration
B-6.   Protocol of progressive arbitration
B-7.   General inter-American convention for trade mark and commercial protection
B-8.   Protocol on the inter-American registration of trade marks
B-9.   Anti-war treaty of non-aggression and conciliation (Saavedra-Lamas Pact)
B-10.   Convention on the repression of smuggling
B-11.   Convention relative to the creation of a Pan American tourist passport and of a transit passport for vehicles
B-12.   Convention relating to the transit of airplanes
B-13.   Convention for the creation of Pan American commercial committees
B-14.   Convention on maintenance, preservation and re-establishment of peace
B-15.   Additional protocol relative to non-intervention
B-16.   Treaty on the prevention of controversies
B-17.   Inter-American treaty on good offices and mediation
B-18.   Convention to coordinate, extend and assure the fulfillment of the existing treaties between the American States
B-19.   Convention on the Pan American highway
B-20.   Convention for the promotion of inter-American cultural relations
B-21.   Convention on interchange of publications
B-22.   Convention concerning artistic exhibitions
B-23.   Convention concerning peaceful orientation of public instruction
B-24.   Convention concerning facilities for educational and publicity films
B-25.   Convention on the provisional administration of European colonies and possessions in the Americas
B-26.   Convention providing for the creation of the Inter-American Indian Institute
B-27.   Convention on the Inter-American University
B-28.   Inter-American convention on the rights of the author in literary, scientific, and artistic works
B-29.   Inter-American treaty of reciprocal assistance
B-30.   Inter-American Convention on facilitation of international waterborne transportation (Convention of Mar del Plata)

B. TREATIES AND CONVENTIONS

	B-1 Electrical Communications MEXICO 1924	B-2 Sanitary Code HAVANA 1924	B-3 (1) Protocol, Sanitary Code LIMA 1927	B-3 (2) Additional Protocol, Sanitary Code HAVANA 1952
ARGENTINA	S	Rd	Rd	
BOLIVIA		ARd	S	
BRAZIL	S	Rd	Rd	Rd
CHILE	.	Rd	ARd	Rd
COLOMBIA	S	Rd	Rd	S
COSTA RICA	S	Rd	S	S
CUBA	S	Rd	S	Rd
DOMINICAN REP.	Rd	Rd	Rd	Rd
ECUADOR	S	ARd	Rd	Rd
El SALVADOR	S	Rd		Rd
GUATEMALA	S	Rd	S	S
HAITI		Rd	S	Rd
HONDURAS		Rd	S	
MEXICO	Rd	Rdr	ARd	Rd
NICARAGUA	S	Ad	S	S
PANAMA	Rd	Rd	Rd	S
PARAGUAY	Rd	Rd	Rd	S
PERU	S	Rd	Rd	S
UNITED STATES		Rd	Rd	
URUGUAY	S	Rd	Rd	S
VENEZUELA		Rd	Rd	S

SIGNED AT SPECIAL CONFERENCES

	WASHINGTON 1929			WASHINGTON 1929		RIO DE JANEIRO 1933	BUENOS AIRES 1935			
	B-4 Inter-American Conciliation	B-5 Inter-American Arbitration	B-6 Progressive Arbitration	B-7 Trade Mark & Commercial Protection	B-8 Protocol - Trade Marks	B-9 Saavedra-Lamas Pact	B-10 Repression of Smuggling	B-11 Passport, Tourist, Transit	B-12 Transit of Airplanes	B-13 Pan American Commercial Committees
						Rd	S	S	S	S
	S	Sr	S	S	S		S	S	S	S
	Rd	Rd	S	S	S	Rd	Rd	S	S	R
	Rd	Rdr	Rd	Sr		Rdr	Rd	S	Rdr	S
	Rd	Rdr	S	Rd	S	ARdr	S	S	S	S
	S	Sr	S	S	S	A	S	S	S	S
	Rd	Rd	S	Rd	Rd	ARd	S		S	S
	Rd	Rdr	Rd	S	S	ARd	S	S	S	Rd
	Rd	Rdr	Rd	S	S	ARdr	Rd	S	Rdr	S
	Rd	Rdr	Rd			ARdr	S	S	S	S
	Rd	Rdr	Rd	Rd		ARd	S	S	S	S
	Rd	Rd	Rd	Rd	D	ARd	S	S	S	S
	Rd	Rdr	Rd	Rd	D	ARdr	S	S	S	S
	Rd	Rdr	Rd	S	S	Rd	S	S	Rd	S
	Rd	Rd	Rd	Rd	S	ARd	S	S	S	S
	Rd	Rd	S	Rd	D	ARd	S	S	S	S
	Rd	Sr	S	Rd	S	Rd	S	Rd	S	S
	Rd	Rd	S	Rd	D	ARdr	S	S	S	S
	Rd	Rdr	S	Rd	D	ARdr	S			S
	Rd	Sr	S	S		Rd	Rd	Rd	Rd	Rd
	Rd	Rdr	Rd	S	S	ARdr	S	S	S	S

B. TREATIES AND CONVENTIONS

BUENOS AIRES 1936

	B-14 Maintenance of Peace	B-15 Protocol, Non-Intervention	B-16 Prevention of Controversies	B-17 Good Offices & Mediation	B-18 Fulfillment, Existing Treaties	B-19 Pan American Highway	B-20 Cultural Relations	B-21 Interchange of Publications	B-22 Artistic Exhibitions	B-23 Peaceful Orientation, Instruction	B-24 Educational Films
ARGENTINA	S	S	S	S	Sr	S	S	S	S	S	S
BOLIVIA	S	S	S	S	S	Rd	Rd	S	S	S	S
BRAZIL	Rd	Rd	S	Rd	Rd	S	Rd	Rd	Rd	Rd	Rd
CHILE	Rd	Rd	Rd	Rd	Rd	Rd	Rd	S	Rd	Rd	Rd
COLOMBIA	Rd	Rd	Rd	Rd	Rdr	Rd	Rd	Rd	Rd	Rd	Rd
COSTA RICA	Rd	Rd	Rd	Rd	S	Rd	Rd	Rd	Rd	Rd	Rd
CUBA	Rd	Rd	Rd	Rd	Rd	S	Rd	S	S	S	S
DOMINICAN REP.	Rd	Rd	Rd	Rd	Rd	S	Rd	Rd	Rd	Rd	Rd
ECUADOR	Rdr	Rdr	Rd	Rd	Rd	S	S	S	S	S	Rd
El SALVADOR	Rd	Rd	Rd	Rd	Rdr	Rd	S	Rd	Rd	Rd	Rd
GUATEMALA	Rd	Rd	Rdr	Rd	Rd	Rd	Rd	Rd	Rd	Rd	Rd
HAITI	Rd	Rd	Rd	Rd	Rd	S	Rd	Rd	Rd	Rd	Rd
HONDURAS	Rdr'	Rd	Rd	Rdr	Rdr	Rd	Rd	Rd	Rd	Rd	Rd
MEXICO	Rd	Rd	Rd	Rd	Rd	Rd	Rd	S	Rd	Rd	Rdr
NICARAGUA	Rd	Rd	Rd	Rd	Rd	Rd	Rd	Rd	Rd	Rd	Rd
PANAMA	Rd	Rd	Rd	Rd	Rd	Rd	Rd	Rd	Rd	Rd	Rd
PARAGUAY	Rdr	S	S	S	Sr	S	Rd	S	S	S	S
PERU	S	S	Sr	S	S	Rd	Rd	Rd	Rd	S	Rd
UNITED STATES	Rd	Rd	Rd	Rd	Rdr	Rd	Rd	Rd	Rd		
URUGUAY	S	S	S	S	S	S	S	S	S	S	S
VENEZUELA	Rd	Rd	S	S	S	S	Rd	Rd	Rd	Rd	Rdr

SIGNED AT SPECIAL CONFERENCES

| B-25 Colonies and Possessions | B-26 Indian Institute | B-27 Inter-American University | B-28 Rights of the Author | B-29 Reciprocal Assistance | B-30 Waterborne Transportation |
HAVANA 1940	MEXICO 1940	PANAMA 1943	WASHINGTON 1946	RIO DE JANEIRO 1947	MAR DEL PLATA 1963
Rdr	A	Sr	Rd	Rd	S
S	Rd	S	Rd	Rd	S
Rd	ARd	S	Rd	Rd	
Sr	A	S	Rd	Rd	Sr
Rd	ARd	S	S	Rd	S
Rd	S	S	Rd	Rd	S
S	S	S	Rd	Rd	
Rd	D	S	Rd	Rd	
Rd	Rd	S	Rd	Rd	
Rd	Rd	S	S	Rd	
Rd	ARd	S	Rd	Rdr	
Rd		S	Rd	Rd	
Rd	Rd	S	Rd	Rdr	S
Rd	Rd	S	Rd	Rd	
Rd	ARd	S	Rd	Rdr	
Rd	ARd	S	S	Rd	S
S	ARd	S	Rd	Rd	S
Rd	Rd	S	S	Rd	S
Rd	Rd	Sr	S	Rd	S
Rd		S	S	Rd	S
Rd	ARd	Rd	S	Rd	

CHART "C"

TREATIES AND CONVENTIONS OPENED FOR SIGNATURE AT THE PAN AMERICAN UNION

C-1.   Convention on the regulation of automotive traffic

C-2.   Agreement on the application of the most-favored-nation clause

C-3.   Treaty on the protection of artistic and scientific institutions and historic monuments (Roerich Pact)

C-4.   Treaty on the protection of movable property of historic value

C-5.   Declaration on the juridical personality of foreign companies

C-6.   Protocol on uniformity of powers of attorney which are to be utilized abroad

C-7.   Convention for the establishment of an Inter-American Bank

C-8.   Convention on nature protection and wild life preservation in the Western Hemisphere

C-9.   Inter-American coffee agreement

C-10.   Protocol to the inter-American coffee agreement

C-11.   Convention on the regulation of Inter-American automotive traffic

C-12.   Convention on the Inter-American Institute of Agricultural Sciences

C-12(1) Protocol of Amendment to the Convention on the Inter-American Institute of Agricultural Sciences

C-13.   Agreement on privileges and immunities of the Organization of American States

C-14.   Protocol to the Convention on duties and rights of States in the event of civil strife

C-15.   Agreement establishing the Inter-American Development Bank

C. TREATIES AND CONVENTIONS OPENED FOR SIGNATURE

	C-1 Automotive Traffic (1930)	C-2 Most-Favored-Nation Clause (1934)	C-3 Roerich Pact (1935)	C-4 Movable Property of Historic Value (1935)	C-5 Juridical Personality (1936)	C-6 Uniformity of Powers of Attorney (1940)	C-7 Inter-American Bank (1940)
ARGENTINA	S		S				
BOLIVIA	S		S			Sr	S
BRAZIL	S		Rd			S	S
CHILE	S		Rd	Rdr	Sr		
COLOMBIA	S	S	Rd			Rdr	S
COSTA RICA	S		S				
CUBA		Rd	Rd				
DOMINICAN REP.	Rd		Rd		Sr		S
ECUADOR	Rd		S	S	S		S
El SALVADOR	S		Rd	Rd	S	Rdr	
GUATEMALA	S	S	Rd	Rd			
HAITI			S				
HONDURAS	Rd		R				
MEXICO	Rd		Rd	Rd		Rdr	R
NICARAGUA	S	S	S	Rd	S	S	S
PANAMA	S	S	S	S		S	
PARAGUAY	S		S				S
PERU	Rd		S		S		
UNITED STATES		Rd	Rd		Rdr	Rd	S
URUGUAY	S		S	S			
VENEZUELA	S		Rd		Rd	Rdr	

C-8 Wild Life Preservation (1940)	C-9 Coffee Agreement (1940)	C-10 Protocol, Coffee Agreement (1941)	C-11 Automotive Traffic (1943)	C-12 Agricultural Sciences Institute (1944)	C-12 (II) Protocol, Agricultural Sciences Institute (1958)	C-13 Privileges & Immunities of the OAS (1949)	C-14 Protocol, Duties and Rights of States (1957)	C-15 Inter-American Bank (1959)
Rdr			Rd	Ad	Ad		Rd	Rd
S			S	Rd	Rd	S		Rd
Rd	Rd	S	Rd	Rd	Rd	Rd	S	Rd
S			Rdr	Rd	S	S		Rd
S	Rd	S	Rd	Rd	Rd			Rd
S	Rd	S	Rd	Rd	Rd	Rd	Rd	Rd
S	Rd	S	S	Rd		Rd	Rd	
Rd	Rd	S	Rdr	Rd	Rd		Rd	Rd
Rd	Rd	S	Rd	Rd	Rd	Rd		Rd
Rd	Rd	S	Rd	Rd	Rd		Rd	Rd
Rd	Rd	S	Rd	Rd	Rd			Rd
Rd	Rd	S	Rd	Ad	Rd	Rd	Rd	Rd
	Rd	S	Rd	Rd	Rd	Rd	Rd	Rd
Rd	Rd	S	Rdr	Rd	Rd			Rd
Rd	Rd	S	Rd	Rd	Rd	ARd		Rd
			Rd	Rd	Rd			Rd
			Rdr	Rd	Rd			Rd
Rd	Rd	S	Rd	Rd	Rd	Rd	S	Rd
Rd	Rd	S	Rdr	Rd	Rd		S	Rd
S			Rd	Rd	ARd			Rd
Rd	Rd	S	Rdr	Rdr	Rd			Rd

25. BIBLIOGRAPHY

ACCIOLY, Hildebrando. Raizes ou causas históricas do pan-americanismo. [Rio de Janeiro] Ministério das Relações Exteriores, Serviço de Publicações [1953]. 77 p.
Bibliographical references included in "Notes" p. [69]–75.

AGUILAR NAVARRO, Mariano. El panamericanismo y el Pacto del Atlántico. (Estudios americanos, Sevilla, 1(4): 729-755, oct. 1949)

AVELLAN VITE, Alberto. Breve estudio sobre la Carta de la Organización de los Estados Americanos. (Revista del Colegio Nacional Vicente Rocafuerte, Guayaquil, 29 (62): 10–24, nov. 1952)

BAQUERO LAZCANO, Emilio. La Unión Panamericana, actual secretaría de la O.E.A.; origen, evolución, régimen actual. Córdoba, República Argentina. Impr. de la Universidad, 1956. 206 p.

BARCIA TRELLES, Milo. Intento de coordinación hemisférica; El tríptico de Bogotá. (Revista de política internacional, Madrid, (64): 59–84, nov./dic. 1962)

BARRERA REYES, Arturo. O.E.A., la Organización de Estados Americanos, medios pacíficos para la solución de conflictos interamericanos. México, 1955. 94 p.

BASANI REILLY, Jorge R. Organización de los Estados Americanos (O.E.A.). Antecedentes—Creación—Desarrollo—Organización—Actuación. (Boletín del Centro Naval, B.A., 73(623):193–227, jul./ag. 1955)

BAYONA ORTIZ, Antonio. Aspectos politico-jurídicos de la organización internacional americana. Bogotá, 1953. 131 p.

BLANCO VILLALTA, Jorge G. La organización de la comunidad internacional. Buenos Aires, Editorial Nova [1958]. 164 p. (Compendios Nova de iniciación cultural, 22).
"Bibliografía": p. [153–157].

BUNKER, Ellsworth. First Special Inter-American Conference provides for admission of new members to Organization of American States. (Department of State Bulletin, Washington, D.C., 52:46–49, Jan. 11, 1965)

CAICEDO CASTILLA, José J. As faculdades do Conselho da Organização dos Estados Americanos. (Boletim da Sociedade Brasileira de Direito Internacional, Rio de Janeiro, 14(27/28): 29–42, jan./dez. 1958)

—. El panamericanismo. Buenos Aires, R. Depalma, 1961. 484 p.

CALZADA FLORES, Miguel. La organización interamericana dentro de la organización mundial. México, 1949. 104 p.

CAMPOS ORTIZ, Pablo. Bases constitucionales de la Organización de los Estados Americanos. (México. Secretaría de Relaciones Exteriores. México en la IX Conferencia Internacional Americana. México, D.F., 1948. p.39–60)

CANYES SANTACANA, Manuel. The Organization of American States and the United Nations. 6th ed. 1963. 57 p.

CARDON, Raul L. La solución pacífica de controversias internacionales en el sistema americano (Revista de Derecho Internacional y Ciencias Diplomáticas, Rosario, vol. 3/5, no. 5/10, ene.–dic. 1953, pp. 153–234)

CASTAÑEDA, Jorge. Pan Americanism and regionalism: A Mexican view. (International organization, Boston, 10(3):373–389, Aug. 1956)

CLARET DE VOOGD, Lilia. La O.E.A. y las Naciones Unidas; contribución de la Organización de los Estados Americanos al afianzamiento de las Naciones Unidas. Prólogo del Dr. Alfredo Palacios. Buenos Aires, Editorial Bibliográfica Argentina 1956. 219 p.

CLAUDE, Inis L., Jr. The OAS, the UN, and the United States. (International conciliation, N.Y., (547): 1–67, Mar. 1964)

CLINE, Howard F. The Inter-American System. (Current history, Philadelphia, Pa., 28(163): 177–184, Mar. 1955)

CONNEL-SMITH, Gordon. Future of the Organization of American States. (World today, London, 18: 112–120, Mar. 1962)

CUEVAS CANCINO, Francisco M. Del Congreso de Panamá a la Conferencia de Caracas 1826–1954; el genio de Bolívar a través de la historia de las relaciones interamericanas. Caracas, 1955. 2v.

—. Práctica en las relaciones entre la Organización de los Estados Americanos y las Naciones Unidas. (Revista de la Facultad de Derecho de México, México, 4(13): 63–77, en./mar. 1954)

D'ANGELO EVANS, Armando. Los conflictos del Caribe y el sistema interamericano de paz. (Revista de derecho internacional y ciencias diplomáticas, Rosario, Arg., 6 (11): 133–149, en./dic. 1954)

DIAZ DOIN, Guillermo. La Organización de Estados Americanos y la no intervención. (Cuadernos americanos, México, 110(3): 73–88, mayo/jun. 1960)

DREIER, John C. The Council of the OAS: performance and potential. (Journal of inter-American studies, Gainesville, Florida, 5(3): 297–312, July 1963)

—. The Organization of American States and the hemisphere crisis. 1st. ed. New York. Published for the Council on Foreign Relations by Harper & Row. 1962. 147 p.

DUPUY, René Jean. Le nouveau panaméricanisme; l'évolution du système inter-américain vers le fédéralisme. Paris, Editions A. Pedone, 1956. 256 p. (Bibliothèque de la Faculté de Droit d'Alger, v. 19).
Bibliography: p. [251]–254.

FACIO, Gonzalo J. Impulso democrático al Sistema Interamericano. (Combate, San José,C.R., 2(10): 48–56, mayo/jun. 1960)

FENWICK, Charles G. Inter-American regional procedures for the settlement of disputes (International organization, v. 10, No. 1, Feb. 1956, pp. 12–21)

—. The Organization of American States; the inter-American regional system. [Washington, 1963] 601 p.

FERNANDEZ-SHAW Y BALDASANO, Felix G. La Organización de los Estados Americanos (O.E.A.) una nueva visión de América. Madrid, 1963. 989 p.

FISCHLOWITZ Estanislau. A O.E.A. no sistema político interamericano. (Revista de direito público e ciência política, Rio de Janeiro, 4(2): 62–80, maio–ag. 1961)

FREEMAN, Alwyn V. La competencia general del Consejo de Organización de los Estados Americanos con respecto a cuestiones de índole política. (Revista peruana de derecho internacional, Lima, 10(33): 3–35, en./abr. 1950)

FURNISS, Edgar S. Inter-American System and recent Caribbean disputes. (International organization, Boston, 4: 585–587, Nov. 1950)

GARCIA AMADOR, F. V. El desenvolvimiento del derecho internacional público en América. (Revista de derecho internacional, Habana, 44: 43–115, 1943)

—. Latin American Integration. (Americas, Vol. 17, No. 4, April 1965: 50–53.

—. The Dominican Situation. The jurisdiction of the Regional Organization. (Americas, Vol. 17, No. 7, July 1965: 1–3)

GOMEZ ROBLEDO, Antonio. Idea y experiencia de América. México, Fondo de Cultura Económica 1958. 250 p.

—. La Seguridad Colectiva en el Continente Americano. (Universidad Nacional Autónoma de México, Escuela Nacional de Ciencias Políticas y Sociales). México, 1960. 226 p.

GOMEZ DE LA TORRE, Mario A. Derecho constitucional interamericano. Quito, 1964. 2 v.

GONZALEZ DITTONI, Enrique. Antecedentes de la Organización de los Estados Americanos. (Revista de la Universidad Católica del Perú, Lima, 15(1): 116–128, 1955)

HADLEY, Paul E. Organization of American States: A regional system within the United Nations. (World affairs interpreter, Los Angeles, 22(1): 31–43, Spring–Apr. 1951)

HERTER, Christian. Inter-American cooperation moves forward. (The Department of State Bulletin, Washington, D.C., 42(1089): 754-757, May 9, 1960)

HOYO ALGARA, Francisco del. Estudio de la Organización de los Estados Americanos. México, 1952. 108 p.

INMAN, Samuel G. The Pan American system: an illustration of regional organization for peace. (International conciliation, N.Y., (369): 348-358, Apr. 1941)

KEY, David McK. The Organization of American States and the United Nations: Rivals or partners? (The Department of State Bulletin, Washington, D.C., 31(787): 115–118, July 26, 1954)

KUNZ, Josef L. The Bogotá Charter of the Organization of American States. (American journal of international law, Washington, D.C., 42: 568–589, 1948)

LOPEZ MALDONADO, Ulpiano. Del Congreso de Panamá a la Conferencia de Caracas, 1826–1954. El genio de Bolívar a través de la historia de las relaciones interamericanas. Quito

LUNA SILVA, Armando. La O.E.A. y sus orígenes. (Cuadernos hispanoamericanos, Madrid, no.109, 16 suppl. pages, en. 1959)

LLERAS CAMARGO, Alberto. The Organization of American States; an example for the world. Lewisburg, Pa. Bucknell University Press, 1954. 16 p.

—. The inter-American way of life; selections from the recent addresses and writings of Alberto Lleras. Washington, Pan American Union, 1951, 46 p.

—. Discurso pronunciado ante la X Conferencia Interamericana, reunida en Caracas, [Washington, Pan American Union, 1954] 11 leaves (Issued also in English.)

—. The Inter-American System today. (Annals of the American Academy of Political and Social Sciences, Philadelphia, 282: 97–103, Jul. 1952)

MANGER, William. Pan America in crisis; the future of OAS. With an introd. by Alberto Lleras Camargo and a foreword by Hector David Castro. Washington, 1961. 104 p.

MARINHO, Ilmar Penna. O funcionamento do sistema interamericano dentro do sistema mundial. Rio de Janeiro, 1959. 198 p.

MECHAM, John Lloyd. The United States and inter-American security, 1889–1960. Austin, 1961.

MacQUARRIE, Heath Nelson. Pan Americanism: pattern of regional cooperation. (Dalhousie review, Halifax, Nova Scotia, 34(3):223–234, Autumn 1954)

MORALES, Cecilio. Acción de la OEA en el campo económico y social. (Boletín informativo, Consejo Interamericano de Comercio y Producción, Montevideo, 129: 35–40, mar./abr. 1960)

MORA OTERO, José Antonio. Fortalecimiento del sistema interamericano; exposición del Secretario General, Dr. José A. Mora, [presentada al Consejo de la OEA el 21 de octubre de 1964]. Washington, D.C., Unión Panamericana, 1964. 22 p. (Issued also in English)

—. The Organization of American States. (International organization, Boston, 14(4): 514–523, Autumn 1960)

NAVARRO ANDRADE, Ulpiano. Unión de las naciones americanas. (Anales, Quito, 76: 63–209, en./dic. 1948)

NORTHWESTERN UNIVERSITY, Evanston, Ill., Dept. of Political Science. United States-Latin American relations: The Organization of American States. A study prepared at the request of the Subcommittee on American Republics Affairs of the Committee on Foreign Relations, United States Senate . . . No. 3. Washington, U.S. Govt. Print. Off., 1959. 87 p.

ORGANIZATION of American States. (International organization, Boston, 1947–date) Summary of activities appearing . . . (Cont.) Title in the first issue, Nov. 1947, is "The Inter-American System," in subsequent issues "Organization of American States."

OSSA G., Jorge. Organización de los Estados Americanos. (Revista de marina, Valparaíso, 67(5): 631–651, sept./oct. 1951; 67(6): 803–814, nov./dic. 1951)

PICCIRILLI, Rodolfo. La Novena Conferencia Internacional Americana. (Revista de derecho internacional y ciencias diplomáticas, Rosario, Arg. 1(1/2): 9–58, abr./dic. 1949)

PRADA JAIMES, Luz M. Paralelo entre la ONU y la OEA; solución pacífica de las controversias. Bogotá, 1960. 93 p.

QUINTANILLA, Luis. La convivencia americana. (Ciencias políticas y sociales, México, D.F., 8(27): 1–13, en./mar. 1962)

SANDERS, William. The Bogotá Conference: The Organization of American States. (International conciliation, N.Y., (442):383–417, 1948.

—. The OAS in a time of change; an evaluation; speech made by William Sanders, Assistant Secretary General of the OAS, at the Tenth Annual Meeting of the Pacific Coast Council on Latin American Studies, San Diego State College, October 23, 1964. Washington, 1964. 14 l. (Issued also in Spanish.)

SEOANE, Manuel. Proyección histórica de la Organización de Estados Americanos (O.E.A.); conferencias. Quito, Ediciones CIESPAL 1963. 40 p.

SILVA, Geraldo E. do N. e. Estrutura e funcionamento da Organização dos Estados Americanos. (Boletim da Sociedade Brasileira de Direito Internacional, Rio de Janeiro, 12(23/24): 38–61, jan./dez. 1956)

TERCERO CASTRO, David. Contribución de la O.E.A. al derecho internacional. Guatemala 1955. 86 p.

THOMAS, Ann Van Wynen and A. J., Jr. The Organization of American States. Dallas, Southern Methodist University Press, 1963. 530 p.

TRAVIS, Martin B. The Organization of American States: a guide to the future. (Western political quarterly, Salt Lake City, 10(3): 491–511, Sept. 1957)

TORRES BODET, Jaime. Transformación del panamericanismo. (Anuario jurídico interamericano, Washington, D.C., p. 61–70, 1948)

URRUTIA HOLGUIN, Francisco. Sentido y alcance de la Organización de Estados Americanos. Caracas, 1952. 11[2] p.

VALLE, Rafael. La idea inter-americana. (Revista de la Universidad, Tegucigalpa, 17(15): 73–76, abr./dic. 1954)

VAZQUEZ CARRIZOSA, Alfredo. La crisis del derecho americano. (Foro internacional, México, D.F., 2(7): 423–439, en./mar. 1962)

VERGARA DONOSO, Germán. La Conferencia de Caracas. (Finis terrae, Santiago de Chile, 1(1): 5–19, 1er. trimestre 1954)

WHITAKER, Arthur. Development of American regionalism; the Organization of American States (International conciliation, N.Y. (469): 121–164, Mar. 1951)

WIENCKE GUALTIERI, Enrique. La función regional de la Organización de los Estados Americanos y su importancia. México, 1962. 127 p.

YEPES, Jesús. Del Congreso de Panamá a la Conferencia de Caracas, 1826–1954; el genio de Bolívar a través de la historia de las relaciones interamericanas. Caracas, 1955. 2 v.
Bibliography: v.2, p. 317–322.

ZANOTTI, Isidoro. Organizaçao dos Estados Americanos. (Revista do Serviço Público, Rio de Janeiro, 3(1/2): 147-171, set./out. 1948)

OTHER PUBLICATIONS OF THE INSTITUTE

Roundtable of Western Hemisphere International Law Scholars, San José, Costa Rica, March 31-April 5, 1963, Final Report. (In cooperation with the Carnegie Endowment for International Peace), 125 p. (Also in Spanish)

Material de Referencia sobre la Enseñanza del Derecho Internacional y Materias Afines en Latinoamérica y Canadá (Publicación Provisional), 1964, 157 p.

Organizaciones Internacionales No Americanas, Instrumentos Constitucionales (1964), 567 p.

Instrumentos Relativos a la Integración Económica en América Latina (1964), 345 p. (English edition in preparation)

Inaugural Meeting, Bogotá, March 18-23, 1964, Report of the General Secretariat (1964). (Also in Spanish)

Special Meeting on Legal and Institutional Aspects of Foreign Private Investment, Rio de Janeiro, March 25-28, 1964, Report of the General Secretariat (1964). (Also in Spanish)

Seminar on Legal and Institutional Aspects of Central American Integration, Center for Advanced International Studies, University of Miami, 17-21 August 1964, Report of the General Secretariat (1964). (Also in Spanish)

Outline for a Basic Course on Public International Law, Report of the Special Committee (1964), 97 p. (Also in Spanish)

Quién es Quién en Latinoamérica en Derecho Internacional y Materias Afines (Publicación Provisional), 1965, 172 p.

Instrumentos Relativos a la Integración Europea, Tratado que Establece la Comunidad Económica Europea y otros Instrumentos (1965), 333 p.

Instrumentos Relativos a la Integración Europea, Tratado que Establece la Comunidad Europea del Carbón y del Acero y otros Instrumentos (1965), 196 p.

Instrumentos Relativos a la Integración Europea, Tratado que Establece la Comunidad Europea de Energía Atómica y otros Instrumentos (1965), 178 p.

Seminar on Legal and Institutional Aspects of the Latin American Free Trade Association, LAFTA Secretariat, Montevideo, October 18-22, 1965, Report of the General Secretariat (1966). (Also in Spanish)

Meeting on Teaching and Research Regarding Legal and Institutional Problems of Latin American Integration, Institute for the Integration of Latin America, Buenos Aires, November 25-29, 1965, Report of the General Secretariat (1966). (Also in Spanish)

Second Special Meeting on Legal and Institutional Aspects of Foreign Private Investment, Rio de Janeiro, November 1-5, 1965, Report of the General Secretariat (1966). (Also in Spanish)

Esquema para la Enseñanza e Investigación de la Problemática Jurídica e Institucional de la Integración Latinoamericana. (In preparation)

Introducción al Estudio del Derecho de la Integración Latinoamericana. (In preparation)